Niśvāsamukhatattvasaṃhitā

A Preface to the Earliest Surviving Śaiva Tantra

(on non-Tantric Śaivism at the Dawn of the Mantramārga)

Critical Edition, with Introduction & Annotated Translation

and an Appendix Containing Śivadharmasaṅgraha 5–9

L'Institut Français de Pondichéry (IFP), UMIFRE 21 CNRS-MAE, est un établissement à autonomie financière sous la double tutelle du Ministère français des Affaires Etrangères (MAE) et du Centre National de la Recherche Scientifique (CNRS). Il est partie intégrante du réseau des 27 centres de recherche de ce Ministère. Avec le Centre de Sciences Humaines (CSH) à New Delhi, il forme l'USR 3330 du CNRS « Savoirs et Mondes Indiens ». Il remplit des missions de recherche, d'expertise et de formation en Sciences Humaines et Sociales et en Ecologie en Asie du Sud. Il s'intéresse particulièrement aux savoirs et patrimoines culturels indiens (langue et littérature sanskrite, histoire des religions, études tamoules...), aux dynamiques sociales contemporaines, et aux écosystèmes naturels de l'Inde du Sud.

The French Institute of Pondicherry (IFP), UMIFRE 21 CNRS-MAE, is a financially autonomous institution under the joint supervision of the French Ministry of Foreign Affairs (MAE) and the French National Centre of Scientific Research (CNRS). It is a part of the network of 27 research centres under this Ministry. It also forms part of the research unit 3330 "Savoirs et Mondes Indiens" of the CNRS, along with the Centre de Sciences Humaines (CSH) in New Delhi. It fulfils its missions of research, expertise and training in Human and Social Sciences and Ecology in South Asia. It works particularly in the fields of Indian cultural knowledge and heritage (Sanskrit language and literature, history of religions, Tamil studies...), contemporary social dynamics and the natural ecosystems of South India.

French Institute of Pondicherry, 11, St. Louis Street, P.B. 33, Pondicherry—605001, India
Tel: (413) 2231600, Email: ifpdir@ifpindia.org Website: http://www.ifpindia.org

L'École française d'Extrême-Orient (EFEO), fondée en 1900 à Hanoï, est un établissement relevant du ministère français de l'Enseignement supérieur et de la Recherche dont la mission scientifique est l'étude des civilisations classiques de l'Asie. Son champ de recherches s'étend de l'Inde à la Chine et au Japon et, englobant l'ensemble du Sud-Est asiatique, comprend la plupart des sociétés qui furent indianisées ou sinisées au cours de l'histoire. Autour de ses dix-sept centres et antennes, installés dans douze pays d'Asie, se sont constitués des réseaux de chercheurs locaux et internationaux sur lesquels l'École a pu s'appuyer pour construire son essor. L'EFEO aborde l'Asie par des recherches pluridisciplinaires et comparatistes, associant l'archéologie, l'histoire, l'anthropologie, la philologie, et les sciences religieuses. À Pondichéry, les projets de l'EFEO portent essentiellement sur l'« indologie » classique : sanskrit, tamoul ancien, histoire, histoire de l'art et des religions.

The mission of The French School of Asian Studies (EFEO), founded in 1900 in Hanoi and today under the aegis of the French Ministry of Higher Education and Research, is to study the classical civilizations of Asia. Stretching from India, in the West, across the whole of South-East Asia to China and Japan, the EFEO's research areas cover most of the societies which have been 'Indianised' or 'Sinicised' over the course of history. A network of international scholars working at the EFEO's seventeen centres and branch offices, which are spread across twelve Asian countries, has been essential in the development of the School's research programme. Interdisciplinary projects bring together leading scholars in the fields of anthropology, archaeology, history, philology, and religious studies. In Pondicherry, the projects of the EFEO focus mainly on classical Indology: Sanskrit, Old Tamil, History, and History of art and of religions.

École française d'Extrême-Orient,
22, avenue du Président Wilson,
75116 Paris, France.
Tel: (33) 1 53 70 18 60
Website: http://www.efeo.fr/

Pondicherry Centre of the EFEO
16 & 19, Dumas Street,
Pondicherry—605 001, India.
Tel: (91) (413) 2334539/2332504
Email: administration@efeo-pondicherry.org

THE EARLY TANTRA SERIES

Tantric scriptures form the basis of almost all the various theistic schools of theology and ritual in post-Vedic India, as well as of a major strand of Buddhism (Vajrayāna). Among these schools, those centred on the Hindu deities Śiva and Viṣṇu spread well beyond the Indian subcontinent to Kambuja (Cambodia/Laos/Thailand), Champa (Vietnam) and Indonesia, while Buddhist tantrism quickly became pan-Asian.

With this mini-series, launched within the 'Collection Indologie', we are releasing some of the fruits of a Franco-German project funded from 2008 to 2011 by the Agence Nationale pour la Recherche *and the* Deutsche Forschungsgemeinschaft. *The series takes its name from the project's title: 'Early Tantra: Discovering the interrelationships and common ritual syntax of the Śaiva, Buddhist, Vaiṣṇava and Saura traditions'. Our aim was to study the interrelationships between the tantric traditions on the basis of fundamental source-material, which we would edit and publish for the first time. For this we made use of some of the exceptionally rich manuscript resources gathered in the twentieth century and studied by German and French research institutes at opposite poles of the sub-continent.*

In recent centuries, the Tamil-speaking South is the only area where a vast corpus of Sanskrit texts of what was long the dominant school of tantric Śaivism continued being copied and so transmitted to the present day. So when, in 1956, Jean Filliozat secured a foothold in Pondicherry for French indological research, he created an ideal institutional base for the study of a forgotten chapter in the religious history of Asia. Gradually, the largest specialised manuscript collection of texts relating to the Śaiva Siddhānta was amassed, recognised in 2005 by UNESCO as a "Memory of the World" collection: The Śaiva Manuscripts of Pondicherry.

At the other end of the subcontinent, the cool climate of Nepal has preserved ancient manuscripts of texts of virtually every branch of Indian learning. Much of the early history of tantrism is thus preserved in the vast archive of Nepalese manuscripts microfilmed over more than three decades by the Nepal-German Manuscript Preservation Project *(NGMPP), then partly catalogued by the* Nepalese German Manuscript Cataloguing Project *(NGMCP), run from Hamburg and from the NGMCP's base in Kathmandu, the Nepal Research Centre (NRC). One Nepalese treasure, also included, in 2013, in UNESCO's register, formed the corner-stone of our project: the ninth-century manuscript of the* Niśvāsatattvasaṃhitā.

The Early Tantra Series *is not a closed collection: as well as the editions and translations promised as part of the 'Early Tantra' project, studies of numerous related works were inspired or further advanced during the project's workshops.*

TO DIWAKAR ACHARYA

GURU AND FRIEND

COLLECTION INDOLOGIE 145
EARLY TANTRA SERIES 6

NIŚVĀSAMUKHATATTVASAṂHITĀ

A PREFACE TO THE EARLIEST SURVIVING ŚAIVA TANTRA

(ON NON-TANTRIC ŚAIVISM AT THE DAWN OF THE MANTRAMĀRGA)

CRITICAL EDITION, WITH INTRODUCTION & ANNOTATED TRANSLATION

AND AN APPENDIX CONTAINING ŚIVADHARMASAṄGRAHA 5–9

EDITED BY

NIRAJAN KAFLE

with a foreword by Dominic Goodall

INSTITUT FRANÇAIS DE PONDICHÉRY
ÉCOLE FRANÇAISE D'EXTRÊME-ORIENT
ASIEN-AFRIKA-INSTITUT, UNIVERSITÄT HAMBURG

Typeset by Nirajan KAFLE in Latin Modern and Velthuis' Devanāgarī, using EDMAC, TEX and XeLATEX.
Cover design: Ink & Paper, Pondicherry.
Cover photo by Andrey KLEBANOV: detail of a coverboard from a Nepalese palm-leaf manuscript of the *Śivadharma* held in the National Archives, Kathmandu, NGMPP B 7/3, dated to 1170 CE, showing a *liṅga* of fire flanked by Brahmā and Viṣṇu.
Printed at the Sri Aurobindo Ashram Press, Pondicherry.

Contents

FOREWORD

I am delighted to have been asked by Nirajan KAFLE to furnish a foreword to this precious edition and translation of a text of very great interest for the history of Śaivism.

When Nirajan KAFLE first came to Pondicherry in 2007, at the suggestion of Diwakar ACHARYA, it was to participate in reading-sessions and to help preparing for the first workshop on the *Niśvāsatattvasaṃhitā*, an event that Alexis SANDERSON's presence made particularly inspiring to many, and that encouraged Harunaga ISAACSON and myself to launch the Franco-German 'Early Tantra' Project. Nirajan KAFLE's assistance was invaluable, for instance in helping Nibedita ROUT, R. SATHYANARAYANAN, S. A. S. SARMA and myself to complete an electronically searchable transcription of related materials, such as the *Niśvāsakārikā* and *Dīkṣottara*. Once the 'Early Tantra' Project was launched, inviting Nirajan KAFLE to come for a longer stay and participate in the project by producing a doctorate in Pondicherry seemed a natural choice. That doctorate was eventually completed and examined at the University of Leiden some years later, under the guidance of Peter BISSCHOP, and has now resulted in the book that you hold in your hands.

I confess that when, towards the beginning of Nirajan KAFLE's doctoral studies, after some weeks of reading together, I asked him which part of the large *Niśvāsa*-corpus he wished to focus upon, I was surprised at his answer and not at once enthusiastic about his choice. From all the intriguing range of possible themes treated in the corpus transmitted in the ninth-century manuscript — yogic meditiation, initiations, magical rites — it seemed to me strange that he should choose the introductory portion, the *Niśvāsamukha*. The exciting discoveries which that introductory portion had to offer had already, as it seemed to me, been drawn out of the text by SANDERSON's important article of 2006 on 'The Lākulas...' What remained seemed to be a screed of pronouncements about non-Mantramārga devotional practice that could surely be found in many a *Purāṇa*.

But of course I soon discovered that the devotional practices recorded by the *Niśvāsamukha* are in fact of considerable intrinsic interest — all the more so as they can be dated within a corpus whose relatively early place in time, while not particularly precise, is nonetheless rather more secure than that of most sections of most *Purāṇas*. Furthermore, I also came to realise that the *Niśvāsamukha* provides invaluable help in mapping the contours of the relations between four different traditions of early Śaivism. Those traditions are: firstly, that of the Pāñcārthika Pāśupatas, hitherto known to us principally from the *Pāśupatasūtra* and Kauṇḍinya's commentary; secondly, another Atimārga school identified by SANDERSON (2006) as the Somasiddhānta, about whom we knew very little before; thirdly, the emerging Mantramārga, whose teachings are expounded in the other books transmitted in the same manuscript; and fourthly, the tradition of what might be called pre-Mantramārga "lay" practices that are reflected in the earliest layers of the corpus of *Śivadharma* texts. In short, it would be difficult to exaggerate how useful this primary source is for the history of the Śaiva religions.

An edition in this series of the *Niśvāsamukha* thus forms a bridge between one of the primary research areas in Pondicherry over the last sixty years, namely the Śaiva Siddhānta, and a newly emerging focus of research, the Śaivism of devotees who were not religious professionals, nor necessarily sectarian initiates.[1]

The Śaiva traditions have been hugely varied, encompassing antinomian practices that harnessed the power of transgressive sexual and charnel-ground rituals, as well as philosophically sophisticated defences of a range of both dualist and non-dualist theological positions. Recently, what has been most studied amongst the Sanskrit works reflecting these traditions,

[1] One important body of non-sectarian Śaiva literature that has long been a focus of research in Pondicherry is that of the hymns of the *Tēvāram*, for they were long supposed in some sense to be works of the Śaivasiddhānta, even though this was certainly not how they were regarded in the period in which they were composed (GOODALL 2014: xxxiii). One day, a longer demonstration of this contention should be provided, showing for instance that many of the supposedly Saiddhāntika technical terms that occur in the *Tēvāram* are not in fact narrowly distinctive of the Śaiva Siddhānta (terms such as *pācam*, *pantam*, and even *cadācivam*). An important exception here is the use of a *cakaḷī ceytu* by Sundarar, apparently as a synonym of the term *sakalīkaraṇa* in 7.65.5 (references to the hymns here follow SUBRAMANYA AIYAR, CHEVILLARD & SARMA 2007), which is indeed distinctive of the Mantramārga. Otherwise, one struggles to find distinctively Saiddhāntika theological or liturgical notions, or Śaiva terms deployed in contexts that imply a Saiddhāntika understanding of those terms. Furthermore, when Śaiva religious professionals are mentioned, for instance in descriptions of temple processions, they are often in mixed groups and no particular importance is accorded to followers of the Śaiva Siddhānta. In 4.20.3 (translated by TÖRZSÖK 2004: 15), for example, we find a mixture of followers of observances characterised by spreading matted locks (*viricaṭaiviratikaḷ*), brahmins (*antaṇar*), Śaivas (*caivar*), Pāśupatas (*pācupatar*) and Kāpālikas (*kapālikaḷ*). The Śaivas may be Saiddhāntikas, but they do not stand out from the list. Elsewhere, in similar passages, we find Śaivas and Pāśupatas together (1.66.4), or Mahāvratins alone (4.21.1), and Rudras (*uruttirarkaḷ*, in 2.29.4), who may be followers of the Atimārga (thus the suggestion of TÖRZSÖK 2004: 13, fn. 49). In other words, there seems to me nothing in this body of hymns to suggest a privileged position of the Śaiva Siddhānta in the socioreligious world that they reflect.

particularly in the last sixty years (and particularly in the French institutions of research in Pondicherry), is overwhelmingly the huge and fascinating literary corpus of doctrines and liturgies produced by an initiated elite of "professionals" whose professed aims were enjoyment of extraordinary powers (*bhoga*) and ultimate personal liberation characterised by the realisation of omniscience and omnipotence (*mokṣa*). These are arguably not the sorts of goals that one might expect to be those of a religious mainstream, and indeed the social dimensions of a large institutionalised religion seem to be absent from the earliest literature of the Mantramārga.[2] Over time, the social base of what came to be called the Śaiva Siddhānta appears gradually to have broadened, to the point where it claimed authority over the large South Indian temple-complexes ringed with multiple enclosure walls that began to proliferate in the Cōḻa period, a phase reflected in the extensive twelfth- and post-twelfth-century corpus of South Indian Temple Āgamas, which appear intended to describe every aspect of the life of such temples as seen primarily from the perspective of the priests.[3] But this body of literature belongs to a much later period and seems in any case not to have spread its influence much beyond the Tamil-speaking South.

And yet there are older sources that give us a picture of what seems to have been a socially much broader lay Śaiva religiosity. And perhaps most important of these sources is the largely still unpublished body of Sanskrit works known as the *Śivadharma*-corpus, the works expounding the "Religion of Śiva", produced between the sixth and ninth centuries CE. Here we find that ultimate liberation is presented as a more distant goal, as DE SIMINI explains (2016: 50):

> The religion promoted by the *Śivadharmaśāstra* and the *Śivadharmottara* is thus mainly a religion of *bhukti* ('enjoyment'), in which devotees strive to secure a very long afterlife in one of the celestial worlds, after which those who have generated the utmost merits can be reborn on Earth as powerful kings or wise Brahmins. Only in a future rebirth will they have the opportunity to become initiated, and will thus attain final emancipation (*mukti*) from the cycle of existence (*saṃsāra*).

---

2 See the section entitled 'Archaism in the realm of social religion' in the introduction to the edition of the earliest *sūtras* of the *Niśvāsatattvasaṃhitā* (GOODALL, SANDERSON, ISAACSON et al. 2015: 47–66).

3 For a relatively recent discussion touching on this development and this corpus, see GOODALL's introduction to SATHYANARAYANAN 2015, in particular the section entitled 'Trilocana and the South Indian Temple' (pp. 37–48).

Furthermore, we find that, instead of theology and liturgy, the principal focus is on public piety and generosity towards the religion, as DE SIMINI continues (2016: 5):

> The main pillar of this worldly religion is the worship of Śiva in his aniconic representation of the *liṅga*—although the use of iconic forms is also well attested —and in the performance of gifts (*dāna*), either to support the community of initiated Śaiva yogins and teachers (*ācārya*), or in favour of other lay followers.

In what may be the first discussion of the *Śivadharma*-corpus in a work published in the Collection Indologie (GOODALL 1998: 375–376, fn. 616), it is implied that the *Śivadharma*-corpus was produced "for non-initiates" by an initiated elite. The tenth-century Kashmirian Saiddhāntika exegete Bhaṭṭa Rāmakaṇṭha tells us in his *Kiraṇavṛtti* (on verses 11d–12 of chapter 6) that those incapable of following the intensive religious life entailed by a regular initiation into the Śaivasiddhānta — diseased persons, the elderly, women and such — may receive an inititation that will liberate them at death, but that will not bind them to the usually obligatory post-initiatory observances. With liberation guaranteed, what they do after initiation is soteriologically irrelevant, but he suggests that they may thereafter express their devotion to Śiva, the guru and Śiva's devotees, either in a worldly way (*laukikena rūpeṇa*),[4] or in a manner taught by the *Śivadharma*. Rāmakaṇṭha's presentation had suggested to me that the *Śivadharma*-corpus was diluted scripture deliberately produced by theologians who were knowingly generating an exoteric — and therefore necessarily only half-true — body of teachings, primarily for pious folk in need of religious encouragement, but unable, for whatever reason, to receive the one soteriologically effective remedy for the ills of *saṃsāra*, namely salvific *dīkṣā*.

Such a model now seems flatly implausible, for a start because the *Śivadharmaśāstra* and *Śivadharmottara* contain numerous allusions that connect them to Atimārga religion (see DE SIMINI 2016:51ff), not to the Mantramārga. In other words, it seems now quite clear (*pace* Rāmakaṇṭha and GOODALL 1998) that the *Śivadharmaśāstra* and *Śivadharmottara* were not deliberately produced as an ancillary bowdlerising scripture for the uplift or social control of pious non-initiates. The testimony of the *Niśvāsamukha*, which incorporates a lengthy account of the sorts of practices that those texts prescribe in its account of the religious context into which the Mantramārga

4 In other words, in a manner congruent with the well recognised exoteric brahmanical sources of *dharma*, namely *śruti* and *smṛti*: see GOODALL 1998: 375, fn. 615.

was born, suggests that they reflect instead a vigorous independent tradition of devotion to Śiva.

The Pondicherry Centre of the EFEO is now a participating beneficiary of a five-year project funded by the European Research Council that has been awarded to Florinda DE SIMINI (« L'Orientale », Naples) to address this literature: 'Translocal Identities: The *Śivadharma* and the Making of Regional Religious Traditions in Premodern South Asia' (ERC grant agreement n° 803624). This new *Śivadharma* project, in which Nirajan KAFLE is also involved, aims to open up more of this primary source material to scholarship and to document better the huge spread of its influence across the Sanskrit cosmopolis (discernible primarily through epigraphs, translations, quotations, borrowings and commentaries). In so doing, it will inevitably also throw further light on the genesis of the complex nexus of ideas and practices that are called "Hinduism", as Nirajan KAFLE has done in this important volume.

Dominic Goodall,
EFEO, Pondicherry

PREFACE

This work is one of the results of a larger, collaborative, three-year project on *Early Tantra* (2008-2010), co-funded by the Agence Nationale pour la Recherche and the Deutsche Forschungsgemeinschaft (DFG); it was jointly directed by Dominic GOODALL and Harunaga ISAACSON. The Japan Student Services Organization and the Jan Gonda Fund Foundation, in collaboration with the International Institute for Asian Studies, also supported my efforts to finalise the present work by providing scholarships of three months[5] and six months[6] respectively, allowing me to carry out research and finalize my doctoral dissertation in 2015.[7] Subsequently, in continuation of my previous research in the field of 'early lay Śaivism', I continued to carry out research in the subject area as part of the NWO project 'From Universe of Viṣṇu to Universe of Śiva', directed by Peter BISSCHOP, University of Leiden.[8] As a result, I had the opportunity to deepen, refine, and expand upon my initial findings to the degree that they reached the present format.

Were it not for Dominic GOODALL, this work would never have seen the light of day. First and foremost, I would therefore like to express my gratitude to him for having taught me what I know about Śaivism, for inviting me to Pondicherry to work with him, and, in particular, for sharing the results of his research—both published and unpublished. During our joint research sessions at the École française d'Extrême Orient, he analysed—with incredible attention to detail—the complete draft of this work, including the translation, offering decidedly beneficial corrections. I am extremely indebted to him for his innumerable suggestions and illuminating comments on all parts of the text. Meanwhile, it goes without saying that the author takes full responsibility for any errors which undoubtedly remain—be they hidden or apparent, and wish to invoke the reader's leniency in this regard.

I also owe a great debt of gratitude to Peter C. BISSCHOP for accepting me as his doctoral student and for providing essential support of practical and administrative nature during my enrolment process at the university of Leiden. During my stay, he scrutinized my entire thesis and made many

5 The scholarship spanned the period from March to May, 2013.

6 Financial support was granted from September 2014 to February 2015.

7 The title of the thesis is 'The *Niśvāsamukha*, the introductory book of the *Niśvāsatattvasaṃhitā*: critical edition, with an introduction and annotated translation appended by *Śivadharmasaṅgraha* 5–9'.

8 `https://www.nwo.nl/onderzoek-en-resultaten/onderzoeksprojecten/i/44/13544.html`

insightful observations that allowed me to improve it considerably. In particular, he kindly invested great efforts in helping me improve the structure and mode of argumentation of the introductory section of this volume, despite his manifold teaching and research obligations.

I am very grateful to Diwakar ACHARYA for long years of teaching the Sanskrit language, for reading the entirety of the precursor to this work, and for inviting me to his home with heart-warming frequency during my stay at Kyoto. He too shared both published and unpublished work, for which I remain thankful to this day. Without his help a great number of seemingly intractable textual difficulties would have remained unresolved.

I would also like to thank Yuko YOKOCHI and Somdev VASUDEVA for proposing constructive changes to the text while ameliorating it during my three-month stay at Kyoto.

My sincere thanks also go to Bhim KANDEL and Kashinath NYUPANE, for having taught me Sanskrit over the years with unfailing energy. Furthermore, I am grateful to Harunaga ISAACSON for his insightful suggestions at different stages of this project. I would also like to express my gratitude to Sasha LUBOTSKY, who kindly took the time to read the language-section of this work and share his incisive observations regarding grammatical analysis.

Marion RASTELLI (IKGA, University of Vienna) and Timothy LUBIN (Washington and Lee University), originally anonymous reviewers of a mature draft of this work submitted for evaluation, have kindly revealed their identities. Although errors and shortcomings without doubt remain, their generosity and specialist knowledge has improved away many structural and factual shortcomings of the earlier draft, for which kind support I would like to express my gratitude.

I thank in particular my friends Esther-Maria GUGGENMOS, Rajan KHATIWODA Nina MIRNIG, Florinda DE SIMINI, Marco FRANCESCHINI, Giovanni CIOTTI, Daniele CUNEO and Andrey KLEBANOV for their strong encouragement throughout, and also for providing me with relevant materials.

I also owe a debt of gratitude to my friends Ven. GYALTEN Jigdrel, Philip PIERCE, Mary PREMILA, Thomas Fulton O'GARA, Suganya ANANDAKICHENIN, Leah COMEAU and Timothy C. CAHILL for proofreading sections of this study at different stages of its development and offering their valuable feedback.

I thank the Pondicherry Centre of the EFEO and its librarian Shanty RAYAPOULLÉ, who was most helpful in the provision of primary and secondary sources; the French Institute of Pondicherry and its librarian NAREN-

DRAN, who showed the same generosity; the National Archives of Kathmandu, and the Nepalese-German Manuscript Cataloguing Project.

I would also like to thank the group of scholars who participated in the *Workshop on Early Śaivism*: the Testimony of the Niśvāsatattvasaṃhitā held in 2007 at the EFEO in Pondicherry, during which we analysed and debated verses 1.1 to 1.88. Among them were: Alexis SANDERSON, Dominic GOODALL, Harunaga ISAACSON, Diwakar ACHARYA, Peter BISSCHOP, Arlo GRIFFITHS, Jun TAKASHIMA, Kei KATAOKA, Anil Kumar ACHARYA, Nina MIRNIG, Nibedita ROUT, Andrea ACRI, R. SATHYANARAYANAN and S.A.S. SARMA. For the preparation of this work, I have drawn on digital materials from the following electronic resources:

1. Muktabodha Indological Research Institute
2. Digital Library of India
3. GRETIL (Göttingen Register of Electronic Texts in Indic Languages).

INTRODUCTION

A sole 9th-century[9] Nepalese palm-leaf manuscript preserved in the National Archives, Kathmandu (NAK) transmits what appears to be the oldest surviving Śaiva tantra, called the *Niśvāsatattvasaṃhitā*. This manuscript consists of five separate books—in order of appearance within the manuscript, these are the *Niśvāsamukha*, the *Mūlasūtra*, the *Uttarasūtra*, the *Nayasūtra* and the *Guhyasūtra*.[10] Various scholars have referred to this manuscript in the past, beginning with ŚĀSTRĪ (1905: lxxvii, 137–140), BAGCHI (1929: 757 ff.), GOUDRIAAN & GUPTA (1981: 33–36), SANDERSON (2006: 152), GOODALL & ISAACSON (2007: 4) and, most recently, GOODALL et al. (2015: 103–108).

Since the *Niśvāsamukha* has not yet been published in full,[11] it is with great joy that we herewith present the first critical edition and annotated translation of the work. We also present an edition of five chapters—chapters five to nine—of the *Śivadharmasaṅgraha* as an appendix. These chapters are closely linked with the *Niśvāsamukha*,[12] provide a host of text-historically relevant information, and hence merit special attention. A critical edition and annotated translation (GOODALL et al. 2015) of the three books which together comprise the *Niśvāsatattvasaṃhitā*—i.e. the *Mūlasūtra*, the *Uttarasūtra*, and the *Nayasūtra*—has been published by Dominic GOODALL, Alexis

9 For an analysis of the evidence relating to the likely date of composition of the text, the reader is referred to pp. 28 ff.

10 In addition to the five books of the *Niśvāsatattvasaṃhitā*, a text called *Niśvāsakārikā* has been detected. This text contains a large section that is referred to as the *Dīkṣottara*, presumably an originally separate Śaiva work (see GOODALL et al. 2015: 23–26). The *Niśvāsakārikā* is not contained in the Nepalese manuscript but survives independently in three South Indian transcripts preserved in the French Institute of Pondicherry (T. 17, T. 127 and T. 150). It is to be noted that *Guhyasūtra* 18.15 refers to a work called *Kārikā*, presumably a reference to the *Niśvāsakārikā*. Besides, there exists a Śaiva *pratiṣṭhā* text—the *Niśvāsākhyamahātantra*—traced to a Nepalese manuscript (NGMPP reel number A 41/13), which, however, bears no apparent connection to the *Niśvāsa* corpus. As far as we are aware, these are the texts that have survived to date under the title *Niśvāsa*. From other Śaiva sources we learn that a number of other texts may have existed under this same title (GOODALL et al. 2015: 23–30). The existence of different works under the same title leads to the assumption that the *Niśvāsa* may have developed in the fashion of the *Kālottara*, undergoing more than one recension. (D. ACHARYA is to be credited for first advancing this theory; for the various recensions of the *Kālottara*, see GOODALL 2007: 125–127).

11 SANDERSON 2006 contains extracts from the *Niśvāsamukha*.

12 For more details, see the section 'Borrowings from the *Niśvāsamukha* by the *Śivadharmasaṅgraha*' (p. 101).

SANDERSON and Harunaga ISAACSON in a joint effort, a process in which we have been involved as well.

The *Niśvāsatattvasaṃhitā* is consistently presented as one of the eighteen Rudratantras in all the lists of the Mantramārgic (Saiddhāntika) Śaiva canon.[13] This canon consists altogether of twenty-eight principal scriptures, falling into two categories: ten Śivabheda (Śiva-divisions) and eighteen Rudrabheda (Rudra-divisions), along with scriptures that claim to be sub-recensions (*upabheda*) of these.[14] All these scriptures, including sub-recensions, are works of authority for the Śaiva Siddhānta.[15] The *Niśvāsatattvasaṃhitā* is an important text for tracing the early history of tantric Śaivism: it may be the oldest surviving text of the 'Mantramārga' (the path of mantras), the term by which the *Niśvāsamukha* (4.132) refers to tantric Śaivism. The tantric tradition, or more specifically, "the scriptural revelations of the Śaiva mainstream" (SANDERSON 1988: 660), is believed to have developed in South Asia from about the 6th century CE.[16] This religious system presents itself as a superior and more powerful form of religion and promises supernatural powers (*bhukti*) and liberation (*mukti*) to its followers, who are encouraged to rely on the power of spells (*vidyā*, *mantra*), which in turn require initiation (GOODALL et al. 2015: 15). The *Niśvāsamukha*, in its four chapters, is devoted to relating the religious context in which the Mantramārga, purportedly the 'highest stream of religion', evolved.[17] The Mantramārga is thereupon taught in the subsequent four books of the *Niśvāsatattvasaṃhitā*. The *Niśvāsamukha* is the earliest extant source to present a five-fold framework known as the 'Five Streams'. This framework envelops the entirety of the *Niśvāsatattvasaṃhitā* in a dialogue between Śiva and his consort Devī; the success of this scheme is reflected in the fact that subsequent early Śaiva treatises have adopted versions of this taxonomy for the framing of their own respective works.[18]

The 'Five Streams' (*pañca srotāḥ*) are subjected to a hierarchical strat-

13 The reader is referred to GOODALL (2004: x ff.).

14 An early list of these scriptures is already attested in the *Uttarasūtra* (1.23 ff.), the second book of the *Niśvāsatattvasaṃhitā*. For other lists, see the appendix to GOODALL (1998).

15 SANDERSON (1988: 668).

16 GOODALL & ISAACSON (2011: 122).

17 Alexis SANDERSON (2006: 145) was the first Western scholar to introduce the term Mantramārga as a designation of tantric Śaivism. For a detailed discussion of tantric Śaivism, see SANDERSON (2006: 145ff).

18 The framework of the *Niśvāsamukha* is apparent in the structural makeup of the *Pauṣkarapārameśvara*, the *Svacchanda*, the *Mṛgendratantra*, the *Jayadrathayāmala*, the *Pūrvakāmika*, and the *Śataratnasaṅgraha*.

ification which, graded from 'lowest' to 'highest', comprise the following elements: the Laukika (worldly), Vaidika (vedic), Ādhyātmika (relating to the soul), Atimārga (transcendent), and Mantramārga streams. The *Niśvāsamukha* (= *Mukha*) functions both as a pithy summary of the first four streams, presented as exoteric tenet systems, and as a preface to the Mantramārga, which is to be expounded in the ensuing volumes of the compilation. It is worth noting that the text of the *Niśvāsamukha* does not expound the 'lower streams' in equal measure—in fact, as we shall see, quite the contrary holds true. The first, Laukika, stream constitutes the largest part of the text and extends over the first three chapters in their entirety. This has the effect that subject-wise, the majority of the text is devoted to the lay Śaiva religion. As regards the sources of the Laukika section, parts of it have been traced to the *Manusmṛti*. There are some passages for which we find parallels in early *Purāṇas*, such as the *Skandapurāṇa*. Although we have singled out a diversity of other passages in the Laukika section that we suspect of likewise containing borrowed material, we have not yet been able to establish fully which of the external sources might have served as templates. The second, Vaidika 'stream', also, receives relatively thorough treatment, spanning forty-one verses (4.1–41), all of which are partly traceable to the *Manusmṛti*. The Ādhyātmika tream encompasses the teaching of Sāṅkhya (verses 4.42–48a) and Yoga (4.48b–69), yet receives altogether scant attention—in particular the Sāṅkhya system is related rather briefly. The Atimārga stream covers the system of the Pāśupatas at some length and is structurally divided into two subsections: the first is referred to as the Atyāśrama subsection, spanning from 4.70b to 88c; the second (4.88d–131d) provides an account of the teaching of the cosmological system of the Lokātīta, particularly as devised by the Kāpālikas.

Unlike the case of the first three streams, whose sources are only partially evident, it is apparent that the teaching of the Atyāśramins as contained in the first sub-section Atimārga constitutes, for the greatest part, a paraphrase of the *Pāśupatasūtra*.[19] That being the case, it is quite possible that, likewise, the second sub-section—elaborating upon the cosmological system of the Kāpālikas—might have drawn from an undefined Kāpālika source, quite likely a source which is no longer extant. As it stands, the fourth section, on the Atimārga, is exceptional insofar as it contains a considerable number of the preciously few extant textual references that—through the act of borrowing—indirectly hail from the tradition of the Kāpālika-Pāśupatas. Since this material is—to the current state of our limited knowledge—not

19 See SANDERSON 2006.

readily available elsewhere, it is, without doubt, an inordinately important source for further research on the otherwise sparsely known 'proto-Śaiva' Pāśupata-school.[20] The Mantramārga is not taught in the *Niśvāsamukha* itself,[21] which only prefaces it. However, the *Niśvāsamukha* makes passing references to the Mantramārga in the inceptive and final sections of the work.[22] The frame narrative of the *Niśvāsamukha* thus finally presents us the Mantramārga teaching in relation to the teachings of the Laukika, Vedic, Ādhyātmika and the Atimārga systems. However, it is expounded, in profound detail, in the ensuing volumes of the *Niśvāsatattvasaṃhitā*. One of the most noteworthy characteristics of the Mantramārga as presented in the *Mūlasūtra*, the *Uttarasūtra*, the *Nayasūtra* and the *Guhyasūtra*, is that it contains no antecedent parallels that we have been able to trace. It therefore comprises the oldest surviving exposition of the Mantramārga amongst all presently known textual sources.

Concerning the typology of the *Niśvāsamukha*'s content, as well as that of the other books of the *Niśvāsa*, two distinct types of teachings become discernible. While the former presents non-tantric traditions, the latter is devoted to tantric Śaivism, which, as we have briefly mentioned above, requires initiation. Given this discrepancy, it is worth noting that they all are contained in a single manuscript. This is indeed a unique feature in the textual history of the early Śaiva tradition—none of the other pre-10th-century canonic Śaiva scriptures, such as the *Kiraṇa*, the non-eclectic and eclectic versions of the *Kālottara*, and the *Svāyaṃbhuvasūtrasaṅgraha*, commences with non-tantric content. Thus, the *Niśvāsamukha*, as the opening book of the *Niśvāsatattvasaṃhitā*, is unique not only in the context of the *Niśvāsa*, but also with regards to the larger history of early Mantramārga Śaivism. Judging from textual indicators that will emerge in more detail as the present study progresses, it appears that the *Niśvāsamukha* was likely composed in order to introduce the Mantramārga to other major 'Hindu' traditions,[23] including branches of Śaivism. We suppose that the tradition of Śaiva tantra had already developed a clear identity distinct from that of

---

20 The text of parts of this last section has already been published and discussed at length by SANDERSON in his 2006 article, '*The Lākulas*: New Evidence of a System Intermediate between Pāñcārthika Pāśupatism and Āgamic Śaivism'.

21 We do nevertheless learn, by way of the frame-story of the *Niśvāsamukha*, that supreme knowledge is only possible through initiation (*dīkṣā*), which destroys worldly existence (1.22). This initiation falls into two categories, that relating to *vidyā* 'supernatural enjoyment' on the one hand, and to *nirvāṇa* 'final liberation' (1.27–28) on the other. See GOODALL et al. 2015: 50–51.

22 These are 1.27, 1.56, 4.132, 4.134 and 4.135.

23 We are here wielding the term 'Hindu' in the broader sense of the word.

other Śaiva traditions. Now, for the first time, the author of the *Niśvāsamukha* expends effort to associate tantric Śaivism with other contemporaneous *mārgas* (paths) of mainstream 'Hindu' traditions—perhaps coining the term 'Mantramārga' in the process. Thus, it may well have been composed in partial subservience to an effort to provide a point of connection between Mantramārga Śaivism and the religious communities it primarily interacted with. Hence it appears quite likely that the *Niśvāsamukha* played a noteworthy part in introducing tantric Śaivism to the diverse Hindu communities during the early stages of the history of Śaivism.

Author, Origin, Date, and Title of the Text

Author of the Text

Although we do not know who the author of the compendium might be, we can nevertheless make a number of relevant, corroborated hypotheses, based on the 9th-century manuscript of the *Niśvāsatattvasaṃhitā* which we have used for this publication. The manuscript contains the oldest extant version of the *Niśvāsamukha*[24] and is written by a singular scribe who presents the five individual volumes in a format which suggests that they form a coherent unit, that of the *Niśvāsa*-'compendium'. The way of presentation of the individual teachings therein may well be indicative of the milieu from which the author of the text hailed, clearly a preponderantly Śaiva background.

Place of Origin

It is, at present, nigh-on-impossible to ascertain, beyond doubt, where and under what circumstances the *Niśvāsamukha* was composed. Nevertheless, we can draw on rudimentary geographical textual evidence: the toponyms Naimiṣāraṇya 'Naimiṣa forest' (1.2, 1.5) and Devadāruvana 'pine forest' (1.11), for example,[25] are in all likelihood situated in the northern part of India. Peter BISSCHOP has offered the plausible suggestion that the Naimiṣa forest may have been situated on the bank of the river Gomatī, in what nowadays is the region of Uttar Pradesh.[26] Although we do not know the

[24] Note that the issue regarding the precise title of the work is somewhat complex, as we shall further investigate from p. 32 ff. We have opted here to refer to the work by the provisional title '*Niśvāsamukha*'.

[25] For a more elaborate discussion, consult p. 53.

[26] See BISSCHOP (2006: 217).

exact location of the Devadāruvana, BISSCHOP,[27] pointing to the evidence of the *Skandapurāṇa*, suggests that this place is probably situated somewhere in the region of the Himavat, the 'snow[capped] mountains.'[28]

Besides these two illustrious woodland areas, the *Niśvāsamukha* makes mention of 'Mahālaya' (situated in the Himālayan region) (3.27) and 'Kedāra' (3.28), known to be located in modern-day Uttarakhand. Note that all of the aforementioned places are renowned, well-attested holy sites. Textually, this is borne out by the description of the Mahālaya as innately brimming with soteriological benefits available to anyone willing to frequent it:

> *mahāpralayasthāyī ca sraṣṭānugrahakārakaḥ* |
> *darśanād eva gacchante padan divyaṃ mahālaye* || 3.27 ||
>
> He who stands in Mahāpralaya (*mahāpralayasthāyī*)[29] [is] the creator and agent of grace; from merely (*eva*) seeing him [=Śiva] in [the sacred site of] Mahālaya, people will attain (*gacchante*) [in the next life] a celestial state of being.

Mahālaya is the summit of the Himavat where Mahādeva, according to Purāṇic traditions, planted his foot-print, for which reason this location had become one of the holiest places for the Śaivas of ancient times.[30] Although the exact location of Mahālaya remains obscure, it is most likely located in the Himālayas.

Likewise, the fame of Kedāra as a worthy pilgrimage site is reflected in our text by its presentation as a special place infused with extraordinary features.[31] As shall be shown in more detail below,[32] it is stated that by dying in the vicinity of any site of the *pañcāṣṭaka*, a group of forty pilgrimage places, one penetrates the shell of the egg of Brahmā and ascends to the world associated with the site of one's demise; one will not be reborn in this world. Moreover, by merely drinking water from the sacred site of Kedāra one can obtain a result identical to the fruit of attaining the five divine sets of eight sacred places. Kedāra also appears in *Guhyasūtra* 7.115, and the

---

27 BISSCHOP (2006: 255).

28 BISSCHOP (2006a: 195) explains: "Most of the Purāṇic sources agree that it is a Himalayan mountain."

29 Perhaps this is to be understood in two ways: 'he who remains [even] in a period of total resorption [of the universe]' and 'he who stands in [the sacred site called] Mahā(pra)laya'.

30 BISSCHOP 2006: 66.

31 *Niśvāsamukha* 3.28a–29a.

32 See p. 72.

elaborate legend of its origin and significance is recounted in chapter 16 of the *Guhyasūtra*.[33]

What is striking regarding Kardamāla is that, although Kardamāla is a minor, regional holy site, fit for the performance of bath rituals,[34] it is here mentioned as being amongst much more famous places for bathing.[35] If the passage is not borrowed from (an) earlier source(s), this would imply that the author treats it as if it were of equal standing to the towering, famed hallmarks of sacred geography. To our mind, this considerably strengthens the importance of Kardamāla as an indication of the provenance of our text, since its relatively limited renown suggests that the author, in all likelihood, must have been intimately acquainted with that area—otherwise he would have scarcely been aware of its existence.

In sum, Peter BISSCHOP plausibly concludes that the evidence culled from the list of toponyms suggests that the place of origin where the *Niśvāsamukha* was composed could be narrowed down to a stretch of land located between the Himavat and modern-day Gujarat.[36]

---

33 For the full treatment of Kedāra, see p. 73 onwards.

34 *Niśvāsamukha* 3.12–13 reads:

> *śoṇapuṣkaralohitye mānase sindhusāgare |*
> *brahmāvartte karddamāle snātvā ca lavaṇodadhau* || 3.12 ||
> *sarvapāpaviśuddhātmā pitṛdevāṃś ca pūjayet |*

> Having bathed in the Śoṇa [river], Puṣkara [lake] or Lohitya [river], in [lake] Mānasa, in the place where the Indus, meets the ocean or in Brahmāvartta, or Kardamāla or in the salty ocean, one [becomes] free from all sins [and] one should [then] worship one's ancestors and the gods.

35 Peter BISSCHOP, during the second International Workshop on Early Tantra, July 2009, Pondicherry, whilst presenting a paper on 'Purāṇic Topography in the Niśvāsa', suggested that this location may have had some connection with the Pāśupatas.

36 During the 'Early Tantra' Workshop, July 2009, at Pondicherry, Peter BISSCHOP showed how the presentation of the *śrāddha*-rites listed in the *Matsyapurāṇa* (22.77) contains evidence for this hypothesis. Likewise, Peter BISSCHOP referred to the *Prabhāsakhandha* (3.53) of the *Skandapurāṇa*, as well as to extracts from the *Viṣṇudharma* (36.13) professing Kardamāla to be a pilgrimage site consecrated especially for Viṣṇu's incarnation as a boar (*varāha*). Following Peter BISSCHOP's lead, we have found, moreover, that the same connection between Kardamāla and the *varāha*-incarnation of Viṣṇu is made in the *Padmapurāṇa* (170.6,7,10). This indicates that Kardamāla—about which little else is known—must have been a significant place of pilgrimage for both Vaiṣṇavites and Śaivas. In the *Nāradapurāṇa*, Kardamāla appears in two distinct contexts: (a) as a pilgrimage site of Śaiva interest (2.70:79 and 1.104:189); (b) as a place for performing the ancestral (*śrāddha*) rites (2.47:38). The

Let us investigate, somewhat more closely, the list of forty pilgrimage sites briefly referred to above. These are known as the *pañcāṣṭaka*, "the group of five ogdoads".[37] In all likelihood, the *Niśvāsamukha* simply adopted this list of 'five sets of eight' *pañcāṣṭaka* from an earlier source,[38] in which case its own origin need not have anything to do with the list. We cannot, thus, take the list as evidence to locate the origin of the text. In addition, we encounter a list of rivers in *Niśvāsamukha* 3.2–8. This list also cannot be taken as evidence for the location of the origin of the text, as the *Niśvāsamukha* once again may have borrowed it from some earlier source, since lists of rivers appear in a vast range of texts.

The Prākṛtic words in the text might serve as a further, although limited, indicator of its origin. The text uses Prākṛtic vowels, such as *sāyojya* for *sāyujya*, in many a case.[39] Similarly, it records a further Prākṛtic vowel, *vāgeśyām* for *vāgīśvaryām* in 4.95a and 4.126c. There are some more conspicuous instances of Prākṛtic influence in the *Niśvāsamukha*. For example, the omission of the final *t* in optatives; and word formations particular to the language, for example *catālīśa*.[40] Such Prākṛtic forms once again invite the conclusion that the language employed in these instances is more likely indicative of a northern than a southern origin.[41] If the text had a more southern origin, we would expect other characteristic types of deviations from standard Sanskrit: masculine nouns, for instance, might be treated as neuter in gender; Prākṛtisms like *catālīśa* would be rare. Prākṛitic phonetic shifts are much less likely to be found in the non-standard Sanskrit written in Dravidian-language-speaking areas, in which Prākṛits were not spoken. All in all, we can conclude that a North Indian origin of the text appears most plausible.

Dating of the Text

The dating of the *Niśvāsamukha* remains an open question, since the sole manuscript of the *Niśvāsatattvasaṃhitā* to survive has been copied from an

śrāddha-context, as noted above, has been traced already by Peter BISSCHOP in the *Matsyapurāṇa*.

37 Literally 'five [sets] of eight', the term has been translated as "the group of five ogdoads" by GOODALL (2004: 15, fn. 617). For a detailed treatment on the *pañcāṣṭaka* see GOODALL 2004: 315, BISSCHOP 2006: 27–37 and TAK2 s.v. *guhyāṣṭaka*.

38 Despite our best efforts, we have not, as of yet, been able to trace the exact source.

39 i.e. 1.41d, 1.79c, 1.79a, 1.83a, 1.86c, 1.89d, 1.91a, 1.94c, 1.96b, 1.99b, 2.18c, 3.29a, 3.86d, 3.145c, 3.150c, 3.191b and 4.87d.

40 See the footnote on verse 4.107 for the form *catālīśa*.

41 See also GOODALL et al. 2015: 72–73.

unknown source in 9th-century Nepal. Although the manuscript is not dated, the script used to write it, 'Licchavi', is characteristic of the 9th century.[42] This provides us with a workable *terminus ante quem.* We note two instances where blank spaces purposefully feature in the manuscript—presumably in places where letters in the source-manuscript had become illegible or were missing to begin with.[43] If these gaps indeed reflect damage to the exemplar, this would mean that the scribe of the extant manuscript was working from a manuscript that was already worn—and therefore, most likely, not of recent origin.

GOODALL et al. (2015: 474) mention the possibility that the scribe of the manuscript failed to copy at least one folio of the source text. Were this indeed the case, this state of affairs would show that the manuscript we presently have recourse to is not the autograph, but a later witness. In other words, this would lead us to suppose that there existed at least one manuscript before the present one. This leads us to recalibrate the *terminus ante quem* of the original and settle it in the somewhat more distant past, and yet it is not possible to discern how much older the autograph would have been than the extant, 9th-century source that forms the basis of this study.

The dating of the other books of the *Niśvāsatattvasaṃhitā*, also, might serve as a valuable indicator for the time-frame of the *Niśvāsamukha*'s composition. GOODALL assumes that the whole corpus of the *Niśvāsa* was in all likelihood composed between the middle of the 5th and end of the 7th century. Hence for GOODALL et al (2015: 35), the text

> ... begins ... with the *Mūlasūtra* (c. 450-550 AD) and is completed with the *Niśvāsamukha* and *Guhyasūtra* probably by the end of the 7th century. The pointers may be broadly grouped under the (partially overlapping) heads of palaeography; iconography; terminology; theology; social religion; and intertextuality (allusion within the *Niśvāsa* to other literature and allusions in other literature to the *Niśvāsa*).

BAKKER (2014: 9), however, prior to having had the possibility of consulting GOODALL et al.'s completed edition, expressed doubts about GOODALL's dating of the *Mūlasūtra*, and instead believed it to be a century younger.

---

[42] See GOODALL et al. 2015: 103 ff. For more details, see the discussion of the manuscript of the *Niśvāsa*, p. 142 ff. below.

[43] These are fol. 50^v, line 4 and fol. 52^r, line 4.

He voiced the possibility that the *Mūlasūtra* and the *Skandapurāṇa* might have evolved in the same period.

However, at present, these deliberations contribute only in minor ways to our quest for the likely time-frame of the date of composition of the *Niśvāsamukha*. Had it been possible to establish the direction of borrowing between the *Guhyasūtra* and the *Niśvāsamukha*, we could have dated the *Niśvāsamukha* more precisely. Since evidence suggests[44] that the passage on the pilgrimage site of Kedāra, as rendered in the *Guhyasūtra* and the *Niśvāsamukha*, has very likely been composed by the same person, we can at least state that these two portions of text might have been composed at around the same time.

There are some parallels shared by the *Niśvāsamukha* and Purāṇic sources. For example, *Niśvāsamukha* 1.2ab (*aṣṭāśītisahasrāṇi ṛṣīṇām ūrdhvaretasām*) is paralleled in the *Brahmāṇḍapurāṇa* (1.7:180ab and 1.21:170cd) and the *Viṣṇupurāṇa* (1.6:36ab). Similarly, *Niśvāsamukha* 1.126c–127b (*bukasya karavīrasya arkkasyonmattakasya ca* || *caturṇṇāṃ puṣpajātīnāṃ sarvam āghrāti śaṅkaraḥ* |) is almost an exact parallel of *Skandapurāṇa* 28.31abcd (*caturṇāṃ puṣpajātīnāṃ gandham āghrāti śaṃkaraḥ* || *arkasya karavīrasya bilvasya ca bukasya ca* |). *Niśvāsamukha* 1.71ab (*śataṃ sanmārjane puṇyaṃ sahasram upalepane*) is closely paralleled by *Skandapurāṇa* 27.24ab (*saṃmārjanaṃ pañcaśataṃ sahasram upalepanam*). Although the first *pāda* is slightly different, we have found *sahasram upalepane*/*sahasram upalepanam* nowhere else except in these two texts and the *Śivadharmasaṅgraha*, which is known to have borrowed from the *Niśvāsamukha*.

It transpires that the parallels between the *Niśvāsamukha* and Purāṇic sources could help shed light on this issue if we could determine the direction of borrowing. With a clear indication of the definite source from which borrowing occurred yet missing, we cannot ascertain whether these verses were extracted from a shared, third source, or whether they found their way into the *Niśvāsamukha* and the Purāṇas by dint of having been widely current, ubiquitously recited verses that had no obvious singular source. Be that as it may, the *Niśvāsamukha*'s connection with these old Purāṇic sources may testify to the antiquity of the *Niśvāsamukha* if we are somehow able to substantiate an argument of contemporaneity—yet for this, we would need further corroborative evidence. Since we can neither ascertain the direction of borrowing of textual parallels, nor therefore the relative antiquity of the

---

44 The reader here is referred also to indicators presented on p. 73 ff.

Niśvāsamukha, it would be ambitious to hypothesise about the absolute date of the *Niśvāsamukha* based on the above evidence alone.

There is, however, one important case of overlapping material in which the direction of borrowing can be determined. We have noted (pp. 101 ff.) that chapters 5–9 of the *Śivadharmasaṅgraha* and the text of the *Niśvāsamukha*[45] are closely related. Having examined this relation in greater detail, we have concluded that the *Śivadharmasaṅgraha* has been composed after the *Niśvāsamukha*, as we will explain below. A. K. ACHARYA, in a recent study (2009: 91) places the date of the *Śivadharmasaṅgraha* between the 9th and 10th centuries. This establishes that the pre-9th *Niśvāsamukha* predates the *Śivadharmasaṅgraha*.[46]

Another important locus of investigation is the *Pāśupatasūtra*, not least because the *Niśvāsamukha* (4.70c–88) paraphrases substantial sections of the work—which *ipso facto* must precede the *Niśvāsamukha*. If it could be established that Kauṇḍinya's commentary on the *Pāśupatasūtra* had any direct or indirect bearing on the *Niśvāsamukha*, a more precise dating would be possible. As we shall see in the course of this study,[47] there is indeed a considerable amount of additional information in the Pāśupata-section of the *Niśvāsamukha* to complement the content of the *Pāśupatasūtra*. Yet we cannot discern any manifest influence of Kauṇḍinya's 6th-century commentary to the *Pāśupatasūtra* reflected in these textual passages. One occasionally encounters borrowings from the *Manusmṛti*, both in the *Niśvāsamukha*'s Vedic section (4.2–41), which borrows from the third chapter of the *Manusmṛti*, and in the third chapter of the Laukika section of the *Niśvāsamukha*, where borrowings from Manu's chapters 2, 3, and 11 are traceable.[48]

Since OLIVELLE (2005: 24–25 ff.), on the basis of textual, historical, and numismatic evidence, dates the *Manusmṛti* to the 2nd–3rd century CE, his findings serve as a dependable *terminus post quem* for the dating of the *Niśvāsamukha*.

Let us scrutinize another relevant piece of evidence that is worthwhile investigating. It is likely that the *Svacchandatantra* was redacted after the *Niśvāsa* corpus, for the former borrows a large amount of text from the latter.[49] For example, SANDERSON (2006: 160), commenting on the account of Atimārga in the *Svacchandatantra*, writes,

---

45 The introductory part of the first chapter and the section on Ādhyātmika and Atimārga (i.e. after verse 4.41) are not attested to in the *Śivadharmasaṅgraha*.

46 See p. 29.

47 Refer to p. 82.

48 The Laukika section spans the first three chapters of the *Niśvāsamukha*.

49 See SANDERSON (2006: 160 ff.).

> ... I propose that this explanation of the term Atimārga is not that of the *Svacchanda* itself, and that on the contrary his source exactly confirms the use of the *Niśvāsamukha*. This conclusion rests on *Svacchanda* 11.179c–184.

More recently (2009: 50), SANDERSON argued the following:

> it is clear in my view that the *Svacchandatantra* was redacted after the formation of the *Niśvāsa* corpus, the *Tantrasadbhāva* after the *Svacchanda*, the *Kubjikāmatatantra* after the *Tantrasadbhāva*, the hexad of the *Jayadrathayāmala* after the *Kubjikāmatatantra*, and the remaining three hexads after the first.

On the basis of SANDERSON's arguments, it is evident that the *Niśvāsamukha* was composed before the *Svacchandatantra*. Since the date of the *Svacchandatantra* is an open question, the exact dating of the *Niśvāsamukha* remains a complicated issue, as pointed out by GOODALL et al. (2015: 22):

> More problematic is the relative date of the *Niśvāsamukha* in the corpus. Being professedly an introduction, it presupposes the existence of at least one *sūtra* for it to introduce, but because it does not discuss the subject matter of the *sūtras*, it is difficult to judge whether or not it was written when all of them were already in existence and constituted together a *Niśvāsatattvasaṃhitā*.

In the end, we agree with the proposition of GOODALL et al. (2015: 35) that the *Niśvāsamukha* was redacted before the 8th century, probably some time during the seventh century. The precise date of the text, however, still needs further investigation.

The Title of the Work

Exactly what is meant by the title of the work *Niśvāsamukhatattvasaṃhitā* is difficult to assess clearly. Let us begin by trying to understand the meaning of the name *Niśvāsatattvasaṃhitā*, which is given as the title for the other four books of the *Niśvāsa* in the respective chapter colophons. This title seems to be less problematic in terms of the meaning concerned.

The *Uttarasūtra* (5.50–51) provides us with the etymology (*nirvacana*) of the *Niśvāsa* as follows:

> *anadhītyatha niśvāsaṃ niśvasanti punaḥ punaḥ |*
> *adhītvā caiva niśvāsan na punar nniśvasanti te ||*
> *niśvāsa eva vikhyātas sarvatantrasamuccayaḥ |*
> *yaṃ jñātvā mucyate jantuḥ saṃsārabhavabandhanāt ||*
>
> Now ('*tha*) those who do not study the *Niśvāsa* will go on sighing and sighing. And those who do study the *Niśvāsa*, they will not sigh again. [For this reason] it is known as the *Niśvāsa*, the compendium of all Tantras, on knowing which a creature will be released from the bondage of being in *saṃsāra*. GOODALL et al. (2015: 400)

On the basis of this passage we may render the title of the work as 'compendium (*saṃhitā*) of the essence (*tattva*) of sighing (*niśvāsa*).' The same work (5.53) uses the term *saṃhitā* to refer to the twenty-eight scriptures of the Śaiva canon:[50]

> *aṣṭāviṃśati yā proktā* ***saṃhitāḥ*** *parameṣṭhinā |*
> *teṣāṃ vyākhyā tu karttavyā upariṣṭāt samantataḥ ||*
>
> Of the twenty-eight scriptures taught by the Supreme One commentary will have to be offered (*kartavyā*) later (*upariṣṭāt*) in full (*samantataḥ*). GOODALL et al. (2015: 400)

In the *Mūlasūtra* (8.10), we come across the term *tattvasaṃhitā*, where it refers to this particular work:

> *adhyāpayitvā etaṃ tu* ***tattvasaṃhitam*** *uttamam |*
> *buddhvā bhaktimayaṃ śiṣyam ācāryatve niyojayet ||*
>
> Having taught him this supreme *tattvasaṃhitā*, if he realises that his disciple is full of devotion, he may appoint him as an *ācārya*. GOODALL et al. (2015: 330)

The same *sūtra* once again uses the same term in the same way in 8.20:

> *samyag eṣa samākhyāto* ***tattvasaṃhita-m-****uttamaḥ |*
> *sagotrā eva mucyante yasya lekhye 'pi tiṣṭhati ||*

50 In the consecutive verse (5.54), this book, on its own, is identified as the *Niśvāsottarasaṃhitā*. It appears that the term here is likewise employed to refer to a tantric text rather than to a compendium of any kind—after all, it is referring to a single work: *śate dve daśa ślokānāṃ* ***niśvāsottarasaṃhitā*** *| ekaviṃśatkulān devi adhītya hy uddhariṣyati |*.

> This supreme *tattvasaṃhitā* has been fully taught. All the members of one's *gotra* are liberated if one has it even [only] in [the form of] a manuscript. GOODALL et al. (2015: 335)

In the *Guhyasūtra* (1.4) the compound ***tattvasaṃhitā*** does not feature; however the shorter term *saṃhitā* is used in congruence with the above connotations.[51] It hence appears that these phrases feature in somewhat interchangeable contexts, which would downgrade the indicative significance of the component *tattva*; the omission of *tattva* appears to be attributable to metrical demands of versification. Furthermore, the use of the term *tattvasaṃhitā* to refer to a Śaiva tantra is also attested by Hṛdayaśiva in a passage copied from the *Mṛgendratantra*, where he refers to the text as the *Mṛgendratattvasaṃhitā*.[52] This suggests that in a Śaiva context, both words, namely *tattvasaṃhitā* and *saṃhitā*, may refer to a work of tantric nature. Taken in that sense, the conjunction of either term with the word *niśvāsa*—which means 'sighing'—could impel us to render the phrase *Niśvāsatattvasaṃhitā* as 'tantra of sighing'. In other words, it may refer to a tantra that originated from the sighing of Śiva, that is to say, a tantra that originated from the *speech* of Śiva.

At first blush, it seemed tricky to analyse *Niśvāsamukhatattvasaṃhitā*, which might look as though it were intended to mean 'compendium (*saṃhitā*) of the essence (*tattva*) of the sighing (*niśvāsa*) face (*mukha*)'. But since it is the first book in the manuscript-compendium, it would be reasonable for it be referred to as the 'face' of the *Niśvāsatattvasaṃhitā*. For that sense, one might perhaps have expected instead the order *niśvāsa-tattvasaṃhitā-mukha*. But now that we know that *saṃhitā* and *tattvasaṃhitā* can be used interchangeably to refer to a 'scripture', we can mentally remove *tattvasaṃhitā* and understand *Niśvāsamukha* to mean 'the [pre]face to the Niśvāsa'. We therefore follow SANDERSON (2006) in frequently referring to the book as the *Niśvāsamukha*. A complete translation of the complete title *Niśvāsamukhatattvasaṃhitā* might be 'the scripture that is the [pre]face to the [scripture called the] Sigh'.

---

51 For the full quotation and translation, the reader is referred to p. 35.

52 Cambridge University Library, Add. 2833, folio. 65^{v}3–4: *mṛgeṃdratat[t]vasaṃhitāyāṃ prāyaścittaṃ likhyate*; fol. 67^{v}4–5: *iti mṛgendratat[t]vasaṃhitāyāṃ prāyaścittapaṭalam iti* |.

The position of the *Niśvāsamukha* in the corpus of the *Niśvāsa*

Delving further into the question regarding the *Niśvāsamukha*'s identity vis-à-vis the *Niśvāsatattvasaṃhitā*, the following passage of the *Guhyasūtra* (1.1–5b) indicates that its author regards the *Niśvāsamukha* as an independent text in itself:

> *upariṣṭāc caturthan tu sūtram ārabhyate punaḥ* |
> *tatra sūtratrayaṃ proktaṃ boddhavyam anupūrvaśaḥ* ||
> *mūlañ cottarasūtraṃ* [[((*ca nayasūtraṃ tathaiva*))]] *ca* |
> *guhyasūtrañ caturthan tu procyamānaṃ nibodha me* ||
> *tenaiva saha saṃyuktā saṃhitaikā prapaṭhyate* | [53]
> *niśvāseti ca nāmena*[54] *sampūrṇṇā tu tato bhavet* || [55]
> *niśvāsasaṃhitā hy eṣā mukhena saha saṃyutā* |
> *pañcasrotās tu ye proktā mukhena parikīrtitāḥ* ||
> *tena yuktā bhavet puṣṭā sarvasūtreṣu paṭhyate* |

> Now (*punaḥ*) below (*upariṣṭāt*) begins the fourth *sūtra*. Among those [*sūtras*], it should be understood that three have been taught in order: the *Mūla*, the *Uttarasūtra* and the *Nayasūtra*. Hear from me the *Guhyasūtra*, the fourth, being taught. Joined with that [*sūtra*], one *saṃhitā* is promulgated: it then becomes complete, [known] by the name *Niśvāsa*. This, joined with the *Mukha*, is the *Niśvāsasaṃhitā*. The Five Streams that are spoken of are proclaimed by the *Mukha*. Joined with that, it becomes full: [the full *saṃhitā*] is taught in all [these] *sūtras*.[56] (GOODALL et al. 2015: 21)

The above-quoted passage indicates that the *Mūlasūtra*, *Uttarasūtra* and *Nayasūtra* are the first three *sūtras*. The extract, moreover, informs us that the fourth *sūtra* is the *Guhyasūtra*. We can therefore safely assume that the former three were already in existence by the time the *Guhyasūtra* was

---

53 prapaṭhyate] NK; prapadhyate W.

54 niśvāseti ca nāmena] NW; niḥśvāseti nāmena K.

55 sampūrṇṇā tu tato bhavet] NWK^{pc}; sampūrṇṇāṃ ca tato bhavet K^{ac}.

56 Given the cryptic nature of the above passage and the lack of further comparative materials, the translation quoted here should be regarded as tentative.

composed.[57] This in turn suggests that the *Guhyasūtra* is the fourth book also with regards to the date of its composition.[58] In fact, in the section cited above, the term *anupūrvaśaḥ*, 'in due order', appears to be implying the relative chronology of the first three *sūtras*. The text mentions that the *Niśvāsa* is 'complete' (*saṃpūrṇā*), provided these four *sūtras* are joined. Note that the text neither refers to the *Mukha* (i.e. the *Niśvāsamukha*) as a *sūtra*, nor even as the fifth text of the compendium. It merely mentions that the compendium becomes enriched, literally 'nourished' (*puṣṭa*), if consulted in conjunction with the *Mukha*. Therefore, perhaps, we should understand that the *Mukha* is somehow related to all the *sūtras* while at the same time remaining an independent treatise.

Moreover, *Guhyasūtra* 18.15 tacitly suggests a separate identity for the *Niśvāsamukha*. It refers to the *Kārikā* (i.e. the *Niśvāsakārikā*) as the fifth *sūtra*, without, however, classifying the *Niśvāsamukha* as belonging to the same category:

> *catvāro*[59] *kathitā sūtrā samukhādyā varānane* |
> *pañcamaṃ tu paraṃ*[60] *sūtraṃ kārikā nāma nāmataḥ* ||
>
> The four *sūtras* have been taught, the *Mukha* being [their] beginning, o lovely-faced lady! The fifth is the highest *sūtra*, called *Kārikā* by name.

In addition, the post-colophon statement of the *Niśvāsatattvasaṃhitā* supports our assumption of a separate identity of the *Niśvāsamukha*. The post-colophon counts only the number of verses of the four *sūtras* and explicitly refers to the collection as a group of four. It thereby excludes the *Niśvāsamukha*: *asmin sūtracatuṣṭaye sahasracatuṣṭayaṃ ślokaṃ śatāni*

57 GOODALL et al. (2015: 22) advance an altogether dependable theory concerning the relative chronology of the *Niśvāsa*-corpus in stating that

> We are ... confident that the *Mūlasūtra* was followed by the *Uttarasūtra*, which was followed by the *Nayasūtra*, which was in turn followed by the *Guhyasūtra*, exactly the order in which those works are transmitted in the manuscript.

58 It hence seems plausible to assume that the phrase *tatra sūtratrayaṃ proktaṃ boddhavyam anupūrvaśaḥ* indicates that one should understand the chronology of these three texts in due order: first, the *Mūlasūtra*, second the *Uttarasūtra*, and third the *Nayasūtra*. The fourth *sūtra*, the *Guhyasūtra*, in conjunction with the previous three texts comprise a compendium that is referred to as the *Niśvāsa*.

59 catvāro] NW; catvāro(ḥ) K

60 pañcamaṃ tu paraṃ] K; pañcaman tu para NW

pañca ca iti |, 'in this fourfold collection *sūtras* there are four thousand and five hundred verses.' The stated number roughly matches the total sum of verses of these four *sūtras*, thereby providing further textual evidence for an originally separate, though eventually associated identity of the *Niśvāsamukha*. Had the *Niśvāsamukha*'s verses been included in the verse-number counted by the scribe, the numbering would have easily exceeded five thousand.[61]

The theory attesting an originally separate identity to the *Niśvāsamukha* gains further momentum if we consider the textual evidence provided by the colophons and chapter-colophons of the relevant witnesses. There is a substantial difference between the chapter-colophons of the *Niśvāsamukha* and the colophons to the other books of the *Niśvāsa*-corpus, and we shall therefore present these separately. The first chapter's colophon contains the phrase *laukike dharme* 'worldly religion'; the second and third reduce this segment to the term *laukike* 'worldly'; the fourth chapter colophon contains neither of these two expressions, since it does not treat worldly religion. Each begins with the phrase *iti niśvāsamukhatattvasaṃhitāyāṃ*, providing clear evidence that all four chapters have been regarded as belonging to a work entitled ***Niśvāsamukhatattvasaṃhitā***. Here are the chapter colophons of the *Niśvāsamukha* in full:

- *iti niśvāsamukhatattvasaṃhitāyāṃ laukike dharmme prathamaḥ paṭalaḥ* |.
- *iti niśvāsamukhatattvasaṃhitāyāṃ laukike dvitīyaḥ paṭalaḥ* |.
- *iti niśvāsamukhatattvasaṃhitāyāṃ laukike tṛtīyaḥ paṭalaḥ* |.
- *iti niśvāsamukhatattvasaṃhitāyāṃ caturthaḥ paṭalaḥ* |.

The colophons of the other four books of the *Niśvāsa*, however, differ both by way of formulation and classification of its referent text. In particular, these are the colophons of the first chapters of the *Mūlasūtra*, *Uttarasūtra*, *Nayasūtra* and *Guhyasūtra*. Note that these colophons categorize those works as separate *sūtras*, together comprising the *Niśvāsatattvasaṃhitā*:[62]

61 Note that the *Niśvāsamukha* contains roughly 640 verses in total, extending over four chapters.

62 The complete colophon at the end of the first chapter of the *Mūlasūtra* in fact reads: *iti niśvāsatatvasaṃhitāyāṃ mūlasūtre prathamaḥ paṭalaḥ ślo* [sic] 23 'thus is the first chapter of the *Mūlasūtra* in the *Niśvāsatattvasaṃhitā*', followed by the number of verses. The second chapter colophon of the *Mūlasūtra*, however, runs: *iti mūlasūtre dvitīyaḥ paṭalaḥ* 'thus is the second chapter of the *Mūlasūtra*.' This is also the way the

- *iti niśvāsatatvasaṃhitāyāṃ mūlasūtre prathamaḥ paṭalaḥ* | .
- *iti niśvāsatattvasaṃhitāyām uttarasūtre prathamaḥ paṭalaḥ* | .
- *iti niśvāsatattvasaṃhitāyāṃ nayasūtre pāśaprakaraṇaṃ prathamaḥ paṭalaḥ* | .
- *iti niśvāsatattvasaṃhitāyāṃ*[63] *guhyasūtre prathamaḥ paṭalaḥ* | .

As regards the most fundamental difference, the chapter-colophons of the *Niśvāsamukha* do not associate the *Niśvāsamukha* with the ***Niśvāsatattvasaṃhitā*** as closely as the colophons of the remaining four books associate their respective 'parent'-work with the compendium. This is indicative of a basic discrepancy between the textual histories of the *Mūlasūtra*, *Uttarasūtra*, *Nayasūtra*, and *Guhyasūtra* on the one hand, and the *Niśvāsamukha* on the other—at least as regards their respective history *before* their conjunction as constitutive elements of the compendium.

Note that the chapter-colophons of the *Niśvāsamukha* state that the work professedly belongs to the ***Niśvāsamukhatattvasaṃhitā*** whereas the remaining four books in their colophons attest to belong to the ***Niśvāsatattvasaṃhitā***.

Secondly, the colophons of the *Niśvāsamukha* do not identify their referent text as an exponent of the *sūtra*-genre, whereas the colophons of the other four books do. Textual evidence shows that the term *sūtra* features in reference to titles of some of the works pertaining to the Mantramārga, such as the *Rauravasūtrasaṅgraha* or the *Svāyaṃbhuvasūtrasaṅgraha*. This, in turn, suggests that the term *sūtra*, as it features in the colophons of the four books of the *Niśvāsa*, might possibly serve to identify the latter as a tantric text. The chapter colophons of the *Niśvāsamukha*, by contrast, refer to the latter as the ***Niśvāsamukhatattvasaṃhitā***.

In deliberately refraining from employing the term '*sūtra*' in the titular compound, they fortify our conception regarding the identity of the *Niśvāsamukha* as distinct from the other books of the *Niśvāsa*. Whereas the latter is identified as tantric material, the *Niśvāsamukha* remains exoteric in nature.

colophons of the *Uttarasūtra*, *Nayasūtra*, and *Guhyasūtra* appear in our manuscript. In other words, the first colophon of each of these books appears in its complete form, including the name of the compendium, the *Niśvāsatattvasaṃhitā*, while in the succeeding colophons this name is not mentioned, the chapter names appearing directly in the locative: °*sūtre ... paṭalaḥ*.

63 iti niśvāsatattvasaṃhitāyāṃ] NW; iti śrīniḥśvāsatattvasaṃhitāyāṃ K

The term *svargāpavarga* is a brahmanical term[64] particular to the mode of expression in the *Niśvāsamukha* (1.52, 4.1); this becomes especially clear when contrasted with the remaining works of the *Niśvāsatattvasaṃhitā*. The first three books, the *Mūlasūtra*, *Uttarasūtra*, and *Nayasūtra* do not use this term. However, it appears once in conjunction with *niraya* ('hell') at *Guhyasūtra* 6.14 to describe the 'sphere of actions' (*karmabhūmi*). This may suggest that this term was not a distinctly Mantramārgic term. The unique term *svargāpavarga* appears to reflect and reinforce the distinct nature of the *Niśvāsamukha*, and emphasises its historical genesis as a work of probably separate origin.

The *Niśvāsamukha*'s introduction of the Mantramārga through the 'Five Streams'

As the 'face' of the compendium, the *Niśvāsamukha* heralds the Five Streams of (supra)mundane knowledge. In doing so, it recapitulates appropriated exoteric systems. At the same time, it announces the distinguishing features of the Mantramārga as supreme path of practice (to be expounded in the ensuing volumes of the *Niśvāsatattvasaṃhitā*).

The concept of the Five Streams (*pañca srotāḥ*) is hence figuratively correlated both (1) to the five faces of Śiva as source and authority over the tenet-systems expounded, as well as (2) to the tenet-systems themselves. Therefore the *pañca srotāḥ* are instrumental in structuring the philosophical and religious systems presented in the *Niśvāsamukha* (1.26–27a) by means of the following five-fold taxonomy:

> *nandikeśvara uvāca* |
> *śṛṇvantu ṛṣayas sarve pañcadhā yat prakīrtitam* |
> *laukikaṃ vaidikañ caiva tathādhyātmikam eva ca* |
> *a[[timārgaṃ ca mantrākhyaṃ]]* --- |
>
> Nandikeśvara said: all you sages, listen to that which is said to be five-fold: [1] worldly (*laukikam*), [2] Vedic (*vaidikam*), [3] relating to the soul (*ādhyātmikam*), [4] transcendent (*atimārgam*), and [5] Mantra (*mantrākhyam*) [...].

The Laukika stream, as depicted in later passages of the *Niśvāsamukha*, springs from the western face, Sadyojāta, (3.196cd); the Vaidika originates

[64] The term is employed in these and other brahmanical textual sources: *Viṣṇupurāṇa* 1.6.10; *Brahmāṇḍapurāṇa* 1.16.15 and *Bhāgavatapurāṇa* 4.24.37.

from the northern face, Vāmadeva, (4.41); the Ādhyātmika flows forth from the southern face, Aghora, (4.42); the Atimārga issues forth from the eastern face, Tatpuruṣa, (4.131cd); and finally the Mantramārga is emitted from the upper face, Īśāna (4.135).

The account of the *Niśvāsamukha* is special in that it is comparatively elaborate, as we shall find in the following in-depth presentation of the four exoteric, preliminary streams:[65]

1. **The Laukika dharma**, as taught in the *Niśvāsamukha*, is framed and presented as a system of practice befitting uninitiated householders devoted to Śiva. It teaches this path of practice as follows:

   kūpavāpīgṛhodyāna --- |
   --- *tha maṇḍapāḥ* |
   dānatīrthopavāsāni vratāni niyamāni ca || 1.53
   bhakṣyābhakṣyaparīhārañ japahoman tathārcanam |
   jalāgnibhṛgupāto hi tathānaśanam eva ca || 1.54
   vidyamānanivṛttiś ca guruvṛddhābhipūjanam |
   laukikaṃ kathitaṃ hy etad | 1.55c

   [Attending to] wells, ponds, houses, gardens [[...]] [and] pavilions (*maṇḍapāḥ*), [making] donations, [going on] pilgrimages (*tīrtha*), fasting, [adhering to] religious observances and restraints; [eating] what may be eaten and avoiding what may not (*bhakṣyābhakṣyaparīhāram*); [engaging in] mantra recitations, sacrifices (*japahomam*) and worship; [committing suicide by] throwing oneself into water or fire or from a cliff; fasting, renouncing possessions (*vidyamānanivṛttiḥ*) and honouring teachers and aged people; this is what I have taught as *laukika*.

   As the above extract itself professes in its last line, this is what the *Niśvāsamukha* presents as a brief summary of Laukika dharma, which is more extensively presented in the ensuing chapters (1–3).

   The first chapter calls for the making of a water-fountain, lotus-pond, temple-garden, and the offering of a house; bathing a *liṅga* in milk, clarified butter, curds, and water; the offering of flowers, fragrant items, incense, clothing, ornaments, edibles, banners, mirrors, and

[65] The fifth stream, the Mantramārga, is mentioned, yet merely briefly alluded to, as we shall see in the ensuing sections.

awnings; the offering of lamps and umbrella(s), cows, goats, sheep, buffaloes, horses and elephants; the offering of servants and maids; the offering consisting in cleansing and besmearing a *liṅga*; the offering of singing, dancing, and playing a lute and other musical instruments in the vicinity of a *liṅga*; keeping vigil on the eighth and fourteenth days of the dark half of the month; fasting and taking refuge in Śiva. This chapter also records a tradition of offering a certain *muktimaṇḍapa* to Śiva (1.114c–115b). A *muktimaṇḍapa* as an object of offering is little known elsewhere.[66]

The second chapter calls for the making of a *liṅga* and installing it in a temple; constructing a temple and installing a figure of one of the following deities therein: Viṣṇu, Brahmā, Skanda, Rudrāṇī, Gaṇeśa, the mother goddesses, the Sun (conceived of as deity), Agni, Indra, Kubera, Vāyu, Dharma or Varuṇa; making a bridge; making a causeway on a muddy path; digging a water channel; making a hut, an abode or a pavilion; and giving different kinds of donations. A striking feature of this chapter is that its text provides us with material on traditions that are otherwise little known, or sometimes even not knowable through other sources at all. For instance, at 2.64, we come across a passage which records the practice of offering a woman. The text does not specify to whom the woman is to be offered, but the recipient is probably either a Brāhmin or Śiva, as the text constantly mentions these two recipients throughout.[67] If Śiva was the intended recipient here, then the text would allude to the practice of offering a Devadāsī, a [female] 'servant of god'. If a Brāhmin was intended as recipient, this would be unusual practice. However, because the text proceeds (2.65) with the offering of lovemaking with beautiful women —presented as a physical and not a symbolic act —,[68] this also does not seem impossible. Whoever the intended recipient may have been, and whether or not the text is recording an actual practice, this custom is not known to us from other sources. The text teaches the worship of Kāmadeva (3.142c–146) on the thirteenth day of a fortnight. Although, the worship of Kāmadeva is not unknown,[69] the emphasis on his worship among other major gods, such as Brahmā, Viṣṇu and Śiva,

66 See 1.114c–115b and our annotation thereon (p. 265).

67 On one occasion the text (2.117 ff.) mentions other recipients too, but it does so while presenting a stratified hierarchy of recipients.

68 To wit: *ratisatran tu satataṃ varanārīṣu dāpayet.*

69 See BENTON 2006.94.

considerably elevates the status of the deity Kāmadeva. This suggests that the place of Kāmadeva as a divinity to be worshipped was relatively lofty during this period, or at least in the specific milieu where the text originated.

The third chapter, for its part, calls for the following: bathing in prescribed rivers or lakes; committing suicide in a river or in a fire; going on pilgrimage to places sacred to Śiva; and to those sacred to Viṣṇu; upholding observances; following procedures[70] for fasting and performing worship of Śiva and other deities that are perceived through a lens of individually assigned, and differing, degrees of worthiness;[71] each of these has a particular day of the lunar fortnight dedicated to their worship.[72] The text informs us about various appropriate offerings such as a golden carriage, a weapon, or an emblem of each

[70] These procedures are observed during both halves of a month for the duration of one year.

[71] These deities (or deified beings) are Brahmā, Agni, Kubera, Gaṇeśa, the Nāgas, Skanda, the Sun, Śiva, Mahādevī, Yama, Dharma, Keśava, Kāmadeva, Śiva (a second time) and one's ancestors.

[72] Twelve names are to be used for each of these deities during twelve months, starting from Mārgaśīrṣa to Kārttika for each fortnight on their respective *tithis*. In the case of some deities, the number of names does not match twelve (Agni, the Nāgas, Yama). We present here the names as attested in the text:

- Brahmā: [1] Brahmā, [2] Svayambhū, [3] Viriñci, [4] Padmayoni, [5] Prajāpati, [6] Caturmukha, [7] Padmahasta, [8] Oṃkārākṣara, [9] Caturvedadhara, [10] Sraṣṭṛ, [11] Gīrvāṇa, and [12] Parameṣṭhin.
- Agni: [1] Vaiśvānara, [2] Jātavedas, [3] Hutabhuk, [4] Havyavāhana, [5] Devavaktra, [6] Sarvabhakṣa, [7] Ghṛṇin, [8] Jagadāhaka, [9] Vibhāvasu and [10] Saptajihva. *Since* Agni *is to be worshipped throughout the year, one form per month, the listing lacks two names.*
- Kubera: [1] Dhanada, [2] Yakṣapati, [3] Vitteśa, [4] Nidhipālaka, [5] Rākṣasādhipati, [6] Piṅgalākṣa, [7] Vimānaga, [8] Rudrasakhā, [9] Kubera, [10] Paulastyakulanandana, [11] Lokapāleśvara, and [12] Yakṣendra.
- Gaṇeśa: [1] Vighneśvara, [2] Gaṇapati, [3] Ekadanta, [4] Gajānana, [5] Gajakarṇa, [6] Tryakṣa [7] Nāgayajñopavītin, [8] Caturbhuja, [9] Dhūmrākṣa, [10] Vajratuṇḍa, [11] Vināyaka, and [12] Mahodara.
- The Nāgas: [1] Ananta, [2] Vāsuki, [3] Takṣaka, [4] Trirekhin, [5] Padma, [6] Mahābja, [7] Śaṅkha, and [8] Kulika.
- Skanda: [1] Viśākha, [2] Trivarṇa, [3] Umānanda, [4] Agnigarbhaja, [5] Gaṅgāgarbha, [6] Śaradgarbha, [7] Kṛttikāsuta, [8] Ṣaṇmukha, [9] Śaktihasta, [10] Mayūravāhana, [11] Pañcachaṭa, and [12] Kumāra.
- Sun: [1] Āditya, [2] Savitṛ, [3] Sūrya, [4] Khaga, [5] Pūṣan, [6] Gabhastimat, [7] Hiraṇyagarbha, [8] Triśiras, [9] Tapana, [10] Bhāskara, [11] Ravi, and [12] Jagannetra.

deity with that deity's name engraved on it (see 3.160ff). It also records a custom of offering 'a golden man' (*puruṣa*) with the name of one's ancestor(s) on it on the new-moon and full-moon days (3.193–196). This injunction is not known from other sources.

Day of fortnight	Deity worshipped	Gift to be offered
Pratipad	Brahmā	golden lotus
Dvitīyā	Agni	golden goat
Tṛtīyā	Yakṣa	golden mace
Caturthī	Gaṇeśa	golden elephant
Pañcamī	Nāgas	golden lotus
Ṣaṣṭhī	Skanda	golden peacock
Saptamī	Āditya	golden horse
Aṣṭamī	Śaṅkara	[golden] bull
Navamī	Mahādevī	[golden] lion
Daśamī	Yama	[golden] buffalo
Ekādaśī	Dharma	[golden] bull
Dvādaśī	Viṣṇu	[golden] Garuḍa
Trayodaśī	Kāmadeva	golden bow
Caturdaśī	Pārameśvara	[golden] bull
Amāvaśī *and* Pūrṇimā	Pitṛs	golden man

Table 1: Deities, their days, and appropriate offerings

- Śiva: [1] Śaṅkara, [2] Devadeva, [3] Tryambaka, [4] Sthāṇu, [5] Hara, [6] Śiva, [7] Bhava, [8] Nīlakaṇṭha, [9] Piṅgala, [10] Rudra, [11] Īśāna, and [12] Ugra.
- Mahādevī: [1] Umā, [2] Kātyāyinī, [3] Durgā, [4] Rudrā, [5] Subhadrikā, [6] Kālarātrī, [7] Mahāgaurī, [8] Revatī, [9] Bhūtanāyikā, [10] Āryā, [11] Prakṛtirūpā, and [12] Gaṇanāyikā.
- Yama: [1] Yama, [2] Dharmaraja, [3] Mṛtyu, [4] Antaka, [5] Vaivasvata, [6] Kāla, [7] Sarvalokakṣaya, [8] Ugradaṇḍadhṛt, [9] Mahiṣāsanayāyin, [10] Śāsitṛ, and [11] Narakādhipati. *Since* Yama *is to be worshipped throughout the year, one form per month, the listing lacks one name.*
- Dharma: [1] Dharma, [2] Satya, [3] Dayā, [4] Kṣānti, [5] Śauca, [6] Ācāra, [7] Ahiṃsā, [8] Adambha, [9] Rakṣā, [10] Lokasākṣin, [11] Vṛṣabha, and [12] Adṛṣṭa.
- Viṣṇu: [1] Keśava, [2] Nārāyaṇa, [3] Mādhava, [4] Govinda, [5] Viṣṇu, [6] Madhusūdana, [7] Trivikrama, [8] Vāmana, [9] Śrīdhara, [10] Hṛṣīkeśa, [11] Padmanābha, and [12] Dāmodara.
- Kāmadeva: [1] Anaṅga, [2] Manmatha, [3] Kāma, [4] Īśvara, [5] Mohana, [6] Pañcabāṇa, [7] Dhanurhasta, [8] Unmāda, [9] Vaśaṃkara, [10] Ratipriya, [11] Prītikara, and [12] Hṛdayāpahārin.
- Śiva: [1] Hara, [2] Śarva, [3] Bhava, [4] Tryakṣa, [5] Śambhu, [6] Vibhu, [7] Śiva, [8] Sthāṇu, [9] Paśupati, [10] Rudra, [11] Īśāna, and [12] Śaṅkara.

The Kashmirian Saiddhāntika commentator Bhaṭṭa Nārāyaṇakaṇṭha[73] — and also the South Indian author of the *Mṛgendrapaddhatiṭīkā*[74] — seem to share the same understanding of Laukika dharma as constituting socially meritorious deeds. For Kṣemarāja, however, author of a non-dualist commentary on the *Svacchandatantra*, it carries a diversity of connotations and encompasses the following topics: (admissable modes of) livelihood; law; the art of government; Āyurveda; Dhanurveda etc.[75] The *Niśvāsamukha*'s understanding of Laukika dharma is different: as is clear from the above discussion, it is not presented merely as primarily comprising of socially meritorious deeds, nor does it embrace Āyurveda, Dhanurveda, and law.

2. ***Vaidika dharma*** outranks Laukika in the five-fold hierarchy presented in the *Niśvāsamukha* and pertains to the four *āśramas*.[76] The *Niśvāsamukha* (4.1–41) teaches that observing the prescriptions pertaining to the four life-stages results in a rebirth in the abode of Brahman.[77] Meanwhile, it should be noted that according to 4.24, a householder (*gṛhastha*) who merely performs rites, and does not cultivate *ātmadhyānam* (meditation on the Self) attains heaven only, which, technically speaking, counts as a 'worldly abode', since it belongs to the domain of *saṃsāra*—in that regard the fruits are identical to those of the practice of Laukika dharma.[78] SANDERSON (2006: 157) observes:

> The distinction between this and the Vaidika religion (*vaidiko dharmaḥ*) is that the latter is the practice of the celibate life-stages. It comes above the Mundane in the hierarchy of paths because we are told that while the Mundane leads only to heaven (*svargaḥ*), this may go beyond that transient reward to bestow [...] liberation.

---

73 See the commentary of Bhaṭṭa Nārāyaṇakaṇṭha on *Mṛgendrakriyāpāda* 8.79: *tatra laukikāni tāvat karmāṇi vāpikūpaprapādīni pūrtākhyāni* | .

74 T. 1021, pp. 217, line, 15: *kūpataṭākādikaraṇaṃ paraṃ pūrtam ucyate* | .

75 Kṣemarāja's commentary on *Svacchandatantra* 11.44: *laukikaṃ vārtādaṇḍanītyāyurvedadhanurvedanāṭyavedādipratipādyakṛṣinayānayacikitsādivijñānam* | .

76 *Niśvāsamukha* 1.55d: *vaidikaṃ cāturāśramam.*

77 *Niśvāsamukha* 4.39: *evaṃ yo varttate nityaṃ sa yāti brahmalaukikam* | *brahmaṇā saha modeta brahmaṇi sa tu līyate* || .

78 *Niśvāsamukha* 1.52cd: *laukikaṃ sampravakṣyāmi yena svargaṃ vrajanti te* | .

Bhaṭṭa Nārāyaṇakaṇṭha,[79] and the author of the *Mṛgendrapaddhati-ṭīkā*[80] see the Vaidika stream as being concerned primarily with *soma* sacrifices 'and the like' (*somasaṃsthādirūpāṇi*). This understanding—as noted above—differs considerably from that of the *Niśvāsamukha*. Kṣemarāja, again, reiterates the categories of *yajña* taught in (some of) the *Kalpasūtras*,[81] focussing on *nitya*, *naimittika* and *kāmya* sacrifices.[82]

3. **Ādhyātmika dharma** is understood as the teaching of Sāṅkhya and Yoga:

> *ādhyātmikaṃ pravakṣyāmi dakṣiṇāsyena kīrttitam* |
> *sāṃkhyañ caiva mahājñānaṃ yogañ cāpi mahāvrate* || 4.42 ||
>
> [Now] I will teach the [*dharma*] called *ādhyātmika* with [my] southern face: [namely] the great knowledge of Sāṅkhya and Yoga, o you who observe the *mahāvrata*.

Let us consider a noteworthy taxonomical irregularity: the classification of the teachings of the Sāṅkhya and Yoga as forming part of the Ādhyātmika system is unusual — all the more so since the Upaniṣads, conventionally hailed as pivotal exponents of the Ādhyātmika religion, curiously are not listed in the *Niśvāsamukha* as such. We do not, at present, have a ready explanation for this state of affairs. Medhātithi[83] and Kullūka,[84] commenting on a verse of the *Manusmṛti* (2.117) — which, as we shall see, is probably the original impetus for the development of the fivefold scheme of the *Niśvāsamukha* — understand Ādhyātmika in the conventional sense: for Medhātithi, it is the knowledge of *brahman*,[85] and for Kullūka, it is something related to the

---

79 In his commentary on *Mṛgendrakriyāpāda*, Nārāyaṇakaṇṭha writes (8.79): *āmnāyo vedaḥ* | *taduktāni tu karmāṇy api karmakṛcchrajanyāni somasaṃsthādirūpāṇi iṣṭa-śabdena prasiddhāni* | .

80 *Mṛgendrapaddhatiṭīkā* T. 1021, p. 217: *tat kṛcchraśabdena somasaṃsthādyātmakam iṣṭam ucyate* | .

81 This presentation is generally in line with the threefold classification found in Bhaṭṭa Nārāyaṇakaṇṭha's *Mṛgendratantra*, and the *Mṛgendrapaddhatiṭīkā*.

82 The commentary on *Svacchandatantra* 11.44: *vaidikaṃ nityanaimittikakāmyayajñādi-svarūpam* | .

83 See JHĀ (1932: 136).

84 See N. R. ACHARYA (1946: 58).

85 *ādhyātmikaṃ brahmajñānam* | .

Upaniṣadic knowledge of the Self.[86] Bhaṭṭa Nārāyaṇakaṇṭha[87] follows the orthodox interpretation in stating *abhisandhirūpāṇi vairāgyātmakāni* | . The interpretation of Nārāyaṇakaṇṭha is moreover echoed by the author of the *Mṛgendrapaddhatiṭīkā*,[88] and Kṣemarāja,[89]both of whom treat the term as referring to the teachings of Yoga and Sāṅkhya.

4. ***Atimārga*** refers to the Pāśupata system, which, in this text, is said to be twofold.[90] That is to say, it refers to Atyāśramins and Lokātītas.[91] The first section paraphrases the *Pāśupatasūtras* in a fully versified form. The second section teaches the observances of the Kapālavratins and provides a systematic account of Kāpālika cosmology.[92] SANDERSON (2006: 158) writes:

> ... the *Niśvāsamukha* holds it ([i.e. Atimārga]) to be of two kinds (*dviprakārakaḥ*). It outlines the first, which it calls 'the Observance of those beyond the Estates' (*Atyāśramavrata*) in a rendering of the enigmatic prose *Pāśupatasūtra* into verses that are clear (where they are not lacunose by dint of physical damage) and adds a small amount of information found neither in the Sūtras nor in Kauṇḍinya's commentary. The first level of the Atimārga, then, is that of the Pāñcārthikas. The remainder of the section on the Atimārga introduces us to a new form of devotion to Rudra, which it calls Kapālavrata ('the observance of the skull'), the Lokātītavrata ('the observance of those beyond the world') and the Mahāpāśupatavrata ('the observance of the Greater Pāśupatas'). It also refers to those who adopt this observance as the Mahāvratas.

The *Svacchandatantra* too (11.45–45) takes the Atimārga as inextri-

---

86 *ādhyātmikavidyā ātmopaniṣadvidyā* | .

87 Bhaṭṭa Nārāyaṇakaṇṭha, commenting on *Mṛgendrakriyāpāda* 8.79.

88 T. 1021.217: *vairāgyaśabdenādhyātmikāny abhisaṃdhirūpāṇi pātañjalasāṃkhyāni* (*conj.*; *pātapañalāsaṃdhyāni* MS) *karmāṇy ucyante* | .

89 The commentary on *Svacchandatantra* 11.44: *ādhyātmikaṃ sāṃkhyayogādipratipāditaprakṛtipuruṣavivekajñānasarvavṛttinirodhajñānādikam* | .

90 *Niśvāsamukha* 4.131: *atimārggaṃ samākhyātaṃ dviḥpra*[[*kāraṃ va*(*rā*)]]*nane* || 4.131.

91 *Niśvāsamukha* (4.88).

92 As we have noted on p. 63, the account given in the *Niśvāsamukha* may indeed be systematically rendered, but the truthfulness of its content can as of yet not be fully ascertained, since there is no further extant source material to compare and contrast it against.

cably linked to the Pāśupata system, and this is further spelled out in *Svacchandatantra* 11.179–184.[93] The *Siddhāntasamuccaya*[94] of Trilocana also makes this identification: *atimārgaṃ punaḥ pāśupatādiḥ* |. But SANDERSON (2006: 158) points out that when Kṣemarāja comments on *Svacchandatantra* 11.43–45 and 11.179–184, he does not distinguish the Atimārga and the Mantramārga in terms of non-Āgamic Śaivism and Āgamic Śaivism:[95]

> Thus when Kṣemarāja comments on the same list of five when it occurs at *Svacchanda* 11.43c–45b he does not see its distinction between the 'Atimārga' and the fifth as a distinction between non-Āgamic and Āgamic Śaivism. According to him – and he is, after all, one of the most influential of Āgamic authorities – the knowledge of the 'Atimārga' mentioned in the text is knowledge of the externals of Āgamic Śaivism itself, while the fifth level is knowledge of the core of the same system.

SANDERSON proceeds by cogently inferring (2006: 162–163) why the redactor(s) of the *Mṛgendratantra* and the commentator Bhaṭṭa Nārāyaṇakaṇṭha failed to associate the Atimārga with non-Āgamic Śaivism.[96] We observe a complete misunderstanding of the sense of Atimārga in the *Tantrālokaviveka* of Jayaratha, who, commenting on the tantra at 13.346, asserts that the Atimārga refers to such systems as Sāṅkhya and Yoga, which, in his work, are elevated above the Laukika religion: *atimārgo laukikamārgātītaṃ sāṃkhyapātañjalādi* |. It is not clear what Abhinavagupta, for his part, may have thought about the matter. SANDERSON (2006: 163) concludes:

> The term Atimārga, which I suggest we use for the non-Āgamic Śaivism of the Pāśupatas and related systems, is extracted, then, from a stage of the tradition which predates our famous commentators and perhaps even some of the Āgamas themselves. But I make no apology for putting it

93 See SANDERSON (2006: 158–160).

94 T. 284, pp. 153, lines 1–2.

95 Note that 'non-Āgamic Śaivism' and 'Āgamic Śaivism' are SANDERSON's translations for the terms 'Atimārga' and 'Mantramārga' respectively.

96 Note that for the author of the *Mṛgendrapaddhatiṭīkā* (T. 1021, p. 217), too, followers of the Atimārga are identified as Pāśupatas.

back to use: the dominion of these commentaries over later tradition need not extend to us.

As we have seen above, the Atimārga is elevated above the Ādhyātmika in the *Niśvāsamukha*, the *Svacchandatantra* and the *Pūrvakāmika*; yet in the *Mṛgendratantra*, their positions are reversed. Bhaṭṭa Nārāyaṇakaṇṭha (ad loc.), however, notes that the Atimārga should technically eclipse the Ādhyātmika, advancing the contention that a sequencing according to the loftiness of the *purpose* (*arthakrama*) surpasses an order mirroring simply the chronological progression in which individual sections are to be read (*pāṭhakrama*).[97] It is worth noting that the *Mṛgendrapaddhatiṭīkā*[98] quotes verses 8.78–79 from the *Mṛgendratantra*, but, in commenting on them, alters the constellation of the hierarchy found therein.[99]

5. The **Mantramārga** is identified as coterminous with Āgamic Śaivism. The *Niśvāsamukha* (1.56c) plainly enunciates: *mantrākhyāś ca tathā śaivāḥ* 'and the followers of the *mantra*[-path] are Śaivas.' For the author of the *Mṛgendratantra*[100] and *Kāmika*,[101] the term conveys the same meaning. It is not clear, however, whether it is understood in the same way by Bhaṭṭa Nārāyaṇakaṇṭha, when he comments on *Mṛgendrakriyāpāda* 8.79, or whether Kṣemarāja[102] understands it thus, or whether the author of the *Mṛgendrapaddhatiṭīkā* does.[103]

The above account sketches how the five major traditions discussed in the *Niśvāsamukha* are presented through an equation with the 'Five Streams'. These, in turn, are structurally embedded in the notion of five faces of Sadāśiva being their source. Can it be ascertained, however, whether the concept of the *Niśvāsamukha*'s five streams is an innovation of the *Niśvāsamukha* or not? There is a distinct possibility that it was influenced by a passage in the *Manusmṛti*, for we encounter a related concept already attested in the *Manusmṛti* (2.117), which has been adopted later by the *Viṣṇusmṛti* (30.43):[104]

---

97 See SANDERSON 2006: 162.

98 *Mṛgendrapaddhatiṭīkā* (T. 1021, pp. 217–218).

99 The *Mṛgendrapaddhatiṭīkā* describes the Atimārga as excelling the Ādhyātmika.

100 See *Mṛgendrakriyāpāda* 8.78.

101 See *Pūrvakāmika* 3.20 ff.

102 Kṣemarāja's gloss on *Svacchandatantrodyota* 22.44.

103 T. 1021.218.

104 Peter BISSCHOP is to be credited with the reference to this item of evidence.

> *laukikaṃ vaidikaṃ vāpi tathādhyātmikam eva ca* |
> *ādadīta yato jñānaṃ taṃ pūrvam abhivādayet* ||
>
> He should greet first the person from whom he received knowledge—whether it is the knowledge of worldly matters, of the Veda, or of the inner self. (OLIVELLE 2005: 101)

We have grounds to assume that *Niśvāsamukha* 1.26cd (*laukikaṃ vaidikaṃ caiva tathādhyātmikam eva ca*) is formulated on the basis of the *Manusmṛti* (2.117ab), because the formulation in the *Niśvāsamukha*—in its complete form—is very similar to its counterpart in the *Manusmṛti*: the only difference is the *Niśvāsamukha*'s *caiva* in place of *vāpi* in the *Manusmṛti*—the meaning of these two expressions, however, remains the same. Thus, we think, it is likely that the conceptual framework of the five streams of the *Niśvāsamukha* is based on the model of the three categories of knowledge as expounded in the *Manusmṛti*, with an addition of two more elements: the Atimārga and the Mantramārga. It is therefore quite possible that the *Niśvāsamukha* first developed the notion of Five Streams in expansion of the basic notions of the *Manusmṛti*.

Furthermore, a scheme of Five Streams features in the *Guhyasūtra* (12.17–18), although with significant discrepancies vis-à-vis the *Niśvāsamukha*. On one hand, the fact that Śaiva Siddhānta is revealed by Īśāna presents a point of congruence between the two expositions. On the other, the remaining four streams differ from those presented in the *Niśvāsamukha*. In the account of the *Guhyasūtra*, the remaining four streams exclusively refer to Pāśupata schools and are associated with the four faces of Śiva as follows: Vaimala is revealed by Tatpuruṣa; Pramāṇa by Aghora; Kāruka by Vāmadeva; and the doctrine of Lakulīśa by Sadyojāta:[105]

> *pañcabhis tu tataḥ sarvaṃ yad bhūtaṃ yac ca bhāvyati* |
> *īśāne*[106] *śaivam utpannaṃ vaimalaṃ puruṣāt*[107] *smṛtam* ||
> *pramāṇaṃ hṛdayāj jātaṃ vāmadevāt tu kārukam* |[108]
> *sadyāc ca lakulīśāntaḥ*[109] *pañcabhedāḥ prakīrttitāḥ* ||

105 For discussion of these four divisions of Pāśupata sects, see SANDERSON (1988: 664–667).

106 īśāne] N; īśānaṃ K; iśāne W

107 puruṣāt] *conj.*; puruṣā NW; puruṣaṃ K

108 hṛdayāj jātaṃ vāmadevāt tu kārukam] *conj.*; hṛdayāj jātaṃ vāmade --- n tu kārakam N; hṛdayā ⊔n tu kārakam K; hṛdayā jātaṃ vāmade ⊔n tu kārakam W

109 sadyāc ca lakulīśāntaḥ] *conj. Sanderson*; sadyāc ca lakulīśāntāḥ NK^{pc}; sadyoc ca lakulīśāntāḥ K^{ac}; sadyāmba lakulīśāntāḥ W

> Thus all creation, as well as what is in the future to be created, [is effected] by the[se] five [**Brahmamantras/faces**]. It is on [the basis of] Īśāna, [that] Śiva came into being; the Vimala [school] is understood to be [emanated] from the Puruṣa; the Pramāṇa [school] springs from the Hṛdaya; from Vāmadeva, however, the Kāruka [came to be]; from the Sadyojāta, the doctrine of Lakulīśa [is proclaimed]—these five divisions have been taught.

Given the congruities between the system of revelation of Śaiva clusters of knowledge as extrapolated both in the *Guhyasūtra* and in the *Niśvāsamukha*, it appears possible that a common source, drawn from earlier Śaiva works, informed the conception of five streams of knowledge as they (re)appear in the *Guhyasūtra* and the *Niśvāsamukha*. It cannot, as of yet, be established with a reasonable degree of certainty, whether earlier sources already depicted Īśāna as the supreme herald of the Mantramārga, which is the account given in the *Niśvāsamukha*.[110]

What is striking about the way this taxonomy is relayed is that the *Niśvāsamukha* is amongst the earliest extant textual sources presenting Śiva as a five-headed divinity. Hans BAKKER (2002), for example, has already noted that Śiva is not presented as a five-headed deity in the *Mahābhārata*. In the same vein, TÖRZSÖK (2013) mentions that a five-headed form of Śiva is absent in the early layer of the *Niśvāsa*-corpus and other relatively early Śaiva sources. Instead, TÖRZSÖK posits (2013: 152–153) that a four-faced depiction is attested to in source material associated with the Atimārga; mention of a fifth face emerges in the context of the revelation of tantric Śaivism through the Śaiva Siddhānta. This has subsequently been adopted also by the non-Saiddhāntika traditions. As BAKKER shows, it is conceivable that the idea of Śiva's having five faces may have developed under the influence of the concept of the five Brahmamantras,[111] which are attested to in the *Taittirīyāraṇyaka* (10.43–46) and the *Pāśupatasūtra*, works which predate the *Niśvāsamukha*. The five mantras are known as 'Sadyo-

---

110 The model of revelation presented in the figurative garb of the Five Streams of tantric Śaiva knowledge is found in a broad range of later scriptures. According to this model, the *Siddhāntatantra* are proclaimed by the Īśāna face; the Bhairavatantras from Aghora; the Vāmatantras from Vāmadeva; the Bhūtatantra from Sadyojāta; and the Gāruḍatantra from Tatpuruṣa (see HATLEY 2010: 3). Since we are, at this point, primarily concerned with sources antecedent to the *Niśvāsa*, we do not actively pursue anything other than a tangential mention of the model as it features in later sources.

111 See BAKKER (2002: 400).

jāta', 'Vāmadeva', 'Tatpuruṣa', 'Aghora', and 'Īśāna'—effectuating an exact correspondence between the names of the five faces of Śiva and the five Brahmamantras as presented in the *Niśvāsamukha*. We can therefore regard the notion that the five faces of Śiva were based on the literature and traditions centred around the five Brahmamantras as both credible and established, for the identification of the five faces with the five Brahmamantras appears to be a relatively late development in Śaivism.[112]

The textual evidence for the emergence of the fifth face as supreme enunciator of the Mantramārga is somewhat complex. In the account of the *Niśvāsamukha*, the fifth, Īśāna-face is associated with the Śaiva Siddhānta.[113] That section, however, does not specify whether the five Brahmamantras are identified with the Five Faces of Śiva—or rather of 'Sadāśiva', as he is known in his five-headed form. The *Guhyasūtra* (12.17–18), on the other hand, introduces the idea that five forms of knowledge are derived from the five Brahmamantras; it is not clear, however, from that account, to what degree they are to be associated with the five faces of Sadāśiva.[114]

GOODALL et al. (2015: 38), after extensive scrutiny of the textual evidence regarding a connection of the five Brahmamantras with Sadāśiva in the *Niśvāsa*-corpus, conclude:

> ... it appears that the notion of a five-headed figure known as Sadāśiva ... whose five heads are the *brahmamantras*, is absent from the earliest *sūtras* of the *Niśvāsa* but is beginning to take shape in the latest layer of the text, namely that constituted by the *Niśvāsamukha* and *Guhyasūtra*.

Later works which feature the concept of 'Five Streams of knowledge'[115]

---

112 Consult BAKKER (2002: 400). As regards the textual evidence within the *Niśvāsamukha*, it merely mentions that Śiva has Five Faces, without further questioning or explaining that state of affairs: *Niśvāsamukha* 3.196cd: ***paścimenaiva vaktreṇa** laukikaṃ gaditaṃ sadā*; *Niśvāsamukha* 4.41: *vedadharmmo mayā proktaḥ svarganaiśreyasaḥ paraḥ* | ***uttareṇaiva vaktreṇa** vyākhyātaś ca samāsataḥ*; *Niśvāsamukha* 4.42: *ādhyātmikaṃ pravakṣyāmi **dakṣiṇāsyena** kīrttitam* | *sāṃkhyañ caiva mahājñānaṃ yogañ cāpi mahāvrate*; *Niśvāsamukha* 4.131: *atimārggaṃ samākhyātaṃ dviḥprakāraṃ varānane* | ***pūrveṇaiva tu vaktreṇa** sarahasyaṃ prakīrttitam* | ; *Niśvāsamukha* 4.135: ***pañcamenaiva vaktreṇa** īśānena dvijottamāḥ* | *mantrākhyaṃ kathayiṣyāmi devyāyā gaditaṃ purā* || .

113 *Niśvāsamukha* (4.135).

114 GOODALL et al. (2015: 36) likewise did not locate the five-faced form of the deity Sadāśiva in the *sūtras* of the *Niśvāsa*.

115 Although all the ensuing sources refer to the same five streams—with the exception of the *Svacchandatantra*—they do not feature an association of the five faces of Śiva with the Five Streams.

include the *Svacchandatantra*,[116] the *Pūrvakāmika*,[117] and the *Jayadratha-yāmala*.[118] In contrast with these three texts, the five domains of religious activity listed in the *Mṛgendrakriyāpāda*[119] and *Mṛgendrapaddhatiṭīkā* have undergone a significant process of transmogrification—both in wording and with regards to sentence-structure. The stratification in the *Mṛgendratantra* (8.79) is as follows: [1] the mundane (*loka*); [2] the Vedic (*āmnāya*); [3] the transcendent (Atimārga); [4] the internal (*abhisaṃdhi*); and [5] the Śaiva.

The *Niśvāsamukha* as a preface to the Mantramārga

In order to assess the type and scope of the *Niśvāsamukha*'s contribution to the Mantramārga at large, we will more closely investigate the narrative framework of the *Niśvāsamukha*.[120] Unfortunately, the text is lacunose, for which reason we are not able to represent every structural aspect with a fully satisfactory degree of precision. Although, as we shall see in a separate section, the *Śivadharmasaṅgraha* provides an abundance of textual parallels for the greater part of the *Niśvāsamukha*, there is an acute lack of textual parallels in the *Śivadharmasaṅgraha* from which to draw in substitution for deprecated sections of the frame-story.[121] That being said, we can nevertheless make a number of relevant observations regarding the narrative framework on the basis of the surviving textual evidence.

First of all, the overarching structure of the *Niśvāsamukha* is cast in the form of a narrative that presents the different tenet-systems by way of divine dialogue between Īśvara and Devī. This setting unmistakably insinuates that whatever is being announced is sanctioned by divine authority and judgment. Since the Mantramārga is presented as the 'highest form of religion' in this particular context, the narrative framework of the *Niśvāsamukha* directly conveys the idea of the supremacy of the Mantramārga.

[116] *Svacchandatantra* 11.43c–45b: *laukikaṃ devi vijñānaṃ sadyojātād vinirgatam | vaidikaṃ vāmadevāt tu ādhyātmikam aghorataḥ || puruṣāc cātimārgākhyaṃ nirgataṃ tu varānane | mantrākhyaṃ tu mahājñānam īśānāt tu vinirgatam ||* .

[117] *Pūrvakāmika* 3.17c–18b: *laukikaṃ vaidikaṃ caiva tathādhyātmikam eva ca || atimārgaṃ ca mantrākhyaṃ tantram etad anekadhā |* .

[118] SANDERSON (2006: 157, fn. 7).

[119] *Mṛgendrakriyāpāda* 8.78–79: *lokāmnāyātimārgābhisandhiśaivātmakāṇyaṇoḥ | karmāṇi kṣetrikādīśagaṇakāṅgāntakāni tu || karmatatkṛcchravairāgyajanyāni triṣu dhāmasu | yogavijñānajanyāni parataḥ parato mune ||* .

[120] It is worth noting that the great majority of references to the Mantramārga occur in the frame-story of the *Niśvāsamukha*.

[121] For a comparative list of the parallels between the *Śivadharmasaṅgraha* and the *Niśvāsamukha*, see page 106 ff.

Secondly, in elevating the Mantramārga above the other tenet-systems, the text makes skilful use of insinuative symbolism, both allegorical and topographical in nature.[122] For example, the Vedic and pro-Vedic sacred topography is directly and emphatically juxtaposed with that of the ascendant Śaiva school. The underlying 'power-struggle' is resolved by an astonished Ricīka witnessing a score of sages, originally residents of the indisputably brahmanical Naimiṣāraṇya (Naimiṣa forest),[123] relocating to the Devadāruvana (Pine Forest), a holy Śaiva site.[124] Upon consulting Mataṅga, Ricīka learns that the sages were inspired to do so upon having learnt that Brahmā and Viṣṇu themselves were initiated in the Pine Forest (1.16–18).

Religious activities associated with the Naimiṣa forest have been described in passages contained in the *Mahābhārata*[125] and in some of the *Purāṇas*.[126] The sages of the Naimiṣa forest are also presented as being engaged in performing extensive sacrifices, which evokes an unmistakenly Vedic atmosphere in the context of the *Niśvāsamukha*; all the more so since it is precisely the Vedic sages of the Naimiṣa forest being engaged in elaborate rituals which we most easily associate with this holy site. In fact, the *Mahābhārata* itself, as well as many a *Purāṇa*, is traditionally presented as having been recited here for the first time—in brief, this place is imbued with special significance in brahmanical traditions.

The Devadāruvana, by contrast, is imbued with deep-rooted cultural associations that, to the common mind, are inextricably linked to the Śaiva traditions. After all, it is the place where, according to Śaiva lore, *liṅga*-worship originated. We encounter the myth of the Devadāruvana for the

---

122 For example, the way the system of initiation in the Śaiva religion (1.18) differs from the Vedic initiatory system (1.8) is emphasized in a context that gives clear preference to the former.

123 The Naimiṣa forest is known to us from the contexts of the *Mahābhārata* and the *Purāṇas* as one of the places of origin for the brahmanical tradition. Indeed, the very narrative of the *Mahābhārata* itself begins "with the arrival of the *sūta* in the Naimiṣa forest" (ROCHER 1986: 81). More extensive information of descriptions of the Naimiṣa forest as they feature in the *Mahābhārata* can be gleaned from ROCHER (1986: 70, 71, 81, 141, 161, 164, 168, 185, 226 and 232) and HILTEBEITEL (2001), in particular the third chapter (pp. 92 ff.).

124 For a rendition of the myth related to the Devadāruvana, see JAHN (1915, 1916), DEUSSEN (1917: 119–120), and GONDA (1963: 211–212).

125 See HILTEBEITEL (2001: 131).

126 Consult, for example, *Brahmāṇḍapurāṇa* 1.1:165 and *Bhāgavatapurāṇa* 1.1:4. See also BISSCHOP (2006: 217).

first time in the *Skandapurāṇa*.[127] BISSCHOP (2006: 80) summarises the myth as follows:

> ... as they[, the sages,] were practising *tapas* in Devadāruvana, some person appeared, engulfed in *tejas*, in the form of a twice-born, a naked man, with a skull in his hand, his body covered with ashes and with an erect penis. At this sight they got angry and went after him, impelled by jealousy. The man, frightened and beaten by them, did not really get angry, but the blows and sticks that they raised were repelled and fell on their sons, wives and themselves in particular. The *liṅga* of that Lokapa fell down, after which he disappeared. With the falling of that *liṅga* in the middle of their hermitage, the virility of the four classes of beings was damaged. They have come to Deva for protection, that he may make them successful again.

To our knowledge the *Niśvāsamukha* is the first text to render Śaiva teachings against the backdrop of the Devadāruvana, thereby contextualising it as counter-model to the traditional setting in the Naimiṣa forest. We assume that in rendering the exodus of the sages to the Devadāruvana, thus favouring it over the Naimiṣa, the *Niśvāsamukha* may be fielding an allegorical ploy to illustrate the emergence of a new, professedly superior, religion with an identity that is to be perceived as distinct from the mainstream traditions.

What is striking in this rendition is that parts of the *Niśvāsamukha* make claims about Vedic deities and associated protagonists that would not only appear uncharacteristic in their original Vedic setting, but outright heterodox, such as the idea that Brahmā, Viṣṇu and all the sages (1.19, 1.27–28) were initiated in the Śaiva system of initiation (1.18), especially in the alien setting of the Devadāruvana.

The *Niśvāsamukha*: A Mirror to Early Śaivism

When discussing textual parallels in the source material to the *Niśvāsamukha*,[128] we have noted that the text draws upon a substantial number of earlier works. Let us now dissect the particular *modus operandi* by which the *Niśvāsamukha* appropriates previous systems of thought. It does so chiefly

127 Note that the account of the Devadāruvana in the *Śivapurāṇa* postdates the rendition in the *Niśvāsamukha*.

128 Refer to p. 22 above.

by granting limited authority to the latters' textual exponents by way of subsumption into the lower four echelons of the five-fold taxonomy of tantric Śaivism. As we shall see, this stratagem becomes apparent upon scrutiny of recontextualized and reframed passages borrowed from the *Manusmṛti*, as well as the 'profile of ideas'[129] expressed therein.

First of all, besides a long passage on the procedures of *liṅga*-worship and other Śaiva teachings, there is a host of standard practices readily traceable to established brahmanical traditions: pilgrimage (3.1 ff.); offering water and sesame seeds to ancestors (2.39); offering a two-faced cow (2.49); offering land (2.56); constructing gardens 1.61); planting trees (2.25); making food offerings (2.37) etc. The fact that the *Niśvāsamukha* is directly borrowing from the *Manusmṛti*, without any change in content, further demonstrates a close affiliation with the brahmanical traditions. For instance, the *Niśvāsamukha* (3.155) gives a list of the ancestors of the four castes (*varṇa*) as follows:

> *pitaras somapā vipre kṣatriye tu havirbhujāḥ* |
> *ājyapā vaiśyayonau tu śūdrāṇān tu sukālinaḥ* ||
>
> In the case of a Brāhmin, the ancestors are [called] Somapās; in the case of a Kṣatriya, Havirbhujas; in the case of a Vaiśya, Ājyapas; and for Śūdras, [they are called] Sukālins.

A close juxtaposition of the *Manusmṛti* (3.197) testifies to an act of borrowing on the part of the *Niśvāsamukha*:

> *somapā nāma viprāṇāṃ kṣatriyāṇāṃ havirbhujaḥ* |
> *vaiśyānām ājyapā nāma śūdrāṇāṃ tu sukālinaḥ* ||
>
> The ancestors of Brāhmins are called Somapas; of Kṣatriyas, Havirbhujs; of Vaiśyas, Ājyapas; and of Śūdras, Sukālins.[130] (OLIVELLE 2005: 118)

In choosing to appropriate[131] textual source material from the *Manusmṛti*, the *Niśvāsamukha* is implicitly accepting the former as an authoritative source. Thereby, we should be inclined to argue, the *Niśvāsamukha*

129 The term 'profile of ideas' (*Ideenprofil*) has been adapted from GRÜNENDAHL in SCHREINER, ed. (1997: 234), and is here employed with comparable connotations.

130 In the same way, *Manusmṛti* 11.214 defines the *atikṛcchra* observance as *ekaikaṃ grāsam aśnīyāt tryahāṇi trīṇi pūrvavat* | *tryahaṃ copavased antyam atikṛcchraṃ caran dvijaḥ* ||, which is echoed in *Niśvāsamukha* 3.40 as follows: *ekaikaṃ bhakṣayed grāsaṃ trīṇy ahāni jitendriyaḥ* | *trirātropavasec caiva atikṛcchraṃ viśodhane* ||.

131 For a detailed list of parallels in the *Niśvāsamukha* that have been traced to the *Manusmṛti*, see p.86 ff.

tacitly assents to the social system that was conceived by the brahmanical tradition, and formulated in the *Manusmṛti.*

This above constellation results in what one might call the brahmanical-śaiva hybrid-nature of the tenet system presented in the *Niśvāsamukha*. This can be well-illustrated by the many passages which relate donative practices, for example. First of all, in all instances the recipient is either a Brāhmin or the deity Śiva (*e.g.* at 2.54 and 2.98) himself, albeit in his symbolical representation as a *liṅga*. The way Brahmanism is presented as subordinate and adjuvant to Śaivism, moreover, is well illustrated by a passage of the *Niśvāsamukha* (2.115–121) which presents a stratified hierarchy of worthiness of recipients of gifts—as we shall see, this schema clearly favours the Śaiva perspective. The prelude to this teaching is wrapped in divine dialogue, with Devī inquisitive about the most deserving recipient of munificent acts, a question that is directly addressed by Śiva (2.115) himself. Śiva, having given a general statement about the act of giving—the merit of which endures for eternity (2.116)—lists the degree of worthiness of the respective recipients (2.117–121) in hierarchical sequence.[132]

This passage attests to the fact that individuals granted high social standing in the brahmanical traditions feature as worthy recipients of donative practices, yet the most worthy recipient remains the knower of Śiva (*śivajñānī*). This is an indicator that Śaivism builds its theoretical framework on the legacy of its brahmanical predecessors, a view that has first been voiced in SANDERSON's influential and extensive contribution '*The Śaiva Age: The Rise and Dominance of Śaivism during the Early Medieval Period*' (2009).[133] In that chapter, SANDERSON developed the theory that Śaivism appropriated major aspects of brahmanical culture. He convincingly argues (2009: 302) that the model of Śaivism is a combination of Śaivism and Brahmanism:

> The religion of the Śaivas, then, was not Śaivism alone but an expression of religious syncretism propelled by Śaivism and Brahmanism. This fact is born[e] out not only by Śaiva literature but also by the biographical data and the epigraphic records of the activities of Śaiva kings.[134]

132 See p. 97 for a detailed presentation.

133 Contained in *Genesis and Development of Tantrism*, ed. Shingo EINOO, 2009, pp. 9-350.

134 SANDERSON (2009: 201 ff.) puts forward the conceptual edifice of a Śaiva-Brahmanical order—a system that corresponds very closely to the model presented in the *Niśvāsamukha*.

In order to establish the Mantramārga as the supreme avenue of religious practice, the *Niśvāsamukha* renders the religious framework by way of Five Streams, therein making skilfull use of potent allegorical symbolism. The depiction of Śaiva religion as embodied by Śiva displaying 'five faces' presents each of the faces as source and legitimizing authority of an equally valid 'stream of teaching'. At the same time, the faces (together with the respectively associated 'streams of teaching') nevertheless differ as to their respective rank and soteriological fruit. This mirrors well our assessment that the *Niśvāsamukha* grants scriptural and traditional authority to all systems presented whilst reserving supremacy for the Mantramārga, extolled as being the highest path of practice. As we learn in the text, this 'highest stream' of the Mantramārga issues forth from the fifth, uppermost face (Īśāna):

> *adhunā tad ato viprās saṃvādam umayā saha* |
> *īśvarasya tu devasya mantramārgaṃ vyavasthitam* || 4.134 ||
> *pañcamenaiva vaktreṇa īśānena dvijottamāḥ* |
> *mantrākhyaṃ kathayiṣyāmi devyāyā gaditaṃ purā* || 4.135 ||
> *catuḥsrotā mayā pūrvaṃ śrutā devyāḥ prasādataḥ* |
> *te sarve kathitās tubhyaṃ nissandigdhā dvijottamāḥ* || 4.136 ||
> *pañcaman tu paraṃ srotaṃ śi* --- |
>
> Now, then (*tad ato*), o Brāhmins, the discourse of the god Śiva (*īśvarasya*) with Umā [is as follows]; the Mantramārga is settled with the fifth face, [that is to say] the Īśāna [face], o Brāhmins! I shall tell [you of] the [path] of *mantra* which was formerly related to Devī. I heard [about] the four streams before by the grace of Devī: all those I have told you of, o best of Brāhmins, you who are free of doubt. The fifth is the highest stream, [[...]]

The process we witness here is a nascent precursor to what came to be known as 'inclusivism', a term originally coined by the German scholar Paul HACKER[135] to denote a strategy of 'subjugation via appropriation' of other systems of thought and practice. This concept has been refined by a number of subsequent scholars who have shown that, though at first glance marked by tolerance, an 'inclusivist' approach to alien systems of thought and practice contains the underhand implication of 'benign' annexation. In the *Niśvāsamukha*, the welcoming aspect on the surface level of this approach is well laid out in the following extract:[136]

135 Consult HACKER (in OBERHAMMER, ed. 1983: 11–28).

136 Note that the pluralistic veneer of the inclusivist approach taken in the *Niśvāsamukha*

prāsādaṃ kārayitvā tu viṣṇuṃ ye sthāpayanti hi || 2.27 ||
viṣṇulokaṃ vrajanty ete modante viṣṇunā saha |
brahmāṇaṃ skaṃdaṃ rudrāṇīṃ gaṇeśaṃ mātaraṃ ravim || 2.28 ||
vahniṃ śatakratuṃ yakṣaṃ vāyuṃ dharmmañ jaleśvaram |
yo yasya sthāpanaṅ kuryāt prāsāde tu suśobhane || 2.29 ||
pūjaye parayā bhaktyā so 'mṛto hy asya lokatām | 2.30ab |

> Those who install Viṣṇu, having had a temple constructed [for him], will go to the world of Viṣṇu and rejoice with Him. If someone worships [whomsoever among] Brahmā, Skanda, Rudrāṇī, Gaṇeśa, the Mothers (*mātaram*), Sun, fire, Indra (*śatakratum*), Kubera (*yakṣam*), Vāyu, Dharma or Varuṇa (*jaleśvaram*) with highest devotion, having installed them in a beautiful temple, he becomes immortal and [achieves] the world of that [particular deity].

Our contention that the term 'inclusivism' is applicable to the approach taken in the *Niśvāsamukha* in particular, and to the Śaiva community at large, is shared by SANDERSON (2009: 301) who contends that the Śaiva 'attitude':[137]

---

is recurrently accentuated to the effect that further illustrative examples can be easily invoked. Let us consider Devī's question (3.60) regarding salvific methods, and Śiva's reply (3.61 ff.), for instance, which is a case in point. As a prelude, Devī asks Śiva:

> By resorting to which god will fasting bear great fruit? And how should [the god] be worshipped? Tell [me this] by your grace. (3.60)

In his reply, Śiva does not only refrain from directly claiming a monopoly of authority, nor from demanding the installation of himself as the solitary and exclusive object of worship; he does not even condemn the worship of other godheads, which is a striking feature in itself. Besides Śiva-worship (3.146 ff., 188 ff. and 3.92 ff., 175 ff.), he recommends the worship of different godheads, however, and thus, accepts their (subservient and restricted) authority.

137 In his recent study, *'Unifying Hinduism'*, NICHOLSON (2010: 185) has argued that the term 'inclusivism' not only accurately describes the intellectual and spiritual milieu of remote mediæval India, but even forms part and parcel of modern-day 'Hinduism':

> The word "inclusivism", popularised in Hindu studies by Paul Hacker, is a better approximate of the process in India by which a multitude of various sects, philosophies, gods, and modes of worship are united under a single overarching concept, whether the late mediæval idea of six *āstika darśanas* [orthodox philosophies] or the modern term Hinduism.

> elaborated an inclusivist model of revelation that ranked other religious systems as stages of an ascent to liberation in Śaivism.

It is apparent that, in presenting the four 'lower streams' as preliminary, foundational tenets of tantric Śaivism, the *Niśvāsamukha* implies their tangential, ancillary position vis-à-vis the more portentous Mantramārga. The tantric 'path of mantra', for its part, is expounded at great length in the subsequent volumes of the *Niśvāsatattvasaṃhitā*. The *Niśvāsamukha* quite clearly subordinates these supposedly 'inferior' belief-structures to the path of tantric Śaivism (as borne out in the following extract):

> *laukikaṃ kathitaṃ hy etad vaidikañ cāturāśramam* || 1.55 ||
> --- |
> --- *proktā lokātītā mahāvratāḥ* |
> *mantrākhyāś ca tathā śaivā ato 'nye kupathe sthitāḥ* || 1.56 ||
>
> This is what I have taught as Laukika. The four-*āśrama* system is called Vaidika, [...][138] [...][139] The world-transcenders are the Mahāvratas and those who are called *mantra*[-path-follower]s are Śaivas. [Any] others apart from these are situated on a wrong path.

If we cast a sober glance at the bottomline mechanics of the argument voiced in the *Niśvāsamukha*, we can swiftly ascertain that some strands of religio-philosophical practice are appropriated into the Śaiva tenet system with the remainder simply being declared invalid. This has the effect that—though presented in the garb of pluralistic open-mindedness—syncretic Śaivism alone remains as the exclusively unmistaken path. Who, we should ask, are these 'others, situated on a wrong path' (*anye kupathe sthitāḥ*)? First of all, without mentioning these explicitly, the 'inclusivistic' teaching of the *Niśvāsamukha* excludes two well-known religions of India from its ambit of soteriological legitimacy: Buddhism and Jainism.[140] In

---

138 The lost part of the text, with a substantial degree of certainty, must have listed the Sāṅkhya and Yoga streams, which, as we recall, together constitute the Ādhyātmika stream.

139 In this lacunose section, we should, in all likelihood, expect the term Atimārga to feature in 56a.

140 Von STIETENCRON's contribution (1995) may be helpful for arriving at a more specific delimitation of which the traditions are that are denied validity. First of all, the primary evidence he consults is more extensive. Secondly, he opts not to view the primary evidence in the context of inclusivism and thereby offers a contrasting interpretation of the nature and the purport of the textual evidence itself. Von

fact, these two distinguished religions are not mentioned in the 'revelation of the Five Streams' in any overt manner. Likewise, the other so-called 'heterodox' (lit. *nāstika*) religions are excluded, which to our mind gives credibility to the contention that early Śaivism as presented in the *Niśvāsamukha* developed around the teaching of brahmanical principles. As we shall see below, the *Niśvāsamukha* constitutes an early platform representative of a model that, with varying degrees of intensity, remains an intrinsically operative feature both of modern day 'Hinduism' as well as of its antecedent traditions.

The *Niśvāsamukha* as a precursor to modern 'Hinduism'

As the reader will know, many a study of the concept of 'Hinduism' has been published in recent years, with the consequence that, presently, divergent and conflicting interpretations with regards to the origins of the umbrella-term of 'Hinduism' abound.[141] Studies in the pre-colonial religious history of 'Hinduism', postcolonial critiques of the term, as well as 'post-critical' assessments of the latter offer an initially bewildering multiplicity of perspectives that the neophyte will find difficult to navigate. Peter BISSCHOP[142] relates how we

> have gone a long way to show that already prior to the arrival of the British a notion of a 'unified Hinduism' had taken shape, even though the term itself may not yet have been in use, and that it is therefore not the British Orientalists who are to be credited with the 'creation of Hinduism'.

In debating the question of the degree to which the *Niśvāsamukha*'s world-view might foreshadow 'modern-day Hinduism', one cannot avoid defining the term 'Hinduism' more distinctly. As Peter BISSCHOP (2016: 41) noted, one of the pivotal insights we have gained "from the discussion about the origins of the notion of Hinduism as a single religion is that it shows that the British Orientalists were clearly building on earlier notions that had

---

STIETENCRON mentions the eleventh-century *Somaśambhupaddhati*'s assigning of religious traditions to different levels, in accordance with their respective levels of attainment, along the path of thirty-six Śaiva *tattvas*. Unsurprisingly, Śaiva texts feature at the apex, yet Buddhists, and Jains still supersede the Śāktas, Smārtas and Naiyāyikas.

141 See HALBFASS 1997, LORENZEN 1999, SWEETMAN 2001, 2003, NICHOLSON 2010, BISSCHOP 2016, and FISHER 2017.

142 BISSCHOP 2016: 39.

been developed not so much under a colonial regime but by missionaries and ministers who tried to make sense of the, in their eyes, heathen religion they encountered in India." The early conception of a unified 'Hinduism' might well have come about partly as an effect of the interpretative lenses of European visitors and missionaries during the 17th and 18th centuries, all "men of faith, with a strong belief in their own intellectual competence" (*ibid.*). Meanwhile, we should not discard outright the possibility that the concept of a unitary religion concocted by these early pioneers might have in fact been based on at least partially correct assumptions, or might have accurately reflected some traits of a rudimentary self-presentation found among some members of the socio-religious milieu contemporaneous to the alien observer. NICHOLSON (2010: 2), in this regard, presents a balanced account, that echoes our own contention closely:

> The idea of Hindu unity is neither a timeless truth nor a fiction wholly invented by the British to regulate and control their colonial subjects.

If, as established, unificatory tendencies in the religious domain in fact predate the orientalists' accounts,[143] is it perhaps worthwhile to investigate whether such currents were nascent—or possibly thriving—even prior to the advent of alien missionaries and religious functionaries? Since it is this very question that we seek to answer, we shall take to a somewhat reductionist[144] definition of the term 'Hinduism' that sidesteps the complications which early 20th-century nationalist innovations, for example, would inject it with. If we relate to it as 'a spiritual and cultural system marked, *inter alia*, by an

[143] See BISSCHOP (*op. cit.* 41–48) and SWEETMAN (2003) for a clear and pithy presentation of the 17th to 18th century textual evidence regarding the formation of the concept of a unitary South Asian religion that eventually came to be associated with the term 'Hinduism'.

[144] For a more intricate discussion of the various religious identities, their group-affiliations, beliefs, corresponding godheads, philosophies, rituals, modes of worship and other distinguishing features, the reader is referred to NICHOLSON (2010: 185 ff.). We are aware that a multiplicity of other, relevant characteristics could have been included in our definition of the term 'Hinduism', characteristics that would likewise have remained fundamentally intact for several millennia. One example would be the concept of *sanātana dharma*—supratemporal (lit. 'eternal') religion—as opposed to religions 'established' at a certain point in time by their respective 'founder' (*e.g.* as in Islam). We could also have included the primacy of Śiva and Viṣṇu as supreme deities in our definition of the term 'Hinduism', since it is textually attested to in the *Niśvāsamukha* and likewise persists as a characteristic feature until the present day. Since these aspects are, however, not central to our discussion of inclusivism, they are consciously omitted in our (admittedly functional and minimalistic) definition.

inclusivist approach to other religious and cultural systems of thought and practice', we are capable of explaining how modern-day 'Hinduism' functions as an umbrella term that subsumes otherwise mutually exclusive religious models—polytheistic, monotheistic, or pantheist tenet-systems, for example. This 'conglomerate entity' as a new conceptual unit is then contrasted with 'outside' systems. Modern day 'Hinduism' hence functions as a taxonomical 'meta-model' for a diversity of systems in the very same way syncretic Śaivism provided the superstructure for the brahmanical-śaiva hybrid system laid out in the *Niśvāsamukha.* The continuity of the inclusivist model, we argue, persists from its earliest explicit formulations, textually verifiable in the *Niśvāsamukha*, right until the ascent of modern-day 'Hinduism' (as we have defined it)—albeit the traction of the inclusivist framework would have fluctuated in accordance with the vagaries of regional and epochal developments.

Parallels and Borrowings

As already indicated above, the *Niśvāsamukha* seems to be largely dependent on outside sources to create its body of text. We know by now that the *Niśvāsamukha* mentions five religious systems—[1] Laukika, [2] Vaidika, [3] Ādhyātmika, [4] Atimārga, and [5] Mantramārga—and elaborates upon the first four in depth, while only alluding to the fifth. Since the *Niśvāsamukha* concerns itself with the introduction of the first four types of religious systems, it is only natural that it draws from the relevant sources of these systems. Although we do not find parallels to what the *Niśvāsamukha* teaches in all cases, it is likely that in many an instance the *Niśvāsamukha* borrowed from other sources.

A large part of the Laukika section of the *Niśvāsamukha* may have been composed on the basis of previous or contemporaneous sources—we do encounter similar materials in other texts, both Śaiva and non-Śaiva. Thus, the *Aṣṭamūrti* hymn (1.30–41), the list of the *pañcāṣṭaka* (3.19–22), the list of rivers (3.2–8) and the famous *Liṅgodbhava*-myth (1.172–185) are probably not inventions *ex nihilo*, ascribable to the author of the *Niśvāsamukha* alone. The descriptions of the Cāndrāyaṇa (3.43), Yaticāndrāyaṇa (3.45), Śiśucāndrāyaṇa observances (3.46), and the names of the ancestors of the four castes (3.155) are borrowed from the *Manusmṛti.*[145] The Vedic section

[145] Likewise, shorter, individual sections incorporated into the fabric of the *Niśvāsamukha* also testify to the fact that the text has drawn from earlier sources: *Niśvāsamukha* 1.167c–168b is exactly paralleled by *Śivadharmaśāstra* 1.14c–15b; *Niśvāsa-*

(4.2–41) of the *Niśvāsamukha* as well has partly borrowed from the *Manusmṛti*. As we have discussed above,[146] the Ādhyātmika section, presenting the systems of Sāṅkhya and Yoga, appears to be modelled on the basis of earlier sources that were possibly originally disjunct. The Atimārga sections (the presentation of teachings of the Pāñcārthas and Kāpālikas) are also fashioned by drawing from sources pertaining to those traditions.[147]

This fact has significant implications for the way that one should engage with the external source-material which has found its way into the textual fabric of the *Niśvāsamukha*. On the one hand, parallels abound; on the other, borrowed insertions are, more often than not, recontextualised—at times even contorted. In some cases, external sources render the original context of the source material and thereby provide contrasting reference points, against which to gauge the degree of distortion in the corresponding presentation of the *Niśvāsamukha*.

Although it is certainly of value for cultural and religious historians to find that the text of the *Niśvāsamukha* preserves some archaic materials which are otherwise unknown to us, we nevertheless have to tread cautiously in our effort to pursue a balanced and dependable extraction of information from the work. The cosmological system of the Kapālavratins—a division of the archaic Pāśupata branch of Śaivism—is a case in point. On the one hand, the *Niśvāsamukha* is the only existing source to preserve a systematic account of the cosmology of the Kāpālikas (SANDERSON 2006: 163) that we know of; on the other, that very fact makes it nigh-on-impossible to verify

---

mukha 2.2 is closely paralleled by *Śivadharmaśāstra* 3.77c–78b; *Niśvāsamukha* 2.91cd is redolent of *Śivadharmaśāstra* 12.72; the notion of a gradation of recipients (*pātra*) in the *Niśvāsamukha* 2.117–19 also appears to have a connection with the account in *Śivadharmaśāstra* 7.69–71. (See p. 94 for further details) *Niśvāsamukha* 1.2ab is paralleled by *Brahmāṇḍapurāṇa* 1.7:180ab and 1.21:170cd, and *Viṣṇupurāṇa* 1.6:36ab; *Niśvāsamukha* 1.126c–127b is paralleled by *Skandapurāṇa* 28.31abcd; *Niśvāsamukha* 1.71ab is closely paralleled by *Skandapurāṇa* 27.24ab (See p. 30 above).

146 Refer to p. 23.

147 There are a few texts that have citable parallels with the *Niśvāsamukha* and that, being unquestionably younger than the *Niśvāsamukha*, we are not going to discuss individually: the division into five streams of knowledge found in *Niśvāsamukha* 1.26c–27b is paralleled in *Pūrvakāmika* 1.17c–18b; the *Aṣṭamūrti*-hymn in *Niśvāsamukha* 1.32–39 is paralleled in *Prayogamañjarī* 1.19–26, *Tantrasamuccaya* 1.16–23, and *Īśānagurudevapaddhati* 26.56–63; and *Niśvāsamukha* 2.82c–86b is paralleled by *Somaśambhupaddhati* 1.6:5–8, *Kriyākramadyotikā* (§ 67, p.134), and *Ātmārthapūjāpaddhati* (attributed to *Suprabhedāgama*). While the first two lines (*Niśvāsamukha* 2.82c–83b) are found in the *Jñānaratnāvalī* fol. 126b, the last two lines (*Niśvāsamukha* 2.85c–86b) have also been attributed there to the *Suprabhedāgama* (GOML MS R 14898, p. 144).

the accuracy of the portrayal. We should therefore hesitate to prematurely draw any definite conclusions regarding the ways of the Kāpālikas in particular, and the Pāśupata school at large, based solely on the rendition of the *Niśvāsamukha*.[148]

Parallels with other Books of the *Niśvāsatattvasaṃhitā*

Among the textual parallels that we shall examine more closely, let us commence with the *Niśvāsamukha* and the other books of the *Niśvāsatattvasaṃhitā*. We shall begin with the first three *sūtras*: the *Mūlasūtra*, *Uttarasūtra* and *Nayasūtra*. Comparing the *Niśvāsamukha* against the bodies of text in these works, it becomes apparent that the *Niśvāsamukha* has no textual parallels in the *Uttarasūtra*, few in the *Mūlasūtra*,[149] some in the *Nayasūtra*, and substantial amounts in the *Guhyasūtra*. As a general rule, these textual parallels, are quite explicit and readily identifiable, although in the section topiclizing cosmology, phrasing differs to a wavering degree between the *Mūlasūtra* and the *Niśvāsamukha*.

As we noted, GOODALL presents a well-founded argument regarding the likely chronological order wherein the individual works of the *Niśvāsatattva-*

---

148 On the other hand, the Pāśupatas, and their subschool, the Kāpālikas, as a corollary of being proto-Śaiva groups hence differ inherently less intensely from the 'new orthodoxy' advanced in the *Niśvāsamukha* than the brahmanical elements absorbed therein originally did. It might therefore be argued that the account of the Kāpālikas and Pāśupatas in the *Niśvāsamukha* is less likely beset by stark distortion, and one can concede some ground to that objection. Still, we will only be able to ascertain the probity of the descriptions in the *Niśvāsamukha* once further material will have surfaced; after all, we have noted significant alterations elsewhere, *e.g.* in instances where a supposedly close commentary inverts the taxonomical framework of its reference text. (I am alluding here to the way the *Mṛgendrapaddhatiṭīkā* (T. 1021, pages 217–218) quotes verses 8.78–79 from the *Mataṅga*.)

149 For example, the textual basis of the cosmology taught in the *Niśvāsamukha* (4.100 ff.) and the cosmology of the *Mūlasūtra* (5.3 ff.) are quite akin. GOODALL (2016: 106–8) notes that the cosmology presented in the *Niśvāsatattvasaṃhitā* was not originally uniform (p. 106), since "there were (at least) two different early tantric extensions of the Sāṅkhyas' *tattvakrama*", and that the account displayed in the work was hence gradually conceived. In sum, GOODALL shows that

> what the testimony of the *Niśvāsatattvasaṃhitā* shows is that even some of those theological features of the Śaivasiddhānta which we have become accustomed to thinking of as defining characteristics of the religion were either absent entirely in early times (e.g. *āṇava-mala*) or have been evolving steadily (the *tattvakrama*, the *bhuvanakrama*).

saṃhitā were probably composed.[150] In theory, this would have allowed us to infer rudimentary generalities with regards to likely directions of borrowing. As the ensuing investigation of textual parallels shall bear out, however, we do not have solid evidence to prove that any of the works within the *Niśvāsatattvasaṃhitā*-compendium borrowed from another work of the corpus, one significant instance excluded.[151] As we shall presently attempt to demonstrate, it is much more likely that the works of the *Niśvāsatattvasaṃhitā*—irrespective of their relative age—have borrowed from outside, antecedent source(s). After all, GOODALL[152] shows "that the sequence of thirty-six *tattvas* may have developed in the *Niśvāsa*-corpus itself, in part by borrowing specifically from the *Rauravasūtrasaṅgraha*"; therefore a theory based on more widespread borrowing appears not too far fetched.

Let us investigate, first of all, the textual parallels the *Niśvāsamukha* shares with the *Nayasūtra*. The sections on Yoga in the *Niśvāsamukha* (4.50ff) and the *Nayasūtra* (4.105ff) are strikingly alike. The phrase in 4.60ab *pṛthvī kaṭhinarūpeṇa śṛṇu dehe yathā sthitā* in the *Niśvāsamukha* matches the *Nayasūtra*'s verse 2.23 nearly to the letter. Another noteworthy parallel is the list of eight yogic postures in the *Niśvāsamukha* and the *Nayasūtra*. By name, these are: Svastika, Padmaka, Bhadra, Ardhacandra, Prasārita, Sāpāśraya, Añjalika and Yogapaṭṭa.

The verse which records this list in the *Niśvāsamukha* (4.50) reads:

> *svastikaṃ padmakaṃ bhadraṃ tv arddhacandraṃ prasāritam |*
> *sāpāśrayam añjalikaṃ yogapaṭṭaṃ yathāsukham ||*
>
> After facing north and then assuming a yogic posture, [such as one of the following:] [1] *svastika*, [2] the lotus-posture (*padmaka*), [3] *bhadra*, [4] *arddhacandra*, [5] *prasārita*, [6] *sāpāśraya*, [7] *añjalika*, [8] *yogapaṭṭa*, in whatever posture is comfortable [for him] ....

The corresponding verse in the *Nayasūtra* (4.14c–15b) is almost identical:[153]

---

150 Refer to footnote 57 on page 36.

151 As we shall see at a slightly later stage (p .76), it appears that the author—or editor—of the *Niśvāsamukha* might have played a role in the redaction of chapter sixteen of the *Guhyasūtra*, the section where the Kedāra myth is expounded. In that specific instance, we hold, textual borrowing could have occurred between those two works of the *Niśvāsatattvasaṃhitā*-compendium.

152 GOODALL 2016: 108.

153 Later on, the *Nayasūtra* presents the eight yogic postures in a slightly different phrasing: *āsanaṃ padmakaṃ baddhvā svastikaṃ bhadracandrakam | sāpāśrayaṃ yogapaṭṭam āsīnañ ca yathāsukham* || 4.105 || .

svastikaṃ padmakaṃ bhadram arddhacandraṃ prasāritam ||
sāpāśrayaṃ añjalikaṃ yogapaṭṭaṃ yathāsukham |

'The *svastika*, the lotus-posture (*padmaka*), the *bhadra*, the half-moon posture (*ardhacandra*), the stretched out posture (*prasārita*), the back-rest-assisted posture (*sāpāśrayam*), the *añjalika*, the yoga-band[-assisted] posture (*yogapaṭṭam*), at ease .... GOODALL et al. (2015: 469)

The only difference is that where the *Nayasūtra* reads *arddhacandram*, the *Niśvāsamukha* reads *tv arddhacandram*. In this context, *Niśvāsamukha* 4.65c–66d and *Nayasūtra* 3.21c–22d[154] may also serve as evidence for the definite affinity between the two texts. Since this is a well-known list of yogic postures that would be textually rendered in other sources, it is possible that both texts have borrowed it from another source or from two different sources.

The descriptions of *prāṇāyāma* in the *Niśvāsamukha* and in the *Nayasūtra*[155] are also closely related. We see that both texts teach three types of *prāṇāyāma*: *kumbhaka*, *recaka* and *pūraka*. The definitions of *kumbhaka*, *recaka* and *pūraka* are fundamentally the same in both texts, the *Niśvāsamukha*'s being more elaborate and the *Nayasūtra*'s more concise. Further, there are two additional categories relating to *prāṇāyāma* taught in the *Nayasūtra*: external and internal.[156] The *Nayasūtra* (4.113d) states that the internal *prāṇāyāma* is of four kinds, the fourth being *supraśānta*—this detail is not found in the *Niśvāsamukha*, despite the latter's generally more exhaustive treatment of the matter.

However, we do find a close connection between these two texts in the section on *dhāraṇā*, 'fixation.' *Niśvāsamukha* 4.57c–61 teaches four types of fixation, in the following order: those of air, fire, earth, and water. The *Nayasūtra*, for its part, teaches five types of *dhāraṇā*, which sequentially

154 The *Niśvāsamukha*'s version runs as follows: *divyadṛṣṭiḥ prajāyeta yadā tanmayatāṅ gataḥ* || *sarvavidyāḥ pravartante sarvaṃ pratyakṣato bhavet* | *siddhaiś ca saha sambhāṣaṃ yadā tanmayatāṅ gataḥ* ||. The version of the *Nayasūtra*, in turn, is constituted thus: *siddhaś caiva svatantraś ca divyasṛṣṭiḥ prajāyate* || *ṣaṇmāsād dhyānayogena divyasiddhiḥ prajāyate* | *trailokye yaḥ pravartteta pratyakṣan tasya jāyate* ||.

155 The rendition in the *Niśvāsamukha* displays *prāṇāyāmaṃ pravakṣyāmi triṣprakāraṃ samabhyaset* || 4.54 || *virecyāpūrya saṃruddhaṃ kumbhakaṃ parikīrttitam* | *pūrayec ca svakaṃ dehaṃ yāvad āpūritaṃ bhavet* || 4.55 || *pūrakas tu samākhyāto prāṇāyāmo dvitīyakaḥ* | *niṣkrāmayati yo vāyuṃ sva[[dehā]]* --- || 4.56 || *sa recakas samākhyātaḥ prāṇāyāmas tṛtīyakaḥ* || 4.57ab. The *Nayasūtra*'s version is as follows: *recanāt pūraṇād rodhāt prāṇāyāmas trayaḥ smṛtaḥ* | 4.111ab.

156 *Nayasūtra* 4.111cd: *sāmānyād bahir etāni punaś cābhyantarāṇi ca* ||.

are defined as those of air, fire, earth, water and ether.[157] Both texts show their account of meditative fixation relating to the same first four elements, but the *Nayasūtra* adds 'ether'. With this unusual sequence, these two texts stand apart from other Śaiva sources.[158]

Another topic treated by both texts in their yoga-section, and commonly taught in the Śaiva yoga system, is *karaṇa*. *Karaṇa* is a technical term for what the yogin does with his upper body once his lower limbs have assumed a yogic posture and he is about to engage in the practice of *prāṇāyāma* ('breath control').[159] What is taught in the *Niśvāsamukha* (4.51) and in the *Nayasūtra* (4.106ab) is effectively the same procedure; the wording of the verses differs slightly, with neither text employing the term *karaṇa*.[160]

Cosmographical descriptions are also shared by the *Niśvāsamukha* and the *Guhyasūtra*, including accounts of the forty Śaiva sites with corresponding homonymous heavens known as the *pañcāṣṭaka*, the 'five ogdoads', which seem closely related. It is striking, for instance, that *Niśvāsamukha* 3.22ab is hypermetrical, as is the corresponding hemistich of *Guhyasūtra* 7.116ab. Both texts present their listings of these places in congruence with regard even to the order of the individual items, with only negligible variation in the names: *Niśvāsamukha* 3.23a calls one world *vastrāpada*, while the corresponding reading of the *Guhyasūtra* (7.117c) is *bhadrāpada*. *Vastrāpada* is attested in a wide range of relevant sources, such as *Mahābhārata* 3.80:108b, *Svacchandatantra* 10.887a *Īśānagurudevapaddhati* 17.197, and *Uttarakāmika* 23.136. The occurrence of *bhadrāpada* as a place particularly sacred to Śiva and his followers, however, is not. We assume therefore that the list of the *Guhyasūtra* in this instance must have been subjected to (wilful or inadvertent) corruption. Although *vastrāpada* transpires in many sources, the original name might have been Bhastrāpada,[161] although it occurs only in a handful of sources, such as *Skandapurāṇa* 125-128, *Śivadharmaśāstra*

---

157 *Nayasūtra* 4.115–116: *vāyavīṃ dhāraye 'ṅguṣṭhe āgneyīṃ nābhimadhyataḥ | māhendrīṃ kaṇṭhadeśe tu vāruṇīṃ ghaṇṭikeṣu ca* || 4.115 || *ākāśadhāraṇā mūrdhni sarvasiddhikarī smṛtā | ekadvitṛścatuḥpañca udghātaiś ca prasiddhyati* || 4.116 ||.

158 We find a different sequence of meditative fixation taught in *Rauravasūtrasaṅgraha* 7.6–10, *Svāyaṃbhuvasūtrasaṅgraha* 20.4–28, *Mataṅgayogapāda* 35c–65, *Kiraṇa* 58.18c–26b, etc., which follow instead this order: fire, water, sovereign (*īśa*) and nectar (*amṛta*). For more details, see TAK3 s.v. *dhāraṇā*.

159 See TAK2 s.v. *karaṇa* for further details.

160 The *Niśvāsamukha* runs as follows: *baddhvā yogāsanaṃ samyak ṛjukāyaḥ samāhitaḥ | jihvān tu tāluke nyasya dantair dantān na saṃspṛśet* ||; and the *Nayasūtra*: *tālujihvo dantāsparśī samako nāsadṛṣṭigaḥ* |.

161 BISSCHOP 2006: 31 and 186.

12.108a,[162] and *Śivadharmasaṅgraha* 7.22a. For the *Śivadharmaśāstra*'s testimony concerning the form of this toponym we consulted two early Nepalese witnesses—one[163] records *bhastrāpada* whereas the other[164] has *vastrāpada*. To many South Asian ears these words are almost homophonous, and this no doubt explains the discrepancy in transmission.[165] Many further such instances of small variation occur: where the *Niśvāsamukha* (3.25b) reads *thaleśvara*, the *Guhyasūtra* (7.120d) attests to *sthaleśvara*. This seems again an insignificant variation, *thaleśvara* being a local variant attributable to the regional pronunciation in the mind(s) of the scribe(s).

All in all, the *Guhyasūtra* follows standard orthography more closely than the *Niśvāsamukha*. It is, however, not always the case that the readings of the *Guhyasūtra* are consistently superior to those of the *Niśvāsamukha*. For instance, in the case of *amrātikeśvara*, the *Guhyasūtra* seems to attest to *ambrātikeśvara*, which has been emended to *amrātikeśvara* (see below)—which is the reading the *Niśvāsamukha* provides. As the *pañcāṣṭaka* is a common topic in Śaiva sources, this list, shared by both texts, does not entitle us to conclude that the *Niśvāsamukha* borrowed this textual portion from the *Guhyasūtra*. It appears more likely that both texts are dependent on an earlier, most probably non-tantric, Śaiva work for the provision of this list. If we are right in our interpretation, in borrowing the list from an earlier, external source, the *Guhyasūtra* adds an extra hemistich, marked in bold, as the concluding remark for each group of eight. This is done in order to summarize the soteriological significance of each ogdoad in the context of Śaiva cosmology. We present the two lists juxtaposed below:

---

162 Refer to the Nepalese manuscript with the reel № B 7/3, fol. 44v. line: 4.

163 A 1028/4, fol. 46v. line 4.

164 A 1082/3, fol. 40v. line 4.

165 Hans Bakker, in a personal communication dated 16th of October 2015, noted that a "similar variant is found in *Mahābhārata* 3.80.108b, where the critical text has Vastrāpada (with wriggle), while the Southern Recension has Bhadrāpada (not Bhastrāpada)". He further remarks: "Bhastrāpada is only found in the *Śivadharma*, the *Skandapurāṇa*, and some pre-angkorean inscriptions", for which reason the original name "might indeed have been Bhastrāpada. But this name, 'original' or not, is not found in the *Guhyasūtra*, nor in the *Niśvāsamukha*".

<table>
<tr><th>NIŚVĀSAMUKHA 3.19–25</th><th>GUHYASŪTRA 7.112–121</th></tr>
<tr><td>*amareśaṃ prabhāsañ ca*
naimiṣaṃ puṣkaran tathā |
āṣāḍhan diṇḍimuṇḍiñ ca
bhārabhūtiñ ca lākulim ||</td><td>*amareśaṃ prahāsañ ca*
naimiṣaṃ puṣkaran tathā |
āṣāḍhin diṇḍimuṇḍiñ ca
bhārabhūtiṃ salākulim ||
pratyātmike mṛtā ye tu
te vrajanty eva tatpadam |
pratyātmike] *conj.*; pratyātmikā NKW</td></tr>
<tr><td>*hariścandraṃ paraṃ guhyaṃ*
guhyaṃ madhyamakeśvaram |</td><td>*hariścandraṃ paraṃ guhyaṃ*
guhyaṃ madhyamakeśvaram ||
guhyaṃ guhyaṃ] K; guhyaṃ guhya° NW</td></tr>
<tr><td>*śrīparvataṃ samākhyātañ*
jalpeśvaram ataḥ param ||</td><td>*śrīparvataṃ samākhyātañ*
jalpeśvaram ataḥ param |
jalpeśvaram ataḥ] N; jāleśvaram ataḥ K; jalpaśvaram ataḥ W</td></tr>
<tr><td>*amrātikeśvarañ caiva*
mahākālan tathaiva ca |</td><td>*amrātikeśvaraṃ caiva*
mahākālaṃ tathaiva ca ||
amrātikeśvaraṃ] *em.*; ambrā --- N; amdhrā ⊔ K; ambrātike ⊔ W, mahākālaṃ] *em.*; mahākāla NW; mahākālas K</td></tr>
<tr><td>*kedāram uttamaṅ guhyaṃ*
mahābhairavam eva ca ||</td><td>*kedāram uttamaṃ guhyaṃ*
mahābhairavam eva ca |
guhyaṃ] NW; śuddhaṃ K
guhyāṣṭake mṛtā ye tu
te vrajantīha tatpadam ||</td></tr>
<tr><td>*gayāñ caiva kurukṣetraṃ*
nakhalaṅ kanakhalan tathā |</td><td>*gayāñ caiva kurukṣetran*
nakhalaṃ kanakhalan tathā |
gayāñ caiva] NW; gayā caiva K</td></tr>
<tr><td>*vimalañ cāṭṭahāsañ ca*
māhendraṃ bhīmam aṣṭamam ||</td><td>*vimalañ cāṭṭahāsañ ca*
māhendraṃ bhīmam aṣṭamam ||
atiguhye mṛtā ye tu
atiguhyaṃ vrajanti te |
te] NW; ca K</td></tr>
</table>

vastrāpadaṃ rudrakoṭim
avimuktam mahābalam |

bhadrāpadaṃ rudrakoṭim
avimuktaṃ mahābalam ||

rudrakoṭim avimuktaṃ] *em.*; rudrakoṭim avimukta NW; rudrakoṭi avimuktaṃ K

gokarṇaṃ bhadrakarṇṇaṃ ca
svarṇṇākṣaṃ sthāṇum aṣṭamam ||

gokarṇaṃ rudrakarṇṇañ ca
svarṇākṣaṃ sthāṇur aṣṭamam |

gokarṇaṃ bhadrakarṇṇaṃ] *em.*; gokarṇa --- karṇṇañ NW; gokarṇa rudrakarṇṇañ K, svarṇākṣaṃ sthāṇur aṣṭamam] *em.*; svarṇā --- raṣṭamam NK; svarṇa ⊔ raṣṭamam W

eteṣv api mṛtās samyag
bhittvā lokam aśeṣataḥ |
dīpyamānās tu gacchanti
atra sthāneṣu ye mṛtāḥ |

chagalaṇḍaṃ dviraṇḍañ ca
mākoṭaṃ maṇḍaleśvaram |
kālañjaraṃ samākhyātaṃ
devadāruvanan tathā ||

chagalaṇḍaṃ dviraṇḍañ ca
mākoṭaṃ maṇḍaleśvaram ||
kālañjaraṃ samākhyātan
devadāruvanan tathā |

śaṅkukarṇṇan tathaiveha
thaleśvaram ataḥ param |
snānadarśanapūjābhir
mucyate sarvakilbiṣaiḥ ||

śaṅkukarṇṇan tathaiveha
sthaleśvaram ataḥ param ||
eteṣv api mṛtā ye tu
bhittvā lokam aśeṣataḥ |
dīpyamānās tu gacchanti
sthānāṣṭakam idaṃ priye ||

sthānāṣṭakam idaṁ] *em.*; sthā --- midam NK; sthāṇva ⊔ W

The list of the *pañcāṣṭaka* in the *Niśvāsamukha* appears in the Laukika section, more precisely, the section wherein the text conveys the religious duties of uninitiated lay followers. The locations listed in connection with the *pañcāṣṭaka* clearly correspond to famous Śaiva pilgrimage sites. As we can see from the extract above, the listing of the 'five sets of eight' as they are displayed in the *Niśvāsamukha* does not provide the names for each group of eight; conversely, they do feature in the case of the *Guhyasūtra*[166]

166 Each ogdoad in the *Guhyasūtra* (7.123–124) has been assigned its particular name: *pratyātmika, guhya, atiguhya, pavitra,* and *sthāṇu.*

and in other significant Śaiva tantric works (in *Svāyambhuvasūtrasaṅgraha* 4.47–55, for example). The list in the *Niśvāsamukha*, however, does display the epithets 'most secret' (*paraṃ guhyaṃ*) in reference to Hariścandra; Madhyamakeśvara, in turn, is referred to as secret (*guhyaṃ*).[167] Further, Kedāra and Mahābhairava are here given the epithet 'extreme[ly] secret' (*uttamaṃ guhyaṃ*).[168]

Regarding the direction of borrowing amongst the two works, Hans BAKKER argued, in short, that the author of the *Guhyasūtra* must have borrowed the list from the *Niśvāsamukha*, adding hemistiches[169] after the description of each ogdoad; he would have done so in order to recast the original list in accordance with the dogmatic particularities of the *Guhyasūtra*. But we suspect that the *Guhyasūtra* did not borrow this list from the *Niśvāsamukha*, since there is evidence to suggest that the *Guhyasūtra* may have been composed before the *Niśvāsamukha*.

We base this contention regarding the relative dating on the grounds that the *Guhyasūtra* (1.1–4) considers the compendium to be complete (*saṃpūrṇa*) without the *Niśvāsamukha*, which is therein described as merely 'informing' or 'complementing' (*puṣṭa*) the *Niśvāsa*-corpus. This would mean that the *Guhyasūtra* antedates the *Niśvāsamukha*, which in turn indicates that at a previous stage, the *Niśvāsa*-compendium would have consisted of the *Guhyasūtra* and the other three *sūtras* alone. This is all the more plausible if we remember that the *Guhyasūtra* and the other three

167 *Niśvāsamukha* 3.20 ff. HansBAKKER, in a personal communication dated 16 October 2015, opined that the use of the terms (*guhyam, paraṃ guhyaṃ* and *uttamaṃ guhyam*) might not refer to any further, particular group of sites, but instead reflects a more generic use which is employed merely to emphasize the *gravitas* of the sites they already qualify.

168 Hans BAKKER, (*ibid.*), notified us that "*Guhyasūtra* 7.115a does not qualify Kedāra as *atiguhya*—indeed one of the five names of the ogdoads—but as *uttamaṃ guhyaṃ*." Yet we would like to point out that the *Śivadharmaśāstra* lists the five sets of ogdoads with specific naming (see BISSCHOP 2006: 30–32).

169 *Guhyasūtra* 7.113ab, 115cd, 117ab, and 118cd–119ab. Hans BAKKER, however, (*ibid.*), conveyed his belief that the *Guhyasūtra* is the younger text, and that its redactor might also have recast individual portions of the *Niśvāsamukha* to streamline it in deference to the profile of ideas expressed in the *Guhyasūtra*. In his own words, he deems it more

> likely that the hemistiches given in bold in *Guhyasūtra* 7.113ab, 115cd, 117ab, and 118cd–119ab ..., which are missing in the *Mukha* text, are additions through which the author of the *Guhyasūtra* adapted the *Mukha* text to the later doctrine.

sūtras have tantric content and are hence also topically distinct from the *Niśvāsamukha*. What is more, as we have seen above, the references to the *Niśvāsamukha* in the *Guhyasūtra* are situated at the very beginning and end of the latter and are therefore likely to be later insertions included with the intent to craft a retroactive link between the *Niśvāsamukha* and the other books of the *Niśvāsa*-corpus.

There is an additional line at the end of the section in the *Niśvāsamukha* (3.25cd) which reminds us of the pre-tantric connotations of the *pañcāṣṭaka*. The writer of this line does not appear to regard these places as counterparts to the respective Śaiva worlds (*bhuvana*) known, from a list of cosmic correlatives, by the same name: *snānadarśanapūjābhir mucyate sarvakilbiṣaiḥ* 'by bathing, beholding or performing worship [there] one becomes free from all sins.' Immediately after that (*Niśvāsamukha* 3.26), however, the text suggests that the divine ogdoads (*pañcāṣṭaka*) are located above the egg of Brahmā (*brahmāṇḍa*). It also mentions that those who die in one of the pilgrimage sites of the worldly *pañcāṣṭaka* will proceed to the corresponding world of the same name in the divine *pañcāṣṭaka*, from which they shall not have to return.[170] Thereby a correlation is established of the earthly pilgrimage sites known as the *pañcāṣṭaka* with the cosmic *pañcāṣṭaka*.[171] The textual evidence for a connection between cosmic and earthly pilgrimage sites in the *Niśvāsamukha* is briefer than the more elaborate presentation in the *Guhyasūtra*, yet it is no less explicit.[172]

The extra lines inserted at the end of each group of eight in the extract of the *Guhyasūtra* above also reflects the correlation of the divine *pañcāṣṭakas* with their forty mundane counterparts. For instance, explaining the properties of the first group, the text mentions: *pratyātmike mṛtā ye tu te vrajanty eva tatpadam* 'whoever dies in [the fivefold set of eight known as] Pratyātmikā certainly ventures forth to the corresponding world.' Thus, the five ogdoads, as presented in the context of the *Guhyasūtra*, reflect a tantric view of the cosmos. The *Guhyasūtra* itself, however, cannot readily be credited with incorporating these ogdoads into Śaiva cosmology. in our view,

---

170 Cf., for example in *Guhyasūtra* 7.113ab.

171 The *Guhyasūtra*, for its part, gives a detailed presentation of a fully developed hierarchy of cosmic counterparts to the earthly *pañcāṣṭakas*.

172 *gacchanti bhitvā brahmāṇḍam eṣu sthāneṣu ye mṛtāḥ | pañcāṣṭakam idan divyaṃ yaṃ gattvā na nivartate* || 3.26 || . 'Those who die in these places ascend, penetrating the [shell of the] egg of Brahmā (*brahmāṇḍam*), to [the respective world in] this divine set of five groups of eight [worlds bearing the same names as the pilgrimage sites], upon reaching which (*yaṃ gatvā*) he will not be reborn [in this world].'

the Lokātīta-Pāśupatas[173] are more likely to have been the first to propel this development; only thereafter did the followers of the Mantramārga proceeded to gradually integrate these places in their cosmology.[174]

In this vein, it is to be noted that the *Śivadharmaśāstra*[175] also records a list of *pañcāṣṭaka*, albeit with some variation in naming. The list in the *Śivadharmaśāstra* likewise refers to the pilgrimage centres and in like manner provides a label for each group.[176]

Another significant point of topical overlap between the *Niśvāsamukha* and the *Guhyasūtra* is the praise of qualities ascribed to the pilgrimage site of Kedāra. The *Niśvāsamukha* (3.28a–29a) presents it thus:

> *kedārodakapānāc ca gatiṃ pañcāṣṭamīṃ dhruvam* |
> *vidyayā saṃyutā ye tu pibante ca jalaṃ śubham* ||
> *śivasāyojyatāṃ yānti* |

> Also, by drinking the water of Kedāra one certainly obtains the realm of rebirth of (*gatim*) [of attaining] the five sets of ogdoads (i.e. all forty *bhuvanas*) (*pañcāṣṭamīm*). As for those who possess (*saṃyutāḥ*) the Vidyāmantra (*vidyayā*) and who drink [this] pure water [of Kedāra], they will obtain (*yānti*) union with Śiva.

The *tīrtha* Kedāra occurs twice in the *Niśvāsamukha*: once in the list of forty sacred places (3.21) and once at this point (3.28), where drinking the

173 Presented in *Niśvāsamukha* 4.88ff.

174 The Śaiva cosmos begins with the world of Kālāgnirudra and reaches up to the *parama* ('highest') Śiva, that is to say: the ultimate reality in and of the system (*Mūlasūtra* 5.1–2). Dominic GOODALL defines the structure of Śaiva cosmology (email of 5th November 2014) as follows:

> The Śaiva cosmology is the 'order of the universe' according to the Śaivas. In other words, it refers to the levels of hells, *pātālas* 'netherworlds' and other *bhuvanas* 'worlds' that are described, for instance in chapter 5 of the *Parākhya*, or chapter 8 of the *Kiraṇa*, or chapters 4–7 of the *Guhyasūtra*, or chapter 10 of the *Svacchanda*. Some people might prefer to refer to a Śaiva cosmography, a description of the cosmos. What makes it Śaiva is that no other group makes the claim that the universe has quite this shape. The Purāṇic cosmography, for example, is much more limited, since it restricts itself to the *brahmāṇḍa* 'egg of Brahmā.'

175 *Śivadharmaśāstra* 12.108 ff (A 1082/3, fol. 40v4–41r2). Refer to p. 99.

176 Note that BISSCHOP (2006: 27–28) argues that this list may represent an archaic phase of its history.

water of Kedāra is emphasised: 'those who possess (*saṃyutāḥ*) the Vidyāmantra (*vidyayā*) and who drink [this] pure water [of Kedāra] will obtain (*yānti*) union with Śiva.' The Vidyāmantra, in all likelihood, refers to the ten-syllable *vidyāmantra* (also referred to as Daśākṣaradeva) taught in chapter 16 of the *Guhyasūtra*.[177] This implies that the Laukika teaching of the *Niśvāsamukha* is partly infused with knowledge of the Mantramārgic teachings. This suspicion hardens when considering the account of Kedāra as presented in the *Guhyasūtra*:

> *ṛṣaya ū*[178] |
> *devadāruvane ramye*[179] *ṛṣayaḥ saṃśitavratāḥ* |
> *nandīśam upasaṃgamya praṇipatya muhur muhuḥ* || 16.1 ||
> *ūcus te ṛṣayaḥ sarve stutvā nandiṃ*[180] *śivātmajam* |
> *sarvadharmātiriktas tu kedāras tu kathaṃ bhavet* || 16.2 ||
> *utpattiñ ca vidhānañ ca pītasyaiva tu yat phalam* |
> *kedārasya samāsena tattvato vaktum arhasi*[181] || 16.3 ||
> *nandir uvāca* |
> *himavacchikharāsīnaṃ deva*[[(*devaṃ jagadguruṃ*)]] |
> *brahmādyādisurāḥ sarve saṃsārabhayapīḍitāḥ* || 16.4 ||
> *śaraṇaṃ śaṃkaraṃ jagmuḥ*[182] *stutvā ca vividhaiḥ stavaiḥ* |
> *padbhyāṃ nipatitāḥ sarve kṛtvā cāñjalisaṃpuṭam*[183] || 16.5 ||
> *vijñāpayaṃ haraṃ caivaṃ*[184] *sarve tatra divaukasāḥ* [185] |
> *yā te rudra śivā mūrtiḥ sā kathaṃ prāpyate vibho*[186] || 16.6 ||
> *aśivaiś ca suraiḥ sarvair brahmaviṣṇupurogamaiḥ* |
> *tataś ca sa haro devaḥ*[187] ((*sa*)) --- [[*kā*]]*rakaḥ*[188] || 16.7 ||
> *vi*[[*dyayā* (*saṃ*)]]*puṭaṃ retaṃ surāṇām agratas tyajan*[189] |

[177] For a summary of the legend, see also TAK 3, s.v. *daśākṣara*.
[178] ṛṣaya ū] *conj.*; ṛ--- NW; ⊔ K
[179] devadāruvane ramye] *conj.*; ---mmye N; ⊔ msK; ṛ ⊔ W
[180] nandiṃ] K; nandi° NW
[181] vaktum arhasi] K; vāktum arhasi NW
[182] śaṃkaraṃ jagmuḥ] KW; śaṃkaraṇ jagmuḥ N
[183] cāñjalisaṃpuṭam] WK^{pc}; cāñjalisaṃpuṭām N; cāñjalisaṃpuṃṭam K^{ac}
[184] vijñāpayaṃ haraṃ caivaṃ] W; vijñāpayaṃ haran cevaṃ N; vijñāpaṃyan haraṃ tvevaṃ K
[185] divaukasāḥ] W; divaukasā N; divaukasaḥ K
[186] mūrtiḥ sā kathaṃ prāpyate vibho] *em.*; mūrtti sā kathaṃ prāpyate vibhoḥ N; mūrtti sā kathaṃ prāpyate vibho KW
[187] devaḥ] K; deva NW
[188] kārakaḥ] K; --- N; dārakaḥ W
[189] °gratas tyajan] *conj.*; °gratas tyajat N; °gratas tyajet KW

bho surendrā pibasvedaṃ[190] *reta vidyāsamanvitam* || 16.8 ||
mama retasya pānena śivatvaṃ prāpyate dhruvam |
etac chrutvā tu vacanaṃ[191] *sarve tatra divaukasāḥ*[192] || 16.9 ||
prādudruvan[193] *tataḥ sarve apītvā tu tadāmṛtam* |
devīṃ[194] *māṃ ca bravīd devo pāsyatāṃ jalam uttamam* || 16.10 ||
na ca devī pibet tat tu ---[195] |
--- ((*vet*)) |
aham eva hi pāsyāmi devī vacanam abravīt || 16.11 ||
nandi nandi mahāprajña[196] *rakṣasva -m- amṛtaṃ*[197] *jalam* |
na deyaṃ devatānāṃ tu naitat pānaṃ kadācana[198] || 16.12 ||
mānuṣā[[*nugra*(*haṃ kāryaṃ paśupakṣi*)]]*mṛgādiṣu*[199] |
vidyāhīnā gaṇeśāś[200] *ca sāyojyaṃ vidyayā yutāḥ*[201] || 16.13 ||

In the beautiful Devadāru forest, the sages [who abided] under stringent vows approached Nandīśa and prostrated [before him] again and again. All the sages, having first praised Nandi, a son of Śiva, asked: "how is it that Kedāra is excelling over all *dharmas*? What is the origin [of its water], what is the [proper] procedure for drinking it and what is the result of drinking it? Pray tell [us all] about Kedāra in brief." Nandi replied: "All the foremost gods, beginning with Brahmā, oppressed by fear of the world, sought refuge with Śaṅkara, god of gods, [and] teacher of the world, who was sitting at the top of the snow[-capped] mountain. The [gods] praised [Śaṅkara] with various panegyrics, [and then,] folding their hands, they all fell at his feet. Then, introducing [themselves] to Hara, the gods [asked]: 'how can, o Rudra, [oneness with] your peaceful form be attained by all [us] anxious gods, headed by Brahmā and Viṣṇu?' Then the god Hara [answered] [...] discharging [his] semen, concealed

190 surendrā pibasvedaṃ reta] NW; surendrāḥ pibasvedaṃ retaṃ K
191 vacanaṃ sarve] NW; sarve K
192 divaukasāḥ] NW; divaukasaḥ K
193 prādudruvan] *conj.*; prādudravan NKW
194 devīṃ] K; devī NW
195 pibet tat tu] W; pibe --- N; pibet ta ⊔ K
196 mahāprajña] K; mahāprajñā NW
197 amṛtaṃ] NW; amṛtaṃ K
198 kadācana] KW; kadācanaḥ N
199 mānuṣānugrahaṃ kāryaṃ paśupakṣimṛgādiṣu] K; mānuṣā _ ga _ ṃ --- mṛgādiṣu N; mānuṣānugrahaṃ kṛtvā tathā pakṣimṛgādiṣu W
200 gaṇeśāś ca] N; gaṇegaṇeśāś ca K; gaṇesāś ca W
201 yutāḥ] K^{pc}; yatā NW; yutām K^{ac}

> by the Vidyā-[mantra], in front of the gods: 'o excellent gods! Drink this [thus] connected with the Vidyā-[mantra]. By drinking my semen, [you] certainly [will] attain Śiva-hood.' As soon as they heard this instruction, all the gods flew away from there without drinking that nectar. God said to Devī and me: '†Drink [this] excellent water; Devī may not drink it [...].' †Devī said the [following] words: 'I myself drink this [semen].' [Then the god said:] 'o Nandi of great intelligence! Protect [this] water, [this] nectar. [You] should never give this water to gods. [You] should [instead] favour human beings, domesticated animals, birds, and forest animals. [All who drink this water] without possessing the Vidyāmantra (*vidyayā*), [will become] lords of the Gaṇas. As for those who possess the Vidyāmantra (*vidyayā*), they will attain oneness [with me].' "

Particularly telling of a certain degree of Laukika-Mantramārga syncretism is the following extract from *Guhyasūtra* 16.15:

> *vidyāyā lakṣaṇaṃ vakṣye yathāha parameśvaraḥ* |
> *nyāsapānavidhānañ ca vidyāmāhātmyam eva ca* ||
>
> I will relate [to you] a description of the Vidyā-[mantra] as the highest god related it [to me], the *nyāsa* procedure [relating to the mantra], the procedure for drinking the [Kedāra water] and also the greatness of the Vidyā-[mantra].

If we consider the above extracts in conjunction with *Niśvāsamukha* 3.28–29b, it appears possible that chapter sixteen of the *Guhyasūtra* influenced the *Niśvāsamukha*, specifically because of the tantric influence on a principally Laukika segment.[202] The *Niśvāsamukha* might have borrowed from the *Guhyasūtra* the idea of achieving union with Śiva by means of the Vidyāmantra and by drinking the Kedāra water.

It is conceivable that a late author/editor was involved *both* in the redaction of the *Niśvāsamukha*, as well as in the generation of the final chapters

[202] There is a further instance where the text of the *Niśvāsamukha* appears to be influenced by the tantric teachings, viz. *Niśvāsamukha* 1.27c–28b: (*dīkṣitā nandinā sarve nirvvāṇe yojitāḥ pare* || *vidyābhikāṅkṣiṇaś cānye vidyāyāṃ te tu yojitāḥ* |). These two lines appear just after Nandin names the Five Streams (1.26a–27a) and states two types of initiation, *vidyādīkṣā* and *nirvāṇadīkṣā*, which actually fall under the fifth stream, the Mantramārga.

of the *Guhyasūtra*, chapter sixteen in particular:[203] rather than remoulding either text to fit the other's idiosyncrasies, that author might have penned the sections containing the reference to the water of Kedāra, the praise of *vidyā*, and the tantric connotations thereof in both texts—to the effect that they originally harmonized.[204]

As we have already observed,[205] *Guhyasūtra* 1.4 refers to the *Niśvāsamukha* in the very beginning of the work; likewise, the very end of the *Guhyasūtra* (18.15) displays a cross-reference of similarly doubtful authenticity.[206]

If the above mentioned cross-references to the *Niśvāsamukha* (in *Guhyasūtra* 1.4 and 18.15) are not subsequent insertions, but instead were original components of the work, then the *Niśvāsamukha* must chronologically precede the *Guhyasūtra*. Yet, given their positions at the very beginning and the very end of the text, the likelihood is that both of them were added subsequently during a late stage of the composition of the *Guhyasūtra*. We therefore hesitate to take these cross-references at face value, and choose to refrain from considering them in our calculations regarding the relative dating of these two texts.[207]

The *Niśvāsamukha*'s Borrowings from the *Pāśupatasūtra*

The *Pāśupatasūtra* is one of the earliest sources from which the composer(s) of the *Niśvāsamukha* drew—it also appears to be the work on which the *Niśvāsamukha* draws most extensively. We recall that the *Pāśupatasūtra* is the earliest extant scripture traceable to the oldest known school of Śaivism, that of the Pāśupatas. In the *Niśvāsamukha*, the Pāśupata system is referred

---

203 The *Guhyasūtra* may quite possibly contain a multiplicity of textual layers, in which case a number of authors may have been involved in the composition of a text that in its youngest version eventually came to span eighteen chapters. Consult GOODALL et al. (2015: 20, 44 and 71–73) for more details.

204 The possibility that the *Niśvāsamukha* and the *Guhyasūtra* were both fashioned after an unknown, external source, certainly remains.

205 See p. 35.

206 'Doubtful' in the sense that both of these verses may be retroactive insertions by a scribe attempting to reinforce the internal cohesion of the compendium by crafting a link between the *Niśvāsamukha* and the four *sūtras*. Consult p. 36 for the full quotation of this extract.

207 Hans BAKKER in a personal communication dated to 16th October 2015, attributes a greater degree of credibility to the cross-references than we are inclined to adopt: "Finally, the *Guhyasūtra* mentions the *Mukha* twice (1.4 & 18,13, 15), the *Mukha* never the *Guhyasūtra*. ... the odds are that the *Guhyasūtra* knew the *Mukha* and not the other way [a]round."

to as the Atimārga—'the outer path.'[208] On the one hand, pivotal practices of the Pāśupata school are reserved for the brahmanical elite—ascetics have to be male brahmins for example.[209] On the other hand, the Pāśupata tenet system intentionally inverts traditional brahmanical observances in many instances[210]—this indicates the antinomian streak of the Pāśupatas. The fact that the *Niśvāsamukha*'s author(s) adopted extensive segments of the *Pāśupatasūtra* reveals that the Pāśupatas were still a prominent presence in contemporaneous society. It also shows, SANDERSON posits, that certain aspects of Mantramārga Śaivism comprise a continuation of core components of the tenet system of the Atimārga.[211]

The fourth section of the *Niśvāsamukha*, relating the ideas and practices of the Atimārga, commences at 4.70c and extends until 4.130d. It presents two distinct types of the Pāśupata system (4.123), namely the Atyāśrama (4.70c–88d) and the Lokātīta (4.89–130). The first, Atyāśrama, is offered in the guise of a fully versified paraphrase of the *Pāśupatasūtra*. In the following section, we shall investigate the precise way in which the *Niśvāsamukha* draws on the *Pāśupatasūtra*, for which task we will be presenting passages of correspondence between these two texts with an analytical emphasis on apparent alterations.[212]

Of course we cannot expect the *Pāśupatasūtra* to reappear verbatim in the textual fabric of the *Niśvāsamukha*: the fact that the *Niśvāsamukha* is in *anuṣṭubh* verse precludes any such possibility. What is more, textual fragments had to be rearranged in accordance with the stylistic and semantic

208 SANDERSON (1988: 664) renders Atimārga as the "outer path" because the latter system operates outside—both in implied, and overt, contradiction to—the brahmanical establishment; in particular, the Atimārga defies the teachings concerning the four stages of life (*caturāśrama*) central to the brahmanical system. Etymologically, however, Atimārga could also be translated as 'transcendent path'.

209 One of the bases for ascertained congruence between the Pāśupata school and the brahmanical tradition is the Pāśupata observance. SANDERSON mentions (1988: 664) that the latter is reserved for a brahmin who has already undergone the *upanayana* rite, in which the boy is invested with the sacred thread and hence qualified to learn the Veda.

210 This becomes evident when ruminating upon the following injunctions: *bhasmani śayīta* 'one should sleep in ashes,' ...' *unmattavad eko vicareta loke* 'one should stroll around in the world alone like a mad person,' *śmaśānavāsī* ... 'one should live in a cremation ground' (*Pāśupatasūtra* 1.3, 4.4 and 5.20).

211 The reader is here referred to SANDERSON (2006: 199 ff.).

212 Other than for the most significant findings, which are presented below, the reader is encouraged to consult the translation and accompanying notes of the section in question (*Niśvāsamukha* 4.70c–88d). We have followed the system of numbering of the *Pāśupatasūtra* which is based on Kauṇḍinya's commentary (i.e. in accordance with ŚĀSTRĪ's edition); this does not accord with the *sūtrapāṭha* of BISSCHOP (2007).

dictates of the *Niśvāsamukha*. Still, despite the agenda with which the composers of the *Niśvāsamukha* approach the content of the *Pāśupatasūtra*—namely to compile a compendium which re-contextualizes earlier related systems as ancillary and subservient to tantric Śaivism—one can nevertheless speak of an affinity in perspective.[213] Let us proceed to investigate the extant evidence.

In some cases, the fact that a fragment comprises borrowed text that has been altered and expanded upon is clear and conspicuous. For example, *Pāśupatasūtra* 1.18 *akaluṣamateḥ* 'of one [who is] of unclouded mind' is rendered in *Niśvāsamukha* 4.75ab as *akāluṣyeṇa bhāvena jantuṃ paśyeta sarvataḥ*: 'one should see all living beings with an unclouded disposition.' We suppose that this text grew not just as a corollary of the dictates of metre, but mostly out of the need to make explicit and clarify the meaning of a source text that by dint of its genre-specific parameters—those of the *sūtras*—tends to be notoriously terse.

First of all, let us turn to cases where the text of the *Niśvāsamukha* deviates significantly from the *Pāśupatasūtra*, although the intended meaning remains largely identical:

PĀŚUPATASŪTRA	NIŚVĀSAMUKHA
• *carataḥ* 1.19	*evaṃ yo varttate nityaṃ* 4.86a
Of somebody who wanders [thus]	[If] somebody always remains thus
• *kāma-rūpitvam* 1.24	*yathepsitam* 4.87b
capability of shapeshifting	whatever he desires
• *avamataḥ* | *sarvabhūteṣu* 3.3–4	*viparītāni karmmāṇi kurvaṃl lokajugupsitaḥ* | 4.78cd
being insulted amidst all beings	performing transgressive acts censured by people

213 We hold that the embedding of the content of the *Niśvāsa*-corpus in a stratified scheme of five streams indicates that the author was driven, at least in part, by an 'inclusivistic' approach that sought to elevate the Mantramārga above its appropriated counterparts. For a brief reaquaintance with the five streams, refer to pp. 22ff).

• *paribhūyamāno hi vidvān kṛtsnatapā bhavati* 3.19	*paribhūtaḥ kṛcchratapā sarvalokeṣu ninditaḥ* | *mahātapāś ca bhavate* 4.81c–82a
For, a wise person being humiliated becomes someone who has undergone all penances	humiliated, practising severe *tapas*, and blamed everywhere, he becomes great in *tapas*
• *sarvaviśiṣṭo 'yaṃ panthāḥ* | *satpathaḥ* 4.16–17	*sanmārggavratacāriṇe* 4.84d
The path is distinguished above all others, [it is the] good path (HARA 1966: 367)	For the one who practises the observances of the right path

Although the intended meanings for each of the above-listed pairs of expressions are largely identical, the redactor still introduces noteworthy changes in formulation. In our view, these stylistic changes were made with the aim of streamlining the tone of the appropriated section in order to harmonize it with the wider textual body of the *Niśvāsamukha*.

That being said, we also encounter semantic discrepancies between Pāśupata injunctions and their reformulations in the *Niśvāsamukha*. In the following example we find a reference to the *liṅga*, the icon of Śiva, in the textual fabric of the *Niśvāsamukha* which is absent both in the *Pāśupatasūtra* and in Kauṇḍinya's commentary—evidently, the inclusion of the *liṅga* in the *Niśvāsamukha* constitutes an act of innovation. If unintentional innovation is a possibility to be considered, then it is conceivable that the paraphrased text may have appeared as the result of relatively loose paraphrasing. Perhaps, due to quasi-synonymous use of the terms *āyatana* ('temple' or 'abode') and *liṅgasyāyatana* ('temple [housing a] *liṅga*') in common parlance, the redactor saw no difference between *āyatana* and *liṅgasyāyatana* ('the abode of the *liṅga*'). In opting for the rendition of *liṅgasyāyatana* in the *Niśvāsamukha* the author might have sought to render explicit what he considered to be an implicit shade of meaning in the *Pāśupatasūtra*.[214] Therefore he may not have been aware of having introduced a potentially significant modification:

[214] Kauṇḍinya states, in his commentary on *Pāśupatasūtra* 1.7, that since people worship at that place, it is called an *āyatana* (*yajanāc cāyatanam*); but he makes no mention of a *liṅga*.

PĀŚUPATASŪTRA 1.7	NIŚVĀSAMUKHA 4.72a
āyatanavāsī	*liṅgasyāyatane vāsaḥ*
resident of a temple	he [should take up his] abode in the house of a *liṅga* [i.e. a temple]

Another conspicuous modification concerns mantra recitation. At 1.17, the *Pāśupatasūtra* and Kauṇḍinya's commentary thereto, attest to two valid alternatives of performing recitation: one can opt either to recite the *raudrī gāyatrī* or the *bahurūpī gāyatrī*. Conversely, *Niśvāsamukha* 4.74d enjoins the recitation of the *bahurūpī gāyatrī* mantra without giving any sanctioned alternative. We cannot as of yet determine whether or not the *Niśvāsamukha* is responsible for abolishing the option of reciting the *raudrī gāyatrī*, as there is a possibility that the *Niśvāsamukha* simply borrowed the passages from a third source.

PĀŚUPATASŪTRA 1.17	NIŚVĀSAMUKHA 4.74d
raudrīṃ gāyatrīṃ bahurūpīṃ vā japet	*bahurūpan tato japet*
he should recite the *gāyatrī* of appeal to Rudra or the *aghora* [mantra]	then he should recite the *aghora* [mantra]

In the following passage, the *Niśvāsamukha* surprisingly replaces *hasita*, 'laughter,' with *stava*, 'eulogy,'—this idea is not traceable in the *Pāśupatasūtra*. If the modification was executed intentionally, this might suggest that by the time of composition of the *Niśvāsamukha*, the offering (*upahāra*) of laughter to Śiva was far less widespread. Instead, a new, less radical, custom of worship may have begun to emerge in its stead. Furthermore, as we shall see at present, the ordering of the individual elements in the verse of the *Niśvāsamukha* differs from the sequencing in the *Pāśupatasūtra*, and the word *upahāra* is missing in the *Niśvāsamukha*. This, however, may simply be attributable to the constraints of metre:

PĀŚUPATASŪTRA 1.8	NIŚVĀSAMUKHA 4.72b–72d
hasitagītanṛtya- huḍḍuṅkāranamaskāra- japyopahāreṇopatiṣṭhet	*huḍḍuṅkārastavais tathā* | *gītanṛtyanamaskārair* *brahmabhir japasaṃyutaḥ* |

he should honour with laughter, songs, dance, the sounds of HUḌḌUṄ, homage by the word *namas*, mantra recitation, and gifts	he [should praise] with the sound HUḌḌUṄ, sing, dance, [pay] homage with the word *namas* and recite the [five] *brahma* [mantras]

Nowhere in the *Pāśupatasūtra* do we encounter any reference to the concept of *pūjā*, 'worship', yet the *Niśvāsamukha*, for its part, mentions it in several instances. This constitutes a substantial change of perspective, since the Pāśupatas were considered to be practising a form of religion that transcends the established traditions, especially in the domain of structured ritual. But we could assume that the author of the *Niśvāsamukha* treated the terms *yajana* and *pūjā* interchangeably. Thus, we cannot exclude the possibility that this change too, was the unpremeditated result of loose paraphrasing:

Pāśupatasūtra 2.9–11	Niśvāsamukha 4.76ab
tasmād ubhayathā yaṣṭavyaḥ; *devavat pitṛvac ca;* *ubhayaṃ tu rudre devāḥ pitaraś ca*	*pitṛpūjāṃ devapūjām* *ubhe devāya kalpayet* |
thus, he should be venerated in both ways; like the gods and the ancestors; as both the gods and the ancestors are certainly [present] in Rudra	worship as performed for ancestors and worship as performed for gods: one should perform [them] both for the great god (i.e. Rudra)

This is not, however, the only instance of the word *pūjā* in the Pāśupata section of the *Niśvāsamukha*, for it occurs again in 4.71b–71d,[215] which has no parallel in the *Pāśupatasūtra*. *Niśvāsamukha* 4.81d (***pūjā****lābhavivarjitaḥ*) once more includes *pūjā* among the injunctions of the Pāśupatas. The offering of withered flowers, which is described in the *Niśvāsamukha* (4.73cd) and also forms part of *pūjā* ritual, implies a Pāśupata concept even though it is not attested in the *Pāśupatasūtra* itself.[216] There is a possibility that the version of the *Pāśupatasūtra* available to the author of the *Niśvāsamukha* was different from that which is available to us through Kauṇḍinya's commentary. Further, we find non-standard *aiśa* grammar strewn[217] among the verses of the *Niśvāsamukha*, while the corresponding passages of the

215 ... *guhyasthānaṃ parivrajet* | *darśanārthan tu īśasya pūjān tatraiva kalpayet* | .
216 This will be further investigated on p. 84.
217 On the significance of *aiśa* grammar, see p. 129.

Pāśupatasūtra follow standard grammar. In the first instance, when two *Pāśupatasūtras* featuring the neuter *s*-stem *vāsas* are paraphrased in the *Niśvāsamukha*, the word is treated as a masculine *a*-stem, *vāsa*. In the second instance, the standard optative singular *avekṣet* of the *Pāśupatasūtra* has been replaced with its common equivalent, but irregularly in the *ātmanepada*, resulting in the form *paśyeta*:

PĀŚUPATASŪTRA	NIŚVĀSAMUKHA
• *ekavāsāḥ* | *avāsā vā* 1.10–11	*ekavāso hy avāso vā* 4.73a
he [should wear] one garment or [be] without garment	he should wear one garment or [be] naked
• *mūtrapurīṣaṃ nāvekṣet* 1.12	*mūtrāmedhyan na paśyeta* 4.74a
he should not look at urine and excrement	he should not look at urine and excrement

There are some sections in the *Niśvāsamukha* that, as SANDERSON has explained,[218] could possibly constitute innovative additions to paraphrased material borrowed from external sources. Amongst the sources that we now know of, there are four independent Pāśupata ritual texts ascribed to a certain Gārgya. These are the *Saṃskāravidhi*,[219] *Antyeṣṭividhi*,[220] *Pātravidhi*,[221] and the *Prāyaścittavidhi*, all of which have come to light due to the efforts of D. ACHARYA, who has published three of the works (with the fourth announced as forthcoming in the foreseeable future). In these sources also, we did not find what appear to be addenda. Our search in the fifth principal source consulted for this task, the *Pampāmāhātmya*,[222] a text which contains components of the *Pāśupatasūtras* in a paraphrased form, also did not yield any results.

Why were the paraphrased borrowings interpolated with addenda during the process of integration into the *Niśvāsamukha*? First of all, we should bear in mind that we are analyzing a fully versified text. It is undoubtedly,

218 Cf. SANDERSON (2006: 158).
219 D. ACHARYA (2007).
220 D. ACHARYA (2010).
221 D. ACHARYA (2011).
222 FILLIOZAT (2001: 91–152).

at least partially, the case, that in the process of drafting verses, transit-words and other items of textual inflation (verse-fillers) found their way into the textual fabric of the *Niśvāsamukha*. For example, a phrase like *jitendriya*, 'with the senses subjugated' appears both in the *Niśvāsamukha* 4.70d as (*bhasmaśāyī jitendriyaḥ*) and in 4.83a (*jitendriyaś ca dāntaś ca*). While one of these mentions in the *Niśvāsamukha* is certainly a parallel for *Pāśupatasūtra* 5.11,[223] the other is a repetition, most likely serving as mere verse-filler, reiterated so as to not distort the fundamental meaning of the passage, but certainly without adding any semantic content.[224]

There are, however, some other sections in the text which might constitute unaltered, or at least minimally distorted, Pāśupata injunctions. For example, *Niśvāsamukha* 4.73cd *suśīrṇapatitaiḥ puṣpair ddevadevaṃ samarccayet* 'he should worship the god of gods with withered, fallen flowers.' This passage is reminiscent of the important Pāśupata concept of *ahiṃsā*, 'non-harm.' Since the Pāśupata are conscious of the subtle implications of *hiṃsā*, 'harmfulness,' they may have regarded the culling of living flowers as an act to be avoided.[225] In this regard, Kauṇḍinya's commentary on the *Pāśupatasūtra* leads its readers to conclude that *ahiṃsā* is a core-concept of the Pāśupata tenet system, to be rigorously applied in ritual practices. Kauṇḍinya explains that the concept of *ahiṃsā* is fundamental to the practice of a Pāśupata ascetic. In order to avoid harming creatures he is enjoined to eat the food prepared by others (*parakṛta*), live in a temple prepared by others, wear *nirmālya*, 'the discarded garlands of god' and bathe in *bhasma*, 'ashes', instead of water, so as to avoid direct harm to living creatures.[226] This effectively means that in theory he deliberately avoids, at least according to Kauṇḍinya, every possibility of harm inflicted upon any creature. Since the *ahiṃsā* concept is thus an ubiquitous and foundational principle of the Pāśupata school, we assume that *suśīrṇapatitaiḥ puṣpair ddevadevaṃ samarccayet* is not just a verse-filler, but quite likely an authentic Pāśupata injunction, although we have not yet been able to trace it in Pāśupata sources. Moreover, it is probable that a wealth of Pāśupata materials have been lost, so our not finding it may not be conclusive evidence that it did not come from a lost Pāśupata source.

---

223 *Pāśupatasūtra* 5.11 includes *jitendriyaḥ* ('somebody who has conquered his sense-faculties') only once.

224 A similar example may be the phrase *prāṇāyāma* 'breath control' that occurs in 4.85a. As this term has already been used in 4.74ab and is paralleled by *Pāśupatasūtra* 1.16, the second occurrence in 4.85a must have served as reiterative verse-filler.

225 The reader is here referred to SANDERSON 2014: 10, fn. 38.

226 See HARA 2002: 71–73.

The passage of the *Niśvāsamukha* (4.83d) *naikānnādaḥ kadācana*, 'he [should] never eat food [that is obtained] from a singular [household]' might also not have a direct parallel in the limited, extant literature available to us; however, it does not appear to be an addendum resulting from the dictates of metre—and indeed the *Prāyaścittavidhi* (v. 81), one of the recently rediscovered Pāśupata texts, prescribes atonement for eating food collected from a single household in certain conditions.

Likewise, the following verse of *Niśvāsamukha* 4.77 is without traceable textual parallel in the *Pāśupatasūtra*:

> *śītātapaparikleśair jalam aśrū --- sibhiḥ* |
> *japadhyānaparo nityaṃ sarvadvandvasahiṣṇutā* || 4.77 ||
>
> Through the hardships of cold and heat; water [[...]] He should always be dedicated to mantra recitation and meditation, and should [have] the capacity for patient endurance of all kinds of pairs [of opposites].

Although we have not found any parallel for this in the *Pāśupatasūtra*, the elements of the verse may have been original components of the borrowed content. We know that enduring the hardships of cold and heat is a widespread practice of asceticism (cf. for example *Yājñavalkyasmṛti* 3.52) and therefore does not present any semantic 'criterion of incoherence',[227] for which reason the meaning conveyed, also, does not imply later redactory influence. Finally, as regards the specific mode of expression of this injunction, we find the compound *°dvandvasahiṣṇutā/dvandvasahiṣṇutva* attested to in Pāśupata sources, such as the *Pāñcārthabhāṣya* (=*Pāśupatasūtrabhāṣya*, p. 121). For these reasons, we believe that the above verse, taken from the *Niśvāsamukha*, may reflect an authentic injunction of the original Pāśupata tradition.[228]

---

227 'Criteria of incoherence' is a term OBERLIES (1997: 76) explained to be indicators for textual accretion: "*Inkohärenzkriterien* ... sind Indizien für ein Wachstum des Textes."

228 As regards the remaining noteworthy innovations we have detected in the Pāśupata-section of the *Niśvāsamukha*, they are listed below. We assume that these addenda, though likely subjected to stylistic (and possibly semantic) inflation, may reflect authentic Pāśupata injunctions, some of which could have entered the tradition after the time of composition of the *Pāśupatasūtra*.

- 4.78a *japaniṣṭhaikāntaratiḥ* 'being intent upon mantra recitation and enjoying solitude.'
- 4.80a *vikrośen* 'he should tremble.'
- 4.80cd *viruddhaceṣṭitaṃ vākyaṃ viruddhañ cāñjanaṃ sadā* '[he should engage

Most striking is that the Pāśupata section of the *Niśvāsamukha* does not display the five Brahmamantras in the order we expect to encounter them in. Since these mantras feature prominently in the *Pāśupatasūtra*, with each one inserted at the end of each of the five chapters, it is worth inspecting the cause of their absence in the *Niśvāsamukha*. Were these mantras not a part of the *Pāśupatasūtra* which the author of the *Niśvāsamukha* drew upon? If this is the case, was perhaps Kauṇḍinya responsible for the division of the *Pāśupatasūtra* into five chapters, adding one of these mantras to each chapter as a quasi-marker? Finally, were these mantras an original element of the *Pāśupatasūtra* and the person who paraphrased it deliberately left them out? At this point, we are only able to raise these issues and guess at explanations.

Not only are the Brahmamantras not included in the account of the *Niśvāsamukha*, but the salvific rewards of following the injunctions are also not contained in the rendition of the *Niśvāsamukha*, although they directly precede the presentation of Brahmamantras in the account of the *Pāśupatasūtra*.

The *Niśvāsamukha*'s Borrowings from the *Manusmṛti*

As we have mentioned in passing, another work upon which the author of the *Niśvāsamukha* evidently drew was the *Manusmṛti*—one of the most influential works of the brahmanical tradition.[229] This work has substantially influenced the profile of the *Niśvāsamukha*—in particular the injunctions regarding donative practices (2.37 ff.), practising observances (3.37 ff.), worshipping ancestors (2.39–41), using the five products of the cow, the ritual handling of *kuśa*-grass[230] and the like. The majority of these individual instances of borrowing occur in the Laukika section of the *Niśvāsamukha*, which are hence strongly influenced by the brahmanical tradition. Let us

in] inappropriate behaviour, inappropriate speech, [and] always [apply] inappropriate ointments.'

- 4.81ab *viruddhamaṇḍanaṁ gātre sarvadā samupakramet* | 'he should always apply inappropriate ornaments on his body.'
- 4.83ab ... *dāntaś ca kṣamī kāmavivarjitaḥ* | '[he should] be restrained, be forgiving, [and] free from desire.'
- 4.86b *dambhalobhavivarjitaḥ* 'devoid of pride and greed.'

229 For the *Manusmṛti* and its place in the brahmanical tradition, see OLIVELLE's introduction to the *Manusmṛti* (2005).

230 See, for example, 3.37 in the *Niśvāsamukha*.

consider the possibility that the *Niśvāsamukha* borrowed directly from the *Manusmṛti* rather than via a third source that was itself influenced by the latter. This remains rather difficult to assess. On the one hand, the *Niśvāsamukha* being a comparatively early work, it would not have been able to draw on a great number of *Purāṇas*, simply because these had not yet been composed in great number. On the other hand, any assimilated text would be expected to lose its original texture upon being transplanted into a novel linguistic or structural environment. Since the *Niśvāsamukha* has generally made modifications to any textual borrowings that were originally in standard Pāṇinian grammar, it becomes even more difficult to assess whether the source of borrowing had been the *Manusmṛti* itself or a later related source. In the *Niśvāsamukha*'s section listing Laukika religious observances, we encounter the following verse concerning the *atikṛcchra* (3.40) observance:

> *ekaikaṃ bhakṣayed grāsaṃ trīṇy ahāni jitendriyaḥ* |
> *trirātropavasec caiva atikṛcchraṃ viśodhane* ||
>
> Having subdued one's sense faculties, one should, for three days, eat [only] a mouthful and one should fast for three nights. [This kind of religious observance is called] *atikṛcchra*, o pure lady!

If we compare this to the definition in the *Manusmṛti* (11.214) we find changes of content and style:

> *ekaikaṃ grāsam aśnīyāt tryahāṇi trīṇi pūrvavat* |
> *tryahaṃ copavased antyam atikṛcchraṃ caran dvijaḥ* ||
>
> A twice-born, observing the *atikṛcchra*, should, eat [only] a mouthful at each of the three times for three days, as before for three-days and during the last three days.

Apart from minimal changes of vocabulary, such as replacing *aśnīyāt* with *bhakṣayed*, and alterations in word-order, the *Niśvāsamukha* replaces *pūrvavat* with *jitendriyaḥ* and *caran dvijaḥ* with *viśodhane*. In the *Manusmṛti* these two words—*pūrvavat* and *caran dvijaḥ*—fit the particular context. The word *pūrvavat* refers to nine-day periods, as taught in verse 11.212 of the *Manusmṛti*, where a twice-born man, practising the *prājāpatya*-penance, is supposed to eat in the morning for three days; in the evening for three days; the following three days he should eat unsolicited food. As the preceding section of the *Niśvāsamukha* concerns the *sāntapana*-penance, the procedure of practising this observance is different to that of the *prājāpatya*. The text hence replaces this word, according to the demands of the context, by *jitendriyaḥ*, a term which appears to perform the function of a verse-filler. Similarly *caran dvijaḥ* makes perfect sense in the context of the *Manusmṛti*, as this type of penance is listed among others which are meant to be practised by twice-born people. Such a restriction is not fitting to the context of the *Niśvāsamukha*.

Moreover, the *Niśvāsamukha*'s grammar is less standard and as such accords with the style of the language of the *Niśvāsa*. As will be shown in a separate section,[231] the overall language of the *Niśvāsamukha* is a mixture of Pāṇinian and non-Pāṇinian *aiśa* forms. The *Niśvāsamukha* replaces *tryahaṃ copavased* with a less standard compound *trirātropavaset*, where the ending of the expected accusative *trirātram* has been irregularly elided with the following word.

In the same section of the *Niśvāsamukha*, we find a verse which relates the *sāntapana*-observance. If we compare the version of the *Niśvāsamukha* with that of the *Manusmṛti*, apart from negligible other changes, the *Niśvāsamukha* also introduces a half a line to herald the result of carrying out the *sāntapana* observance. Since the *Manusmṛti*-segment is transplanted into a textual environment that is embedded in a schematic structure whereby rewards for the various observances are systematically, the compiler must have felt inclined to supply such information, despite the fact the original segment of the *Manusmṛti* does not specify any rewards. The version of the *Manusmṛti* (11.213) reads as follows:

> *gomūtraṃ gomayaṃ kṣīraṃ dadhi sarpiḥ kuśodakam* |
> *ekarātropavāsaś ca kṛcchraṃ sāntapanaṃ smṛtam* ||
>
> Subsisting on cow's urine, cow dung, milk, curd, ghee, and water boiled with Kuśa grass, and fasting during one day—tradition calls this *Sāntapana* penance.[232]

The *Niśvāsamukha*'s text (3.37a–38b), however, appears as follows:

> *māse māse tu yaḥ kuryād ekarātram upoṣitaḥ* |
> *pañcagavyaṃ śucir bhūtvā pītvā sāntapanaṃ bhavet* ||
> *samvatsareṇa śuddhātmā brahmaloke mahīyate* |
>
> If someone observes (*kuryāt*) fasting for one night every month (*māse māse*) after consuming [only] the five products of the cow having first purified himself—[this] would be *Sāntapana*. [By observing this vow of *Sāntapana*] for a year, one [becomes] pure and will be honoured in the world of Brahmā.

---

231 See p. 129 ff.

232 Olivelle 2005: 226.

Similarly, the *Manusmṛti* (11.217), defining the *cāndrāyaṇa* observance, says:

> *ekaikaṃ hrāsayet piṇḍaṃ kṛṣṇe śukle ca vardhayet |*
> *upaspṛśaṃs triṣavaṇam etat cāndrāyaṇaṃ smṛtam ||*
>
> He should decrease his food by one rice-ball a day during the dark fortnight and increase it likewise during the bright fortnight, bathing three times a day—tradition calls this *cāndrāyaṇa* (the lunar penance).[233]

This appears in *Niśvāsamukha* 3.43–44 thus:

> *ekaikaṃ varddhayed grāsaṃ śukle kṛṣṇe ca hrāsayet |*
> *triṣkālasnāyī māsan tu candravṛddhyā vratañ caret ||*
> *cāndrāyaṇam idaṃ śreṣṭhaṃ sarvapāpāpanodanam |*
> *pāpī mucyeta pāpena apāpaḥ svarggago bhavet ||*
>
> One should increase [one's food] by a mouthful [a day in the days of] the bright fortnight and should decrease it [during the days] of the dark fortnight [by a mouthful a day] and should bathe three times a day; [one should] observe this observance for a month in accordance with the changing of the moon (*candravṛddhyā*). This is the excellent lunar observance (*cāndrāyaṇa*), which removes all sins. A sinner will be freed from sin [by performing it], and one who has not committed sin will go to heaven.

The *Niśvāsamukha* here refers to two types of people practicing this observance: on the one hand, there is the *pāpī*, 'sinful one', on the other, it mentions the *apāpaḥ*, 'one without sin'. The text emphasizes this distinction throughout the section on *upavāsa*, 'fasting.' Accordingly, it describes two types of rewards, one for the sinful person and the other for the practitioner 'without sin'. Such a distinction of agent and reward is absent in the *Manusmṛti*, for which reason one could argue for the account in the *Niśvāsamukha* being conceptually somewhat more sophisticated in this regard. The two adjectives, *śreṣṭhaṃ* and *sarvapāpāpanodanam*, are not present in the original text of the *Manusmṛti*. Once again, the fruit of observing this *cāndrāyaṇa* is an additional element, only mentioned in the *Niśvāsamukha*.[234]

Let us next examine a parallel concerning the rules for householders in the *Niśvāsamukha*'s Vaidika section, where a change of choice of vocabulary

233 Olivelle 2005: 226–227.

234 There are comparable, relevant examples that are here reproduced for illustrative purposes:

Manusmṛti	Niśvāsamukha
caturaḥ prātar aśnīyāt *piṇḍān vipraḥ samāhitaḥ* | *caturo 'stamite sūrye* *śiśucāndrāyaṇaṃ smṛtam* || 11.220	*caturo bhakṣayet piṇḍān* *pūrvāhne tu vicakṣaṇaḥ* || *sūryasyāstamane vāpi* *caturo bhakṣayet punaḥ* | *śiśucāndrāyaṇaṃ hy etad* *upapātakanāśanam* || *māsenaikena śuddhātmā* *apāpī svargatiṃ vrajet* | 3.46c–3.48b
A Brāhmin should eat four rice-balls in the morning with a collected mind and four after sunset—tradition calls this the lunar penance of children. (Olivelle 2005: 227)	A wise man should eat four lumps of rice in the forenoon, and again he should [eat] four lumps of rice after the setting of the sun; this observance which [is called] *śiśucāndrāyaṇa* destroys [the demerit accrued from] minor transgressions. By observing it for a month (*māsenaikena*) one becomes pure-souled; if someone who is [already] free of sin performs it for three nights, he will go to heaven.
aṣṭāv aṣṭau samaśnīyāt *piṇḍān madhyaṃdine sthite* | *niyatātmā haviṣyasya* *yaticāndrāyaṇaṃ caran* || 11.219	*aṣṭāv aṣṭau samaśnīyāt* *piṇḍān madhyandine sthite* | *haviṣyeṇa samāyuktān* *mucyate sarvapātakaiḥ* || *apāpī svarggam āyāti* *yaticāndrāyaṇena tu* | 3.45a–46b
A man practicing the lunar penance of ascetics should eat each day at noon eight rice-balls from the sacrificial oblation, controlling his self. (Olivelle 2005: 227)	One should eat eight rice-lumps each noon from the sacrificial oblation (*haviṣyeṇa samāyuktān*). By [this religious observance which is called] *yaticāndrāyaṇa* one will be freed from all crimes (*sarvapātakaiḥ*); [but] if he is sinless, he will go to heaven.

In the first example, the *Niśvāsamukha* states that the Śiśucāndrāyaṇa observance ('lunar observance of children') removes secondary sins, allowing people to purify themselves within a month. Having attained a state of purity, they will go to heaven. This has no equivalent in the *Manusmṛti*. In the second example, too, the *Niśvāsamukha* asserts that by practising the *Yaticāndrāyaṇa* observance, one becomes free from all sins and, being sinless, goes to heaven. This again stands in contrast with the *Manusmṛti*.

may have entailed a total rearrangement of word-order. The original reading *upaskaraḥ* of the *Manusmṛti* is replaced by the synonymous term *pramārjanī* in the *Niśvāsamukha*. Moreover, *badhyate yās tu vāhayan* is replaced by *kathitās tava śobhane* to fit the context of the *Niśvāsamukha*. The result is, at least superficially, an entirely new verse in the *Niśvāsamukha*:

MANUSMṚTI	NIŚVĀSAMUKHA
pañca sūnā gṛhasthasya *cullī peṣaṇy upaskaraḥ* | *kaṇḍanī codakumbhaś ca* *badhyate yās tu vāhayan* || 3.68	*peṣaṇī kaṇḍanī cullī* *udakumbhaḥ pramārjanī* | *pañca sūnā bhavanty ete* *kathitās tava śobhane* || 4.19
A householder has five slaughter-houses: fireplace, grindstone, broom, mortar and pestle, and water pot. By his use of them, he is fettered. (OLIVELLE 2005: 112)	Mortar and pestle, fireplace, water-pot and broom are the five slaughter-houses of [a house-holder]; these have been taught to you, o beautiful one!

There are some instances of the *Niśvāsamukha* employing *aiśa* language[235] while lightly modifying the original formulation of the *Manusmṛti*—be it intentionally or inadvertently.[236] The *Niśvāsamukha* recurrently uses grammatical forms that from the standpoint of standard Pāṇinian grammar are incorrect. Consider, for instance, how the *Manusmṛti* (3.197) presents the list of the ancestors of the four *varṇas* in standard Pāṇinian grammar:

> *somapā nāma viprāṇāṃ kṣatriyāṇāṃ havirbhujaḥ* |
> *vaiśyānām ājyapā nāma śūdrāṇāṃ tu sukālinaḥ* ||
>
> The ancestors of Brāhmins are called Somapas; of Kṣatriyas, Havirbhujs; of Vaiśyas, Ājyapas; and of Śūdras, Sukālins. (OLIVELLE 2005: 118)

[235] For a more detailed account on *aiśa* use, refer to p. 129 ff.

[236] Tim LUBIN, in a personal communication, dated 31st of March, 2018, reminded us that although "it is possible that the author of the *Niśvāsamukha* deliberately changed the *Manusmṛti* to conform to *aiśa* 'norms', it is not the only way to explain textual discrepancies." As a matter of fact, he argues that "the very fact that past scholars take note of this irregularity would be due to their own familiarity with Pāṇinian rules. In all likelihood, it is thus a form of apologetics." Note that a further possible alternative Tim LUBIN presents as explanation for this irregularity is "that the author of the *Niśvāsamukha* was citing stanzas from memory—stanzas that may have been circulating under Manu's name, but not necessarily in the form of the text handed out to us in printed editions."

This is how the same verse appears in the version of the *Niśvāsamukha* (3.155):

> *pitaras somapā* ***vipre kṣatriye*** *tu havirbhujāḥ* |
> *ājyapā* ***vaiśyayonau*** *tu* ***śūdrāṇān*** *tu sukālinaḥ* ||
>
> In the case of a Brāhmin, the ancestors will be [called] Somapās; in the case of a Kṣatriya, Havirbhujas; in the case of a Vaiśya, Ājyapas; and for Śūdras, [they are called] Sukālins.

The author of the *Niśvāsamukha* does not make changes of vocabulary here, but the genitives, namely, *viprāṇāṃ, kṣatriyāṇāṃ* and *vaiśyānām* of the *Manusmṛti* have been replaced by locatives *vipre, kṣatriye* and *vaiśyayonau* in the *Niśvāsamukha*. At the end of the verse, however, the *Niśvāsamukha* retains the original genitive form (*śūdrāṇān*), rendering the construction unbalanced and surprising. This usage could be considered to be one of the features of *aiśa* language—although syntactically either genitive or locative is permissible, the combination in what are otherwise parallel phrases is disturbing. Other *aiśa* transformations include the following:

MANUSMṚTI	NIŚVĀSAMUKHA
ṣaṭtriṃśadābdikaṃ caryaṃ gurau *traivedikaṃ vratam* | *tadardhikaṃ pādikaṃ vā grahaṇāntikam eva vā* || 3.1	***ṣaṭtriṃśadabdikā caryā guros*** *traivedikaṃ vratam* | *tadardhikaṃ pādikaṃ vā grahaṇāntikam eva vā* || 4.5c–6b
He should carry out the observance relating to the three Vedas at his teacher's house, an observance lasting thirty-six years, or one-half or one-quarter of that time, or else until he has learnt them. (OLIVELLE 2005: 108)	The [aforementioned] observance [should last] thirty-six years, and [this] commitment, based on the tripartite Veda, [should be carried out] at his teacher's [house]. Alternatively, [it may last] half of that [time] (i.e. eighteen years), or a quarter (i.e. nine years), or until he has learnt them [i.e. the Vedas]

*adhyāpanaṃ brahma**yajñaḥ***
*pitṛ**yajñas** tu tarpaṇam* |
homo daivo balir bhauto
nṛyajño 'tithipūjanam ||
*pañcaitān yo mahā**yajñān***
na hāpayati śaktitaḥ |
sa gṛhe 'pi vasan nityaṃ
sūnādoṣair na lipyate || 3.70–71

The sacrifice to the Veda is teaching; the sacrifice to ancestors is the quenching libation; the sacrifice to gods is the burnt offering; the sacrifice to beings is the Bali offering; and the sacrifice to humans is the honoring of guests. If a man never fails to offer these five great sacrifices to the best of his ability, he remains unsullied by the taints of his slaughter-houses in spite of living permanently at home.
(OLIVELLE 2005: 108)

*adhyāpanaṃ brahma**yajñaṃ***
*pitṛ**yajñan** tu tarppaṇam* |
homo daivo balir bhauto
nṛyajño 'tithipūjanam ||
*pañcaitāṃs tu mahā**yajñāṃ***
na hāpayati śaktitaḥ |
svagṛhe 'pi vasan nityaṃ
sūnādoṣair na lipyate || 4.17–18

The sacrifice to the Veda is teaching; the sacrifice to the ancestors is the quenching libation; the sacrifice to gods is the burnt offering; the sacrifice to beings is the Bali offering; and the sacrifice to humans is the honouring of guests. If a man never fails to offer these five great sacrifices to the best of his ability, he remains unsullied by the taints of his slaughter-houses in spite of living permanently at home.

In the first example, we observe that the *Niśvāsamukha* renders an irregular grammatical construction, an *aiśa* form, by employing the feminine *ṣaṭtriṃśadabdikā caryā* in qualification of the neuter *traivedikaṃ vratam*. The *Manusmṛti*, in turn, displays the segment in accordance with the expected neuter case: *ṣaṭtriṃśadābdikam* to qualify *caryam*. In the second example, the *Niśvāsamukha* furnishes an irregular neuter noun *°yajñam*, whereas the *Manusmṛti* records the regular masculine form, *°yajñaḥ*.

In sum, the *Niśvāsamukha*'s borrowing from the *Manusmṛti* is significant for the history of early Śaivism, as it demonstrates that some features of orthodox brahmanical teaching were adopted by the Śaivas in the creation of their own corpus of teachings. This fact, yet again, buttresses SANDERSON's theory (2009) that, in essence, the religion of the Śaivas consists of a hybrid of Śaivism and Brahmanism.

The *Niśvāsamukha* and the *Śivadharmaśāstra*

The *Śivadharmaśāstra* is the first in a group of non-tantric Śaiva works that is commonly called the *Śivadharma*-corpus.[237] A number of Nepalese palm-leaf manuscripts transmit eight works of this corpus together. As regards the ordering principle,[238] the *Śivadharmaśāstra*—being the oldest work of the group—generally features as the first text[239] in these manuscripts:[240]

1. the *Śivadharmaśāstra*
2. the *Śivadharmottara*
3. the *Ṣaḍdarśanasaṅgraha*
4. the *Śivopaniṣad*
5. the *Umāmaheśvarasaṃvāda*
6. the *Uttarottaramahāsaṃvāda*, also known as the *Umottara*
7. the *Vṛṣasārasaṅgraha*
8. the *Dharmaputrikā*[241]

Until recently, the *Śivopaniṣad* was the only work published from amongst this corpus, but there is now a printed version (albeit based on a single manuscript and full of errors) published by Yogi Narahari NĀTHA: all the previously listed texts are printed therein (omitted is the *Lalitavistara*, which is not transmitted in most manuscripts).[242] Recently, Florinda

237 For a summary of its chapters, see HAZRA 1952–53, and A. K. ACHARYA 2009: 28 ff.

238 Note that DE SIMINI (2016b) has recorded individual instances of structural disparity between the individual multi-text manuscripts.

239 The following listing reflects the most common order of presentation of the texts of the corpus. For an overview of the manuscript transmission of the *Śivadharma*-corpus, see DE SIMINI 2016a.

240 According to GOODALL (1998: 375), the first two texts have, in the course of time, been transmitted from North to South India.

241 DE SIMINI & MIRNIG (2017) investigated an 11th-century Nepalese palmleaf manuscript in the Asiatic Society of Calcutta (G4077) which contains a longer text by the name of *Lalitavistara*. In the MS investigated by de DE SIMINI & MIRNIG (2017), this latter text—not to be confused with the Buddhist work by the same name—features in place of the *Dharmaputrikā* of our present listing. Note that there is a possibility that the *Lalitavistara* may also have been incorporated during the later stages of the textual history of the *Śivadharma*-corpus.

242 See GOODALL 1998: 375-376, for a brief outline of this corpus; for a summary of each chapter of the texts of the *Śivadharma*-corpus including the *Lalitavistara*, see A. K. ACHARYA 2009: 22–82.

DE SIMINI has published a monograph that includes an edition and translation of the second chapter of the *Śivadharmottara* (2016a). More recently still, Peter BISSCHOP (2018) has published a monograph on the sixth chapter of the *Śivadharmaśāstra*, the 'Chapter on Appeasement' (*Śāntyadhyāya*), a work comprising a critical-edition-cum-translation with an annotated commentary of that section. There is now also an edition of the complete text of the *Śivadharmaśāstra*, that of JUGNU & SHARMA (2014), which shows a general predilection towards the readings found in what BISSCHOP refers to as the 'Pondicherry-Transcript'.[243] "The preface of the edition mentions, however, that it was based on a manuscript from Adyar" (Library),[244] while the 'Pondicherry-Transcript' was copied from a manuscript in Kilvelur. Finally, as we shall have occasion to mention below, there is A. K. ACHARYA's 2009 edition of the first three chapters of the *Śivadharmasaṅgraha*.

R.C. HAZRA, in two articles[245] published in the 1940s and 1950s in the journal *Purana*, proposed approximate dates for the first two works of the corpus—the *Śivadharmaśāstra* and the *Śivadharmottara*. He suggests that the former was composed between 200 and 500 CE, while the latter must have been composed much later, between 700 and 800 CE, on the grounds that it makes use of expressions such as *āgama* and *śivatantra*, which HAZRA assumes to refer to tantric *Śaiva* scriptures.

This assumption, however, is far from certain. It is perhaps worth mentioning that the *Śivadharmottara* prescribes the installation of an image of Lakulīśa, a deity of no importance in the Mantramārga, yet indicative of a Pāśupata background. BISSCHOP (2014) has presented the view that some of the information in chapter six of the *Śivadharmaśāstra* cannot predate the 6th century. More recently, upon examination of the sixth chapter of the *Śivadharmaśāstra*, BISSCHOP (2018: 21) concludes that evidence[246]

243 BISSCHOP (2018) mentions the 'Pondicherry-Transcript' on p. 57 fn. 107, being housed at the Institut Français de Pondichéry (IFP), T 32, 156 folios, being a Devanāgarī paper transcript of a manuscript belonging to Kilvelur and bearing the title of *Śivadharmaśāstra*. `http://muktalib7.org/IFP_ROOT/IFP/transcripts_data/T0032/PDF/T0032.pdf`.

244 JUGNU & SHARMA 2014: ix.

245 HAZRA (1940; 1952–3).

246 For a more detailed discussion of the evidence consulted by Peter BISSCHOP which is indicative of the dating of the *Śivadharmaśāstra*, refer to BISSCHOP 2018: 20–21. There BISSCHOP discusses the developmental stage of the concept of the Dikpālas as presented in the sixth chapter of the work, the four-faced form of Śiva (as contrasted with the later five-faced depiction of the deity), the inclusion of Ketu amongst the nine planets (Navagrahas), which "has only been attested to from 600 CE onwards", etc.

> suggest[s] that the text may have been composed towards the end of the 6th century at the earliest. In the light of Goodalls's dating of the *Śivadharmottara* to the 7th century, the Atimārga milieu of the text, ... and the quotation in the *Kāraṇḍavyūhasūtra*, it will not have been much later than this. The *terminus ante quem* is the date of the incomplete *Śivadharmottara* manuscript, which was most probably written in the early 9th century.[247]

The *Niśvāsamukha* has sizeable parallels with the *Śivadharmaśāstra*. The presence of parallels was to be expected, as we have seen above that the *Niśvāsamukha* is teaching lay Śaiva religious duties to common householders in its Laukika section—yet, one may ask, can we ascertain the direction of borrowing and situate these texts chronologically?

Let us first consider a telling example of a shared verse teaching the reward of recalling Śiva (*virūpākṣa*) which occurs verbatim as *Niśvāsamukha* 1.167c–168b and as *Śivadharmaśāstra* 1.14c–15b:

> *ekakālaṃ dvikālaṃ vā triṣkālaṃ vāpi nityaśaḥ* ||
> *ye smaranti virūpākṣaṃ vijñeyās te gaṇeśvarāḥ* |

> Those who always remember the oddly-eyed (*virūpākṣam*) once, twice or three times [a day], they are to be known as lords of Gaṇas.

Since both textual units are identical, it is likely that the borrowing between the two works occurred directly, rather than via a third source. Furthermore, there is no such Śaiva source known to us that predates the *Niśvāsamukha* and teaches lay Śaivism other than the *Śivadharmaśāstra*.BISSCHOP has proposed a tentative dating for the sixth chapter of the *Śivadharmaśāstra*, which, he believes, belongs to the late 6th century CE at the earliest.[248] If this credible hypothesis holds true, then the *Śivadharmaśāstra* probably predates the *Niśvāsamukha*, which appears to originate from the end of the 7th century. For this reason, we may posit that the latter borrowed from the former.

---

247 Note that Florinda DE SIMINI (2016a, ch. 2) presents a detailed treatment of the *Śivadharma*-corpus and offers her analysis regarding the date of the first two works. In further pursuit of this question, the reader is hence referred to her more detailed discussion on the date of these texts, in particular pp. 28–66 (or more briefly, pp. 63–63).

248 See fn. 246.

We may further note that both the *Niśvāsamukha* and the *Śivadharmaśāstra* share recommendations for constructing temporary *liṅgas* out of diverse substances.[249] One notable example is that of the making of a dust *liṅga* in *Śivadharmaśāstra* 3.77c–78b, which is echoed in *Niśvāsamukha* 2.2. Although this example does not present an instance of verbatim repetition, the concept is presented in a comparable manner:

NIŚVĀSAMUKHA	ŚIVADHARMAŚĀSTRA
krīḍamānās tu ye bālā *liṅgaṁ kurvanti pāṃśunā* | *labhanty ekāntato rājyaṃ* *nissapatnam akaṃṭakam* ||	*pāṃśunā krīḍamāno 'pi* *liṅgaṃ kuryāt tu yo naraḥ* || *pratyante labhate rājyam* *asapatnam akaṇṭakam* |
Those children who make a *liṅga* at play will definitely obtain an unrivalled kingdom without enemies.	Any man at play, who erects a *liṅga* out of dust will obtain a universal kingdom without contest, without enemies.

Another distinctive recommendation is found in *Niśvāsamukha* 2.91cd: anyone who offers tooth-cleaning sticks, will receive a beautiful wife as reward. The causal connection between offering tooth-cleaning sticks and obtaining a beautiful wife in return features also in *Śivadharmaśāstra* 12.72:

NIŚVĀSAMUKHA	ŚIVADHARMAŚĀSTRA
dantadhāvanadātā ca *bhāryāṃ labhati śobhanām*	*dantadhāvanam uddiṣṭaṃ* *nivedya śivayogine* | *divyastrībhogasaṃyuktaṃ* *divi ramyaṃ puraṃ labhet* ||
And one who offers teeth-cleaning sticks (*dantadhāvanadātā*) will obtain a beautiful wife.	By offering promised teeth-cleaning sticks to a Śivayogin, one will obtain a beautiful city in heaven conjoined by the enjoyments of celestial ladies.

A further example illustrative of the close textual ties between the *Niśvāsamukha* and the *Śivadharmaśāstra* is the following account regarding a gradation of recipients (*pātra*) in accordance with their perceived merit. Note how *Niśvāsamukha* 2.117–119 is closely paralleled by *Śivadharmaśāstra* 7.69–71:

249 The reader is referred here to *Niśvāsamukha* 2.2 ff. and *Śivadharmaśāstra* 3.63 ff.

NIŚVĀSAMUKHA

mūrkhaviprasahasrebhyo
vedādhyāyī paraḥ smṛtaḥ |
vedādhyāyisahasrebhyo
hy āhitāgnis tato 'dhikaḥ ||
āhitāgnisahasreṣu
agnihotrī varaḥ smṛtaḥ |
agnihotrīsahasreṣu
brahmavettā tato 'dhikaḥ ||

One learned in the Vedas is considered to outweigh thousands of foolish Brāhmins, one who has installed the Vedic fires is considered to be superior to thousands of men learned in the Vedas. Among the thousands of those who have installed the Vedic fires (*āhitāgni*) an *agnihotrī* (one who maintains the sacrificial fire) is considered to excel. Among the thousands of *agnihotrī*s, he who knows *brahman* (*brahmavettā*) is considered to be superior.

ŚIVADHARMAŚĀSTRA

brahmacārisahasrebhyo
vedādhyāyī viśiṣyate |
vedādhyāyīsahasrebhyo
hy agnihotrī viśiṣyate ||
agnihotrisahasrebhyo
yajñayājī viśiṣyate |
yajñayājisahasrebhyaḥ
satrayājī viśiṣyate ||
satrayājisahasrebhyaḥ
sarvavidyāntapāragaḥ ||
sarvavidyāvidkoṭibhyaḥ
śivabhakto viśiṣyate ||

One learned in the Vedas excels thousands of Brahmacarins; Certainly an *agnihotrī* (one who maintains the sacrificial fire) surpasses thousands of men learned in the Vedas; he who has performed sacrifices (*yajñayājin*) surpasses thousands of *agnihotrins*; he who has performed the *soma* sacrifice (*satrayājin*) surpasses thousands of (*yajñayājin*)s; he who has reached the end of the other shore of knowledge surpasses thousands of *soma*-sacrificers (*satrayājins*); a devotee of Śiva surpasses ten[s of] millions of the knowers of all [ancillary objects of] knowledge.

Further illustrations could be multiplied: compare for example *Śivadharmaśāstra* 11.71cd and *Niśvāsamukha* 2.122cd:

NIŚVĀSAMUKHA

akṣayan tad bhaved dānaṃ
yad dattaṃ svalpam alpapi ||

ŚIVADHARMAŚĀSTRA

atyalpam api kāruṇyād
dattaṃ bhavati cākṣayam ||

That [effect of] offering will be indestructible, even if (*api*) what is offered is very little (*svalpam alpapi*).

If someone, out of compassion, were to make even a trifle offering, [its effect] becomes indestructible.

Note also that the version of the *Liṅgodbhava* myth of *Niśvāsamukha* 1.72 ff. is close to that of *Śivadharmaśāstra* 3.2 ff.;[250] the list of rivers (3.2 ff.) in the *Niśvāsamukha* is also close to *Śivadharmaśāstra* 6.201 ff. and 12.108 ff.

One topic in which close correspondence between these texts might have been expected has been alluded to earlier in our introduction, namely the section listing the *pañcāṣṭaka*. For this list of the *pañcāṣṭaka* recorded in *Śivadharmaśāstra*, we have collated two old Nepalese sources:[251]

bhastrāpadaṃ[252] *rudrakoṭir avimuktaṃ*[253] *mahālayam* |
gokarṇaṃ bhadrakarṇaṃ ca suvarṇākṣo 'tha dīptimān ||
sthāneśvaraś[254] *ca vikhyātas triṣu lokeṣu viśrutaḥ* |
sthānāṣṭakam idaṃ jñeyaṃ rudrakṣetraṃ mahodayam ||
bhastrāpadādisthāṇvantam[255] *rudrasāyojyakāraṇaṃ* |
chagaraṇḍaṃ[256] *diraṇḍaṃ ca*[257] *mākoṭaṃ maṇḍaleśvaraḥ* ||
kālañjaraṃ[258] *śaṅkukarṇaṃ sthaleśvaraḥ*[259] *sthūleśvaraḥ*[260] |
pavitrāṭakam ity etat mahāpuṇyavivardhanaḥ[261] ||
mṛtāḥ prayānti tatriva[262] *śivasya paramaṃ padam*[263] |
gayā caiva kurukṣetraṃ nakhalaṃ kanakhalaṃ tathā ||
vimalaṃ cāṭṭahāsaṃ ca māhendraṃ bhīmam aṣṭakam[264] |
etad guhyāṣṭakaṃ nāma sarvapāpavimocanam ||

---

250 See KAFLE (2013) for more details.

251 These are MS 1028/4 (=N^{K}_{28}), 46v6–47r3 and MS 1082/3 (= N^{K}_{82}) 40v6–41r1. One may compare the text with *Niśvāsamukha* 3.19 ff. See also p. 68 ff. of this study.

252 bhastrāpadaṃ N^{K}_{82}; vastrāpadaṃ N^{K}_{28}

253 °koṭir N^{K}_{82}; °koṭim N^{K}_{28}

254 sthāneśvaraś N^{K}_{28}; sthālīśvaraś N^{K}_{82}

255 °vantaṃ N^{K}_{82}; °vanta° N^{K}_{28}

256 chagaraṇḍaṃ N^{K}_{82}; chatalaṇḍaṃ N^{K}_{28}

257 *conj.*; vilaṇḍaṃ ca N^{K}_{28}; duraṇḍaś ca N^{K}_{82}

258 kālañjaraṃ *em.*; kāliñjaraṃ N^{K}_{28}; kālajjaraṃ N^{K}_{82}

259 sthaleśvaraḥ N^{K}_{82}; sthāleśvaraṃ N^{K}_{28}

260 sthūleśvaraḥ N^{K}_{82}; sthūleśvaraṃ N^{K}_{28}

261 °vivardhanaḥ N^{K}_{82}; --- N^{K}_{28}

262 mṛtāḥ prayānti tatriva N^{K}_{82}; lac N^{K}_{28}

263 śivasya paramaṃ padaṃ N^{K}_{82}; śivasya parama pa _ N^{K}_{28}

264 mā --- N^{K}_{28}; mahendraṃ N^{K}_{82}

gatvā tu puruṣaḥ strīmān prāpnoti śivamandiram |
śrīparvataṃ hariścandraṃ jalpam amrātikeśvaram[265] ||
madhyamaṃ ca mahākālaṃ kedāraṃ bhairavaṃ tathā[266] |
etad guhyātiguhyaṃ ca[267] *aṣṭakaṃ parikīrttitam*[268] ||
santārya ca[269] *pitṝn sarvān śivaṃ yānti param padam* [270] |
amareśvaraṃ[271] *prabhāsaṃ ca naimiśaṃ*[272] *puskaraṃ tathā* ||
aṣāḍhaṃ[273] *diṇḍimuṇḍiś ca bhārabhūtiṃ bhavāntakam* |
lakulīśvarañ ca[274] *vikhyātas tathā pratyātmiko mahān* ||
pratyāmikāṣṭakam idaṃ kṣatraṃ rudrasya kāmikam[275] |
tara yānti mṛtāḥ sarve rudrasya paramaṃ padam[276] ||
dānāny āvasathaṃ kūpam udyānaṃ devatākulam |
tīrtheṣu yāni yaḥ kuryāt so 'kṣayaṃ phalam āpnuyāt ||

It immediately becomes apparent that the order here differs from that of the *Niśvāsamukha*. Instead, it reveals close links to the list of the *Mālinīvijayottaratantra* and the *Svāyaṃbhuvasūtrasaṅgraha* (see GOODALL 2004: 315). It seems that the list in the *Śivadharmaśāstra* has not served the *Niśvāsamukha* as source for adaptation. An important feature of this list of ogdoads in the *Śivadharmaśāstra* is that it attributes a different name to each set of eight pilgrimage sites, which are inserted by way of an additional line after each set of eight. As we have seen earlier, the *Guhyasūtra* proceeds in a similar, though not entirely identical, manner. Although stratification of the cosmological system is current in the tantric milieu, subdivision into 'levels' is traceable to both tantric and non-tantric Śaiva sources. Hence we cannot attribute such lists to one or other genre simply on the basis of a stratified cosmology.

While the list of the *pañcaṣṭaka* does not constitute a close point of connectivity between the *Niśvāsamukha* and the *Śivadharmaśāstra*, the other

265 jalpama° N^{K}_{82}; jalpa _ N^{K}_{28}
266 madhya° N^{K}_{82}; ma --- ya° N^{K}_{28}
267 °tiguhyaṃ N^{K}_{82}; °diguhyakam N^{K}_{28}
268 aṣṭakaṃ N^{K}_{28}; aṣṭakāṃ N^{K}_{28}
269 ca N^{K}_{28}; tu N^{K}_{82}
270 yānti N^{K}_{28}; śānti N^{K}_{82}
271 amareśvaraṃ N^{K}_{28} (hypermetrical); amreśvaram N^{K}_{82}
272 naimiśaṃ N^{K}_{82}; naimiśa N^{K}_{28}
273 aṣāḍhaṃ N^{K}_{82}; aṣāḍhi° N^{K}_{28}
274 °śvarañ ca N^{K}_{28}; °śvaro 'tha N^{K}_{82}
275 kṣatraṃ rudrasya kāmikaṃ N^{K}_{28}; kṣatraṃ rudrasya hitakāmikaṃ N^{K}_{82}
276 padam N^{K}_{82}; pamaṃ N^{K}_{28}

cases listed above do imply close textual affinity, and it seems likely that the *Niśvāsamukha* borrowed these portions of text from the *Śivadharmaśāstra* for the reasons listed above. If the *Śivadharmaśāstra* was indeed the basis for these parallels as they appear in the *Niśvāsamukha*, then the *Niśvāsamukha* must have been composed after the compilation of the *Śivadharmaśāstra* in the sixth or seventh century.[277]

Borrowings from the *Niśvāsamukha* by the *Śivadharma-saṅgraha*

Let us now consider the textual development which the *Niśvāsamukha* underwent after its composition. Thanks to the initial observations of Mr. SAMBANDHAŚIVĀCĀRYA and A. K. ACHARYA, we have been able to gather clear evidence that the *Niśvāsamukha* also served as template from which a later text, the *Śivadharmasaṅgraha*, borrowed. The title of the *Śivadharmasaṅgraha* is directly indicative of the nature of the text it contains, since *Śivadharmasaṅgraha* literally means 'collection of teachings of Śiva', suggesting that it comprises teachings gathered from earlier Śaiva sources. This initial impression is directly reinforced by an explicit attestation, penned by the author (1.3), that it is on the basis of the kernel of the compositions of Śaṃbhu, Sanatkumāra, Vāyu and Dvaipāyana that he composed (*kriyate*) the ensuing compendium of teachings *Dharmasaṅgraha* (i.e. the *Śivadharmasaṅgraha*):

> *śambhoḥ sanatkumārasya vāyor dvaipāyanasya ca* |
> *granthasāraṃ samuddhṛtya kriyate dharmasaṃgrahaḥ* || 1.3 ||
>
> The [*Śiva*]*dharmasaṅgraha* is composed upon having extracted the essence of the scriptures of Śambhu, Sanatkumāra, Vāyu and Dvaipāyana.

Among the twelve chapters of the *Śivadharmasaṅgraha*, the first three chapters, which have now been edited by A. K. ACHARYA,[278] comprise moralising or sermonising counsel, in the form of'well-spoken advice' (*subhāṣitas*). Chapter 4 then gives a description of the hells, the *narakas*, which exhibits a certain degree of correspondence with the *Skandapurāṇa*: some of its verses are identical with their counterparts in chapters 37–47 of the *Skandapurāṇa*.[279] Chapters 5 to 9 closely parallel parts of the *Niśvāsamukha*. Chapters 10 to 12 present the Purāṇic cosmography; chapter 10 is

---

[277] See fn. 246.
[278] A. K. ACHARYA (2009*).
[279] See BAKKER, BISSCHOP & YOKOCHI (2014: 82–95).

nearly identical to the fifth chapter of the *Guhyasūtra*; chapter 11 of the *Śivadharmasaṅgraha* has considerable overlap with parts of the sixth and seventh chapters of the *Guhyasūtra*;[280] finally, chapter 12 corresponds to verses 209–355 of the thirty-ninth chapter of the *Vāyupurāṇa*.

Clearly it makes sense to take the above-quoted introductory verse seriously—and to try and locate the texts upon which the compendium has drawn. To begin with, we may note that the scripture 'of Śambhu' may refer to the *Niśvāsatattvasaṃhitā*, which we know to be ascribed to Śiva, since the *Śivadharmasaṅgraha* demonstrably draws on the *Niśvāsamukha* and *Guhyasūtra*. As for the second author mentioned, Sanatkumāra, it appears likely that the author of the compendium had the *Skandapurāṇa* in mind, since this *Purāṇa* was supposedly narrated by Sanatkumāra. Regarding the textual evidence for this contention, the fourth chapter of the *Śivadharmasaṅgraha* displays parallels with the *Skandapurāṇa*. The third mention, Vāyu, plainly refers to the *Vāyupurāṇa*. As regards the final reference, since [Kṛṣṇa-]dvaipāyana (i.e. Vyāsa) is the purported author of the *Mahābhārata*, 'Dvaipāyana' could be a reference to the epic. However, this remains to be investigated.

Extent and type of borrowing

It is important to mention here that, as we will show in the section below, the *Śivadharmasaṅgraha* is not merely copying verbatim from the *Niśvāsamukha*. Instead, it standardises irregular forms and corrects awkward syntax. The underlying source text consulted by the author of the *Śivadharmasaṅgraha*, it should be noted, comprises the Laukika and Vaidika sections of the *Niśvāsamukha*, from which, as we shall presently see, the *Śivadharmasaṅgraha* draws heavily. The *Śivadharmasaṅgraha* did not appropriate the Ādhyātmika and Atimārga portions of the *Niśvāsamukha*.

The following comparative table shows the locations and scope of the textual parallels between the *Niśvāsamukha* and the *Śivadharmasaṅgraha*:

280 The *Śivadharmasaṅgraha* appears to be the first text of the *Śivadharma*-corpus to incorporate tantric material. It does so by drawing intensively from chapter five, six, and seven of the *Guhyasūtra*.

Niśvāsamukha	**Śivadharmasaṅgraha**
1.1–1.57	—
—	5.1–5.14
1.58–1.63	5.15–5.20
1.64	—
1.65–1.87	5.21–5.43
1.88–1.92	—
—	5.44ab
1.93a–1.98b	5.44c–5.49
—	5.50ab
1.98c–1.100b	5.50c–5.52b
—	5.52c–5.54
1.100c–1.107b	5.55–5.61
1.107c–1.114b	—
1.114c–1.124b	5.62–5.71
1.124c–1.125b	5.72
—	5.73–5.75
1.125c–1.127b	5.76–5.77
1.127c–1.154	5.83a–5.110b
1.155ab	—
1.155c –1.156b	5.110cd
1.156c–1.158b	5.111a–5.112
1.158c–1.150b	—
—	5.113–5.119
1.150c–1.159b	—
1.159c–1.160	5.120a–5.121b
1.161ab	—
—	5.121cd
1.161c–1.162b	5.122
—	5.123
1.162c–1.165b	5.124–5.126
—	5.127
1.165c–1.169b	5.128–5.131
—	5.132
1.169c–1.171	5.133–5.135
1.172	5.136
1.173–1.176	5.137–5.140
1.177ab	—

—	5.141a–5.143b
1.177cd	5.143c–5.144b
1.178	5.144c–5.145b
—	5.145c–5.149
1.179–1.185	5.150–5.156
2.1a–2.18b	6.1a–6.17f
—	6.18–6.38
2.18c–2.35	6.39a–6.56b
2.36	—
2.37a–2.38b	6.56c–6.57
—	6.58
2.38c–2.39b	6.59
—	6.60–64
2.39c–2.41b	6.65–6.66
—	6.70c–6.76b
2.41c–2.42b	6.76c–6.77b
—	6.77c–6.78b
2.42c–2.43b	6.78c–6.78f
2.43c–2.46	6.67a–6.70b
—	6.79–6.88
2.47–2.48	6.89–6.90
—	6.91–6.94
—	6.97
—	6.105
—	6.107–6.117
2.49	6.118
2.50	6.106
—	6.119–6.122
2.51	6.123
2.53a–2.56b	—
—	6.138–6.153b
2.56cd	—
2.57–2.70	6.124–6.137
2.71a–2.80b	6.153c–6.162
2.80c–2.82b	6.95–6.96
2.82c–2.86b	6.98–6.101
2.86c–2.88b	6.103–6.104
2.88c–2.115	6.163–6.189
2.116	6.190

2.117
2.118
2.119a–2.120b
2.120c–2.121b
2.121c–122
—
3.1a–3.13b
3.13c–3.14b
3.14c–3.15d
—
3.16
3.17–3.18
3.19–3.22
3.23
3.24ab
3.24c–3.25b
3.25c–3.30b
—
3.30c–3.34b
3.35c–3.36b
3.36c–3.37
3.38–3.42
—
3.43a–3.56f
—
3.57–3.69
—
3.60–3.83
3.84ab
3.84cd
3.85ab
3.85cd
3.86ab
—
3.86c–3.151
3.152–3.153
—
3.154
3.155
6.191
6.192ab
6.192c–6.193d
6.194
—
6.195
7.1a–7.13b
7.13cd
7.14a–7.15b
7.15c–7.16b
7.16c–7.17b
—
7.17c–7.21b
7.22
7.21cd
—
7.23–7.27
7.24–7.40
7.41–7.44
—
7.45a–7.46b
—
7.46c–7.52
7.53a–7.67b
7.67c– 7.69b
7.69c–7.72b
7.72c–7.124
8.1a–8.25b
8.25c–8.26b?
8.26cd
8.26ab
8.27ab
8.27cd
8.28ab
8.28c–8.93
—
8.94–8.108
8.110
8.109

3.156a– 3.158b	—
—	8.111–8.114
3.158c–3.163	8.115a–8.120b
3.164	8.120c–8.121b
3.165a–3.177b	8.121c–8.133
3.177c–3.179b	8.134–8.135
3.179c–3.194b	8.136–8.150
3.194cd	8.151
3.195a–3.196b	8.152a–8.152f
3.196cd	—
4.1–4.7b	9.1–9.7b
4.8–4.12	9.7c–9.12b
4.13–4.14	—
4.15–4.16	9.12c–9.14b
4.17–4.19	—
—	9.14c–9.23b
4.20a–4.31b	9.23c–9.34d
4.31cd	—
4.32a–4.36b	9.35a–9.39b
4.36c–4.37b	9.39c–9.40
4.37c–4.41	9.41–9.44
4.42–4.137	—

Table 2: Comparative table of parallels between the *Niśvāsamukha* and *Śivadharmasaṅgraha*

From this table we can see that the *Śivadharmasaṅgraha* draws particularly on the first three chapters of the *Niśvāsamukha* quite intensively. Other than that, the *Śivadharmasaṅgraha* also evidently borrows the first part of the fourth chapter from the Vedic section of the *Niśvāsamukha*. As we have noted in the opening sections of this study, the latter offers a stratified scheme of Five Streams, four of which are presented as inferior, yet conducive, preliminary stages which culminate in the soteriologically most rewarding path, the Mantramārga. No such idea—nor indeed any structured stratification of the content at all—is present in the *Śivadharmasaṅgraha*. Instead, the *Śivadharmasaṅgraha*, a text of lay Śaivism, overtly declares its much more limited ambition of simply compiling materials drawn mostly from Śaiva sources in order to present a coherent overview over the materials assembled. The rationale behind the impulse of composition of the two texts is therefore fundamentally dissimilar. Thus, the *Śivadharmasaṅgraha* omits a number of passages pivotal to the intentions of the *Niśvāsamukha*. Amongst these omissions are the following:

1. The frame story of the *Niśvāsatattvasaṃhitā* (1.1–57).

2. Passages that do not accord with the setting of the *Śivadharmasaṅgraha* are omitted because the *Śivadharmasaṅgraha* is not framed as a dialogue between Śiva and Devī reported by Nandikeśvara. *Niśvāsamukha* 1.64 presents an illustrative example:

   evaṃ śrutam mayā pūrvvan devyāṃ kathayato harāt |
   tat sarvvaṅ kathitan tubhyaṃ yat phalaṃ liṅgapūraṇe ||

   This is what I heard from Hara, as he was telling it to the goddess, and I have told it all to you, namely what the fruit of covering the *liṅga* (*liṅgapūraṇe*) is.

3. Those passages that directly reflect the conceptual framework of the Five Streams have also been omitted—with the noteworthy exception of the Vedic section.[281]

At present, we cannot fully comprehend the principles of selection of the *Śivadharmasaṅgraha*. For example, the passage in the *Niśvāsamukha* which speaks of offering a black woollen garment and a buffalo (2.52–53), has been reduced to two lines when incorporated into the *Śivadharmasaṅgraha*. While this could be the result of a slip in transmission, it is possible that the redactor felt it was unnecessary to adopt it, although it is difficult to fathom why, for the section in question fits the context and is readily comprehensible. Other comparable cases could be cited.

Additions in the *Śivadharmasaṅgraha*

As the *Śivadharmasaṅgraha* is a compendium which draws on a multiplicity of pre-existing sources, it is to be expected that it features both interpolated and original material that does not originate from the *Niśvāsamukha*. In the following example, we see that the *Śivadharmasaṅgraha* integrates a substantial passage, of twenty-one verses, which is inserted in the middle of what is verse 2.18 of the *Niśvāsamukha* and which introduces both a

[281] The passage of *Śivadharmasaṅgraha* 9.44cdef reads: *vedadharmo mayā proktaḥ svarganaiśreyasaḥ padam* | *uttareṇaiva vaktreṇa vyākhyātaś ca samāsataḥ* ||. This, we think, is the inadvertent result of careless borrowing: the *Śivadharmasaṅgraha* does not claim to be sourced in any of Śiva's faces.

new topic—the procedure for worshipping a *liṅga* made of sand—and a new speaker (Dadhīci). Most probably the *Śivadharmasaṅgraha* borrowed this segment from another source where Dadhīci was the narrator. In doing so, the compiler-author effectively split a verse of the *Niśvāsamukha* in two. We have not been able to identify the source of the borrowed passage. There are further such examples, but we will restrict ourselves to just this one. *Niśvāsamukha* 2.18 reads:

> *lakṣeṇaikena gaṇatāṃ koṭim abhyarcya gacchati* |
> *svaśarīreṇa sāyojyaṃ punaś ca na nivarttate* ||
>
> By worshipping [it] ten thousand times, he will obtain the state of Gaṇa, and by worshipping [it] one hundred thousand times, he will obtain (*gacchati*) union with [Śiva] in his own body (*svaśarīreṇa*) and will never come back [to worldly existence] again.

In the *Śivadharmasaṅgraha* this becomes (6.18–39b):

> *lakṣeṇaikena gaṇatāṃ koṭyām abhyarcya gacchati* ||
> ***dadhīcir uvāca*** |[282]
> ***kiṃ phalaṃ bālukāliṅgasyārccanād api kiṃ bhavet*** |
> ***kathaṃ vā pūjayet karma vratañ caiva katham bhavet*** ||
> ***maheśvara uvāca*** |
> ***śṛṇu me kathayiṣyāmi bālukāliṅgam arcanam*** |
>
> [...]
>
> ***etat purā mayā khyātaṃ na deyaṃ yasya kasyacit*** |
> *svaśarīreṇa sāyojyaṃ punaś ca na nivarttate* |
>
> By worshipping [it] ten thousand times, one will obtain the state of Gaṇa, and by worshipping [it] one hundred thousand times, one will obtain (*gacchati*)
>
> ...

282 Note that Dadhīci does not appear in the *Niśvāsamukha*. Either Devī poses questions to Śiva or the sages entreat Nandikeśvara to share his knowledge. In the *Śivadharmasaṅgraha*, Dadhīci appears in this isolated instance only.

Dadhīci spoke:

What fruit does one obtain from worshipping a *liṅga* made of sand? How is one supposed to worship it? What is the procedure [of worship]? And how should one practise the observance?

Maheśvara spoke:

Listen to me. I will tell [you] the [procedure of] worshipping the *liṅga* made of sand.

[...]

This [knowledge that] I taught earlier (*purā*) should not be given to everybody. ... [he will obtain] union with [Śiva] in his own body and will never come back [to worldly existence] again.

Grammatical Changes

One of the characteristics of the *Niśvāsamukha*[283] is that it shares features of *aiśa* language with the rest of the *Niśvāsatattvasaṃhitā*. We will show that the *Śivadharmasaṅgraha* has removed these archaic irregularities and replaced them with what are considered 'standard' Sanskrit forms. As the rest of the text of the *Śivadharmasaṅgraha* is mostly written in Pāṇinian Sanskrit, we believe these changes were implemented in the *Śivadharmasaṅgraha* to smoothen out the text. This process of 'streamlining' grammar is typically more likely to be a shift from *aiśa* language to standardized Sanskrit—not the reverse. As a rule of thumb, textual parallels between texts displaying *aiśa*-grammar and texts with standardized Sanskrit should raise the suspicion that the standardised version is likely to be the 'younger' text and has borrowed from the non-standard one.[284]

We present here five types of grammatical modification in the parts of the text borrowed from the *Niśvāsamukha* by the *Śivadharmasaṅgraha*. These involve verb-forms, nominal forms, regularisation of *sandhi*, compounds and gender. We are confronted with changes of this type time and again throughout the text, and the examples quoted below are characteristic of a more widespread phenomenon:

283 For a more detailed account of *aiśa* grammar, refer to p. 129 ff.

284 Note however, that the *Manusmṛti*'s standard Sanskrit being reformulated along *aiśa*-lines in the *Niśvāsamukha* can readily be cited as counter-example to this general rule.

Regularisation of Verb-forms

- Correction of irregular optative: *dadet* (NM 1.60b) to *dadyāt* (ŚiDhS 5.17ab)
- Correction of irregular optative: *pūjye* (NM 2.30a) to *pūjayet* (ŚiDhS 6.50c)
- Correction of irregular *lyap*: *pūjya* (NM 3.160c) to *saṃpūjya* (ŚiDhS 8.117a)

Regularisation of Nominal Forms

- Correction of irregular nominative: *kṛṣṇāṣṭamicaturddaśī* (NM 1.69d) to *kṛṣṇāṣṭamyāṃ caturdaśyāṃ* (ŚiDhS 5.25c)
- Correction of irregular numerical form: *triṃśabhir lakṣaiḥ* (NM 2.7c) to *triṃśallakṣaiḥ* (ŚiDhS 6.7c)
- Correction of irregular nominative singular: *parameṣṭhinaḥ*[285] (NM 3.65ab) to *parameṣṭhī* (ŚiDhS 3.65b)

Regularisation of *Sandhi*

- Correction of double *sandhi*: *yoddharet* (NM 1.87b) to *uddharet* (ŚiDhS 5.43b)
- Correction of irregular extended ending: *kuruteti*[286] (NM 3.58d) to *kurute tu* (ŚiDhS 7.70cd).
- Correction of irregular *sandhi* of the pronoun: *so dhruvam* (NM 4.16d) to *sa dhruvam* (ŚiDhS 9.14ab)

Regularisation of Compounds

- Correction of inflected form: *śaṣkulyāmodakāni* (1.164b) to *śaṣkulīmodakāni* (ŚiDhS 5.125cd)
- Justifying an otiose *sa* : *guḍakṣīrasapāyasaiḥ* (NM 3.80d) to *guḍakṣīraiḥ sapāyasaiḥ* (ŚiDhS 8.21d)

---

285 This form is the same in accusative plural and genitive singular too. Consulting other instances (*Niśvāsamukha* 1.58b, 1.115d, 2.34d etc.) we could derive that this is more likely to be a nominative singular.

286 Cf. Goodall et al. 2015: 122.

REGULARISATION OF GENDER

- Correction of irregular masculine to standard neuter: *°puṣpaḥ* (NM 1.147d) to *°puṣpam* (ŚiDhS 5.103b)
- Correction of irregular neuters to regular masculines: *kumbhīpākan tu nirayan* (NM 2.44c) to *kumbhīpākas tu nirayo* (ŚiDhS 6.68a)

SYNTACTICAL CHANGES

The *Śivadharmasaṅgraha* does not merely correct obvious grammatical mistakes in the borrowed text, but also changes the syntax substantially with the intention of clarifying the original text. There are many instances of this type of syntactical change, and most of these will be discussed in the notes to the translation of the *Niśvāsamukha*. But let us quote one example showing how the *Śivadharmasaṅgraha* corrects awkard syntax and irregular morphology:

> *Niśvāsamukha* (4.15c–16b)
>
> *asvayaṅkṛtavāṇijye bhūtādroheṇa jīvate* ||
> *japti juhoti vā nityaṃ sa svarggaphalabhāg bhavet* |
>
> Without engaging in trade, he lives without harming living beings. He should regularly do mantra-recitation (*japti*) and (*vā*) perform oblations; [by doing so] he will partake of the fruit of heaven.
>
> *Śivadharmasaṅgraha* (9.13)
>
> *vāṇijyādi tyajet karma bhūtadrohañ ca sarvadā* |
> *japāgnihomasaṃyuktaḥ sa svarggaphalabhāg bhavet* ||
>
> He should avoid participating in such activities as trade, and [should] always [avoid] harming living beings. Engaged in mantra-recitation and fire-oblations, he will partake of the fruit of heaven.

Here the *Śivadharmasaṅgraha* corrects *asvayaṅkṛtavāṇijye*, apparently used as a foreshortened instrumental, to *vāṇijyādi tyajet karma*, then replaces *bhūtādroheṇa jīvate*, with *bhūtadrohañ ca sarvadā*. As for *japti juhoti vā nityaṃ* (where *japti* is used for *japati* and both verbs should be optative or marked in some way as being part of a conditional clause), it is replaced by *japāgnihomasaṃyuktaḥ*.

Alteration of Content

Comparing the *Śivadharmasaṅgraha* and the source passages of the *Niśvāsamukha*, in some cases, we detect a modification of the meaning in the borrowed passages. These may be grouped in two categories, which we shall examine below:

1. deliberate alteration concerning rewards and
2. deliberate alteration of the essential meaning.

Modifications Concerning Rewards

Especially with regards to the descriptions of rewards promised for engaging in religious practice, the *Śivadharmasaṅgraha* has considerably altered the passages it has borrowed. Typically, the religious practices themselves remain identical, whereas the results ascribed to them are significantly different. In a few cases, it is possible that such changes are the result of graphic confusion while copying, as in the case of *śivālayam* (NM 1.82d) ≈ *surālayam* (ŚiDhS 5.83d).

- Change of 'Brahma-hood' to 'Skanda-hood': *brahmatvam* (NM 2.7b) to *skandam*[287] (ŚiDhS 6.7b)
- Change from 'attaining the world of the moon' to 'attaining the world of Indra': *somapuraṃ* (NM 2.59c) to *śakrapuraṃ* (ŚiDhS 6.126c)
- Change of 'the fruit of rejoicing in heaven' to attaining the 'world of Kāmadeva': *divi* (NM 2.65d) to *kāmadevapuram* (ŚiDhS 6.132c)

Modifications of the Fundamental Meaning

Occasionally, small changes make significant alterations to the essential meaning of the borrowed text, as in this example:

Niśvāsamukha (2.110)

atidānavidhiḥ khyāto *lokānāṃ hitakāmyayā* |
dine dine ca ***yo dadyād*** *dāna**n*** ***tañ ca*** *nibodha me* ||

I have taught the injunction of consummate offering (*atidānavidhiḥ*) for the benefit of the worlds. If someone makes an offering every day, listen to the fruit of that offering too.

[287] We have taken Skanda in the sense of Skanda-hood here.

> *Śivadharmasaṅgraha* (6.184c-185b)
>
> ***iti** dānavidhiś **cokto** lokānāṃ hitakāmyayā* ||
> *dine dine ca **yad dānaṃ tac cāpi hi** nibodha me* |
>
> I have thus taught the injunction of offering (*iti dānavidhiḥ*) for the benefit of the worlds. [If someone makes] an offering every day, listen to the fruit of that offering too.

Here the pronouncement of the *Niśvāsamukha* is about a 'consummate offering' (*atidāna°*), a problematic term, as its meaning may differ from context to context.[288] The *Śivadharmasaṅgraha*, by writing *iti dāna°* 'thus offering, makes this kind of offering disappear, and ends up with a different and more banal sense.

In sum, the *Śivadharmasaṅgraha* has often rephrased, replacing uncommon words, structures, and syntax. In doing so, it has banalised the text, but it has also often clarified it. The fact that the *Śivadharmasaṅgraha* chose to borrow from the *Niśvāsamukha* suggests that the *Niśvāsamukha* had acquired and still enjoyed some authority among Śaivas at the time the *Śivadharmasaṅgraha* was composed.[289] If not, the redactor of the *Śivadharmasaṅgraha* would presumably have been less likely to draw upon it.

Noteworthy Irregularities in the *Niśvāsamukha*

As noted towards the beginning of this introduction, the text of the *Niśvāsamukha* depends on outside sources to furnish a substantial part of its textual fabric. This becomes evident also stylistically, since the mode of expression varies greatly throughout the text. Some of the unevenness of the text may have been caused by the uneven process of recontextualization of loaned passages.[290] At the same time, the process of transmission may have added to the textual inconsistencies, as would have the introduction of '*aiśa*' forms.[291] However, what might be worth considering is the possibility that at least some of the uncertainties about the text and its interpretation may be attributable to our limited knowledge of the community which produced the work.

---

288 See footnote to verse 2.105d on page 297.

289 A. K. ACHARYA (2009: 91) argues that the *Śivadharmasaṅgraha* can be dated to the 9th and 10th centuries CE.

290 SCHREINER, ed. (1997), in this regard, speaks of 'textual interstices' (*Textfugen*) and 'textual hinges' or 'transition points' (*Schaltstellen*), which constitute disruptive factors in interpolated materials, and moreover mark the contours of the borrowed passages.

291 See p. 129.

As a first example, let us invoke *Niśvāsamukha* 1.51–52, which presents the five streams of knowledge and their goals in accordance with the Mantramārgic perspective:

> *īśvara uvāca* |
> *pañca srotā mayā khyātā lokānāṃ hitakāmyayā* |
> *tān pravakṣyāmi sarvāṃs tu śṛṇuṣva vahitā priye* || 1.51 ||
> *svarggāpavarggahetoś ca tan nibodha yathārthataḥ* |
> *laukikaṃ sampravakṣyāmi yena svargaṃ vrajanti te* || 1.52 ||
>
> Īśvara spoke:
> I have [elsewhere] taught Five Streams [of knowledge] on account of my desire for the welfare of the worlds. I will explain (*pravakṣyāmi*) all of them, o beloved one! Please listen attentively. And for the sake of heaven and liberation (*svargāpavargahetoḥ*), understand this (*tan*) exactly. I shall teach [first] the worldly [stream] (*laukikam*), by which people attain heaven (*svargam*).

Viewed from a logical perspective, the above passage (*Niśvāsamukha* 1.51–52) contains a somewhat problematic statement, particularly as regards the Laukika stream and the Mantramārga. First of all, the fifth stream, which is not the subject matter of the *Niśvāsamukha*, does not topicalize either *svarga* ('heaven') or *apavarga* ('final beatitude'). Instead, it presents the somewhat parallel but nonetheless different concepts of *bhukti* ('enjoyment of supernatural powers') and *mukti* ('liberation').[292] Secondly, this passage clearly mentions that the Laukika stream professes to lead to heaven, and 'heaven' is designated as being (merely) a 'worldly' [293] state. Despite that, we encounter a passage (1.86) in the same Laukika section that declares that union with Śiva (*sāyojyam*)—usually a supramundane state—results from bathing a *liṅga* with ghee for two years.[294]

It thus appears that the soteriological contours of the Laukika stream and the Mantramārga have been presented in a manner that has been not

---

[292] GOODALL et al. 2015: 15, 32, 59 and 73.

[293] Refer to §2 on page 44 above.

[294] From this passage alone, one might doubt whether union with Śiva (*sāyojyam*) refers to a supramundane state of liberation, yet this is how it is used in another passage of the *Niśvāsamukha* (2.17–18): that latter section intimates that by obtaining union with [Śiva] one is never reborn, showing that there is no difference between union with Śiva and final liberation:

> *saccakena tu liṅgāni pārthivāni tu kārayet* |
> *sahasrapūjanāt so hi labhate īpsitaṃ phalam* ||

made fully consistent, and that there are instances of conceptual imbrication. To cite another instance, the passage spanning 1.118c–119b in the same Laukika section states that if one worships Śiva by offering a *muktimaṇḍapa* with devotion, no rebirth ensues—which again implies that the final goal of the Mantramārga can be achieved by means of a Laukika practice.[295] As in the case of the mention of 'union with Śiva', such passages in the Laukika section seem to contradict the statement of 1.52cd above that the Laukika stream leads merely to heaven. This inconsistency here may have resulted from the attempt of the author of the *Niśvāsamukha* to present these teachings of the Laukika stream within a Mantramārgic framework. In doing so, the author appears to attempt to confine the benefits offered by the Laukika stream to those of an inferior, preliminary stage, presumably in order to highlight the supremacy of the Mantramārga teachings. This attempt, however, leaves traces of doctrinal tension within the text as its corollary.

Another passage displaying a degree of logical inconsistency is the list of hells in 4.100a–105b. Because this extract is taught in a section that relates the views and practices of the Kapālavratins, it seems likely that this passage was borrowed from a now lost Kāpālika source. Although thirty-five named hells are listed, the list is followed by the assertion that there are thirty-two (4.105cd). Since thirty-two is a standard number featuring abundantly in the Mantramārga system,[296] it is possible that the author of this passage therefore favoured that number. We therefore guess that the last line (4.105cd) in the following passage might have been added without previously counting the number of items in the list—or possibly with a generous *laissez-faire* attitude that would allow for a few of the individual hells to be grouped together under one rubric. The passage reads as follows:

---

lakṣeṇaikena gaṇatāṃ koṭim abhyarcya gacchati |
svaśarīreṇa sāyojyaṃ punaś ca na nivarttate ||

If someone makes [and worships] earthen *liṅgas* made from a mould (*saccakena*) a thousand times, he will certainly (*hi*) obtain the desired fruits. By worshipping [it] ten thousand times, he will obtain the state of Gaṇa, and by worshipping [it] one hundred thousand times, he will obtain (*gacchati*) union with [Śiva] in his own body (*svaśarīreṇa*) and will never come back [to worldly existence] again.

295 *Niśvāsamukha* 1.118c–119b: *muktimaṇḍapadānena bhaktyā tu yo 'rcayec chivam* ||
na tasya punar āvṛttir gganaś caivottamo bhavet |

296 See SANDERSON 2003-4: 422 and GOODALL 2004: 282–283, fn. 487.

avīcī kṛminicayo vaitaraṇī kūṭaśālmalī |
giriryamala ucchvāso nirucchvāso hy athāparaḥ || 4.100 ||
pūtimānsadravaś caiva trapus taptajatus tathā |
paṃkālayo 'sthibhaṅgaś ca krakacacchedam eva ca || 4.101 ||
medo'sṛkpūyahradaś ca tīkṣṇāyastuṇḍam eva ca |
aṅgārarāśibhuvanaḥ śakuniś cāmbarīṣakaḥ || 4.102 ||
--- *'nyā hy asitālavanas tathā* |
sūcīmukhaḥ kṣuradhāraḥ kālasūtro 'tha parvataḥ || 4.103 ||
padmaś caiva samākhyāto mahāpadmas tathaiva ca |
apāko sāra uṣṇaś ca sañjīvanasujīvanau || 4.104 ||
śītatamondhatamasau mahārauravarauravau |
dvātriṃśad ete narakā mayā devi prakīrttitāḥ || 4.105 ||

[1] Avīcī, [2] Kṛminicaya, [3] Vaitaraṇī, [4] Kuṭaśālmalī, [5] Giriryamala, [6] Ucchvāsa, and then [7] Nirucchvāsa [8], Pūtimāṃsadrava, [9] Trapu, [10] Taptajatu then [11] Paṃkālaya, [12] Asthibhaṅga, [13] Krakacaccheda and [14] Medo'sṛkpūyahrada, [15] Tīkṣṇāyastuṇḍa, then [16] Aṅgārarāśibhuvana, [17] Śakuni, [18] Ambarīṣaka, [19] Asitāladruma, [20] Asitālavana, then [21] Sūcīmukha, [22] Kṣuradhāra, [23] Kālasūtra, then [24] Parvata, then [25] Padma is taught, then [26] Mahāpadma, then [27] Apāka, [28] Sāra, [29] Uṣṇa, [30] Sañjīvana, [31] Sujīvana, [32] Śītatamas, [33] Andhatamas, [34] Mahāraurava and [35] Raurava; **I have taught, o goddess, these thirty-two hells.**

It is to be noted that a list of thirty-two hells found in the inscription of the Angkor Vat bas-relief is particularly close to the list of the hells of the *Niśvāsamukha* both in names and ordering principle applied.[297]

The *Aṣṭamūrti*-hymn in *Niśvāsamukha* 1.30–41 arguably does not smoothly fit the context in which it occurs and is perhaps also interpolated from a different source. Note, first of all, that the hymn features a *phalaśruti*, which is typically included at the end of self-contained texts. Secondly, were this portion removed—as will be shown in the following extract—the preceding (1.29) and the following textual segment (1.42) of the *Niśvāsamukha* appear to interlock seamlessly, with Nandin first introducing a question of the goddess and then supplying that question:

297 See SANDERSON 2003-4: 422. The list of hells found in Angkor Vat may therefore be further evidence of knowledge of the *Niśvāsa*-corpus being transmitted beyond the Indian subcontinent (SANDERSON 2001: 7–8, fn. 5), for we already know from Khmer inscriptions that the *Niśvāsa* was known and employed among royalty in rituals.

mahādevyā yathā pṛṣṭas sarvvaduḥkhaharo haraḥ |
tathā vakṣyāmi viprendrāḥ praṇipatya śivaṃ śuciḥ || 1.29 ||

[...]—**[ostensibly interpolated passage]**

devy uvāca |
anādinidhano devo hy ajam akṣaram avyayaḥ |
sarvagas sarvarūpo 'si sarvajñaś caikakāraṇaḥ || 1.42 ||

I will teach, o best among Brāhmins, just as Śiva, the destroyer of all suffering [did], when requested by the great goddess after prostrating before Śiva and purifying myself.

[...]—**[ostensibly interpolated passage]**

Devī spoke: You are the god [having] no beginning, nor end (*anādinidhano*), devoid of birth and destruction, imperishable, all-pervading and having all forms. You are omniscient [and] the sole cause [of the whole universe].

At first glance, not all the unevennesses in the text appear to have arisen due to textual borrowing—some may rather have occurred during the course of the subsequent transmission of the text. To cite one possible example: in a passage where the rewards for worshipping different deities are indicated, the verse relating the worship of Kubera on the third day of the fortnight lacks such an explanation of the reward for worshipping the deity:

tṛtīyāyāṃ tu sampūjya yakṣaṃ hemamayīṅ gadām |
nāmāny ālikhya dātavyā bhājane ghṛtapūrite || 3.164 ||
caturtthyān dantinan dadyāt sauvarṇṇan nāma-cāṅkitam |
vighneśvarasya devasya ghṛtapūrṇṇodumbare sthitam || 3.165 ||

Having [first] worshipped Kubera (*yakṣam*) on the third day [of the fortnight], one should give a golden mace [to a Brāhmin], writing the names of [Kubera on it and putting it] in a vessel filled with clarified butter. On the fourth day [of the fortnight], one should give a golden elephant marked with the names of the god Vighneśvara placed in [a vessel made of] *udumbara* wood.

Instead of relating the reward for performing the worship of Kubera, as expected, the text proceeds at once to relate the worship of Vighneśvara. Since we are presumably missing a single line here, one possible explanation is that it might have been left out by a transmitter as a result of eye-skip. However, the fact that the very same segment—mention of the rewards for worshipping a particular deity—is again missing in the instance of the worship of Devī,[298] we should mention another possible scenario. Since such a coincidence would be arguably unlikely to occur accidentally when copying, it is perhaps just as likely to be an authorial feature. Perhaps the author drew the exposition of performing the worship of diverse deities from one source and the respective rewards from another source, from oral tradition, from floating verses, or from his own inventiveness. In the process, the exposition of the worship of two deities—Kubera and Devī—may, because of oversight, never actually have been supplied with the corresponding rewards.

We may conclude our lengthy discussion of borrowings and parallels with the observation that the *Niśvāsamukha* is plainly a syncretic composition—one whose hybrid nature, by the way, cannot simply be described by the label 'Mantramārgic Śaivism'. But it is hard to judge to what extent irregularities of the text are authorial, and to what extent they are caused by scribal error during the process of transmission. This is all the more difficult since we have only a single manuscript witness to the text.

Structural Overview and Summary of Content

The *Niśvāsamukha* is divided into four chapters (*paṭalas*). The first begins with the frame story in which the entirety of the *Niśvāsatattvasaṃhitā* is enveloped. Thereafter, the Five Streams of knowledge are briefly taught, after which lay religious duties are expounded, ending with the worshipping of the *liṅga* and the rewards of doing so. The second chapter relates how to fashion different kinds of *liṅgas*, installing them and worshipping them on a daily basis, the rewards of such worship and various affiliated donative practices. The third chapter discusses sacred places of pilgrimage, the benefits of worshipping various gods and performing different religious observances.

---

298 Here is the account in question of the worship of Devī (3.177c–178):

> *navamyāṃ siṃha nāmena devyāś cābhyarcitena ca* |
> *ghṛtatāmrasya dānāc ca bhakṣaiḥ payaghaṭānvitaiḥ* ||
> *yamāya mahiṣan dadyān nāmāṅkan tu ghṛtaplutam* |
>
> On the ninth day [of a fortnight], [one should offer a statuette of] a lion [after first] worshipping Devī by [calling out] her name[s], [and] also by giving a copper [container] of ghee and [some] eatables, together with pots filled with milk, [to a Brāhmin]. For [the worship of] Yama (*yamāya*), one should give [a statuette of] a buffalo covered in ghee, marked with the names [of Yama to a Brāhmin].

Instead of mentioning the expected rewards for performing this act of worship, the text instead immediately proceeds to describe the procedure for worshipping Yama.

The fourth chapter relates the so-called Vedic, Ādhyātmika and Atimārga streams.

Chapter One

[Frame story: the Five Streams]

Ricīka (=Ṛcīka) inquires of Mataṅga about a miracle that he had seen in the Naimiṣa forest. (1–4)

Mataṅga answers Ricīka (=Ṛcīka) in brief that Brahmā and Viṣṇu were initiated, and, upon hearing this, sages gathered in the forest of Devadāruvana/ (5–13)

Nandin is granted the authority to teach the sages. (14–17)

Ricīka (=Ṛcīka) asks Mataṅga how Nandin could be the teacher of the sages and how he could grant initiation to them. (18)

Mataṅga relates how the sages praised Nandikeśvara. (19–25)

Nandin initiates the sages and promises to impart to them the Five Streams of knowledge as they were revealed to Devī by Hara. (26–29)

Nandin bows down to Śiva and praises him in what is called an *Aṣṭamūrti*-hymn. (30–41)

Devī recites a hymn to Śiva. (41–45)

Devī informs Śiva about her compassion for afflicted beings and proceeds to ask how they can be freed from affliction. (45–50)

Īśvara gives a brief account of the Five Streams of knowledge. (51–56)

Devī asks Īśvara to describe the five streams of knowledge in detail. (57)

[The Laukika stream]

Īśvara teaches the fruits of making a fountain of drinking water, creating a lotus pond, offering a house to a Brāhmin, making a garden at a temple, offering the gift of a flower or a garland, and covering a *liṅga* with flowers. (58–63)

Nandin reiterates what he had heard when Hara was teaching Devī regarding the fruit of covering a *liṅga* with flowers. (64)

The sages inquire about how the god is to be pleased and about the fruits of worshipping him by different means and with diverse substances. (65–70)

[Worship of the *liṅga*]

Nandin tells of the fruits of cleansing a *liṅga*, worshipping it with different substances on a daily basis, such as leaves, flowers, fruits, curd, milk, ghee, *pavitra* (i.e. *kuśa* grass), and the sounding of 'HUḌḌUṄ'. (71–76)

The fruits of bathing a *liṅga* with water, curds, ghee, milk, honey and with the five products of a cow. (76–97)

The fruits of besmearing a *liṅga* with sandal paste mixed with camphor, burning *guggulu* in front of a *liṅga*, offering clothes, banners or awnings to the *liṅga*. (98–107b)

The fruits of offering a golden bell made of different substances, a yak-tail fly-whisk, a girdle and waist-cord, a crown, an ear-ring and a multicoloured fabric, a turban, gems, ornaments, adornments, and a *muktimaṇḍapa* to the *liṅga*. (107c–119b)

The fruits of performing the rite of besmearing with different substances, offering bracelets, armbands, gems, scentless flowers, and covering a *liṅga* with flowers. (119c–123b)

The beginning of the teaching of worshipping the *liṅga* with fragrant flowers. (123c–124b)

The fruits of offering a fragrant flower, the names of flowers, whose fragrance Śaṅkara [delights in], and the fruits of worshipping Śiva with them. (124c–128b)

The fruits of worshipping a *liṅga* with different flowers and the rewards for doing so. (128c–156b)

The fruits of offering leaves, flowers, fruit, water, grass, and milk to Śaṅkara daily. (1156c–158b)

Ranking of various types of flowers. (158c–159)

The fruits of offering different foods and songs. (160–165b)

The fruits of offering lute music, the sound 'HUḌḌUṄ', dance, mouth music ('*mukhavādya*'), and loud laughter to Śiva. (165c–169b)

The fruits of worshipping Śiva for those who have not received Śaiva initiation and for those who have. (169cdef)

Nandi tells the sages the significance of the *liṅga*, and states that this is what he heard from Hara as he related it to the goddess. (170–171)

[The *Liṅgodbhava* myth]

Nandi relates the famous *Liṅgodbhava* myth to the sages. (172–184)

The chapter concludes with the warning that prosperity is not possible for mortals who do not worship Śiva in the form of the *liṅga*. (185)

Chapter Two

[Temporary *liṅgas*]

The question of the sages to Nandi about the fruits of making a *liṅga* and installing it. (1)

The fruits of making a *liṅga* and worshipping it. (2–7)

The fruits of making a *liṅga* out of different substances, and thereupon worshipping it. (6–20b)

[Donations]

The fruits of making a Śiva temple with marked bricks, and the fruits of making and worshipping the *liṅga* made of different metals. (20c–24b)

The fruits of planting trees and cultivating a garden. (24c–27b)

The fruits of constructing a temple and installing deities. (27c–30b)

The fruits of making a bridge, causeway, water-channel, hut, abode or pavilion, and of making donations. (30c–36)

The fruits of offering food and water. (37–39b)

The fruits of offering sesame and water to gods and ancestors. (39c–41b)

The fruits of offering the hide of a black buck. (41c–43b)

The fruits of performing *śrāddha* rites to ancestors. (43c–45b)

The fruits of offering a lamp and cows to gods and ancestors. (45c–48)

The fruits of offering a calving cow and a bull to a Brāhmin. (49–50)

The fruits of offering a goat, a garment and a buffalo to a Brāhmin. (51–55)

The fruits of offering land, gems, clothes, and silver. (56–57)

The fruits of donating sesame seeds, gold, pearls, or gems of various kinds and quality. (58–59)

The fruits of offering treacle, milk, curds, ghee, sandalwood, agallochum, camphor, cloves etc. (60–61)

The fruits of offering a virgin girl, grains and protection to living beings. (62–63)

The fruits of offering a woman and providing a feast of lovemaking with women. (64–65)

The fruits of offering a cane-seat, a couch, fuel, shelter, straw, a blanket and food. (66–68)

The fruits of regularly offering songs, musical instruments and vehicles to the gods, and of offering a horse to Brāhmins. (69–71)

The fruits of offering an umbrella, a pair of shoes, a chariot drawn by an elephant, a horse and a bullock cart. (72–80b)

The fruits of offering a mouthful of grass (*grāsa*) to cows. (80c–86b)

The fruits of letting a black bull, or any bull, free. (86c–88b)

The reward of offering various kinds of fruits. (88b–91b)

The fruits of offering tooth-cleaning sticks, fragrant betel, flowers and other fragrant substances. (91c–92)

The fruits of offering cushions made of *kuśa*-grass, different weapons, and vessels. (92–97)

The fruits of offering servants and maids to the gods or to Brāhmins; sea salt, piper longum, ginger, pepper, and dry ginger; and remedies for the sick. (98–100)

The fruits of offering sweet, sour, pungent, bitter, astringent and salty objects; oil, sugar or treacle, and thickened curd or buttermilk. (101–102)

The fruits of offering pearls or nacreous shells, cowrie shells, a mirror, nourishment, expressions of compassion or alms. (103–105)

[Hierarchy of recipients]

The magnificence of the donor and the characteristics of a true donor. (106–109)

The end of the description of the highest form of offering. (110)

The fruits of offering objects that are applied in daily use, cosmetics and food;. (111–114)

Devī's queries to Īśvara about the best recipient, and Īśvara's answer about the best types of recipients of gifts. (115–116)

Ranking of recipients. (117–122)

Chapter Three

[Sacred sites]

Devī questions Īśvara about the merits of pilgrimage. (1)

[Rivers]

A list of river names. (2–8)

The fruits of bathing in different bodies of water, the mantra that is to be recited while bathing and its fruits. (9–13b)

The fruits of bathing while remembering Agni as the womb, Viṣṇu as the seminal fluid, Brahmā as the father, and water as a form of Rudra. (13c–14)

The fruits of suicide by abandoning one's body in rivers. (15a–16b)

The fruits of always recalling a certain pilgrimage site and of entering a fire (with the intent to perish therein). (16c–18)

[The *pañcāṣṭakas* and other sacred sites]

A list of five groups of eight pilgrimage places, and the fruits of bathing, seeing or performing worship and dying at any of them. (19a–26)

The fruits of seeing the god in Mahālaya and drinking the water of Kedāra with and without reciting the *vidyāmantra*. (27a–29b)

The fruits of visiting other secret (*guhyāḥ*) places and of passing away at those locations. (29c–30)

The places where Hari is said to perpetually reside, and the fruits of of passing away at those locations. (31–32)

The fruits of being a devotee of various divinities. (33a–34b)

[Observance of fasts]

The fruits of undertaking a fast until death. (34c–36)

The description of the fasts known as Sāntapana, Parāka, Atikṛcchra, Taptakṛcchra, Cāndrāyaṇa, Yaticāndrāyaṇa and Śiśucāndrāyaṇa observances, and the fruits of practising them. (37a–50b)

The fruits of fasting every other day, every other fortnight and every other month for a year. (50c–53)

The fruits of an observance restricting the intake of food to the night-time. (54–55)

The reward of not consuming honey and meat. (56)

The significance of celibacy. (57)

The significance of giving up all wealth. (58)

A list of unacceptable food items that are not to be offered to Brāhmins. (59)

Devī's question about the fruits of resorting to and worshipping different divinities. (60)

[Worship of different divinities]

Śiva's reply about the rewards of worshipping Brahmā, Agni, Kubera, Gaṇeśa, the Nāgas, Skanda, and Āditya—all in twelve forms (except the Nāgas)—on the first, second, third, forth, fifth, sixth and seventh days respectively of each month, starting from Mārgaśīrṣa and ending in Kārttika. (61–91)

The fruits of fasting and worshipping Śaṅkara, Devadeva, Tryambaka, Sthāṇu, Hara, Śiva, Bhava, Nīlakaṇṭha, Piṅgala, Rudra, Īśāna and Ugra, on the eighth day of each month from Mārgaśīrṣa to Kārttika. (92–106b)

The fruits of fasting and worshipping twelve different forms of Mahādevī on the ninth day. (106c–113b)

The fruits of fasting and worshipping the mother goddess for nine consecutive ninth lunar days. (113c–116b)

The fruits of worshipping twelve forms of Yama on the tenth day of each month, beginning with Mārgaśiras. (116c–121b)

The fruits of worshipping twelve forms of Dharma on the eleventh day. (121c–126b)

The fruits of fasting and worshipping Keśava, Nārāyaṇa, Mādhava, Govinda, Viṣṇu, Madhusūdana, Trivikrama, Vāmana, Śrīdhara, Hṛṣīkeśa, Padmanābha and Dāmodara on the twelfth day of each month for a year. (126c–138b)

The fruits of worshipping Viṣṇu for a year and for a lifetime. (138c–141b)

The fruits of worshipping the twelve forms of Anaṅga on the thirteenth lunar day. (141c–145)

The fruits of worshipping *Pārameśvara* in his twelve forms on the fourteenth lunar day. (146–150)

The fruits of satisfying the needs of the ancestors on the new and full moon days of Mārgaśiras. (151–154)

The names of the ancestors of the four castes. (155)

The fruits of fasting and worshipping Agni on a full moon day. (156–157)

The fruits and procedure of worshipping Prajāpati on a new moon day. (158–160b)

The fruits and procedure of worshipping Agni on the second day. (160c–163)

The procedure of worshipping Kubera on the third day; (164)

The fruits and procedure of worshipping Vighneśvara on the fourth day. (165–166)

The fruits and procedure of worshipping Nāgas on the fifth day. (167–169)

The fruits and procedures of worshipping Skanda on the sixth day. (170–172)

The fruits and procedure of worshipping the Sun god [on the seventh day]. (173–174)

The fruits and procedure of worshipping Śiva on the eighth day. (175–177b)

The fruits and the procedure of worshipping Devī on the ninth day. (177c–178b)

The fruits and the procedure of worshipping Yama on the tenth day. (178c–180)

The fruits and the procedure of worshipping Dharma on the eleventh day. (181–182)

The fruits and the procedure of worshipping Viṣṇu on the twelfth day. (182–185)

The fruits and the procedure of worshipping Kāmadeva on the thirteenth day. (186–188b)

The fruits and the procedure of worshipping *Pārameśvara* on the fourteenth day. (188c–191b)

The injunction for honouring the ancestors on the new and full-moon days. (191c–195b)

The end of the section on worshipping gods and ancestors in Nandin's words, stating that this is what Śaṅkara taught Devī with his western face. (195c–196)

Chapter Four

[The Vaidika stream]

Devī's question about Vedic *dharma* to Īśvara. (1)

[Injunctions for Vedic students]

The god's description of the observance of a *brahmacārin*. (2–6)

[Injunctions for householders]

The duties of the householder and the distinguishing characteristics of a Brāhmin. (7–12)

The fruits of reciting the [Vedic] *saṃhitās*.13–14)

The proper form of livelihood for a householder. (15)

The significance of reciting mantras, making oblations, and the consequences of not performing the five mandatory sacrifices. (16)

The list of the five sacrifices and the five slaughter-houses of a householder. (17–19)

The defining characteristic of an expert in the Vedic *dharma*. (20)

The fruits of meditating while intoning the *praṇava*. (21)

The conclusion of the observances of a householder. (22–24)

[Injunctions for forest-dwellers]

The observances of the forest-dwelling stage of life.(25)

Further injunctions for a forest-dweller. (26–31)

[Injunctions for ascetics]

The procedures for renunciation and the injunctions for an ascetic. (32a–40)

The end of the Vedic section, taught by Śiva's Southern face. (41)

[The Ādhyātmika stream]

The beginning of the *ādhyātmika* section, taught by Śiva's Northern face. (42)

[Sāṅkhya]

The cause of everything coming into being, according to the Sāṅkhya view. (43)

The emanation of the three qualities, the twenty-five *tattvas*, and the distinctive features of *puruṣa*. (44–46)

The conditions determining whether one is content or remains bound, according to the Sāṅkhya system. (47)

The end of the section on the Sāṅkhya view and beginning of the section on Yoga. (48ab)

[Yoga]

The definition of a *yogin*, the right direction to face when assuming a yogic posture, the eight yogic postures, and assuming correct upper-body posture. (48c–51)

The definition of *pratyāhāra*, the purpose of practising meditation, the three breath-controlling exercises and their definitions. (52a–57b)

The section on the fixations (*dhāraṇā*) of air, fire, earth and water, followed by the sections on *tarka* and *samādhi*. (57c–67)

The result of practising contemplation. (68–69)

[The Atimārga stream]

The Atimārga stream comprises the following two schools of thought:

[Atyāśrama]

The teaching of the first type of Pāśupata practice, called the Atyāśramavrata.[299] (70–88c)

[Lokātīta]

The teaching of the second type of Pāśupata practice, called Lokātīta.[300] (88d–130)

---

299 For more details, see our translation and the accompanying footnotes.

300 The reader is here referred to the translation of our text and footnotes thereon.

Conclusion by Śiva that he has taught the Atimārga in two forms with his Eastern face. (131)

Devī's query regarding the Mantramārga. (132)

Nandin's promise to pass on to sages the supreme knowledge of the Mantramārga that he heard while Śiva spoke to Devī with his fifth face, the Īśāna face. (133–137)

Language of the *Niśvāsamukha*

The Sanskrit employed to write the *Niśvāsamukha* is often anomalous with regards to syntax and morphology, for it does not strictly to adhere to all the rules of standard Pāṇinian Sanskrit grammar. This type of slightly irregular language when used in Śaiva tantric texts is framed by the later tradition as '*aiśa*' (*īśvaraprokta*), in other words '*that spoken by the Lord.*' The underlying supposition is that, although such language is ungrammatical from the vantage point of human grammarians such as Pāṇini, it is nonetheless authoritative, since it is said to reflect the mode of expression of Lord Śiva himself. Kṣemarāja, the 11th-century Kashmirian author, for the first time, in his commentary *Svacchandatantrodyota*, refers to such linguistic oddities as *aiśa*.[301]

We find such non-standard usages of language in the Epics and *Purāṇas* as well. OBERLIES (2003: xxxi) observes that the "Epic language presents itself as a mixture of correct and incorrect forms, always met with side by side, within one and the same stanza." In the case of the Purāṇas, such irregularities have also been discussed, for instance with regard to the *Skandapurāṇa*. The editors of the different volumes of the *Skandapurāṇa*[302] have listed numerous non-Pāṇinian forms which they find spread throughout the text. Similar linguistic features have been studied and discussed by SALOMON (1986) with regard to the *Viṣṇupurāṇa*. Such irregularities in the Epics and the Purāṇas are known as *ārṣa* (*ṛṣiprokta*), in other words 'spoken by sages', by commentators of the Epics.[303] Franklin EDGERTON

301 See GOODALL 1998: lxv–lxx (discussing the *Kiraṇatantra*) and TÖRZSÖK 1999: xxvi ff. (discussing the language of the *Siddhayogeśvarīmata*). Two further lists of such deviations from classical Sanskrit grammar have appeared recently in this series, namely those of GOODALL et al. (2015: 113 ff.) of KISS (2015:77–90), covering the more stridently deviant language of the *Brahmayāmala*.

302 See ADRIAENSEN, BAKKER & ISAACSON 1998: 26–51; YOKOCHI 2013: 67–72; BAKKER, BISSCHOP & YOKOCHI 2014: 21–23; BISSCHOP & YOKOCHI 2018: 18.

303 OBERLIES 2003: xxviii.

(1953) has carried out extensive research on deviant Sanskrit as it appears in Indian Buddhist Sanskrit texts.[304] His stance towards such 'drifting forms' of Sanskrit is that these are not incorrect forms but simply belong to a different register of the language.

How does this manifest in the *Niśvāsamukha*? This is most easily understood by listing types of non-standard usage. Some peculiar features of the *Niśvāsamukha* that may be described as *aiśa* are equally shared by the other books of the *Niśvāsatattvasaṃhitā*. We have indicated such shared characteristics with reference to the deviations noted in the edition offered by GOODALL et al. (2015: 113 ff.) in the list of morphological, orthographical and grammatical deviations from standard Sanskrit below.

A number of *aiśa* forms in the *Niśvāsamukha*, and indeed, in a large number of texts pertaining to the Mantramārga,[305] can be explained as resulting from the constraints of metre. Metre-dependent instances of *aiśa*-forms are commonly observed in several tantric texts, such as in the other books of the *Niśvāsa*, the *Svacchandatantra*, the *Brahmayāmala*, different recensions of the *Kālottara*, the *Mataṅga* etc.

In a few cases, we must consider the possibility that some forms are due to scribal variation, and did not originally form an intrinsic part of the composition of the text.[306] The foremost among these variations is *āṃ* used for *ān* in substitution of an accusative plural. For example in *Niśvāsamukha* 2.98, which speaks about the way to offer female and male slaves, it employs the phrase *dāsīdāsāṃ ca yo dadet*, where the *āṃ* ending features in place of *ān*. Other masculine accusative plurals with a final *anusvāra* instead of the standard *n*, such as in 2.39c (*devān* ***pitṝṃ*** *samuddiśya*) and in 2.56cd (*yāvat* ***sūryakṛtāṃ lokāṃ***), may also be similarly attributable to the same type of scribal style.[307] We have, however, decided to keep such scribal variations in the text, rather than emending them, and have done so in deference to the editorial policies established by GOODALL et al. (2015). Since our text is based on a single manuscript, we are hesitant to apply conjecture too broadly, and limit ourselves to the most obvious and compelling instances

---

304 EDGERTON refers to this type of grammar as 'Buddhist hybrid Sanskrit'.

305 This is a feature that is already fairly well-established with respect to other texts, as shown by OBERLIES's (2003) analysis of the Epics.

306 Some such scribal variations are discussed with reference to the *Skandapurāṇa* by ADRIAENSEN, BAKKER & ISAACSON (1998: 49–50). The editors of the *Skandapurāṇa* considered such readings to be traceable to the regionally coloured linguistic background of the scribes and did not form an intrinsic part of the original constitution of the text.

307 For more examples see 2.63a, 2.98b, 3.166a, 3.171a, 3.187a, 3.187b, 4.8b (twice), 4.18a, 4.62a, 4.62b, and 4.111b. Cf. also GOODALL et al. 2015: 133.

calling for editorial intervention. Thus we attempt to present the text mostly in congruence with the way it has been transmitted in the manuscript, and only deviate from that principle when good reason impels us to emend a reading.

Here we present an exhaustive list of types of unusual linguistic forms of the *Niśvāsamukha*, some of which are also shared by the Epics and the Purāṇas; note that we have left out deviant forms that we consider with some confidence to be scribal variations. Note also that we have not exhausted listed all instances of all types! For the discussion of individual cases see our translation and accompanying notes.

Morphology of Nominal Forms

Syncopation of a *visarga*

1.70d (*upasannāḥ* ***sma*** *te vayam*) and 4.41b (*°**naiśre**yasa* for *°**naiḥśre**yasa*)

Syncopation of a vowel

1.58a (*utpānam* for *udapānam*) and 4.16 (*japti* for *japati*)[308]

Elongation of a vowel

1.118a, 1.162a, 3.104d and 3.105d (*gāṇāpatyam* for *gāṇapatyam*), 4.8d (*hāvanam* for *havanam*) and 1.11d and 1.13b (***brahmā**viṣṇumaheśvarāḥ*)[309]

Prākṛtic vowel-shifts

1.79c, 1.79a, 1.83a, 1.86c, 1.91a, 1.94c, 1.99b, 2.18c, 3.86d, 3.145c, 3.150c and 3.191b (*sāyojya* for *sāyujya*), and 4.95a and 4.126c (*vāgeśyām* for *vāgīśvaryām*)[310]

Prākṛtic vowel with double abstract

1.41d, 1.89d, 1.96b, 3.29a and 4.87d (*śiva**sāyojyatā**m*)[311]

Shortening of vowels

3.81a (*śarka**ra*** for *śarkarā*)

---

[308] Cf. GOODALL et al. 2015: 118–119 and 123.

[309] Cf. GOODALL et al. 2015: 119.

[310] Cf. GOODALL et al. 2015: 127.

[311] Cf. GOODALL et al. 2015: 128.

Singular for plural

1.64c (*tat sarvvaṅ kathitan* ***tubhyam***) and 1.170c (*mayāpi kathitaṃ* ***tubhyaṃ***),[312] and 2.45b (*śrāddhakāra**yitā** narāḥ*)

Plural for singular

1.58b (*pāpātmā* ***duṣṭacetasaḥ***), 1.115d (*citrapaṭṭapradā**yinaḥ***), 2.34b (*nālīmārgaprayā**yinaḥ***), 2.34d (*maṇḍapasya ca* ***kāriṇaḥ***), 2.45b (*śrāddhakārayitā* ***narāḥ***), 2.45d (*nityan dīpapradā**yinaḥ***), 3.89d (*nirujo dīrghajī**vinaḥ***), 4.78b (*vyaktāvyaktaika**liṅginaḥ***), and 3.7cd (*tāmrā caiva trisandhyā ca* ***mandākinyaḥ parāḥ smṛtāḥ***)

Plural for dual

1.17ab (*yathā* ***te*** *sarvaśāstrāṇāṃ dīkṣājñānasya vedakau*) and 4.33b (*dikṣu* ***śrotrāṇi*** *vinyaset*)

Instrumental for locative

4.123b *mūrdhn**ā**bhibhavapañcakam*[313]

Locative for instrumental

2.102 (*gavāḍhyo* ***goprapūjane***), and 3.76b and 3.166d (***yāvajjīve*** *gaṇottamaḥ*)

Nominative for locative

3.75d (***caturtthy*** *ubhayapakṣayoḥ*) and 3.158c (***pratipad*** *bhojayed viprān*)[314]

Nominative for accusative

1.124d (*aśītikalpakoṭayaḥ*) and 3.11a (***ayaṃ*** *mantram anusmṛtya*)[315]

Locative for dative 1.24d (*tryakṣāya* ***ṛṣisambhave***), 1.31d (***śive*** *namaḥ*), 1.157a (*pratyahaṃ* ***śaṅkare*** *dadyān*), three times in 2.38ab (*yastu grīṣme prapān dadyāt* ***tṛṣṇārtte pathike jane***), 2.50b (*yaḥ prayacched* ***dvijottame***), 2.53b (*mahiṣīṃ yo daded* ***dvije***), 2.54d (*athavāpi* ***dvijottame***), 2.75ab (*gajarathan tu yo dadyād brāhmaṇāya* ***guṇānvite***), 2.100ab (*dattvā nirujatāṃ yāti* ***āture*** *oṣadhāni ca*),

312 In both cases, *tubhyam* refers to the sages *ṛṣayaḥ*, for which reason we would expect *yuṣmabhyam* instead of *tubhyam*.

313 Cf. Goodall et al. 2015: 124.

314 Cf. Goodall et al. 2015: 125–126.

315 Cf. Goodall et al. 2015: 126. Note that in addition to serving as a nominative masculine pronoun, *ayaṃ* also is used as a nominative neuter pronoun.

2.119d (*ekan dadyāt tu* ***jñānine***), 3.59c (*tad* ***brāhmaṇe*** *na dātavyam*), 3.118c (***ugradaṇḍadhṛte*** *nityam*), 3.119ab (*śāsitre ca namas tubhyaṃ* ***narakādhipate*** *namaḥ*), 3.162c (*dadyād viprāya* ***śobhane***), 3.175ab (*aṣṭamyāṃ vṛṣabhan dadyād bhavanāmāṅkitaṃ* ***dvije***) and 3.181b (*vṛṣan dadyād* ***dvijottame***)[316]

Vocalic *ri* for *ṛ*

1.1, 1.7 and 1.18 (***ri****cīka*)[317]

Feminine *ī*-stem as *ā*-stem 1.107c (*hemamayāṅ*) and 1.109a (*mṛnmay****āṃ***)[318]

Feminine *ī* stem singular treated as a *yā*-stem

1.14c (***devyāyās*** *tu tathā pūrvam*) and 4.135d (***devyāyā*** *gaditaṃ purā*)[319]

Masculine for neuter

1.147d (***javāpuṣpas*** *tathaiva ca*), 4.8c (*svādhyāyaṃ* ***pratyahaḥ*** *kuryāt*), 1.10c: (***taṃ*** *śrutvā āgatāḥ sarve*), 2.14 (*labhen* ***mahāntam*** *aiśvaryam*), 4.45d (*bhūtastanmātrasambhavaḥ*), 1.139a (*tān puṣpān*), 2.90a (***anyāmṛtaphalā ye*** *ca*), 1.140c (*saugandhikādyā jalajā*), 1.155a (*nīlaraktās tu ye puṣpāḥ*), and 2.120cd (*yasya dāne na duḥkhāni* ***narakapretasambhavāḥ***)[320]

Neuter for masculine

1.21c–22b (*devyāśaṅkara****saṃvādaṃ śrutaṃ*** *pūrvvan tvayānagha* || *saṃsārocchitti****karaṇaṃ*** *sarvajñānāmṛ****tottamam***) and 3.67c–68c: *vaiśvānaraṃ jātavedaṃ hutabhugghavyavāhanam* || *devavaktraṃ sarvabhakṣaṃ ghṛṇī ca jagadāhakam* | *vibhāvasuṃ saptajihvaṃ* (except *hutabhuk*, and *ghṛṇī*)[321]

The feminine stem *ap* 'water' irregularly treated as an *a*-stem masculine in accusative singular

---

316 Cf. GOODALL et al. 2015: 125.
317 Cf. GOODALL et al. 2015: 133.
318 Cf. GOODALL et al. 2015: 118.
319 Cf. GOODALL et al. 2015: 118.
320 Cf. GOODALL et al. 2015: 116.
321 Cf. GOODALL et al. 2015: 116.

3.100c (*āpam/apam* for *apaḥ*)[322]

Non-thematic ending

4.23b (*°homasu*)[323]

Compounds

Member(s) in inflected form

1.21c (***devyā****śaṅkarasaṃvādam*), 1.130d (***bṛhatyā****gastipuṣpakaiḥ*), 1.164b (***śaṣkulyā****modakāni*), 2.21d (***sphaṭir****mmarakatāni*), 3.33c (***devyāmātara****yakṣeṣu*), and 3.34b (*japahom****ādya****pūjanaiḥ*)[324]

Otiose letter in the middle of a compound

3.165b (*sauvarṇṇan nāma-****cā****ṅkitam*), 3.80d (*guḍakṣīra****sa****pāyasaiḥ*), and 3.82c (*gandhapuṣpa****sa****dhūpena*)

Shortening of a vowel

4.13c (*tryabdād* ***gāyatri****siddhis tu*) and 4.14a (*ṛgyajuḥ****sāma****tharvāṇām*)

Omission of a vowel

4.29d (***parāk****cāndrāyaṇais sadā*)

Lengthening of a vowel

1.178c (***anā****nurūpaṃ yasmād dhi*) and 3.11b (*kuryān* ***nadyā****vagāhanam*)

Reversal of the members in a compound

1.33b (*mūrtyākāśa* for *ākāśamūrte*) and 3.140d (*maṇiratnavicitrakaiḥ* for *vicitramaṇiratnakaiḥ*)

Dvandva followed by conjunction

2.11c (*arccayen naranārī* ***vā***) and 4.1 (*svargāpavargahetoś* ***ca***)[325]

---

[322] Cf. GOODALL et al. 2015: 115. Sasha LUBOTSKY opines that it is theoretically possible to take *āpam/apam* as a regular feminine accusative. For further discussion, see our translation and accompanying footnote.

[323] Cf. GOODALL et al. 2015: 116.

[324] Cf. GOODALL et al. 2015: 129.

[325] Cf. GOODALL et al. 2015: 129.

Elision of a word

1.67c (*dīpacchatraphalaṃ brūhi* for *dīpacchatra**dāna**phalaṃ brūhi*), 1.68b (*dāsīdāsasya yat phalaṃ* for *dāsīdāsa**pradāna/dāna**sya yat phalaṃ*)[326]

Morphology of the Verb

ktvā for *lyap*

2.62a (***alaṅkṛtvā** tu yo dadyāt*)[327]

ktvā for optative

3.168ab (*pañcamyāṃ hemajaṃ padmaṃ* ***dattvā*** *viprāya bhojite*)

Singular for dual

1.176ab (*punaś caiva samāgamya stotreṇa* ***tuṣṭuve*** *haram*)[328]

Plural for dual

2.46b (*tāmisramandhatāmisrau* ***narakā*** *na* ***bhavanti*** *hi*)

The root *vid* (VII) 'to find' in the sense of *vid* (II) 'to know'

3.14a *vindyāt* for *vidyāt* and 4.47d *vindati* for *vetti*

Omission of final *t*[329]

2.30a (***pūjaye*** *parayā bhaktyā*), 2.119a (*tasya dattaṃ* ***bhave*** *nantaṃ*), and 4.80b (*maṃṭe kuṇṭeti vā punaḥ*)[330]

Perfect for optative

3.95c (*aśvamedhaphalaṃ* ***lebhe***) and 3.11d (*dehatyāge divaṃ* ***yayau***)

---

326 Apart from these, there are other irregular compounds in the text, which do not fall into some specific category. These we list here: 1.54a (*bhakṣyābhakṣyaparīhāram*), 3.121a (*yāvajjīvārcanam*), 3.192d (*yāvajjīvakṛtenaiva*), 4.2c (*homajāpī*), 4.45a (*budhyahaṃkāras saṃbhūtaḥ*) and 4.122b (*harirudradaśeśakam*).

327 Cf. GOODALL et al. 2015: 122.

328 Cf. GOODALL et al. 2015: 134.

329 Cf. GOODALL et al. 2015: 132.

330 Here *kuṇṭeti* presumably stands for *kuṇṭet iti*. After omitting the final *t* in *kuṇṭet* it becomes *kuṇṭe iti*. Finally, *kuṇṭeti* is the result of *aiśa sandhi* performed thereon.

Optative for past tense

1.172b (*pūrvvavṛttaṃ hi yad* ***bhavet***) and 1.173d (*kim etac cādbhutaṃ* ***bhavet***)

Irregular optative singular

1.60b, 1.100d 2.42b, 2.52b, 2.98b and 2.104d (*dadet* for *dadyāt*), and 1.137b, 2.65b, 3.159d, 3.179d and 3.187b (*dāpayet* for *dadyāt*)

Causative for simplex

2.8b (*mṛdā liṅgan tu* ***kārayet***), 2.17b (*saccakena tu liṅgāni pārthivāni tu* ***kārayet***), and 2.107c (*jīvaṃ* ***rakṣayate*** *yo hi*)[331]

Simplex for causative

1.91c *snaped* for *snāpayed*

Gerund for infinitive

1.176d (*varan* ***dattvā*** *ubhāv api*)

Active for passive

3.76d (*yo* ***'rcayeta*** *gaṇādhipam*)[332]

Sandhi

Hiatus within a *pāda*

1.176d (*varan datt**vā** **u**bhāv api*), 1.188c (*sendrair ddevaiś **ca** **a**suraiḥ*), 1.185d (*ye martyā na naman**ti** **ī**dṛśam ajaṃ kṣemas tu teṣāṃ kutaḥ*), 2.8d (*labha**te** **ī**psitaṃ phalam*),[333] 2.20b (*krīḍan**te** **a**ṇimādibhiḥ*), 2.52b (*kṛṣṇāṃ **vā** **ā**vikān dadet*), 2.62b (*kanyāñ cai**va** **a**yācitām*), 2.63d (*ye cāny**e** **a**bhayapradāḥ*), 2.74d (*yo dadā**ti** **u**pānahau*), 2.87c (*nīlasyai**va** **a**lābhe tu*), 2.100b (*ātur**e** **o**ṣadhāni ca*), 3.123a (*ahiṃsā **ca** **a**dambhaś ca*), 3.127d 3.128d, 3.129d, 3.130d, 3.132d and 3.134d (***tu*** ***u**poṣitaḥ*), 4.2d (*bhaikṣāśī **ca** **a**maithunī*) and 4.38b (*anāraṃbh**ī** **a**hiṃsakaḥ*)[334]

so **for *sa* when followed by a voiced consonant**

2.31a and 2.33 (*so hi*), 3.195b (*so bhavet*) and 4.89 (*so bhramet*)[335]

331 Cf. GOODALL et al. 2015: 122.

332 Cf. GOODALL et al. 2015: 122.

333 The same irregularity occurs in 2.13b and 2.17d.

334 Cf. GOODALL et al. 2015: 134.

335 Cf. GOODALL et al. 2015: 132.

as-stem turned into a-stem

1.44d (*piśācāpsararākṣasāḥ*) and 1.183b (*apsaroragakinnaraiḥ*)

as-stem treated as an-stem

4.81c (*paribhūtaḥ kṛcchratapā*) and 4.82a (*mahātapā ca bhavate*)

No *vṛddhi* when *a* is followed by *e*

1.19d (*śṛṇuṣvekamanā dhunā*)

Double *sandhi*

1.87b (*yoddharet kulasaptakam*), 2.90a (*anyāmṛtaphalā ye ca*), 3.58b (*kuruteti*), 4.80b (*kuṇṭeti*), 4.115c (*svarlokan tu tatordhvan tu*), 4.116a (*satyaṃ caiva tatordhvaṃ tu*), 4.118c (*tattvasargaṃ atordhvan tu*), 4.121c (*gahanañ ca tatordhvan tu*) and 4.121d (*vigraheśaṃ tatordhvataḥ*)[336]

Hiatus-breakers

***m*:** 1.11a: (*te dṛṣṭvā tvayi-**m**-āyāntā*), 1.38b twice (*hy aja-**m**-* and *akṣara-**m**-avyayaḥ*), 2.46a (*tāmisra-**m**-andhatāmisrau*), 2.31cd (*nadīṃ vaitaraṇīṃ caiva-**m**-uṣṇatoyāṃ mahāravām*) and 4.89d (*sa jaṭī muṇḍa-**m**-eva vā*)[337]

***r*:** 1.185c (*varārthino -**r**-ahar*)

Syntax

Anacoluthon

1.72–76 (starts with an optative and ends with a conditional; it is also an incomplete sentence); 1.77, 1.78–79, 2.38c–39b, 2.43c–44b, 2.56, 2.65 (start with a singular structure and end with a plural); and 3.178c–180b (starts with a singular structure and ends with a plural and also constitutes an incomplete sentence)[338]

---

336 Cf. GOODALL et al. 2015: 131.
337 Cf. GOODALL et al. 2015: 133.
338 Cf. GOODALL et al. 2015: 136.

Cumbersome syntax

1.87, 1.95, 1.135, 1.148–149, 1.152c–154b, 1.172–173, 1.178, 2.1, and 2.3ab, 2.33c–34b, 2.37d, 2.45c–46b, 2.56–57, 2.66, 2.65, 2.69, 2.85a–86b, 3.1, 3.69ab, 3.101c, 3.145cd, 3.148ab, 164, and 4.123ab[339]

Two correlative pronouns for a single relative

2.32c–33b: *setubandhan tu* ***yaḥ*** *kuryāt karddame pathi dāruṇe* | *dharmmarājapure* ***so*** *hi durggame sukhayāyy* ***asau*** ||

Omission of relative and correlative pronouns

1.88 (*kṣīreṇa snāpayel liṅgaṃ kṛṣṇāṣṭamicaturdaśī* | *yāvajjīvakṛtāt pāpān mucyate nātra saṃśayaḥ* ||)

Omission of a relative pronoun

2.52, 2.65, 2.68, 3.100, and 3.197

Absence of case-ending for days of the fortnight

1.69d, 1.80b, 1.88b, 1.93b (*kṛṣṇ**āṣṭamicaturddaśī***), and 3.114 (*labhate sarvakāmāṃs tu* ***navamī****navamoṣitaḥ* | *maricaprāśanaṃ kṛtvā* ***navamīnava*** *yo 'rccayet* ||)

Otiose repetition

1.110c–1011 (*śvetaṃ raktaṃ tathā pītaṅ kṛṣṇaṃ vā* ***cāmaran dadet*** || *hemadaṇḍan tu raupyaṃ vā raityan trāpuṣam eva vā* | ***īdṛśañ cāmaraṃ datvā*** *rudraloke mahīyate* |), 1.130c–131 (*mantrasiddhim avāpnoti bṛhatyāgastipuṣpakaiḥ* || ***yo rccayet*** *parameśānaṃ siddhakena samāhitaḥ* | *sarvakāmān avāpnoti* ***yo rcayed*** *gandhapuṣpakaiḥ* ||), 1.142c–143b (*jayārthe damanakaṃ syād* ***yo rccayet parameśvaram*** || *nirjitāḥ śatravas tena* ***yo rccayeta vṛṣadhvajam*** |), 2.90 (*anyāmṛtaphalā ye ca dattvā tu* ***subhago*** *bhavet* | *bahuputraś ca rūpāḍhyas* ***subhagaś*** *caiva jāyate* ||), 3.73c–74 (*lokapāleśvaraś caiva* ***yakṣendraḥ*** *parikīrtitaḥ* | *abdaṃ pūjayate yas tu yakṣaṃ bhaktisamanvitaḥ* || *dhanadhānyasamṛddhaś ca yāvajjīvena* ***yakṣarāṭ*** |), and 4.36c–36b (*tridaṇḍakuṇḍī cakrī ca naikānnādas sa* ***bhaikṣabhuk*** || *na tv asvam upabhuñjīta* ***bhaikṣavṛttisamāśritaḥ*** |)

---

339 For particular awkwardness in the syntax in these cases, see the translation and footnotes accompanying these verses.

Ordinal instead of Cardinal Numbers

3.114b (*navamī**navamo**ṣitaḥ*)

Other Irregular Numbers

There are some cases of irregular formations with regards to numbers as well: 1.86c: *dvirabdena* for *dvyabdena*, 1.167a and 1.167d *triṣkāla* for *trikāla*, 2.7b *viṃśabhiḥ* for *viṃśatibhiḥ*, and 2.7c *triṃśabhiḥ* for *triṃśatibhiḥ*

Unfamiliar Words

There are also some lexical items the meaning of which we are not able to define:

- NM 1.51b *apsara* (denoting a flower)
- NM 1.151c *ḍitvākṣī* (denoting a flower)
- NM 2.102c *marjjitā* (denoting a flower)

Aiśa Forms Unattested Elsewhere

Note that there are four types of irregularities in the above list of *aiśa* forms that had not been included in the overview of *aiśa* forms and usages published by GOODALL et al. (2015):

- **Gerund (*dattvā*) for infinitive *dātuṃ***: the occurrence is at 1.176d (*varan* ***dattvā*** *ubhāv api*). The context tells us that the gerund *dattvā* here fulfils the function of the infinitive *dātum*.
- **Optative for past tense**: In verse 1.172b (*pūrvvavṛttaṃ hi yad* ***bhavet***) and 1.173d (*pūrvvavṛttaṃ hi yad* ***bhavet***) the optative is used, although the contextual requires past sense.
- **Perfect for optative**: In 3.11d (*dehatyāge divaṃ* ***yayau***) and 3.95c (*aśvamedhaphalaṃ* ***lebhe***), where one would expect an optative instead of the past perfect form attested to in this section.[340]
- **Absence of case-endings for days of the fortnight**: 1.69d, 1.80b, 1.88b, 1.93b (*kṛṣṇāṣṭamicaturddaśī*), and 3.114 (*labhate sarvakāmāṃs tu* ***navamī****navamoṣitaḥ* | *maricaprāśanaṃ kṛtvā* ***navamīnava*** *yo rc-cayet* ||)

[340] It is to be noted that our text uses simple present and optative interchangeably.

Metre

The text is written in *ślokas* (*anuṣṭubh* metre) with the exception of the concluding verse of the first chapter, which is written in the *śārdūlavikrīḍita* metre. The style of the *ślokas* is defined by an abundant use of *vipulās*. GOODALL (1998: lxxi) observes in his discussion of metrical features of certain early Śaiva tantras, such as the *Kiraṇa* and the *Svāyaṃbhuvasūtrasaṅgraha*, that they are metrically plain and scarcely make use of *vipulās*. The *Pārameśvara*, *Mataṅga* and *Parākhya*, however, show more variation and make use of *vipulās* on occasion. Metrically, the versification of the *Niśvāsamukha* stands out, just like the other books of the *Niśvāsa*, when we compare it with other tantras. We even observe some use of *sa-vipulās* in the *Niśvāsamukha*. Instances of the *sa-vipulā* are expected to be rare, and their inclusion (instead of seeking to emend them away) may be questioned. Still, this form of metrical variation is also shared by the other books of the *Niśvāsa* and by the *Mahābhārata*.[341] Moreover, we noticed a few instances of hypermetry, hypometry and of lines that are in other ways unmetrical, which we have listed below. All of these instances deviate from the standard *pathyā* pattern:

- **na-vipulā**: 1.4c, 1.22a, 1.85a, 1.120c; 1.144c, 1.158c, 2.18a, 2.33c, 2.39a, 2.44a, 2.44c, 2.50a, 2.65a, 2.91a, 2.92c, 2.95c, 2.114a, 3.10a, 3.77a, 3.88a, 3.105c, 3.159a, 3.171a, 3.177a, 3.194c, 4.32c, 4.36c, 4.37a, 4.82a, 4.86c, 4.100a (with irregular preamble),[342] 4.102c, 4.105c, 4.109a, 4.109c, 4.112a, 4.118a, and 4.132c
- **ma-vipulā**: 2.49a, 3.17a, 3.26a, 3.43c (with irregular preamble), 3.89c, 3.116c, 3.128a (with irregular preamble), 3.132a (with irregular preamble), 3.138a, 3.147c (with irregular preamble), 3.161c, 3.177c (with irregular preamble), 4.32a, 4.35c, 4.40c, 4.45a (with irregular preamble), 4.71a, 4.90c, 4.94c, and 4.99a
- **bha-vipulā**: 1.140c, 1.153c (with irregular preamble), 3.5c (with irregular preamble), 3.34c, 3.72a (with irregular preamble), 3.90c 3.143c, 3.151a, 4.17a, 4.27a, 4.46c, 4.69a, 4.78a (with irregular preamble), 4.81c (with irregular preamble), and 4.105c
- **ra-vipulā**: 3.23a, 3.31a, 3.63a, 3.64c, 3.67c, 3.68a, 3.102c, 3.103c, 3.133a, 4.6a, 4.67a, 4.75c, 4.82c, 4.85a, and 4.102a

341 See GOODALL et al. 2015: 238–239.

342 We have not considered verse-quarters to have an 'irregular preamble' when all that is irregular is that the caesura (*yati*) is not in its expected place.

- **sa-vipulā**: 1.142c, 3.31c, 3.115c, 4.103c, and 4.122a
- **hypermetry**: 1.37a, 2.101a, 3.6a, and 3.67a
- **hypometry**: 1.84c and 3.64a
- **otherwise unmetrical**: 1.3d, 2.49a, 2.98c, 4.100b, 4.126a (the second and the third syllables are short), 3.93a, and 3.94c (the seventh syllable is short)

Manuscripts

Sources for the *Niśvāsamukha*

The Manuscript N

The principal source for the present edition is a palm-leaf manuscript transmitting the *Niśvāsatattvasaṃhitā*, preserved in the National Archives, Kathmandu (NAK). The NAK accession number is 1-277. The Nepal-German Manuscript Preservation Project (NGMPP) have microfilmed it and the microfilm reel number is A 41/14. The size of the leaves of the manuscript is 50 cm x 4 cm. The manuscript consists of 114 folios written in the Nepalese 'Licchavi' script. Both the recto and verso sides contain six (occasionally five[343]) lines. The manuscript contains two binding holes, one to the left and one to the right of the centre. The manuscript is considerably damaged in the margins. The leaves were originally numbered in letter-symbols in the right-hand margin of the versos. These leaves have been paginated again at a later stage above the first binding hole in a different hand. There is a third hand that inserted correction marks to the second run of foliation below the same binding hole.

Although the manuscript is not dated, on the basis of palæographic evidence we can assign it, with reasonable confidence, to the 9th century. Various scholars have taken note of the manuscript, on account of its antiquity, and put forward tentative dates.[344] It has been variously dated from the middle of the 8th to the very beginning of the 10th century. GOODALL et al. (2015: 103–108) have a lengthy discussion that is based on comparisons with other early Nepalese manuscripts, and in conclusion they propose the date of the manuscript to be situated somewhere between 850–900 CE, which is also the date earlier proposed by SANDERSON (2006: 152). We, for our part, suspect that this is a little too early, for we think that the date of the *Niśvāsa* manuscript is probably to be placed after the date of an old Nepalese manuscript of the *Suśrutasaṃhitā* that is dated to 878 CE.[345]

The only independent witness is the old manuscript N, but there are three twentieth-century apograph copies:

Apograph W

At the time of writing of this study, W is housed in the Wellcome Insti-

343 F.4r,v ,100r,v and 114v.

344 ŚĀSTRĪ (1905), BAGCHI (1929), GOUDRIAAN & GUPTA (1981), SANDERSON (2006), GOODALL & ISAACSON (2007), and most recently GOODALL et al. (2015).

345 See HARIMOTO 2014.

tute, London, bearing the Wellcome Institute Sanskrit MS number I.33. It is written in Devanāgarī script and also covers 114 folios. Both the recto and verso sides contain five to six lines. The foliation is located in the right-hand margin of the verso, and is erroneous in a few cases. The scribe supplies raised dashes in substitution for damaged or illegible letters. This apograph is dated *vikramasamvat* 1969 (=1912 CE). The colophon states that the manuscript was copied in Nepal by a certain Bauddhasevita Vajrācārya. The post-colophon runs as follows:

> *ida[sic] pustaka[sic] tāra[sic]patraguptākṣarapustake dṛṣṭvā nepālavāsibauddhasevitavajrācāryyena[sic] likhitam* || *śubham* || | *śrīsamvat* 1969 *sālam iti āṣāḍhaśukla-aṣṭamyām.*

This manuscript retains more letters than apograph K succeeded in gleaning from the damaged portions of the original manuscript. This is most likely due to the fact that it was prepared at a time when the original manuscript was less damaged. The copyist appears to have remained as faithful to the original as possible, and unlike the scribe of K, avoided conjectures.

Apograph K

This apograph is preserved in the NAK and is dated Vikrama *samvat* 1982 (=1925 CE). The colophon states that it was prepared at the request of Rājaguru Hemarāja Śarma during the reign of King Tribhuvana, when Candra Śamśera served as prime minister.[346]

The NGMPP reel number ascribed to the apograph is A 159/18, whereas the NAK accession number has been recorded as 5-2406. The text is written in Devanāgarī script on 114 folios and is of the following dimensions: 49 cm x 13 cm. Both the recto and verso sides contain between six to ten lines. The recto side of folio 104 is blank. The regular foliation is placed in the middle of the right-hand margin of each verso, with instances of erroneous numbering occasionally crossed out and corrected. There are three deviating foliations: in the extreme lower right-hand margin, in

346 The post-colophon reads as follows: *likhitam idaṃ purātanajarattāḍapatralivitaḥ samuddhṛtya vikramābde* 1982 *pramite śrāvaṇaśuklaikādaśyāṃ samāpya sāmbaśivāya samarpitaṃ* [[*ka*]]*virājani nepālabhūmaṇḍalādhīśvare śrīpaṃcakasaṃpanne tribhuvanavīravikramavarmaṇi samabhiśāsati* [[*ca*]] *taddhīsacive śrītritayasampanne mahārājacandrasaṃśerajaṅgavahādūrarāṇāvarmaṇi mahāmahodaye tadīyaguruvaragururājaśrīmaddhemarājapaṇḍitamahodayānujñayā tadīyasarasvatīsadane niveśitaṃ ca bhūyāl lekhakapāṭhakayor mude* | *śubham* | *maṃgalam* | *hariharau śaraṇīkaravāmi* | *iti śubham* | .

the extreme upper right-hand margin and in the extreme upper left-hand margin of the verso. The scribe leaves gaps for unrecovered letters, and provides dots when only a small portion of letters is visible. In damaged places, the scribe attempts to restore letters. Frequently he also provides conjectures, replacing irregular or non-Pāṇinian Sanskrit forms with their standardized counterparts, enveloping uncertain readings in parentheses. In a few cases, parenthesis-markers ( ) enclose empty space, sometimes in conjunction with dots (· · ·).

Apograph T

This apograph is preserved in the Tucci collection in Italy. It is written in Devanāgarī script. The manuscript number is 3.7:1 and the folio size is 48.5 cm x 9.5 cm. There are 94 folios, fols. 1, 4, 5 and 98–104 of which are missing. Both the recto and verso sides generally contain five to six lines. The foliation is located in the lower right-hand margin of the verso (see SFERRA 2008: 60, fn. 132). The scribe provides dots · · · to indicate either damaged portions or unreadable letters. In contradistinction to K, these are not enclosed by brackets. Since the manuscript does not have a final colophon, its date cannot be determined from a textual declaration. Nonetheless, since the scribe has recorded fewer letters in the margins, one can surmise that N had deteriorated further by the time the scribe of this apograph began the process of copying it. It is therefore likely to be slightly younger than K and W. The scribe obviously had difficulty reading N, and given the large number of scribal errors, we have not drawn upon this manuscript, instead opting to discard its testimony.

Sources for the *Śivadharmasaṅgraha*

Since chapters 5–9 of the *Śivadharmasaṅgraha* closely mirror the *Niśvāsamukha*, we have included an edition of these chapters in an Appendix to this study. For this preliminary edition,[347] we have collated two Nepalese manuscripts and one printed edition. To provide a more detailed description of the sources, let us briefly introduce them at this point:

[347] We refer to our edition as 'preliminary' since there are many more sources that deserve consultation and collation. The three sources used for this preliminary draft do not suffice for a fully 'critical' edition.

Manuscript A

This manuscript, dated to [Nepāla] Saṃvat 156 (=1035/36 CE),[348] is stored in the premises of the Asiatic Society of Bengal, Kolkata. It is a palm-leaf manuscript written in Newari script and is damaged in the margins. The manuscript number is G 4077/3. There are 324 folios, and both the recto and verso sides contain five lines. The folios measure 53 cm x 4.5 cm in size and have two binding holes. The original foliation is placed in the left-hand margin of each verso, marked in letter-symbols. A later foliation, apparently in pencil, has been added in arabic numerals both on the obverse and reverse (distinguished as 'a' and 'b') below the left-hand string-hole. The manuscript contains nine separate texts: the *Śivadharmaśāstra*, *Śivadharmottara*, *Śivadharmasaṅgraha*, *Umāmaheśvarasaṃvāda*, *Śivopaniṣad*, *Uttarottaramahāsaṃvāda*, *Vṛṣasārasaṅgraha*, *Dharmaputrikā*, and an otherwise unknown *Lalitavistara*.[349] Some archaic Prākṛtic forms, such as *sāyojya* for *sāyujya* are also preserved. Since this manuscript is ancient—just short of a thousand years old—it might have been expected to be more accurate than its apographs (or than younger witnesses of other transmission lines). Nevertheless, it contains numerous slips of the pen.

Manuscript C

This is another multi-text manuscript, currently housed in the University Library, Cambridge, England. It is dated to Nepal *saṃvat* 256 (=1136 AD). The manuscript shelf number is MS Add. 1645, and the script is Newari.[350] There are 247 folios, and both the recto and verso sides of it usually contain six lines. Fols. 87-131 cover the *Śivadharmasaṅgraha*. The foliation is given on the verso, in letter-numerals in the left-hand margin and in Newari numerals on the right-hand margin. It contains all the texts found transmitted in Manuscript A, with the exception the *Lalitavistara*. This is the more reliable source of the two manuscripts collated for the present edition of the *Śivadharmasaṅgraha*, as it contains markedly less scribal errors.

Printed edition

The printed edition, E_N, is in some sections accompanied by a

---

[348] For the details of the stated date, see Bisschop (2018: 29, 56), De Simini (2017: 1–2) & Mirnig (2016a: 63).

[349] A. K. Acharya first identified the latter text (which, as we have mentioned before, is not to be confused with the Buddhist text of the same name).

[350] The complete manuscript is accessible online at: `https://cudl.lib.cam.ac.uk/view/MS-ADD-01645/1`.

translation into Nepali, and also infrequently furnished by the editor's commentary. It was produced by Narahari NĀTHA in the year 2055 VS (=1998 CE) under the editorial leadership of Viṣṇu Prasād Aryāl ĀTREYA and Śrīśa THĀPĀ. The title of the book, *Paśupatimatam śivadharmaśāstram paśupatināthadarśanam*, is a fancy of the editors. The tome contains the same eight texts as are included in the Cambridge manuscript C. It is poorly edited, and its text is construed on the basis of a single manuscript. The *Śivadharmasaṅgraha* is to be found here on pages 323–433. See A. K. ACHARYA 2009: 114–115 for more details.

Editorial Policies

Since a body of conventions for producing critical editions of the *Niśvāsa* corpus has already been established in the companion volume to this publication,[351] we intend to apply the same conventions in the present edition, both for the sake of consistency and because we hold those editorial conventions in high regard. There is, however, one major difference that needs to be noted: as mentioned above, the *Niśvāsamukha* has been copied by the author(s) of the *Śivadharmasaṅgraha*—and we have decided to include its readings into our edition of the *Niśvāsamukha*. This adds an element of complexity to the constitution of the edited text of the critical edition.

We have resorted to four sources in our production of a critical edition of the *Niśvāsamukha*: N, K, W and those chapters of the *Śivadharmasaṅgraha* which we have provisionally edited (chapters 5–9). It is the readings of the text of the *Śivadharmasaṅgraha* as constituted in that provisional edition that are marked in our apparatus with the siglum '*ŚiDhaSaṅ*'.

The critically edited text appears as the main text, i.e. the running text. The apparatus is fully positive and is divided into two registers. On pages that display both registers, the upper register records testimonia and parallels and the bottom register records the variants found in the manuscripts. Each entry begins with a chapter-and-verse number in boldface (e.g. **1.97**). Then follows the adopted textual segment as displayed in the main text, capped by a lemma sign]. Immediately thereafter, the siglum (or sigla) referencing the source (or sources) of this reading is (or are) displayed. At this point, a semicolon separates the preferred (and adopted) reading (to its left) from the variants (to its right). The variants to its right are again separated from each other by semicolons.

Any siglum that is followed by superscript *ac* indicates the reading of a source before correction (=*ante correctionem*) and a siglum followed by superscript *pc* indicates the reading of a source after correction (=*post correctionem*).

When a reading is unmetrical, that is recorded after the sigla denoting the source.

351 GOODALL et al. 2015.

When a portion of text is lacunose in manuscript N, we have marked it thus: ---.

If a portion of the text is missing in all sources except manuscript K, the segment in question is enclosed in two double square brackets [[...]].

When the scribe of manuscript K has expressed his own doubt concerning a specific reading as he had found it in the exemplar from which he copied, he marked these by use of single, round brackets. We have preserved this convention only in relation to this manuscript (=K).

If a textual portion is lost in all sources except manuscript W, that segment is rendered in between two double round brackets ((...)). If the reading is lost in manuscript N but preserved in both K and W, then its rendition is enveloped between two double square and round brackets: [[((...))]]. If a section of the text has perished in all manuscripts consulted, yet is retrievable from the *Śivadharmasaṅgraha*, the relevant passage has been adopted from the edited text of the *Śivadharmasaṅgraha* and marked as such in the apparatus.

The readings adopted from the *Śivadharmasaṅgraha* are by definition insecure, since we have established that the *Śivadharmasaṅgraha* modifies the text considerably when borrowing passages from the *Niśvāsamukha*.[352] Nevertheless, we have preferred to insert the readings of the *Śivadharmasaṅgraha* into the missing sections of the *Niśvāsamukha* in order to allow for continuity in the unfolding of the text in a way that probably retains its basic meaning. We have, however, enclosed the reading of the *Śivadharmasaṅgraha* between double angled brackets (≪...≫) to alert the reader concerning those portions of the texts that have been supplied from the *Śivadharmasaṅgraha*.

When the text is omitted in one particular source we have placed *om.* just before the siglum of that source; for example: *om.* N. Textual segments enclosed within single square brackets '[ ]' are supplied by us; each folio-change and line-change in the manuscript is marked and placed within the same bracket; for example [3] stands for third line in the manuscript and [3^v] indicates that this is the beginning of the third folio.

352 See p. 113 above.

When we are not certain as to whether a reading that we record has been correctly deciphered, we have indicated this by putting a question mark (?) after the reading.

When the text is judged by us to be corrupt (which often means that it seems uninterpretable to us), we have put it between crux marks: †...†.

When apographs leave long dashes, we have marked them: ¯. If there appear two long dashes in one of the apographs it is marked thus: ¯ ¯.

Portions of text lost to damage from the original manuscript have been marked with ---, whereas gaps deliberately left by the scribes of the apographs to indicate that the text was lost or illegible to them have been marked with ⊔.

Where the gap is large and there is a possibility of counting the number of letters lost, we have printed an underscore-mark to indicate a hypothetical letter slot. For example, if five letters are lost, this is presented in this way: _ _ _ _ _.

Any *akṣara*(s) that are enclosed between plus-signs (+ ... +) were added later—either by the same or by a different hand.

Any *akṣara*(s) displayed between two 'x ... x' signs in the critical edition had been written in the respective manuscript and cancelled later.

The sign ⊗ (*puṣpika*) stands for ornamental signs in manuscripts written before or after colophons. A list of all these symbols is provided at the start of the edition, on p. 151.

When there are scribal errors and other conspicuous mistakes, we have introduced emendations, marked with *em.*; 'bolder' corrections are marked *conj.* (conjecture). Of course, the difference is somewhat subjective. Conjectures occur when there is a complete lacuna in the text or when litte is legible. When these conjectures have been proposed by other scholars, this is mentioned in the apparatus. When an *avagraha* is missing in our sources, we have silently supplied it.

The verse-numeration is more or less arbitrary. In most of the text, verses are divided up into four *pādas*. Occasionally, a verse is divided into six, either because there is a lacuna in the text (e.g. 1.17), or the context demands it (for instance because of a change of speaker).[353] At times, we have felt compelled to arrange the verses differently to the four-*pāda* system: since the semantics of verse 1.169, for example, spread over six *pādas*, we have chosen to format that unit accordingly, in order better to reflect the intended meaning.

The middle register contains testimonia, i.e. passages from other sources, older or younger, that display textual parallels and are sufficiently close to our text to merit our attention. The entry first lists the verse number. Testimonia are preceded by 'cf.' if the passage is sufficiently similar to the *textus criticus* of the *Niśvāsamukha*, or can contribute to its elucidation.

In our preliminary edition of the relevant chapters of the *Śivadharmasaṅgraha* in Appendix I, we have followed the same editorial conventions extrapolated above. Since what is signified by the use of square and round brackets does not feature in the MSS of the *Śivadharmasaṅgraha*, square and round brackets are not employed in the appended edition of the latter work.

[353] For example, at 1.56.

Symbols and Abbreviations in the Apparatus

≪ ... ≫	Enclosed text is drawn from the *Śivadharmasaṅgraha*.
+ ... +	Enclosed text was added later by the same or by a different hand.
x ... x	Enclosed text was first written and then cancelled later.
–	A number of letters lost in the manuscript.
⊔	Gap left by the scribes of the apographs.
---	Text lost due to damage in the original manuscript.
—	Long dashes in the apographs.
† ... †	The text between these signs is corrupt (and typically uninterpretable to us).
?	Used when we are not certain about the reading.
[...]	Enclosed text supplied by us.
[[...]]	Enclosed text survives only in K.
((...))	Enclosed text survives only in W.
[[((...))]]	Enclosed text survives in both K and W but is lost in N.
(...)	Enclosed text is the reading of K where the scribe is not certain about the reading. The round brackets are used in the manuscript itself.
⊗	Ornamental signs in manuscripts written before or after colophons.

conj.	conjecture
em.	emendation
ac	before correction
pc	after correction
f.	folio
cf.	conferatur
r	recto
v	verso
om.	omit(s)
Ex conj.	based on conjecture
m.c.	*metri causa* (=as dictated by metre)

Sigla of the Manuscripts Used

N National Archives, Kathmandu, NGMPP reel number is A 41/14, the NAK accession number is 1-277 and the size of the manuscript is 50 cm x 4 cm. The manuscript consists of 114 folios written in the Nepalese "Licchavi" script. Although the manuscript is not dated, on the basis of paleographic evidence we can assign it, with a reasonable margin of error, to 850–900 CE. Both the recto and verso sides contain six (occasionally five) lines.

W Wellcome Institute, London: Wellcome Institute Sanskrit MS number I. 33, Devanagari script, 114 folios. This apograph is dated *vikramasamvat* 1969, which corresponds to 1912 CE. Both the recto and verso sides contain five to six lines.

K National Archives, Kathmandu, NGMPP reel number A 159/18, NAK accession number 5-2406. The text is written in Devanagari script on 114 folios of 49 cm x 13 cm in size. Both the recto and verso sides contain six to ten lines. The recto side of folio 104 is blank. This apograph is dated to Vikrama *samvat* 1982 (1925 CE).

T Apograph from the Tucci collection in Italy. It is written in Devanāgarī script. The MS number is 3:7:1 and the folio size is 48.5 cm x 9.5 cm. There are 94 folios, of which 1, 4, 5 and 98–104 are missing. Both the recto and verso sides usually contain five to six lines. We have not used this apograph as it contains many scribal errors.

निश्वासमुखतत्त्वसंहितायां प्रथमः पटलः॥

रिचीक उवाच।
गतो ऽहं पूर्व्वमाशायां पुष्पाणां समिधैस्तथा।
अपूर्व्वन्दृष्टमाश्चर्यन्तन्दृष्ट्वा कौतुकान्वितः॥ 1:1॥

अष्टाशीतिसहस्राणि ऋषीणामूर्ध्वरेतसाम्।
नैमिषारण्य ⏑̱ ⏑̱ ⏑̱ ⏑̱ ⏑̱ ⏑̱ ⏑̱ ⏑̱ ⏑̱ ⏑̱ ⏑̱॥ 1:2॥

--- [-16-] ---।
भ[2]गवन्सर्व्वमेतत्तु कथय मम पृच्छतः॥ 1:3॥

त्वं वेत्ता सर्व्वशास्त्राणां वेदानाञ्च विशेषतः।
तेन पृच्छामि भगवन्येन वेत्सि मतङ्ग त्वम्॥ 1:4॥

मतङ्ग उवाच।
शृणु वत्स समासेन प्रवक्ष्यामि तवाखिलम्।
नैमिषे वसमानैस्तु श्रुतं ((स)) --- [-5-] ---॥ 1:5॥

---

1 The palm-leaf manuscript and apographs K and W begin with ॐ नमः शिवाय। Apograph T is available only from folio 2^r.

2 Cf. *Brahmāṇḍapurāṇa* 1.7:180ab, 1.21:170cd and *Viṣṇupurāṇa* 1.6:36ab: अष्टाशीतिसहस्राणि ऋषीणामूर्ध्वरेतसाम्।

1:1 पुष्पाणां समिधैस्तथा] *conj.*; पुष्पा णा समिधेस्तथा N; पुष्पाणि समिधेस्तथा K; पुष्पाणा समि ⁻ स्तथा W **1:1** तन्दृष्ट्वा] N; तद्दृष्ट्वा KW **1:2** °सहस्राणि ऋषी°] K; सहस्राणामृषी° NW **1:2** मूर्ध्वरेतसाम्] KW; मू ⏑̱ रेत ⏑̱ म् N **1:3** भगवन्सर्व्वमेतत्तु] *em.*; ---वन्सर्वमेतत्तु] N; ⊔ व सर्वमेतत्तु K; ⊔ ण्वत्सर्वमेतत्तु W **1:4** वेदानाञ्च] *conj.*; देवानाञ्च NKW

--- [-16-] --- ।
--- [-8-] नैमि[3]षारण्यवासिभिः ॥ 1:6॥

तत्रैव दीक्षितो ब्रह्मा केशवश्च रिचीकक।
कौतूहलान्वितास्सर्व्वे विस्मयं परमङ्गताः॥ 1:7॥

परस्परं वदन्त्येवं सर्व्वशास्त्रविशारदाः।
कथम्दीक्षां प्रपद्येत मुक्त्वा वेदोक्तमागमम्॥ 1:8॥

न हि वेदात्परञ्ज्ञान्यद्योग --- [-6-] --- ।
--- [-13-] --- [4] [[प]]द्यते॥ 1:9॥

साङ्ख्ययोगस्य वेत्तासौ कथं विष्णुश्च दीक्षितः।
तं श्रुत्वा आगताः सर्वे ऋषयः संशितव्रताः॥ 1:10॥

ते दृष्ट्वा †त्वयि मायान्ता†देवदारुवनं वनम्।
प्रविष्टास्तत्र ते सर्व्वे ब्रह्माविष्णुमहेश्वराः॥ 1:11॥

समुदायेन पश्यामो दीक्षा --- [-6-] --- ।
--- [-16-] ---॥ 1:12॥

--- [-4-] --- [5] ततस्ते तु ब्रह्माविष्णुमहेश्वराः।
स्वस्थानन्तु गताः सर्व्वे आज्ञान्दत्त्वा तु नन्दिने॥ 1:13॥

त्वमनुग्रहकर्ता तु ऋषीणां सर्व्वप्राणिनाम्।
देव्यायास्तु तथा पूर्वमधिकारस्समर्पितः॥ 1:14॥

दी --- [-15-] --- ।
--- [-16-] ---॥ 1:15॥

--- [-16-] --- ।

16 This long gap is due to considerable damage to the end of the fifth as well as the beginning of the sixth line.

1:6 नैमिषारण्य°] *em.*; --- रण्य° NW; ⊔ षा रण्य° K **1:7** रिचीकक] *em.*; रिचीककः NKW **1:8** दीक्षां] *conj.*; दीक्षा NKW **1:9** °द्योग] NK; °द्योगी न W **1:9** पद्यते] N(?); पमते K; ⊔ते W **1:10** संशित] *em.*; सम्सित NKW **1:11** ब्रह्माविष्णुमहेश्वराः] *conj.*; ब्रह्माविष्णुर्म्महेश्वराः NW; ब्रह्मविष्णुमहेश्वराः K **1:12** समुदायेन पश्यामो] N; सम्प्रदायेन पश्यामो K; समुदायेन यस्यायो W **1:13** ब्रह्मा°] NW; ब्रह्म° K **1:15** दी] NW; ⊔ K

[6]अस्माकं कथय सर्वं ब्रह्माविष्णू तु दीक्षितौ॥ 1:16॥

यथा ते सर्वशास्त्राणां दीक्षाज्ञानस्य वेदकौ।
तथा कथय सर्वन्तु सर्वज्ञ नन्दिकेश्वर।
((एवं ते)) --- [-13-] ---॥ 1:17॥

रिचीक उवाच।
[2ʳ] ((कथं व))क्ता भवेत्तेषाम्भगवान्नन्दिकेश्वरः।
दीक्षितास्तु कथन्ते तु शास्त्रे ऽस्मिञ्छिवसन्मते॥ 1:18॥

मतङ्ग उ।
ते स्तुन्वन्ति यथा नन्दिं दीक्षाज्ञानस्य चार्त्थिनः।
तथा वक्ष्यामि विप्रेन्द्र शृणुष्वेकमनाधुना॥ 1:19॥

देवदारुवने रम्ये --- [-8-] ---।
--- [-16-] ---॥ 1:20॥

[2] [[सु]]((महा))तप रुद्रांश सर्वज्ञ शिवतेजसा।
देव्याशङ्करसंवादं श्रुतम्पूर्व्वन्त्वयानघ॥ 1:21॥

संसारोच्छित्तिकरणं सर्वज्ञानामृतोत्तमम्।
दीक्षामात्रेण कथितं शिवेनाशिवहारिणा॥ 1:22॥

त्वत्प्रसादाद्यथा सर्व्वे मुच्यन्ते ऋषिसत्तमाः।
तथा कुरु [[प्रसा]]दा वा कु? --- [-7-] ---॥ 1:23॥

---

17 W, which always faithfully copies the manuscript, hints only at the loss of two *pādas* of a verse. We have accepted this since in other cases too, the last line does not run right up to the end of the leaf of the mansuscript.

20 Cf. *Guhyasūtra* 16.1–2b: देवदारुवने रम्ये ऋषयः संशितव्रताः। नन्दीशमुपसंगम्य प्रणिपत्य मुहुर्मुहुः॥ ऊचुस्ते ऋषयः सर्वे स्तुत्वा नन्दिं शिवात्मजम्।

1:16 कथय सर्वं] K; कथय सर्व्वं N; कथयः सर्व W **1:17** सर्वज्ञ नन्दिकेश्वर] N; सर्वज्ञ नन्दिकेश्वरः K; सर्वज्ञो नन्दिकेश्वरः W **1:18** रिचीक उवाच] *conj.*; *om.* NKW **1:18** कथं वक्ता भवेत्तेषाम्] *em.*; --- क्त भवेत्तेषाम् N; स भवेत्तेषां K; कथं वक्ता सवेत्तेषान् W **1:18** °सन्मते] *conj.*; °सम्मते NKW **1:19** तथा] NK; तेषां W **1:21** सुमहातप] *em.*; ---तप N; सुमहांतप K; ⊔महातप W **1:21** पूर्वन्त्वयानघ] NK; पूर्व्वं ˉयोनघ W **1:22** °ज्ञानामृतोत्तमम्] *em.*; °ज्ञानामृतोतमम् NW; °ज्ञानामृतोपमम् K **1:23** त्वत्प्रसादाद्] K; त्वत्प्रसादा NW **1:23** प्रसादा वा कु] *conj.*; --- दा वा कु? N; प्रसादा ⊔ K; ˉदा वा ⊔ W

--- [-13-] --- [3] रूपिणे।
नमस्ते शूलहस्ताय त्र्यक्षाय ऋषिसम्भवे॥ 1:24॥

तपःखेदितगात्राय उद्धरस्व प्रसादतः।
नान्यस्त्राता भवेद्देव त्वदृते नन्दिकेश्वर॥ 1:25॥

नन्दिकेश्वर उवाच।
शृण्वन्तु ऋषयस्सर्वे पञ्चधा यत्प्रकीर्तितम्।
लौकिकं वैदिकञ्चैव तथाध्यात्मिकमेव च॥ 1:26॥

अ[[तिमार्गं च मन्त्राख्यं]] --- [-8-] ---।
दीक्षिता न[4]न्दिना सर्वे निर्व्वाणे योजिताः परे॥ 1:27॥

विद्याभिकाङ्क्षिणश्चान्ये विद्यायां ते तु योजिताः।
दीक्षयित्वा यथान्यायम्प्रवक्तुमुपचक्रमे॥ 1:28॥

महादेव्या यथा पृष्टस्सर्व्वदुःखहरो हरः।
तथा वक्ष्यामि विप्रेन्द्राः प्रणिपत्य शिवं शुचिः॥ 1:29॥

प्रणम्य शिरसा देवञ्चन्द्रार्द्धकृतशेख[[((रम्))]]।
मूर्ध्नि कृत्वाञ्जलिं भक्त्या स्तोत्रमेवमु[5]दीरयेत्॥ 1:30॥

सगणाय नमस्तुभ्यं सपत्नीक नमो ऽस्तु ते।
सदाशिव नमस्ते ऽस्तु परमात्म शिवे नमः॥ 1:31॥

क्षितिर्द्धारयते लोकांल्लोकाः क्षितिमयाः स्मृताः।

---

27 Cf. *Pūrvakāmika* 1.17c–1.18b: लौकिकं वैदिकं चैव तथाध्यात्मिकमेव च। अतिमार्गं च मन्त्राख्यं तन्त्रमेतदनेकधा॥

32 Cf. *Prayogamañjarī* 1.18ff: तानष्टमूर्तीरथ मूर्तिपांश्च सङ्कल्प्य संपूज्य यथाक्रमेण। मन्त्रैरमीभिः प्रणिपत्य पूर्वं सन्तोषयेदंशुकभूषणाद्यैः॥ 18॥ क्षितिर्वै धार्यते लोकान् लोकाः क्षितिमयाः स्मृताः। सर्वगं क्षितिरूपं ते क्षितिमूर्ते नमोस्तु ते॥ 19॥ अग्निर्वै धार्यते लोकान् लोकाश्चाग्नि-

---

1:24 °रूपिणे] K; ---पिणे N; रूपिणां W **1:24** ऋषिसम्भवे] N; ऋषिसम्भुवे K; ऋषिसम्भव W **1:25** प्रसादतः] KW; प्रसादत N **1:27** अतिमार्गं च मन्त्राख्यं] *em.*; अ--- N; अतिमार्गश्च मन्त्राख्यं K; अतोमार्गश्च मन्त्राख्य W **1:27** दीक्षिता नन्दिना] *conj.*; --- न्दिना NKW **1:29** हरः] K; हः NW **1:30** °शेखरम्] K; °शेख--- N; °शेषरम् W **1:30** मूर्ध्नि कृत्वाञ्जलिं भक्त्या स्तोत्रमेवमुदीरयेत्] *conj.*; --- येत् N; मूर्ध्नि कृ ⊔ दीरयेत् KW **1:31** °स्तु] K; °तु NW **1:31** शिवे नमः] *em.*; शिवे नमः N; शिव नमः KW **1:32** लोकांल्लोकाः क्षितिमयाः] K; लोकाल्लोकाः क्षितिमयाः N[pc]W; लोकाल्लोकाः क्षितिमया N[ac]

सर्वगं क्षितिरूपन्तु क्षितिमूर्त्ति नमो ऽस्तु ते॥ 1:32॥

जलन्धारयते लोकांल्लोका जलमयाः स्मृ[[((ताः))]] ।
[[सर्वगं ज]]लरूपन्तु जलमूर्त्ति नमो ऽस्तु ते॥ 1:33॥

[[वायुर्धारयते लोकां[6]ल्लोका वायुमयाः स्मृ]]ताः।
सर्वगं वायुरूपन्तु वायुमूर्त्ति नमोऽस्तु ते॥ 1:34॥

अग्निर्द्धारयते लोकांल्लोका अग्निमयाः स्मृताः।
सर्वगमग्निरूपं तु अग्निमूर्त्ति नमो ऽस्तु ते॥ 1:35॥

आत्मा यजति यज्ञानि लोका यज्ञमयाः स्मृ[[((ताः))]] ।
[[((सर्वगं यज्ञरूपं तु यज्ञमूर्ति नमो ऽस्तु ते))]] ॥ 1:36॥

[[आकाशं धारयते लोकांल्लोका [2^v] व्योममयाः स्मृताः॥]]
आकाशं सर्वगं रूपं मूर्त्या[[((काश नमो ऽस्तु))]] ते॥ 1:37॥

सोमो धारयते लोकांल्लोकाः सोममयाः स्मृताः।

मयाः स्मृताः। सर्वगञ्चाग्निरूपं ते अग्निमूर्ते नमोस्तु ते॥ 20॥ यज्ञो वै धार्यते लोकान् लोका यज्ञमयाः स्मृताः। सर्वगं यज्ञरूपं ते यज्ञमूर्ते नमोस्तु ते॥ 21॥ सूर्यो धारयते लोकान् लोकाः सूर्यमयाः स्मृताः। सर्वगं सूर्यरूपं ते सूर्यमूर्ते नमोस्तु ते॥ 22॥ जलं वै धार्यते लोकान् लोका जलमयाः स्मृताः। सर्वगं जलरूपं ते जलमूर्ते नमोस्तु ते॥ 23॥ वायुर्वै धार्यते लोकान् लोका वायुमयाः स्मृताः। सर्वगं वायुरूपं ते वायुमूर्ते नमोस्तु ते॥ 24॥ सोमो धारयते लोकान् लोकाः सोममयाः स्मृताः। सर्वगं सोमरूपं ते सोममूर्ते नमोस्तु ते॥ 25॥ आकाशो धार्यते लोकान् लोका आकाशमयाः स्मृताः। आकाशं सर्वगं रूपं मूर्त्याकाश नमोस्तु ते॥ 26॥ क्षमाग्निय-जमानार्कवारीरणनिशाकराः। व्योमान्ता मूर्तयो ह्येता निर्दिष्टास्त्रिजगत्पतेः॥ 27॥ शर्वो रुद्रः पशुपतिरीशानो भव एव च। तथैवोग्रो महादेवो भीमान्ता मूर्तिपाः स्मृताः॥ 28॥

1:32 क्षितिमूर्त्ति नमो] N; क्षितिमूर्तिर्नमो KW **1:33** लोकांल्लोका जलमयाः स्मृताः] K; लोकाल्लोका जलमया स्मृ--- N; लोकाल्लोका जालमया स्मृताः W **1:33** सर्वगं जलरूपन्तु जलमूर्त्ति नमो ऽस्तु ते] *em.*; सर्वगं जलरूपन्तु जलमूर्त्तिर् नमो ऽस्तु ते] K; ---लरूपन्तु जल--- N; ⊔ शं जालरूपं तु जाल ⊔ W **1:34** वायुर्धारयते लोकांल्लोका वायुमयाः स्मृताः] K; ---ताः N; ⊔ स्मृताः W **1:34** वायुमूर्ति नमोऽस्तु ते] W; वायुमूर्ति नमोस् --- N; वायुमूर्तिर् नमोऽस्तु ते K **1:35** लोकांल्लोका] K; लोकाल्लोका NW **1:35** अग्निमूर्त्ति] NW; अग्निमूर्त्तिर् K **1:36** स्मृताः] KW; स्मृ --- N **1:36** सर्वगं यज्ञरूपं तु यज्ञमूर्ति नमो ऽस्तु ते] W; --- N; सर्वगं यज्ञरूपं तु यज्ञमूर्तिर्नमो ऽस्तु ते K **1:37** आकाशं धारयते लोकांल्लोका व्योममयाः स्मृताः] K; --- N; आकाश W **1:37** आकाशं सर्वगं रूपं मूर्त्याकाश] K; आकाश सर्वग रूपम्मूर्त्त्या ⌓ ⌓ N (tops missing in N); काशं आकाश सर्वग रूपम्मूर्त्त्याकाशं W **1:38** लोकांल्लोकाः सोममयाः] K; लोकाल्लोका सोमयाः N; लोकाल्लोका सोममयाः W

सर्वगं सोमरूपं तु सोममूर्त्ति नमो ऽस्तु ते॥ 1:38॥

सू [[((र्यो धारयते लोकांल्लोकाः सूर्यमयाः स्मृताः।
सर्वगं सूर्यरूपं तु सूर्यमूर्त्ति नमो ऽस्तु ते))]] ॥ 1:39॥

अष्टमूर्त्ति --- [-12-] ---।
[2] [[((अने))]]न सत्यवाक्येन संसारादुद्धरस्व माम्॥ 1:40॥

अष्टमूर्त्तिमिदं स्तोत्रं यः पठेत्सततं शुचिः।
सर्व्वपापविनिर्म्मुक्तः शिवसायोज्यताम्व्रजेत्॥ 1:41॥

देव्युवाच।
अनादिनिधनो देवो ह्यजमक्षरमव्ययः।
सर्वगस्सर्वरूपो ऽसि सर्वज्ञश्चैककारणः॥ 1:42॥

स्रष्टा धर्त्ता च हर्त्ता च परमेष्ठी महे[[((श्वरः))]]।
--- [-11-] --- [3] [[ग]]तिरुत्तमा॥ 1:43॥

त्वामाश्रित्य गतास्सर्वे सिद्धिमृषिसुरासुराः।
नागगन्धर्व्वयक्षाश्च पिशाचाप्सरराक्षसाः॥ 1:44॥

त्वत्प्रसादाद्वरं लब्ध्वा क्रीडन्ते च गतिङ्गताः।
अपुनर्भवनिर्वाणं यद्गत्वा न निवर्त्तते॥ 1:45॥

अहं हि शोकसंतप्तान्दृष्ट्वा लोकान्सुपीडितान्।
पश्यामि परिवर्त्तन्तं [[((कालचक्रं सुदा))रुणम्]] ॥ 1:46॥

--- [-3-] --- देव देवेश लोकानुग्रहकारणात्।
यथा मुच्यन्ति ते मर्त्त्या जन्ममृत्युजरादिभिः॥ 1:47॥

1:38 सर्वगं सोमरूपं तु सोममूर्त्ति नमो ऽस्तु ते] N; सर्वगं सोमरूपं तु सोममूर्त्तिर् नमो ऽस्तु ते K; सर्वगसोमरूपं तु सोममूर्त्ति नमो ऽस्तु ते W **1:39** लोकांल्लोकाः सूर्यमयाः] K; --- लोका सूर्य म --- N; लोकाल्लोकाः W **1:39** सर्वगं] K; --- N; सर्वग W **1:39** सूर्यमूर्त्ति] *em.*; --- N; सूर्यमूर्त्तिर् K; सूर्यरूप W **1:40** अष्टमूर्त्ति] *conj.*; --- N; अष्टमू K; अष्टसू; W **1:40** माम्] NK; मा W **1:41** स्तोत्रं] KW; स्त्रोत्रं N **1:41** °सायोज्यताम्] NW; °सायुज्यतां K **1:42** देवो ह्यजमक्षर] NK; वा ⩳जामक्षर W **1:43** स्रष्टा धर्त्ता च] *conj.*; स्रष्टा --- N; स्रष्टा पाता च K; श्रष्टा कर्त्ता च W **1:43** परमेष्ठी] *conj.*; परमिष्टो NK; परमिष्टा W **1:44** त्वामाश्रित्य] K; त्वमाशृत्य NW **1:46** सुपीडितान्] N; प्रपीडितान् K; अपीडितान् W **1:46** परिवर्त्तन्तम्] *conj.*; परिवर्त्तन्त ⩳ N; परिवर्त्तन्ते K; परिवर्त्तन्तु W **1:47** देवदेवेश] *conj.*; ---देवेश N; केनोपायेन देवेश K; ⊔वदेवस W

क्षुत्तृष्णाशीततोष्णेन कामक्रोधभयेन च।
इष्टानां विप्रयोगैश्च सर्वरोगसमावृताः॥ 1:48॥

अनाथाशरणा देव दम्भमायासमन्विताः।
परहिंसारता दुष्टा त्राहि तान्परमेश्वर॥ 1:49॥

कथमेते दुराचाराः शुद्ध्यन्ते --- [-5-] --- ।
[5] [[येनो]]पायेन देवेश तदुपायं वदस्व मे॥ 1:50॥

ईश्वर उवाच।
पञ्च स्रोता मया ख्याता लोकानां हितकाम्यया।
तान्प्रवक्ष्यामि सर्वांस्तु शृणुष्ववहिता प्रिये॥ 1:51॥

स्वर्गापवर्गहेतोश्च तन्निबोध यथार्थतः।
लौकिकं सम्प्रवक्ष्यामि येन स्वर्गं व्रजन्ति ते॥ 1:52॥

कूपवापीगृहोद्यान --- [-8-] ---।
--- [-12-] --- [6]थ मण्डपाः।
दानतीर्थोपवासानि व्रतानि नियमानि च॥ 1:53॥

भक्ष्याभक्ष्यपरीहारञ्जपहोमन्तथार्चनम्।
जलाग्निभृगुपातो हि तथानशनमेव च॥ 1:54॥

विद्यमाननिवृत्तिश्च गुरुवृद्धाभिपूजनम्।
लौकिकं कथितं ह्येतद्वैदिकञ्चातुरा[[((श्रमम्))]] ॥ 1:55॥

--- [-16-] ---।
--- [-6-] ---। [3r] [[((प्रोक्ता))]] लोकातीता महाव्रताः।
मन्त्राख्याश्च तथा शैवा अतो ऽन्ये कुपथे स्थिताः॥ 1:56॥

1:48 क्षुत्तृष्णाशीततोष्णेन] N; क्षुड्तृष्णाशीततोष्णेन K; क्षुत्तृष्णासीततोष्णान W **1:48** इष्टानां विप्रयोगैश्च] *conj.*; इष्टानां विप्रियैर्न्नित्यं NKW **1:49** दम्भमायासमन्विताः] K; दम्भमायास --- न्विताः N; द ⁻मायास ⁻ स्थिताः W **1:49** दुष्टा] NK^{ac}W; दुष्टा+ः+ K **1:49** तान्] *em.*; मां NKW **1:50** कथमेते दुराचाराः शुद्ध्यन्ते] *conj.*; --- N; कथमेते दुराचारा ⊔ K; कथमेते दुराचारा मुद्ध ⊔ W **1:50** येनोपायेन] K; ---पायेन N; ⊔खोगेयेन W? **1:51** उवाच] K; उ NW **1:51** शृणुष्ववहिता प्रिये] N; शृणुष्वावहिता प्रिये K; शृणुष्ववेहिता प्रिय W **1:52** लौकिकं] K; लोकिकं NW **1:53** कूपवापीगृहोद्यान] *conj. Sanderson*; कूपवा ⏑̲ गृहाहो --- N; ⊔ K; कुप ⊔ मालयान W **1:53** थ मण्डपाः] W; --- मण्डपाः N; ⊔ था K **1:54** °अनशनम्] NK; °अनसनम् W **1:55** चातुराश्रमम्] K; चातुरा--- N; चान्तराश्रमम् W **1:56** कुपथे] NW; कुपथि K

देव्युवाच।
पञ्च स्रोतास्त्वया देव सूचिता न तु वर्ण्णिताः।
तांस्तु विस्तरतो मे ऽद्य प्रसादाद्वक्तुमर्हसि॥ 1:57॥

ईश्वर उवाच।
उत्पानं कुरुते यस्तु पापात्मा दुष्टचेतसः।
स विधूय --- पितृभिस्सह मोदते॥ 1:58॥

≪पुष्करिण्याश्च यः कर्ता ≫दिवं व्रजेद्वि[2]कल्मषः।
कुलैस्तु सप्तभिर्युक्तो यावत्कीर्त्तिर्न नश्यते॥ 1:59॥

गृहन्द्रव्यसमोपेतङ्कृत्वा विप्राय यो ददेत्।
तस्य हेममयन्दिव्यङ्गृहं स्वर्ग्गे प्रजायते॥ 1:60॥

उद्यानङ्कुरुते यस्तु देवदेवस्य चालये।
तस्य पुण्यफलं यत्तत्पुष्पे पुष्पे निबोध मे॥ 1:61॥

दशसौवर्णिकं पुष्पं माला लक्षेण संमिता।
कोटिर्माला≪शतेनाहुरनन्तं लिंग≫पू[3]रणे॥ 1:62॥

एवङ्कुर्व्वन्ति ये नित्यन्ते गणा मम चाक्षयाः।
न तेषाम्मर्त्यभावो ऽस्ति कल्पकोटिशतैरपि॥ 1:63॥

एवं श्रुतम्मया पूर्व्वन्देव्यां कथयतो हरात्।

---

58 *Niśvāsamukha* 1.58–1.63 is parallel with *Śivadharmasaṅgraha* 5.15–5.20.

64 Cf. *Śivadharmasaṅgraha* 5.134ab: श्रुतमेतत् मया विप्रा देव्यै कथयतो हरात्।

1:57 त्वया] NW; च या K **1:57** तांस्तु] NW; तास्तु K **1:58** उवाच] K; उ NW **1:58** उत्पानं कुरुते यस्तु] NK^{ac}; उद्यानं कुरुते यस्तु K^{pc}; उत्पान कुरुते यस्तु W; उदपानं तु यः कुर्यात् *ŚiDhaSaṅ* **1:58** पापात्मा] KW, *ŚiDhaSaṅ*; --- पात्मा N **1:58** स विधूय] *conj.*; स विधू --- NKW; विधूय पापसंघातं *ŚiDhaSaṅ* **1:58** पितृभिस्सह मोदते] W, *ŚiDhaSaṅ*; --- NK **1:59** पुष्करिण्याश्च यः कर्ता] *ŚiDhaSaṅ*; --- NKW **1:59** दिवं व्रजेद्विकल्मषः] *conj.*; --- ल्मषः NK; ⊔ कल्मषः W; मोदते दिवि शक्रवत् *ŚiDhaSaṅ* **1:59** कुलैस्तु] NW; कुलैश्च K, *ŚiDhaSaṅ* **1:59** नश्यते] NKW; नश्यति *ŚiDhaSaṅ* **1:60** कृत्वा विप्राय यो ददेत्] NKW; दद्याद्विप्राय यो नरः *ŚiDhaSaṅ* **1:61** चालये] NKW; मंदिरे *ŚiDhaSaṅ* **1:61** पुण्यफलं यत्तत्] NKW; तस्य दानफलं यत्तत् *ŚiDhaSaṅ* **1:61** पुष्पे पुष्पे] KW, *ŚiDhaSaṅ*; ---॰ष्पे पुष्पे N **1:62** दशसौवर्णिकं] *ŚiDhaSaṅ*; लससौवर्णिकं N; लसत्सौवर्णिकं K; लससौवर्णकं W **1:62** माला लक्षेण संमिता] KW, *ŚiDhaSaṅ*; माला लक्षे --- N **1:62** कोटिर्मालाशतेनाहुरनन्तं लिंगपूरणे] *ŚiDhaSaṅ*; --- रणे N; कोटि ⊔रणे K; कोटिमाला ⊔ रणे W **1:63** भावो ऽस्ति] NKW; भावो हि *ŚiDhaSaṅ*

तत्सर्व्वङ्कथितन्तुभ्यं यत्फलं लिङ्गपूरणे॥ 1:64॥

ऋषय ऊचुः।
पृच्छन्ति ऋषयो भीतास्संसारभयपीडिताः।
तुष्यते च कथन्देव अर्चितस्य च ≪किं फलम्≫॥ 1:65॥

≪क्षीराज्यद≫धि[4]तोयेन स्नापितस्य च किम्फलम्।
पुष्पाणाञ्चैव सर्व्वेषां गन्धधूपस्य किं फलम्॥ 1:66॥

वस्त्रालङ्कारनैवेद्यध्वजादर्शवितानकैः।
दीपच्छत्रफलं ब्रूहि गोजाविमहिषीषु च॥ 1:67॥

अश्वदन्तिप्रदानस्य दासीदासस्य यत्फलम्।
सन्मार्जने फलं किं स्यात्तथा चैवोपलेपने॥ 1:68॥

गीतनृत्यफलं ब्रूहि तन्त्री≪वाद्यफलञ्च यत्≫।
[5]जागरस्य फलं ब्रूहि कृष्णाष्टमिचतुर्द्दशी॥ 1:69॥

उपवासस्य यत्पुण्यं देवदेवाश्रितस्य च।
एतत्सर्वं समाख्याहि उपसन्नाः स्म ते वयम्॥ 1:70॥

नन्दीश उ।
शतं सन्मार्जने पुण्यं सहस्रमुपलेपने।

---

65 *Niśvāsamukha* 1.65–1.87 is parallel with *Śivadharmasaṅgraha* 5.21–5.43.

1:64 °पूरणे] *conj. Sanderson*; °पूजने NKW **1:65** पृच्छन्ति] KW, *ŚiDhaSaṅ*; पच्छन्ति W **1:65** °पीडिताः] NKW; °विह्वलाः *ŚiDhaSaṅ* **1:65** अर्चितस्य च किं फलम्] *ŚiDhaSaṅ*; --- N; अर्चितस्य च दा ⊔ K; अर्चितस्य च प ⊔ W **1:66** क्षीराज्यदधितोयेन] *ŚiDhaSaṅ*; --- तोयेन N; (पञ्चगव्येन) तोयेन K; ⊔ धितोयेन W **1:66** च] K, *ŚiDhaSaṅ*; *om.* NW **1:66** गन्धधूपस्य] K, *ŚiDhaSaṅ*; गन्धाधूपस्य NW **1:67** °वेद्य°] KW; °वेद्ये N; °वेद्यैर् *ŚiDhaSaṅ* **1:67** दीपच्छत्रफलं ब्रूहि गोजावि°] K; दीपच्छत्रफलं ब्रूहि गैजावि° NW; किं फलं च्छत्रदीपैश्च गवादि° *ŚiDhaSaṅ* **1:68** अश्वदन्तिप्रदानस्य] NKW; अजवारणदानस्य *ŚiDhaSaṅ* **1:69** गीतनृत्यफलं ब्रूहि] KW, *ŚiDhaSaṅ*; गीतनृत्य --- N **1:69** तन्त्रीवाद्यफलञ्च यत्] *ŚiDhaSaṅ*; --- N; तंत्री ⊔ K; तन्त्र ⊔ W **1:69** जागरस्य फलं ब्रूहि कृष्णाष्टमिचतुर्दशी] *em.*; --- रस्य फलं ब्रूहि कृष्णाष्टमिचतुर्द्दशी N; ⊔ रस्य फलं ब्रूहि कृष्णाष्टमीचतुर्द्दशी K; जागरस्य फलं ब्रूहि कृष्णाष्टमिचतुर्द्दसी Wकृष्णाष्टम्यां चतुर्दश्यां जागरस्य फलं वद *ŚiDhaSaṅ* **1:70** °श्रितस्य च] K; °शृतस्य च NW; °श्रितस्य तु *ŚiDhaSaṅ* **1:70** उपसन्नाः स्म] *ŚiDhaSaṅ*; उपसन्ना स्मस् N; उपसन्ना स्म KW **1:71** नन्दीश उ] NKW; नन्दिकेश्वर उवाच *ŚiDhaSaṅ* **1:71** पुण्यं] NKW; दानं *ŚiDhaSaṅ*

निष्काणाम्प्राप्नुयाच्चैव शिवभक्तिसमन्वितः॥ 1:71॥

उपलिप्य शिवागारं शुचिर्भूत्वा समाहितः।
≪अर्चयेत्ससततं देवं≫[6] शिवदीक्षाविवर्जितः॥ 1:72॥

पत्रपुष्पफलैश्चैव दधिक्षीरघृतादिभिः।
पवित्रैर्भक्तिपूतैश्च यः पूजयति नित्यशः॥ 1:73॥

वस्त्रनैवेद्यच्छत्रैश्च ध्वजादर्शवितानकैः।
घण्टाचामरदामैश्च अलंकारोदकेन च॥ 1:74॥

≪सुवर्ण्णमणिवस्त्रैश्च गन्धधूपोपलेपनैः।
गीतवादित्रनृत्तैश्च हुड्डुङ्कारस्तवेन च॥ 1:75॥

[3^v] वक्ष्यामि सर्व्वमेवन्तु ≫अपरिज्ञातकारणे।
केवलां भक्तिमापन्नाः शृणुध्वं पूजनात्फलम्॥ 1:76॥

तोयेन स्नापयेल्लिङ्गं गन्धदिग्धेन चैव हि।
एकरात्रेण मुच्यन्ते मानसा≪त्किल्बिषान्नराः॥ 1:77॥

दशरात्रात्कायिकेन महापापेन पक्षतः।
मासेन स्वर्गमाप्नोति अब्दाद्गाणेश्वरीं गतिम्॥ 1:78॥

त्र्यब्देन पितृतां याति पञ्चभिः कुलमु≫द्धरे[2]त्।

1:71 निष्काणां प्राप्नुयाच्चैव] NW; निष्काणं प्राप्नुयादेव K; निष्काणां प्राप्नुयात्पुण्यं *ŚiDhaSaṅ* **1:71** °भक्तिसमन्वितः] KW; °भक्ति --- N; °भक्त्या समन्वितः *ŚiDhaSaṅ* **1:72** उपलिप्य शिवागारं शुचिर्भूत्वा समाहितः] K, *ŚiDhaSaṅ*; --- N; ⊔ लिप्य शिवागारं W **1:72** शुचिर्भूत्वा समाहितः] K; --- N; शुचिभूत्वा समाहितः W; शुचीभूय समाहितः *ŚiDhaSaṅ* **1:72** अर्चयेत्ससततं देवं] *ŚiDhaSaṅ*; --- NKW **1:72** शिवदीक्षाविवर्जितः] W; --- ि ⏑ ⏑ र्जितः N; सर्व्वदीक्षादिवर्जितः K; ज्ञानदीक्षाविवर्जितः *ŚiDhaSaṅ* **1:73** पवित्रैर्भक्तिपूतैश्च] NKW; विचित्रैर्भक्तिपूतैश्च *ŚiDhaSaṅ* **1:74** वस्त्र°] NKW; यस्तु *ŚiDhaSaṅ* **1:74** °दामैश्च अलंकारोदकेन च] KW; °दामैश्च --- N; °दानेन अलङ्कारौदनेन वा *ŚiDhaSaṅ* **1:75** सुवर्ण्णमणिवस्त्रैश्च गन्धधूपोपलेपनैः।] *ŚiDhaSaṅ*; --- NKW **1:75** गीतवादित्रनृत्तैश्च हुड्डुङ्कारस्तवेन च] *ŚiDhaSaṅ*; --- NKW **1:76** वक्ष्यामि सर्व्वमेवन्तु] *ŚiDhaSaṅ*; --- N; ⊔ त्र K; ⊔ तन्तु W **1:76** अपरिज्ञातकारणे] KW *ŚiDhaSaṅ*; --- ज्ञातकारणे N **1:76** केवलां भक्तिमापन्नाः] *conj.*; केवला भक्तिमापन्ना N; केवलां भक्तिमापन्न K; वला भक्तिमापन्नो W; केवलम्भक्तिमापन्ने *ŚiDhaSaṅ* **1:76** शृणुध्वं पूजनात्फलम्] *conj.*; शृणु व? पूजना फ ⏑ म् N; शृणुष्वं पूजनात्फलम् K; शृणुध्वं पूजनां फलम् W; शृणुध्वं पूजने फलम् *ŚiDhaSaṅ* **1:77** तोयेन स्नापयेल्लिङ्गं ···कुलमुद्धरेत्] N, *ŚiDhaSaṅ*; --- K; तोयेन स्नापयेल्लिंगं गन्धदि ⏑ न चव हि W **1:77** एकरात्रेण मुच्यन्ते मानसात्किल्बिषान्नराः] *ŚiDhaSaṅ*; --- NK; एकरात्रेण मुच्यन्ते मानसा ⊔ W **1:79** त्र्यब्देन पितृतां याति पञ्चभिः कुलमुद्धरेत्] *ŚiDhaSaṅ*; --- त् NK; ⊔ द्धरेत् W

द्विषद्भादीशसायोज्यं यावज्जीवं शिवम्व्रजेत्॥ 1:79॥

सुदध्ना स्नापयेल्लिङ्गङ्कृष्णाष्टमिचतुर्दशी।
यावज्जीवकृतात्पापान्मुच्यते नात्र संशयः॥ 1:80॥

सततं स्नापयेद्यस्तु मासमेकं शुचिर्न्नरः।
प्रत्यहं क्रतुमाप्नोति भिन्ने देहे शिवालयम्॥ 1:81॥

षण्मासं स्नापयेद्यस्तु स गणश्चोत्तमो भवेत्।
≪अब्दस्ना≫नेन [3] पितरस्तस्य यान्ति शिवालयम्॥ 1:82॥

त्र्यब्देन रुद्रसायोज्यं द्वादशाब्दैः स्वकङ्कुलम्।
घृतेन स्नापयेल्लिङ्गमेकाहं यदि मानवः॥ 1:83॥

दग्ध्वा तु सर्व्वपापानि अश्वमेधफलं लभेत्।
दशरात्रात्स्वर्ग्गतिम्मसाद्गाणेश्वरीङ्गतिम्॥ 1:84॥

नरकस्थाश्च पितर उद्धृतास्तु न संशयः।
षण्मासं ≪स्नापयेद्यस्तु नित्यं चाभग्न≫ [4] योगतः॥ 1:85॥

तस्यापि पितरो यान्ति नित्यं गाणेश्वरीङ्गतिम्।
द्विरब्देनैव सायोज्यं गच्छते पितृभिस्सह॥ 1:86॥

घृतस्नानात्परन्नास्ति योद्धरेत्कुलसप्तकम्।

1:79 द्विषद्भादीशसायोज्यं] NK; द्विषद्भादिससायोज्यं W; द्विषद्भैरीशसायुज्यं *ŚiDhaSaṅ* **1:79** व्रजेत्] NKW; विशेत् *ŚiDhaSaṅ* **1:80** सुदध्ना स्नापयेल्लिङ्गङ्कृष्णाष्टमिचतुर्दशी] *em.*; सुदध्ना स्नापयेल्लिङ्गङ्कृष्णाष्टमिचतुर्दशीम् N; सुदध्ना स्नापयेल्लिङ्गङ्कृष्णाष्टमीचतुर्दशीम् K; सुदध्ना स्नापयेल्लिङ्गङ्कृष्णाष्टमिचतुर्दशीम् W; कृष्णाष्टम्याश्चतुर्दश्यां यो दध्ना स्नापयेच्छिवम् *ŚiDhaSaṅ* **1:80** °कृतात्पापान्मु°] NKW; °कृतैः पापैर्मु° *ŚiDhaSaṅ* **1:81** सततं] NKW; प्रत्यहं *ŚiDhaSaṅ* **1:81** प्रत्यहं क्रतुमाप्नोति भिन्ने देहे शिवालयम्] KW; प्रत्य ⏑⏑⏑⏑⏑ ति भि ⏑--- N; क्रतूनां फलमाप्नोति भिन्ने देहे सुरालयम् *ŚiDhaSaṅ* **1:82** षण्मासं स्नापयेद्यस्तु] *ŚiDhaSaṅ*; --- N; षण्मासं स्नापये यस्तु K; षण्मास स्नापयेद्यस्तु W **1:82** स गणश्चोत्तमो भवेत्] *conj.*; --- N; स गणश्चो ⊔ KW; सुराणां चोत्तमो भवेत् *ŚiDhaSaṅ* **1:82** अब्दस्नानेन] *ŚiDhaSaṅ*; --- NK; ⊔ नेन W **1:82** शिवालयम्] NKW; सुरालयम् *ŚiDhaSaṅ* **1:83** °सायोज्यं] K *ŚiDhaSaṅ*; °सायोज्य NW **1:83** स्वकङ्कुलम्] NKW; कुलैः स्वयम् *ŚiDhaSaṅ* **1:83** °काहं यदि] NW; °काहमपि K, *ŚiDhaSaṅ* **1:84** °मेधफलं लभेत्] NKW; °मेधमवाप्नुयात् *ŚiDhaSaṅ* **1:84** स्वर्ग्गतिम्म्र्मा°] NW (unmetrical); स्वर्गतिं मा° K (unmetrical); स्वर्ग्गगतिम् *ŚiDhaSaṅ* **1:85** नरकस्थाश्च पितर उद्धृतास्तु न संशयः] NW; नरकस्थास्तु पितर उद्धृतास्तु न संशयः K; पितॄन्नरकगर्तस्थानुद्धरत्यविकल्पतः *ŚiDhaSaṅ* **1:85** षण्मासं स्नापयेद्यस्तु नित्यं चाभग्नयोगतः] *ŚiDhaSaṅ*; --- योगतः N; षण्मास ⊔योगतः KW **1:86** सायोज्यं] NKW; सायुज्यं *ŚiDhaSaṅ* **1:86** गच्छते] NKW; व्रजन्ति *ŚiDhaSaṅ* **1:87** योद्धरेत्कु°] NKW; उद्धरेत्कु° *ŚiDhaSaṅ*

त्रिनेत्राः शूलहस्ताश्च वृषाङ्काश्चन्द्रशेखराः॥ 1:87॥

क्षीरेण स्नापयेल्लिङ्गं कृष्णाष्टमिचतुर्दशी।
यावज्जीवकृतात्पापान्मुच्यते नात्र संशयः॥ 1:88॥

[5] मासैकं [[((स्नाप))]]येद्यस्तु सर्वपापसमन्वितः।
मुच्यते तैस्तु पापैस्तु शिवसायोज्यतां व्रजेत्॥ 1:89॥

षण्मासान्स्नापयेद्यस्तु स गणश्चोत्तमो भवेत्।
अब्दस्नानेन तस्यैव उद्धरेत्कुलसप्तकम्॥ 1:90॥

त्र्यब्देन रुद्रसायोज्यम् †उद्धरेण शिवात्मकम्†।
द्वादशाब्दान्स्नयेद्यस्तु सततं भक्तिसंयुतः॥ 1:91॥

कुलकोटिशतं साग्रं नरकात्तारयिष्य[6]ति।
क्षीरस्नानफलं ह्येतद्घृतस्नानोपरि स्थितम्॥ 1:92॥

मधुना स्नापयेल्लिङ्गङ्कृष्णाष्टमिचतुर्द्दशी।
राजसूयस्य यज्ञस्य फलं प्राप्नोति मानवः॥ 1:93॥

प्रत्यहम्फलमाप्नोति अब्देनैव गणेश्वरः।
पञ्चाब्देनैव सायोज्यं गच्छते पितृभिः सह॥ 1:94॥

---

92 Cf. Niśvāsakārikā (T. 127, p. 298 and T. 17, p. 252): कुलकोटिशतं साग्रं नरकात्तारयिष्यति।

93 *Niśvāsamukha* 1.93a–1.98b is parallel with *Śivadharmasaṅgraha* 5.44c–5.49.

93 Cf. *Mahābhārata* 3.82:113ef, *Saromāhātmya* of the *Vāmanapurāṇa* 13.34cd, *Śivadharmasaṅgraha* 5.45ab and *Umāmaheśvarasaṃvāda* 21.33cd: राजसूयस्य यज्ञस्य फलं प्राप्नोति मानवः।

1:87 त्रिनेत्राः] K, *ŚiDhaSaṅ*; त्रिनेत्रा NW **1:88** क्षीरेण स्नापयेल्लिङ्गं कृष्णाष्टमिचतुर्दशी] N; क्षीरेण स्नापयेल्लिङ्गं कृष्णाष्टमीचतुर्दशी K; क्षीरेण स्नापयेल्लिङ्गं कृष्णाष्टमिचतुर्दसी W **1:88** यावज्जीवकृतात्पापान्मुच्यते नात्र संशयः] KW; यावज्जीवकृतात्पापान्मु --- N **1:89** मासैकं] *conj.*; --- NKW **1:90** षण्मासान्] N; षण्मासात् KW **1:91** स्नयेद्यस्तु] NK; स्तुपेद्यस्तु W **1:92** कुलकोटिशतं साग्रं नरकात्तारयिष्यति] *conj.*; कु --- ति N; कुलकोटिशतै (युक्त) ⊔ K; कुलकोटिसत स ⊔ ि ॑ष्यति W **1:93** मधुना स्नापयेल्लिङ्गङ्कृष्णाष्टमिचतुर्द्दशी] NW; मधुना स्नापयेल्लिङ्गङ्कृष्णाष्टमीचतुर्दशी K; कृष्णाष्टम्यां चतुर्द्दश्यां मधुना स्नापयेच्छिवम् *ŚiDhaSaṅ* **1:94** फलमाप्नोति अब्देनैव] NKW; स्नापयेद्यस्तु वर्षेणैव *ŚiDhaSaṅ* **1:94** पञ्चाब्देनैव सायोज्यं गच्छते पितृभिः सह] *conj.*; पञ्चाब्देनैव सायोज्यं गच्छते पितृ --- NKW; पञ्चाब्देन तु सायोज्यं प्रयाति पितृसंयुतः *ŚiDhaSaṅ*

[[((पञ्चगव्येन स्नानं तु प्रत्यहम्))]] ---।
[4^r] ≪†न तस्य दृश्यते चान्तं†देवलोकञ्च ≫गच्छति॥ 1:95॥

संवत्सरेण शुद्धात्मा शिवसायोज्यतां व्रजेत्।
वर्षद्वयेन पितरः सप्त चैवोद्धृताः स्मृताः॥ 1:96॥

गन्धैश्च लेपयेल्लिङ्गन्दिव्यैश्चैव सुगन्धकैः।
वाजपेयस्य यज्ञस्य फलम्प्राप्नोति मानवः॥ 1:97॥

कर्पूरव्यतिमिश्रेण चन्दनेन ≪तु लेपयेत्≫।
[2] अश्वमेधफलञ्चैव दशरात्रेण प्राप्नुयात्॥ 1:98॥

मासेन गणतां याति अब्दात्सायोज्यमाप्नुयात्।
अभग्नयोगो यो दद्यात्प्रत्यहं लिङ्गलेपनम्॥ 1:99॥

पितरस्तस्य ते सर्व्वे गतिं यास्यन्ति चोत्तमाम्।
गुग्गुलुन्दहते यस्तु देवदेवस्य सन्निधौ॥ 1:100॥

सकृद्धूपेन प्राप्नोति अग्निष्टोमस्य यत्फलम्।
सततं दहते यस्तु ≪धूपं गुग्गुल≫[3]मुत्तमम्॥ 1:101॥

मासेनैकेन प्राप्नोति क्रतूनां शतमेव तु।

---

98 *Niśvāsamukha* 1.98c–1.100b is parallel with *Śivadharmasaṅgraha* 5.50c–5.52b.

100 *Niśvāsamukha* 1.100c–1.107b is parallel with *Śivadharmasaṅgraha* 5.55–5.61.

1:95 (पञ्चगव्येन स्नानं तु प्रत्यहम्] KW; --- N; प्रत्यहं पञ्चगव्येन यः शिवं स्नपयेन्नरः *ŚiDhaSaṅ* **1:95** कारयेन्नरः] *ŚiDhaSaṅ*; --- NKW **1:95** न तस्य दृश्यते चान्तं देवलोकञ्च गच्छति] *ŚiDhaSaṅ*; --- ति N; ⊔ K; स गच्छति W **1:96** संवत्सरेण शुद्धात्मा] *ŚiDha-Saṅ*; सम्बत्सरण ⍽ द्धामा N; संवत्सरेण ⊔ K; ⊔ W **1:96** °सायोज्यतां] N *ŚiDhaSaṅ*; °सायुज्यतां K; °सायोज्य सो W **1:96** वर्षद्वयेन पितरः सप्त चैवोद्धृताः स्मृताः] NKW; द्विवर्षेण पितॄन्सप्त समुद्धृत्य शिवं व्रजेत् *ŚiDhaSaṅ* **1:97** लेपयेल्लिङ्गन्] NKW; स्नापयेल्लि-ङ्गं *ŚiDhaSaṅ* **1:97** सुगन्धकैः] NKW; सुगन्धिभिः *ŚiDhaSaṅ* **1:98** कर्पूरव्यतिमिश्रेण] K, *ŚiDhaSaṅ*; कर्पूरव्यति --- N; कर्पूर ⊔ W **1:98** तु लेपयेत्] *ŚiDhaSaṅ*; --- NKW **1:98** दशरात्रेण प्राप्नुयात्] NKW; दशरात्रेण चाप्नुयात् *ŚiDhaSaṅ* **1:100** ते सर्व्वे] NK; ते सर्व W; सर्वे ते *ŚiDhaSaṅ* **1:100** गुग्गुलुन्दहते यस्तु देवदेवस्य सन्निधौ] NKW; एकाहं दहते यस्तु देवदेवस्य संनिधौ *ŚiDhaSaṅ* **1:101** सकृद्धूपेन प्राप्नोति अग्निष्टोमस्य यत् फलम्] NK; सकृद्धूपेन प्राप्नोति अग्निष्टामस्य यत् फलम् W; सर्वपापविशुद्धात्मा अग्निष्टोममवाप्नुयात् *ŚiDhaSaṅ* **1:101** सततं दहते यस्तु] K; --- N; सततं दहते ⊔ W; भक्तिमान् प्रदहेद्यस्तु *ŚiDhaSaṅ* **1:101** धूपं गुग्गुलमुत्तमम्] *ŚiDhaSaṅ*; --- मुत्तमम् NKW **1:102** मासेनैकेन प्राप्नोति] NKW; मासैकेन समाप्नोति *ŚiDhaSaṅ* **1:102** क्रतूनां शतमेव तु] NK; कुह्नानां शतमेव तु W; क्रतूनां शतमुत्तमम् *ŚiDhaSaṅ*

षण्मासन्तन्दहेद्यस्तु स गणश्चोत्तमो भवेत्॥ 1:102॥

न तस्य सम्भवो मर्त्ये पितृभिस्सह मोदते।
अब्दमेकन्दहेद्यस्तु शुचिर्भूत्वा दिने दिने॥ 1:103॥

स्वकुलञ्चोद्धृतन्तेन शिवभक्तेन धीमता।
वस्त्रध्वजवितानं वा यो दद्याल्लिङ्गसन्निधौ॥ 1:104॥

स लभेत्परमैश्वर्यं जायते चोत्त[4]मे कुले।
सकृद्दानफलं ह्येतद्विस्त्रिधा गतिरुत्तमा॥ 1:105॥

प्राप्नुयान्मानवः शीघ्रं सोमलोकन्न संशयः।
शतसाहस्रदानेन गतिर्गाणेश्वरी भवेत्॥ 1:106॥

पितृभिस्संयुतश्चैव लक्षदानान्न संशयः।
घण्टां हेममयाङ्कृत्वा यो ददाति शिवस्य तु॥ 1:107॥

तेन पुण्यफलेनैव शिवलोके महीयते।
रौप्यान्ताम्रान्तथा कांस्यां रै[5]त्यां वा त्रापुषामपि॥ 1:108॥

मृन्मयां वा तथा कुर्यात्सुलोलां सुस्वरां पुनः।
शिवागारे तु यो दद्यात्स सर्वः स्वर्गगोचरः॥ 1:109॥

स्वर्गलोकात्परिभ्रष्टो जायते पृथिवीपतिः।
श्वेतं रक्तं तथा पीतङ्कृष्णं वा चामरन्ददेत्॥ 1:110॥

हेमदण्डन्तु रौप्यं वा रैत्यन्त्रापुषमेव वा।
ईदृशञ्चामरं दत्वा रुद्रलोके [[((महीयते॥ 1:111॥

रुद्रलोका))]][6]त्परिभ्रष्टो वायुलोकमु[[((पाग))]]तः।

1:102 षण्मासन्तन्] NKW; वर्षमेकन् *ŚiDhaSaṅ* **1:103** अब्दमेकन्दहेद्यस्तु] NKW; द्व्यब्दं दहति यो देवि *ŚiDhaSaṅ* **1:103** शुचिर्भूत्वा] NKW; शुचीभूय *ŚiDhaSaṅ* **1:105** स लभेत् परमैश्वर्यं जायते चोत्तमे] *conj.*; स लभेत्प --- मे N; स लभेत्परमैश्व ⊔ मे K; स लभेत्परमैश्वर्य ⊔ मे W; लभते परमैश्वर्यं जायते चोत्तमे *ŚiDhaSaṅ* **1:105** ह्येतद्विस्त्रिधा] K; ह्येतद्विस्तृधा NW; हि तद्विस्त्रिधा *ŚiDhaSaṅ* **1:106** मानवः] K *ŚiDhaSaṅ*; मानव NW **1:107** संयुतश्चैव] NKW; संयुतं चैव *ŚiDhaSaṅ* **1:107** हेममयां] NW; हेममयीं K **1:108** रौप्यान् ताम्रान् तथा कांस्यां रैत्यां वा त्रापुषामपि] *conj.*; रौ --- त्यां वा त्रापुसानपि N; रौप्यान् ताम्रान् तथा ⊔ वा त्रपुसानपि K; रूप्यान् न्त्यां वा त्रापुसानपि W **1:109** सुलोलां सुस्वरां] *conj.*; सुलोलां सुस्वरान् N; सुलोलान् सुस्वरान् K; सुलालां सुस्वरान् W **1:110** परिभ्रष्टो] NK; परिभ्रष्टा W **1:110** ददेत्] NW; ददत् K **1:111** °दण्डं K; °दण्डान् NW **1:112** परिभ्रष्टो] NK; परिभ्रष्टा W

वायुलोकात्परिभ्रष्टो वह्निलोकमुपागतः॥ 1:112॥

वह्निलोकात्परिभ्रष्टो जायते पृथिवीपतिः।
ब्राह्मणो राज्यसम्पन्नो विद्वांश्च ज्ञानपारगः॥ 1:113॥

तेन पुण्यफलेनैव सर्वमेतद्भवेदिह।
मेखलां कटिसूत्रञ्च यो दद्याल्लिङ्गमूर्धनि॥ 1:114॥

चतुस्सागरसंयुक्तपृथिव्या भवतीश्वरः।
[4v] मुकुटङ्कुण्डलञ्चैव चित्रपट्टप्रदायिनः॥ 1:115॥

सकलान्तु महीम्भुङ्क्ते अङ्गाभरणदायकः।
मुखकोशे तथैवेह पट्टे प्रादेशिको नृपः॥ 1:116॥

विचित्रैश्चित्रभोगानि निःसपत्नानि भुंजते।
पुनः पुनश्च यो [[द]]द्याद्रत्नाभरणभूषणम्॥ 1:117॥

गाणापत्यमवाप्नोति अक्षयं ध्रुवमव्ययम्।
मुक्तिमण्डपदानेन भक्त्या तु यो ऽर्च[2]येच्छिवम्॥ 1:118॥

न तस्य पुनरावृत्तिर्गणश्चैवोत्तमो भवेत्।
रोचनाङ्कुङ्कुमञ्चैव लिङ्गस्योपरि यो नरः॥ 1:119॥

प्रत्यहं लेपनन्दद्यात्स विद्याधरतां व्रजेत्।

---

114 *Niśvāsamukha* 1.114c–1.124b is parallel with *Śivadharmasaṅgraha* 5.62a–5.71.

1:112 परिभ्रष्टो] NK; परिभ्रष्टा W **1:113** परिभ्रष्टो] NK; परिभ्रष्टा W **1:113** ज्ञानपारगः] NW; वेदपारगः K **1:115** चतुस्सागरसंयुक्तपृथिव्या भवतीश्वरः] *conj.*; चतुस्सा --- N; चतुस्सागरसंयुक्ता पृथिव्या भवतीश्वरः K; चतुस्स ⊔ तां ⊔ W; चतुःसागरपर्यन्तक्ष्मायास्तु स भवेन्नृपः *ŚiDhaSaṅ* **1:115** मुकुटङ्कु°] K, *ŚiDhaSaṅ*; ⏓ कुटङ्कु° N; मुकुटाङ्कु° W **1:115** चिन्त्रपट्टप्रदायिनः] NW; चित्रपट्टं प्रदायिनः K; चित्रपट्टकदायकः *ŚiDhaSaṅ* **1:116** °दायकः] NKW; °दानतः *ŚiDhaSaṅ* **1:116** पट्टे प्रादेशिको नृपः] N; यष्टा प्रादेशिको नरः K; प ⁻ प्रादेशिको नृपः W; पट्टात् प्रादेशिको नृपः *ŚiDhaSaṅ* **1:117** विचित्रैश्चित्रभोगानि निःसपत्नानि भुंजते] K; विचित्रैश्चित्र --- N; विचित्रैश्चित्रसागानि निःसपत्नानि भुंजते W; चित्रके चित्रभोगानि निस्सपत्नमवाप्नुयात् *ŚiDhaSaṅ* **1:117** दद्याद्रत्नाभरणभूषणम्] *ŚiDhaSaṅ*; ⏓ द्याद्रत्नाभरणभूषणम् N; दद्याद्द्रव्याभरणभूषणम् K; दद्याद्रत्नारुरणभुषणम् W **1:118** गाणापत्यमवाप्नोति] NW *ŚiDhaSaṅ*; गाणपत्यमवाप्नोति K **1:118** अक्षयं ध्रुवमव्ययम्] NK; अक्षय ध्रुवमव्ययम् W; अक्षयं परमं ध्रुवम् *ŚiDhaSaṅ* **1:118** मुक्तिमण्डपदानेन भक्त्या तु योऽर्चयेच्छिवम्] *conj.*; म --- येच्छिवम् N; म ⊔ यंमदामेन ⊔ येच्छिवम् KW; मुक्तिमण्डपिकां भक्त्या दत्वा यो ऽर्च्चयते शिवम् *ŚiDhaSaṅ* **1:120** विद्याधरतां] NW, *ŚiDhaSaṅ*; विद्याधरता K

द्वादशाब्देन गणतां कर्प्पूरागरुलेपनैः॥ 1:120॥

कटकेयूरदानेन आधिपत्यं मनोमतम्।
प्राप्नुवन्ति नरा लोके शिवभक्तिपरायणाः॥ 1:121॥

[[((रत्नदा))]] --- [-3-] --- [3] कन्तु यो ददाति शिवस्य तु।
दशसौवर्ण्णिकं पुष्पन्निर्गन्धञ्चैव यद्भवेत्॥ 1:122॥

शतसाहस्रिका माला अनन्तं लिङ्गपूरणे।
निर्ग्गन्धकुसुमैरेष विधिः ख्यातो द्विजोत्तमाः॥ 1:123॥

शोभनैर्दिव्यगन्धाद्यैः शृणु तस्यापि यत्फलम्।
एकपुष्पप्रदानेन अशीतिकल्पकोटयः॥ 1:124॥

दुर्गतौ नाभिजायेत लिङ्गार्चायास्तु तत्फलम्।
[4] अकामादर्च्चिते लिङ्गे ह्येतदुक्तम्महत्फलम्॥ 1:125॥

कामेनाभ्यर्च्यमानस्य शृणु तस्यापि यत्फलम्।
बुकस्य करवीरस्य अर्क्कस्योन्मत्तकस्य च॥ 1:126॥

चतुर्ण्णाम्पुष्पजातीनां सर्वमाघ्राति शङ्करः।

---

124 Cf. *Śivadharmasaṅgraha* 5.72: एकपुष्पप्रदानेन लिंगेषु प्रतिमासु वा। अशीतिकल्पकोटीनां दुर्गतिं न नरो व्रजेत्॥

125 *Niśvāsamukha* 1.125c–1.127b is parallel with *Śivadharmasaṅgraha* 5.76–5.77.

126 Cf. *Skandapurāṇa* 28.32c–33b: चतुर्णां पुष्पजातीनां गन्धमाघ्राति शंकरः॥ अर्कस्य करवीरस्य बिल्वस्य च बुकस्य च।

1:121 मनोमतम्] NKW; महेच्छताम् *ŚiDhaSaṅ* **1:121** ॰परायणाः] KW, *ŚiDhaSaṅ*; प-रा --- N **1:122** --- कन्तु] NW; ⊔ न्तु K; रत्नदानानि दिव्यानि *ŚiDhaSaṅ* **1:122** ददाति] KW, *ŚiDhaSaṅ*; दंदाति N **1:122** दशसौवर्ण्णिकं पुष्पन्निर्गन्धञ्चैव यद्भवेत्] N; दशसौवर्णिक पुष्प निर्गन्धं चैव यद्भवेत् K; दससौवर्णिकं पुष्पन्निर्गन्धं चैव यत् भवेत् W; दशसौवर्णिकं पुष्पं निर्ग्गन्धि यदि भाविनि *ŚiDhaSaṅ* **1:123** निर्गन्धकुसुमैरेष विधिः] N^{pc}K; निर्गन्धकुसुमैरेष विधि N^{ac}W; निर्गन्धिकुसुमस्यायं विधिः *ŚiDhaSaṅ* **1:124** शोभनैर्दिव्यगन्धाद्यैः] *ŚiDhaSaṅ*; शोभने दिव्यगन्धाढ्ये NK; सोभने दिव्यगन्धाढ्य W **1:124** शृणु तस्यापि] NKW; शृणु तत्र तु *ŚiDhaSaṅ* **1:125** लिङ्गार्चायास्तु तत्फलम्] *conj.*; --- N; लिङ्गार्चायास्तु ⊔ K; लिङ्गार्चा-यास्तु तत्फ् (?) W **1:125** अकामादर्च्चिते लिङ्गे ह्येतदुक्तम्महत्फलम्] N; अकामादर्चिते लिङ्गे ह्येतदुक्तमहत्फलम् K; अकामादर्च्चिते लिङ्ग ह्येतदुक्तम्महत्फलम् W; अकामाभ्यर्च्चिते लिङ्गे एत-दुक्तं मया फलम् *ŚiDhaSaṅ* **1:126** बुकस्य करवीरस्य अर्क्कस्योन्मत्तकस्य च] NKW; अर्क्कस्य करवीरस्य बुकस्योन्मत्तकस्य च *ŚiDhaSaṅ* **1:127** चतुर्ण्णाम्] NW *ŚiDhaSaṅ*; चतुर्णा K **1:127** सर्वमाघ्राति शङ्करः] NK; सर्वमाघ्राति संकरः W; गन्धं जिघ्रति शंकरः *ŚiDhaSaṅ*

बुकेन वरदो देवः करवीरैर्द्धनप्रदः॥ 1:127॥

अर्क्केण प्रियमन्विच्छन्मोक्षं धुत्तूरकेण तु।
नीलोत्पलैर्भ ((([[वेद्योगी]]))[5] यो ≪ऽर्चयेल्लि≫ङ्गमुत्तमम्॥ 1:128॥

पद्मेन तु तथा राज्यं पुण्डरीकैश्च चक्रिणः।
चम्पकैस्सर्वकामानि पुन्नागैर्न्नागकेशरैः॥ 1:129॥

ईप्सितांल्लभते कामांस्तथा केसरदामकैः।
मन्त्रसिद्धिमवाप्नोति बृहत्यागस्तिपुष्पकैः॥ 1:130॥

यो ऽर्च्चयेत्परमेशानं सिद्धकेन समाहितः।
सर्वकामानवाप्नोति यो ऽर्चयेद्गंधपुष्पकैः॥ 1:131॥

[6]≪कुब्जकैर्व्विपुलो लाभः≫सौभाग्याय च वारुणी।
कन्याकामस्तु जातीभिर्यो ऽर्च्चयेत्परमेश्वरम्॥ 1:132॥

स लभेदुत्तमां कन्यां षण्मासेन न संशयः।
मल्लिकैर्ज्ज्ञानकामाय अर्च्चयन्यो महेश्वरम्॥ 1:133॥

लभेत परमञ्ज्ञानं संसारभयनाशनम्।
पुत्रकामाय कुन्दैस्तु ≪अर्च्चयीत शुचिर्नरः≫॥ 1:134॥

≪लभते बहुपुत्रत्वं धनवन्तश्चिरायुषम्≫।

---

127 *Niśvāsamukha* 1.127c–1.154 is parallel with *Śivadharmasaṅgraha* 5.83a–5.110b.

1:128 प्रियमन्विच्छन्] *conj.*; प्रियमन्विच्छम् N; प्रियमवीक्ष K; प्रियमस्थिच्छम् W; श्रियमाप्नोति *ŚiDhaSaṅ* **1:128** धुत्तूर°] N, *ŚiDhaSaṅ*; धत्तूर° K; धत्तुर° W **1:128** भवेद्योगी] KW; भ --- N; भवेद्योगो *ŚiDhaSaṅ* **1:128** यो ऽर्च्चयेल्लिङ्गमुत्तमम्] *ŚiDhaSaṅ*; --- ङ्गमुत्तमम् NK; यो ⊔ ङ्गमुत्तमम् W **1:129** पद्मेन तु तथा राज्यं] NK; पद्मेन तु तथा राज्यां W; रक्ताब्जैः प्राप्नुयाद्राज्यं *ŚiDhaSaṅ* **1:129** चक्रिणः] NKW; चक्रिणम् *ŚiDhaSaṅ* **1:129** न्नागकेसरैः] N, *ŚiDhaSaṅ*; नागकेसरैः KW **1:130** ईप्सितांल्लभते] K, *ŚiDhaSaṅ*; ईप्सितां लभते NW **1:130** केसर°] N; केशर° KW, *ŚiDhaSaṅ* **1:131** सिद्धकेन समाहितः] NKW; सिद्धकेन तथैव हि *ŚiDhaSaṅ* **1:131** योऽर्चयेद्गंधपुष्पकैः] KW, *ŚiDhaSaṅ*; यो ऽर्चये --- N **1:132** कुब्जकैर्व्विपुलो लाभः] *ŚiDhaSaṅ*; --- NKW **1:132** सौभाग्याय च वारुणी] W, *ŚiDhaSaṅ*; --- ग्याय च वारुणी N; ⊔ य च वारुणी K **1:133** लभेदुत्तमां] NKW; लभेच्चोत्तमां *ŚiDhaSaṅ* **1:133** मल्लिकैर्ज्ज्ञानकामाय] NK; मल्लिकैर्ज्ञानकोमाय W; मल्लिका ज्ञानकामाय *ŚiDhaSaṅ* **1:133** अर्च्चयन्यो] N; अर्च्चयेद्यो KW *ŚiDhaSaṅ* **1:134** लभेत] NW; लभते K; लभन्ते *ŚiDhaSaṅ* **1:134** कुन्दैस्तु अर्चयीत शुचिर्नरः] *ŚiDhaSaṅ*; कुन्दै --- NK; कुन्दैस्तु ⊔ W **1:135** लभते बहुपुत्रत्वं धनवन्तश्चिरायुषम्] *ŚiDhaSaṅ*; --- NKW

[5^r] आरोग्यं कुशपुष्पैस्तु अशोकैः प्रियसङ्गमम्॥ 1:135॥

कर्णिकारैर्द्धनं विन्द्याद्वश्यार्थे द्रोणपुष्पिका।
कदम्बेनार्चयेल्लिंगं सततन्नियतव्रतः॥ 1:136॥

शत्रूणां वशकामाय नित्यमेव प्रदापयेत्।
नश्यन्ति व्याधयस्तस्य यो ऽर्चयेद≪रिमुस्तकैः≫॥ 1:137॥

≪सिंदुवारस्य पुष्पेण बद्धो मुच्येत बन्धनात् ≫।
[2]अङ्कोटकाश्च निर्ग्गन्धाः कृष्णाश्चैव तु ये स्मृताः॥ 1:138॥

तान्पुष्पाञ्छत्रुनाशाय देवदेवाय कल्पयेत्।
पीतकानि तु पुष्पाणि पुष्ट्यर्थे विजयाय च॥ 1:139॥

नित्यमेवन्तु यो दद्यात्सर्व्वकामानवाप्नुयात्।
सौगन्धिकाद्या जलजा वश्यार्थे तु प्रकल्पयेत्॥ 1:140॥

नीलरक्तानि पुष्पाणि नित्याकर्षकराणि तु।
सर्वकामप्रदो बिल्वो [3] दारिद्रस्य प्रणाशकः॥ 1:141॥

बिल्वपत्रात्परन्नास्ति येन तुष्यति शङ्करः।

1:135 आरोग्यं कुशपुष्पैस्तु] K, *ŚiDhaSaṅ*; --- कुशपुष्पैस्तु N; आरोग्यं कुशपुष्पं तु W **1:136** कर्ण्णिकारैर्द्धनं विन्द्याद्वश्यार्थे द्रोणपुष्पिका] N, *ŚiDhaSaṅ*; कर्णिकारैर्धनं विद्याद्वश्यार्थे द्रोणपुष्पिका K; कर्णिकारै ⁻ न विन्द्याद्वश्यार्थे द्रोणपुष्पिका W **1:136** कदम्बेनार्चयेल्लिंगं] KW, *ŚiDhaSaṅ*; यदम्बेनाचयेल्लिङ्ग N **1:137** शत्रूणां वशकामाय नित्यमेव] W, *ŚiDhaSaṅ*; शत्रूणा वशकामाय नित्यमेव N; शत्रूणां वसकामाय नित्यमेकं K **1:137** नश्यन्ति व्याधयस्तस्य यो ऽर्चयेदरिमुस्तकैः] *ŚiDhaSaṅ*; नश्यन्ति --- N; नश्यन्ति व्याधयस्तस्य यो ऽर्चयेद ⊔ K; नश्यन्ति व्याधयस्तस्य यो ऽर्चयेदति ⊔ W **1:138** सिंदुवारस्य पुष्पेण बद्धो मुच्येत बन्धनात्] *ŚiDhaSaṅ*; --- NKW **1:138** अङ्कोटकाश्च निर्ग्गन्धाः कृष्णाश्चैव तु ये स्मृताः] *conj.*; --- काश्च निर्ग्गन्धाः कृष्णाश्चैव तु ये स्मृताः NK; ⊔ ज (?) काश्च निर्ग्गत्वा कृष्णाश्चैव तु ये स्मृताः W; अंकोटासितवर्ण्णानि निर्गन्धिकुसुमानि च *ŚiDhaSaṅ* **1:139** तान् पुष्पाञ्छत्रुनाशाय] NKW; तानि शत्रुविनाशाय *ŚiDhaSaṅ* **1:139** पीतकानि तु पुष्पाणि पुष्ट्यर्थे विजयाय च] NKW; पीतकानि तु पुष्ट्यर्थे पुष्पाणि विजयाय च *ŚiDhaSaṅ* **1:140** नित्यमेवन्तु यो दद्यात् सर्व्वकामानवाप्नुयात्] NW; नित्यमेव तु यो दद्यात् सर्व्वकामानवाप्नुयान् K, *ŚiDhaSaṅ* **1:140** सौगन्धिकाद्या जलजा वश्यार्थे] NW; सौगन्धिकाद्या जलजा वंस्यार्थे K; जलजानि तु पुष्पाणि वश्यार्थे *ŚiDhaSaṅ* **1:141** नीलरक्तानि पुष्पाणि] K; --- N; नीलरक्तानि पुष्पानि W; नीलरक्तानि यो दद्यात् *ŚiDhaSaṅ* **1:141** नित्याकर्षकराणि तु] *conj.*; ---क (?) ष (?) N; ⊔ K; नित्याकय ⊔ W; तानि वश्यकराणि तु *ŚiDhaSaṅ* **1:141** सर्वकामप्रदो बिल्वो] *conj.*; --- N; ⊔ KW; सर्वकामप्रदं बिल्वं *ŚiDhaSaṅ* **1:141** दारिद्रस्य प्रणाशकः] NK; दारिद्रस्य प्रणासकः W; दारिद्र्यभयनाशनम् *ŚiDhaSaṅ*

जयार्थे दमनकं स्याद्यो ऽर्च्चयेत्परमेश्वरम्॥ 1:142॥

निर्जिताः शत्रवस्तेन यो ऽर्च्चयेत वृषध्वजम्।
मरुवः सर्वसौख्यानि जम्बुतः सर्वकामदः॥ 1:143॥

तिलको धनकामाय गोकामाय च आंकुली।
सौभाग्यदश्च तगरः किंकिराटश्च कामदः॥ 1:144॥

[4] आरोग्यञ्च धनञ्चैव प्रियङ्गुश्चैव ईप्सितम्।
शालः प्रियङ्करश्चैव किंशुको ह्यायुवर्द्धनः॥ 1:145॥

हस्त्यश्वपशुकामाय कुटजेनार्च्चयेद्धरम्।
कर्प्पूरदमकौ योज्यौ शत्रूणाञ्च विनाशने॥ 1:146॥

नश्यन्ति शत्रवः शीघ्रन्देवदेवस्य पूजनात्।
श्यामा चारोग्यदा नित्यञ्जवापुष्पस्तथैव च॥ 1:147॥

केरञ्जकश्च वश्यार्थे नित्यं लिङ्गं प्रपू[5]जयेत्।
विद्वेषे यूथिका प्रोक्ता अर्चायां परमेश्वरे॥ 1:148॥

केतकी शत्रुनाशाय क्रुद्धो लिङ्गन्तु यो ऽर्चयेत्।
सर्वकामप्रदो ह्येष व्याघ्रो देवि प्रकीर्त्तितः॥ 1:149॥

1:142 जयार्थे दमनकं स्याद्] *conj.*; जयार्थे मदनकं स्याद् N; जयार्थे मदनकं स्यात् K; जर् ⁻ थे मदनकं स्याद् W; विजयार्थे दमनकं *ŚiDhaSaṅ* **1:142** यो ऽर्च्चयेत् परमेश्वरम्] NKW; योजयेन्नियमस्थितः *ŚiDhaSaṅ* **1:143** निर्जिताः शत्रवस्तेन] NK; निर्जिताः सत्रवस्तेन W; विजिताः शत्रवस्तेन *ŚiDhaSaṅ* **1:143** यो ऽर्च्चयेत वृषध्वजम्] NKW; यो ऽर्चयेद्वृषभध्वजम् *ŚiDhaSaṅ* **1:143** मरुवः सर्वसौख्यानि] NKW; सुखं मरुवकन्दद्याज् *ŚiDhaSaṅ* **1:143** जम्बुतः] N *ŚiDhaSaṅ*; जंबू ⊔ K; जंबुटास्° W **1:144** आंकुली] N (?); ⁻⁻ली K; ⁻कुली W; वंकुली *ŚiDhaSaṅ* **1:144** सौभाग्यदश्च तगरः] W; सौभाग्यदश्च तगर N; सौभाग्यंदस्तु तगर K; सौख्यदश्चापि तगरः *ŚiDhaSaṅ* **1:144** किंकिराटश्च कामदः] W; --- NK; किङ्करातश्च कामदः *ŚiDhaSaṅ* **1:145** आरोग्यञ्च] *ŚiDhaSaṅ*; --- ग्यञ्च NKW **1:145** प्रियङ्गुश्चैव ईप्सितम्] NKW; फलिनी कामदा स्मृता *ŚiDhaSaṅ* **1:145** शालः प्रियङ्करश्चैव] NW; सालः प्रियङ्करश्चैव K; शालः प्रियकरश्चैव *ŚiDhaSaṅ* **1:145** किंशुको ह्यायुवर्द्धनः] NK; किंशुका ह्यायुवर्द्धनः W; किंशुकादायुराप्नुयात् *ŚiDhaSaṅ* **1:146** धरम्] NK; वरम् W **1:146** कर्प्पूरदमकौ योज्यौ शत्रूणाञ्च विनाशने] NK; कर्प्पूरदमकौ योज्यै शत्रूणाञ्च विनाशये W; कर्पूरदमनं दद्याच्छत्रूणाञ्च विनाशने *ŚiDhaSaṅ* **1:147** °पुष्पस्तथैव] N; °पुष्पं तथैव KW, *ŚiDhaSaṅ* **1:148** केरञ्जकश्च वश्यार्थे] K; के⏑ ञ्जकश्च वस्या ⏑ NW; कुरण्टकस्य वश्यार्थं *ŚiDhaSaṅ* **1:148** नित्यं लिङ्गं प्रपूजयेत्] *conj.*; --- जये N; ⊔ पूजयेत् K; नित्यं लिङ्गं ⁻ पूजने W; नित्यं लिङ्गस्य पूजनात् *ŚiDhaSaṅ* **1:148** प्रोक्ता अर्चायां परमेश्वरे] NKW; योज्या देवदेवे महेश्वरे *ŚiDhaSaṅ* **1:149** सर्वकामप्रदो ह्येष] NW; सर्वदामप्रदो ह्येष K; सर्वकामप्रदा ह्येषा *ŚiDhaSaṅ* **1:149** व्याघ्रो देवि प्रकीर्त्तितः] N; व्याघ्रा देवि प्रकीर्त्तितः KW; व्याघ्री देवि प्रकीर्त्तिता *ŚiDhaSaṅ*

ज्योत्स्नाकारी तथैवेह नित्यमेव हि कामदा।
वासकेनार्च्चयेद्देवं बलमायुश्च वर्द्धते॥ 1:150॥

झण्टिका सुखदा नित्यन्तथा चाप्सरचम्पकम्।
डित्वाक्षी व्याधिना [6] शाय अश्वकर्ण्णस्तथैव च॥ 1:151॥

जयन्ती जयकामाय श्वेता च गिरिकर्ण्णिका।
विद्वेषोच्चाटनार्थाय निम्बपुष्पैस्तु यो ऽर्चयेत्॥ 1:152॥

भटीमाकर्षणे प्रोक्ता मदयन्ती च या भवेत्।
ऋषिपुष्पो रुद्रजटा नाशयेत उपद्रवान्॥ 1:153॥

शणपुष्पी च या प्रोक्ता कोकिलाक्षा तथैव च।
सर्वे [5^{v}] शुक्लास्तु शान्त्यर्थे सर्व्वे पीतास्तु पौष्टिके॥ 1:154॥

नीलरक्तास्तु ये पुष्पा अर्च्चने परिकल्पिताः।
वश्याकर्षणमेवं हि सर्व्वन्तैः परिकल्पयेत्॥ 1:155॥

कृष्णांश्चैवाभिचारे तु देवदेवाय कल्पयेत्।
पत्रम्पुष्पं फलन्तोयन्तृणञ्चैव तथा पयः॥ 1:156॥

प्रत्यहं शङ्करे दद्यान्नासौ दुर्ग्गतिमाप्नुयात्।

---

156 Cf. *Śivadharmasaṅgraha* 5.110cd: सर्वरक्तन्तु वश्यार्थे कृष्णं चैवाभिचारुके॥

156 *Niśvāsamukha* 1.156c–1.158b is parallel with *Śivadharmasaṅgraha* 5.111a–5.112.

1:150 ज्योत्स्नाकारी] N, *ŚiDhaSaṅ*; ज्येकारी K; ज्यत्स्नाकारी W **1:151** झण्टिका] N; मल्लिका K (?); ⏓ श्विका W; झिण्टिका *ŚiDhaSaṅ* **1:151** डिम्बाक्षी व्याधिनाशाय] *em.*; डि --- N; ⊔ K; डित्वाक्षी का ⊔ W; डिम्बाक्षी व्याधिनाशार्थम् *ŚiDhaSaṅ* **1:152** श्वेता च] N, *ŚiDhaSaṅ*; श्वेता K (unmetrical); ¯ता च W **1:152** निम्बपुष्पैस्तु] NKW; निम्बपुष्पेण *ŚiDhaSaṅ* **1:153** भटीमाकर्षणे प्रोक्ता मदयन्ती च] N^{pc}W; भटीमाकर्षणे प्रोक्ता मदयन्तीव N^{ac}; भदीमाकर्षणे प्रोक्तो दमयन्ती च K; भण्डी चाकर्षणे योज्या मदयन्ती तु *ŚiDhaSaṅ* **1:153** ऋषिपुष्पो रुद्रजटा नाशयेत उपद्रवान्] K; ऋषिपुष्पो रुद्रजाटा नाशयेत उपद्रवान् N; ऋषिपुष्पो रुद्रजाव्य नाशयेत उपद्रवान् W; ऋषिपुष्पी रुद्रजटी हन्ति सर्वानुपद्रवान् *ŚiDhaSaṅ* **1:154** शणपुष्पी च या प्रोक्ता] NKW; शणपुष्पञ्च यत्प्रोक्तं *ŚiDhaSaṅ* **1:154** कोकिलाक्षा तथैव च] *em.*; ⏓⏓⏓ ⏓ ⏓⏓⏓⏓ N; ⊔ KW; कोकिलाक्षस्तथैव च *ŚiDhaSaṅ* **1:154** सर्वे शुक्लास्तु] W; --- शुक्लास्तु NK; सर्वशुक्लं तु *ŚiDhaSaṅ* **1:154** सर्व्वे पीतास्तु पौष्टिके] W; सर्व्वे पीतास्तु --- ष्टिके N; सर्वपीतास्तु पौष्टिके K; सर्वपीतन्तु पौष्टिके *ŚiDhaSaṅ* **1:155** सर्वन्तैः] NW; सर्वतः K **1:156** कृष्णांश्चैवाभिचारे] *conj.*; कृ ष्णाच्चेवाभिचारे N (tops missing); कृष्णांस्तु व्यभिचारे K; कृष्णा ¯वाभिचारे तु W **1:157** शङ्करे] NKW; शम्भवे *ŚiDhaSaṅ*

यस्य वृक्षस्य पत्राणि पुष्पाणि [2] च फलानि च॥ 1:157॥

महादेवाय युक्तानि सो ऽपि याति पराङ्गतिम्।
करवीराच्छतगुणमर्क्कम्बिल्वस्तथैव च॥ 1:158॥

बिल्वाद्धुकं सहस्रेण बुकाद्धुत्तूरको वरः।
एवमभ्यर्च्य देवेशन्नैवेद्यञ्च प्रकल्पयेत्॥ 1:159॥

अन्ननैवेद्यदानेन लभते सुखमक्षयम्।
देवलोकमनुप्राप्तिर्भक्षदानात्तथैव च॥ 1:160॥

लभते शिवमैश्वर्यं [3] [[((भ))]]क्षनैवेद्यदायकः।
सघृतम्पायसन्दद्यान्नैवेद्यं शम्भवे सदा॥ 1:161॥

गाणापत्यं लभेच्छीघ्रं द्वादशाब्दं कुलैस्सह।
खण्डखाद्यकृतं दद्यात्प्राप्नुयाद्गतिमुत्तमाम्॥ 1:162॥

भक्ष्यभोज्यानि दत्त्वा वै सर्व्वकामानवाप्नुयात्।
यवागूङ्कृसराम्पूपान्दत्त्वा तु सुखभाग्भवेत्॥ 1:163॥

मण्डकां सुसुमालांश्च शष्कुल्यामोदकानि च।
[4] अन्यानि फलमूलानि लेह्यचोष्याणि यानि च॥ 1:164॥

---

159 *Niśvāsamukha* 1.159c–1.160 is parallel with *Śivadharmasaṅgraha* 5.120a–5.121b.

161 *Niśvāsamukha* 1.161c–1.162b is parallel with *Śivadharmasaṅgraha* 5.122.

162 *Niśvāsamukha* 1.162c–1.165b is parallel with *Śivadharmasaṅgraha* 5.124–5.126.

1:157 पत्राणि पुष्पाणि च] *conj.*; पत्राणि --- NK; पत्राणि पु ⊔ च W; पुष्पाणि पत्राणि च *ŚiDhaSaṅ* **1:158** महादेवाय युक्तानि] NKW; महादेवोपयुक्तानि *ŚiDhaSaṅ* **1:158** परां गतिम्] K, *ŚiDhaSaṅ*; पराङ्गंतिम् N; परङ्गतिम् W **1:158** बिल्वस्तथैव] NW; बिल्वं तथैव K **1:159** सहस्रेण] NW; सहस्रण K **1:159** धुत्तूरको] NW; धत्तूरको K **1:159** च प्रकल्पयेत्] NKW; परिकल्पयेत् *ŚiDhaSaṅ* **1:160** देवलोकमनुप्राप्तिर्भक्षदानात्तथैव च] NKW; देवलोकमनुप्राप्तो भक्ष्यदानान्नरोत्तमः *ŚiDhaSaṅ* **1:161** शिवमैश्वर्यं] *conj.*; शिव --- NK; शिवमै ⊔ W **1:162** लभेच्छीघ्रं द्वादशाव्दं] K; लभेच्छीघ्रं द्वादशाव्य (?) N; लभेच्छीघ्रं द्वादशाब्दाङ्° W; भवेच्छीघ्रं द्वादशाब्दात्कुलैः *ŚiDhaSaṅ* **1:162** °कृतं दद्यात्] NKW; कृतान्दत्त्वा *ŚiDhaSaṅ* **1:163** भक्ष्यभोज्यानि दत्त्वा वै] NKW; भक्ष्यभोज्यादिकं दत्वा *ŚiDhaSaṅ* **1:163** यवागूङ्कृसराम्पूपान्] N, *ŚiDhaSaṅ*; यवागूङ्कृसरान्पूपान् K; यवा ⁻⁻सराम्पूर्यान् W **1:163** सुख°] NW, *ŚiDhaSaṅ*; स्वर्ग° K **1:164** मण्डकां सुसुमालांश्च शष्कुल्यामोदकानि च] *em.*; मण्डकां सुसुमालांश्च शष्कुल्यामोदकानि --- N; मण्डकान् सुसुमालांश्च शष्कुल्यामोदकानि च K; मण्डकां सुसुमालांश्च स ⁻ ल्यमोदकानि च W; मण्डकां सिद्धिपिण्डांश्च शष्कुलीमोदकानि च *ŚiDhaSaṅ* **1:164** अन्यानि फलमूलानि] *em.*; --- न्यानि (?) फलमूलानि N; ⊔ न्यानि फलमूलानि K; ⊔ नि फलमूलानि W; दत्वान्यफलमूलञ्च *ŚiDhaSaṅ*

दत्त्वा सर्वसुखावाप्तिरनन्तं गीतवादिते।
सकृत्कृत्वा फलं ह्येतत्तन्त्रीवाद्यस्य मे शृणु॥ 1:165॥

कृत्वासौ गणतां याति तन्त्रीवाद्यस्य वादकः।
हुडुङ्कारस्य नृत्यस्य मुखवाद्याट्टहासयोः॥ 1:166॥

त्रिष्कालञ्चैव कुर्वाणो भवेद्गणः स चोत्तमः।
एककालं द्विकालं वा त्रि[5]ष्कालं वापि नित्यशः॥ 1:167॥

ये स्मरन्ति विरूपाक्षं विज्ञेयास्ते गणेश्वराः।
षष्टितीर्थसहस्राणि षष्टिकोटिस्तथैव च॥ 1:168॥

लिङ्गप्रणामस्यैकस्य कलां नार्हति षोडशीम्।
एवं यः पूजयेदज्ञः शिवदीक्षाविवर्ज्जितः।
तस्येदं फलमुद्दिष्टमपवर्ग्गाय दीक्षिते॥ 1:169॥

≪श्रुतमेतन्मया विप्रा देव्यै [6]कथयतो≫हरात्।
मयापि कथितं तुभ्यं सत्यमीशानभाषितम्॥ 1:170॥

ऋषय ऊ॥
किं लिङ्गस्येह माहात्म्यं यत्त्वया चातिवर्ण्णितम्।
कृत्वा चैव फलं ब्रूहि यः करोति दिने दिने॥ 1:171॥

नन्दिकेश्वर उ॥

---

165 *Niśvāsamukha* 1.165c–1.169b is parallel with *Śivadharmasaṅgraha* 5.128–5.131.

169 *Niśvāsamukha* 1.169c–1.171 is parallel with *Śivadharmasaṅgraha* 5.133–5.135.

1:165 गीतवादिते] NKW; गीतवादने *ŚiDhaSaṅ* **1:165** सकृत्कृत्वा] K, *ŚiDhaSaṅ*; सकृङ्कृत्वा NW **1:166** हुडुङ्कारस्य नृत्यस्य] NK^{pc}; हुन्तुङ्कारस्य नृत्यस्य K^{ac}W; हुंदुंकारादिकं नित्यं *ŚiDhaSaṅ* **1:166** मुखवाद्याट्टहासयोः] NK; मुखवाद्या ⁻हासयाः W; मुखवाद्याट्टहासताम् *ŚiDhaSaṅ* **1:167** त्रिष्कालञ्चैव कुर्वाणो भवेद्गणः स चोत्तमः] K; त्रिष्कालञ्चैव कुर्वाणो भवेद्गण स चोत्तमः NW; त्रिकालञ्चैव कुर्वाणः स भवेदुत्तमो गणः *ŚiDhaSaṅ* **1:167** एककालं द्विकालं वा त्रिष्कालं वापि नित्यशः] K, *ŚiDhaSaṅ*; --- ष्कालं वापि नित्यशः N; एककाल द्विकाल ⊔ लं चापि नित्यशः W **1:169** कलां नार्हति] K, *ŚiDhaSaṅ*; कलानार्घन्ति NW **1:169** अपवर्ग्गाय दीक्षिते] KW; अ --- ग्गाय दीक्षि --- N; निर्वाणं दीक्षितस्य तु *ŚiDhaSaṅ* **1:170** श्रुतमेतन्मया विप्रा देव्यै कथयतो हरात्] *ŚiDhaSaṅ*; ⏑̆ रात् N; शंकरात् K; ⊔ हरात् W **1:171** ऊ] NW; ऊचुः K, *ŚiDhaSaṅ* **1:171** लिङ्गस्येह] NK; लिङ्गस्येक W; लिङ्गस्य हि *ŚiDhaSaṅ* **1:171** यत्त्वया चातिवर्ण्णितम्] NKW; त्वया यदिति वर्ण्णितम् *ŚiDhaSaṅ* **1:172** उ] NW; उवाच K, *ŚiDhaSaṅ*

[[((ब्रह्मविष्णुविवादन्तु [6^r] पू))]]र्व्ववृत्तं हि यद्भवेत्।
अहं कारणकर्त्तेति जले तेजस्समुत्थितम्॥ 1:172॥

तेजोमध्ये स्थितं लिङ्गम्पर्व्वाङ्गुष्ठप्रमाणतः।
उभौ तौ विस्मितौ तत्र किमेतच्चाद्भुतम्भवेत्॥ 1:173॥

उभौ तौ द्रष्टुमारब्धौ ततो लिङ्गं विवर्द्धितम्।
आश्चर्यमिति सञ्चिन्त्य अधश्चोर्ध्वङ्गतावुभौ॥ 1:174॥

≪अधो गतस्ततो विष्णुर्≫ऊ[2]र्ध्वम्ब्रह्मा ततो गतः।
अन्तं चास्य न पश्यन्तौ खिन्नावेतावुभावपि॥ 1:175॥

पुनश्चैव समागम्य स्तोत्रेण तुष्टुवे हरम्।
ततस्तुष्टो महादेवो वरन्दत्त्वा उभावपि॥ 1:176॥

पुरुषरूपी स्थितो भूत्वा यदभीष्टन्ददामि ते।
ब्रह्मा वदति पुत्रस्तु त्वमेव भव सुव्रत॥ 1:177॥

---

172 Cf. *Śivadharmasaṅgraha* 5.136: ब्रह्माब्रवीदहं कर्त्ता तथैवाह गदाधरः। इत्येवं वदतोरग्रे प्रादुरासीज्जले विभुः॥

173 *Niśvāsamukha* 1.173–1.176 is parallel with *Śivadharmasaṅgraha* 5.137–5.140.

177 Cf. *Śivadharmasaṅgraha* 5.143c–5.144b: यदा ते सम्भवेत्पुत्रो भवानेव तदा प्रभुः। तथैवाह तथा ब्रह्मा पुत्रो मे भव इत्यमुम्॥

1:172 हि] NW; तु K **1:172** कारणकर्त्तेति] K; कारणकंर्त्तेति N; कारणकंर्त्तति W **1:172** जले तेजस्समुत्थितम्] *conj.*; जले तेजस्ममुत्थितम् NW; जलतेजस्ममुत्थितम् K **1:173** लिङ्गम्पर्व्वाङ्गुष्ठप्रमाणतः] K; लि ⏑ म्पर्व्वङ्गुष्ठप्रमाणतः N; लिङ्गम्पर्व्वङ्गुष्ठप्रमाणतः W; लिङ्गम्पर्व्वाङ्गुष्ठप्रमाणकम् *ŚiDhaSaṅ* **1:173** किमेतच्चाद्भुतम्भवेत्] NKW; किञ्चेदमिति चाहतुः *ŚiDhaSaṅ* **1:174** द्रष्टुमारब्धौ] N, *ŚiDhaSaṅ*; द्रटुमारब्धौ K; द्रष्टमारब्धौ W **1:174** ततो लिङ्गं विवर्द्धितम्] W; ततो लिङ्ग विवद्धितम् N; ततो लिङ्ग विवर्द्धितम् K; वर्द्धमानस्ततो विभुः *ŚiDhaSaṅ* **1:174** आश्चर्यमिति सञ्चिन्त्य] *ŚiDhaSaṅ*; आश्चर्यमिति सञ्चि --- य N; ⊔ K; आश्चयं मिति स ⊔ W **1:174** अधश्चोर्ध्वङ्गतावुभौ] *conj.*; अधश्चोध्व --- N; ⊔ KW; अध ऊर्ध्वङ्गतावुभौ *ŚiDhaSaṅ* **1:175** अधो गतस्ततो विष्णुरूर्ध्वं] *ŚiDhaSaṅ*; --- र्द्धम् NW; ऊर्ध्वं K **1:175** ततो गतः] NKW; जगाम च *ŚiDhaSaṅ* **1:175** अन्तं चास्य] K, *ŚiDhaSaṅ*; अन्तचास्य N; अन्त ⁻स्य W **1:175** °तावुभावपि] NKW; °तौ सुरोत्तमौ *ŚiDhaSaṅ* **1:176** स्तोत्रेण तुष्टुवे हरम्] NK; स्तोत्रेण तुष्टुव हरम् W; स्तोत्रैस्तुष्टुवतुर्हरम् *ŚiDhaSaṅ* **1:176** वरन्दत्त्वा उभावपि] NKW; ब्रह्माणमिदमब्रवीत् *ŚiDhaSaṅ* **1:177** यदभीष्टन्ददामि] N; यदभीष्ट ददामि K; यदभीष्टन्ददायि W **1:177** सुव्रत] K; सुव्रतः NW

एवमस्त्वब्रवीद्देवः ≪किंत्वपूज्यो भविष्य[3]सि ≫।
अनानुरूपं यस्माद्धि वरन्ते काङ्क्षितं द्विज॥ 1:178॥

विष्णो ददामि ते ह्यद्य वरमिष्टं वदस्व मे।
मम वाक्यममिथ्यं हि ब्रूहि यत्ते ऽभिकाङ्क्षितम्॥ 1:179॥

विष्णुरुवाच।
यदि तुष्टो ऽसि मे देव वरं मे दातुमिच्छसि।
त्वद्भक्तस्त्वत्प्रियश्चैव भविष्यामि न संशयः॥ 1:180॥

ईश्वर उवाच।
एवं भवतु ≪भद्रन्ते≫[4]रुद्रनारायणी प्रजा।
उभयोरन्तरन्नास्ति केशवस्य हरस्य च॥ 1:181॥

एष एव हि लिङ्गन्तु स्थापितं ब्रह्मविष्णुना।
सेन्द्रैर्देवैश्च असुरैः सयक्षोरगराक्षसैः॥ 1:182॥

सिद्धैर्विद्याधरैर्भूतैरप्सरोरगकिन्नरैः।
पिशाचैर्ग्रहनक्षत्रैस्तथा च मुनिसत्तमैः॥ 1:183॥

संपूज्य वरदं देवं वरं लब्ध्वा तु रेमि[5]रे।

---

178 *Niśvāsamukha* 1.178 is parallel with *Śivadharmasaṅgraha* 5.144c–5.145b.

179 *Niśvāsamukha* 1.179–1.185 is parallel with *Śivadharmasaṅgraha* 5.150–5.156.

1:178 एवमस्त्वब्रवीद्देवः] *conj.*; एवम ⏑ ⏑ f --- N; ⊔ K; ⊔ मु ˉ यौ ⊔ W; तथास्त्वित्यब्रवीद्देवः *ŚiDhaSaṅ* **1:178 किंत्वपूज्यो भविष्यसि**] *ŚiDhaSaṅ*; --- सि NK; ⊔ अपू ⊔ सि W **1:178 अनानुरूपं**] N *ŚiDhaSaṅ*; अंभोनुरूपं K; अनान्नरूपं W **1:179 विष्णो ददामि ते ह्यद्य**] K; विष्णोर्द्दादामि ते ह्यद्य N; विष्णोर्द्ददामि ते ह्यद्य W; विष्णो ददामि ते वत्स *ŚiDhaSaṅ* **1:179 वाक्यममिथ्यं**] NKW; वाक्यममिथ्या *ŚiDhaSaṅ* **1:180 वरं मे दातुमिच्छसि**] K^{pc}; वरमे दातुमिच्छसि NW; वरं दातुमिच्छसि K^{ac}; वरं दातुमिहेच्छसि *ŚiDhaSaṅ* **1:180 संशयः**] NW, *ŚiDhaSaṅ*; सशयः K **1:181 ईश्वर उवाच**] KW; ईश्वर उव --- N; महेश्वर उवाच *ŚiDhaSaṅ* **1:181 एवं भवतु भद्रं ते**] *ŚiDhaSaṅ*; --- NK; एवं भवन्तु ⊔ W **1:181 उभयोरन्तरन्नास्ति**] NKW; आवयोरन्तरं नास्ति *ŚiDhaSaṅ* **1:181 केशवस्य हरस्य च**] NW; केशवस्य शिवस्य च K; वरदंवरयोरिव *ŚiDhaSaṅ* **1:182 एष एव हि लिङ्गन्तु स्थापितं**] NW; एतच्चैव हि लिङ्गं तु स्थापित K; एष एव हि लिङ्गो हि स्थापितं *ŚiDhaSaṅ* **1:182 सेन्द्रैर्देवैश्च असुरैः**] NKW; इन्द्रादिभिः सुरैर्दैत्यैः *ŚiDhaSaṅ* **1:183 तथा च**] NKW; तथैव *ŚiDhaSaṅ* **1:184 संपूज्य वरदं देवं वरं लब्ध्वा तु रेमिरे**] *ŚiDhaSaṅ*; सम्पू वरद --- रे N; सम्पूवरय ⊔ K; सम्पू वरदन्देवं वरं ल ⊔ रे W

सर्वकामप्रदं लिङ्गमेतदुक्तो मयानघाः॥ 1:184॥

ब्रह्माविष्णुमहेन्द्रनागमुनयो यक्षास्सविद्याधराः
संसारार्णवदुःखभीतमनसो लिङ्गार्च्चने तत्पराः।
स्तुन्वन्ते च वरार्थिनो -र्-अहरहः कृत्वाञ्जलिम्मस्तके
ये मर्त्या न नमन्ति ईदृशमजं क्षेमस्तु तेषां कुतः॥ 1:185॥

॥ ⊗॥ [[((इति))]] निश्वासमुखतत्त्वसं [6]हितायां लौकिके धर्म्मे प्रथमः पटलः॥ ⊗॥

श्लोकशतं सप्ताशीत्यधिकम्॥ ⊗॥

1:184 सर्वकामप्रदं लिङ्गमेतदुक्तो मयानघाः] *conj.*; सर्वकामप्रदं लिङ्गमेतदुक्तो मयानघ N; सर्वकामप्रदं लिङ्गमेतदुक्तो मयानघ K; सर्वकामप्रदं लिङ्गमेतद्दुक्ता मयानघः W; सर्वकामप्रदो लिङ्ग एष उक्तो मयानघाः *ŚiDhaSaṅ* **1:185** ब्रह्माविष्णुमहेन्द्रनागमुनयो] NK; ब्रह्माविष्णुमहेन्द्रागमुनयो W; ब्रह्मोपेन्द्रमहेन्द्रनागमुनयो *ŚiDhaSaṅ* **1:185** °मनसो] N[pc]W, *ŚiDhaSaṅ*; °मसो N[ac]; °मनसा K **1:185** स्तुन्वन्ते च वरात्र्थिनो -र्-अहरहः] N; स्तुन्वन्ते च वरार्थिनो ह्यहरहः K; स्तुत्वन्ते च वरार्थिनो -र्-अहरहः W; भक्तिप्रह्वधिय स्तुवन्त्यहरहः *ŚiDhaSaṅ* **1:185** ईदृशमजं क्षेमस्तु तेषां कुतः] NKW; तं सुरगुरुं ते घ्नन्ति स्वं मुष्टिभिः *ŚiDhaSaṅ* **1:185** निश्वासमुखतत्त्वसम्] K; --- N; ⊔ W

निश्वासमुखतत्त्वसंहितायां द्वितीयः पटलः॥

ऋषय ऊ॥

कृतस्यैव तु लिङ्गस्य स्थापितस्य तु यत्फलम्।
प्रत्यहं कुरुते यस्तु किं वा [6^{v}] तस्य फलम्भवेत्॥ 2:1॥

नन्दिरुवाच।
क्रीडमानास्तु ये बाला लिङ्गङ्कुर्वन्ति पांशुना।
लभ्यन्त्येकान्ततो राज्यं निस्सपत्नमकंटकम्॥ 2:2॥

प्रत्यहं कुरुते यस्तु विधिमेतदजानता।
केवलं भक्तिमालम्ब्य शृणु तस्यापि यत्फलम्॥ 2:3॥

धनम्भोगान्तथा राज्यं यः कृत्वा पूजयेच्छिवम्।
लिङ्गपूजयिता नित्यं महतीं [2] श्रियमश्नुते॥ 2:4॥

---

1 *Niśvāsamukha* 2.1a–2.18b is parallel with *Śivadharmasaṅgraha* 6.1a–6.17f.

2 Cf. *Śivadharmaśāstra* 3.77c–78b: पांशुना क्रीडमानोऽपि लिङ्गं कुर्यात्तु यो नरः॥ प्रत्यन्ते लभते राज्यमसपत्नमकण्टकम्।

2:0 ऊ] NW; ऊचुः K, *ŚiDhaSaṅ* **2:1** स्थापितस्य तु] KW, *ŚiDhaSaṅ*; स्थापितस्य स्तु N **2:1** प्रत्यहं कुरुते यस्तु किं वा तस्य] K; प्रत्यं कुरु ⏓⏓⏓ किं वा --- स्य N; प्रत्यं कु ⊔ किं वा तस्य W; प्रत्यहं कुरुते यस्तु किन्तस्यापि *ŚiDhaSaṅ* **2:2** नन्दिरुवाच] NKW; नन्दिकेश्वर उवाच *ŚiDhaSaṅ* **2:2** क्रीडमानास्तु] NKW; क्रीडन्तो ऽपि च *ŚiDhaSaṅ* **2:2** लभ्यन्त्येकान्ततो] NK; लभ्यन्त्येकोन्ततो W; लभन्ते राज्यमेकान्ते *ŚiDhaSaṅ* **2:3** प्रत्यहं कुरुते यस्तु विधिमेतदजानता] NKW; प्रत्यहम्विधिहीनं तु लिङ्गं यः कुरुते नरः *ŚiDhaSaṅ* **2:4** भोगान्तथा] भोगान्तथा NW; भोगांस्तथा K; भोग्यम्तथा *ŚiDhaSaṅ* **2:4** कृत्वा पूजयेच्छिवम्] K; कृत्वा ⏓ जयेच्छिवम् N; कृ -पूजयेच्छिवम् W; कृत्वा पूजयेत्सदा *ŚiDhaSaṅ* **2:4** लिङ्गपूजयिता नित्यं महतीं] *conj. Acharya*; लिङ्ग --- N; लिङ्गं पूजयिता ⊔ K; लिङ्गपूजयित W; लिङ्गं पूजयिता नित्यं महतीं *ŚiDhaSaṅ*

सहस्रमर्च्चयन्विद्यान्निरयन्न तु पश्यति।
रुद्रलोकमवाप्नोति भुक्त्वा भोगाननिन्दितान्॥ 2:5॥

लक्षन्तु कुरुते यस्तु तस्यैकं ज्वलते ध्रुवम्।
दृष्ट्वा लिङ्गञ्ज्वलन्तन्तु सिद्धो देवत्वमाप्नुयात्॥ 2:6॥

लक्षैर्द्दशभिरिन्द्रत्वं ब्रह्मत्वं विंशभिः स्मृतम्।
विष्णुत्वन्त्रिंशभिर्लक्षै रुद्रत्वं तु चतुर्गुणैः॥ 2:7॥

[3] पञ्चगव्येन संमार्ज्य मृदा लिङ्गन्तु कारयेत्।
अन्नलिङ्गन्तु कुर्वाणो लभते ईप्सितं फलम्॥ 2:8॥

गुडलिङ्गं समभ्यर्च्य लभेत्सौभाग्यमुत्तमम्।
कन्याशतपतिश्चैव प्रातिराज्येश्वरो भवेत्॥ 2:9॥

नारी च स्त्रीसहस्रेण समन्तात्परिवारिता।
लभेत्सौभाग्यमतुलं सर्वेषामुपरि स्थिता॥ 2:10॥

[4] नन्दते पुत्रपौत्रैस्तु सुखञ्चात्यन्तमश्नुते।
अर्च्चयेन्नरनारी वा गुडलिङ्गन्तु नित्यशः॥ 2:11॥

सितेन कृत्वा लिङ्गन्तु प्रत्यहं यस्समर्च्चयेत्।
सर्वकामानवाप्नोति मासैः षड्भिर्न्न संशयः॥ 2:12॥

नवनीतमये लिङ्गे लभते ईप्सितं फलम्।

2:5 भोगाननिन्दितान्] K, *ŚiDhaSaṅ*; भोगाननि ⏑̆ ि तान् NW **2:6** ज्वलते] NKW; ज्वलति *ŚiDhaSaṅ* **2:6** ज्वलन्तन्तु] NKW; ज्वलन्तञ्च *ŚiDhaSaṅ* **2:7** ब्रह्मत्वं विंशभिः स्मृतम्] NK; ब्रह्मत्वं विंशतिः स्मृतम् W (unmetrical); स्कन्दं विंशतिभिः स्मृतम् *ŚiDhaSaṅ* **2:7** विष्णुत्वन्त्रिंशभिर्लक्षै] *conj.*; विष्णुत्वन्त्रिंभिर्लक्षै N; विष्णुत्वं त्रिभिर्लक्षैस्तु K; विष्णुत्वन्त्रिभिर्ल्लक्षै W; त्रिंशल्लक्षैः सुरारित्वं *ŚiDhaSaṅ* **2:7** रुद्रत्वं तु चतुर्गुणैः] *ŚiDhaSaṅ*; --- NK; रुद्रत्वं तु चतु ⊔ W **2:8** संमार्ज्य] *ŚiDhaSaṅ*; संमर्ज्य NW; संमर्द्य K **2:8** मृदा लिङ्गन्तु कारयेत्] NKW; यदा लिङ्गं तु पूजयेत् *ŚiDhaSaṅ* **2:8** अन्नलिङ्गन्तु] NKW; अन्नलिङ्गञ्च *ŚiDhaSaṅ* **2:8** लभते ईप्सितं फलम्] NWK; लभते कामिकं फलम् *ŚiDhaSaṅ* **2:9** लभेत्सौभाग्यमुत्तमम्] NKW; परं सौभाग्यमाप्नुयात् *ŚiDhaSaṅ* **2:10** समन्तात्परिवारिता] NKW; सापत्नैः परिवारिता *ŚiDhaSaṅ* **2:10** सर्वेषामुपरि स्थिता] *ŚiDhaSaṅ*; सर्वे --- N; सर्व ⊔ K; सर्वासामुपरि स्थिता W **2:11** नन्दते] *conj.*; --- न्दते; NW; मोदते K; रमते *ŚiDhaSaṅ* **2:11** सुखञ्चात्यन्तमश्नुते] NK; सुखञ्चात्यन्तमस्तुते W; सुखमानंत्यमश्नुते *ŚiDhaSaṅ* **2:11** अर्चयेन्नरनारी वा] NW, *ŚiDhaSaṅ*; अर्चये ना च नारीं वा K **2:11** गुडलिङ्गन्तु] NKW; खण्डलिङ्गञ्च *ŚiDhaSaṅ* **2:12** मासैः षड्भिर्न्न] NKW; षड्भिर्मासैर्न *ŚiDhaSaṅ* **2:13** ईप्सितं] NKW; चेप्सितं *ŚiDhaSaṅ*

षण्मासेनैव युक्तात्मा शिवलोकं स गच्छति॥ 2:13॥

प्र≪त्यहं पत्रलि≫[5]ङ्गन्तु तु यः कृत्वा तु समर्चयेत्।
लभेन्महान्तमैश्वर्यम्भुङ्क्ते च निरुजः सदा॥ 2:14॥

पृथिव्या आधिपत्यन्तु पुष्पलिङ्गस्य पूजनात्।
लभते निस्सपत्नस्तु भुङ्क्ते चैव ददाति च॥ 2:15॥

लावणेन तु लिङ्गेन लभेत्सौभाग्यमुत्तमम्।
नित्यैश्वर्यमखण्डञ्च प्रत्यहं यो ऽभिपूजयेत्॥ 2:16॥

सच्चकेन ≪तु लिङ्गानि≫पा[6]र्थिवानि तु कारयेत्।
सहस्रपूजनात्सो हि लभते ईप्सितं फलम्॥ 2:17॥

लक्षेणैकेन गणतां कोटिमभ्यर्च्य गच्छति।
स्वशरीरेण सायोज्यं पुनश्च न निवर्त्तते॥ 2:18॥

एतान्येव समभ्यर्च्य सदेवासुरमानुषाः।
[7r]सर्वकामसमृद्धाश्च सुखदुःखविवर्जिताः॥ 2:19॥

ईश्वरस्य प्रसादेन क्रीडन्ते अणिमादिभिः।
अष्टेष्टकसमायुक्तं ये कुर्व्वन्ति शिवालयम्॥ 2:20॥

तावत्ते दिवि तिष्ठन्ति यावदिन्द्राश्चतुर्द्दश।
मणिरत्नप्रवालानि स्फटिम्र्म्मरकतानि च॥ 2:21॥

---

18 *Niśvāsamukha* 2.18c–2.35 is parallel with *Śivadharmasaṅgraha* 6.39a–6.56b.

2:13 युक्तात्मा] K, *ŚiDhaSaṅ*; मुक्त्यात्मा NW **2:13** स गच्छति] K; ⏑̄ --- N⊔ W; च गच्छति *ŚiDhaSaṅ* **2:14** प्रत्यहं पत्रलिङ्गन्तु] *ŚiDhaSaṅ*; --- ङ्गन्तु NK; प्र ⊔ W **2:14** लभेन्महान्तमैश्वर्यम्भुङ्क्ते च] NK; लभेन्महान्तमैश्वर्यम्भुंक्ता च W; लभेच्चोत्तममैश्वर्यं स भुंक्ते *ŚiDhaSaṅ* **2:14** निरुजः] K, *ŚiDhaSaṅ*; निरुजाः NW **2:15** पृथिव्या आधिपत्यन्तु] NKW; पृथिव्यामाधिपत्यञ्च *ŚiDhaSaṅ* **2:15** निस्सपत्नस्तु] NKW; निःसपत्नन्तु *ŚiDhaSaṅ* **2:16** यो ऽभिपूजयेत्] W, *ŚiDhaSaṅ*; यो ऽभि --- NK **2:17** सच्चकेन तु लिङ्गानि पार्थिवानि] *ŚiDhaSaṅ*; --- र्त्थिवानि N; ⊔ पार्थिवानि K; सच्चकेन ⊔ र्त्थिवानि W **2:17** ईप्सितं] NKW; चेप्सितं *ŚiDhaSaṅ* **2:17** फलम्] K, *ŚiDhaSaṅ*; --- NW **2:18** लक्षेणैकेन] NW, *ŚiDhaSaṅ*; लक्षेनैकेन K **2:18** कोटिमभ्यर्च्य गच्छति] NKW; कोट्यामभ्यर्च्य गच्छति *ŚiDhaSaṅ* **2:19** एतान्येव] NW, *ŚiDhaSaṅ*; एतांश्चैव K **2:19** सुखदुःख°] NKW; सर्वदुःख° *ŚiDhaSaṅ* **2:20** क्रीडन्ते अणिमादिभिः] NKW; प्रक्रीडंत्यणिमादिभिः *ŚiDhaSaṅ* **2:20** अष्टेष्टकसमायुक्तं] *ŚiDhaSaṅ*; अष्टेष्टकसमायुक्त NW; अष्टेष्टकसमायुक्ता K **2:21** स्फटिम्र्म्मरकतानि च] *conj.*; स्फटिम्र्म्मरकतानि --- N; स्फटी मारकती ⊔ K; स्फाटिम्र्म्मरकतानि च W; स्फटिकं मरकतानि च *ŚiDhaSaṅ*

काचहेम≪जरौप्याणि ≫ताम्रकांस्यानि ≪यानि तु।
रैत्यलोहक≫[2]सैस्यानि त्रापुषाणि तथैव च॥ 2:22॥

पुनश्चैतानि चाभ्यर्च्य भुत्का कामाञ्छिवम्व्रजेत्।
न तस्य पुनरावृत्तिर्यो लिङ्गं स्थापयेद्भुवि॥ 2:23॥

कृत्वा प्रासादमध्ये तु स शिवो नात्र संशयः।
दशाम्रवापी घोराणि नरकाणि न पश्यति॥ 2:24॥

आरामस्यैव यः कर्ता स्वर्गे मोदति चेन्द्रवत्।
ल्रक्षादींश्च तथा[3] वृक्षां पथि कुर्वन्ति ये नराः॥ 2:25॥

छायाभिः शीतलाभिश्च ते यान्ति यमसादनम्।
याम्यदुःखानि घोराणि न च तेषाम्भवन्ति हि॥ 2:26॥

वृक्षवापनधर्म्मो ऽयमेष ते परिकीर्त्तितः।
प्रासादं कारयित्वा तु विष्णुं ये स्थापयन्ति हि॥ 2:27॥

विष्णुलोकं व्रजन्त्येते मोदन्ते विष्णुना सह।
ब्रह्माणं स्कंदं[4] रुद्राणीं गणेशम्मातरं रविम्॥ 2:28॥

वह्निं शतक्रतुं यक्षं वायुम्धर्म्मञ्जलेश्वरम्।
यो यस्य स्थापनङ्कुर्यात्प्रासादे तु सुशोभने॥ 2:29॥

पूजये परया भक्त्या सो ऽमृतो ह्यस्य लोकताम्।

2:22 काचहेमजरौप्याणि ताम्रकांस्यानि यानि तु] *ŚiDhaSaṅ*; काचहेम --- ताम्रकास्यानि --- N; ⊔ KW **2:22** रैत्यलोहकसैस्यानि] *ŚiDhaSaṅ*; --- सैस्यानि NKW **2:23** पुनश्चैतानि चाभ्यर्च्य] NKW; पुनश्चैतान्समभ्यर्च्य *ŚiDhaSaṅ* **2:23** भुत्का] N, *ŚiDhaSaṅ*; भुंक्ता K; भुक्ता W **2:24** दशाम्रवापी] *ŚiDhaSaṅ*; दशास्रवापी NKW **2:24** घोराणि नरकाणि न] K; घोराणि नरकानि न N; द्योराणि नरकानि W; नरकानतिघोरान्न *ŚiDhaSaṅ* **2:25** आरामस्यैव] NKW; आरामस्य च *ŚiDhaSaṅ* **2:25** चेन्द्रवत्] NK; चन्द्रवत् W; इन्द्रवत् *ŚiDhaSaṅ* **2:25** ल्रक्षादींश्च तथा] *ŚiDhaSaṅ*; --- N; ल्रक्षादाश्च ⊔ K; ल्रक्षादींश्च त ⊔ W **2:25** वृक्षां] NW; वृक्षार K; वृक्षान् *ŚiDhaSaṅ* **2:26** छायाभिः] N[pc], *ŚiDhaSaṅ*KW; छायाभि N[ac] **2:26** ते यान्ति यमसादनम्] NKW; न ते यान्ति यमालयम् *ŚiDhaSaṅ* **2:28** सह] K, *ŚiDhaSaṅ*; ⏑̱ --- N; ⊔ W **2:28** ब्रह्माणं स्कंदं रुद्राणीं] *conj.*; --- रुद्राणीं N; ब्रह्माणं स्कं ⊔ रुद्राणीं K; ब्रह्माणं स्क ⊔ रुद्राणीं W; ब्रह्माणीस्कन्दरुद्राणीं *ŚiDhaSaṅ* **2:28** गणेशम्मातरं रविम्] NKW; मातॄन् गणपतिं रविम् *ŚiDhaSaṅ* **2:29** यो यस्य स्थापनङ्कुर्यात्प्रासादे तु] NW; यो यस्य स्थापने कुर्यात्प्रासादे तु K; यो यं स्थापयते धीमान्प्रासादे च *ŚiDhaSaṅ* **2:30** पूजये] NW; पूजयेत् K, *ŚiDhaSaṅ* **2:30** सो ऽमृतो ह्यस्य लोकताम्] NKW; स मृतस्तत्पदं व्रजेत् *ŚiDhaSaṅ*

असङ्क्रमपथे यस्तु सङ्क्रमङ्कारयिष्यति॥ 2:30॥

धर्म्मराजपथे सो हि सुपथेनैव गच्छति।
नदीं वैतरणीं चैव [5]-म्-उष्णतोयाम्महारवाम्॥ 2:31॥

गम्भीरावर्त्तदुस्तारां सन्तरेत्सङ्क्रमेण तु।
सेतुबन्धन्तु यः कुर्यात्कर्द्दमे पथि दारुणे॥ 2:32॥

धर्म्मराजपुरे सो हि दुर्ग्गमे सुखयाय्यसौ।
पङ्कलेपश्च नरकस्तप्तत्रपुजतुश्च यः॥ 2:33॥

सन्तरेन्नरकान्घोरान्नालीमार्गप्रयायिनः।
मठस्यावसथस्यैव मण्डपस्य च [6]कारिणः॥ 2:34॥

धर्म्मराजपुरङ्गत्वा स्वर्ग्गे हेममयङ्गृहम्।
तप्ताङ्गारशिलावर्षे न भयन्तस्य विद्यते॥ 2:35॥

मठस्यावसथस्यैव मण्डपस्य च यत्फलम्।
कथितं सर्वमेतत्तु दानस्य तु फलं शृणु॥ 2:36॥

अन्नदाता नरो यो हि नासौ दुर्ग्गतिमाप्नुयात्।
अक्षयं सुखमाप्नोति ब्रह्मलोकगतो भवेत्॥ 2:37॥

---

37 *Niśvāsamukha* 2.37a–2.38b is parallel with *Śivadharmasaṅgraha* 6.56c–6.57.

2:30 असङ्क्रमपथे] NKW; अचंक्रमपथे *ŚiDhaSaṅ* **2:31** धर्मराजपथे] NKW; धर्मराजपथं *ŚiDhaSaṅ* **2:31** नदीं वैतरणीं चैव] K; --- N; नदी वैतरणीम्चा ⊔ W; नदीं वैतरणीं घोराम् *ŚiDhaSaṅ* **2:31** मुष्णतोयां महारवाम्] NKW; उष्णतोयां महार्ण्णवाम् *ŚiDhaSaṅ* **2:32** गम्भीरावर्त्तदुस्तारां] *ŚiDhaSaṅ*; गम्भीरावर्त्तदुस्तारा NW; ⊔ म्भीरावत्तदुस्तारा K **2:32** सेतुबन्धन्तु] NKW; सेतुबन्धञ्च *ŚiDhaSaṅ* **2:33** धर्म्मराजपुरे] NW, *ŚiDhaSaṅ*; धर्म्मराज ⊔ K **2:33** सो हि] NKW; मार्ग्गे *ŚiDhaSaṅ* **2:33** सुखयाय्यसौ] N; सुखं यात्यसौ K; सुखमाप्यसौ W; स सुखं व्रजेत् *ŚiDhaSaṅ* **2:33** तप्तत्रपुजतुश्च यः] NK; तप्ते त्रपुजतुश्च यः W; तप्तत्रपुजतूनि च *ŚiDhaSaṅ* **2:34** सन्तरेन्नरकान्घोरान्] *em.*; सन्तरेन्नर्कान्घोरो N; सन्तरेन्नरका घोरान् K; सन्तरेन्नरकात् घोरा W; सन्तरेत्तानि घोराणि *ŚiDhaSaṅ* **2:34** नालीमार्गप्रयायिनः] NW; नातीमार्गप्रयायिनः K; नदीमार्ग्गप्रदायकः *ŚiDhaSaṅ* **2:34** मठस्यावसथस्यैव मण्डपस्य च] *ŚiDhaSaṅ*; मठस्यावसथस्यैव मण्डपस्य ⊔ K; मठ --- N; ⊔ थस्यैव मते पस्य W **2:34** कारिणः] *em.*; --- णः NK; कारकः *ŚiDhaSaṅ* **2:35** धर्म्मराजपुरङ्गत्वा स्वर्ग्गे हेममयङ्गृहम्] NKW; त्यक्त्वा यमपुरं स्वर्ग्गे तस्य हेमगृहं भवेत् *ŚiDhaSaṅ* **2:35** तप्ताङ्गारशिलावर्षे न] W, *ŚiDhaSaṅ*; तप्ताङ्गारशिलावेषे न NK **2:35** विद्यते] NKW; जायते *ŚiDhaSaṅ* **2:37** दुर्ग्गति°] NKW; नरक° *ŚiDhaSaṅ* **2:37** ब्रह्मलोकगतो भवेत्] KW; --- N; ब्रह्मलोकगतो नरः *ŚiDhaSaṅ*

[7^v] न तस्य सम्भवो मर्त्ये यावद्ब्रह्मा न नश्यति।
यस्तु ग्रीष्मे प्रपान्दद्यात्तृष्णार्त्ते पथिके जने॥ 2:38॥

ते तृप्ताः प्रेतभवने तृषाद्वन्द्वविवर्ज्जिताः।
देवान्पितॄं समुद्दिश्य यो ददाति तिलोदकान्॥ 2:39॥

तृप्तास्तु पितरस्तस्य वर्ज्जिता नरकैस्त्रिभिः।
सपूयासृग्मेदह्रदे न निमज्जन्ति ते नराः॥ 2:40॥

पितरस्तु ≪विमुक्ताः स्युः≫[2]तिलोदकफलेन तु।
अजिनं तिलपूर्ण्णन्तु रौप्यक्षुरसमन्वितम्॥ 2:41॥

हेमशृङ्गं सचैलाङ्गं कान्सदोहन्तु यो ददेत्।
अक्षयांल्लभते लोकांस्तिलधेनुप्रदाय्यसौ॥ 2:42॥

युगान्ते च परिभ्रष्टो जायते विपुले कुले।
श्राद्धङ्कुर्वन्ति ये नित्यं पितृभक्ता हि मानवाः॥ 2:43॥

---

38 *Niśvāsamukha* 2.38c–2.39b is parallel with *Śivadharmasaṅgraha* 6.59.

39 *Niśvāsamukha* 2.39c–2.41b is parallel with *Śivadharmasaṅgraha* 6.65–6.66.

41 *Niśvāsamukha* 2.41c–2.42b is parallel with *Śivadharmasaṅgraha* 6.76c–6.77b.

42 *Niśvāsamukha* 2.42c–2.43b is parallel with *Śivadharmasaṅgraha* 6.78c–6.78f.

43 *Niśvāsamukha* 2.43c–2.46 is parallel with *Śivadharmasaṅgraha* 6.67a–6.70b.

2:38 न तस्य सम्भवो मर्त्ये] *ŚiDhaSaṅ*; न सम्भवो मर्त्ये K; --- म्भवोम्मर्त्ये N; ⊔ स्य सम्भवोर्म्मर्त्ये W **2:38** यस्तु] KW, *ŚiDhaSaṅ*; यस्तुं N **2:38** तृष्णार्त्ते] NW; तृषार्ते K, *ŚiDhaSaṅ* **2:39** प्रेतभवने] NW, *ŚiDhaSaṅ*; प्रेतभावेन K **2:39** तिलोदकान्] NKW; तिलोदकम् *ŚiDhaSaṅ* **2:40** तृप्तास्तु] NKW; तृप्यन्ति *ŚiDhaSaṅ* **2:40** नरकैस्त्रिभिः] *ŚiDhaSaṅ*; नरकैस्तृभिः NW; नरकै ⊔ भिः K **2:40** सपूयासृग्मेदह्रदे] NKW; मेदोऽसृक्पूयगर्तेषु *ŚiDhaSaṅ* **2:40** ते नराः] KW, *ŚiDhaSaṅ*; --- N **2:41** पितरस्तु] KW; --- N; पितरश्च *ŚiDhaSaṅ* **2:41** विमुक्ताः स्युः] *ŚiDhaSaṅ*; --- N; दि ⊔ K; ि ⊔ W **2:41** तिलोदकफलेन तु] KW; --- लोदकफलेन तु N; तिलोदकफलेन वै *ŚiDhaSaṅ* **2:41** अजिनं] N, *ŚiDhaSaṅ*; अस्विन्नं K; अ ि - नं W **2:41** रौप्यक्षुरसमन्वितम्] NK^pc W; रौप्यखुरसमन्वितम् K^ac; दद्याद्रौप्यमयं खुरम् *ŚiDhaSaṅ* **2:42** सचैलाङ्गं] *conj.*; सचैलङ्गा NW; सचैलं गां K; सुचैलाङ्गं *ŚiDhaSaṅ* **2:42** कान्सदोहन्तु यो ददेत्] NW; कंसदोहं यो ददेत् K (unmetrical); कांस्यदोहं द्विजन्मने *ŚiDhaSaṅ* **2:42** अक्षयांल्लभते लोकांस्तिलधेनुप्रदाय्यसौ] K; अक्ष्याल्लभते लोकान्तिलधेनुप्रदाय्यसौ N, W; अक्षयं लभते लोकन्तिलधेनुप्रदायकः *ŚiDhaSaṅ* **2:43** युगान्ते च] NW, *ŚiDhaSaṅ*; युगान्तरे K **2:43** विपुले कुले] NKW; पृथिवीपतिः *ŚiDhaSaṅ* **2:43** पितृभक्ता हि] NKW; पितृभक्ताश्च *ŚiDhaSaṅ*

तेषान्तृप्ता हि पितरः स च तृप्तो [3]यमालये।
कुम्भीपाकन्तु निरयन्न च तस्य भविष्यति॥ 2:44॥

पितृलोकञ्च यास्यन्ति श्राद्धकारयिता नराः।
पितॄन्देवान्समुद्दिश्य नित्यन्दीपप्रदायिनः॥ 2:45॥

तामिस्रमन्धतामिस्रौ नरका न भवन्ति हि।
लोचने शोभने तस्य दृक्छक्तिश्च न नश्यते॥ 2:46॥

रौप्यक्षुरां हेमशृङ्गां रत्नाङ्गीं कांस्यदोहनीम्।
[4]चैलगण्डान्तु यो दद्याङ्गूयो भूयो गुणान्विताम्॥ 2:47॥

गोलोके स्वगर्गलोके वा वासस्तेषाम्भविष्यति।
सर्वद्वन्द्वविनिर्मुक्तो वसते गोप्रदायकः॥ 2:48॥

प्रसवतीं यो गान्दद्याद्वक्त्रोभयसुसंस्थिताम्।
पृथ्वीदानफलं ह्येतत्स्वर्गलोकञ्च गच्छति॥ 2:49॥

अनड्वाहानि बहुशो यः प्रयच्छेद्विजोत्तमे।

---

47 *Niśvāsamukha* 2.47–2.48 is parallel with *Śivadharmasaṅgraha* 6.89–6.90.

49 *Niśvāsamukha* 2.49 is parallel with *Śivadharmasaṅgraha* 6.118.

50 *Niśvāsamukha* 2.50 is parallel with *Śivadharmasaṅgraha* 6.106.

2:44 पितरः स च तृप्तो यमालये] *ŚiDhaSaṅ*; पि --- ये N; पितरः स च तृप्तो य ⊔ ये KW **2:44** कुम्भीपाकन्तु निरयन्न] NKW; कुम्भीपाकस्तु निरयो *ŚiDhaSaṅ* **2:44** च तस्य भविष्यति] NKW; न तेषां प्रभविष्यति *ŚiDhaSaṅ* **2:45** नराः] NW, *ŚiDhaSaṅ*; नरः K **2:46** तामिस्रमन्धतामिस्रौ] N; तामिस्रमन्धतामिस्रो K; तामिश्रमन्धतामिश्रौ W; तामिस्रश्चा-न्धतामिस्रो *ŚiDhaSaṅ* **2:46** नरका न भवन्ति हि] NKW; नरकौ न भविष्यतः *ŚiDhaSaṅ* **2:46** तस्य] NKW; तेषां *ŚiDhaSaṅ* **2:46** दृक्छक्तिश्च न नश्यते] N; दृग्शक्तिश्च न नश्यते K; दृक्कुक्तिश्च न नस्यते W; दृक्शक्तिश्च न नश्यति *ŚiDhaSaṅ* **2:47** रौप्यक्षुरां हेमशृङ्गां] NW; रौप्यखुरां हेमशृङ्गां K; रौप्यक्षुरां हेमशृङ्गै W; हेमशृंगां रौप्यक्षुरां *ŚiDhaSaṅ* **2:47** रत्नाङ्गीं कांस्यदोहनीम्] K, *ŚiDhaSaṅ*; रत्न् --- N; रत्नाङ्गीं कांस्यदाहिनी W **2:47** चैलगण्डान्तु यो दद्याङ्गूयो भूयो गुणान्विताम्] NK; चेलगण्ठान्तु यो दद्याङ्गूयो भूयो गुणान्विताम् W; सचैलघण्टाङ्गान्दद्याच्छिवभक्तद्विजन्मने *ŚiDhaSaṅ* **2:48** °मुक्तो वसते गोप्रदायकः] NK; °मुक्तो वसते गौप्रदायकः N; मुक्ता वसेयुर् गोप्रदायिनः *ŚiDhaSaṅ* **2:49** प्रसवतीं यो] NK; प्रसवती यो W; प्रसवन्तीश्च *ŚiDhaSaṅ* **2:49** ह्येतत्स्वर्ग°] KW, *ŚiDhaSaṅ*; ह्येत् स्वर्ग° N (unmetrical) **2:49** °लोकञ्च गच्छति] K; °लोकञ्च सच्छति N; °लोकञ्च स गच्छति W; °लोकाभिकांक्षिणाम् *ŚiDhaSaṅ* **2:50** अनड्वाहानि] N; अनड्वाहोति K; अनन्द्वाहानि W; अनड्वाहो ऽपि *ŚiDhaSaṅ* **2:50** प्रयच्छेद्विजोत्तमे] K, *ŚiDhaSaṅ*; प्रयच्छेद्विजो --- N; प्रयच्छद्विजोत्तमे W

तेन पुण्यफ[5]लेनैव स्वर्ग्गलोके महीयते॥ 2:50॥

अजां सुवर्ण्णरोमाम्वा यः प्रयच्छति नित्यशः।
अग्निलोकमवाप्नोति बहुपातकिको ऽपि यः॥ 2:51॥

श्वेतां रक्तान्तथा पीताङ्कृष्णां वा आविकान्ददेत्।
देवान्पितॄन्समुद्दिश्य सोमलोकं स गच्छति॥ 2:52॥

पितॄन्देवान्समुद्दिश्य महिषीं यो ददेद्द्विजे।
तेन पुण्य[[((फलेनैव))]] [6] [[विष्णुलोके म]]हीयते॥ 2:53॥

श्वेताङ्कृष्णां सुशीलां च सुधेनुं भ्रमराकृतिम्।
देवानां यः प्रयच्छेत अथवापि द्विजोत्तमे॥ 2:54॥

ईदृशीम्महिषीन्दत्त्वा शिवलोके महीयते।
शिवलोकात्परिभ्रष्टो जायते च महीपतिः॥ 2:55॥

फालकृष्टां महीन्दद्यात्सबीजां सस्यमालिनीम्।
[[या]]वत्सूर्यकृतां लोकां तावत्तिष्ठति सूर्यवत् ॥ 2:56॥

[8r] भूमिदानाद्भवेत्स्वर्ग्गो रत्नदानाद्रवेः पुरम्।
वस्त्रदः शशिलोके तु तारदो वैष्णवे पुरे॥ 2:57॥

---

51 *Niśvāsamukha* 2.51 is parallel with *Śivadharmasaṅgraha* 6.123.

56 Cf. *Niśvāsamukha* 2.78ab below, and also *Śivadharmasaṅgraha* 6.160ab: यावत्सूर्यकृता लोकास्तावत्तिष्ठेत्स सूर्यवत्।

57 *Niśvāsamukha* 2.57–2.70 is parallel with *Śivadharmasaṅgraha* 6.124–6.137.

2:50 तेन पुण्यफलेनैव] W, *ŚiDhaSaṅ*; --- नैव N; तेन पुण्यबलेनैव K **2:51** अजां सुवर्ण्णओमाम्वा यः प्रयच्छति नित्यशः] N; अजां सुवर्ण्णरोमांश्च सुंप्रप्रच्छति (?) नित्यशः K; अजं सुवर्णरामाम्वा य प्रयछति नित्यसःW; हेमवर्ण्णमजं दत्वा शिवभक्तद्विजन्मने *ŚiDhaSaṅ* **2:51** यः] NKW; सन् *ŚiDhaSaṅ* **2:53** द्विजे] NW; द्विजः K **2:53** विष्णुलोके महीयते] *conj.*; --- हीयते N; विष्णुलोकं महीयते KW **2:54** सुशीलां च] *conj.*; सुशीलांश्च NKW **2:55** जायते च] NK; जायते स W **2:56** सबीजां] N[pc]K; सबिजां N[ac]; सुचिजं W **2:56** सस्यमालिनीम्] W; सस्यमालि ी N; शस्यशालिनीम् K[ac]; शस्यमालिनी K[pc] **2:56** यावत्सूर्यकृतां] K; --- वत्सूर्यकृतां N; यावत्सूर्य ⊔ W **2:56** लोकां तावत्तिष्ठति सूर्यवत्] *em.*; लोका --- N; लोकां (तावत्तिष्ठति सूर्यवत्) म्स्ख्; ⊔ W **2:57** भूमि°] KW, *ŚiDhaSaṅ*; ⏓ मि° N **2:57** शशिलोके तु] NK; शशिलोकं तु *ŚiDhaSaṅ*; ससिलोके तु W **2:57** तारदो वैष्णवे पुरे] N; नारदो वैष्णवं पुरम् K; तारदा वैष्णवे पुरे W; तारदो वैष्णवं पुरम् *ŚiDhaSaṅ*

तिलकांचनदातारो यान्ति रुद्रस्य चालयम्।
कांसताम्रप्रवालानि दत्त्वा याति वसोः पुरम्॥ 2:58॥

मुक्तामणिविचित्राणि हारजातानि यान्यपि।
दत्त्वा सोमपुरं याति तिलहोमान्न संशयः॥ 2:59॥

गुडक्षीरदधिसर्पि[2]र्यः प्रयच्छति नित्यशः।
यक्षलोकपुरं याति मधुदानात्तथैव च॥ 2:60॥

चन्दनागरुकर्प्पूरकक्कोलकलवङ्गकान्।
दत्त्वान्यानि सुगन्धानि व्रजेद्गन्धर्वतान्नरः॥ 2:61॥

अलङ्कृत्वा तु यो दद्यात्कन्याञ्चैव अयाचिताम्।
स नरः स्वर्ग्गमायाति यश्च धान्यप्रदायकः॥ 2:62॥

माषमुद्गादिकां व्रीहीन्नित्यमेव प्रदायिनः।
[3]ते ऽपि स्वर्ग्गम्प्रयास्यन्ति ये चान्ये अभयप्रदाः॥ 2:63॥

रूपयौवनसम्पन्नां वस्त्रालङ्कारभूषिताम्।
स्त्रियञ्चैव प्रयच्छन्ति यान्ति वैद्याधरम्पदम्॥ 2:64॥

रतिसत्रन्तु सततं वरनारीषु दापयेत्।

2:58 तिलकांचनदातारो] K; तिलकोचनदातारो NW; तिलहेमप्रदातारो *ŚiDhaSaṅ* **2:58** कांसताम्र°] *ŚiDhaSaṅ*; कान्सतांम्व्र° N; कांसताम्रा× ⏓ × ° K^{ac}; कांस्यताम्र° K^{pc}; कान्सतांम्र° W **2:58** दत्त्वा याति वसोः पुरम्] NKW; दत्त्वैति वसुमन्दिरम् *ŚiDhaSaṅ* **2:59** हारजातानि] W; हानजातानि N; होमजातानि K; हीनजातानि *ŚiDhaSaṅ* **2:59** दत्त्वा सोमपुरं याति] KW; ⏓ ⏓ ⏓ ⏓ ⏓ ⏓ ⏓ ⏓ N; दत्वा शक्रपुरं यांति *ŚiDhaSaṅ* **2:59** तिलहोमान्न संशयः] KW; तिलहोमान्न ⏓ ⏓ यः N; तिलहोमाच्च मानवाः *ŚiDhaSaṅ* **2:60** गुडक्षीरदधिसर्पिर्यः] *conj.*; --- N; गुड ⊔ यः K; गुडक्षारदधिस ⊔ W; दधि क्षीरं गुडं सर्पिर्यः *ŚiDhaSaṅ* **2:60** मधुदानात्तथैव च] *conj.*; मधदानात्तथैव च N; गन्धदानात्तथैव च K; ⊔ W; मधुदानेन चैव हि *ŚiDhaSaṅ* **2:61** °कक्कोलकलवङ्गकान्] *em.*; °कक्कोल्लकलवङ्गकान् N; ककोलबालवङ्गकान् K; °कक्कोल्लकलपङ्गकान् W; कक्कोलकलवङ्गकम् *ŚiDhaSaṅ* **2:61** सुगन्धानि] NKW; सुगन्धीनि *ŚiDhaSaṅ* **2:62** अलङ्कृत्वा तु यो दद्यात्कन्याञ्चैव] NKW; अलङ्कृत्य च ये कन्यां प्रयच्छन्ति *ŚiDhaSaṅ* **2:62** अयाचिताम्] NW; अयाचितान् K; त्वयाचिताम् *ŚiDhaSaṅ* **2:62** स नरः स्वर्ग्गमायाति यश्च धान्यप्रदायकः] NKW; ते नराः स्वर्गमेष्यन्ति ये च धान्यप्रदायिनः *ŚiDhaSaṅ* **2:63** माषमुद्गादिकां] NW; माषमुद्गादिकान् K, *ŚiDhaSaṅ* **2:63** व्रीहीन्नित्यमेवप्रदायिनः] K; प्र --- N; व्रीहि ⊔ प्रदायिने W; व्रीहीन् ये ददत्यसकृन्नराः *ŚiDhaSaṅ* **2:63** ते ऽपि] K, *ŚiDhaSaṅ*; --- पि NW **2:63** स्वर्ग्गम्प्रयास्यन्ति] NW; स्वगर्स्यं यास्यन्ति K; स्वर्गङ्गमिष्यन्ति *ŚiDhaSaṅ* **2:63** अभयप्रदाः] NK; अभयप्रदां W; ह्यभयप्रदाः *ŚiDhaSaṅ* **2:64** स्त्रियञ्चैव] NKW; युवतीम्ये *ŚiDhaSaṅ* **2:65** रतिसत्रन्तु सततं] NKW; रतिसत्रञ्च यो दद्याद् *ŚiDhaSaṅ* **2:65** वरनारीषु दापयेत्] NKW; वराभिः प्रमदाजनैः *ŚiDhaSaṅ*

ते ऽप्यप्सरसां संघेषु मोदन्ते दिवि मानवाः॥ 2:65॥

वेत्रासनञ्च शय्याञ्च प्रतिवर्षप्रदायिनः।
यक्षलोके तु मोदन्ते [4] यक्षिणीभिस्सहस्रशः॥ 2:66॥

इन्धनानि तु यो दद्याद्द्विप्रेभ्यः शिशिरागमे।
धनवान्रूपसम्पन्नो जायते सुभगस्तथा॥ 2:67॥

प्रतिश्रयन्तृणं शय्यां प्रावरान्नं हुताशनम्।
प्रतिदिनम्प्रयच्छन्ते ते नराः स्वर्ग्गगामिनः॥ 2:68॥

गीतवादित्रयानानि देवानान्नित्यदायिनः।
ते जायन्ते महाभोगा गीतवादित्रबोधिताः॥ 2:69॥

रू[5]पयौवनसम्पन्नं सप्तिं हेमविभूषितम्।
प्रयच्छेद्द्विजमुख्येभ्यो ब्रध्नस्याप्नोति विष्टपम्॥ 2:70॥

शारीसंयोगसंयुक्तमिभं काञ्चनमालिनम्।
दत्त्वा शक्रपुरं याति भ्रष्टो जायति भोगवान्॥ 2:71॥

आतपत्रप्रदानेन श्रीमाञ्जायत्यसौ नरः।
धर्म्मराजपुरं गच्छन्नातपेन तु पीड्यते॥ 2:72॥

---

71 *Niśvāsamukha* 2.71a–2.80b is parallel with *Śivadharmasaṅgraha* 6.153c–6.162.

2:65 ते ऽप्यप्सरसां संघेषु मोदन्ते दिवि मानवाः] NKW; कामदेवपुरं याति जातो ऽनङ्गसमो भवेत् *ŚiDhaSaṅ* **2:66** प्रतिवर्षप्रदायिनः] NKW; प्रत्यब्दं यः प्रयच्छति *ŚiDhaSaṅ* **2:66** यक्षलोके तु (मोदन्ते)] K; यक्षलोके तु --- NW; मोदते यक्षलोकेषु *ŚiDhaSaṅ* **2:66** सहस्रशः] NK; सहस्रसः W; समन्वितः *ŚiDhaSaṅ* **2:67** तु] NKW; च *ŚiDhaSaṅ* **2:67** जायते सुभगस्तथा] NKW; दीप्ताग्निः सुभगो भवेत् *ŚiDhaSaṅ* **2:68** प्रावरान्नं हुताशनम्] NK; प्रावरान्नं हुतासनम् W; पुण्याग्निं शुद्धमानसाः *ŚiDhaSaṅ* **2:68** प्रतिदिनम्प्रयच्छन्ते] NKW; प्रत्यहं ये प्रयच्छन्ति *ŚiDhaSaṅ* **2:69** ते जायन्ते महाभोगा] NKW; जायन्ते ते च भोगाढ्या *ŚiDhaSaṅ* **2:69** गीतवादित्रबोधिताः] K; गीतवादित्रबोधि --- NW; गीतवादित्रबोधकाः *ŚiDhaSaṅ* **2:70** रूपयौवन॰] K; --- वन॰ N; ⁻पयौवन॰ W; जवे यौवन॰ *ŚiDhaSaṅ* **2:70** प्रयच्छेद्द्वि॰] *ŚiDhaSaṅ*; प्रयच्छेद्वि॰ N; प्रचच्छन्द्वि॰ K; ⊔ द्वि॰ W **2:70** विष्टपम्] NKW; पिष्टपम् *ŚiDhaSaṅ* **2:71** शारी॰] N, *ŚiDhaSaṅ*; सारी॰ KW **2:71** ॰मालिनम्] NWK; ॰मालया *ŚiDhaSaṅ* **2:71** जायति] NKW; भवति *ŚiDhaSaṅ* **2:72** श्रीमाञ्जायत्यसौ नरः] N; श्रीमांञ्जायत्यसौ नरः K; श्रीयां जायत्यसौ नरः W; जायेत मानवः *ŚiDhaṢaṅ* **2:72** गच्छन्नातपेन तु पीड्यते] KW; ग --- न्नातपेन तु पीड्यते N; गच्छन्नातपेनानुपीड्यते *ŚiDhaSaṅ*

उपानहौ तु यो दद्यात्सर्वान्मु [6] च्यति किल्बिषात्।
धर्म्मराजपथे तस्य अश्वो जायति शोभनः॥ 2:73॥

तप्तवालुकदुःखैस्तु कण्टकैश्च सुदारुणैः।
न च तस्य भवेत्पीडा यो ददाति उपानहौ॥ 2:74॥

गजरथन्तु यो दद्याद्ब्राह्मणाय गुणान्विते।
तेन पुण्यफलेनैव स्वर्ग्गलोके महीयते॥ 2:75॥

तावन्न च्यवते ≪स्वर्गाद्यावद्देवास्सवासवाः≫।
ततश्चैव [8^{v}] परिभ्रष्टो राजा भवति धार्मिकः॥ 2:76॥

दत्त्वा चाश्वरथन्दिव्यं बहुद्रव्यसमन्वितम्।
सूर्यलोकमवाप्नोति तेनैव सह मोदते॥ 2:77॥

यावत्सूर्यकृतांल्लोकान्तावत्तिष्ठति सूर्यवत्।
तत्र चैव परिभ्रष्टो धनवाञ्जायते पुनः॥ 2:78॥

अनड्वाहरथन्दत्त्वा ≪सर्वद्रव्यसमन्वितम्।
दासीदाससमोपेतः स्वर्ग≫ [2] माप्नोति मानवः॥ 2:79॥

परिभ्रष्टो ह्यतो भूयो धनवाञ्जायते सदा।

---

76 Cf. *Kūrmapurāṇa* 1.36:12cd: ततस्तस्मात्परिभ्रष्टो राजा भवति धार्मिकः।. In said work, the same line occurs at 2.38:18ab, reading ततः स्वर्गात् instead of ततस्तस्मात्।

2:73 तु यो दद्यात्सर्वान्मुच्यति] *conj.* (K); --- ति N; तु यो (दद्यात्सर्वान्मुच्यति) K; तु यो दद्या ⊔ ति W; तु यो दद्यात्स तु मुच्येत *ŚiDhaSaṅ* **2:73** किल्बिषात्] NW, *ŚiDhaSaṅ*; किल्बिषम् K **2:73** अश्वो जायति शोभनः] NK; अश्वा जायति सासनः W; जायते शोभनो हयः *ŚiDhaSaṅ* **2:74** °वालुकदुःकैस्तु] NKW; °सैकतदुःखाग्रैः *ŚiDhaSaṅ* **2:74** ददाति उपानहौ] NKW; हि दद्यादुपानहौ *ŚiDhaSaṅ* **2:75** गजरथन्तु यो दद्याद्] NW; गजं रथं यो दद्याद् K; दद्याद्राजरथं यस्तु *ŚiDhaSaṅ* **2:75** महीयते] KW, *ŚiDhaSaṅ*; मही --- N **2:76** तावन्न च्यवते स्वर्गाद्यावद्देवास्सवासवाः] *ŚiDhaSaṅ*; तावन्न च्यवते ⊔ W; --- NK **2:76** ततश्चैव परिभ्रष्टो] *ŚiDhaSaṅ*; --- परिभ्रष्टो N; स्वर्गलोकात्परिभ्रष्टो K; ⊔ व परिभ्रष्टा W **2:77** बहुद्रव्यसमन्वितम्] N^{pc}KW; बहुद्र+व्य+समन्वितम् N **2:78** °कृतांल्लोकान् K; °कृताल्लोकान् NW; °कृता लोकास् *ŚiDhaSaṅ* **2:78** तिष्ठति] NKW; तिष्ठेत्स *ŚiDhaSaṅ* **2:79** अनड्वाहरथन्दत्त्वा] *conj.*; अनत्वाहरथन्द --- N; आनड्वाहरथं ⊔K; अनत्ताहर ⊔ W; बलीवर्दरथं दत्वाम् *ŚiDhaSaṅ* **2:79** दासीदाससमोपेतः स्वर्गमाप्नोति मानवः] *ŚiDhaSaṅ*; --- नोति मानवः N; ⊔ प्राप्नोति मानवः K; ⊔ मायाति मानवः W **2:80** परिभ्रष्टो ह्यतो भूयो] NK; परिभ्रष्टा ह्यतो भूयो W; परिभ्रष्टस्तु तद्भूयो *ŚiDhaSaṅ*

गवां ग्रासन्तु यो दद्यात्प्रातरुत्थाय मानवः॥ 2:80॥

मन्त्रेणैव समायुक्तम्मुच्यते सर्वकिल्बिषैः।
स्वर्गगामी च भवते परिभ्रष्टो महाधनः॥ 2:81॥

गवाढ्ये तु कुले जन्म गवाढ्यश्च भविष्यति।
अमृतमथनोत्पन्ना सुरभी लोकधारि[3]णी॥ 2:82॥

इदङ्ग्रासङ्गृहाण त्वमिदम्मे व्रतमुत्तमम्।
गवां ग्रासं यथा देयं सौरभेये तथैव च॥ 2:83॥

तुल्यमेतत्फलन्दृष्टं किन्तु मन्त्रम्पृथक्पृथक्।
सर्वलोकधरा ह्येते जीवितान्नप्रदायकाः॥ 2:84॥

ग्रासङ्गृह्णन्तु हृष्टास्तु एतन्मे व्रतमुत्तमम्।
नित्यम्परगवे दद्याद्गृहीत्वा दुर्लभं व्रतम्॥ 2:85॥

रक्षन्ति च भयाद्घोरात् [4] स्पर्शने पापनाशनाः।
पुण्यकाले तु संप्राप्ते वृषोत्सर्गङ्करोति यः॥ 2:86॥

---

80 *Niśvāsamukha* 2.80c–2.82b is parallel with *Śivadharmasaṅgraha* 6.95a–6.96.

82 *Niśvāsamukha* 2.82c–2.86b is parallel with *Śivadharmasaṅgraha* 6.98a–6.101.

82 Cf. *Somaśambhupaddhati* (1.6:5–8), *Kriyākramadyotikā* (§ 67, p.134), *Ātmārthapūjāpaddhati* fol.126b (attribution to *Suprabhedāgama*), the first two lines are found in *Jñānaratnāvalī* (R 14898, p.144), also with the attribution to the *Suprabhedāgama*:
अमृतमथनोत्पन्ने सुरभे लोकधारिणि। इमं ग्रासं गृहाण त्वमिदं मे व्रतमुत्तमम्॥ गवां ग्रासो यथा देयः सौरभेयाय चैव तु। तुल्यमेतत्फलं दृष्टं किंतु मन्त्रः पृथक् पृथक्॥ सर्वलोकधरा ह्येते जीवितान्नप्रदायिनः। ग्रासं गृह्णन्तु हृष्टास्ते ह्येतन्मे व्रतमुत्तमम्॥ नित्यं परगवे दद्याद्गृहीत्वा दुर्लभं व्रतम्। रक्षन्ति च भयाद्घोरात्स्पर्शने पापनाशनम्॥

86 *Niśvāsamukha* 2.86c–2.88b is parallel with *Śivadharmasaṅgraha* 6.103–6.104.

2:80 तु यो दद्यात्प्रातरुत्थाय मानवः] NKW; दरिद्रेण कर्तव्यं प्रातरेव हि *ŚiDhaSaṅ* **2:81** समायुक्तम्] NKW; समायुक्तो *ŚiDhaSaṅ* **2:81** भवते] NKW; भवति *ŚiDhaSaṅ* **2:81** महाधनः] NKW; महाधनी *ŚiDhaSaṅ* **2:82** गवाढ्ये तु कुले जन्म] NKW; गवाढ्ये च भवेज्जन्म *ŚiDhaSaṅ* **2:82** गवाढ्यश्च भविष्यति] KW; गवाढ्यश्च --- विष्यति N; गवाढ्यश्च भवत्यसौ *ŚiDhaSaṅ* **2:82** अमृतमथनोत्पन्ना] NKW (unmetrical); उत्पन्नामृतमथने *ŚiDhaSaṅ* **2:82** लोकधारिणी] K, *ŚiDhaSaṅ*; ल --- N; तोलो ⊔ णी W **2:83** व्रतमुत्तमम्] KW, *ŚiDhaSaṅ*; व्रतमुत्तमन्नं N **2:84** मन्त्रम्] W; म्मन्त्रम् N; मेद्यं K; मन्त्रः *ŚiDhaSaṅ* **2:85** हृष्टास्तु] NKW; तुष्टास्तु *ŚiDhaSaṅ* **2:85** गृहीत्वा] K, *ŚiDhaSaṅ*; गृही ⏑̲ N; गृहीयाद् W **2:86** रक्षन्ति च भयाद्घोरात्] *ŚiDhaSaṅ*; रक्षन्ति च भय --- N; रक्षन्ति च भयाद्घोरा ⊔ KW **2:86** स्पर्शने] NK; स्पसन्न W; दर्शने *ŚiDhaSaṅ* **2:86** पुण्यकाले तु संप्राप्ते] NW, *ŚiDhaSaṅ*; पुण्यकालं तु संप्राप्य K

स याति रुद्रलोकन्तु यदि नीलो भविष्यति।
नीलस्यैव अलाभे तु पितृभिस्सह संयुतः॥ 2:87॥

स्वर्गलोकमवाप्नोति भ्रष्टो जायति भोगवान्।
कपित्थन्दाडिमञ्चाम्रं जम्बु बिल्वं तथैव च॥ 2:88॥

पनसम्मातुलुङ्गञ्च नारिकेलं समोचकम्।
[5] प्राचीनामलनारङ्गन्द्राक्षा खर्जूरमेव च॥ 2:89॥

अन्यामृतफला ये च दत्त्वा तु सुभगो भवेत्।
बहुपुत्रश्च रूपाढ्यस्सुभगश्चैव जायते॥ 2:90॥

सम्पूर्णाङ्गश्च निरुजो भवेत्फलप्रदायकः।
दन्तधावनदाता च भार्यां लभति शोभनाम्॥ 2:91॥

ताम्बूलं सुरभिं पुष्पान्दत्त्वा जायति पण्डितः।
सुगन्धास्य«श्च भवति»[6]वाग्मी गन्धप्रदायकः॥ 2:92॥

उपवीतं बृसीन्दत्त्वा जायते ब्रह्मयोनिषु।
खड्गञ्चक्रायुधन्दत्त्वा शक्तिकुन्तपरश्वधान्॥ 2:93॥

असिपत्रवनाद्घोरान्न भयन्तस्य जायते।
असंस्कृतस्य लोहस्य दानाद्बन्धभयन्न च॥ 2:94॥

---

88 *Niśvāsamukha* 2.88c–2.115 is parallel with *Śivadharmasaṅgraha* 6.163–6.189.

2:87 नीलस्यैव अलाभे तु] NKW; अलाभे नीलषण्डस्य *ŚiDhaSaṅ* **2:88** जायति] NKW; भवति *ŚiDhaSaṅ* **2:88** कपित्थन्दाडिमञ्चाम्रं जम्बु बिल्वं तथैव च] NKW; कपित्थं दाडिमञ्चैव पनसं बीजपूरकम् *ŚiDhaSaṅ* **2:89** पनसम्मातुलुङ्गञ्च नारिकेलं समोचकम्] *conj.*; पनसम्मातुलुङ्गञ्च नारिकेलं समे--- N; पनसम्मातुलुङ्गञ्च नारिकेलं समो ⊔ K; पनस ˉतुलु ˉञ्च नारिकेलं समोच ⊔ W; नालिकेरकनारङ्गं प्राचीनामलमोचकम् *ŚiDhaSaṅ* **2:89** प्राचीनामलनारङ्गन्द्राक्षा खर्जूरमेव च] NW; प्राचीनामलनारङ्गद्राक्षा खर्जूरमेव च K; श्रीफलं चूतजम्बीरन्द्राक्षा खर्जूरमेव च *ŚiDhaSaṅ* **2:90** अन्यामृतफला ये च दत्त्वा तु]] NKW; अन्यानि च फलान्येवं दत्वा तु *ŚiDhaSaṅ* **2:90** सुभगो भवेत्] NKW; सुखभाग्भवेत् *ŚiDhaSaṅ* **2:91** भवेत्फलप्रदायकः] NKW; भवेच्च फलदायकः *ŚiDhaSaṅ* **2:91** दन्तधावनदाता च] K; दन्तधावनदात्ता च N; दन्तधावनदान्ता च W; दन्तधावनदानाच्च *ŚiDhaSaṅ* **2:91** भार्यां लभति शोभनाम्] NK; भायां लभति शोभनाम् W; भार्या भवति शोभना *ŚiDhaSaṅ* **2:92** सुरभिं पुष्पान्दत्त्वा जायति] NKW; शोभितं पुष्पं दत्वा जायेत *ŚiDhaSaṅ* **2:92** पण्डितः] K, *ŚiDhaSaṅ*; प --- N; पण्डितम् W **2:92** सुगन्धास्यश्च भवति] *ŚiDhaSaṅ*; सगन् ा --- N; सुगन्धास्य ⊔ KW **2:93** बृसीन्दत्त्वा] NKW; वृतं दत्वा *ŚiDhaSaṅ*

घटितोपस्करं लोहं दत्त्वा शस्त्रभयं न च।
[9^r] लोहकारश्च नरको न कदाचिद्भविष्यति॥ 2:95॥

मृन्मयानि कपालानि दत्त्वा चैव कमण्डलुम्।
यतिदानमिदं श्रेष्ठं दत्त्वा सुखमवाप्नुयात्॥ 2:96॥

≪काञ्चनं रजतं ताम्रं भाण्डमायस≫त्रापुषम्।
अक्षयन्तद्भवेद्दानन्दीर्घमायुश्च जायते॥ 2:97॥

≪देवताभ्यो द्विजातिभ्यो ≫दासीदासां च यो ददेत्॥
भवति स महाभागः [2] बहुभृत्यजनावृतः॥ 2:98॥

सिन्धूत्थं लवणन्दत्त्वा रूपवान्सुभगो भवेत्।
पिप्पलीं शृङ्गवेरञ्च मरिचं विश्वभेषजम्॥ 2:99॥

दत्त्वा निरुजतां याति आतुरे ओषधानि च।
आतुरं निरुजङ्कृत्वा निर्व्याधिर्दीर्घमायुषम्॥ 2:100॥

मधुराम्लकटुतिक्तानि कषायलवणानि च।
सर्वक्रीडारसाभिज्ञो जायते पण्डितो नरः॥ 2:101॥

[3] तैलात्सर्वाधिकं तेज आयुः शर्क्करखण्डयोः।

2:95 शस्त्रभयं न च] KW, *ŚiDhaSaṅ*; शस् ⏑ भ ⏑ --- N **2:95** लोहकारश्च नरको] *conj.*; --- कारश्च नरको N; शस्त्रकारंश्च नरके K; होलकार स नरको W; लोहीपाकश्च नरके *ŚiDhaSaṅ* **2:96** सुखमवाप्नुयात्] NKW; तु सुखभाग्भवेत् *ŚiDhaSaṅ* **2:97** काञ्चनं रजतं ताम्रं भाण्डमायसस°] *ŚiDhaSaṅ*; क --- यस° NK; ⊔ स° W **2:97** °त्रापुषम्] NKW; °सीसकम् *ŚiDhaSaṅ* **2:97** दीर्घमायुश्च] NW, *ŚiDhaSaṅ*; दीर्घमायुः प्र° K **2:97** जायते] W, *ŚiDhaSaṅ*; ⏑ --- N; °जायते K **2:98** देवताभ्यो द्विजातिभ्यो] *ŚiDhaSaṅ*; --- NK; नाञ्च ⊔ W **2:98** दासीदासां च यो ददेत्] *conj.*; --- NK; दसो दासीं च यो ददेत् W; दासीदासां ददाति यः *ŚiDhaSaṅ* **2:98** भवति स महाभागः] *conj.*; --- NK; भवति स महाभा ⊔ W; ते लभन्ते महाभोगान् *ŚiDhaSaṅ* **2:98** बहुभृत्यजनावृतः] *conj.*; ---वृतः NK; ⊔ नावृतः W; बहुभृत्यजनावृताः *ŚiDhaSaṅ* **2:99** पिप्पलीं] K, *ŚiDhaSaṅ*; पिप्पलीङ्° NW **2:99** शृङ्गवेरञ्च] K, *ŚiDhaSaṅ*; भृङ्गवेरञ्च NW **2:99** विश्वभेषजम्] NKW; भैषजानि च *ŚiDhaSaṅ* **2:100** निरुजतां] NW, *ŚiDhaSaṅ*; नीरुजतां K **2:100** आतुरे ओषधानि च] N; आतुरे औषधानि K; आतुरे ओषधानि W; आतुरायौषधानि च *ŚiDhaSaṅ* **2:100** कृत्वा निर्व्याधिर्दीर्घमायुषम्] N; कृत्वा निर्व्याधिं दीर्घमायुषम् K; कृत्वा निर्व्याधिदीर्घमायुषम् W; कुर्यादायुष्मान् निरुजो भवेत् *ŚiDhaSaṅ* **2:101** मधुराम्लकटुतिक्तानि] NW (unmetrical); मध्वम्लकटुतिक्तानि K; मधुराम्लानि तिक्तानि *ŚiDhaSaṅ* **2:101** जायते पण्डितो नरः] KW; जायते --- N; विद्वाञ्जायेत मानवः *ŚiDhaSaṅ* **2:102** तैलात्सर्वाधिक् तेज] *conj.*; --- धिको तेज N; तैलासर्वाधिकं तेज K; तैला ⊔ धिको तेजा W; तैलात्प्राणा घृतात्तेज *ŚiDhaSaṅ*

मर्ज्जिततातक्रदानेन गवाढ्यो गोप्रपूजने॥ 2:102॥

मौक्तिकं शङ्खशुक्तीनि दत्त्वा बहुसुतो भवेत्।
कपर्द्दकानि यो दद्याद्दर्प्पणं विमलं शुभम्॥ 2:103॥

रूपवान्धनसम्पन्नो जायते स्त्रीषु वल्लभः।
पोषणं हन्ततिञ्चैव भिक्षां वा प्रत्यहन्ददेत्॥ 2:104॥

धनवान्स तु जायेत अन्यथा दु[4]र्गतिर्भवेत्।
एष दानविधिः ख्यातस्त्वतिदानञ्च मे शृणु॥ 2:105॥

अन्नपानं सदा दद्याद्वस्त्रशय्याप्रतिश्रयम्।
गां सुवर्ण्णञ्च भूमिञ्च धर्म्माणां किमतः परम्॥ 2:106॥

विद्यादानन्तथा श्रेष्ठमतिश्रेष्ठञ्च रक्षणम्।
जीवं रक्षयते यो हि स च दाता परः स्मृतः॥ 2:107॥

सर्वेषामेव दानानां भूतेष्वभयदक्षिणा।
यो ददा[5]ति स दाता हि अन्ये कामविमोहिताः॥ 2:108॥

तस्माद्रक्षेत सर्वाणि प्राणिनां जीवितात्यये।
स दाता स तपस्वी च स याति परमं पदम्॥ 2:109॥

अतिदानविधिः ख्यातो लोकानां हितकाम्यया।

2:102 मर्ज्जिता॰] NW; म ⊔ ता K **2:102** गोप्रपूजने] NW; गोः प्रपूजने K; गोप्रपूजनात् *ŚiDhaSaṅ* **2:103** भवेत्] KW, *ŚiDhaSaṅ*; भवेम् N **2:103** विमलं शुभम्] NKW; निर्मलं तथा *ŚiDhaSaṅ* **2:104** हन्ततिञ्चैव] K; हन्ततिञ्चै NW (unmetrical); हन्तकारञ्च *ŚiDhaSaṅ* **2:104** ददेत्] W; दद --- N; ददत् K; क्षिपेत् *ŚiDhaSaṅ* **2:105** धनवान् स तु जायेत] NKW; धनिनस्ते प्रजायन्ति *ŚiDhaSaṅ* **2:105** अन्यथा] W, *ŚiDhaSaṅ*; अ --- N; अन्येषां K **2:105** दुर्गतिर्भवेत्] *conj.*; --- तिर्भवेत् NK; ⊔ र्ग्गतिर्भवेत् W; दुर्ग्गतिं व्रजेत् *ŚiDhaSaṅ* **2:105** दानविधिः] N^{pc}KW; दानविधि N^{ac} **2:105** त्वतिदानञ्च] NKW; ह्यन्नदानञ्च *ŚiDhaSaṅ* **2:106** वस्त्रशय्याप्रतिश्रयम्] NK; वस्त्रशय्याप्रतिस्रयम् W; वस्त्रं शय्यां प्रतिश्रयम् *ŚiDhaSaṅ* **2:106** गां सुवर्ण्णञ्च भूमिञ्च] NW; गां सुवर्णञ्च भूमिञ्च W; गां सुवर्ण्णन्तथा भूमिं *ŚiDhaSaṅ* **2:106** धर्म्माणां] NKW; धर्मेण *ŚiDhaSaṅ* **2:107** तथा] NKW; परं *ŚiDhaSaṅ* **2:107** जीवं रक्षयते यो हि स च] NKW; जीवं रक्षति यो नित्यं स *ŚiDhaSaṅ* **2:108** ॰दक्षिणा] N; ॰दक्षिणा+:+ K; ॰दक्षिणाम् W, *ŚiDhaSaṅ* **2:108** यो ददाति] K, *ŚiDhaSaṅ*; --- ति स N; ⁻ ददाति W **2:108** अन्ये कामविमोहिताः] NK; अन्ये काम ⁻ ि मोहिताः W; ये चान्ये काममोहिताः *ŚiDhaSaṅ* **2:109** तस्माद्रक्षेत सर्वाणि] NK; तस्माद्रक्षत सर्वाणि W; तस्माद्रक्षन्ति सत्वानि *ŚiDhaSaṅ* **2:109** स दाता स तपस्वी च] NKW; स च दाता तपस्वी च *ŚiDhaSaṅ* **2:110** अतिदानविधिः ख्यातो] NKW; इति दानविधिस्त्वोक्तो *ŚiDhaSaṅ*

दिने दिने च यो दद्याद्दानन्तञ्च निबोध मे॥ 2:110॥

दन्तधावनताम्बूलं स्रग्धूपञ्च विलेपनम्।
रोचना«ञ्जनवस्त्रा»[6]णि दिव्यालङ्कारमण्डनम्॥ 2:111॥

गजाश्वारोहणं यानमभ्यङ्गोद्वर्त्तनन्तथा।
स्नानं दिव्यसुगन्धैश्च चन्दनागरुकुङ्कुमैः॥ 2:112॥

कर्प्पूरव्यतिमिश्रैश्च लेपं धूपं सपुष्पकम्।
मृष्टान्नपानदानञ्च †सुखशय्यानिशीतवान्†॥ 2:113॥

वरनारीरति«सुखं यो ददाति स चाश्नुते»।
[9v]अद«त्त्वा यो ऽभिकांक्षेत स च»दुःखी परो भवेत्॥ 2:114॥

देव्युवाच।
किन्तत्पात्रम्भवेच्छ्रेष्ठं यस्य दत्ते महत्फलम्।
अक्षयन्तु भवेद्दानन्तन्मे ब्रूहि महेश्वर॥ 2:115॥

ईश्वर उ।
मातापितृषु यद्दानं गुरुबन्धुषु कन्ययः।
दीनार्तान्धकृपणिनां तदानन्त्याय कल्पते॥ 2:116॥

---

116 Cf. *Śivadharmasaṅgraha* 6.190: मातापितृषु यद्दानं दीनान्धकृपणेषु च। गुरुबन्धुषु कन्यासु तदान्त्याय कल्प्यते॥

2:110 यो दद्याद्दानन्तञ्च] NKW; यद्दानं तच्चापि हि *ŚiDhaSaṅ* **2:111** दन्तधादनताम्बूलं] *ŚiDhaSaṅ*; द --- ताम्बुलं N; दन्तद्धादनताम्बूलं K; ⊔ W **2:111** स्रग्धूपञ्च विलेपनम्] N, *ŚiDhaSaṅ*; स ⊔ ञ्च विलेपनम् K; ⊔ W **2:111** रोचनाञ्जनवस्त्राणि] *ŚiDhaSaṅ*; रोच --- णि N; रोचना ⊔ K; रोचना ⊔ णि W **2:112** गजाश्वारोहणं] K, *ŚiDhaSaṅ*; --- जाश्वारोहणं N; गजाश्वारोहनं W **2:112** यानमभ्यङ्गोद्वर्त्तनन्तथा] K, *ŚiDhaSaṅ*; यानं मभ्यङ्गै ⏓ र्त्तनन्तथा N; यानं मभ्यङ्गा⁻ र्त्तनन्तथा W **2:113** °दानञ्च] NKW; °दानानि *ŚiDhaSaṅ* **2:113** °निशीतवान्] NK; °निसीतवान् W; °निषीदनम् *ŚiDhaSaṅ* **2:114** वरनारीरतिसुखं] *ŚiDhaSaṅ*; वरनारीरति --- NK; वरनारीर ि ⊔ W **2:114** यो ददाति स चाश्नुते] *ŚiDhaSaṅ*; --- NKW **2:114** अदत्त्वा यो ऽभिकांक्षेत स च] *ŚiDhaSaṅ*; अद --- N; ⊔ KW **2:114** दुःखी परो भवेत्] KW, *ŚiDhaSaṅ*; --- खी परो भवेत् N **2:115** देव्युवाच] KW, *ŚiDhaSaṅ*; देव्यु --- N **2:115** भवेच्छ्रेष्ठं] K; भवेच्छ्रेष्ठ NW; भवेच्छ्रेयं *ŚiDhaSaṅ* **2:115** यस्य] NW, *ŚiDhaSaṅ*; यस्य(स्मिन्) K **2:115** दत्ते] NKW; दत्तम् *ŚiDhaSaṅ* **2:115** अक्षयन्तु] NKW; अक्षयञ्च *ŚiDhaSaṅ* **2:116** कन्ययः] N; कन्ययोः K; कन्यया W **2:116** °कृपणिनां] W; °कृपणि ⏓ N; °कृपणिना K **2:116** तदनन्त्याय कल्पते] *conj.*; तदानन्ताय कल्प्यते NW; तदानन्तं प्रकल्प्यते K

मूर्खविप्रसहस्रेभ्यो वेदाध्यायी परः स्मृतः ।
वेदाध्यायि[2]सहस्रेभ्यो ह्याहिताग्निस्ततो ऽधिकः॥ 2:117॥

आहिताग्निसहस्रेषु अग्निहोत्री वरः स्मृतः ।
अग्निहोत्रीसहस्रेषु ब्रह्मवेत्ता ततो ऽधिकः॥ 2:118॥

तस्य दत्तम्भवे ऽनन्तं स वै त्राता परः स्मृतः ।
एषां लक्षगुणान्दद्यादेकन्दद्यात्तु ज्ञानिने॥ 2:119॥

न तेषां तुल्यमेतत्तु स वै त्राता वरो वरः ।
यस्य दाने न दुःखा[3]नि नरकप्रेतसम्भवाः॥ 2:120॥

न भवन्ति हि दातारो विपापाः स्वर्गगामिनः ।
तस्मात्सर्वेषु पात्रेषु शिवज्ञानी वरो वरः॥ 2:121॥

तस्मिन्पात्रे सदा देयमात्मनः श्रेय इच्छता ।
अक्षयन्तद्भवेद्दानं यद्दत्तं स्वल्पमल्पपि॥ 2:122॥

---

117 *Niśvāsamukha* 2.117 is parallel with *Śivadharmasaṅgraha* 6.191.

117 Cf. *Śivadharmaśāstra* 7.69–71: ब्रह्मचारिसहस्रेभ्यो वेदाध्यायी विशिष्यते। वेदाध्यायिसहस्रेभ्यो ह्यग्निहोत्री विशिष्यते॥ 7:69॥ अग्निहोत्रिसहस्रेभ्यो यज्ञयाजी विशिष्यते। यज्ञयाजिसहस्रेभ्यः सत्रयाजी विशिष्यते॥ 7:70॥ सत्रयाजिसहस्रेभ्यः सर्वविद्यान्तपारगः। सर्वविद्याविल्कोटिभ्यः शिवभक्तो विशिष्यते॥ 7:71॥

118 Cf. *Śivadharmasaṅgraha* 6.192ab: आहिताग्निसहस्राणां ब्रह्मवेत्ता ततो ऽधिकः।

119 *Niśvāsamukha* 2.119a–2.120b is parallel with *Śivadharmasaṅgraha* 6.192c–6.193d.

120 Cf. *Śivadharmasaṅgraha* 6.194: यद्दानशक्त्या दुःखानि नरकप्रेतजान्यपि। अन्यानि च सुघोराणि न भवन्तीह दातरि॥

2:117 मूर्खविप्रसहस्रेभ्यो] K; मू ⏑̲ विप्रस ⏑̲ स्रेभ्यो N; मू ˉ विप्र ˉˉ श्रेभो W; मूर्खविप्रसहस्राणां *ŚiDhaSaṅ* **2:117** परः] N; वरः K, *ŚiDhaSaṅ*; पनः W **2:117** स्मृतः] KW, *ŚiDhaSaṅ*; ⏑̲ --- N **2:117** वेदाध्यायिसहस्रेभ्यो ह्याहि°] K[pc]; --- सहस्रेभ्यो ह्याहि° N; वेदाध्यायीसहस्रेभ्यो ह्याहि° K[ac]; ⊔ यिसहस्रस्या ह्याहि° W; वेदाध्यायिसहस्राणामाहि *ŚiDhaSaṅ* **2:119** तस्य दत्तम्भवे ऽनन्तं] NKW; तस्मै दत्तं भवेद्दत्तं *ŚiDhaSaṅ* **2:119** परः] NKW; वरः *ŚiDhaSaṅ* **2:119** एषां लक्षगुणान्दद्यादेकन्दद्यात्तु] NK; एषां लक्षगुणान्दद्यादेकन्दद्यान्तु W; अन्येषां कोट्गुणितं दद्यादेकं तु *ŚiDhaSaṅ* **2:120** न तेषां] W, *ŚiDhaSaṅ*; ⏑̲ तेषां N; एतेषां K **2:120** तुल्यमेतत्तु] K; ⏑̲ ल्यमेतत्तु N; कल्पमेवन्तु W; तुल्यमेवं हि *ŚiDhaSaṅ* **2:120** वरो वरः] N; ⊔ वरः K; व ˉ वरः W; परो वरः *ŚiDhaSaṅ* **2:120** यस्य दाने न दुःखानि] W; यस्य दाने --- नि N; यस्य दाने ⊔ नि K **2:120** नरकप्रेतसम्भवाः] N; न ⊔ प्रेतसंभवाः K; नभवप्रेतसम्भवाः W; नरकप्रेतजान्यपि *ŚiDhaSaṅ* **2:121** विपापाः] K; विपापा NW **2:122** देयमात्मनः] NW; देय+ः+मात्मन K **2:122** स्वल्पमल्पपि] NW; स्वल्पमण्वपि K

॥ ⊗॥ इति निश्वासमुखतत्त्वसंहितायां लौकिके द्वितीयः पटलः ॥ ⊗॥

श्लो 122

2:122 °संहितायां] K; °सहितायां NW **2:122** श्लो (122)] K; श्लो --- 2 N; श्लो - 22 W

निश्वासमुखतत्त्वसंहितायां तृतीयः पटलः॥

[4] देव्युवाच।
दानधर्म्मस्त्वया ख्यातस्तीर्त्थधर्मञ्च मे वद।
स्नाने पुण्यफलं यत्स्यात्तीर्थे तीर्थे भविष्यति॥ 3:1॥

ईश्वर उ।
गङ्गा सरस्वती पुण्या यमुना गोमती तथा।
चर्मिला चन्द्रभागा च सरयुर्ग्गण्डकी तथा॥ 3:2॥

जम्बुका च शतद्रू च कालिका सुप्रभा तथा।
वितस्ती च विपाशा च नर्मदा च पु[5]नःपुना॥ 3:3॥

गोदावरी महावर्त्ता शर्करावर्त्तमर्जुनी।
कावेरी कौशिकी चैव तृतीया च महानदी॥ 3:4॥

विटङ्का प्रतिकूला च सोमनन्दा च विश्रुता।
करतोया वेत्रवती रेणुका वेणुका च या॥ 3:5॥

आत्रेयगङ्गा वैतरणी कर्म्मारी ह्लादनी तथा।

1 *Niśvāsamukha* 3.1a–3.13b is parallel with *Śivadharmasaṅgraha* 7.1a–7.13b.

3:1 यत्स्यात्] NK; यस्यात् W; किं स्यात् *ŚiDhaSaṅ* **3:1** भविष्यति] NKW; सुरेश्वर *ŚiDhaSaṅ* **3:2** उ] NW; उवाच K, *ŚiDhaSaṅ* **3:2** सरस्वती] K, *ŚiDhaSaṅ*; स्वरस्वती NW **3:2** चर्मिणी] *ŚiDhaSaṅ*; चर्मिला NW; चर्मि () ⊔ K **3:2** सरयुर्ग्गण्डकी] NW; शरयूर्ग्गण्डकी K; सरयूर्ग्गण्डकी *ŚiDhaSaṅ* **3:3** विपाशा] N, *ŚiDhaSaṅ*; विपासा KW **3:3** च पुनःपुना] KW, *ŚiDhaSaṅ*; च --- पुना N **3:4** °मर्जुनी] *ŚiDhaSaṅ*; °मर्जुरी N; °मंर्जुरी K; °मर्जरी W **3:5** विटङ्का] NKW; वटङ्का *ŚiDhaSaṅ* **3:6** कर्म्मारी ह्लादनी तथा] N; कर्म्मारी ह्लादिनी तथा KW; कौशिकी ह्लादनी च या *ŚiDhaSaṅ*

स्नावनी च सवर्ण्णा सा कल्माषा स्रंसिनी शुभा॥ 3:6॥

वसिष्ठा च वि[6]पापा च सिन्धुवत्यारुणी तथा।
ताम्रा चैव त्रिसन्ध्या च मन्दाकिन्यः पराः स्मृताः॥ 3:7॥

तैलकोशी च पारा च दुन्दुभी नलिनी तथा।
नीलगङ्गा च गोधा च पूर्ण्णचन्द्रा शशिप्रभा॥ 3:8॥

उपवासरतस्तासु यः स्नायात्तु सरिद्वराम्।
समभ्यर्च्य पितॄन्देवान्स तु मुच्येत किल्बिषात्॥ 3:9॥

≪नद्येषा≫[10^r] पूतसलिला हरमूर्तिविनिसृता।
स्नातो यैस्तु विमुच्येत जलमूर्ति नमो ऽस्तु ते॥ 3:10॥

अयं मन्त्रमनुस्मृत्य कुर्यान्नद्यवगाहनम्।
सर्वपापविशुद्धात्मा देहत्यागे दिवं ययौ॥ 3:11॥

शोणपुष्करलोहित्ये मानसे सिन्धुसागरे।
ब्रह्मावर्त्ते कर्द्दमाले स्नात्वा च लवणोदधौ॥ 3:12॥

सर्वपापविशुद्धात्मा पितृदेवांश्च पूजयेत्।
[2]अग्निर्योनिर्भवेन्नित्यं विष्णु रेतः प्रकीर्त्तितः॥ 3:13॥

---

13 Cf. *Śivadharmasaṅgraha* 7.13cd: अग्निर्योनिर्विष्णु रेता ब्रह्मणः पिता रुद्रमूर्तिरापः॥

3:6 सवर्ण्णा सा] NW *ŚiDhaSaṅ*; सवर्ण्णाभा K **3:6** कल्माषास्रंसिनी] NK; कल्माषाश्रंसिनी W; कल्माषस्रंसनी *ŚiDhaSaṅ* **3:6** शुभा] W, *ŚiDhaSaṅ*; --- NK **3:7** वसिष्ठा च विपापा च] *conj.*; वसिष्ठा --- पापा च N; वसिष्ठा च विपापापा च K (unmetrical); वसिष्ठा च ⁻ पाया च W; वशिष्ठा च अपापाच *ŚiDhaSaṅ* **3:7** सिन्धुवत्यारुणी] NW, *ŚiDhaSaṅ*; सिन्धुर्वप्तारुणी K **3:7** पराः] W^{ac}, *ŚiDhaSaṅ*K^{pc}; परा $NK^{ac}W^{pc}$ **3:8** तैलकोशी च पारा] N; तैलकाशी च पारा K; तैलकोसी च पारा W; वाग्वती तैलकोशी *ŚiDhaSaṅ* **3:8** गोधा] NKW; बोधा *ŚiDhaSaṅ* **3:9** यः स्नायात्तु सरिद्वराम्] N^{pc}; यः स्नायात्तु सरि+द्+वराम् N; यः स्नाया ×⏓× त्तु सरिद्वराम् K; यः स्ना ⁻न्तु सरिद्वराम् W; यः स्नायाद्धि सरित्स्विह *ŚiDhaSaṅ* **3:9** पितॄन्देवान्] K, *ŚiDhaSaṅ*; पितॄदेवान् N; विष्णुदेवा W **3:9** स तु मुच्येत किल्बिषात्] K, *ŚiDhaSaṅ*; स तु मुच्येत ि --- N; ⊔ W **3:10** नद्येषा] *ŚiDhaSaṅ*; --- NKW **3:10** हरमूर्तिविनिसृता] NKW; हरमूर्तिरियं स्मृता *ŚiDhaSaṅ* **3:10** स्नातो] *ŚiDhaSaṅ*; ⏑̆ तो N; ⊔ तो KW **3:10** जलमूर्ति नमो ऽस्तु ते] *ŚiDhaSaṅ*; जलमूर् ि ⏓ ⏓ मो ऽस्तु ते A; जलमूर्तिर्नमो ऽस्तु ते K; जल ⁻ ⁻ नमो ऽस्तु ते W **3:11** अयं] *conj.*; अय NW; इदं K; इमं *ŚiDhaSaṅ* **3:11** नद्यवगाहनम्] KW, *ŚiDhaSaṅ*; नद्यावगाहनम् N **3:12** °लोहित्ये मानसे] NW, *ŚiDhaSaṅ*; °लौहित्यमानस° K **3:12** स्नात्वा च लवणोददौ] K, *ŚiDhaSaṅ*; स्नावा --- N; ⊔ णोद ⁻ W **3:13** पितृदेवांश्च पूजयेत्] *ŚiDhaSaṅ*; पितॄ --- NW; पितॄन्देवान् (समर्चयन्) K **3:13** अग्निर्योनिर्भवेन्नित्यं विष्णु] *em.*; अग्नियोनिर्भवेन्नित्यं विष्णु N; अग्नि ⊔ भवेन्नित्यं विष्णू K; अग्नि ⊔ वे नित्यं विष्णु W

ब्रह्माणम्पितरं विन्द्याद्रुद्रमूर्त्ति जलं स्मृतम्।
एतानुस्मृत्य यः स्नायात्स याति परमाङ्गतिम्॥ 3:14॥

नदीनदेषु यो देहं कामतो वाप्यकामतः।
समुत्सृज्य विशुद्धात्मा स्वर्ग्गलोकम्व्रजेदिह॥ 3:15॥

स्वर्ग्गलोकात्परिभ्रष्टो जायते विपुले कुले।
यस्तीर्त्थं स्मरते नित्यं [3]मरणं चाभिकांक्षते॥ 3:16॥

अग्निप्रवेशं यः कुर्यान्मानवो नियमे स्थितः।
रुद्रलोकमवाप्नोति तेनैव सह मोदते॥ 3:17॥

रुद्रलोकात्परिभ्रष्टो वह्निलोकमवाप्नुयात्।
भुक्त्वा वह्निमयान्भोगाञ्जायते पृथिवीपतिः॥ 3:18॥

अमरेशम्प्रभासञ्च नैमिषं पुष्करन्तथा।
आषाढन्दिण्डिमुण्डिञ्च भारभूतिञ्च लाकुलिम्॥ 3:19॥

---

14 *Niśvāsamukha* 3.14c–3.15d is parallel with *Śivadharmasaṅgraha* 7.14a–7.15b.

16 *Niśvāsamukha* 3.16 is parallel with *Śivadharmasaṅgraha* 7.16c–7.17b.

19 *Niśvāsamukha* 3.19–3.22 is parallel with *Śivadharmasaṅgraha* 7.17c–7.21b.

19 Cf. *Guhyasūtra* 7.112–121: अमरेशम्प्रहासञ्च नैमिषं पुष्करन्तथा। आषाढिन्दिण्डिमुण्डिञ्च भारभूतिं सलाकुलिम्॥ प्रत्यात्मिके मृता ये तु ते व्रजन्त्येव तत्पदम्। हरिश्चन्द्रं परं गुह्यं गुह्यं मध्यमकेश्वरम्॥ श्रीपर्वतं समाख्यातञ्जल्पेश्वरमतः परम्। अम्ब्रातिकेश्वरं चैव महाकालं तथैव च॥ केदारमुत्तमं गुह्यं महाभैरवमेव च। गुह्याष्टके मृता ये तु ते व्रजन्तीह तत्पदम्॥ गयाञ्चैव कुरुक्षेत्रन्नखलं कनखलन्तथा। विमलञ्चाट्टहासञ्च माहेन्द्रम्भीममष्टमम्॥ अतिगुह्ये मृता ये तु अतिगुह्यं व्रजन्ति ते। भद्रापदं रुद्रकोटिमविमुक्तं महाबलम्॥ गोकर्णं रुद्रकर्ण्णञ्च स्वर्णाक्षं स्थाणुरष्टमम्। एतेष्वपि मृतास्सम्यग्भित्त्वा लोकमशेषतः॥ दीप्यमानास्तु गच्छन्ति अत्र स्थानेषु ये मृताः। छगरण्डं द्विरण्डञ्च माकोटम्मण्डलेश्वरम्॥ कालञ्जरं समाख्यातन्देवदारुवनन्तथा। शङ्कुकर्ण्णन्तथैवेह स्थलेश्वरमतः परम्॥ एतेष्वपि मृता ये तु भित्त्वा लोकमशेषतः। दीप्यमानास्तु गच्छन्ति स्थानाष्टकमिदं प्रिये॥

3:14 °द्रुद्रमूर्ति जलं] N; °द्रुद्रमूर्तिर्जलं K; °द्रु ⁻ मूर्तिजलं W **3:14** एतानुस्मृत्य] *em.*; एतानुत्स्मृत्य NW; एतान्संस्मृत्य K; एताननुस्मृत्य *ŚiDhaSaṅ* (unmetrical) **3:15** स्वर्ग्गलोकम्व्रजेदिह] NKW; सोमलोकमियान्नरः *ŚiDhaSaṅ* **3:16** स्वर्गलोकात्] NKW; सोमलोकात् *ŚiDhaSaṅ* **3:16** यस्तीर्त्थं स्मरते] NK; यस्तीर्थे स्मरते W; तत्तिर्थं संस्मरेन् *ŚiDhaSaṅ* **3:16** नित्यं] *ŚiDhaSaṅ*; --- NK; नि ⊔ W **3:16** चाभिकांक्षते] NKW; चात्र कांक्षते *ŚiDhaSaṅ* **3:18** वह्निमयान्] *conj. Acharya*; वह्नियान् NW; वह्नि( )यान् K **3:19** भारभूतिञ्च] *ŚiDhaSaṅ*; भारभूति NW (unmetrical); भारभूमि ⁻ K

हरिश्च[4]न्द्रं परं गुह्यं गुह्यं मध्यमकेश्वरम्।
श्रीपर्वतं समाख्यातञ्जल्पेश्वरमतः परम्॥ 3:20॥

अम्रातिकेश्वरञ्चैव महाकालन्तथैव च।
केदारमुत्तमङ्गुह्यम्महाभैरवमेव च॥ 3:21॥

गयाञ्चैव कुरुक्षेत्रं नखलङ्कनखलन्तथा।
विमलञ्चाट्टहासञ्च माहेन्द्रं भीममष्टमम्॥ 3:22॥

वस्त्रापदं रुद्रकोटिमविमुक्तम्महाबलम्।
[5]गोकर्णं भद्रकर्ण्णं च स्वर्ण्णाक्षं स्थाणुमष्टमम्॥ 3:23॥

छगलण्डं द्विरण्डञ्च माकोटम्मण्डलेश्वरम्।
कालञ्जरं समाख्यातं देवदारुवनन्तथा॥ 3:24॥

शङ्कुकर्ण्णन्तथैवेह थलेश्वरमतः परम्।
स्नानदर्शनपूजाभिर्मुच्यते सर्वकिल्बिषैः॥ 3:25॥

गच्छन्ति भित्वा ब्रह्माण्डमेषु स्थानेषु ये मृताः।
पञ्चाष्टकमिदन्दिव्यं «यं गत्त्वा»[6] न निवर्तते॥ 3:26॥

महाप्रलयस्थायी च स्रष्टानुग्रहकारकः।
दर्शनादेव गच्छन्ते पदन्दिव्यम्महालये॥ 3:27॥

---

23 *Niśvāsamukha* 3.23 is parallel with *Śivadharmasaṅgraha* 7.22.

24 *Niśvāsamukha* 3.24ab is parallel with *Śivadharmasaṅgraha* 7.21cd.

25 *Niśvāsamukha* 3.25c–3.30b is parallel with *Śivadharmasaṅgraha* 7.23–7.27.

3:20 हरिश्चन्द्रं परं गुह्यं गुह्यं] *ŚiDhaSaṅ*; हरि --- न्दम्परगुह्यङ्गुह्यम् N; हरि ⊔ गुह्यं गुह्यम् K; हरि ⊔ न्द्रपारगुह्यगुह्यम् W **3:21** अम्रातिके°] NK; अस्रातिके° W; आम्रातिके° *ŚiDhaSaṅ* **3:22** भीममष्टमम्] KW, *ŚiDhaSaṅ*; भाममष्टमम् N **3:23** वस्त्रापदं रुद्रकोटिमविमुक्तम्महाबलम्] *em.*; वस्त्रापदं रुद्रकोटिमविमुक्तं म --- N; वस्त्रापदं रुद्रकाशीमवियुक्तं महा ⊔ K; वस्त्र - दंरुद्रकोटिमविमुक्तं महाब ⊔W; भस्त्रापदं रुद्रकाशीमवियुक्तम् महालयम् *ŚiDhaSaṅ* **3:23** गोकर्णं भद्रकर्णं च] W, *ŚiDhaSaṅ*; --- कण्णम्भ +द+कर्ण्णञ्च N; ⊔ र्णम्भकर्णं च K **3:24** छगलण्डन्] *ŚiDhaSaṅ*; छगरण्डं NW; ⊔ गरण्डं K **3:24** कालञ्जरं] *em.*; कारञ्जरं NKW **3:25** थलेश्वर°] NW; स्थलेश्वर° K **3:26** पञ्चाष्टकमिदन्दिव्यं] K; प --- मिदन्दि --- A; प ⊔ मिदं दिव्यं W; पञ्चाष्टकपदं दिव्यं *ŚiDhaSaṅ* **3:26** यं गत्त्वा] *ŚiDhaSaṅ*; --- NKW **3:27** महाप्रलयस्थायी च] NKW; प्रलयस्थायिनो दिव्या *ŚiDhaSaṅ* **3:27** स्रष्टानुग्रहकारकः] NK; श्रष्टा तु ग्रहकारकः W; स्थित्यनुग्रहकारिणः *ŚiDhaSaṅ* **3:27** गच्छन्ते] NKW; गच्छन्ति *ŚiDhaSaṅ* **3:27** महालये] NW, *ŚiDhaSaṅ*; महालयम् K

केदारोदकपानाच्च गतिम्पञ्चाष्टमीं ध्रुवम्।
विद्यया संयुता ये तु पिबन्ते च [10^{v}] जलं शुभम्॥ 3:28॥

शिवसायोज्यतां यान्ति सर्वावस्थापि मानवाः।
गुह्यान्यान्यपि देवस्य दृष्ट्वा मुच्यन्ति किल्बिषैः॥ 3:29॥

प्राप्नुवन्ति गणत्वं हि ये तत्र निधनङ्गताः।
उक्तं हरस्य माहात्म्यं हरेश्चापि निबोध मे॥ 3:30॥

शालग्रामे मल्लकूपे नित्यं ≪सौकरवे≫हरिः।
सन्निधाने मथुरायां श्वेतद्वीपे तथैव च॥ 3:31॥

दृष्ट्वा ⏑̆ [2] ⏑̆ ाव(?)टे(?) विष्णुं मुच्यते सर्वकिल्बिषैः।
स्थानेष्वेषु मृता यान्ति विष्णोस्तत्परमम्पदम्॥ 3:32॥

ब्रह्मस्कन्दगणेशस्य लोकपालग्रहेषु च।
देव्यामातरयक्षेषु पिशाचोरगराक्षसाम्॥ 3:33॥

तद्भक्तास्तद्गतिं यान्ति जपहोमाद्यपूजनैः।
अनाशकं यः कुरुते पापात्मा पापसंयुतः॥ 3:34॥

---

30 *Niśvāsamukha* 3.30c–3.34b is parallel with *Śivadharmasaṅgraha* 7.41–7.44.

3:28 गतिम्पञ्चाष्टमीं ध्रुवम्] *conj.*; गतिम्पञ्चाष्टमीं ध--- N; गतिम्पञ्चाष्टमीं ⊔ K; गतिम्पञ्चाष्ट ⊔ W; गतिः पञ्चाष्टकी ध्रुवा *ŚiDhaSaṅ* **3:28** विद्यया संयुता ये तु] *ŚiDhaSaṅ*; ि ⏑̆ द्यया ⏑̆ ˙ ⏑̆ ता ⏑̆ ⏑̆ N; विद्यया तं प्रगायन्ते K; ⊔ W **3:28** पिबन्ते च जलं शुभम्] K; पिबन्ते च --- शुभम् N; ⊔ जाल श्चरन् W; पिबन्ति च शुभं जलम् *ŚiDhaSaṅ* **3:29** शिवसायोज्यतां] NW; शिवसायुज्यतां K, *ŚiDhaSaṅ* **3:29** सर्वावस्थापि] NW; सर्वावस्थासु K; सर्वावस्थाश्च *ŚiDhaSaṅ* **3:29** गुह्यान्यान्यपि देवस्य] NW; गुह्यान्यान्यपि देवस्य K; गुह्यायतनमीशस्य *ŚiDhaSaṅ* **3:29** दृष्ट्वा मुच्यन्ति किल्बिषैः] NKW; मुच्यते वीक्ष्य किल्बिषैः *ŚiDhaSaṅ* **3:30** माहात्म्यं] K, *ŚiDhaSaṅ*; माहात्म्य NW **3:31** नित्यं] KW, *ŚiDhaSaṅ*; नि ⏑̆ N **3:31** सौकरवे] *ŚiDhaSaṅ*; साकरव N; ⊔ K; ⊔ रव W **3:31** सन्निधाने मथुरायां] *conj.*; सन्निधा ⏑̆ मथुरायां N; सन्निधा ⊔ K; सन्नि ⊔ W; मथुरायां स्थितः साक्षात् *ŚiDhaSaṅ* **3:31** श्वेतद्वीपे तथैव च] *ŚiDhaSaṅ*; श्वेतद्वीपे त --- N; ⊔ KW **3:32** दृष्ट्वा ---ाव(?)टे(?) विष्णुं मुच्यते सर्वकिल्बिषैः] N; ⊔ विष्णुं मुच्यते सर्वकिल्बिषैः K; ⊔ पा ⊔ विष्णुं मुच्यते सर्वकिल्बिषैः W; तं दृष्ट्वा पुरुषवटे विष्णुम्मुच्येत किल्बिषैः *ŚiDhaSaṅ* **3:32** स्थानेष्वेषु मृता यान्ति] NK; स्थानेष्वष्ट मृतो यांति W; स्थानेष्वेषु मृतो यायात् *ŚiDhaSaṅ* **3:32** विष्णोस्तत्परमम्पदम्] NKW; तद्विष्णोः परमं पदम् *ŚiDhaSaṅ* **3:33** °गणेशस्य] NKW; °गणेशानां *ŚiDhaSaṅ* **3:33** देव्यामातरयक्षेषु] NKW; उमाया मातृयक्षाणां *ŚiDhaSaṅ* **3:33** °राक्षसाम्] NW, *ŚiDhaSaṅ*; °रक्षसाम् K **3:34** तद्भक्तास्तद्गतिं] NK; तंद्भक्तास्तद्गतिं W; ये भक्तास्तद्गतिं *ŚiDhaSaṅ* **3:34** जपहोमाद्यपूजनैः] NKW; जपहोमार्चनादिभिः *ŚiDhaSaṅ*

सर्वपापविनिर्मु[[क्तो]] [3]विष्णुलोकञ्च गच्छति।
विष्णुलोकाच्च्युतश्चैष ब्राह्मणः पण्डितो भवेत्॥ 3:35॥

तेनैवाभ्यासयोगेन तच्चैवाभ्यसते पुनः।
एवन्ते सर्वमाख्यातमुपवासविधिं शृणु॥ 3:36॥

मासे मासे तु यः कुर्यादेकरात्रमुपोषितम्।
पञ्चगव्यं शुचिर्भूत्वा पीत्वा सान्तपनम्भवेत्॥ 3:37॥

सम्वत्सरेण शुद्धात्मा ब्रह्मलोके [4] महीयते।
कृत्वा सान्तपनम्चान्यो द्वादशाहमभोजनम्॥ 3:38॥

तङ्कृत्वा मुच्यते पापैर्विप्रत्वाच्च न हीयते।
द्वादशैतानि कृत्वा वै सद्गतिम्प्राप्नुयान्नरः॥ 3:39॥

एकैकम्भक्षयेद्ग्रासन्त्रीण्यहानि जितेन्द्रियः।
त्रिरात्रोपवसेच्चैव अतिकृच्छ्रं विशोधने॥ 3:40॥

प्रतिपक्षन्तु यः कुर्यात्स स्वर्ग्गफलभाग्भवेत्।
[5] जलं क्षीरं घृतञ्चोष्णमेकैकन्तु त्र्यहम्पिबेत्॥ 3:41॥

त्रिःस्नायी च विशुद्धात्मा सर्वपापविवर्जितः।
प्राप्नुयात्स्वर्गतिं विप्रः पापात्मा च विशुध्यति॥ 3:42॥

---

36 *Niśvāsamukha* 3.36c–3.37 is parallel with *Śivadharmasaṅgraha* 7.45a–7.46b.

37 Cf. *Manusmṛti* 11.213: गोमूत्रं गोमयं क्षीरं दधि सर्पिः कुशोदकम्। एकरात्रोपवासश्च कृच्छ्रं सान्तपनं स्मृतम्॥

40 Cf. *Manusmṛti* 11.214: एकैकं ग्रासमश्नीयात् त्र्यहाणि त्रीणि पूर्ववत्। त्र्यहं चोपवसेदन्त्यमतिकृच्छ्रं चरन्द्विजः॥

3:35 ब्राह्मणः] KW; ब्राह्मंणः N **3:36** तच्चैवाभ्यसते] N; तथैवाभ्यसते K; त ⊔ सने W **3:37** मासे मासे तु] NKW; मासि मासि च *ŚiDhaSaṅ* **3:37** °मुपोषितम्] *ŚiDhaSaṅ*; °मुपोषितः NKW **3:37** सान्तपनम्भवेत्] NKW; मुच्येत पातकैः *ŚiDhaSaṅ* **3:38** ब्रह्मलोके महीयते] *conj.*; ब्रह्म --- महीयते N; ब्रह्म तस्य न हीयते K; ब्रह्म ⊔ न हीयते W **3:39** तङ्कृत्वा] NW; तत्कृत्वा K **3:40** अतिकृच्छ्रं विशोधने] K; अतिकृच्छ्रविशोधने N; अतिकृच्छ्रविसोधने W **3:41** °मेकैकन्तु त्र्यहम्पिबेत्] N; °मेकैकं तु अहं पिबेत् K; °मेकैकं तु त्राहम्पिबेत् W **3:42** त्रिःस्नायी] K; त्रिस्नायी NW **3:42** स्वर्गतिं विप्रः] *em.*; सर्ग्गतिं विप्र NW; स्वर्गतिं विप्र K

एकैकम्वर्द्धयेद्ग्रासं शुक्ले कृष्णे च ह्रासयेत्।
त्रिष्कालस्नायी मासन्तु चन्द्रवृद्ध्या व्रतञ्चरेत्॥ 3:43॥

चान्द्रायणमिदं श्रेष्ठं सर्वपापापनोदनम्।
पापी मुच्येत [6] पापेन अपापः स्वर्ग्गगो भवेत्॥ 3:44॥

अष्टावष्टौ समश्नीयात्पिण्डान्मध्यन्दिने स्थिते।
हविष्येण समायुक्तान्मुच्यते सर्वपातकैः॥ 3:45॥

अपापी स्वर्ग्गमायाति यतिचान्द्रायणेन तु।
चतुरो भक्षयेत्पिण्डान्पूर्वा [11^r] ह्णे तु विचक्षणः॥ 3:46॥

सूर्यस्यास्तमने वापि चतुरो भक्षयेत्पुनः।
शिशुचान्द्रायणं ह्येतदुपपातकनाशनम्॥ 3:47॥

≪मासेनैकेन≫शुद्धात्मा अपापी स्वर्गतिं व्रजेत्।
त्रिरात्राणि तु यः कुर्या≪त्सर्वकालं ≫शुचिव्रतः॥ 3:48॥

---

43 *Niśvāsamukha* 3.43a–3.56f is parallel with *Śivadharmasaṅgraha* 7.53a–7.67b.

43 Cf. *Manusmṛti* 11.217: एकैकं ह्रासयेत्पिण्डं कृष्णे शुक्ले च वर्धयेत्। उपस्पृशंस्त्रिषवणमेतत्चान्द्रायणं स्मृतम्॥

45 Cf. *Manusmṛti* 11.219: अष्टावष्टौ समश्नीयात्पिण्डान्मध्यंदिने स्थिते। नियतात्मा हविष्यस्य यतिचान्द्रायणं चरन्॥

46 Cf. *Manusmṛti* 11.220: चतुरः प्रातरश्नीयात्पिण्डान्विप्रः समाहितः। चतुरो ऽस्तमिते सूर्ये शिशुचान्द्रायणं स्मृतम्॥

3:43 ग्रासं] NKW; पिण्डं *ŚiDhaSaṅ* **3:43** त्रिष्कालस्नायी मासन्तु] NW; त्रिकालस्नायी मासन्तु K; त्रिस्नायी मासमेकन्तु *ŚiDhaSaṅ* **3:44** सर्वपापापनोदनम्] N, *ŚiDhaSaṅ*; सर्वपापप्रणोदनम् K; सर्वपापा ⁻ नोदनम् W **3:44** मुच्येत] K, *ŚiDhaSaṅ*; म ⊔ N; मुच्य ⊔ W **3:44** अपापः] NKW; अपापी *ŚiDhaSaṅ* **3:45** समायुक्तान्] N; समायुक्तो K; समायुक्तात् W; समायुक्तं *ŚiDhaSaṅ* **3:46** °मायाति] NKW; °माप्नोति *ŚiDhaSaṅ* **3:46** यतिचान्द्रायणेन तु] N; --- यणेन N; यति ⊔ यणेन W; यतिचान्द्रायणान्नरः *ŚiDhaSaṅ* **3:46** चतुरो भक्षयेत्पिण्डान्पूर्वाह्णे] K, *ŚiDhaSaṅ*; चतुरो भ --- ह्णे N; चतुरो भक्षये ⊔ ह्णे W **3:47** सूर्यस्यास्तमने वापि] NK, *ŚiDhaSaṅ*; सूर्यास्यास्तमने वापि W **3:47** °द्रायणं] K^{pc}, *ŚiDhaSaṅ*; °द्रायण N; °द्रायनं K^{ac}; चान्द्राषणा W^{pc}; चान्द्रोषणा W^{ac} **3:47** °नाशनम्] K, *ŚiDhaSaṅ*; °ना --- NW **3:48** मासेनैकेन] *ŚiDhaSaṅ*; --- केन NW; पापी मुच्यति K **3:48** स्वर्गतिं] K, *ŚiDhaSaṅ*; स्वर्ग्गत N; स्वर्ग्गतम् W **3:48** त्रिरात्राणि तु] K; त्रिरात्रा ⩳ तु N; त्रिरात्रा ि ⩳ W; त्रिरात्राणि च *ŚiDhaSaṅ* **3:48** कुर्यात्सर्वकालं] *ŚiDhaSaṅ*; कु --- NW; कुर्या ⊔ K **3:48** शुचिव्रतः] NK, *ŚiDhaSaṅ*; ⊔ चिव्रतः W

शतेनैकेन पूर्णेन मुच्यते सर्वकिल्बिषात्।
सहस्रेण महापापान्मु[2]च्यते जपसंयुतः॥ 3:49॥

अपापी स्वर्ग्गमाप्नोति च्युतश्च धनभाग्भवेत्।
एकान्तरोपवासानि द्वादशाब्दङ्करोति यः॥ 3:50॥

महतो मुच्यते पापाच्छुद्धात्मा स्वर्ग्गमाप्नुयात्।
पक्षोपवासं यः कुर्याद्द्वादशाब्दान्विकल्मषः॥ 3:51॥

स स्वर्ग्गतिमवाप्नोति पापात्मा तु विकल्मषः।
प्रतिवर्षन्तु यः कुर्यान्मासैकं संयते[3]न्द्रियः॥ 3:52॥

उपवासन्नरो लोके स गतिमुत्तमाम्व्रजेत्।
महापापाद्विशुद्ध्येत धनवानपि जायते॥ 3:53॥

एकान्नञ्चैव भुञ्जानो धनवाञ्जायते नरः।
नक्ते ऽन्नम्भुञ्जते यस्तु यावज्जीवन्नरोत्तमः।
धनधान्यसमृद्धात्मा उत्तमो जायते नरः॥ 3:54॥

अयाचितन्तु भुञ्जानो यावज्जीवं ≪व्रते नरः≫।
[4] मृतो देवत्वमाप्नोति पापान्मुच्यति पातकी॥ 3:55॥

मधु मान्सन्न भक्षेत व्रतमेतदनुत्तमम्।

---

56 Cf. *Manusmṛti* 2.177a: वर्जयेन्मधु मांसं च।

3:49 शतेनैकेन] K, *ŚiDhaSaṅ*; श ⏑⏑ केन N; स ⁻ नैकेन W **3:49 सर्वकिल्बिषात्**] K, *ŚiDhaSaṅ*; सर्व ⏑ बि --- N; स ⊔ W **3:49 सहस्रेण महापापान्मुच्यते**] *em.*; --- च्यते N; ⊔ पापान्मुच्यते KW; सहस्रेण महापापैर्मुच्यते *ŚiDhaSaṅ* **3:50 धनभाग्भवेत्**] NW; धनं भाग्भवेत् K; धनवान् भवेत् *ŚiDhaSaṅ* **3:50 ॰वासानि**] NKW; ॰वासन्तु *ŚiDhaSaṅ* **3:51 दशाब्दान्विकल्मषः**] *conj.*; दशाब्दान्वि ⏑ ल्मशः N; ॰दशाब्दानि नित्यशः K; ॰दशाब्दाद्विकल्मसः W; द्वादशाब्दं विकल्मषः *ŚiDhaSaṅ* **3:52 स्वर्ग्गतिमवाप्नोति**] NKW; स्वर्गगतिमाप्नोति *ŚiDhaSaṅ* **3:52 प्रतिवर्षन्तु**] NW, *ŚiDhaSaṅ*; प्रप्रतिवर्षन्तु K **3:52 यः कुर्यान्मासैकं संयतेन्द्रियः**] *ŚiDhaSaṅ*; य --- न्द्रियः N; यः (कुर्याद्उपवासं जिते)न्द्रियः K; यः कुर्यात्मा ⊔ न्द्रियः W **3:53 गतिमुत्तमाम्**] NKW; गतिञ्चोत्तमां *ŚiDhaSaṅ* **3:53 महापापाद्विशुद्ध्येत**] NW; महापापाद्विमुच्येत K; महत्पापं विशुद्ध्येत *ŚiDhaSaṅ* **3:53 जायते**] NKW; पूजयेत् *ŚiDhaSaṅ* **3:54 नक्ते ऽन्नम्भुञ्जते यस्तु यावज्जीवन्नरोत्तमः**] NKW; यावज्जिवं तु यो भुङ्क्ते नक्तमन्नं नरोत्तमः *ŚiDhaSaṅ* **3:54 धनधान्यसमृद्धात्मा**] NKW; धनधान्यसमृद्धः स्याद् *ŚiDhaSaṅ* **3:55 यावज्जीवं**] K, *ŚiDhaSaṅ*; यावज्जीव KW **3:55 व्रते नरः**] *ŚiDhaSaṅ*; --- NKW **3:55 मृतो**] *em.*; ⏑ तो N; ⊔ KW; मृते *ŚiDhaSaṅ* **3:55 देवत्वमाप्नोति**] NK, *ŚiDhaSaṅ*; ⊔ त्वमाप्नोति W **3:55 पापान्मुच्यति पातकी**] K; पापान्मुच्यति पातका NW; पापान्मुच्येत पातकी *ŚiDhaSaṅ* **3:56 मधु मान्सन्न**] NW, *ŚiDhaSaṅ*; ⊔ न K

एवं यो वर्त्तते नित्यं स याति परमाङ्गतिम्॥ 3:56॥

ब्रह्मचर्यव्रतं कष्टं यश्चरेत्स्त्रीसमन्वितः।
इहामुत्र च सिद्ध्येत गतिं यास्यति चोत्तमाम्॥ 3:57॥

द्रव्यस्य विद्यमानस्य निवृत्तिं कुरुतेति यः।
स महाफलमाप्नो[5]ति तच्चानन्तम्भविष्यति॥ 3:58॥

मत्स्यं मान्सं सुरा सीधु राक्षसान्नमिदं स्मृतम्।
तद्ब्राह्मणे न दातव्यं गतिमिच्छन्महात्मनाम्॥ 3:59॥

देव्युवाच।
कतरं देवमाश्रित्य उपवासफलम्महत्।
कथं वा पूजनीयश्च कथयस्व प्रसादतः॥ 3:60॥

ईश्वर उ।
प्रतिपत्सूपवासी च ब्रह्माणम्पूजयीत यः।
ब्रह्मणे नमो [6]मन्त्रेण उभयोरपि पक्षयोः॥ 3:61॥

गन्धैः पुष्पैश्च धूपैश्च भक्ष्यभोज्यसमन्वितैः।
अब्दमेकं समभ्यर्च्य क्रतूनां प्राप्नुयात्फलम्॥ 3:62॥

अश्वमेधं राजसूयं सौवर्णञ्च गवामयम्।
सप्तभिः सोमसंस्थैश्च नरमेधसमन्वितैः॥ 3:63॥

---

57 *Niśvāsamukha* 3.57–3.69 is parallel with *Śivadharmasaṅgraha* 7.69c–7.72b.

60 *Niśvāsamukha* 3.60–3.83 is parallel with *Śivadharmasaṅgraha* 8.1a–8.25b.

3:57 ब्रह्मचर्यव्रतं] NK; ब्रह्मच ⁻ व्रतं W; ब्रह्मचर्यं व्रतं *ŚiDhaSaṅ* **3:57 स्त्रीसमन्वितः**] NW, *ŚiDhaSaṅ*; त्रीसमन्वितः K **3:57 इहामुत्र च सिद्ध्येत गतिं यास्यति**] NK; इहामुत्र च सिद्ध्ये ⁻ गतिं यास्यति W; इहैव मन्त्राः सिध्यन्ते गतिं व्रजति *ŚiDhaSaṅ* **3:58 कुरुतेति यः**] NKW; कुरुते तु यः *ŚiDhaSaṅ* **3:58 स महाफलमाप्नोति**] *conj.*; मह ⊔ ति NW; महा ⊔ K; स महत्फलमाप्नोति *ŚiDhaSaṅ* **3:59 तद्ब्राह्मणे न**] K; तद्ब्रह्मणे न NW; तच्छाम्भवेन *ŚiDhaSaṅ* **3:59 दातव्यं**] NKW; मोक्तव्यं *ŚiDhaSaṅ* **3:60 देवमाश्रित्य**] K, *ŚiDhaSaṅ*; देवमाशृत्य NW **3:60 पूजनीयश्च**] KW; पूजनीश्च N (unmetrical); पूजनीयास्ते *ŚiDhaSaṅ* **3:60 कथयस्व प्रसादतः**] NKW; ब्रवीहि परमेश्वर *ŚiDhaSaṅ* **3:61 च ब्रह्माणम्पूजयीत यः**] K; च ब्रह्माणम्पूजयी --- NW; तु ब्रह्माणं पूजयेन्नरः *ŚiDhaSaṅ* **3:61 ब्रह्मणे नमो**] *conj.*; --- NKW; ब्रह्मणे नम *ŚiDhaSaṅ* **3:61 मन्त्रेण**] NW; ⊔ ण K; इत्येवम् *ŚiDhaSaṅ* **3:62 गन्धैः पुष्पैश्च**] NK; ⁻ऐः पुष्पैश्च W; गन्धपुष्पैश्च *ŚiDhaSaṅ* **3:62 °समन्वितैः**] K; °समन्वितः NW; °समन्वितम् *ŚiDhaSaṅ* **3:62 प्राप्नुयात्फलम्**] NKW; फलमाप्नुयात् *ŚiDhaSaṅ* **3:63 सोमसंस्थैश्च**] N *ŚiDhaSaṅ*; सोमसंज्ञैश्च K; सोमसं ⁻श्च W

ब्रह्मा स्वयंभूर्विरिञ्चिः पद्मयोनिः प्रजापतिः।
चतुर्मुखः पद्म[11^{v}]हस्त ओमित्येकाक्षरस्तु यः॥ 3:64॥

चतुर्वेदधरः स्रष्टा गीर्वाणः परमेष्ठिनः।
सञ्ज्ञाभिः पूजयेदेभिर्ब्रह्माणममितद्युतिम्॥ 3:65॥

सम्वत्सरेण युक्तात्मा स्वर्ग्गलोके महीयते।
यावज्जीवन्तु कुर्वाणो ब्रह्मलोकं स गच्छति॥ 3:66॥

द्वितीयायां पूजयेदग्निमाज्येनैव तु तर्पयेत्।
वैश्वानरं जातवेदं हुतभु[2]ग्घव्यवाहनम्॥ 3:67॥

देववक्त्रं सर्वभक्षं घृणी च जगदाहकम्।
विभावसुं सप्तजिह्वं वरनामेति कीर्त्तितम्॥ 3:68॥

प्रतिमासं समभ्यर्च्य उभयोरपि पक्षयोः।
वर्षेणैकेन शुद्धात्मा यावज्जीवाग्निलोकता॥ 3:69॥

तृतीयायां पूजयेद्यक्षम्गान्धधूपनिवेदनैः।
उभाभ्यामपि पक्षाभ्यां याव«दब्दं भवेदिह»॥ 3:70॥

[3]धनन्दास्यति यक्षो हि भक्तियुक्तं सुपूजितः।

3:64 **ब्रह्मा स्वयंभूर्विरिञ्चिः**] *ŚiDhaSaṅ*; ब्र ⏑व ⏑ र्वि ⏑ N; ⊔ K; ब्र ˉˉ यम्भु विरिंचिः W **3:64** **पद्मयोनिः प्रजापतिः**] *ŚiDhaSaṅ*; --- NK; ˉ द्मयोनिः प्र ⊔ W **3:64** **चतुर्मुखः पद्म-हस्त**] *conj.*; --- हस्त NW; ⊔ K; गीर्वाणः पद्महस्तश्च *ŚiDhaSaṅ* **3:64** **ओमित्येकाक्षरस्तु यः**] N; ⊔ क्षरस्तु यः K; हस्त उमि ˉकाक्षरस्तु यः W; ओमित्येकाक्षरः प्रभुः *ŚiDhaSaṅ* **3:65** **स्रष्टा**] K, *ŚiDhaSaṅ*; स्रष्टां N; श्रष्टा W **3:65** **गीर्वाणः परमेष्ठिनः**] KW; गीर्वाणः पर्रमेष्ठिनः N; परमेष्ठी चतुर्मुखः *ŚiDhaSaṅ* **3:66** **सम्वत्सरेण**] N^{pc}KW; सम्वत्सरे+ण+ N **3:66** **ब्रह्मलोकं स गच्छति**] NKW; ब्रह्मलोके महीयते *ŚiDhaSaṅ* **3:67** **द्वितीयायां पूजयेद-ग्निम्**] W (unmetrical); द्वितीयायाम्पूजयेदग्नि --- N; ⊔ K; द्वितीये पूजयेदग्निम् *ŚiDhaSaṅ* **3:67** **आज्येनैव तु तर्पयेत्**] *ŚiDhaSaṅ*; --- NK; आज्यनेव तु तर्प्पयेत W **3:67** **वैश्वानरं जातवेदं हुतभुग्घव्यवाहनम्**] *conj.*; --- ग्घव्यवाहनम् NW; घव्यवाहनम् K; वैश्वानरो जातवे-दा हुतभुग्घव्यवाहनः *ŚiDhaSaṅ* **3:68** **देववक्त्रं सर्वभक्षं**] NKW; देववक्त्रः सर्वभक्षो *ŚiDhaSaṅ* **3:68** **जगदाहकम्**] N; जगता ⊔ म् K; जग ⊔ म् W; जगदाहकः *ŚiDhaSaṅ* **3:68** **विभा-वसुं सप्तजिह्वं**] NKW; विभावसुः सप्तजिह्वो *ŚiDhaSaṅ* **3:69** **उभयोरपि पक्षयोः**] NKW; पक्षयोरुभयोरपि *ŚiDhaSaṅ* **3:69** **यावज्जीवाग्निलोकता**] NKW; स गच्छेदग्निलोकताम् *ŚiDhaSaṅ* **3:70** **तृतीयायां पूजयेद्यक्षम्**] NKW (unmetrical); तृतीये पूजयेद्यक्षं *ŚiDhaSaṅ* **3:70** **उभाभ्यामपि पक्षाभ्यां**] *ŚiDhaSaṅ*; उभामपि पक्षाभ्या N; उभाभ्यामपि पक्षाक्भ्या ⏑ K; उभामपि पक्षाभ्यां W **3:70** **यावदब्दं भवेदिह**] *ŚiDhaSaṅ*; --- NK; याव ⊔ W **3:71** **ध-नन्दास्यति यक्षो हि भक्तियुक्तं सुपूजितः**] NK; ⊔ स्येति यक्षो हि भक्षियुक्तं सुपूजितः W; धनन्दास्यन्ति यक्षा हि धनदाद्याः सुपूजिताः *ŚiDhaSaṅ*

यावज्जीवं प्रकुर्वाणो धनदस्य पदम्व्रजेत्॥ 3:71॥

धनदश्च यक्षपतिर्वित्तेशो निधिपालकः।
राक्षसाधिपतिश्चैव पिङ्गलाक्षो विमानगः॥ 3:72॥

रुद्रसखा कुबेरश्च पौलस्त्यकुलनन्दनः।
लोकपालेश्वरश्चैव यक्षेन्द्रः परिकीर्तितः॥ 3:73॥

अब्दं पूज[4]यते यस्तु यक्षम्भक्तिसमन्वितः।
धनधान्यसमृद्धश्च यावज्जीवेन यक्षराट्॥ 3:74॥

गणेशम्पूजयेद्यस्तु गन्धपुष्पसमन्वितः।
भक्षभोज्यसमाकीर्णश्चतुर्थ्युभयपक्षयोः॥ 3:75॥

अब्देनैकेन शुद्धात्मा यावज्जीवे गणोत्तमः।
विनायकैर्नाभिभूयेद्यो ऽर्चयेत गणाधिपम्॥ 3:76॥

[5]विघ्नेश्वरं गणपतिमेकदन्तङ्गजाननम्।
गजकर्णन्तथा त्र्यक्षन्नागयज्ञोपवीतिनम्॥ 3:77॥

चतुर्भुजञ्च धूम्राक्षं वज्रतुण्डं विनायकम्।
महोदरञ्च सञ्ज्ञाभिस्साधकः संयतेन्द्रियः॥ 3:78॥

मोदकैर्ल्लड्डुकैश्चैव मूलकैर्वापि शोभनैः।
न तस्य दुर्ल्लभं किञ्चित्पूजयेद्यो गणाधिपम्॥ 3:79॥

3:71 यावज्जीवं प्रकुर्वाणो] NKW; यावज्जीवन्तु कुर्वाणो *ŚiDhaSaṅ* **3:72** धनदश्च यक्षपतिर्वित्तेशो] NW; धनदश्च यक्षपति वित्तेशो K; धनदो यक्षराजश्च वित्तेशो *ŚiDhaSaṅ* **3:73** रुद्रसखा] K; रुद्र ⏓ खा N; रुद्र ⁻खा W; रुद्रसखः *ŚiDhaSaṅ* **3:73** पौलस्त्य°] K, *ŚiDhaSaṅ*; पौलस् ⏓ N; पौलष्टि° W **3:73** परिकीर्तितः] KW, *ŚiDhaSaṅ*; परिकीर्त्ति --- N **3:74** अब्दं पूजयते यस्तु] *conj.*; --- त यस्तु N; ⊔ पूजयते यस्तु K; ⊔ यस्तु W; अब्दन्तु पूजयेद्यस्तु *ŚiDhaSaṅ* **3:74** °समन्वितः] NKW; °समाश्रितः *ŚiDhaSaṅ* **3:74** धनधान्यसमृद्धश्च यावज्जीवेन यक्षराट्] NK; वेरधा ⁻ समृद्धश्च यावज्जीवेन यक्षराट् W; धनधान्यसमृद्धस्तु यावज्जीवं स यक्षराट् *ŚiDhaSaṅ* **3:75** भक्ष°] N; भक्ष्य° KW, *ŚiDhaSaṅ* **3:76** यावज्जीवे गणोत्तमः] *conj.*; यावज्जीवे गणोत्तमम् NW; यावज्जीवं; गणा+धि+पम् K; स याति गणमन्दिरम् *ŚiDhaSaṅ* **3:76** विनायकैर्नाभिभूयेद्यो ऽर्चयेत गणाधिपम्] NKW; विघ्नैश्च नाभिभूयेत यो ऽर्चयेद्गणनायकम् *ŚiDhaSaṅ* **3:77** विघ्नेश्वरं गण°] *ŚiDhaSaṅ*; --- ण° N; (गणेश्वरं) गण° K; ⊔ श्वरङ्गण° W **3:77** गजाननम्] N[pc]KW, *ŚiDhaSaṅ*; +ग+जाननम् N **3:77** °यज्ञोपवीतिनम्] K, *ŚiDhaSaṅ*; °यज्ञोप्रवीतिनम् N; °यज्ञेप्रवीतिनम् W **3:78** वज्रतुण्डं] NKW; वक्रशुण्डम् *ŚiDhaSaṅ* **3:79** वापि] NKW; चापि *ŚiDhaSaṅ* **3:79** गणाधिपम्] KW, *ŚiDhaSaṅ*; गणाधि --- N

पञ्च[6]म्यां पूजयेन्नागान्पुष्पैः सुरभिशोभनैः ।
धूपैश्चैव सुगन्धैस्तु गुडक्षीररसपायसैः॥ 3:80॥

पुष्पैः शर्क्करमध्वाभिरुभयोरपि पक्षयोः ।
सम्वत्सरेण कामानि लभते ≪कांक्षितानि ≫तु ।
यावज्जीवं समभ्यर्च्य नागलोकमवाप्नुयात्॥ 3:81॥

स्कन्दं षष्ठ्यां पूजयेत्तु [12r] उपवाससमन्वितः ।
गन्धपुष्पसधूपेन भक्षभोज्येन संयुतः॥ 3:82॥

उभाभ्यामपि पक्षाभ्याम्पूजयित्वा समाहितः ।
स्कन्दं विशाखन्त्रिवर्ण्णं उमानन्दाग्निगर्भजम्॥ 3:83॥

गङ्गागर्भं शरद्गर्भङ्कृत्तिकासुतमेव च ।
षण्मुखं शक्तिहस्तञ्च मयूरवरवाहनम्॥ 3:84॥

पञ्चछटङ्कुमारञ्च पूज[[((येन्नाम))]]भिः शुभैः ।
[2]प्रतिमासन्तु युक्तात्मा मार्ग्गशीर्षे समाहितः॥ 3:85॥

---

84 Cf. *Śivadharmasaṅgraha* 8.25c–8.26b: नैगमेशो महासेनस्त्रिवर्णः कृत्तिकासुतः॥ पञ्चशिखः कुमारश्च देवसेनापतिर्गुहः ।

84 *Niśvāsamukha* 3.84cd is parallel with *Śivadharmasaṅgraha* 8.26cd.

85 *Niśvāsamukha* 3.85ab is parallel with *Śivadharmasaṅgraha* 8.26ab.

85 Cf. *Śivadharmasaṅgraha* 8.27ab: नामभिः पूजयेदेभिः संयतो मार्ग्गशीर्षतः ।

3:80 पञ्चम्याम्] KW, *ŚiDhaSaṅ*; --- म् N **3:80** धूपैश्चैव सुगन्धैस्तु गुडक्षीररसपायसैः] NW; धूपैश्चैव सुगन्धैश्च गुडक्षीररसपायसैः K; धूपैः सुरभिगन्धैश्च गुडक्षीरैः सपायसैः *ŚiDha-Saṅ* **3:81** पुष्पैः शर्क्करमध्वाभिरुभयोरपि पक्षयोः] *conj.*; पुष्पैः शर्क्करमध्वांभिरुभयोरपि पक्षयोः N; शर्करगन्धाभैरुभयोरपि पक्षयोः K; शर्क्करमध्वास्नरुभयोरपि पक्षयोः W; शर्क-रामधुपुष्पैश्च पक्षयोरुभयोरपि *ŚiDhaSaṅ* **3:81** सम्वत्सरेण कामानि लभते कांक्षितानि तु] *ŚiDhaSaṅ*; सम्वत्सरेण कामा --- ि लभते --- ि तु N; सम्वत्सरेण कामास्निर्लभते ⊔ K; सम्वत्सरेण कामानि लभते ⊔ W **3:82** स्कन्दं षष्ठ्यां पूजयेत्तु] K; --- NW; स्कन्दं षष्ठ्यां तु संपूज्य *ŚiDhaSaṅ* **3:82** उपवास॰] KW, *ŚiDhaSaṅ*; ⊻ पवास॰ N **3:82** ॰सधूपेन भक्ष॰] NW; ॰सुधूपेन भक्ष्य॰ K, *ŚiDhaSaṅ* **3:83** स्कन्दं विशाखन्त्रिवर्ण्णं उमानन्दाग्निगर्भजम्] *em.*; स्कन्दं विशाखन्तृवर्ण्णं उमानन्दाग्निगर्भजम् N; स्कन्दं विशाखं ⊔ उमानन्दाग्निगर्भजम् K; स्कन्दं विशाखन्तृवर्ण्ण उमानन्दाग्निगर्भजाम् W; स्कन्दो विशाखः क्रोञ्चारिरुमानन्दो ऽग्निगर्भ-जः *ŚiDhaSaṅ* **3:84** षण्मुखं शक्तिहस्तञ्च] NK; खण्मुखशक्तिहस्तञ्च W; षड्मुखः शक्तिहस्तश्च *ŚiDhaSaṅ* **3:84** मयूरवरवाहनम्] K; मयूर --- वाहनम् NW; मयूरवरवाहनः *ŚiDhaSaṅ* **3:85** पञ्चछटङ्कुमारञ्च पूजयेन्नामभिः शुभैः] *conj.*; पञ्चछटङ्कुमारञ्च पूज N; पञ्चछटङ्कुमारञ्च पूजयेन्नाम K; पञ्चछटाङ्कुमारञ्च पूजयेन्नाम W; पञ्चच्छटः कुमारश्च देवसेनापतिर्गुहः *ŚiDhaSaṅ*

सर्वकामानवाप्नोति वर्षेणैकेन मानवः।
यावज्जीवं समभ्यर्च्य स्कन्दसायोज्यमाप्नुयात्॥ 3:86॥

सप्तम्याम्मार्ग्गशीर्षादौ चादित्यं यस्तु पूजयेत्।
उपवासेन युक्तात्मा पुष्पधूपविलेपनैः॥ 3:87॥

भक्षभोज्यैश्च बहुभिस्तथा होमजपादिभिः।
संवत्सरे[3]ण शुद्धात्मा अपापी काममुत्तमम्॥ 3:88॥

सूर्यलोकं व्रजत्येष यावज्जीवन्तु पूजनात्।
च्युतो धनाढ्यो जायेत निरुजो दीर्घजीविनः॥ 3:89॥

आदित्यस्सविता सूर्यो खगः पूषा गभस्तिमान्।
हिरण्यगर्भस्त्रिशिरास्तपनो भास्करो रविः॥ 3:90॥

लोकसाक्षिर्जगन्नेत्रो नामभिस्तु प्रपूजयेत्।
सर्वकामान[4]वाप्नोति पूजयेद्यो दिवाकरम्॥ 3:91॥

अष्टम्यां शङ्करम्पूज्य मासे मार्ग्गशिरे शुभे।
उपवासेन युक्तात्मा गोमूत्रप्राशनेन तु॥ 3:92॥

अतिरात्रफलं लभेदुभयोरपि पक्षयोः।
भक्षभोज्यान्नपानैश्च एतत्फलमवाप्नुयात्॥ 3:93॥

---

86 *Niśvāsamukha* 3.86ab is parallel with *Śivadharmasaṅgraha* 8.27cd.

86 *Niśvāsamukha* 3.86c–3.151 is parallel with *Śivadharmasaṅgraha* 8.28c–8.93.

3:86 स्कन्दसायोज्यमाप्नुयात्] NW; स्कन्दसायुज्यमाप्नुयात् K; स्कन्दसायुज्यतां व्रजेत् *ŚiDhaSaṅ* **3:87** चादित्यं यस्तु पूजयेत्] NKW; भास्करं पूजयेच्छुचिः *ŚiDhaSaṅ* **3:88** भक्ष°] NW; भक्ष्य° K, *ŚiDhaSaṅ* **3:88** होमजपादिभिः] KW, *ŚiDhaSaṅ*; होमजपादिभि --- N **3:88** संवत्सरेण] K, *ŚiDhaSaṅ*; --- ण N; ⊔ रेण W **3:88** अपापी] NKW; निर्मलः *ŚiDhaSaṅ* **3:89** व्रजत्येष यावज्जीवन्तु पूजनात्] NKW; व्रजत्याशु यावज्जीवं प्रपूजनात् *ŚiDhaSaṅ* **3:89** च्युतो धनाढ्यो जायेत निरुजो] NKW; च्युता धनाढ्या जायन्ते निरुजा *ŚiDhaSaṅ* **3:90** सूर्यो] NKW; सूर्यः *ŚiDhaSaṅ* **3:90** त्रिशिरास्त°] K; तृशिरास्त° N; तृसिरास्त° W; त्रिशिखस्त° *ŚiDhaSaṅ* **3:91** लोकसाक्षिर्जगन्नेत्रो] NK[pc]W; लोकसाक्षिर्जगच्चक्षुर् K[ac]; लोकसाक्षी जगन्नेत्रं *ŚiDhaSaṅ* **3:91** नामभिस्तु प्रपूजयेत्] NKW; नाअमभिस्त्वेभिरर्चयेत् *ŚiDhaSaṅ* **3:91** सर्वकामानवाप्नोति पूजयेद्यो] K, *ŚiDhaSaṅ*; --- ⏑̱ ⏑̱ ⏑̱ ि पूजयेद्यो N; सव ⊔ येद्या W **3:92** शङ्करम्पूज्य मासे मार्ग्गशिरे शुभे] NK; शङ्करम्पूज्य मासे मार्ग्गसिरे शुभे W; मार्गशीर्षस्य शिवनामानमर्चयेत् *ŚiDhaSaṅ* **3:92** तु] NKW; च *ŚiDhaSaṅ* **3:93** लभेदुभयोरपि पक्षयोः] NKW; तस्य पक्षयोरुभयोरपि *ŚiDhaSaṅ* **3:93** भक्ष°] NW; भक्ष्य° K, *ŚiDhaSaṅ* **3:93** °पानैश्च एतत्फलमवाप्नुयात्] NKW; °पानाद्यैरेतत्फलमाप्नुयात् *ŚiDhaSaṅ*

देवदेवं तु पौषे च अर्चयेत ह्युपोषितः।
वाजपेयफलं लभेद्गोश[5]कृत्प्राशनेन तु॥ 3:94॥

त्र्यम्बकं पूजयित्वा तु माघे कृष्ण उपोषितः।
अश्वमेधफलं लेभे पयसा प्राशनेन तु॥ 3:95॥

स्थाणुं फाल्गुनकृष्णे तु उपवासेन पूजयेत्।
दधि प्राश्य विशुद्धात्मा नरमेधफलं लभेत्॥ 3:96॥

हरश्चैत्रे तु सम्पूज्य कृष्णाष्टम्यामुपोषितः।
आज्यं प्राश्य शुचिर्भूत्वा [6]राजसूयफलं लभेत्॥ 3:97॥

वैशाखे तु शिवं पूज्य उपवासी कुशोदकम्।
प्राशयित्वा जितात्मासौ सौत्रामणिफलं लभेत्॥ 3:98॥

भवं ज्येष्ठे तु संपूज्य उपवासी शुचिर्न्नरः।
प्राश्य शृङ्गोदकं गोस्तु सर्वयज्ञफलं[12ᵛ] लभेत्॥ 3:99॥

आषाढे नीलकण्ठञ्च कृष्णाष्टम्यां समर्चयेत्।
शङ्खस्यापं स पीत्वा तु गोमेधस्य फलं लभेत्॥ 3:100॥

पिङ्गलं श्रावणे पूज्य कृष्णाष्टम्यामुपोषितः।
सिद्धार्थमुदकम्पीत्वा कन्यादानफलं लभेत्॥ 3:101॥

3:94 तु पौषे च अर्चयेत ह्युपोषितः] NKW; समभ्यर्च्य मासे पौषे उपोषितः *ŚiDhaSaṅ* **3:94** वाजपेयफलं लभेद्] *conj.*; वा --- N; ⊔ K; ⁻जये ⊔ भे ⊔ W; वाजपेयमवाप्नोति *ŚiDhaSaṅ* **3:94** गोशकृत्प्राशनेन] K, *ŚiDhaSaṅ*; --- कृत् प्राशनेन N; गो ⁻कृत्प्रासनेन W **3:95** कृष्ण उपोषितः] NKW; माघे कृष्णे ह्युपोषितः *ŚiDhaSaṅ* **3:95** अश्वमेधफलं लेभे पयसा प्राशनेन तु] NK; अश्वमेधफलं लेभे पयसा प्रासनेन तु W; लभते हयमेधन्तु पयःसंप्राशनेन तु *ŚiDhaSaṅ* **3:96** फाल्गुनकृष्णे तु उपवासेन पूजयेत्] NKW; फाल्गुनमासे तु पूजयेदुपवासितः *ŚiDhaSaṅ* **3:96** प्राश्य] N, *ŚiDhaSaṅ*; चास्य K (there is a correction sign above the word); प्रास्य W **3:96** नरमेधफलं लभेत्] NKW; नृमेधफलमाप्नुयात् *ŚiDhaSaṅ* **3:97** आज्यं प्राश्य शुचिर्भूत्वा] K, *ŚiDhaSaṅ*; ⏑ ⏑ म्प्राश्य --- N; ⊔ भूत्वा W **3:98** वैशाखे] KW, *ŚiDhaSaṅ*; --- N **3:98** कुशोदकम्] K, *ŚiDhaSaṅ*; ⏑ शोदकम् N; ⁻सोदकम् W **3:98** जितात्मासौ] NKW; जितक्रोधः *ŚiDhaSaṅ* **3:99** उपवासी शुचिर्न्नरः] NKW; सोपवासी शुचिव्रतः *ŚiDhaSaṅ* **3:99** शृङ्गोदकं गोस्तु] *ŚiDhaSaṅ*; शृगोदकं गोस्तु NW (unmetrical); शृंगोदकं यस्तु K **3:99** लभेत्] *ŚiDhaSaṅ*; --- NK; लभेत् ⊔ बेत् W **3:100** आषाढे नीलकण्ठञ्च] KW; --- षाढे नीलकण्ठञ्च; आषाढे नीलकण्ठन्तु *ŚiDhaSaṅ* **3:100** कृष्णाष्टम्यां] KW, *ŚiDhaSaṅ*; कृष्ण --- म्यां K **3:100** शङ्खस्यापं स पीत्वा तु] *em.*; ⏑ ख ⏑ ा पं स ी त्वा N; ⊔ पीत्वां तु K; ⊔ तु W; शङ्खस्यापस्ततः पीत्वा *ŚiDhaSaṅ* **3:100** गोमेधस्य फलं लभेत्] NKW; गोसहस्रफलं भवेत् *ŚiDhaSaṅ*

मासे भाद्रपदे रुद्रं पूजयित्वा उपोषितः।
यवोदकम्प्राशयित्वा रुद्रलोके महीयते॥ 3:102॥

ईशानञ्«चाश्विने»मासे कृष्णाष्टम्यां तु [2] पूजयेत्।
तिलोदकं प्राशयित्वा बहुरुग्मफलं लभेत्॥ 3:103॥

उग्रन्तु कार्त्तिके मासे कृष्णाष्टम्यामुपोषितः।
सुवर्णमुदकं पीत्वा गाणापत्यमवाप्नुयात्॥ 3:104॥

सम्वत्सरन्ततः कृत्वा इष्टकामांल्लभेन्नरः।
अकामतः क्रतुफलं गाणापत्यञ्च कामतः॥ 3:105॥

उभाभ्यामपि पक्षाभ्यां विधिरेष [3]प्रकीर्त्तितः।
नवम्यां सम्प्रवक्ष्यामि महादेव्यास्तु पूजनम्॥ 3:106॥

उपवासेन संयुक्तः पूजयेन्नामभिः शुभैः।
उमा कात्यायिनी देवी दुर्ग्गा रुद्रा सुभद्रिका॥ 3:107॥

कालरात्री महागौरी रेवती भूतनायिका।
आर्या प्रकृतिरूपा च गणानाञ्चैव नायिका॥ 3:108॥

नामभिः पूजयेदेभिः पक्षयो[4]रुभयोरपि।
गन्धैः पुष्पैश्च धूपैश्च वस्त्रालङ्कारभूषणैः॥ 3:109॥

नैवेद्यैश्चोपहारैश्च कन्दमूलफलैस्तथा।
प्राशनैश्च विचित्रैश्च वरदाम्पूजयेत्सदा॥ 3:110॥

3:102 उपोषितः] NKW; ह्युपोषितः *ŚiDhaSaṅ*   **3:103** ईशानञ्चाश्विने] *ŚiDhaSaṅ*; ई (?) --- N; ⊔ K; ईशाना ⊔ से W   **3:103** कृष्णाष्टम्यां तु] W, *ŚiDhaSaṅ*; --- न्तु N; ⊔ K   **3:103** बहुरुग्मफलं] *conj.*; बहुरूग्मफलं NKW; बहुसौवर्णिकं *ŚiDhaSaṅ*   **3:104** सुवर्णमुदकं] KW; सुवर्णमुदकंम् N; सौवर्णमुदकं *ŚiDhaSaṅ*   **3:104** गाणापत्य°] NW, *ŚiDhaSaṅ*; गाणपत्य° K   **3:105** इष्टकामांल्लभेन्नरः] *em.*; इष्टकामाल्लभेन्नरः NW; इष्टकामां लभेन्नरः K; इष्टकामांल्लभेत सः *ŚiDhaSaṅ*   **3:105** अकामतः क्र(तुफलं)] K; अकामतः क्र ⏓⏓⏓ ङ् N; अकामतः ⊔ ङ् W; भवेत्क्रतुफलं कामाद् *ŚiDhaSaṅ*   **3:105** गाणापत्यञ्च कामतः] NW; गाणपत्यं तु कामतः K; गाणापत्यमकामतः *ŚiDhaSaṅ*   **3:106** पक्षाभ्यां] K, *ŚiDhaSaṅ*; पक्षाभ् ⏓ N; पक्षाभ्या W   **3:106** विधिरेष] *ŚiDhaSaṅ*; --- N; ⊔ रेष KW   **3:106** महादेव्यास्तु पूजनम्] NKW; महादेव्याः प्रपूजनम् *ŚiDhaSaṅ*   **3:107** सुभद्रिका] NW, *ŚiDhaSaṅ*; सुनन्दिक K   **3:108** कालरात्री म°] NW, *ŚiDhaSaṅ*; कालरात्रिर्म° K   **3:108** आर्या] N, *ŚiDhaSaṅ*; आद्या K; आया W   **3:109** पक्षयोरुभयोरपि] K, *ŚiDhaSaṅ*; --- रुभयोरपि N; ⊔ योरपि W   **3:109** गन्धैः पुष्पैश्च धूपैश्च] NKW; पुष्पैर्धूपैश्च गन्धैश्च *ŚiDhaSaṅ*   **3:110** कन्द°] K, *ŚiDhaSaṅ*; स्कन्द° NW

उदकं कुसुमम्प्राश्य सक्तुं लाजां सधानकाम्।
कृसराञ्च पयो मूलं फलम्पर्ण्णन्तथैव च॥ 3:111॥

शाकानि च तिलाञ्चैव तिलानां च खलि[5]न्तथा।
मुद्गानि च समश्नीयात्तथा चैव निरश्नता॥ 3:112॥

प्राशयित्वा तथैतानि सर्वकामानवाप्नुयात्।
आर्द्रकम्प्राशयित्वा तु शुक्लभोजी निशाक्षये॥ 3:113॥

लभते सर्वकामांस्तु नवमीनवमोषितः।
मरिचप्राशनं कृत्वा नवमीनव यो ऽर्च्चयेत्॥ 3:114॥

सर्वकामानवाप्नोति देवी च वरदा «भवेत्»।
[6]कुशप्रस्तरणशायी पञ्चगव्यकृताशनः॥ 3:115॥

नवमीस्तु नव पूज्य देवी दद्याद्वरोत्तमम्।
यमन्दशम्यां सम्पूज्य [13^r] मासि मार्गशिरे शुभे॥ 3:116॥

पुष्पैर्ग्गन्धैश्च धूपैश्च भक्षभोज्यसमन्वितैः।
यमाय धर्मराजाय मृत्यवे चान्तकाय च॥ 3:117॥

वैवस्वताय कालाय सर्वलोकक्षयाय च।
उग्रदण्डधृते नित्यं महिषासनयायिने॥ 3:118॥

3:111 सक्तुं लाजां] NK; सक्तुं लाजं W; सक्तुलाजं *ŚiDhaSaṅ* **3:111** कृसराञ्च] NW, *ŚiDhaSaṅ*; कृशरांश्च K **3:112** तिलाञ्चैव] N; तिलांश्चैव K; तिलां चैव W; फलञ्चैव *ŚiDhaSaṅ* **3:112** तिलानां च] W, *ŚiDhaSaṅ*; तिलाना --- NK **3:112** खलिन्तथा] *ŚiDhaSaṅ*; ---न्तथा N; ⊔ लिस्तथा K; ⊔ लिन्तथा W **3:112** निरश्नता] N, *ŚiDhaSaṅ*; निरश्रता K; निरसुता W **3:113** तथैतानि] NW, *ŚiDhaSaṅ*; तथौतानि K **3:113** शुक्लभोजी] N, *ŚiDhaSaṅ*; शुक्तभोजी K; शुक्लत्पैजी (?) W **3:113** निशाक्षये] NK^{pc}W; निशात्यये K^{ac}; तथा पुनः *ŚiDhaSaṅ* **3:114** °नवमोषितः] NKW; °समुपोषितः *ŚiDhaSaṅ* **3:114** मरिचप्राशनं] NK (unmetrical); मरिचप्रासनं W (unmetrical); मरिचं प्राशनं *ŚiDhaSaṅ* **3:115** वरदा भवेत्] *ŚiDhaSaṅ*; --- N; वरदा ⊔ KW **3:115** कुशप्रस्तरणशायी] N; कुशप्रस्तरणे शायी K; कुशप्रस्तरणसोयी W; कुशप्रस्तरशायी च *ŚiDhaSaṅ* **3:116** नवमीस्तु नव पूज्य] N; नवम्या (?) तु नव पूज्य K^{pc}W; नवमी तु नव पूज्य K^{ac}; नवमीं नव संपूज्य *ŚiDhaSaṅ* **3:116** वरोत्तमम्] K, *ŚiDhaSaṅ*; वरोत्तमाम् NW **3:116** मासि मार्गशिरे शुभे] K; --- शिरे शुभे N; ⊔ र्ग्गशिरे शुभे W; मासे वै मार्गशीर्षके *ŚiDhaSaṅ* **3:117** भक्ष्यभोज्यसमन्वितैः] K, *ŚiDhaSaṅ*; भक्षभोज्यसमन्वितः N; भक्षभोज्यासमन्वितैः W **3:117** धर्मराजाय] KW, *ŚiDhaSaṅ*; धर्म्मराय N **3:117** चान्तकाय च] N, *ŚiDhaSaṅ*; चान्तकाय K; चोत्तमाय च W **3:118** उग्रदण्डधृते नित्यं] NW; उग्रदण्डधते नित्यं K; उग्रदण्डोग्रहस्ताय *ŚiDhaSaṅ*

शासित्रे च नमस्तुभ्यं नरकाधिपते नमः।
नामभिः पूजयेदेभिस्तर्प्पयेच्च ≪तिलोदकैः≫॥ 3:119॥

≪उभाभ्यामपि≫[2]पक्षाभ्यामब्दमेकं सुयन्त्रितः।
मुच्यते सर्वपापैस्तु न दुःखं नरकोद्भवम्॥ 3:120॥

यावज्जीवार्च्चनङ्कृत्वा स गच्छेत्परमाङ्गतिम्।
एकादश्यान्तु यो धर्म्मम्पूजयेत शुचिव्रतः॥ 3:121॥

गन्धैः पुष्पैश्च धूपैश्च भक्षैर्नानाविधैस्तथा।
धर्म्मस्सत्यन्दया क्षान्तिः शौचमाचारमेव च॥ 3:122॥

अहिंसा च अदम्भश्च रक्षा लोकस्य [3]साक्षिणे।
वृषभाय नमस्तुभ्यमदृष्टाय नमो नमः॥ 3:123॥

नामभिः पूजयेदेभिर्धर्म्मं सत्यं पराक्रमम्।
उभयोः पक्षयोश्चैव वर्षमेकं सुयन्त्रितः॥ 3:124॥

याम्यदुःखैर्विमुक्तस्तु जायते पृथिवीश्वरः।
यावज्जीवं समर्च्चन्तन्तर्पयंश्च तिलोदकैः॥ 3:125॥

उत्तमाङ्गतिमाप्नोति ≪याङ्गत्वा न निवर्त्तते≫।
≪केशवं[4] पूज≫यित्वा तु मासे मार्ग्गशिरे नरः॥ 3:126॥

द्वादश्याम्प्राश्य गोमूत्रमग्निष्टोमफलं लभेत्।
पुष्ये नारायणम्पूज्य द्वादश्यां तु उपोषितः॥ 3:127॥

3:119 नरकाधिपते नमः] W; नरकाधि --- NW; नरकाधिपतये *ŚiDhaSaṅ* (unmetrical) **3:119** नामभिः] *ŚiDhaSaṅ*; --- NK; नामादैः W **3:119** पूजयेदेभिस्तर्प्पयेच्च] W, *ŚiDhaSaṅ*; पूजयेदे --- N; ⊔ K **3:119** तिलोदकैः] *ŚiDhaSaṅ*; --- NKW **3:120** उभाभ्यामपि] *ŚiDhaSaṅ*; --- NK; ⊔ पि W **3:120** दुःखं] NW, *ŚiDhaSaṅ*; दुःख° K **3:121** परमाङ्गतिम्] NW, *ŚiDhaSaṅ*; परमागतिम् K **3:122** गन्धैः पुष्पैश्च धूपैश्च] NKW; गन्धैर्धूपैश्च पुष्पैश्च *ŚiDhaSaṅ* **3:122** भक्षैर्नाना°] NW, *ŚiDhaSaṅ*; भक्ष्यैर्नाना° K **3:122** धर्म्मस्स°] NW, *ŚiDhaSaṅ*; धर्म्म स° K **3:123** अहिंसा च अदम्भश्च रक्षा लोकस्य साक्षिणे] *conj.*; --- साक्षिणे N; अहिंसा च ⊔ स्य साक्षिणे K; अहिंसा च ⊔ स्य साक्षिणा W; अहिंसा चाप्यदम्भश्च रक्षा लोकस्य साक्षिणे *ŚiDhaSaṅ* **3:124** धर्म्मं सत्यं पराक्रमम्] N, *ŚiDhaSaṅ*; धर्म्मसत्यपराक्रमम् KW **3:125** समर्च्चन्तन्तर्पयंश्च] N; समर्च्चन्तत् KW; समभ्यर्च्य तर्पयेच्च *ŚiDhaSaṅ* **3:126** याङ्गत्वा न निवर्त्तते] *ŚiDhaSaṅ*; --- NK; ⊔ निव ⊔ W **3:126** केशवं पूजयित्वा तु] *ŚiDhaSaṅ*; --- त्वा तु N; ⊔ K; ⊔ पित्वा तु W **3:126** मासे मार्ग्गशिरे नरः] NW; मार्ग्गशिरे नरः K^{pc}; मासे मार्ग्गशिरे शुभे K^{ac}; मार्गशीर्षे नरोत्तमः *ŚiDhaSaṅ* **3:127** पुष्ये] KW, *ŚiDhaSaṅ*; षुष्ये N **3:127** द्वादश्यां तु उपोषितः] NKW; द्वादश्यामुपवासितः *ŚiDhaSaṅ*

फलञ्चैवाग्निष्टोमस्य कृत्वा गोमयभक्षणम्।
माधवं माघमासे तु द्वादश्यान्तु उपोषितः॥ 3:128॥

पूजयित्वा पयः प्राश्य उक्थ्यमेधफलं लभेत्।
गोविन्दं फाल्गुने ऽभ्यर्च्य द्वादश्यां तु [5]उपोषितः॥ 3:129॥

षोडशीफलमाप्नोति कृत्वा तु दधिभक्षणम्।
चैत्रे विष्णुं समभ्यर्च्य द्वादश्यान्तु उपोषितः॥ 3:130॥

आज्यं वै प्राशयित्वा तु वाजपेयफलं लभेत्।
उपोषितस्तु वैशाखे पूजयेन्मधुसूदनम्॥ 3:131॥

कुशाम्बु प्राश्य द्वादश्यां ≪अतिरात्रफलं लभेत्≫।
ज्येष्ठे त्रिविक्रमं पूज्य द्वादश्यान्तु उपोषितः॥ 3:132॥

[6]≪तिलोदकं प्राशयित्वा≫आप्तोर्यामफलं लभेत्।
आषाढे वामनम्पूज्य द्वादश्यां सुसमाहितः॥ 3:133॥

फलं प्राश्य विशुद्धात्मा अश्वमेधफलं लभेत्।
श्रावणे श्रीधरम्पूज्य द्वादश्यां तु उपोषितः॥ 3:134॥

≪पर्णं प्राश्य विशुद्धात्मा राजसूयफलं लभेत्।
तथा भाद्रे हृषीकेशं संपूज्य विधिवद्बुधः॥ 3:135॥

गवामयस्य [13v] यज्ञस्य ततः ≫फलमवाप्नुयात्।

3:128 फलञ्चैवाग्निष्टोमस्य] NK; फलञ्चैवाग्निष्टामस्य W; ज्योतिष्टोमफलन्तस्य *ŚiDhaSaṅ* **3:128** द्वादश्यान्तु उपोषितः] NKW; द्वादश्यां समुपोषितः *ŚiDhaSaṅ* **3:129** उक्थ्यमेधफलं लभेत्] *conj.*; उक् ⩲ मेधफलं --- N; उक्तमेधफलं लभेत् K; उक्षमेधफलं ⊔ W; अश्वमेध-फलं लभेत् *ŚiDhaSaṅ* **3:129** गोविन्दं फाल्गुने ऽभ्यर्च्य द्वादश्यां तु उपोषितः] *conj.*; ---पोषितः N; ⊔ उपोषितः K; ⊔ W; गोविन्दं फाल्गुने ऽभ्यर्च्य द्वादश्यामुपवासितः *ŚiDha-Saṅ* **3:130** द्वादश्यान्तु उपोषितः] NKW; द्वादश्यां समुपोषितः *ŚiDhaSaṅ* **3:132** कुशाम्बु प्राश्य द्वादश्यां] K; कुशाम् ⩲ N; कुशाम्बः प्राश्य द्वादश्यां W; द्वादश्यां प्राश्य दर्भोदम् *ŚiDhaSaṅ* **3:132** अतिरात्रफलं लभेत्] *ŚiDhaSaṅ*; --- NKW **3:132** ज्येष्ठे त्रिविक्रमं पूज्य द्वादश्यान्तु उपोषितः] *conj.*; ज्येष्ठे त्रिविक्रमं पूज्य द्वादश्यामुपवासितः *ŚiDhaSaṅ*; --- NKW **3:133** तिलोदकं प्राशयित्वा] *ŚiDhaSaṅ*; --- ि ⩲ ा N; ⊔ KW **3:133** आप्तोर्यामफलं लभेत्] *ŚiDhaSaṅ*; आप्तर्यामफलं लभेत् N; ⊔ फलं K; आप्नुयायफलं W **3:133** सुसमा-हितः] NKW; उपवासितः *ŚiDhaSaṅ* **3:134** प्राश्य] *ŚiDhaSaṅ*; प्राप्य NKW **3:134** तु उपोषितः] NKW; समुपोषितः *ŚiDhaSaṅ* **3:135** पर्णं प्राश्य विशुद्धात्मा राजसूयफलं लभेत्] *ŚiDhaSaṅ*; --- NKW **3:135** तथा भाद्रे हृषीकेशं संपूज्य विधिवद्बुधः] *ŚiDhaSaṅ*; --- NKW **3:136** गवामयस्य यज्ञस्य ततः फलमवाप्नुयात्] *ŚiDhaSaṅ*; --- नुयात् N; ⊔ माप्नुयात् K; ⊔ तु फलमवाप्नुत् W

मासे त्वाश्वयुजे देवं पद्मनाभन्तु पूजयेत्॥ 3:136॥

नरमेधस्य यज्ञस्य फलं लभति मानवः।
≪दामोदरन्तु संपूज्य कार्तिके मासि यो नरः॥ 3:137॥

उपोषितस्तु द्वादश्यां बहुसौवर्ण्णिकं फलम्।
सम्वत्सरन्तु संपूज्य सर्वकामानवाप्नुयात्॥ 3:138॥

अपापी क्रतुमाप्नोति पापात्मा≫[2]मुच्यते नशात्।
यावज्जीवं समभ्यर्च्य पुष्पैर्ग्गन्धैः सुगन्धकैः॥ 3:139॥

भक्ष्यभोज्यैश्च धूपैश्च च्छत्रध्वजवितानकैः।
हेमजैर्भूषणैर्द्दिव्यैर्म्मणिरत्नविचित्रकैः॥ 3:140॥

वस्त्रैः पूजां विचित्राञ्च कृत्वा विष्णुपदम्व्रजेत्।
अनङ्गन्तु त्रयोदश्यां पू≪जयेद्यो विधानवित्॥ 3:141॥

भक्ष्यभोज्यान्नपानैश्च गन्ध≫धू[3]पस्रगादिभिः।
अनङ्गम्मन्मथं काममीश्वरम्मोहनन्तथा॥ 3:142॥

पञ्चबाणन्धनुर्हस्तमुन्मादञ्च वशंकरम्।
रतिप्रियम्प्रीतिकरं हृदयस्यापहारिणम्॥ 3:143॥

नामभिः पूजयेदेभिः कामदेवम्महाबलम्।
मासे मार्गशिरस्यादौ यावत्कार्त्तिकमेव च॥ 3:144॥

≪सौभाग्यं धनधान्यञ्च पुत्रदारा ≫भ[4]वन्ति च।

3:136 मासे त्वाश्वयुजे देवं पद्मनाभन्तु पूजयेत्] NK; मासत्व ⊔ पूजयेत् W; मासे चाश्वयुजे देवं पद्मनाभन्तु पूजयेत् *ŚiDhaSaṅ* **3:137** नरमेधस्य यज्ञस्य फलं लभति मानवः] N, *ŚiDhaSaṅ*; नरमेधस्य ⊔ K; ⊔ W **3:137** दामोदरन्तु संपूज्य कार्तिके मासि यो नरः] *ŚiDhaSaṅ*; --- न्तु पूज्यत? का f --- N; ⊔ KW **3:138** उपोषितस्तु द्वादश्यां बहुसौवर्ण्णिकं फलम्] *ŚiDhaSaṅ*; --- NKW **3:138** सम्वत्सरन्तु संपूज्य सर्वकामानवाप्नुयात्] *ŚiDhaSaṅ*; --- NKW **3:139** अपापी क्रतुमाप्नोति पापात्मा] *ŚiDhaSaṅ*; --- NKW **3:139** मुच्यते नशात्] N; मुच्यते नसात् K; अच्यते रसात् W; मुच्यते ऽंहसा *ŚiDhaSaṅ* **3:141** विचित्राञ्च] NW; विचित्रांश्च K; विचित्रैश्च *ŚiDhaSaṅ* **3:141** त्रयोदश्यां पूजयेद्यो विधानवित्] *ŚiDhaSaṅ*; त्र --- N; त्रयोदश्यां पू ⊔ K; त्रयोदश्यां ⊔ W **3:142** भक्ष्यभोज्यान्नपानैश्च गन्धधूपस्रगादिभिः] *ŚiDhaSaṅ*; --- पस्रगादिभिः N; ⊔ धूपस्रगादिभिः KW **3:142** काममीश्वरम्] NKW; काममीशारिं *ŚiDhaSaṅ* **3:143** धनुर्हस्त॰] NW, *ŚiDhaSaṅ*; चतुर्हस्त॰ K **3:143** वशंकरम्] NW, *ŚiDhaSaṅ*; वसंकरम् K **3:145** सौभाग्यं धनधान्यञ्च पुत्रदारा भवन्ति च] *ŚiDhaSaṅ*; --- वन्ति च N; ⊔ भवन्ति च K; सोसा ⁻धनधा ⊔ वन्ति च W

कामदेवस्य सायोज्यं यावज्जीवस्य पूजनात्॥ 3:145॥

चतुर्द्दश्यामपुनर्देवम्पूजयेत्परमेश्वरम्।
हरं शर्वं भवन्त्र्यक्षं शम्भुञ्चैव विभुं शिवम्॥ 3:146॥

स्थाणुं पशुपतिं रुद्रं ईशानं शङ्करन्तथा।
पूजयेदेभिस्संज्ञाभिर्विधिवत्परमेश्वरम्॥ 3:147॥

मार्ग्गशीर्षस्य मासादौ यावदब्दं «व्रतञ्चरेत्»।
[5] पुष्पैर्गन्धैश्च धूपैश्च भक्षभोज्यैस्तथैव च॥ 3:148॥

अलङ्कारैश्च विविधैश्छत्रध्वजवितानकैः।
उभयोः पक्षयोश्चैव सर्वकामानवाप्नुयात्॥ 3:149॥

सम्वत्सरेण युक्तात्मा निष्कामस्तु गणो भवेत्।
यावज्जीवेन सायोज्यं पापी मुच्यति किल्बिषात्॥ 3:150॥

अमावास्यां मार्गशिरे ((पितॄंस्तर्प्प)) --- [-4-] ---।
[6]कर्म्मणा श्राद्धयुक्तेन पिण्डेन च तिलोदकैः॥ 3:151॥

पौर्ण्णमास्यान्तथैवेह कुर्व्वतस्तु फलं शृणु।
सतिलोदकपिण्डेन यः श्राद्धे तर्प्पयेत्पितॄन्॥ 3:152॥

ते तृप्ताः पितरस्तस्य ये वसन्ति यमालये।
[14ʳ] सम्वत्सरेण पितरो मुच्यन्ते यमयातनात्॥ 3:153॥

यावज्जीवन्तु कुर्वाणो पक्षयोरुभयोरपि।

---

154 *Niśvāsamukha* 3.154 is parallel with *Śivadharmasaṅgraha* 8.110.

3:145 सायोज्यं] NW; सायुज्यं K, *ŚiDhaSaṅ* **3:146** शर्वं] K, *ŚiDhaSaṅ*; शर्व्वं॰ N; सर्व W **3:147** पशुपतिं] NKW; चाप्यथ *ŚiDhaSaṅ* **3:147** विधिवत्परमेश्वरम्] NKW; देवदेवं वृषध्वजम् *ŚiDhaSaṅ* **3:148** मार्ग्गशीर्षस्य मासादौ] W; मार्ग्गशीर्षस्य मा --- NK; मार्गशीर्षात्समारभ्य *ŚiDhaSaṅ* **3:148** यावदब्दं व्रतञ्चरेत्] *ŚiDhaSaṅ*; --- NK; यावद ⊔ W **3:148** पुष्पैर्गन्धैश्च धूपैश्च] W; --- र्गन्धैश्च धूपैश्च N; ⊔ गन्धैश्च धूपैश्च K; पुष्पैर्धूपैश्च गन्धैश्च *ŚiDhaSaṅ* **3:148** भक्षभोज्यैस्तथैव च] NW; भक्ष्यभोज्यैस्तथैव च K; भक्ष्यभोज्यैः सुशोभनैः *ŚiDhaSaṅ* **3:150** निष्कामस्तु] NW, *ŚiDhaSaṅ*; निष्कांमस्तु K **3:150** सायोज्यं] NW, *ŚiDhaSaṅ*; सायुज्यं K **3:151** अमावास्यां मार्गशिरे] K; अ ⪯ ᒥ वास्याम्मार्गशि --- N; अमावास्यां मार्गसिरे W; अमावास्यां पितॄणां हि *ŚiDhaSaṅ* **3:151** पितॄंस्तर्प्प] *conj.*; --- NK; पितृस्तर्प्प W; मासे वै मार्ग्गशीर्षके *ŚiDhaSaṅ* **3:153** सम्वत्सरेण] *em.*; --- NK; ⊔ रेण W **3:154** कुर्वाणो] NW; कुर्वाणः K, *ŚiDhaSaṅ*

पापात्मा मुच्यते पापादपापी स्वर्ग्गगो भवेत्॥ 3:154॥

पितरस्सोमपा विप्रे क्षत्रिये तु हविर्भुजाः।
आज्यपा वैश्ययोनौ तु शूद्राणान्तु सुकालिनः॥ 3:155॥

[[((पौर्णमास्यां पुन)) श्चाग्निं पू]] जयेत --- [-4-] ---।
--- [-3-] --- [2] उपवासेन अग्निलोकमवाप्नुयात्॥ 3:156॥

पापी मुच्यति पापेन धनवान्सम्प्रजायते।
उभयोः पक्षयोर्ह्येष विधिरुक्तो मया द्विजाः॥ 3:157॥

उपवासस्य देवानाम्पूजनं साम्प्रतं शृणु।
प्रतिपद्भोजयेद्विप्रान्पूजयित्वा प्रजापतिम्॥ 3:158॥

सौवर्ण्णञ्चारविन्दन्तु कुर्यान्नामाङ्कितं ततः।
≪ताम्रपात्रे घृतापूर्णे ≫क्षि [3] स्त्वा विप्राय दापयेत्॥ 3:159॥

ईप्सितांल्लभते कामान्निष्कामो ब्रह्मलोकताम्।
अग्निं पूज्य द्वितीयायाम्ब्राह्मणांस्तर्प्पयेन्नरः॥ 3:160॥

सौवर्ण्णवस्त्े नामानि वह्नेरालिख्य यत्नतः।

---

155 *Niśvāsamukha* 3.155 is parallel with *Śivadharmasaṅgraha* 8.109.

155 Cf. *Manusmṛti* 3.197: सोमपा नाम विप्राणां क्षत्रियाणां हविर्भुजः वैश्यानामाज्यपा नाम शूद्राणां तु सुकालिनः॥

158 *Niśvāsamukha* 3.158c–3.163 is parallel with *Śivadharmasaṅgraha* 8.115a–8.120b.

3:154 पापादपापी स्वर्ग्गगो भवेत्] NKW; पापैरपापी स्वर्गमाप्नुयात् *ŚiDhaSaṅ* **3:155** हविर्भुजाः] NW; हविर्भुजः K, *ŚiDhaSaṅ* **3:155** तु शूद्राणान्तु] K, *ŚiDhaSaṅ*; --- द्राणान्तु NW **3:156** °जयेत] *conj.*; --- NKW **3:156** उपवासेन] *em.*; --- वासेन NW; --- पवासेन K **3:157** सम्प्रजायते] NW; स प्रजायते K **3:157** द्विजाः] *em.*; द्विजा K; द्विज NW **3:158** प्रतिपद्भोजयेद्वि°] NKW; प्रतिपदि भोजयेद्वि° *ŚiDhaSaṅ* (unmetrical) **3:159** चारविन्दन्तु] NKW; सौवर्णमरविदन्तु *ŚiDhaSaṅ* **3:159** कुर्यान्नामाङ्कितं ततः] K, *ŚiDhaSaṅ*; कुर्यान्नामा --- NW **3:159** ताम्रपात्रे घृतापूर्णे] *ŚiDhaSaṅ*; --- NK; अ? ⊔ W **3:159** क्षिस्त्वा विप्राय दापयेत्] *conj.*; स्त्वा विप्राय दापयेत् N; ⊔ विप्राय दापयेत् K; ⊔ प्राय दापयेत् W; क्षिप्त्वा दद्याद्विजन्मने *ŚiDhaSaṅ* **3:160** ईप्सितांल्लभते कामान्निष्कामो] K; ईप्सिताल्लभते कामान् निष्कामो N; ईप्सिताल्लभते कामान् निक्रामो W; ईप्सितं लभते कामं निष्कामो *ŚiDhaSaṅ* **3:160** अग्निं पूज्य द्वितीयायाम्] KW; अग्निम्पूज द्वितीयायाम् N; सम्पूज्याग्निं द्वितीयायां *ŚiDhaSaṅ* **3:160** नरः] NKW; पुनः *ŚiDhaSaṅ* **3:161** सौवर्ण्णवस्त्े नामानि] NW; सौवर्ण ⊔ नामानि K; तानि नामानि सौवर्णे *ŚiDhaSaṅ*

उदुम्बरेज्यपूर्ण्णे तु भाजने प्रक्षिपेत्तु तम्॥ 3:161॥

तोयपूर्ण्णे घटे स्थाप्य भक्षभोज्यसमन्विते।
उभाभ्यामपि पक्षाभ्यां दद्याद्विप्रा[4]य शोभने॥ 3:162॥

सर्वकामप्रदो वह्निरब्दैकेन भविष्यति।
यावज्जीवं कृतेनैव त्वग्निलोकं स गच्छति॥ 3:163॥

तृतीयायां तु सम्पूज्य यक्षं हेममयीङ्गदाम्।
नामान्यालिख्य दातव्या भाजने घृतपूरिते॥ 3:164॥

चतुर्त्थ्यान्दन्तिनन्दद्यात्सौवर्ण्णन्नाम-चाङ्कितम्।
विघ्नेश्वरस्य देवस्य घृतपूर्ण्णोदुम्बरे स्थितम्॥ 3:165॥

[5]विप्रां सुभोजिताङ्कृत्वा दत्त्वा भक्षान्घटान्यपि।
सम्वत्सरेण सिद्धिः स्याद्यावज्जीवे गणेशता॥ 3:166॥

पञ्चम्यां हेमजम्पद्म दत्त्वा विप्राय भोजिते।
घृतप्लुतं सनामाङ्कन्ताम्रभाजनसंस्थितम्॥ 3:167॥

---

164 Cf. *Śivadharmasaṅgraha* 8.120c–8.121b: संपूज्य लविलन्तस्य नामाङ्काङ्काञ्चनीं गदाम्॥ क्षिप्त्वा दद्यात्तृतीयायां सघृते ताम्रभाजने।

165 *Niśvāsamukha* 3.165a–3.177b is parallel with *Śivadharmasaṅgraha* 8.121c–8.133.

3:161 उदुम्बरेज्यपूर्ण्णे तु] NW; उदुम्बरेज्यपूर्णा तु K; ताम्रिके सर्पिषा पूर्णे *ŚiDhaSaṅ* **3:161** भाजने प्रक्षिपेत्तु तम्] N; भोजने प्रक्षिपेस्तु तम् K; भोजने प्रक्षिपेत्तु तम् W; भाजने प्रक्षिपेत च *ŚiDhaSaṅ* **3:162** °पूर्ण्णे] NW, *ŚiDhaSaṅ*; °पूर्ण्ण° K **3:162** भक्षभोज्यसमन्विते] N; भक्ष्यभोज्यसमन्वितम् K; भक्ष्यभोज्यसमन्विते W, *ŚiDhaSaṅ* **3:162** पक्षाभ्यां दद्याद्विप्राय शोभने] *ŚiDhaSaṅ*; प ⏓ --- य शोभने N; पक्षाभ्यां ⊔ य शोभने K; पक्षाभ्यां दद्या ⊔ य शोभने W **3:163** यावज्जीवं] *ŚiDhaSaṅ*; यावज्जीव° NKW **3:163** त्वग्निलोकं स गच्छति] NKW; प्रयात्यनलमन्दिरम् *ŚiDhaSaṅ* **3:164** यक्षं हेममयीङ्गदाम्] K; यक्षां हेममयीङ्गदाम् N^{pc}; यक्षां हेमयीङ्गदाम् N^{ac} (unmetrical); यक्षां हेममयीङ्गदाम् W **3:164** भाजने] NW; भोजने K **3:165** चतुर्त्थ्यान्दन्तिनन्दद्यात्सौवर्ण्णन्नाम-चाङ्कितम्] NKW; चतुर्थ्यां रदनं दद्याद्धेमं नामाङ्कितं शुभम् *ŚiDhaSaṅ* **3:165** घृतपूर्ण्णोदुम्बरे स्थितम्] W ((hypermetrical)); घृतपूर्ण्णोदु --- N; घृतपूर्ण्णोदुम्बरस्थितम् K ((hypermetrical)); ताम्रपात्रे घृतान्विते *ŚiDhaSaṅ* **3:166** विप्रां सुभोजिताङ्कृत्वा] NW; विप्रांस्तु भोजितान् K; विप्रान् सुभोजितान् कृत्वा *ŚiDhaSaṅ* **3:166** दत्त्वा भक्षान् घटान्यपि] N; दत्त्वा भक्ष्यान् घटान्यपि K; दत्त्वा भक्षां घटान्यपि W; दद्याद्भक्षं घटानपि *ŚiDhaSaṅ* **3:166** यावज्जीवे] NW; यावज्जीवं K, *ŚiDhaSaṅ* **3:167** पद्म] N; पद्मं KW; सर्पं *ŚiDhaSaṅ* **3:167** दत्त्वा विप्राय] NK^{ac}W; दत्त्वा विप्रे च K^{pc}; दद्याद्विप्राय *ŚiDhaSaṅ*

अनन्तं वासुकिं वापि तक्षकं वा त्रिरेखिणम्।
पद्मं [14^{v}]महाब्जं शङ्खं वा कुलिकं वा महोरगम्॥ 3:168॥

सम्पूज्यान्यतमन्तेषां गन्धधूपस्रगादिभिः।
भक्षभोज्यान्नपानैश्च कामदम्पापहारिणम्॥ 3:169॥

मयूरं हेमजङ्कृत्वा स्कन्दनामाङ्कितं शुभम्।
षष्ठ्यान्दद्यात्तु विप्राय घृतपूर्णोदुम्बरे स्थितम्॥ 3:170॥

तोयपूर्णांश्च कलशान्भक्षभोज्यसमन्वितान्।
≪दत्वा कामानवाप्नो[2]ति ≫पक्षयोरुभयोरपि॥ 3:171॥

सम्वत्सरेण कामांस्तु चिन्तितां लभते नरः।
पापी मुच्यति पापेन शुद्धात्मा स्कन्दमाप्नुयात्॥ 3:172॥

अश्वं हेममयन्दद्याद्रवेर्न्नामाङ्कितं बुधः।
पक्षयोरुभयोश्चैव सघृते ताम्रभाजने॥ 3:173॥

वर्षेणैकेन पापात्मा मुच्यते बहुकिल्बिषात्।
यावज्जीवकृतेनैव आदित्यप[3]दमाप्नुयात्॥ 3:174॥

अष्टम्यां वृषभन्दद्याद्भवनामाङ्कितं द्विजे।
उभाभ्यामपि पक्षाभ्यां सघृते ताम्रभाजने॥ 3:175॥

कलशैर्भक्षसंयुक्तैः पयसा च सुपूरितैः।
सम्वत्सरेण शुद्धात्मा ईप्सितं लभते फलम्॥ 3:176॥

3:168 त्रिरेखिणम्] KW, *ŚiDhaSaṅ*; त्रिरेखि --- N **3:168** पद्मं महाब्जं] *ŚiDhaSaṅ*; --- हाब्जं N; ⊔ महा ⁻⁻ W; अब्जं महाब्जं K **3:168** वा महोरगम्] NKW; च महोरगम् *ŚiDhaSaṅ* **3:169** सम्पूज्यान्यतमन्तेषां] NKW; संपूज्यान्यतमं वापि *ŚiDhaSaṅ* **3:169** भक्ष°] NW, *ŚiDhaSaṅ*; भक्ष्य° K **3:170** दद्यात्तु] NKW; दद्याच्च *ŚiDhaSaṅ* **3:170** घृतपूर्णोदुम्बरे स्थितम्] N ((hypermetrical)); घृतपूर्णादुम्बरे स्थितम् K ((hypermetrical)); घृतपूर्णोंदुम्बरे स्थितम् W; ताम्रपात्रे घृतान्विते *ŚiDhaSaṅ* **3:171** तोयपूर्णांश्च कलशान्] *ŚiDhaSaṅ*; तोयपूर्णां ⏓ कलशान् N; तोयपूर्णां ⊔ कलशान् K; तोयपूर्ण ⁻ कलसा W **3:171** भक्ष°] NW; भक्ष्य° K, *ŚiDhaSaṅ* **3:171** दत्वा कामानवाप्नोति पक्षयोरुभयोरपि] *ŚiDhaSaṅ*; --- ति पक्षयोरुभयोरपि N; ⊔ माप्नोति पक्षयोरुभयोरपि K; ⊔ प्नोति पक्षयोरुभयोरपि W **3:172** चिन्तितां लभते] NW; चिन्तितांल्लभते K, *ŚiDhaSaṅ* **3:172** मुच्यति] NKW; मुच्यते *ŚiDhaSaṅ* **3:172** शुद्धात्मा] N^{pc}KW, *ŚiDhaSaṅ*; शुद्धात्मां N^{ac} **3:174** बहुकिल्बिषात्] NKW; सर्वकिल्बिषैः *ŚiDhaSaṅ* **3:174** आदित्यपद°] K, *ŚiDhaSaṅ*; आ --- द° N; आदि ⊔ पद° W **3:175** वृषभन्दद्याद्भवनामाङ्कितं द्विजे] NKW; भवनामांकं वृषं दद्याद्विजन्मने *ŚiDhaSaṅ* **3:176** भक्ष°] NW; भक्ष्य° K, *ŚiDhaSaṅ* **3:176** ईप्सितं लभते] NKW; प्राप्नुयादीप्सितं *ŚiDhaSaṅ*

यावज्जीवेन गणतां यो ऽर्च्चयेन्नामभिर्हरम्।
नवम्यां सिंहं नामेन देव्याश्चाभ्यर्चिते [[((न च))]] ॥ 3:177॥

[4] घृतताम्रस्य दानाच्च भक्षैः पयघटान्वितैः।
यमाय महिषन्दद्यान्नामाङ्कन्तु घृतप्लुतम्॥ 3:178॥

ताम्रभाजनसंस्थन्तु पयोघटसमन्वितम्।
भक्षैर्युक्तं दशम्यान्तु विप्रान्संभोज्य दापयेत्॥ 3:179॥

याम्यदुःखेन मुच्यन्ते महापातकिनो ऽपि ये।
संवत्सरेण शुद्धात्मा जीवान्ते गतिरुत्तमा॥ 3:180॥

एका [5] दश्यान्तु धर्म्मस्य वृषन्दद्याद्विजोत्तमे।
नामाङ्कं सघृतन्ताम्रं घटं भक्षसमायुतम्॥ 3:181॥

स धर्म्मगतिमाप्नोति शुद्धः संवत्सरेण तु।
कामी लभति कामांश्च निष्कामो धर्म्मलोकताम्॥ 3:182॥

द्वादश्यां गरुडं दद्यान्नामाङ्कं घटमेव वा।
ताम्रभाजनसंस्थन्तु घटान् [15r] तोयेन पूरितान्॥ 3:183॥

---

177 Cf. *Śivadharmasaṅgraha* 8.134–8.135: पूर्वोक्तविधिना सिंहं देव्या नामाङ्कितं शुभम्। दत्वा नवम्यां विप्राय प्रयाति परमाङ्गतिम्॥ यमनामाङ्कितं हेमं महिषं ताम्रभाजने। आज्यपूर्णे विनिक्षिप्य पयोघटसमन्विते॥

179 *Niśvāsamukha* 3.179c–3.194b is parallel with *Śivadharmasaṅgraha* 8.136–8.150.

3:177 सिंहं] N; सिंह KW **3:178** घृततामस्य] W; --- ततामस्य N; ⊔ संप्र° K **3:178** भक्षैः पयघटा°] NW; भक्ष्यैः पयोघटा° K **3:179** भक्षैर्युक्तं दशम्यान्तु विप्रान्संभोज्य दापयेत्] NW; भक्ष्यैर्युक्तं दशम्यान्तु विप्रान्संभोज्य दापयेत् K; दत्त्वा दशम्यां विप्राय भोजिताय तपस्विने *ŚiDhaSaṅ* **3:180** °पातकिनो] K, *ŚiDhaSaṅ*; °पातकिना NW **3:180** ये] N, *ŚiDhaSaṅ*; च KW **3:180** सम्वत्सरेण] KW, *ŚiDhaSaṅ*; संवत् --- ण N **3:180** शुद्धात्मा] NKW; युक्तात्मा *ŚiDhaSaṅ* **3:180** गतिरुत्तमा] K, *ŚiDhaSaṅ*; गति --- N; गतिमुत्तमा W **3:181** एकादश्यान्तु] K, *ŚiDhaSaṅ*; --- दश्यान्तु NW **3:181** द्विजोत्तमे] NKW; द्विजन्मने *ŚiDhaSaṅ* **3:181** ताम्रं घटं भक्षसमायुतम्] *em.*; ताम्रं घटभक्षसमायुतम् NW; ताम्रं घटं भक्ष्यसमायुतम् K; न्यस्य ताम्रपात्रे घृतान्विते *ŚiDhaSaṅ* **3:182** शुद्धः] N^{pc}KW, *ŚiDhaSaṅ*; शुद्ध N^{ac} **3:182** कामी लभति कामांश्च निष्कामो] NKW; कामी च लभते कामान् निष्कामी *ŚiDhaSaṅ* **3:183** नामाङ्कं घटमेव वा] KW; नामाङ्कं घटमेव --- N; नानाभक्ष्यसमन्वितम् *ŚiDhaSaṅ* **3:183** ताम्रभाजनसंस्थन्तु घटान् तोयेन पूरितान्] *conj.*; --- तोयेन पूरितान् N; ताम्र ⊔ तोयेन पूरितान् KW; पूर्वोक्तेन विधानेन पयोघटसमन्वितम् *ŚiDhaSaṅ*

विष्णोर्नाम्ना तु दातव्या पक्षयोरुभयोरपि।
संवत्सरेण शुद्धात्माऽपापी क्रतुफलं लभेत्॥ 3:184॥

यावज्जीवन्तु सम्पूज्य भोजनैश्च सदक्षिणैः।
विष्णुलोकमवाप्नोति विष्णुना सह मोदते॥ 3:185॥

सौवर्णन्धनुषन्दद्यात्पञ्चबाणसमन्वितम्।
कामदेवं समभ्यर्च्य सघृते ≪ताम्रभाजने≫॥ 3:186॥

[2] भक्षाम्बुपूर्ण्णघटकां विप्रां सम्भोज्य दापयेत्।
सौभाग्यन्धनधान्यञ्च अपापी लभते ध्रुवम्॥ 3:187॥

यावज्जीवं तु सम्पूज्य कामदेवपदम्व्रजेत्।
चतुर्द्दश्यां वृषन्दद्यात्सम्पूज्य परमेश्वरम्॥ 3:188॥

तस्य नामाङ्कितङ्कृत्वा ताम्रभाजनसम्स्थितम्।
प्रदद्याद्विप्रमुख्येभ्यो भोजयित्वा यथाविधि॥ 3:189॥

उभाभ्यामपि पक्षा[3]भ्याम्घटाम्भक्षाम्बुपूरिताम्।
अब्दात्पापविशुद्धस्तु द्वादशाब्दैर्ग्गणेश्वरः॥ 3:190॥

यावज्जीवकृतेनैव सायोज्यस्तु महेश्वरे।
अमावास्याम्पौर्ण्णमास्यां पक्षयोरुभयोरपि॥ 3:191॥

श्राद्धपिण्डाप्सुदानेन पितॄन्यस्तु समर्च्चयेत्।

3:184 विष्णोर्नाम्ना तु दातव्या] NW; विक्षुनाम्ना तु दातव्या K; विष्णोर्नाम समुच्चार्य *ŚiDhaSaṅ* **3:184** °पापी क्रतुफलं लभेत्] NKW; विपापः क्रतुमाप्नुयात् *ŚiDhaSaṅ* **3:186** सौवर्णन्धनुषन्दद्यात्पञ्चबाणसमन्वितम्] *conj.*; --- धनु ⏑̱ न्दद्यात्प N; ⊔ KW; सौवर्णन्धनुषं कृत्वा पञ्चबाणसमन्वितम् *ŚiDhaSaṅ* **3:186** कामदेवं समभ्यर्च्य सघृते ताम्रभाजने] *ŚiDhaSaṅ*; --- NK; कामदेवं समभ्यर्च्य सघृ ⊔ W **3:187** भक्षाम्बुपूर्ण्णघटकां विप्रां] NW; भक्ष्याम्बुपूर्णघटकान् विप्रान् K; भक्ष्याम्बुपूर्णघटकां विप्रान् *ŚiDhaSaṅ* **3:187** अपापी] NKW; विपाप्मा *ŚiDhaSaṅ* **3:188** तु सम्पूज्य कामदेवपदम्] NKW; च सम्पूज्य कामदेवपुरं *ŚiDhaSaṅ* **3:189** °भाजन°] *ŚiDhaSaṅ*; °भाज° NW (unmetrical); ⊔ K **3:189** यथाविधि] *ŚiDhaSaṅ*; यथाविधिम् NW; यथाविधिः K **3:190** उभाभ्यामपि पक्षाभ्यां] K, *ŚiDhaSaṅ*; उभा --- भ्यां N; उभो ⊔ भ्याम् W **3:190** घटाम्भक्षाम्बुपूरिताम्] N; भटा+न्+ भक्ष्यांबुपूरिताम् K; भ्याद्याव्यम्भक्षाम्बुपूरिताम् W; घटं भक्ष्याम्बुपूरितम् *ŚiDhaSaṅ* **3:190** अब्दात्पापविशुद्धस्तु] NK; अब्दा ¯¯पविशुद्धस्तु W; अब्दात्पापविशुद्धिः स्याद् *ŚiDhaSaṅ* **3:191** सायोज्यस्तु] NW; सायुज्यस्तु K; सायुज्यन्तु *ŚiDhaSaṅ* **3:191** अमावास्याम्पौर्ण्णमास्यां] NKW; पौर्ण्णमास्याममावास्यां *ŚiDhaSaṅ* **3:192** श्राद्धपिण्डाप्सुदानेन] NW, *ŚiDhaSaṅ*; श्राद्धपिण्डप्रदानेन K **3:192** पितॄन्यस्तु समर्च्चयेत्] NK; पितृन्यस्तु समर्च्चयेत् W; पितॄन् सन्तर्पयेन्नरः *ŚiDhaSaṅ*

सौवर्ण्णम्पुरुषङ्कृत्वा पितृनामाङ्कितं नरः॥ 3:192॥

प्रदद्याद्विप्रमुख्येभ्यो ताम्रस्थं [4] घृतसंप्लुतम्।
भक्षाम्बुपूर्णघटकान्दत्त्वा चैव विकल्मषः॥ 3:193॥

अब्देनैकेन युक्तात्मा विपापी काममीप्सितम्।
यावज्जीवं पितृपदम्भ्रष्टो भवति भोगवान्॥ 3:194॥

धनधान्यसमृद्धस्तु बहुपुत्रश्च सो भवेत्।
देवानाम्पूजने ह्येष विधिरुक्तो मया द्विजाः॥ 3:195॥

देव्याशंकरसंवादे तन्मया परिकीर्त्तितम्।
[5][[(पश्चिमे)]]नैव वक्त्रेण लौकिकं गदितं सदा॥ 3:196॥

॥ ⊗॥ इति निश्वासमुखतत्त्वसंहितायां लौकिके तृतीयः पटलः श्लो 197 ॥ ⊗॥

---

194 Cf. *Śivadharmasaṅgraha* 8.151: यावज्जीवकृतेनैव सुतृप्ताः पितरो भवेत्। पितॄणां पदमाप्नोति भ्रष्टो भवति चोत्तमः॥

195 *Niśvāsamukha* 3.195a–3.196b is parallel with *Śivadharmasaṅgraha* 8.152a–8.152f.

3:192 पितृनामाङ्कितं नरः] K; पितृनामाङ्कि --- : NW; पितृनामाङ्कितं बुधः *ŚiDhaSaṅ* **3:193** °मुख्येभ्यो] KW; प्रदद्याद्विप्रमुख्ये --- N; प्रदद्याद्विप्रमुख्ये *ŚiDhaSaṅ* **3:193** ताम्रस्थं घृतसंपुलुतम्] *conj.*; --- त सपतम् N; ⊔ न संयुतम् K; तस ⁻⁻म् W; ताम्रस्थन्तु घृतप्लुतम् *ŚiDhaSaṅ* **3:193** भक्षाम्बु°] NW; भक्ष्याम्बु° K, *ŚiDhaSaṅ* **3:194** भ्रष्टो] NW; भुंक्त्का K **3:195** बहुपुत्रश्च सो भवेत्] NW; बहुपुत्रश्च स भवेत् K (unmetrical); बहुपुत्रः प्रजायते *ŚiDhaSaṅ* **3:195** मया द्विजाः] NK; मया द्विजः W; मयानघ *ŚiDhaSaṅ* **3:196** देव्याशंकरसंवादे] N; देव्याः शंकरसंवादे K; देव्यासंकरसंवादे W; देव्याशंकरसंवादं *ŚiDhaSaṅ* **3:196** पश्चिमेनैव] K; --- नैव N; प ⊔ नैव W

निश्वासमुखतत्त्वसंहितायां चतुर्थः पटलः॥

देव्युवाच।
वेदधर्म्मः कथन्देव कर्त्तव्यो गतिमिच्छता।
स्वर्गापवर्गहेतोश्च प्रसादाद्वक्तुमर्हसि॥ 4:1॥

ईश्वर उवाच।
मेखली दण्डधारी च संध्योपासनतत्परः।
≪स्वाध्या [6] यी≫होमजापी च भैक्षाशी च अमैथुनी॥ 4:2॥

मधुमांसनिवृत्तश्च सक्षारलवणानि च।
वृक्षरोहणमेकान्तन्ताम्बूलञ्च न भक्षयेत्॥ 4:3॥

वर्जनम्प्रेक्षणं कूपे न नग्नस्नानमाचरेत्।
स्त्रीप्रेक्षणन्न कुर्वीत माल्यधूपञ्च वर्जयेत्॥ 4:4॥

वर्जयेदञ्जनं ≪गन्धन्तथा विषमलंघनम्≫।
≪षट्त्रिंशदब्दिका चर्या≫ [15ᵛ] गुरोस्त्रैवेदिकं व्रतम्॥ 4:5॥

---

1 *Niśvāsamukha* 4.1–4.7b is parallel with *Śivadharmasaṅgraha* 9.1–9.7b.

5 Cf. *Manusmṛti* 3.1: षट्त्रिंशदाब्दिकं चर्यं गुरौ त्रैवेदिकं व्रतम्। तदर्धिकं पादिकं वा ग्रहणान्तिकमेव वा॥

4:1 गतिमिच्छता] NKW; विधिमिच्छता *ŚiDhaSaṅ* **4:1** वक्तुमर्हसि] K, *ŚiDhaSaṅ*; --- क्तुमर्हसि NW **4:2** स्वाध्यायी होमजापी च] *ŚiDhaSaṅ*; --- होमजापी च NK; ⁻⁻ यी होमजपी च W **4:2** भैक्षाशी च अमैथुनी] N; भैक्ष्याशी च अमैथुनी K; भैक्षासी च अ-मैथुनी W; भिक्षाशी त्यक्तमैथुनी *ŚiDhaSaṅ* **4:4** कूपे न नग्नस्नानमाचरेत्] NK; कुपे न नग्ने स्नानमाचरेत् W; कोपमघृष्टा स्नानमाचरेत् *ŚiDhaSaṅ* **4:5** वर्जयेदञ्जनं] K, *ŚiDhaSaṅ*; वर्जयेदञ्ज --- N; वर्जयेद ⊔ W **4:5** गन्धन्तथा विषमलंघनम्] *ŚiDhaSaṅ*; --- तथा --- NKW **4:5** षट्त्रिंशदब्दिका चर्या] *ŚiDhaSaṅ*; --- NKW **4:5** गुरोस्त्रैवेदिकं] W, *ŚiDhaSaṅ*; --- स्त्रैवेदिक व्रतम् N; शुभैस्त्रैवेदिकं व्रतम् K

तदर्धिकं पादिकं वा ग्रहणान्तिकमेव वा।
ब्रह्मचारिव्रतं ह्येतदुक्तन्देवि मया पुरा॥ 4:6॥

विप्लुतो नरकं याति स्वाचरन्स्वर्गगतिम्व्रजेत्।
ब्रह्मचारिविधिः ख्यातो गृहस्थस्य प्रचक्ष्यते॥ 4:7॥

कृतदारो गृहे यस्तु यजेद्यज्ञां सदक्षिणां।
स्वाध्यायं प्रत्यहं कुर्यात्सायं ≪प्रातश्च हावन[2]म् ≫॥ 4:8॥

बलिञ्च वैश्वदेवञ्च अतिथेश्चैव पूजनम्।
दर्शं च पौर्णमासञ्च पशुबन्धेष्टिमेव च॥ 4:9॥

श्राद्धं सदक्षिणङ्कुर्यादृतुकाले व्रजेत्स्त्रियम्।
वर्जयेत्परदारांश्च आचाराद्गतिमाप्नुयात्॥ 4:10॥

अहिंसा निर्ममत्वं च बाधस्तेयविवर्जितः।
कामक्रोधनिवृत्तिश्च गुरुपूजाभिवादनम्॥ 4:11॥

क्षमा दमो दया दा[3]नं सत्यं शौचन्धृतिर्घृणा।
विद्या विज्ञानमास्तिक्यमेतद्ब्राह्मणलक्षणम्॥ 4:12॥

प्रत्यहं संहिताजापी त्वब्देनैकेन सिद्ध्यति।
त्र्यब्दाद्गायत्रिसिद्धिस्तु ब्रह्मलोकमवाप्नुयात्॥ 4:13॥

---

8 *Niśvāsamukha* 4.8–4.12 is parallel with *Śivadharmasaṅgraha* 9.7c–9.12b.

4:6 तदर्धिकं पादिकं] *ŚiDhaSaṅ*; तदर्धिकं पादिकां NW; तदधिकार्याधिकं K **4:6** ह्येतदुक्तन्देवि] NKW; ह्येतदुक्तमेव *ŚiDhaSaṅ* **4:7** स्वाचरन्] NK; आचरेत् W; आचारात् *ŚiDhaSaṅ* **4:8** यजेद्यज्ञां] N; यजेद्यज्ञं KW, *ŚiDhaSaṅ* **4:8** सदक्षिणां] *conj.*; सदक्षिणम् K *ŚiDhaSaṅ*; सद --- N; सदा ⊔ W **4:8** स्वाध्यायं प्रत्यहं] *em.*; स्वाध्यायं सततं *ŚiDhaSaṅ*; ⏓ वाय ⏓ यहः --- N; वेदाध्यायं प्रत्यहः K (unmetrical); ⊔ ध्यायं प्रत्यह W **4:8** कुर्यात्सायं प्रातश्च हावनम्] *ŚiDhaSaṅ*; कुर्या षाय --- म् N; कुर्यात्साय ⊔ म् W; कुर्या ⊔ K **4:9** वैश्वदेवञ्च] NKW; वैश्वदेवानाम् *ŚiDhaSaṅ* **4:9** अतिथेश्चैव पूजनम्] N; अतिथेश्च प्रपूजनम् K; अतिथिं चैव पूजनम् W; अतिथेश्चैव भोजनम् *ŚiDhaSaṅ* **4:9** दर्शं च] K, *ŚiDhaSaṅ*; दर्शनं N; दर्शन W **4:10** व्रजेत् स्त्रियम्] *conj.*; रमेत्स्त्रियम् NKW; स्त्रियं व्रजेत् *ŚiDhaSaṅ* **4:10** परदारांश्च] NKW; परदारादीन् *ŚiDhaSaṅ* **4:11** अहिंसा निर्ममत्वं च] K; अहिन्साभिममत्वञ्च N; अहिन्सो ऽभिममन्धञ्च W; अहिंसा निर्मलत्वं हि *ŚiDhaSaṅ* **4:11** बाधस्तेयविवर्जितः] *conj.*; बाधस्तेयवर्जितः N; ⊔ स्तेयवर्जितः K; ⊔ स्तपवर्जितः W; तप्तस्तेयविवर्जनात् *ŚiDhaSaṅ* **4:11** गुरुपूजाभिवादनम्] NKW; गुरुपूजनमेव च *ŚiDhaSaṅ* **4:12** दमो दया दानं सत्यं शौचं] K, *ŚiDhaSaṅ*; दमो द --- ⏓ सत्यं शौचं N; दमा दया ⊔ चन् W **4:13** गायत्रि°] NW; गायत्री° K

ऋग्यजुःसामथर्वाणां प्रत्यहन्संहिताञ्जपेत्।
जितेन्द्रियो ऽप्रतिग्राही ब्रह्मलोकं स गच्छति॥ 4:14॥

शिलोञ्छेनैव जीवेत प्रमृ[4]तेनैव वा पुनः।
अस्वयङ्कृतवाणिज्ये भूताद्रोहेण जीवते॥ 4:15॥

जप्ति जुहोति वा नित्यं स स्वर्ग्गफलभाग्भवेत्।
पञ्चयज्ञमकुर्वाणो नरकं याति सो ध्रुवम्॥ 4:16॥

अध्यापनं ब्रह्मयज्ञं पितृयज्ञन्तु तर्प्पणम्।
होमो दैवो बलिर्भौतो नृयज्ञो ऽतिथिपूज[[नम्]]॥ 4:17॥

पञ्चैतांस्तु महायज्ञां न हापयति श[5]क्तितः।
स्वगृहे ऽपि वसन्नित्यं सूनादोषैर्न लिप्यते॥ 4:18॥

पेषणी कण्डनी चुल्ली उदकुम्भः प्रमार्जनी।
पञ्च सूना भवन्त्येते कथितास्तव शोभने॥ 4:19॥

यस्तु ब्रह्मार्पणेनैव यजेद्यज्ञान्सदक्षिणान्।
आत्मध्यानरतश्चैव स विद्वान्वेदधर्म्मवित्॥ 4:20॥

---

15 *Niśvāsamukha* 4.15–4.16 is parallel with *Śivadharmasaṅgraha* 9.12c–9.14b.

17 Cf. *Manusmṛti* 3.70–71: अध्यापनं ब्रह्मयज्ञः पितृयज्ञस्तु तर्पणम्। होमो दैवो बलिर्भौतो नृयज्ञो ऽतिथिपूजनम्॥ पञ्चैतान्यो महायज्ञान्न हापयति शक्तितः। स गृहे ऽपि वसन्नित्यं सूनादोषैर्न लिप्यते॥

19 Cf. *Manusmṛti* 3.68: पञ्च सूना गृहस्थस्य चुल्ली पेषण्युपस्करः। कण्डनी चोदकुम्भश्च बध्यते यास्तु वाहयन्॥

20 *Niśvāsamukha* 4.20a–4.31b is parallel with *Śivadharmasaṅgraha* 9.23c–9.34d.

4:14 ऋग्यजुःसामथर्वाणां] *conj.*; ऋग्यजुस्सामर्थर्वाणां NW; ऋग्यजुःसामथर्वाणं K **4:15** शिलोञ्छेनैव जीवेत] NK; शिलाञ्छिनैव जीवेत W; जीवेच्छिलोञ्छवृत्यैव *ŚiDhaSaṅ* **4:15** प्रमृतेनैव] *ŚiDhaSaṅ*; प्र --- तेनैव NKW **4:15** अस्वयङ्कृतवाणिज्ये भूताद्रोहेण जीवते] N; अस्वयङ्कृतवाणिज्य ⊔ ताद्रोहेण जीवते K; अस्वयङ्कृतवाणिज्ये ⊔ ताद्रोहेण जीवते W; वाणिज्यादि त्यजेत्कर्म भूतद्रोहञ्च सर्वदा *ŚiDhaSaṅ* **4:16** जप्ति जुहोति वा नित्यं] NW; जपति जुहोति वा नित्यं K (unmetrical); जपाग्निहोमसंयुक्तः *ŚiDhaSaṅ* **4:16** याति सो ध्रुवम्] NW; याति स ध्रुवम् K; स ध्रुवं व्रजेत् *ŚiDhaSaṅ* **4:17** नृयज्ञो] K; तृयज्ञो N; ˉ यज्ञे W **4:18** महायज्ञां] *em.*; महायज्ञा NK; महायज्ञ W **4:18** न हापयति शक्तितः] *em.*; --- क्तितः NW; ⊔ K **4:19** पेषणी] K; पीषणी NW **4:20** यस्तु ब्रह्मार्पणेनैव] NKW; यज्ञब्रह्मार्पणेनैव *ŚiDhaSaṅ* **4:20** यजेद्यज्ञान् सदक्षिणान्] NKW; यजेद्यज्ञं सदक्षिणम् *ŚiDhaSaṅ* **4:20** स विद्वान्] NKW; सिद्ध्यते *ŚiDhaSaṅ*

ध्यायन्प्रणवयोगेन सर्वगत्वं स चाप्नुयात्।
≪षोडशारे[6]ण≫चक्रेण यदिच्छेत्सिद्धिमात्मनः॥ 4:21॥

श्रद्धया एकचित्तेन सर्वद्वन्द्वसहेन च।
नित्यञ्चालुब्धचित्तेन सर्वमेकत्वदर्शिना॥ 4:22॥

एवं यो वर्त्तते नित्यं जपध्यानार्चहोमसु।
न चासौ दुर्गतिं याति ब्रह्मलोकं स गच्छति॥ 4:23॥

केवलं कर्मकारी स्यादात्मध्यानविवर्जितः।
अगत्वा ≪सर्वगं ब्रह्म स्वर्गमात्र≫[16^r]फलं लभेत्॥ 4:24॥

अत ऊर्ध्वं वनेवासी सभार्यस्तु जितेन्द्रियः।
वसेद्वनगतो विद्वान्वर्त्तनं कुशबिन्दुना॥ 4:25॥

कन्दमूलफलैः शाकैः श्यामनीवारकाङ्गुभिः।
सायम्प्रातश्च तैरेव होमयेज्जातवेदसम्॥ 4:26॥

अफालकृष्टैर्वनजैर्देवब्राह्मणतर्पणम्।
((पितॄणां तर्प्पणं कार्यं)) ≪जपहोमरतः सदा≫॥ 4:27॥

सर्वभूतहि[2]ते युक्तस्सर्वदुःखसहिष्णुश्च।
शीतातपावकाशादि पञ्चाग्निर्जलशायिता॥ 4:28॥

4:21 सर्वगत्वं स चाप्नुयात्] K; सर्वगत्वे चाप्नुयात् N (unmetrical); सर्वगन्ध चाप्नुयात् W **4:21** सर्वगत्वं स चाप्नुयात्] NKW; सर्वगं ब्रह्म सर्वदा *ŚiDhaSaṅ* **4:21** षोडशारेण] *ŚiDhaSaṅ*; --- NKW **4:21** चक्रेण] NW, *ŚiDhaSaṅ*; नक्तेन (?) K **4:22** श्रद्धया] KW, *ŚiDhaSaṅ*; शुद्धया N **4:22** एकचित्तेन] NKW; चैकचित्तेन *ŚiDhaSaṅ* **4:23** जपध्यानार्चहोमसु] NKW; जपध्यानाग्निकर्म्मसु *ŚiDhaSaṅ* **4:23** स गच्छति] W; --- ति N; च गच्छति K, *ŚiDhaSaṅ* **4:24** कर्मकारी] K, *ŚiDhaSaṅ*; कर्म्मका --- N; कर्मकारिः W **4:24** अगत्वा] *conj.*; अग --- N; ⊔ K; ⊔ W; अजित्वा *ŚiDhaSaṅ* **4:24** सर्वगं ब्रह्म स्वर्गमात्रफलं] *ŚiDhaSaṅ*; --- फलं NKW **4:25** सभार्यस्तु जितेन्द्रियः] NK; सभायस्तु जितेन्द्रियः W; जितक्रोधो जितेन्द्रियः *ŚiDhaSaṅ* **4:25** वनगतो] NW, *ŚiDhaSaṅ*; वनं गतो K **4:25** वर्त्तनं कुशबिन्दुना] *conj.*; वर्त्तनं कुरु बिन्दुना NKW; वर्तयन्कुशबिन्दुना *ŚiDhaSaṅ* **4:26** कन्द°] KW, *ŚiDhaSaṅ*; स्कन्द° N **4:26** श्यामनीवारकाङ्गुभिः] N; स्यामनीवारकंगुभिः K; स्यामनीवारकाङ्गुभिः W; श्यामानीवारकङ्गुभिः *ŚiDhaSaṅ* **4:27** °कृष्टैर्वनजैः देवब्राह्मणतर्पणम्] *ŚiDhaSaṅ*; --- द्दएवब्राह्म --- N; कृष्टैर्वनजै ⊔ ब्राह्मणतर्पणम् K; कृष्टैर्वनज द्देवब्राह्मणतर्पणात् W **4:27** पितॄणां तर्प्पणं कार्यं] W; ⏓ ि ॠ णा तपण कर्य --- N; ⊔ K; पितॄणान्तर्प्पणञ्चैव *ŚiDhaSaṅ* **4:27** जपहोमरतः सदा] *ŚiDhaSaṅ*; --- NKW **4:28** सर्वभूतहिते] *conj.*; --- ते NW; ⊔ K; सर्वभूतहितो *ŚiDhaSaṅ* **4:28** युक्तस्सर्वदुःखसहिष्णुश्च] NKW; नित्यं सर्वदुःखसहिष्णुकः *ŚiDhaSaṅ* **4:28** शीतातपावकाशादि] NKW; अभ्रावकाश्यं शीतोष्णे *ŚiDhaSaṅ*

कुशवल्कलवासः स्यात्कृष्णाजिनधरस्सदा।
कृच्छ्रातिकृच्छ्रतप्तादिपराक्चान्द्रायणैस्सदा॥ 4:29॥

शीर्ण्णपर्ण्णाम्बुभोजी च आत्मानम्परिशोषयेत्।
मृगचारी सहावासः कष्टां वृत्तिं समाश्रितः॥ 4:30॥

ब्राह्मणः ≪स्वर्गगामी स्याद्विप्लु[3]तो ≫नरकं व्रजेत्।
वानप्रस्थव्रतं ख्यातञ्चतुर्थञ्चाश्रमं शृणु॥ 4:31॥

कायस्थमग्निङ्कृत्वा तु खमाकाशे तु विन्यसेत्।
विन्यसेद्वायुमनिले त्वनले ऽग्निं पयो ऽम्भसि॥ 4:32॥

कायं भूमौ मनश्चन्द्रे दिक्षु श्रोत्राणि विन्यसेत्।
विष्णौ पादौ बलं रुद्रे अग्नौ वाचं विनिक्षिपेत्॥ 4:33॥

मित्रे पाय्वेन्द्रियं न्यस्य शिश्नं चैव प्र[4]जापतौ।
संन्यासं तु क्रमङ्कृत्वा क्रोधलोभविवर्जितः॥ 4:34॥

अद्रोही सर्वभूतानां सर्वमात्मनि पश्यति।
त्रिदण्डकुण्डी चक्री च नैकान्नादस्स भैक्षभुक्॥ 4:35॥

---

32 *Niśvāsamukha* 4.32a–4.36b is parallel with *Śivadharmasaṅgraha* 9.35a–9.39b.

4:29 कुशवल्कलवासः स्यात्] NKW; कुशवल्कलवासांसि *ŚiDhaSaṅ* **4:29** °पराक्चान्द्रायणैस्सदा] NK; परां चाचणैस्सदा W; पराकैश्चान्द्रायणैस्तथा *ŚiDhaSaṅ* (unmetrical) **4:30** शीर्ण्णपर्ण्णाम्बुभोजी च] NK; शीर्ण्णपर्ण्णाम्बुभोजी च W; शीर्णपर्णोदकाहारैर् *ŚiDhaSaṅ* **4:30** सहावासः] NW; सहावास K; वसेत्तैस्तु *ŚiDhaSaṅ* **4:30** समाश्रितः] NKW; समास्थितः *ŚiDhaSaṅ* **4:31** ब्राह्मणः स्वर्गगामी स्याद्विप्लुतो] *ŚiDhaSaṅ*; ब्राह्म --- तो N; ब्राह्मण ⊔ तो K; ब्राह्मणः श्व ⊔ W **4:32** विन्यसेद्वायुमनिले] NKW; चेष्टायां विन्यसेद्वायुम् *ŚiDhaSaṅ* **4:32** त्वनले ऽग्निं पयो ऽम्भसि] *conj.*; त्वनलाग्निम्पयोम्भसि NW; त्वनलाग्निं पयोम्भसि K; अनले ऽग्निं पयो ऽम्भसि *ŚiDhaSaṅ* **4:33** श्रोत्राणि] NKW; श्रोत्रे तु *ŚiDhaSaṅ* **4:33** विष्णौ पादौ बलं रुद्रे अग्नौ वाचं] *conj.*; विष्णुं पादौ बलं रुद्रे अग्नौ वाचं N; विष्णुं पादौ बलं रुद्रो अग्नौ वाचं K; विष्णं पादों बलं रुद्रो अग्नौ वाचं W; विष्णुं पादे गले रुद्रं अग्निं वाचि *ŚiDhaSaṅ* **4:33** विनिक्षिपेत्] *ŚiDhaSaṅ*; विनिर्नि --- त् NW; विनि ⊔ त् K **4:34** पाय्विन्द्रियं न्यस्य] K *ŚiDhaSaṅ*; पाय्वेन्द्रि --- N; पाय्वेन्द्रियं न्य ⁻ W **4:34** शिश्नं चैव प्रजापतौ] *conj.*; शि --- जापतिम् NKW; शिश्ने चैव प्रजापतिम् *ŚiDhaSaṅ* **4:34** संन्यासं तु] K *ŚiDhaSaṅ*; सन्यासन्तु NW **4:34** क्रमङ्कृत्वा क्रोधलोभविवर्जितः] NK; क्रम कृत्वा क्रोधलाभविवर्जितः W; ततः कृत्वा लोभक्रोधादिवर्जितः *ŚiDhaSaṅ* **4:35** अद्रोही] NKW; अद्रोहः *ŚiDhaSaṅ* **4:35** त्रिदण्डकुण्डी चक्री च] NW; त्रिदण्ड ⊔ ण्डी चक्री च K; त्रिदण्डी कुण्डिपात्री च *ŚiDhaSaṅ* **4:35** नैकान्नादस्स भैक्षभुक्] NKW; भैक्षग्रासाष्टभुक् सदा *ŚiDhaSaṅ*

न त्वस्वमुपभुञ्जीत भैक्षवृत्तिसमाश्रितः।
ग्रामैकरात्रमुषितो नगरे पञ्चरात्रकम्॥ 4:36॥

वर्षास्वेकत्र निवसेद्दम्भकल्कविवर्जितः।
≪ग्रामसङ्गवि[5]वर्ज्जी ≫स्यात्सङ्गदोषविवर्जितः॥ 4:37॥

समस्सर्वेषु भूतेषु अनारंभी अहिंसकः।
आत्मध्यानरतो नित्यं ब्राह्मचभावसमन्वितः॥ 4:38॥

एवं यो वर्त्तते नित्यं स याति ब्रह्मलौकिकम्।
ब्रह्मणा सह मोदेत ब्रह्मणि स तु लीयते॥ 4:39॥

विप्लुतो नरकं याति कामलोभसमन्वितः।
यथोक्तकारी ब्रह्मात्मा ब्रह्मलोकं [6] स गच्छति॥ 4:40॥

वेदधर्म्मो मया प्रोक्तः स्वर्गनैश्रेयसः परः।
उत्तरेणैव वक्त्रेण व्याख्यातश्च समासतः॥ 4:41॥

आध्यात्मिकं प्रवक्ष्यामि दक्षिणास्येन कीर्त्तितम्।
सांख्यञ्चैव महाज्ञानं योगञ्चापि महाव्रते॥ 4:42॥

प्रकृतिं पुरुषञ्चैव उभावेकत्र योजितौ।
⏓ ⏓ ⏓ ⏓ ⏓ हेतुश्च यतस्सर्वं प्रवर्तते॥ 4:43॥

--- [16^v]भूते तु रजःसत्त्वौ प्रजायते।

---

36 Cf. *Śivadharmasaṅgraha* 9.39c–9.40: ग्रामैकरात्रमुषितो न वसेत्पञ्चरात्रिकः॥ वर्षास्वेकत्र संवासी नगरे पञ्चरात्रिकः। दम्भकल्कविनिर्मुक्तः सर्वद्वंद्वसहिष्णुकः॥

37 *Niśvāsamukha* 4.37c–4.41 is parallel with *Śivadharmasaṅgraha* 9.41–9.44.

4:36 त्वस्वमुप॰] NW; स्वस्वमुप॰ K; न शश्वदुप॰ *ŚiDhaSaṅ* **4:36** ॰समाश्रितः] K, *ŚiDhaSaṅ*; ॰समाशृतः N; ॰समासृतः W **4:36** पञ्चरात्रकम्] NW; पञ्चरात्रकः K **4:37** ग्रामसङ्गविवर्ज्जी स्यात्सङ्ग॰] *ŚiDhaSaṅ*; ग्रा --- वर्ज्जी स्यात्सङ्ग N; ग्राम ⊔ त्संग॰ K; ग्राम ⊔ W **4:38** अनारंभी अहिंसकः] *ŚiDhaSaṅ*; त्वनारम्भी त्वहिन्सकः NKW **4:38** अत्मध्यानरतो नित्यं] NKW; आत्मध्यानरतिर्नित्यं *ŚiDhaSaṅ* **4:38** ब्राह्मचभावसमन्वितः] NW; ब्राह्मभावसमन्वितः K; ब्रह्मभावसमन्वितः *ŚiDhaSaṅ* **4:39** ब्रह्मणि स तु लीयते] NK; ब्रह्मणि स तु लीप्यते W; ब्रह्मण्येव तु लीयते *ŚiDhaSaṅ* **4:40** ब्रह्मलोकं स गच्छति] *conj.*; ब्रह्म --- ⏓ ति N; ब्रह्मणो ⊔ तिम् K; ब्रह्मलोक स गच्छति W; ब्रह्मलोकञ्च गच्छति *ŚiDhaSaṅ* **4:41** परः] NKW; पदम् *ŚiDhaSaṅ* **4:43** प्रकृतिं] NW; प्रकृति K **4:43** हेतुश्च] NK; ⏑ ⏑ ⏑ ⏑ व W **4:44** तमोगुणाभिभूते] *conj. Kandel*; --- भूते N; ⊔ भूते KW

एतत्त्रिगुणसंयुक्तं ततो बुद्धिश्च जायते॥ 4:44॥

बुद्ध्यहंकारस्सम्भूतस्तन्मात्राणि ततो ऽभवन्।
इन्द्रियाणि तथैवेह भूतस्तन्मात्रसम्भवः॥ 4:45॥

अचेतनानि सर्वाणि पुरुषश्चेतनः स्मृतः।
यावन्ममत्वं कुरुते [[तावद्ब(द्धस्त्व)सौ पुमान्]]॥ 4:46॥

प्रकृत्या सर्वकर्माणि स --- [-3-] --- सु[2]खी भवेत्।
असंन्यासी तु बध्येत यावन्मायान्न विन्दति॥ 4:47॥

सांख्यज्ञानम्मयाख्यातं योगज्ञानञ्च मे शृणु।
सर्वद्वन्द्वसहो धीरस्सर्वदोषविवर्जितः॥ 4:48॥

संसारोद्विग्नचित्तस्तु स योगी परिकीर्त्तितः।
उत्तराभिमुखो भूत्वा बद्धा योगासनन्ततः॥ 4:49॥

स्वस्तिकं पद्मकं भद्रं त्वर्द्धचन्द्रम्प्रसारितम्।
सापा[3] श्रयमञ्जलिकं योगपट्टं यथासुखम्॥ 4:50॥

बद्धा योगासनं सम्यकृजुकायस्समाहितः।
जिह्वान्तु तालुके न्यस्य दन्तैर्दन्तान्न संस्पृशेत्॥ 4:51॥

शब्दे स्पर्शे च रूपे च रसे गन्धे च पञ्चसु।
अवशश्चेन्द्रियग्रामं सन्निरुन्ध्यात्प्रयत्नतः॥ 4:52॥

प्रतिप्रतिनिरोधाच्च प्रत्याहारः प्रकीर्त्तितः।

---

50 Cf. *Nayasūtra* 1.105: आसनम्पद्मकं बद्धा स्वस्तिकम्भद्रचन्द्रकम्। सापाश्रयं योगपट्टमासीनञ्च यथासुखम्॥ .

The same list is found in *Svacchandatantra* 7.290c–291b thus:
आसनं पद्मकं बध्वा स्वस्तिकं भद्रमासनम्॥
सापाश्रयमर्द्धचन्द्रं योगपट्टं यथासुखम्।

4:44 एतत्त्रिगुणसंयुक्तं] *conj.*; एतत्त्रिगु ⏓ ⏓ ⏓ त्क्तं N; एतत्त्रिगुणसंयुक्तं K; एतत्त्रिगुण ⊔ W **4:44** जायते] KW; जाते⁻ N **4:46** तावद्ब(द्धस्त्व)सौ पुमान्] K; तावद्धध ⏓ त्वसो पुमान् N; ताव ⊔ सो W **4:47** स---] NW; ⊔ K **4:47** सुखी] *em.*; --- NKW **4:47** असंन्यासी] K; असन्यासी NW **4:47** मायान्न] NW; माया न K **4:48** योगज्ञानञ्च मे] NW; योगज्ञानमथ K **4:49** योगासनन्ततः] NW; योगासन ततः K **4:50** सापाश्रय°] *em.*; --- श्रय° NKW **4:52** अवशश्चे°] N; अवसं चे° KW **4:53** निरोधाच्च] K; निरोद्धाच्च N; निरोधाच्चा W

सर्वगमे --- [-3-] --- [4] तु ध्यानरूपमरूपकम्॥ 4:53॥

रागद्वेषविनाशाय चिन्तयेद्ध्यानमेव तु।
प्राणायामम्प्रवक्ष्यामि त्रिष्प्रकारं समभ्यसेत्॥ 4:54॥

विरेच्यापूर्य संरुद्धं कुम्भकम्परिकीर्त्तितम्।
पूरयेच्च स्वकन्देहं यावदापूरितम्भवेत्॥ 4:55॥

पूरकस्तु समाख्यातो प्राणायामो द्वितीयकः।
निष्क्रामयति यो वायुं स्व[[देहा]] --- [-5-] ---॥ 4:56॥

[5] स रेचकस्समाख्यातः प्राणायामस्तृतीयकः।
अङ्गुष्ठाग्रे तु ध्यायीत वायुं सर्वगतञ्चलम्॥ 4:57॥

वायुना पूरयेद्विश्वं कृष्णरेण्वाकुलेन तु।
एवमभ्यसमानस्तु वायुरूपः प्रवर्त्तते॥ 4:58॥

ज्वलन्तञ्चिन्तयेद्वह्निं दहन्तं सर्वतोदिशाम्।
एवमभ्यसतस्तस्य वह्निरूपं प्रजायते॥ 4:59॥

पृथ्वी कठिनरूपे((([[ण]]))) शृणु देहे यथा स्थि[6]ता।
ध्यातव्या सा समुद्रान्ता पीता निश्चललक्षणा॥ 4:60॥

घण्टिकायां स्रवन्तन्तु वरुणञ्चिन्तयेद्धदि।
आपरूपः प्रजायेत धारणादग्धकिल्बिषः॥ 4:61॥

आगमैस्तर्क्कयेत्तर्क्यां योगविज्ञानकारणाम्।
स्वपरिज्ञानमुत्पत्तौ अविषण्णस्तु लक्षयेत्॥ 4:62॥

---

60 Cf. *Nayasūtra* 2.23cd and *Svacchandatantra* 12.3ab: पृथ्वी कठिनरूपेण शृणु देहे यथा स्थिता।

4:53 सर्वगमे ⊔ तु] K; सर्वग --- तु N; सर्वस ⊔ न्त्र W **4:54** त्रिष्प्रकारं] NW; त्रिःप्रकारं K **4:56** समाख्यातो] NW; समाख्यातं K **4:56** द्वितीयकः] K; द्वितीय ⩳ ः N; द्वितीयकं W **4:59** सर्वतोदिशाम्] N; सर्वतोदिशम् KW **4:59** वह्निरूपं] *em.*; वह्निरूपः N[pc]KW; वह्निरूप N[ac] **4:60** पृथ्वी] NW; पृथ्वीं K **4:60** शृणु देहे यथा स्थिता] *em.*; --- ता NK; स ⊔ ता W **4:60** सा] *conj.*; स NKW **4:60** निश्चललक्षणा] NW; निश्चललक्षणां K **4:61** आपरूपः] NW; अपारूपं K **4:62** तर्क्यां योगविज्ञानकारणाम्] N; तर्क्य योगविज्ञान-कारणम् K; तर्क्ां योगविज्ञानकारणाम् W **4:62** स्वपरिज्ञानमुत्पत्तौ] N; सुपरिज्ञानमुत्पत्तौ K; स्वपरिज्ञानम ⁻त्तौ W **4:62** अविषण्णस्तु] N; अविषणस्तु KW

समाधौ संस्थितस्यास्य [[विचित्रदर्शना]] --- [-2-] --- ।
--- [-6-] --- [17r] व्येत यावत्तन्मयतां गतः॥ 4:63॥

शब्दं स्पर्शं च रूपञ्च रसं गन्धञ्च पञ्चमम्।
सर्वाण्येतान्यजानाति यदा तन्मयताङ्गतः॥ 4:64॥

ताडितञ्च न विन्देत चक्षुषा न च पश्यति।
दिव्यदृष्टिः प्रजायेत यदा तन्मयताङ्गतः॥ 4:65॥

सर्वविद्याः प्रवर्तन्ते सर्वम्प्रत्[[((य))]]क्षतो भवेत्।
((सिद्धैश्च सह संभाषं यदा)) तन्मयताङ्गतः॥ 4:66॥

--- [-8-] --- स[2]र्वज्ञश्चैव जायते।
अनेनैव शरीरेण स सृजेच्चैव संहरेत्॥ 4:67॥

ईश्वरं ध्यायमानस्य सर्वमेतत्प्रवर्त्तते।
ईश्वरम्पदमाप्नोति ब्रह्मध्यानाच्च तत्पदम्॥ 4:68॥

विष्णुध्यानाद्विष्णुपदमन्येषामेव तत्पदम्।
येन येन हि भावेन तत्तत्पदमवाप्नुयात्॥ 4:69॥

अध्यात्मिकं समाख्यातमतिमार्गञ्च मे शृणु।
भस्म((ना)) --- [-5-] --- [3] भस्मशायी जितेन्द्रियः॥ 4:70॥

निर्माल्यधारी भिक्षाशी गुह्यस्थानम्परिव्रजेत्।
दर्शनार्थन्तु ईशस्य पूजान्तत्रैव कल्पयेत्॥ 4:71॥

लिङ्गस्यायतने वासो हुड्डुङ्कारस्तवैस्तथा।
गीतनृत्यनमस्कारैर्ब्रह्मभिर्जपसंयुतः॥ 4:72॥

---

70 Cf. *Pāśupatasūtra* 1.2: भस्मना त्रिषवणं स्नायीत। and 1.3: भस्मनि शयीत।

71 Cf. *Pāśupatasūtra* 1.5: निर्माल्यम्।

72 Cf. *Pāśupatasūtra* 1.7: आयतनवासी। and 1.8: हसितगीतनृत्तडुंडुंकारनमस्कारजप्योपहा-रेणोपतिष्ठेत् (read: °हुड्डुङ्कार°)।

4:63 विचित्रदर्शना] K; ि --- र् --- N; ि -ि -त्रदर्शना W **4:63** व्येत] NW; य्येत K **4:66** प्रवर्तन्ते] KW; प्रव ⏓ न्ते N **4:66** तन्मयताङ्गतः] *conj.*; --- NKW **4:67** सर्वज्ञ°] *em.*; --- र्वज्ञ° NKW **4:67** सृजेच्चैव] *conj.*; सृजेंच्चैव N; संसृजंश्चैव K; सशृजेच्चैव W **4:69** विष्णुध्यानाद्] K; विष्णुध्यानाच्च NW (unmetrical) **4:72** हुड्डुङ्कार°] N; हुन्तुङ्कार° K; हुत्तुङ्कार° W **4:72** जपसंयुतः] NW; त्तपसंयुतः K

एकवासो ह्यवासो वा दक्षिणामूर्त्तिमाश्रितः।
सुशीर्णपतितैः पुष्पैर्द्देवदेवं समर्च्च[[((येत्))]] ॥ 4:73॥

मूत्रामे[4]ध्यन्न पश्येत स्त्रीशूद्रन्नाभिभाषयेत्।
प्राणायामञ्च दृष्ट्वा वै बहुरूपन्ततो जपेत्॥ 4:74॥

अकालुष्येण भावेन जन्तुम्पश्येत सर्वतः।
अमङ्गलम्मङ्गलञ्च अपसव्यं प्रदक्षिणम्॥ 4:75॥

पितृपूजां देवपूजामुभे देवाय कल्पयेत्।
अनन्यभक्तिना कार्यं तप उग्रम्महात्मना॥ 4:76॥

शीतातपपरिक्लेशैर्जलमश्रू --- [-2-] --- [5] सिभिः।
जपध्यानपरो नित्यं सर्वद्वन्द्वसहिष्णुता॥ 4:77॥

जपनिष्ठैकान्तरतिर्व्यक्ताव्यक्तैकलिङ्गिनः।
विपरीतानि कर्म्माणि कुर्वंल्लोकजुगुप्सितः॥ 4:78॥

परिभूयमानश्चरेद्व्रतम्पाशुपतं महत्।

---

73 Cf. *Pāśupatasūtra* 1.10: एकवासाः।, 1.11: अवासा वा। and 1.9: महादेवस्य दक्षिणामूर्तेः (Bisschop 2006:5 reads: दक्षिणामूर्तिम्)।

74 Cf. *Pāśupatasūtra* 1.12: मूत्रपुरीषं नावेक्षेत्। and 1.13: स्त्रीशूद्रं नाभिभाषेत्।

74 Cf. *Pāśupatasūtra* 1.16: प्राणायामं कृत्वा।, 1.14: यद्यवेक्षेद्यद्यभिभाषेत्। and 1.17: रौद्रीं गायत्रीं बहुरूपीं वा जपेत्।

75 Cf. *Pāśupatasūtra* 1.18: अकलुषमतेः।

75 Cf. *Pāśupatasūtra* 2.7: अमङ्गलं चात्र मङ्गलं भवति। and 2.8: अपसव्यं च प्रदक्षिणम्।

76 Cf. *Pāśupatasūtra* 2.9: तस्मादुभयथा यष्टव्यः।, 2.10: देववत्पितृवच्च। and 2.11: उभयं तु रुद्रे देवाः पितरश्च।

76 Cf. *Pāśupatasūtra* 2.20: नान्यभक्तिस्तु शङ्करे। and 2.16: अतितप्तं तपस्तथा।

78 Cf. *Pāśupatasūtra* 3.2: व्यक्ताचारः। and 3.1: अव्यक्तलिङ्गी।

78 Cf. *Pāśupatasūtra* 3.3: अवमतः। and 3.4: सर्वभूतेषु।

79 Cf. *Pāśupatasūtra* 3.5: परिभूयमानश्चरेत्।

4:74 मूत्रामेध्यन्न] *conj.*; --- ध्यन्न NW; ⊔ न K **4:75** जन्तुम्] NW; जक्तन् K **4:75** अपसव्यं] NW; अवसव्यं K **4:76** पितृपूजां देवपूजाम्] K; पितृपूजां देवपूजा NW **4:77** जलमश्रू] N(?); जलम ⊔ KW **4:77** °सहिष्णुता] KW; °सहिष्णुंता N **4:78** कुर्वंल्लोक°] K; कुर्वल्लोके NW **4:79** °मानश्चरेद्] NW; °मानश्च चरेद् K

तेभ्यो दुष्कृतमादत्ते सुकृतञ्चापकर्षते॥ 4:79॥

स्पन्दमानस्तु विक्रोशेन्मंटे कुण्टेति वा पुनः।
विरुद्धचेष्टितं वाक्यं विरुद्ध[6]ञ्चाञ्जनं सदा॥ 4:80॥

विरुद्धमण्डनङ्गात्रे सर्वदा समुपक्रमेत्।
परिभूतः कृच्छ्रतपा सर्वलोकेषु निन्दितः॥ 4:81॥

महातपा च भवते पूजालाभविवर्जितः।
गूढव्रतोन्मत्तचेष्टी विलोमी लौकिके व्रते॥ 4:82॥

जितेन्द्रियश्च दान्तश्च क्षमी कामविवर्जितः।
गोधर्म्मा मृगधर्म्मा वा नैकान्नादः कदाचन॥ 4:83॥

लवण ⏑̱ --- [-4-] --- [17^v] च भिक्षायां पतितं सदा।
न दुष्येत तदश्नाति सन्मार्ग्गव्रतचारिणे॥ 4:84॥

प्राणायामैर्धारणाभिरोङ्कारन्तु विचिन्तयेत्।
शून्यागारगुहावासी नित्यमेव श्मशानगः॥ 4:85॥

---

79 Cf. *Pāśupatasūtra* 3.8: पापं च तेभ्यो ददाति। and 3.9: सुकृतं च तेषामादत्ते।

80 Cf. *Pāśupatasūtra* 3.13: स्पन्देत वा। and 3.14: मण्टेत वा।

80 Cf. *Pāśupatasūtra* 3.16: अपितत्कुर्यात्। and 3.17: अपितद्भाषेत्।

81 Cf. *Pāśupatasūtra* 3.19: परिभूयमानो हि विद्वान्कृत्स्नतपा भवति।

82 Cf. *Pāśupatasūtra* 4.2: गूढव्रतः। and 4.6: उन्मत्तवदेको विचरेत लोके।

83 Cf. *Pāśupatasūtra* 5.11: जितेन्द्रियः।

83 Cf. *Pāśupatasūtra* 5.18: गोधर्मा मृगधर्मा वा।

84 Cf. *Pāśupatasūtra* 5.14: भैक्ष्यम्।, 5.15: पात्रागतम्। and 5.16: मांसमदुष्यं लवणेन वा।

85 Cf. *Pāśupatasūtra* 5.25: हृदि कुर्वीत धारणाम्। and 5.24: ओङ्कारमभिध्यायीत।

85 Cf. *Pāśupatasūtra* 5.9: शून्यागारगुहावासी।

4:80 मंटे कुण्टेति] *conj.*; मंठोकुण्टेति NW; संठोकुण्टति K **4:80** विरुद्धचेष्टितं (वाक्यं +विरुद्धं+)] K; विरुद्धचेष्टितं वा --- N; विरुद्धचेष्टितं वाक्यं ⊔ W **4:81** समुपक्रमेत्] N^{pc}; समुपुक्रमेत् N^{ac}; संप्रचक्रमेत् K; स ⁻⁻क्रमेत् W **4:81** परिभूतः] K; परिभू ⏑̱ N; परिभू-त्त W **4:82** °चेष्टी] KW; °चेष्ठी N **4:82** लौकिके] NW; लोकिके K **4:83** नैकान्नादः कदाचन] *em. Acharya*; नैकनादः कदाचनः NKW **4:84** लवण ⏑̱] N; लवण K; लवण W **4:84** च भिक्षायां] NK; स ⁻भिक्षायां W **4:84** °चारिणे] NW; °चारिणः K

एवं यो वर्त्तते नित्यं दम्भलोभविवर्जितः।
सर्वज्ञाता च भवते श्रवणन्दर्शनन्तथा॥ 4:86॥

मननं शोधनं चैव विज्ञानं च यथेप्सितम्।
((महा)) ⏓ ⏓ ⏓ [2] चैवासौ रुद्रसायोज्यताम्व्रजेत्॥ 4:87॥

सिद्धस्तु न निवर्त्तेत विश्रुतो नरकम्व्रजेत्।
अत्याश्रमव्रतं ख्यातं लोकातीतञ्च मे शृणु॥ 4:88॥

आलब्धः पञ्चभिर्गुह्यैर्दीक्षितश्चैव सो भ्रमेत्।
खट्वाङ्गी च कपाली च स जटी मुण्डमेव वा॥ 4:89॥

वालयज्ञोपवीती च शिरोमुण्डैश्च मण्डितः।
कौपीनवासो भस्माङ्गी दिव्याभरण[[भूषितः]]॥ 4:90॥

[3] जगद्रुद्रमयम्मत्वा रुद्रभक्तो दृढव्रतः।
सर्वादस्सर्वचेष्टश्च रुद्रध्यानपरायणः॥ 4:91॥

रुद्रं मुक्त्वा न चान्यो ऽस्ति त्राता मे देवतम्परम्।
विदित्वैकादशाध्वानं निर्विशङ्कः समाचरेत्॥ 4:92॥

प्रथमे जालमेतत्तु द्वितीये मूर्त्तिसञ्ज्ञकम्।
तृतीये पशुराख्यातम्पाशाश्चैव चतुर्थके॥ 4:93॥

पञ्चमे विग्रहः ख्यातः [4] अशुद्धास्ते प्रकीर्त्तिताः।

---

86 Cf. *Pāśupatasūtra* 1.19: चरतः।

86 Cf. *Pāśupatasūtra* 1.22: सर्वज्ञता। and 1.21: दूरदर्शनश्रवणमननविज्ञानानि चास्य प्रवर्तन्ते।

87 Cf. *Pāśupatasūtra* 1.24: कामरूपित्वम्।

87 Cf. *Pāśupatasūtra* 5.26: ऋषिर्विप्रो महानेषः। and 5.33: लभते रुद्रसायुज्यम्।

4:86 सर्वज्ञाता] NK; सर्व ⏓ ता W **4:87** मननं शोधनं] K; मन ⏓ --- धन N; मनं स - साधनं W **4:87** यथेप्सितम्] NW; य ⊔ प्सितम् K **4:87** महा] W; --- NK **4:87** °सा-योज्य°] NW; °सायुज्य° K **4:88** नरकम्व्रजेत्] NW; नगरं व्रजेत् K **4:88** ख्यातं] KW; ख्या ⏓ N **4:89** आलब्धः पञ्चभिर्गुह्यैर्दीक्षितश्चैव सो भ्रमेत्] N; आलब्धं पञ्चभि-र्गुह्यैर्दीभितश्चैव सो भ्रमत् K; आलम्ब पंचभिर्गुह्यैर्दीक्षितश्चैव सो भ्रमेत् W **4:90** °पवीती] NK^{pc}W; पवीति K^{ac} **4:90** कौपीनवासो] NW; कौपीनवासा K **4:90** °भूषितः] K; --- N; भू ⊔ W **4:92** देवतम्परम्] NW; देवतत्परः K **4:92** विदित्वैकादशा°] N; विदि-त्वैकादश° KW **4:93** जालमेतत्तु] N; जलमेतत्तु K; जालमेतन्तु W **4:93** °ख्यातम्पा°] NW; ख्यातः पा° K **4:94** ख्यातः] K; --- या ⏓ --- N; ख्यात ⊔ W **4:94** अशुद्धास्ते] *em.*; --- द्धास्ते NKW

अशुद्धमाग्गर्गो व्याख्यातः शुद्धमार्गञ्च मे शृणु॥ 4:94॥

योनिर्वागेश्वरी देवी प्रणवो यत्र जायते।
तृतीयञ्चैव धातारं ध्यानञ्चैव चतुर्त्थकम्॥ 4:95॥

तेजीशम्पञ्चमङ्ख्यातं ध्रुवं षष्ठम्प्रकीर्त्तितम्।
अवीच्यादि ध्रुवान्तञ्च एतज्ज्ञात्वा विमुच्यते॥ 4:96॥

क्रीडार्थसिद्धये चैव प्रक्रियाध्यानमाश्रितः।
[5]शोध्य वै प्रक्रियाध्वानमथशब्देन दीक्षयेत्॥ 4:97॥

अथशब्दनिपातेन दीक्षितश्चापशुर्भवेत्।
क्रियावांश्च दुराचारो मुच्यते नात्र संशयः।
लोकातीतं समाख्यातं किमन्यत्परिपृच्छसि॥ 4:98॥

देव्युवाच।
एकादशैते तत्त्वास्तु नाममात्रेण मे श्रुताः।
पुनर्विस्तरशो ब्रूहि यथा वेद्मि महेश्वर॥ 4:99॥

महेश्वर उवाच।
[6][[((अ))]]वीची कृमिनिचयो वैतरणी कूटशाल्मली।
गिरिर्यमल उच्छ्वासो निरुच्छ्वासो ह्यथापरः॥ 4:100॥

पूतिमान्सद्रवश्चैव त्रपुस्तप्तजतुस्तथा।
पंकालयो ऽस्थिभङ्गश्च क्रकचच्छेदमेव च॥ 4:101॥

मेदोऽसृक्पूयह्रदश्च तीक्ष्णायस्तुण्डमेव च।
अङ्गारराशिभुवनः शकुनिश्चाम्बरी [[षकः]] ॥ 4:102॥

--- [18^r]न्या ह्यसितालवनस्तथा।

4:96 तेजीशम्] NK^{pc}W; तैजसं K^{ac} **4:96** षष्ठम्] NK^{pc} (?) W; षट् च K^{ac} **4:97** क्रीडार्थसिद्धये] W§; क्रीडार्थं सिद्धये NK **4:97** शोध्य वै प्रक्रियाध्वानमथ॰] *conj. Acharya*; वै प्रक्रियाध्वानंमथ॰ NW; ⊔ ध्वानमथ॰ K **4:99** तत्त्वास्तु] K; तत्ता ⏑̄ NW **4:99** विस्तरशो] K; विस्तरंशो N; विस्तरसा W **4:99** महेश्वर] KW; महेंश्वर N **4:100** महेश्वर उवाच] K; --- NW **4:100** कृमिनिचयो] N; कृमिंनिचयो K; क्रिमिनिचयो W **4:100** कूटशाल्मली] NK; कुटशाल्मली W **4:100** निरुच्छ्वासो] K; निरुश्वासो NW **4:101** पूतिमान्स॰] KW; पूंतिमान्स॰ N **4:101** पङ्कलेपो] N; पंकालयो K; पङ्कलेपा W **4:102** तीक्ष्णायस्तुण्डमेव] NW; ⊔ यस्तुण्डमेव K **4:102** शकुनिश्चाम्बरीषकः] K; शकुनिश्चाम्बरी ⊔ N; सक्तनिश्वाश्वरीपकः W **4:103** न्या] न्या N; ⊔ K; ग ⊔ W

सूचीमुखः क्षुरधारः कालसूत्रो ऽथ पर्वतः॥ 4:103॥

पद्मश्चैव समाख्यातो महापद्मस्तथैव च।
अपाको सार उष्णश्च सञ्जीवनसुजीवनौ॥ 4:104॥

शीततमोन्धतमसौ महारौरवरौरवौ।
द्वात्रिंशदेते नरका मया देवि प्रकीर्त्तिताः॥ 4:105॥

शताष्टा((धिकसंयु))क्ताः --- [-5-] --- [2] संयुताः।
चतालीसशतं ह्येतन्नरकाणाम्प्रकीर्त्तितम्॥ 4:106॥

पातालानि प्रवक्ष्यामि निबोधय यशस्विनि।
आदौ महातलन्नाम कृष्णभौमम्प्रकीर्त्तितम्॥ 4:107॥

रसातलन्द्वितीयन्तु स्फाटिकन्तत्प्रकीर्त्तितम्।
तलातलन्तृतीयन्तु रैत्यभौमम्प्रकीर्त्तितम्॥ 4:108॥

ताम्रभौमन्तु नितलञ्चतुर्थन्तु निगद्यते।
रौप्यभौ[3]मन्तु सुतलम्पञ्चमम्परिपठ्यते॥ 4:109॥

षष्ठं वितलसञ्ज्ञन्तु रत्नशर्क्करसञ्चितम्।
सप्तमन्नितलन्नाम सौवर्ण्णन्तदुदाहृतम्॥ 4:110॥

क्रमेण कथितास्सप्त पातालाधिपतीं शृणु।
नागाश्च गरुडाश्चैव तथा किम्पुरुषाण्डजाः॥ 4:111॥

अग्निर्वायुश्च वरुणो ह्यसुरांपतयस्तथा।
कथितास्तु निवासिन्यो भूलोक[[((मधुना शृ))]][4]णु॥ 4:112॥

सप्तद्वीपसमुद्रान्तं वर्षवृक्षनगैर्युतम्।
वनोपवनगूढञ्च नदीभिस्सागरैर्युतम्॥ 4:113॥

4:104 अपाको सार उष्णश्च] N; अप्रा ⊔ र उष्णस्च K; अद्याको ⁻⁻उष्णश्च W **4:105** महारौरवरौरवौ] NK; महारौरव ⁻ नवौ W **4:105** द्वात्रिंशदेते] K; द्वातृंशदेते N; द्वातृसदेते W **4:105** प्रकीर्त्तिताः] NW; प्रकीर्त्तिता K **4:106** शताष्टाधिकसंयुक्ताः] *conj.*; शताष्टा ि --- N; शताष्टाधिक ⊔ K; शताष्टाधिकसंयु W **4:106** चतालीसशतं] *conj. Sanderson*; सचतालं शतं NW; सचैतालं शतं K **4:109** रौप्यभौमन्तु] *conj.* Sathyanarayanan; --- मन्तु NW; ⊔ भौमं तु K **4:111** °धिपतीं] *conj. Sanderson*; °धिपतिं NKW **4:111** °पुरुषाण्डजाः] *conj.*; °पुरुषान्डजाः N; °पुरुषान्तजा+:+ K^{ac}; °पुरुषाण्+:+ K^{pc}; °पुरुषातुजाः W **4:112** निवासिन्यो] NW; निवासिनो K **4:113** सप्तद्वीप°] $NK^{pc}W$; सप्तद्विप° K^{ac} **4:113** °वृक्ष°] K; °वृर्क्ष° NW **4:113** सागरैर्युतम्] $N^{ac}KW$; सागरैर्युतः N^{pc}

ऋषिदेवगणाकीर्ण्णं गन्धर्वाप्सरसेवितम्।
धर्म्मार्थकाममोक्षन्तु सर्वमस्मिन्प्रतिष्ठितम्॥ 4:114॥

भूर्लोकः कथितो ह्येष भुवर्लोकमतः परम्।
स्वर्लोकन्तु ततोर्ध्वन्तु महर्लोकञ्जनं तपः॥ 4:115॥

सत्यं चैव ततोर्ध्वं तु [[ब्रह्म]][5]लोकन्ततोपरि।
विष्णोश्चैव निकेतन्तु शिवस्य तु पुरन्तथा॥ 4:116॥

ब्रह्माण्ड एष विख्यातः कपाला[[(व)]]रणैर्युतः।
शतरुद्राश्च पञ्चाष्टौ देवयोन्यष्टकन्ततः॥ 4:117॥

योगाष्टकञ्च सुशिवं गुरुपङ्क्तित्रयन्ततः।
तत्त्वसर्गमतोर्ध्वन्तु कथ्यमानञ्च मे शृणु॥ 4:118॥

प्रधानबुद्ध्यहङ्कारतन्मात्राणीन्द्रियाणि च।
[6]भूतानि च तथा पञ्च मनश्चैवोभयात्मकम्॥ 4:119॥

चतुर्विंशति तत्त्वा[[नि पु]]रुषः पञ्चविंशकः।
पञ्चविंशकमेतत्तु षट्कौशिकसमुद्भवम्॥ 4:120॥

मातृजैः पितृजैश्चैव अन्नपानविवर्द्धितम्।
गहनञ्च ततोर्ध्वन्तु विग्रहेशं ततोर्ध्वतः॥ 4:121॥

शिवशङ्करम[18ᵛ]साध्यं हरिरुद्रदशेशकम्।
पञ्च शिष्यास्तथाचार्या महादेवत्रयन्ततः॥ 4:122॥

---

121 Cf. *Guhyasūtra* 1.18–22: गहनं विग्रहेशं च नियति --- भागयोः। शिवशंकरमसाध्यं हरिरुद्रं च कीर्तितम्। दशेशानास्तथा शिष्या गुरवः पञ्च एव च। महादेवत्रयं यच्च गोपतिर्ग्रन्थिसंस्थिताः। मूर्धाभिभवपाशा हि तथा रिषिकुलं च यत्। योनिर्वागेश्वरी देवी प्रणवोङ्कारमेव च। धातारं मदनेशश्च भस्मेशेन समन्वितः। प्रमाणाष्टकविद्याष्टौ माया मायी च विद्ययोः। रूपं चतुर्विधं ज्ञेयं शक्तयस्तिस्रमेव च। ज्ञानशक्तिक्रियाशक्ति तेजीश निधनो ध्रुवम्।

4:114 °प्सरसेवितम्] *em. Sanderson*; °प्सरस्सेवितम् NW (unmetrical); °प्सरसोवितम् K **4:116** सत्यं चैव ततोर्ध्वं तु] K; सत्यञ्चैव ततो --- N; सत्यं चेव ततोर्द्धन्तु W **4:117** कपालावरणै°] K; कपाला⏑ रणै° NW **4:117** देवयोन्यष्टकं] K; देवयोन्याष्टकं NW **4:119** °भयात्मकम्] N; भयात्मकः KW **4:120** चतुर्विंशति तत्त्वानि पुरुषः] K; चतुविंशति तत्त्व --- रुषः N; चतुविंशति तत्त्व ⁻पुरुषः W **4:120** षट्कौशिक°] K; षट्कौषिक° N; षट्काषिक° W **4:121** विग्रहेशं] N; विग्रहेसं KW **4:122** °दशेशकम्] *em. Sanderson*; °दशेषकम् NKW **4:122** °त्रयन्ततः] *conj. Sanderson*; °त्रय --- N; °त्रयं ⊔ तः K; °त्रय ⁻⁻ः W

गोपतेर्ग्रन्थिरूर्ध्वन्तु मूर्ध्नाभिभवपञ्चकम् ।
अनन्तश्चैव पाशाश्च जालमेतत्प्रकीर्त्तितम्॥ 4:123॥

कार्यं दुःखं तथा ज्ञानं साधनन्तत्त्वमेव च ।
षष्ठं साध्यं तथैश्वर्यं कारणञ्च तथाष्टमम्॥ 4:124॥

[2] प्रोक्तं विषयमज्ञानं कारणोर्ध्वी च कथ्यते ।
अशुद्धाध्वा समाख्यातः शुद्धाध्वानञ्च मे शृणु॥ 4:125॥

मुक्त ऋषिकुलेभ्यस्तु संसाराच्च दुरत्ययात् ।
योन्याञ्चाप्यथ वागेश्यां जातः प्रणव उच्यते॥ 4:126॥

धातारन्दमनञ्चैव ईश्वरं ध्यानमेव च ।
भस्मीशञ्च समाख्यातं प्रमाणाष्टकमेव च॥ 4:127॥

विद्याष्टकं च मूर्त्य[3]ष्टौ तेजीशश्च ध्रुवस्तथा ।
इति सङ्ख्याः समासेन शुद्धाध्वानः प्रकीर्त्तिताः॥ 4:128॥

कपालव्रतमाश्रित्य ध्रुवं गच्छन्ति तत्पदम् ।
लोकातीतं समाख्यातं महापाशुपतं व्रतम्॥ 4:129॥

प्रक्रियाचर्यसंयुक्तो ध्रुवं गच्छति तत्पदम् ।
विप्लुतो नरकं याति प्रक्रियाचर्यवर्जितः॥ 4:130॥

अतिमार्ग्गं समाख्यातं द्विःप्र[[कारं व(रा)]][4]नने ।
पूर्वेणैव [[(तु)]] वक्त्रेण सरहस्यं प्रकीर्त्तितम् ।
अत ऊर्ध्वम्महादेवि किं वक्ष्ये परमेश्वरि॥ 4:131॥

देव्युवाच ।
मन्त्रमार्गन्त्वया देव सूचितन्न तु वर्ण्णितम् ।

4:123 मूर्ध्ना°] NW; मूर्धा° K **4:123 पाशाश्च जाल°**] *conj. Sanderson*; ⏑⏑ श्च जाल° NW; ⊔ जल° K **4:124 कार्यं**] N; काय° K; कायं W **4:124 साधनन्त°**] NW; सोधनं त° K **4:125 कारणोर्ध्वी**] N; कारणेर्द्धं K; कारणोद्धी W **4:125 समाख्यातः**] K; समाख्यातं NW **4:126 मुक्त**] *conj. Sanderson*; --- NK; मु ⁻⁻ W **4:126 वागेश्यां**] N; वागेस्यां KW **4:127 दमनञ्चैव**] NW; दमकं चैव K **4:128 विद्याष्टकं च मूर्त्यष्टौ**] *conj. Sanderson*; विद्याष्टक --- ष्टौ N; विद्याष्टकम ⊔ ष्टौ K; विद्याष्टंक च ⊔ ष्टौ W **4:128 सङ्ख्याः**] K^{pc}; सङ्ख्या $NK^{ac}W$ **4:128 शुद्धाध्वानः**] NK; सुद्धाध्वानः W **4:129 °श्रित्य**] K; °शृत्य NW **4:129 महापाशुपतं**] K; महापाशुतम् N; महापाशूतं W **4:130 प्रक्रियाचर्य°**] N; प्रक्रियाचय° KW **4:131 द्विःप्रकारं वरानने**] K; द्विष्प्र --- नने N; द्विष्प्रकार व ⁻नरे W **4:131 पूर्वेणैव तु वक्त्रेण**] K; पूर्वेणैव क्त्रेण NW

संसारोच्छित्तिकरणन्तमाचक्ष्व महेश्वर॥ 4:132॥

एवमुक्तस्तु पार्वत्या सर्वपापहरो हरः।
उवाच मधुरां वाणीम्मन्त्रतन्त्रार्थनिश्चिताम्॥ 4:133॥

अधुना [5] [[तदतो]] विप्रास्संवादमुमया सह।
ईश्वरस्य +तु+ देवस्य मन्त्रमार्गव्यवस्थितम्॥ 4:134॥

पञ्चमेनैव वक्त्रेण ईशानेन द्विजोत्तमाः।
मन्त्राख्यं कथयिष्यामि देव्यायाया गदितम्पुरा॥ 4:135॥

चतुःस्रोता मया पूर्वं श्रुता देव्याः प्रसादतः।
ते सर्वे कथितास्तुभ्यं निस्सन्दिग्धा द्विजोत्तमाः॥ 4:136॥

पञ्चमन्तु परं स्रोतं [[शि]] --- ।
[6] कथितं देवदेवेन किम्भूयः श्रोतुमिच्छथ॥ 4:137॥ ०॥

॥ ⊗ ॥ इति निश्वासमुखतत्त्वसंहितायां चतुर्थः पटलः॥ ०॥

श्लोकशतं सप्तत्रिंशोत्तरम्। चतुःस्रोताः श्लो 643 ॥ ⊗ ॥

4:133 वाणीं] KW; णीं N (unmetrical) **4:134 तदतो**] K; --- N; वदतो W **4:134 तु**] NW; च K **4:134 °व्यवस्थितम्**] NW; °व्यवस्थितः K **4:135 मन्त्राख्यं**] NW; मंत्राख्यो K **4:135 गदितम्पुरा**] NW; गदिता पुरा K **4:136 चतुःस्रोता**] K; चतुस्रोता N; चतु-श्रोता W **4:136 देव्याः**] K; देव्या NW **4:137 स्रोतं**] N; स्रोतस् K[pc]; स्रोतो K[ac]; श्रोत W **4:137 श्रोतुमिच्छथ**] NW; श्रोतुमिच्छथः K **4:137 चतुर्थः पटलः**] NW; चतुर्थपटलः K **4:137 सप्तत्रिं°**] *conj.*; सप्त ⏓ N; सप्तविं° KW **4:137 चतुःस्रोताः**] K; चतुस्रोताः N; चतुश्रोत्रा W

CHAPTER I

[Frame story: the Five Streams]

Ricīka spoke:

1:1 I went to the eastern direction for the sake of [gathering] flowers and kindling.[354] An unprecedented marvel was seen. Having seen that [I became] full of curiosity.[355]

1:2 [There were] eighty-eight thousand sages, whose semen flowed upwards,[356] [living in] the Naimiṣa forest [...].[357]

1:3 [...][358] O Lord! please tell me, who am asking, all [about] this.

1:4 O Lord you are expert in all scriptures and especially in the Vedas.[359] I ask you, o Mataṅga, because (*tena...yena*) you know.

---

354 There is a euphonic glide *m* between the words *pūrva* and *āśā*. Here *samidhaiḥ* is presumably to be understood as meaning 'together with firewood'. Prof. VASUDEVA, by way of personal communication, suggests a possibility of conjecturing *samidhe* (as in any case we need to understand it to be dative). He further points out that there are a handful of instances where *puṣpa* and *samidh* appear together, such as *Divyāvadāna* p. 43, lin. 6, *Kūrmapurāṇa* 2.12:24 etc.

355 Masculine pronoun *tam* is presumably meant for neuter *tat*.

356 The same line appears in *Brahmāṇḍapurāṇa* 1.7:180 and 1.21:170, *Mārkaṇḍeyapurāṇa* 49.79 and *Garuḍapurāṇa* 1.49:26. The same line reading *yatīnām* and *munīnāṃ* instead of *ṛṣīṇām* appears in *Mahābhārata* 2.11:34 and *Skandapurāṇa* 114.14 respectively. Eighty-eight thousand (*aṣṭāśītisahasrāṇi*) appears to be a common cliché in the *Mahābhārata*, (2.48:39, 2.11.34, 4.65:16, 12.34:17 etc.) and Purāṇas (*Bhāgavatapurāṇa* 8.1:22, *Brahmāṇḍapurāṇa* 1.21:164, *Viṣṇudharmottara* 64.22, *Viṣṇupurāṇa* 1.6:36, 2.8:92, *Vāmanapurāṇa* 27.59, *Skandapurāṇa* 114.14, *Agnipurāṇa* 376.32 etc.).

357 In comparison to the other folios, the first folio of the manuscript is markedly damaged in the right-hand margin. The text lost in this and the following line must be describing events surrounding the sages of the Naimiṣa forest, most likely as regards their visit to the Devadāruvana. We know from a somewhat later passage (1.19–20) that these sages have departed for the forest of Devadāru for the purpose of receiving initiation. Our guess is that the 'unprecedented marvel' which Ricīka beheld, and which aroused his curiosity, is the relocation of the sages of the Naimiṣa forest to the Devadāru forest.

358 We are not able to conjecture here since it is not possible to fathom the precise wording of the query which Ricīka posed to Mataṅga.

359 All of our sources read *devānām* instead. Theoretically, we could accept this reading, in which case our translation would be: o Lord you are expert in all scriptures and especially of gods.

Mataṅga said:

1:5 Listen, my child: I will tell you everything briefly. Those [sages] residing in the Naimiṣa forest heard (*śrutam*) that [...][360]

1:6–7 [...][361] by those [sages] residing in the Naimiṣa forest in the very place Brahmā and Keśava were initiated. O Ricīka! [Thus,] they were all full of curiosity [and] were utterly astonished.

1:8–9 Those experts in all scriptures spoke to each other as follows. How could one obtain (*katham...prapadyeta*) an initiation outside (*muktvā*) the Vedic tradition (*vedoktam āgamam*)? For there is nothing higher than the Veda. Yoga [[...]].[362]

1:10 How is it that Viṣṇu also, the knower of the Sāṅkhya and Yoga,[363] was initiated? Having heard that (*taṃ*),[364] all sages of stringent vows came [there].

1:11–12 Seen (*dṛṣṭvā*) [to you] as you were approaching [there] (*tvayi-m-āyāntā*),[365] they entered the forest of Devadāruvana (*devadāru-*

---

360 As a bare minimum, the ensuing deprecated textual portion must have related, what the sages heard. Logically speaking, it is possible that they were told that the gods, including Brahmā and Viṣṇu have gathered in the Devadāru forest where Maheśvara stayed. We are, however, unable to reconstruct the lost text.

361 Three *pāda* of the verse are missing here. It is possible that the lost text included the segment 'it was heard again,' since immediately after the lacuna, the text displays 'by the sages of the Naimiṣa forest'. It is also related what they heard: 'in that very place Brahmā and Keśava were initiated'. Once again we are not able to conjecture the text.

362 Twenty-one syllables of text are missing here and so the last three *pādas* of this verse cannot be translated precisely. However, we assume that the missing text incorporates a question regarding the initiation of Brahmā. The reason for this assumption is that the immediately following line relates a question about Viṣṇu's initiation, stating *kathaṃ viṣṇuś ca dīkṣitaḥ* 'how Viṣṇu also was initiated,' and in doing so, alludes to the initiation of Brahmā. We know that both Brahmā and Viṣṇu were initiated in the Devadāruvana (1.7) and (1.16). As Viṣṇu is said to be the knower of the Sāṅkhya and Yoga, we somehow expect that Brahmā is recognized as the master of Veda (for example see, *Śivadharmaśāstra* 6.29, *Haracaritacintāmaṇi* 1.98).

363 *Guhyasūtra* 1.12cd also states that the Sāṅkhya and Yoga are connected to Viṣṇu: *anviṣet sāṅkhyayogañ ca viṣṇudhyānaratas sadā.*

364 Masculine accusative singular standing for neuter accusative singular.

365 Here the letter *m* has probably been used in order to avoid hiatus, and although all manuscripts read *tvayimāyāntā* perhaps we need to understand *tvayi-m* as a locative functioning as an instrumental. Our interpretation is very tentative. The passage, after all, may be corrupt.

vanaṃ vanaṃ).[366] They there, thinking that they shall see Brahmā, Viṣṇu and Maheśvara[367] together (*samudāyena*) [and request] initiation (*dīkṣā*) [[...]][368]

1:13 [...] Then they all, Brahmā, Viṣṇu and Maheśvara, however, [[...]][369] went [back] to their respective places[370] after having given permission to Nandin [in the following way].

1:14 You are the bestower of favour [not only] upon sages but also upon all living beings[371] and also (*tathā*) you were earlier endowed with authority [to bestow *dīkṣā*?] by Devī.[372]

1:15a–16b [[.... ...]][373]

1:16c–17 Tell us all how (*yathā...tathā*) Brahmā and Viṣṇu were initiated, both of them (*te*)[374] being knowers of knowledge about initiation in all scriptures.[375]

---

366 Although this sentence is not lacunose, the syntax is ambiguous and unwieldy, resulting in an internally incongruous declarative sentence.

367 We require *brahmāviṣṇumaheśvarāḥ* as a compound. One should note that *brahmā-* is often used in this text as a stem-form.

368 The text breaks off after *dīkṣā*. We assume that the lost text here could have mentioned that Śiva himself did not grant initiation to the sages, but he bestowed this authority to Nandikeśvara.

369 Here we may be missing a past participle referring to the gods.

370 The second of the two instances of *tu* seems intended only to pad out the metre (*pādapūraṇa*).

371 The second *pāda* is unmetrical, the fifth letter being long.

372 According to the third chapter, *tantrāvatāra*, of the *Rauravāgama*, Devī teaches tantra to Nandikeśvara and he teaches it to Brāhmins. We are not sure what is referred to in this case. We have assumed here that this is an *aiśa* use of the genitive singular (*devyāyāḥ*) employed (m.c.) in the sense of the ablative: 'authority has been handed down [to you] from the goddess'.

373 Six *pādas* are missing here. Only the first letter *dī* of 15a has been transmitted. Most probably, the complete word would be *dīkṣā*, 'initiation'. If that were the case, could the text describe the initiation of Nandikeśvara by Śiva? After all, Devī granted Nandikeśvara the authority to bestow *dīkṣā*. Alternatively, the text may have stated that Nandikeśvara is capacitated to grant initiation to the sages. Be that as it may, at least in the last part of this lacuna, we expect a change of interlocutors, because after the lacuna we find the sages requesting Nandikeśvara to clear their doubt.

374 Here this masculine plural must either be taken in the sense of a masculine dual pronoun, or simply corrected to *tau*.

375 This line could certainly be interpreted in alternate ways. For instance, it might be assumed instead that they are conversant in all scriptures and have understood initiation and knowledge (assuming a *samāhāradvandva*, for this cf. *Svāyaṃbhuvasūtrasaṅgraha*, *Vidyāpāda* 1.1 and Sadyojyoti's commentary on it.)

Please tell [us] all about it, o omniscient Nandikeśvara! Thus they [[...]][376]

Ricīka spoke:

1:18 How could Lord Nandikeśvara be the teacher of them [i.e. sages]? How were they initiated into this system (*śāstre*), the true doctrine of Śiva (*śivasanmate*)?

Mataṅga spoke:

1:19 Now I will tell you, o best among Brāhmins, how (*yathā...tathā*) they, desirous of initiation and knowledge,[377] venerated (*stunvanti*) Nandi: please listen[378] with one-pointed minds.

1:20 In the beautiful Devadāru forest [[...]][379]

1:21–22 O you of very great austerity! Devotee of Rudra (*rudrāṃśa*)![380]

---

[376] We are not able to conjecture as almost two *pādas* are missing here.

[377] We take *dīkṣājñānasya* as a *samāhāradvandva*.

[378] Here *śṛṇuṣvekamanādhunā* is *aiśa sandhi* for *śṛṇuṣvaikamanādhunā*.

[379] At first glance, the text of *Guhyasūtra* 16.1a–2b appears to provide the missing portion for this lacuna:

devadāruvane ramye ṛṣayaḥ saṃśitavratāḥ |
nandīśam upasaṃgamya praṇipatya muhur muhuḥ ||
ūcus te ṛṣayaḥ sarve stutvā nandiṃ śivātmajam |

In the beautiful Devadāru forest, having approached Nandin and upon bowing down again and again, [and] after praising Nandin, son of Śiva, the sages spoke thus.

However, the damaged portion of the manuscript is to small to have contained all three lines. On the other hand, it would theoretically be possible to include these three lines in the lacunose section by structuring them in the following bipartite fashion:

devadāruvane ramye praṇipatya muhur muhuḥ |
ūcus te ṛṣayaḥ sarve stutvā nandiṃ śivātmajam ||

Given that we are not able to further substantiate this possibility, we have opted not to insert this conjecture in the main text.

[380] The *Svacchandatantra* 8.3d–4b defines *rudrāṃśa* as follows:

... *rudrāṃśaṃ ca nibodha me* ||
rudrabhaktaḥ suśīlaś ca śivaśāstrarataḥ sadā |

Omniscient because of Śiva's power (*śivatejasā*)![381] Sinless one! The dialogue between Devī and Śaṅkara,[382] [which is] the means for destruction of worldly existence [and is] the supreme nectar among all knowledge, was previously heard by you. It is taught only through initiation by Śiva, who removes what is inauspicious (*aśivahāriṇā*).[383]

1:23 Please (*prasādāt*)[384] act in such a way as to ensure that all the excellent sages [here] are liberated through your grace [...].[385]

1:24–25 [...] To [you, who has] the form of [...]![386] Homage to you who hold a spear in your hand,[387] three-eyed, to you who were born from a sage (*ṛṣisambhave*),[388] to you whose body is afflicted by austerity! Please

---

Now listen to me [about] *rudrāṃśa*. [The person called *rudrāṃśa* is] devoted to Rudra, well-disposed and always delighting in Śiva-scriptures.

Cf. *Guhyasūtra* 1.11. Certainly *rudrāṃśa* could equally mean 'part of Rudra' or 'partial incarnation of Rudra' but SANDERSON convincingly says, "In Śaiva terminology a compound formed of the name of a deity followed by the word -*aṃśaḥ* means a devotee of that deity, more precisely a person with a natural inclination (*aṃśaḥ*) towards that deity rather than another." For more details see SANDERSON 2003: 354. fn. 16. Kṣemarāja, commenting on *Svacchandatantra* 8.1ab defines *aṃśaka* as follows: *parasya bodhabhairavasya śaktibhiḥ brāhmyādibhir adhiṣṭhitā brāhmādyās tathābhāvabhāsitā aṃśāḥ, tatas tadanugrāhyā api tadaṃśā ity ucyante*|. Cf. also *Śivadharmaśāstra* 4.9.

381 Alternatively, we could take *śivatejasā* with what follows. In this case our translation would be: 'the dialogue between Devī and Śaṅkara was previously heard by you through the power of Śiva ...'.

382 *devyāśaṃkarasaṃvādam* is assumed to be an *aiśa* compound for *devīśaṃkarasaṃvādam*, but the word could be split by taking *devyā* as an instrumental.

383 This may mean that the above-mentioned knowledge is somehow transmitted through a ritual initiation or that it is only through having received initiation that one is entitled to receive the knowledge.

384 Instead of manuscript K's reading *prasādād* we could retain the reading of N and W, *prasādā*, and treat it as a *aiśa* ablative without a final consonant.

385 We are not able to conjecture 23d.

386 25d might for example have read *namas te śivarūpiṇe*; the translation would then be 'veneration to you [who has] the form of Śiva'. It is clear from the context that we are missing some epithet(s) of Nandin in 25c too.

387 *śūlahastāya* might indeed mean that he holds a trident.

388 *ṛṣisambhave* might be an *aiśa* use of the locative for the dative, but it is a perfectly correct form of the dative singular, since the root *saṃbhu* also exists in the same meant as *saṃbhū*. Alternatively it could simply be corrected, as suggested by Professor SANDERSON, to a vocative, *ṛṣisambhava*. In that case our translation would be 'o you who were born from a sage!'. According to the *Skandapurāṇa* (20.4 ff.), *Śatarudrasaṃhitā* (6.1 ff.) of the *Śivapurāṇa*, *Haracaritacintāmaṇi* (4.32 ff.) etc. Nandikeśvara is the son of the sage Śilāda.

raise [us] up [out of *saṃsāra*] through your compassion (*prasādataḥ*). O Nandikeśvara, there can be no other protector apart from you.

Nandikeśvara spoke:

1:26a–27b All you sages, listen to that which is said to be five-fold: worldly (*laukikam*), Vedic (*vaidikam*), relating to the soul (*ādhyātmikam*), transcendent (*atimārgam*), and mantra (*mantrākhyam*) [...].[389]

1:27c–28 All [the sages] were initiated by Nandin: some (*pare*) were linked to liberation (*nirvāṇe yojitāḥ*); others, being desirous of *vidyā*, were joined to *vidyā*.[390] Having initiated them according to rule, he started to speak.

1:29 "I will teach, o best among Brāhmins, just as Śiva, the destroyer of all

---

389 Perhaps we may conjecture something like *mantrākhyaṃ tantrabhedam anekadhā* (cf. *Śataratnasaṅgraha* p. 8, quoting from the *Kāmika*): *laukikaṃ vaidikaṃ caiva tathādhyātmikam eva ca* | *atimārgaṃ ca mantrākhyaṃ tantrabhedam anekadhā* | or instead *mantrākhyam tantram etad anekadhā* (cf. *Pūrvakāmika* 1.17c–18b: *laukikaṃ vaidikaṃ caiva tathādhyātmikam eva ca* || *atimārgaṃ ca mantrākhyaṃ tantram etad anekadhā* |).

In neither of the above-cited sources, however the Laukika, Vaidika, and the remaining 'streams' are presented as revealed by five different faces of Śiva. We recall that, in contrast, the *Niśvāsamukha* announces the providence of each of the individual Five Streams as each sourced in one of Śiva's faces: the *laukika* is issued forth from the western face, i.e. Sadyojāta (3.197), the *vaidika* from the northern face, i.e. Vāmadeva (4.41), the *ādhyātmika* from the southern face, i.e. Aghora (4.42), the *atimārga* from the eastern face, i.e. Tatpuruṣa (4.132), and the Mantramārga from the upper face, i.e. Īśāna (4.136). SANDERSON (2006: 157) points out that the same kind of division is found in the *Mṛgendra*, the *Puṣkarapārameśvara*, the *Svacchandatantra* and the *Jayadrathayāmala*. See also commentary of Bhaṭṭa Nārāyaṇakaṇṭha on *Mṛgendrakriyāpāda* 8.76.

The first four divisions are treated in this section of the *Niśvāsa*, the *Niśvāsamukha*. They provide the religious context out of which the Tantric religion of Mantramārga arose. The fifth, the Mantramārga, is what is taught in the remainder of the *Niśvāsa*.

390 27c—28 must have been spoken by Mataṅga to Ricīka. Vidyā here may be *vidyādīkṣā*. Throughout the *Niśvāsa*-corpus, there are two basic types of initiation, one of which is called *nirvāṇadīkṣā* and the other *vidyādīkṣā*. GOODALL has suggested (in the paper '*Vidyādīkṣā and Muktidīkṣā in Niśvāsa* corpus' delivered in the First International Workshop on Early Tantra on 19th September 2008) that the first is bestowed to bring about liberation and the second is granted in order to bring about 'supernatural enjoyments'. One possible explanation of the name *vidyādīkṣā* is that it grants entitlement to use mantra (*vidyā*) for the pursuit of *siddhis*. But this passage might be supposed to imply instead that the element *vidyā* refers to a level of the universe.

suffering, when asked by the great goddess". After prostrating before Śiva, purifying oneself,[391]

1:30 One should bow one's head to the god [who has] the crescent moon as his diadem, join one's hands together and raise them to one's forehead with devotion, and proclaim a hymn as follows.[392]

1:31 Veneration to you, together with your attendants. O one with a wife, let there be veneration to you! O Sadāśiva let there be veneration to you! O greatest soul Śiva (*paramātma*)![393] Veneration to you, Śiva (*śive*).[394]

1:32 The earth supports people [so] people are understood to consist of earth. [Your][395] form as earth is all pervading:

---

391 Kṣemarāja, on *Svacchandatantrodyota* Vol.1, p. 26, takes *śuciḥ* 'pure' to mean *śuciḥ kṛtayatheṣṭasnānaḥ* 'who has taken adequate bath(s)'.

392 We assume that the *aṣṭamūrtistava* is a hanging passage here. See introduction (p. 116).

393 *paramātma* is presumably an *aiśa* vocative for the dative.

394 We assume that *śive* is an *aiśa* usage of the locative as a dative.

395 Cf. *Prayogamañjarī* 1.19, *Tantrasamuccaya* 1.15 and *Īśānagurudevapaddhati* 26.56 *kṣitir vai dhāryate lokān lokāḥ kṣitimayāḥ smṛtāḥ | sarvagaṃ kṣitirūpaṃ te kṣitimūrte namo 'stu te ||* . Note that the *Prayogamañjarī*, *Tantrasamuccaya* and *Īśānagurudevapaddhati* have *kṣitirūpaṃ te* ('your form as earth') where our text has *kṣitirūpaṃ tu*. Here starts the description of the eight forms of Śiva. We often find these eight forms of god mentioned in *Purāṇas*, tantras, *Kāvyas*, inscriptions, etc. including the *Śatapathabrāhmaṇa* (6.1:3:9–17). Cf. *Liṅgapurāṇa* 41.29 ff, *Vāyupurāṇa pūrvabhāga* 27.1 ff., *Brahmāṇḍapurāṇa pūrvabhāga* 1.10:1 ff, *Viṣṇupurāṇa* 1.8:1 ff., *Śivapurāṇa uttarabhāga* of the *Vāyavīyasaṃhitā* 3.18–19, *Kūrmapurāṇa* 1.10:23–26, *Rauravasūtrasaṅgraha upodghāta* verse 16 (it appears in the Rauravāgama vol. I, p. 2, verse 16) *Prayogamañjarī* 1.18–28, *Tantrasamuccaya* 1.15–23, *Īśānagurudevapaddhati* 26.56–65, *Somaśambhupaddhati* 4.2:205–206, *Pūrvakāmika*, 66.102–103, *Suprabhedāgama*, 37.74–78, *Abhijñānaśākuntala* 1.1, Vallabhadeva's commentary on Raghuvaṃśa 5.4 and *Kūrmapurāṇa* 41.32, *Śiśupālavadha* 14.18, Bhera-ghat inscription (*Epigraphia Indica* Vol. II, no. 2, p. 10), Bakong Stele inscription of Indravarman I (*Epigraphia Indica* Vol. II, no. 35, p. 439), the inscription of Harsha stone (*Epigraphia Indica* Vol. II, no. 8, p. 120) the inscription of Bhaṭṭa Bhavadeva etc. Note that the inscriptional records are quoted from SATHYANARAYANAN (2007: 401–403).

There are close parallel verses for 27c–35b, in the *Prayogamañjarī* (1.18–26) and *Tantrasamuccaya* (1.16–23), and *Īśānagurudevapaddhati* 26.56–63. It is remarkable that we find this parallel only in the Keralā Tantric tradition. Our sources for the *aṣṭamūrti* are unanimous in recording these eight forms of god except for some variants of one of the names. These forms are: earth, water, wind, fire, oblation/*yajamāna*/*dīkṣita*/*ātmā*, ether, moon and sun. The *Śatapathabrāhmaṇa* (6.1:3:9–17), perhaps the earliest source for these eight names of god, however, records the eight forms as: fire, water, wind, *oṣadhi*, *vidyut*, *parjanya*, moon and sun.

o you who have earth as your form![396] Let there be veneration to you.

1:33 The water supports people [so] people are understood to consist of water. [Your] form as water is all pervading: o you who have water as your form! Let there be veneration to you.

1:34 The wind supports people [so] people are understood to consist of wind. [Your] form as wind is all pervading: o you who have wind as your form! Let there be veneration to you.

1:35 The fire supports people [so] people are understood to consist of fire. [Your] form as fire is all pervading: o you who have wind as your form! Let there be veneration to you.

1:36 The soul performs oblations [so] people are understood to consist of oblation. [Your] form as oblation is all pervading: o you who have oblation as your form! Let there be veneration to you.[397]

1:37 Ether supports people [so] people are understood to consist of ether. [Your] form [as] ether is all pervading: o you who have ether as your form![398] Let there be veneration to you.

1:38 The moon supports people [so] people are understood to consist of moon. [Your] form as a moon is all pervading: o you who have moon as your form! Let there be veneration to you.

---

396 Or perhaps 'o form [of yours] as earth'?

397 *yajña*, being one of the forms of Śiva, is attested to not only in our present text, but also in *Tantrasamuccaya* (1.18), the *Prayogamañjarī* (1.21) and *Īśānagurudevapaddhati* (26.58).

A number of variants of this form of Śiva appear in our sources, the most common being *yajamāna*, as attested in *Abhijñānaśākuntala* 1.1, *Liṅgapurāṇa* 41.32, Vallabhadeva's commentary on *Kumārasaṃbhava* 1.55, *Śiśupālavadha* 14.18, *Somaśambhupaddhati* 4.2:205, the Bhera-ghat inscription, (quoted from SATHYANARAYANAN 2007: 401). The *Viṣṇupurāṇa* (1.8:7), the *Vāyupurāṇa pūrvabhāga* (27.19) and the *Brahmāṇḍapurāṇa pūrvabhāga* (1.10:20) use the term *dīkṣito brāhmaṇa* for *yajamāna*; *dīkṣita* (see Vallabhadeva's commentary on Raghuvaṃśa 5.4 and *Kūrmapurāṇa* 41.32, commentary on *Netratantra* 18.61, *Viṣṇupurāṇa* 1.8:7 etc.). See also GOODALL & ISAACSON 2003: 263–264 on this point; *ātman*, cf. *Rauravasūtrasaṅgraha*, *upodghāta*, verse 16, *uttarabhāga* of *Vāyavīyasaṃhitā* 3.19 of the *Śivapurāṇa*, *Ajitāgama* 54.2, *Mahimnastava* 26 and various inscriptional records (see SATHYANARAYANAN 2007: 401 etc.)

398 *pāda* 32c is hypermetrical and *mūrtyākāśa* is an *aiśa* compound for *ākāśamūrti* (m.c.) unless we analyse, as suggested by Prof. Bhim KANDEL by way of *personal communication*, the compound as *mūrtiḥ ākāśaṃ iva*.

1:39 The sun supports people [so] people are understood to consist of sun. [Your] form as sun is all pervading: o you who have sun as your form! Let there be veneration to you.

1:40 Eight form [[...]][399] By this true sentence please draw me out from worldly existence.

1:41 Whoever is pure (*śuciḥ*) and constantly recites (*paṭhet*) this hymn consisting of eight forms [of Śiva], [becoming] free from all sins, he will attain union[400] with Śiva.

Goddess spoke:

1:42 You are the god [having] no beginning and end (*anādinidhanaḥ*), devoid of birth and destruction,[401] imperishable, all pervading and hav-

---

399 Twelve letters are missing here. It is likely from the context of the following line that the lost text would have included a praise of Śiva. However, the gap is too small to allow for a full enumeration of the names of the eight forms of Śiva mentioned above (27c–35b)—earth, water, and so forth—which is the insertion we normally would have expected at this point.

In its theomorphic aspect, the 'eight forms of Śiva' are also known as the 'eight guardians of the forms', the *mūrtipāḥ* (or *mūrtiśvarāḥ*), although SATHYANARAYANAN (2007: 401–402) rightly points out that the correlation between the two sets of eight names of Śiva is not consistent. It is therefore certainly warranted—had more space in the MS been originally allotted to this section—to alternatively expect a listing of the latter at this juncture. As for the individual names of the 'guardians', these are: Śarva, Bhava, Rudra, Paśupati, Īśāna, Ugra, Mahādeva, and Bhīma. Note that *Śatapathabrāhmaṇa* mentions 'Aśani' in place of 'Bhīma' (6.1.3:11) and 'Sarva', in place of Śarva (6.1.3:14). Close textual parallels in the *Prayogamañjarī* (1.28), *Tantrasamuccaya* (1.15) and *Īśānagurudevapaddhati* (26.65), record the eight forms of Śiva in direct proximity with the 'eight guardians of the forms'.

The *Liṅgapurāṇa* 2.13:1 ff. and *Viṣṇupurāṇa* 8.8 ff. give the eight names along with the corresponding wives and sons, the *Īśānagurudevapaddhati uttarārddha* 12.40 ff. presents the iconography of these eight forms of Śiva, and the *Śatapathabrāhmaṇa* (6.1:3:8–17), *Vāyupurāṇa pūrvabhāga*, 27.1 ff. =*Brahmāṇḍapurāṇa pūrvabhāga* 1.10:1 ff. and *Viṣṇupurāṇa* 1.8:1 ff. gives a detailed account as to how Śiva became the *aṣṭamūrti* (note that *Kūrmapurāṇa* 1.10:23, too, alludes to the story). It is likely that this story can be traced to the *Śatapathabrāhmaṇa* (6.1:3:8–17).

400 *sāyojyatām* is a common *aiśa* form, with Prakritic *guṇa*-grade of the vowel, for *sāyujyatām*.

401 The first *pāda anādinidhano devaḥ* is a common cliché. The first half of this verse seems to be somewhat similar to *Vākyapadīyam* 1.1ab: *anādinidhanaṃ brahma śabdatattvaṃ yad akṣaram.* We have assumed that the sense is that of *ajo 'kṣaro 'vyayaḥ*, although the transmitted text is *ajam akṣaram avyayaḥ*, where the *m* functions as a euphonic glide sound.

ing all forms. You are omniscient [and] the sole cause [of the whole universe].

1:43 [You are] the creator, maintainer and destroyer, the chief (*parameṣṭhī*)[402] and the supreme god. [[...]][403] highest goal (*gatiḥ*).

1:44 Having taken refuge in you, sages, gods and demons, snakes, Gandharvas, Yakṣas, Piśācas, Apsaras and Rākṣasas have all obtained accomplishment (*siddhi*).[404]

1:45 Having obtained a boon by your grace, they play after having reached the [highest realm of] rebirth,[405] which is liberation after which one is not reborn (*apunarbhavanirvāṇam*), from which, once one has reached it, one does not return [to this world].[406]

1:46 Indeed (*hi*), I watch the spinning, dreadful wheel of time, seeing people tormented by sorrows and extremely afflicted.

1:47–49 O Lord of gods! [...][407] on account of your compassion for the world, how mortals may be released from birth, death, old age etc.

---

402 The term *parameṣṭhī* generally is an epithet of Brahmā, not of Śiva.

403 Certainly the lost text speaks in praise of Śiva, but we are not able to conjecture what it would be.

404 The compound *piśācāpsararākṣasāḥ* involves an *aiśa sandhi* between *apsaras* and *rākṣasāḥ*.

405 I would like to express my gratitude to my friend Ven. GYALTEN Jigdrel for pointing out, during the final revision process of this volume, the semantic connotations of the term '*gati*' in the Buddhist Abhidharma-context. Had he not shared his ongoing doctoral research findings *by way of personal conversation, dated 8th May, 2018*, I would not have been able to make the relevant adaptations in translating the term. Cf. KRAGH (2016, fn. 290, p. 197) for the textual attestation of '*gati*' as 'course of rebirth' in glosses gleaned from the *Mūlasarvāstivādin Pratimokṣasūtra*.

406 'They play' (*krīḍante*) is a somewhat startling expression. We think that the term refers to the 'play' of supernatural powers (*siddhi*) in which a practitioner would be able to assume infinitesimal forms (*aṇimā*) and other such feats. This becomes clearer somewhat later in the text (2.20ab), when it states that the practioners engage in play by drawing on the *aṇimā* and other such [feats]: *īśvarasya prasādena krīḍante aṇimādibhiḥ*. Cf. also *Svacchandatantra* 7.225b. This, in the context of the *Niśvāsa*, is bestowed by the *bhukti-/vidyā-dīkṣā*, an initiation that upon fruition leads to the acquisition the 'enjoyment' of supernatural powers.

407 Three letters are missing, which would have had to be calibrated in order to convey something along the lines of 'please teach [me]'. Some fitting expression might have been *vadasva*, *ācakṣva*, *brūhi me* etc.

and also from hunger, thirst, cold, heat, desire, anger, fear,[408] and separations from loved ones (*iṣṭānām*), [they who are] enveloped by all [kinds of] diseases. Helpless, destitute of refuge, o god, [they are] treacherous and deceitful, delighting in harming others and malevolent (*duṣṭāḥ*). o great god! Please protect them.

1:50 O Lord of the gods! how and by which [specific] means will these [malevolent ones], devoid of pure conduct be purified [[...]];[409] please tell me that means.

God spoke:

1:51 I have taught Five Streams [of knowledge] on account of my desire for the welfare of the world. I will explain (*pravakṣyāmi*) all of them, o beloved one! Please listen attentively.[410]

1:52ab And for the sake of heaven and liberation (*svargāpavargahetoḥ*), understand this (*tan*)[411] precisely.

1:52cd I shall teach [first] the worldly [stream] (*laukikam*), by which people attain heaven (*svargam*).

1:53–56 Wells, ponds, houses, gardens [[...]][412] [and] pavilions (*maṇḍapāḥ*), donations, pilgrimages (*tīrtha*), fasting, religious observances and restraints, [eating] edibles and avoiding inedibles (*bhakṣābhakṣa-parīhāram*),[413] mantra recitation and sacrifice (*japahomam*), [committing suicide by] throwing oneself into water, into fire or from a cliff, and abstaining from food, renouncing possessions (*vidyamānanivṛttiḥ*),[414] honouring teachers and elderly people, this is what I have taught as

[408] We take all these instrumentals in the meaning of the ablative case.

[409] *Ex conj.* The *Śivadharmasaṅgraha* (5.15) clarifies that what we are missing is a word—or words—or a compound that topicalizes sins. There are several plausible avenues of conjecture. Prof. D. ACHARYA, to cite a pertinent possibility, has suggested *sarvakilbiṣaiḥ*.

[410] Note an elision instead of ordinary *sandhi*, in *śṛṇuṣv' avahitā*. One could, undoubtedly, consider adopting the reading of apograph K: *śṛṇuṣvāvahitā*.

[411] *tam* may refer to *hetu*; alternatively, it could be *tān*, or might be intended to mean 'therefore'. If *tan* is intended in the sense of *tān*, it would refer to the Five Streams.

[412] A considerable portion of the text is missing here, consisting of 20 letters. The perished section must have topicalized the construction of gardens, cross-ways, and the like, for the public good. See 2.25 ff.

[413] We assume that *bhakṣābhakṣaparīhāram* is an *aiśa* compound construed thus *metri causa*. Its intended meaning, we gather, is: *bhakṣaṃ ca abhakṣaparīhāraṃ ca*.

[414] To locate this expression as embedded in the text, cf. 3.58 below.

Laukika. The four-*āśrama* system is called Vaidika, [...][415] [...][416]. The world-transcenders are *mahāvratins* and those who are called *mantra*[-path-follower]s are Śaivas. [Any] others apart from these are situated on a wrong path.

Goddess spoke:

1:57 O god! You have indicated the Five Streams but not described them, now you should (*arhasi*) teach (*vaktum*) them to me at length by your grace.

[1. The Laukika stream]

God spoke:

1:58 [Even] a bad, evil-minded (*duṣṭacetasaḥ*) person,[417] who constructs a drinking-fountain,[418] will shake off [...][419] and rejoice with ancestors.[420]

1:59 One who creates a lotus pond, becoming free from blemishes, will go to heaven[421] together with seven generations [of his family] until his fame fades away.[422]

---

415 The lost part of the text must have listed 'Sāṅkhya' and 'Yoga' (which together constitute the *ādhyātmika* section of the text).

416 We expect the term '*atimārga*' to occur here in 56a.

417 We understand this genitive singular *duṣṭacetasaḥ* to be used as a masculine nominative singular *duṣṭacetāḥ*. This kind of use is quite common throughout the *Niśvāsa*-corpus. See *Nisvāsamukha*: 1.110, 1.124, 2.34; *Niśvāsaguhya:* 1.10, 3.15, 3.80 etc.; *Niśvāsamūla:* 1.16; *Niśvāsanaya:* 2.58, 4.59 and *Niśvāsottara:* 5.23.

418 It is not inconceivable that this means instead: 'who offers drinking water [to others']; *utpānaṃ* is an *aiśa* usage (m.c.), with the sense of *udapānaṃ*, as is confirmed by the reading of the *Śivadharmasaṅgraha* (5.15).

419 On the basis of the *Śivadharmasaṅgraha* (5.15), namely *pāpasaṃghātam*, we could conjecture something like *vidhūya pāpasaṃgham* 'will shake off a multitude of sin'. Since it is not possible to ascertain how the word-order was arranged in the lost textual portion, we did not inject it into the text itself. The other likely conjecture could be *vidhūya svakaṃ pāpaṃ* 'will shake off his own sin'. We could have adopted the reading of the *Śivadharmasaṅgraha*, namely, *pāpasaṃghātam*, but that would have rendered the *pada* hypermetrical.

420 Here begins the treatment of *laukika* religion, the first of the five *srotas*.

421 *Ex conj.*

422 For this idea, see *Mahābhārata* 5.35:4:

yāvat kīrtir manuṣyasya puṇyā lokeṣu gīyate |
tāvat sa puruṣavyāghra svargaloke mahīyate ||

1:60 Whoever offers a house, having filled it with possessions,[423] to a Brāhmin, for that person there will be a celestial golden house in heaven.

1:61 If one makes a garden in a temple of the lord of lords (*devadevasya cālaye*),[424] then hear from me the reward of the merit that one gains from each different flower [offered from that garden(?)].

1:62 [The offering] of one flower [to the *liṅga*] is of the value of ten gold coins; a garland is equivalent to one lakh [of gold coins]; one crore, they say, [is obtained] from a hundred garlands; if one covers the *liṅga* [with flowers, then the reward is] infinite.[425]

1:63 Those who always act in this manner [viz. by making offerings of flowers] become my troops (*gaṇāḥ*), never to fall [from that state]:[426] they will not become mortals [again], even after a hundred crores of *kalpas*.

1:64 This is what I heard from Hara, who was telling the goddess, and I have told it all to you (*tubhyaṃ*),[427] namely that which is the fruit of covering the *liṅga* (*liṅgapūraṇe*).[428]

[1.1 Worship of the *liṅga*]

The sages spoke:[429]

1:65–70 The sages, fearful, oppressed by the fear of the world, ask: How is god to be pleased?[430] What is the fruit of worshipping him? What

Here *naśyate* is an *aiśa ātmanepada* for *naśyati* (m.c.). It is conceivable, as has been suggested by Prof. D. ACHARYA, that the text enunciates that the devotee remains in heaven until the lotus-pond—the physical basis for his fame—perishes.

423 Alternatively, we could take *kṛtvā* as only intended to pad out the metre.

424 *ca* is functioning as a hiatus breaker.

425 Cf. below 1.123 ff.

426 Once again *ca* is functioning as a hiatus breaker.

427 This dative singular *tubhyaṃ* is perhaps being used here (m.c.) in the sense of dative plural *yuṣmabhyaḥ*.

428 *Ex conj.* *liṅgapūraṇe* (cf. 1.57 below) is a proposition of Professor SANDERSON, forwarded on the grounds that the merits of *liṅgapūjana* will be taught at a posterior point, and that Nandin has just (1.62) taught the merit of *liṅgapūraṇa*.

429 *ṛṣayaḥ ūcuḥ* is, strictly speaking, not necessary, and D. ACHARYA suggests removing this phrase. It is possible, however, that it is original, even though its sense is repeated in the following verse.

430 Note an *aiśa ātmanepada*.

is the fruit of bathing him with milk, clarified butter, curds, and water?[431] And what is the fruit of [offering] all kinds of flowers, fragrance, incense,[432] cloths, ornaments, edibles, banners, mirrors, and awnings? Tell us the fruit of [offering] lamps and an umbrella, (*dīpacchatraphalam*)[433] cows, goats, sheep and buffalo (*go'jāvimahiṣīṣū*),[434] offering of horses and elephants, the fruit of [offering] servants and maids; what is the fruit of cleansing and likewise besmearing? Tell [us] the fruit of singing and dancing, and the fruit [of playing] the lute and [other] musical instruments. Tell [us] the fruit of keeping vigil on the eighth and fourteenth days of the dark half of the month.[435] What is the merit of fasting and taking refuge in the Lord of gods?[436] Please tell us all this properly; we have approached you.[437]

Nandīśa spoke:

1:71 If somebody endowed with devotion to Śiva cleanses [the *liṅga*], he will certainly get [the fruit of offering] a hundred pure golden coins (*niṣkāṇāṃ*),[438] and if he besmears [it], he will obtain [the fruit of offering] a thousand of them.

1:72 One who has not had Śaiva initiation (*śivadīkṣāvivarjitaḥ*)[439] should

---

431 Note that K's reading, *pañcagavyena toyena* is a conjecture, and that the reading adopted from the *Śivadharmasaṅgraha* (5.22) is confirmed by W.

432 *gandhadhūpa* is an *aiśa samāhāradvandva*.

433 We understand *dīpacchatraphalam* to be used in the sense of *dīpacchatradānaphalaṃ*.

434 Presumably *go'jāvimahiṣīṣū* stands for *gojāvimahiṣīnāṃ dānasya phalam*. The reading of the *Śivadharmasaṅgraha* (5.23) *gavādimahiṣīṣu ca* is intended as an improvement on this.

435 For this expression *kṛṣṇāṣṭamicaturdaśī*, see 1.80, 88 and 93 below, which is an *aiśa* compound for *kṛṣṇāṣṭamyāṃ kṛṣṇacaturdaśyāṃ*; for this grammatically correct form see *Guhyasūtra* 3.46, 14.33 and 14.103.

436 This particular phrase—*devadevāśritasya*—gives a nuance similar to that of *Pāśupatasūtra* 1.9 (*mahādevasya dakṣiṇāmūrtim*) 'on the southern side of the great god.' We come across the peculiar practice of the Pāśupatas distinctly one more time in the *Niśvāsamukha* (1.75 and 1.166). In both cases it mentions offering the *huḍḍuṅ* sound to god, reflecting *Pāśupatasūtra* 1.8. These pieces of evidence show that some of the particular practices of the Pāśupatas were shared with the lay Śaiva religion by the time the *Niśvāsamukha* was composed.

437 *sma* here is presumably intended not as the particle, but rather as the 1st person plural present indicative verb-form: the *visarga* has been irregularly dropped, ostensibly for metrical reasons.

438 The syntax of the sentence is awkward. *niṣka* can also refer to a golden ornament for the neck or breast. This may then refer to the fruit of offering such ornaments.

439 The same expression occurs once again in 1.165d. We are not absolutely clear which type of initiation it is referring to; it might be either refer to Mantramārgic Śaiva

always worship god attentively after having purified himself and anointed the Śiva temple [with clay mixed with cow-dung].[440]

1:73–76 If someone (*yaḥ*) daily (*nityaśaḥ*) worships with leaves, flowers, fruits, curds, milk, ghee and so forth, and with *pavitras*,[441] that have been rendered pure with devotion,[442] clothes, edibles, parasols, banners, mirrors, awnings, bells, yak-tail whisks, garlands, ornaments, and water, with gold, jewels and garments, with fragrances, incense and unguents, with songs, instrumental music and dances, and with the sound HUḌḌUṄ[443] and with eulogies, o you [who have] obtained exclusive devotion (*kevalāṃ bhaktim*) to the god whose origin is

initiation or its Atimārgic counterpart. In this case, it is more likely to refer to Mantramārgic Śaiva initiation since the *Niśvāsamukha* prefaces the *Niśvāsatattvasaṃhitā*, a compendium expounding the Mantramārga. On the other hand, in both instances, the *Pāśupatasūtra* (1.8) presents the term *śivadīkṣāvivarjitaḥ* in close association with the injunction of offering the bellowing sound 'HUḌḌUṄ' to Śiva. Certainly hence, one could also posit that the reference is made in indication of Pāśupata-initiation.

A further thing to note is that this passage insinuates that the teaching of the worldly (*laukika*) path is intended for cultivation by uninitiated lay people (only). This impression gains further traction by 1.169ab: *evaṃ yaḥ pūjayed ajñaḥ śivadīkṣāvivarjjitaḥ* | 'If someone who is unaware [of the rules] and has not received Śaiva initiation worships [the *liṅga*] in this fashion (*evam*)'. Yet the following line informs us that the teaching is not for exclusive practice by the uninitiated, but also accessible to initiates—the inverse situation, it needs be stated, most certainly was not declared to be applicable; an uninitiated devotee would not carry out initiates' religious duties: *tasyedaṃ phalam uddiṣṭam apavarggāya dīkṣite* || 1.169cd 'for him these fruits have been taught (*uddiṣṭam*); in the case of an initiate, [the same act of worship] will contribute to liberation (*apavargāya*)'. What hence transpires is that the initiated were entitled to perform lay practices, albeit their elevated status effectuated that the identical mode of worship would bear different fruit, contributing to an initiates' procession towards liberation.

440 The underlying idea is that non-initiates are nevertheless worthy of performing temple duties (refer to the previous footnote).

441 *pavitra* can refer to a ring made of *kuśa*-grass which is worn on the fourth finger when sprinkling water, or ghee, during the act of purification in a ritual setting. In this context, it is possible that it refers to the cords that are lain on the *liṅga*, according to various *paddhatis*, during a ceremony of *pavitrāropaṇa*: see, e.g., *Somaśambhupaddhati* volume 2, pp.3–193.

442 Note that it would be possible also to emend this to *bhaktipūtaś ca*, qualifying the worshipper.

443 We know from the *Pāśupatasūtra* (1.8) that this is one of the offerings that a Pāśupata is supposed to offer to Śiva. This occurrence here, among lay Śaiva teaching, is significant as it tells us that this particular practice of Pāśupatas was also a part of lay Śaivism at the time of composition of the *Niśvāsamukha*. The reading *huḍḍuṅ* is of *Śivadharmasaṅgraha* 5.31 (the oldest manuscript of the *Śivadharmasaṅgraha*—

A—reads *huḍukāra*; another manuscript, C, reads *huṃḍuṃkāra*; the Nepalese edition of the text reads *huhuṅkāra* whereas our manuscript and both apographs do not transmit the text), and the particular word *huḍḍuṅkāra* is our emendation based on *Niśvāsamukha* 4.72:

liṅgasyāyatane vāso huḍḍuṅkārastavais tathā |
gītanṛtyanamaskārair brahmabhir japasaṃyutaḥ ||

where the *Niśvāsamukha* has paraphrased the *Pāśupatasūtra* 1.8:

hasitagītanṛtyahuḍḍuṅkāranamaskārajapyopahāreṇopatiṣṭhet |

• °huḍḍuṅkāra°] *em.*; °huḍuṃkāra° BISSCHOP; °ḍuṃḍuṃkāra° ŚĀSTRĪ

ŚĀSTRĪ's edition of the *Pāśupatasūtra* and *ad loc.* Kauṇḍinya's *bhāṣya* (see *Pāśupatasūtra* 1.8 cum commentary) read *ḍuṃḍuṃkāra*; Kauṇḍinya's description of the word is—*huḍḍuṅkāro* (corr; *ḍuṃḍuṃkāro* ed.) *nāma ya eṣa jihvātālusaṃyogān niṣpadyate puṇyo vṛṣanādasadṛśaḥ saḥ*. Whereas Kṣemarāja's description (*Svacchandatantra* p. 99) is—*bhaktivaivaśyenoccaran āntaraḥ śabdo huḍḍuṅkāraḥ* (corr; *huḍuṃkāraḥ* ed.).

BISSCHOP (2006: 4–5) retains the reading of the *Pāśupatasūtra* as *huḍuṃkāra*. Since *Niśvāsamukha* 4.72, which is the paraphrase of the related *sūtra* 1.8, gives the reading *huḍḍuṅkāra*; and since *Svacchandatantra* 2.182 and Kṣemarāja's commentary *ad loc.* also have the reading *huḍḍuṅkāra*, I feel *huḍḍuṅkāra* is the original reading. (Although in the printed edition of *Svacchandatantra* 10.588 and *ad loc.*, Kṣemarāja also has the reading *huḍuṅkāra*. Thus we are tempted to correct it to *huḍḍuṃkāra* since the old Nepalese manuscript, B28/18 fol. 106r, li. 6, reads *huḍḍūkāra*). Cf. also *Tīrthakāṇḍa* of *Kṛtyakalpataru*, p. 82 *huḍḍuṅkāranamaskāraiḥ* (corr; *huḍukkāra* BISSCHOP & GRIFFITHS 2007: 34, fn. 155; *huḍuṅkāra* ed.) *nṛtyagītais tathaiva ca* (corr; *huḍḍuṅkāra*. I have drawn this information from BISSCHOP & GRIFFITHS 2007: 34, fn. 155). SANDERSON (2002: 30, fn. 32) has also claimed that the original reading should be *huḍḍuṅkāra*.

Furthermore, there is another reading—*huḍukkāra*—which is also commonly attested in early sources. See *Niśvāsamukha* 1.166: *huḍukkārasya nṛtyasya mukhavādyāṭṭahāsayoḥ*. Cf. also *Ratnaṭīkā* p. 18–19, where it occurs four times: *tadanu pūrvoktavidhinopaviśya śivaṃ dhyāyan eva huḍḍukkāraṃ kṛtvā namaskāraṃ kuryāt tadanu japam iti | atra japanamaskārau mānasāv eva, nṛtyaṃ kāyikam eva, hasitagītahuḍukkārā vācikā eveti tatra dīrghocchvāsatrayaṃ* (corr; *dīrghocchvāsa°* ed.) *yāvad dhasitaṃ, daṇḍakatrirāvartanaṃ yāvad gītanṛtye gambhīrahuḍukkāratrayam* [...] *tad evaṃ nirvartyopahāraṃ dhyāyan īśaṃ hasitagītanṛtyahuḍukkāranamaskārajapyaiḥ ṣaḍaṅgopahāraṃ bhagavan mahādeva*, *Sarvadarśanasaṅgraha* (p. 169) where it occurs twice: *tad uktaṃ sūtrakāreṇa—hasitagītanṛtyahuḍukkārajapyaṣaḍaṅgopahāreṇopatiṣṭheteti* [...] *huḍukkāro nāma jihvātālusaṃyogān niṣpādyamānaḥ puṇyo vṛṣanādasadṛśo nādaḥ |*. These pieces of evidence suggest that there was another well attested orthography, i.e. *huḍukkāra*. However, BISSCHOP (2006: 4–5) argues that the vocalization *huḍuṃ* (*huḍuṃkāra*) is original.

unknown [i.e. Śiva] (*aparijñātakāraṇe*),[444] listen[445] to the fruit [obtained] by worshipping [the *liṅga*]—I will tell [you], everything [about it], thus:

1:77–79 One should bathe the *liṅga* with water mixed with fragrance; [by doing so] men will be freed from mental sin in one night,[446] from bodily [sin] in ten nights, and from a capital sin[447] in fifteen nights. In one month one attains heaven (*svargam*); in one year the sphere of existence (*gatim*) of a lord of *gaṇas*;[448] in three years one attains the state of being ancestor-divinities (*pitṛtām*); in five years, one may save one's [entire] family; in twelve years one attains union with Īśvara;[449] and after a lifetime[450] one attains union with Śiva.[451]

1:80–81 One should bathe the *liṅga* with pure curds on the eighth and fourteenth day of the dark half of the month:[452] [one who does so] will be freed from sins committed in his lifetime, there is no doubt. If a man, [being] pure, bathes [the *liṅga*] daily for one month, he will get

---

444 Cf. *Kumārasaṃbhava* 5.71 (*vapur virūpākṣam alakṣyajanmatā* [...]). We have taken *aparijñātakāraṇa* to mean whose cause of birth (i.e. the parents) is not known. We could also translate (*aparijñātakāraṇe*) to 'who do not know any instrumentality'. This, however, does not make much sense. Professor ISAACSON suggests that we may understand °*kāraṇa* to mean °*karaṇa* '[proper] procedure'; if so, this orthography °*kāraṇa* is retained for metrical reasons. He also pointed out to me that reading °*karaṇa* does not completely solve the problem since what follows is also a procedure.

445 Note that *śṛṇudhvam* is an *aiśa* use of *ātmanepada* imperative second person plural for *śṛṇuta*.

446 *ekarātreṇa* means one day and night. Note that *ekāham* (1.83) is a synonym for the same. This sentence is anacoluthic, beginning with a singular and ending with a plural subject.

447 Presumably *mahāpāpa* means the same as *mahāpātaka*: see, e.g., *Manusmṛti* verse 55, p. 847:

brahmahatyā surāpānaṃ steyaṃ gurvaṅganāgamaḥ |
mahānti pātakāny āhuḥ saṃsargaś cāpi taiḥ saha |

448 For the expression *gāṇeśvarī gatiḥ*, cf. *Revākhaṇḍa* of the *Vāyupurāṇa* (previously assigned to *Skandapurāṇa*) 23.8, 215.2 *Niśvāsamukha* 1.97, 81, 1.101 and *Śivadharmasaṅgraha* 5.34, 40, 42 and 61.

449 *īśvara* is the lowest level of Śiva (just above *vidyā*) both in the *Niśvāsa* and in the theology of the developed Śaiva Siddhānta.

450 *yāvajjīvam* alone as clause of a sentence is incomplete. We would expect something like *yāvajjīvaṃ kṛte* where *sati* is understood.

451 *śivaṃ vrajet* has been translated as though it were the same as *śivasāyujyatāṃ vrajet*.

452 See footnote on verse 69 about *kṛṣṇāṣṭamicaturdaśī*.

the [fruit of performing] sacrifice daily;[453] [and] when he departs from the body, he will attain the abode of Śiva.[454]

1:82a–83b If someone bathes [the *liṅga*] for six months, he will become a supreme Gaṇa. By bathing [it] for one year his ancestors attain the abode of Śiva (*śivālayam*); [by bathing it] for three years [he will attain] union with Rudra; [by his bathing it for twelve years] his own lineage [will attain union with Rudra].

1:83c–85b If a man bathes the *liṅga* with ghee for one day, destroying all sins, he will obtain the fruit of performing an Aśvamedha sacrifice. By [bathing it for] ten nights he goes to heavenly plane of existence (*svargagatiḥ*);[455] for one month, sphere of existence of a lord of Gaṇas (*gāṇeśvarīṃ gatim*); and ancestors in hell will be lifted out, there is no doubt.

1:85c–86 If he bathes [the *liṅga*] daily with uninterrupted focus (*abhagnayogataḥ*) for six months, his ancestors, too, will always (*nityam*) obtain the sphere of existence of a lord of Gaṇas. By [bathing it for] two years,[456] he will obtain (*gacchate*)[457] union [with Śiva] together with his ancestors.

1:87 There is nothing higher than bathing [a *liṅga*] with ghee, [by which] one can draw out seven generations [of his family from hell].[458] [His ancestors will become] three-eyed, having trident in hand, bull-marked and moon-diademed.[459]

---

453 *kratum āpnoti* presumably means *kratuphalam āpnoti*, but what kind of sacrifice is intended? Perhaps a Vedic *soma*-sacrifice?

454 Once again, the exact nature of the reward is not clear.

455 84c is a hypometrical *pāda*.

456 One might think that *dvirabdena* is used here (m.c.) for *dvyabdena*. Yet *dvirabdena* is a grammatically attested form (see the Pāṇinian *dvitricaturbhyaḥ suc* 5.4:18).

457 Note an *aiśa* use of the *ātmanepada*.

458 The syntax is ambiguous; there is no mention of the correlative pronoun, *sa*, for *ya*. Furthermore, there is an *aiśa* sandhi between *ya* and *uddharet*. Although these two grammatical problems (an *aiśa sandhi* and hanging relative pronoun) have been edited out in *Śivadharmasaṅgraha* 5.43 by the reading *ghṛtasnānāt paran nāsti uddharet kulasaptakam*, the problem of understanding the line remains unsolved. We may therefore have to understand the line as follows:

ghṛtasnānāt param anyat snānaṃ nāsti |
yo ghṛtena liṅgaṃ snāyāt sa kulasaptakam uddharet |

459 Presumably this is the reward of *sārūpya*, but the phrase is incomplete or ana-

1:88 If one bathes the *liṅga* with milk on the eighth and fourteenth days of the dark half of the month,[460] one will be freed from the sin made in [his] lifetime; there is no doubt on this point.

1:89 If one who possesses all kinds of sin bathes [the *liṅga* with milk] for one month,[461] he will be freed from all those sins and obtain union with Śiva (*śivasāyojyatām*).

1:90a–91b If one bathes [the *liṅga* with milk] for six months, he will be the best of Gaṇas. By bathing [it] for one year he will certainly lift out seven generations [of his family from hell]; by bathing [it] for three years [he will obtain] union with Rudra and † *uddhareṇa śivātmakaṃ* †.[462]

1:91c–92 If one bathes [it with milk] daily (*satatam*) for twelve years with devotion, he will raise a whole hundred crores of [members of one's] family and beyond (*sāgram*)[463] out of hell. This is the fruit of bathing

---

colouthic. Note again that the *Śivadharmasaṅgraha* (5.43–44) has improved the construction here mainly by supplying the finite verb *bhavanti*. The *Śivadharmasaṅgraha* (5.43c–44b) reads

trinetrāḥ śūlahastāś ca vṛṣāṅkāś candraśekharāḥ |
sarvajñāḥ sarvagā nityā bhavanti jagadīśvarāḥ ||

460 See note on verse 69 for *kṛṣṇāṣṭamicaturdaśī*. The *Śivadharmasaṅgraha* (5.44) tries to make this compound regular by reading *kṛṣṇāṣṭamyāṃ caturddaśyāṃ*, but for metrical reasons the complete regularization is not possible in this place in the *Śivadharmasaṅgraha*.

461 *Ex conj.* An alternative reading might be *māsena*.

462 Prof. SANDERSON points out that *śivātmakam* is perplexing and that we might rather expect *śivaṃ vrajet* or *śivātmatām*. Prof. D. ACHARYA, however, suggests *pañcābdena* or *ṣaḍabdena* in the place of *uddhareṇa*. The *Śivadharmasaṅgraha* (5.38a–39c) rephrases it (86–87) avoiding the problem as follows:

ṣaṇmāsaṃ snāpayed yas tu surāṇāṃ cottamo bhavet |
abdasnānena pitaras tasya yānti surālayam ||
tryabdena rudrasāyujyaṃ dvādaśābdaiḥ kulaiḥ svayam |

In light of this reading of the *Śivadharmasaṅgraha* we may interpret the reading *uddhareṇa śivātmakaṃ* thus: *uddhareṇa* meaning having raised [his ancestors from hells], and *śivātmakaṃ* (assuming as Professor SANDERSON suggests, that is a corruption for *śivātmatā*) meaning '[he obtains] the state of being Śiva' [together with his ancestors].

463 92ab is paralleled by the *Niśvāsakārikā* (consult our edition) and 92a is also paralleled by *Revākhaṇḍa* of the *Vāyupurāṇa* 172.79c.

[the *liṅga*] with milk, [which] is higher than that of bathing it with ghee (*ghṛtasnānopari sthitam*).[464]

1:93 If a man bathes the *liṅga* with honey on the eighth and fourteenth days of the dark half of the month, he will obtain the fruit of having performed the Rājasūya sacrifice.

1:94 [By bathing it] daily for one year [one will become] a lord of Gaṇas [and?] obtain a fruit(?);[465] by [bathing it for] five years he will obtain union [with Śiva], together with his forefathers.

1:95 Somebody who [...][466] bathes [the *liṅga*] daily with the five products of the cow, †his death does not occur†: he obtains the world of gods (*devalokam*).

1:96 By [bathing it for] one year, being pure, he will obtain union with Śiva, and [by bathing it for] two years seven generations (*pitaraḥ*) [of his family] are considered to be raised out [of the hells].

1:97a–99b If a man besmears the *liṅga* with fragrances that are sweet-smelling and divine,[467] he will obtain the fruit of performing the Vājapeya sacrifice, and if he besmears [it] with sandal paste mixed with camphor for ten nights he gets the fruit of an Aśvamedha; [if he does so] for one month, he becomes a Gaṇa; [by doing so] for one year, he will achieve union with [Śiva]

1:99c–100b If someone performs [the rite of] besmearing *liṅga* [with sandal paste mixed with camphor] daily with uninterrupted focus, all his ancestors will go to the supreme sphere of rebirth (*gati*).

---

464 It is slightly bewildering that this text registers bathing the *liṅga* by milk as higher than bathing it with ghee. Perhaps detecting this problem, the *Śivadharmasaṅgraha* does not render this particular section.

465 We expect the usual sequence of one month, six months, one year, but in the *Śivadharmasaṅgraha* (5.45) too, no longer sequence occurs in this context. It is possible nonetheless that the text is corrupt and became so before it was used by the redactor of the *Śivadharmasaṅgraha*. There is a further difficulty here in that the expression *phalam āpnoti* appears to be left hanging without sufficient context. Probably in the course of transmission a scribe has by mistake copied *phalam āpnoti* from the preceding line, replacing the actual words fitting in the context.

466 We could perhaps conjecture something like *kārayen naraḥ*.

467 Is it conceivable that this instead means: 'If a man besmears the *liṅga* with [ordinary] fragrance and with divine fragrances ...'

1:100c–101b He who burns[468] *guggulu* once in the vicinity of the supreme god (*devadevasya*) [by the merit of giving that] incense, he will obtain the fruit of having performed an Agniṣṭoma.

1:101c–102b If someone burns incense of the best *guggulu* [in the presence of the supreme god/the *liṅga*] continuously for one month, he will obtain [the fruit] of a hundred sacrifices.[469]

1:102c–103b If someone burns them for six months, he will become an excellent (*uttamaḥ*) Gaṇa. For him there is no possibility of being reborn (*sambhavaḥ*) in the mortal [world] (*martye*); he rejoices with [his] ancestors.

1:103c–104b If someone, having purified himself, burns [them] daily for one year, as a wise Śiva-devotee (*tena śivabhaktena dhīmatā*), he will lift out [his] own family [from hells].

1:104c–105b If someone offers cloths, banners or awnings to the *liṅga*, he will obtain sovereignty (*paramaiśvaryam*) and will be born in an excellent family.

1:105c–106b This will be the fruit of offering [them] once; by [offering them] twice or three times (*dvis tridhā*) he will have an excellent rebirth (*gatiḥ*); [namely] the man will attain the moon-world (*somalokam*) without delay:[470] there is no doubt regarding this point.

1:106c–107b By offering [them] hundreds [or] thousands of times, the realm of rebirth of a lord of Gaṇas (*gatir gāṇeśvarī*) would ensue [for him], and by offering [them] one hundred thousand times, there is no doubt that, together with his ancestors, [he will obtain position of a lord of Gaṇas].[471]

---

468 *ātmanepada* remains for *parasmaipada*.

469 Obtaining the fruit of a hundred sacrifices presumably means that he becomes equal to Indra.

470 Prof. YOKOCHI thinks *somaloka* is odd here. She thinks that it could be *śivaloka* instead.

471 *śatasāhasra* and *lakṣa* should be equivalent and so we could, as suggested by Professor SANDERSON, conjecture *daśasāhasradānena*. But because this awkwardness is also to be found in the *Śivadharmasaṅgraha* (5.61), we have assumed it to be authorial and have accordingly interpreted *śatasāhasra-* to mean 'hundreds or thousands'.

1:107c–108b If, having made a golden bell, someone offers [it] to Śiva,[472] by the fruit of that merit [he] will be honoured in the world of Śiva.

1:108c–109 He who gives [a bell with] a good clapper (*sulolāṃ*)[473] as well as (*punaḥ*) well-sounding [bell] made of silver, copper, bell-metal, brass,[474] tin or clay to a Śiva-temple (*śivāgāre*), such a person will fully (*sarvaḥ*)[475] abide in heaven.

1:110ab Once that person falls from heaven (*svargalokāt*), he will be born a king on earth.

1:110c–111 If someone offers (*dadet*)[476] a white, red, yellow or black yak-tail fly-whisk having a golden handle, or [having] a silver, brazen or tin [handle], [he] will be honoured in the world of Rudra.[477]

1:112–113 [When he has] fallen from the world of Rudra, he reaches (*upāgataḥ*)[478] the world of Vāyu; [when he has] fallen from the world of Vāyu, he reaches the world of Agni; [and when he has] fallen from the world of Agni, he is born as a king on earth [and/or][479] a Brāhmin, possessed of a kingdom, wise (*vidvān*) and profoundly learned.

1:114ab All this [sort of status] in this world comes about through the fruit of such merit.

1:114c–115b If someone offers a girdle and waist-cord on the head of the *liṅga*, [he] will be the lord of the earth bounded by the four seas.

1:115c–116b Someone who offers a crown, an ear-ring (*kuṇḍalaṃ*) and a multicoloured turban (*citrapaṭṭam*) [to the *liṅga*, that] giver of body ornaments will [also] enjoy the entire earth.[480]

---

472 Here Śiva presumably means a Śiva-*liṅga*, in other words, a Śiva-temple.

473 It is conceivable that the adjective *sulolāṃ* is intended to mean 'well-swinging'.

474 *Ex conj.* For a comparable hierarchical list of metals, see *Guhyasūtra* 1.59.

475 The precise force of the word *sarvaḥ* here is doubtful.

476 *dadet* is an *aiśa* optative third person singular for *dadyāt*.

477 In verse 106a, the word *hemadaṇḍan* is assumed to be a *bahuvrīhi* compound, which means that *raupyaṃ*, *raityaṃ* and *trāpuṣaṃ* stand for *raupyadaṇḍam*, etc. The word *īdṛśaṃ cāmaraṃ datvā* seems only to pad out the meter.

478 Past participle used for present.

479 It is not clear whether he becomes both a king and a Brāhmin or whether he may become either of the two.

480 *pradāyinaḥ* has the appearance of a plural adjective, but is intended as a masculine nominative singular. See our note on the word *duṣṭacetasaḥ* in the verse 58b above.

1:116c–117b [If someone offers] a turban onto the [metal] covering [decorated] with a face (*mukhakośe*) [of the *liṅga*],[481] he will [become] a

[481] The sentence is elliptical and the present translation reflects our best attempt at conjecture. It is not yet clear in which place 116d should be construed. The *Śivadharmasaṅgraha* (5.64) modifies the text, perhaps losing the original sense, by reading *yaṣṭā prādeśiko nṛpaḥ*. We find the occurrence of the *mukhakośa* in Bāṇa's *Harṣacarita* pp. 151–152 thus: *kailāsakūṭadhavalaiḥ kanakapatralatālaṅkṛtaviṣāṇakoṭibhir mahāpramāṇaiḥ saṃdhyābalivṛṣaiḥ sauvarṇaiś ca snapanakalaśair arghabhājanaiś ca dhūpapātraiś ca puṣpapaṭṭaiś ca maṇiyaṣṭipradīpaiś ca brahmasūtraiś ca mahārhamāṇikyakhaṇḍakhacitaiś ca* ***mukhakoṣaiḥ*** *paritoṣam asya manasi cakruḥ* |. The translation of COWELL & THOMAS, p. 85, is paired with a footnote (fn. 3) that reads: 'It is difficult to see what this word means'. The commentary of glosses ***mukhakoṣaiḥ***, *mukhayuktāḥ kośā ye liṅgopari dīyante* 'Those coverings, consisting of faces [of god], that one puts on the top of a *liṅga*'. Cf. also *Kubjikāmatatantra* 17.83–84:

lalāṭakaṇṭhavakṣastham guhyāṅghrau ratnapañcakam |
ślokadvādaśabhir mālā pādādau cūlikāvadhim ||
brahmasūtrojjvalā devyāḥ skandhobhau tadgrahānvitau |
pañcabījair ***mukhakoṣaṃ*** *pañcauṃkāraiḥ khilaṃ nyaset* ||.

Mukhakośa is also known as *mukhaliṅgakośa*. For this, see C. 38, inscription No. 2 in GOLZIO (2004: 35):

śrīsatyavarmmācyutasatyavarmmā |
daivasvabhāvapravikīrṇṇakīrttiḥ |
bhāsvatmukhaṃ ***śrīmukhaliṅgakośam*** |
prāsthāpayat sadguṇakarmmaśuddhyā

Sometimes it is plainly known as *kośa*. BAGCHI (1930: 102) commenting on the word *kośa* in the inscriptional verse *tasyaiva sthāpitaṃ tena dvayaṃ kośaṃ carasthiram* | *samukhaṃ carakośaṃ hi śāke śaśiyamādrige* | says "*kośa* here, as in many other cases in these [Campa] inscriptions, should be taken in the sense of *liṅga-kośa*"). Cf. also the Nepalese 10th century inscription *kṛtvā caturmukhaṃ kośaṃ sauvarṇaṃ ratnamaṇḍitam* (BHAṬṬĀCĀRYA 1966: 6, fn. 7, quoting C. BENDALL 1886: 85).

BAGCHI (1930: 102), on the strength of the Champa inscription, says "these *kośa*s were often golden and decorated with costly gems" (cf. also GUY 2009: 139, 2018: 89). Since we are also told in Bāṇa's description (see above) and the Nepalese inscription (see above) that *kośa* is decorated with precious gems, we may be correct in assuming that decorating in such a way is common custom. GUY (2009: 138) says in that regard

> A number of examples of *liṅgakośa* have been recovered in recent years, most notably from the Mỹ Sơn area of Quảng Nam province. A series of Sanskrit inscriptions in Champa, dating from the sixth to ninth centuries, are the first to make explicit reference to the commissioning and installation of golden *liṅga*-covering. They are described four- or five faced in form. To date, the *liṅga-kośa* recovered appear to belong to single-faced assemblages (*ekamukhaliṅga*).

BAGCHI (1930: 102), however, also mentions that in Champa inscriptions, there are two references to six-faced *liṅga* coverings. He mentions an occurrence of an *ūrddhvakośa* which he thinks is a detachable one. It is clear from the Champa inscriptional verse quoted by BHAṬṬĀCĀRYA 1966: 7, that there are two types of *kośas*: moveable and immovable:

asyaiva sthāpitaṃ tena dvayaṃ kośaṃ carasthiram |
samukhaṃ carakośaṃ hi śāke śaśiyamādrige

BHAṬṬĀCĀRYA points out that this verse also prevents us from thinking that all *kośas* necessarily are formed in the image of a face. GUY (2009: 139) notes that the moveable *kośa* was provided with one or several faces. On the strength of this we may say that there are two types of covering of the *liṅga*, with face(s) or without face(s). In the case of six-faced *kośas*, BHAṬṬĀCĀRYA informs us:

> This custom recalls a well-known philosophical conception. In Sāṃkhya and Vedānta, in fact, the word *liṅga* (= *liṅgaśarīra* = *sūkṣmaśarīra*) means the 'subtle body', enclosed in the 'sheath' (*kośa*) of the 'gross body' (*sthūlaśarira*). This word, moreover has given rise to various speculations, and it is interesting to note that a certain etymology of the word was current in Śaiva as well as in Sāṃkhya circles: *layanāl liṅga* (here he gives reference to this phrase from the *Liṅgapurāṇa*, *Suprabhedāgama* and the rest). We can, therefore, safely assert that the Śaivas, when they invented the custom of enclosing the *liṅga* in a sheath, had in mind this philosophical conception—Śiva was conceived as a person with his *liṅga* (-*śarīra*) enclosed in the *kośa* of this "gross body" (BHAṬṬĀCĀRYA 1966: 7) [[...]] Finally, in the enunciations of dates contained in the epigraphy of Champa and Kambuja, the word *kośa* is sometimes used in the numeric sense of six (see his footnote 34). This is well attested in India itself (see his footnote 35); so it should not surprise us. [[...]] According to a physiological theory, adopted by Sāṃkhya and Vedānta, the 'gross body' (*sthūlaśarīra*), i. e. the *annamayakośa*, itself composed of six elements, called *kośa*. These are: skin (or, according to another tradition, hair), blood, flesh, tendons (or, according to another tradition, fat), bones, and marrow. The first three, it is said, derive from the mother, and the last three from the father (see also his footnote 35; BHAṬṬĀCĀRYA 1966: 12–13)

From BAGCHI, BHAṬṬĀCĀRYA, and GUY we understand that there are plenty of examples of *kośa* or *liṅga-kośa* found in Champa and Kambuja inscriptions. The occurrence of the term is quite broadly attested, with '(*liṅga*)-*kośa*' featuring in the *Niśvāsamukha*, *Harṣacarita*, the Nepalese inscriptions as well as in the record of Vijayanagar King Kṛṣṇadevarāja's gift to the presiding deity of Virupākṣa temple, at Hampi. Hence, we feel inclined to agree with GUY's (2009: 140) contention, viz. that the practice of offering *kośa* to a *liṅga* was in fact common practice in India at the time of writing of these diverse sources.

On the strength of these pieces of evidence we can say without doubt that there are two types of covering of the *liṅga*—with face(s) and without faces; *mukhakośa* in

regional king; by offering multicoloured [turbans] he will partake of wonderful kinds of unrivalled enjoyments.

1:117c–118b If someone again and again offers gems, ornaments and adornments, he will obtain the indestructible, eternal and imperishable state of being a leader of Gaṇas.

1:118c–119b If one worships Śiva by offering a *muktimaṇḍapa*[482] with devotion, there is no rebirth for him; he will become an excellent Gaṇa.

---

particular is an outer covering consisting of face(s) of god that is put on the *liṅga* for decorative purposes. GUY (2009: 138) and BAGCHI (1930: 102) both observe the fact that the offering of the outer covering to *liṅga* is considered as the highest gift to the deity. BAGCHI (1930: 102) further says, "the cult objects, installed during the performance of *liṅgapūjā*s were a major feature of Śaivite temple worship in Champa."

482 This may be, as its name suggests, a pavilion that is employed in a devotional act geared towards the attainment of liberation. In the present context, it appears to be an offering to the *liṅga*. We are not entirely certain as to how it should be offered. Is the pavilion to be constructed over the *liṅga*? Or should the pavilion be constructed conventionally in the southern side of the temple as an offering to Śiva? The evidence of *Śivadharmaśāstra* (5.174c–175b) seems to suggest that it is something to be constructed or offered unto the *liṅga*:

> *śivasyopari yo dadyāt sarvaratnopaśobhitam* || 5.174 ||
> *maṇḍapaṃ mauktikaṃ śrīmān tasya puṇyaphalaṃ śṛṇu* |
>
> Listen to the fruit for him, who, a fortunate person, offers a liberating pavilion (*muktimaṇḍapa*) decorated with all precious jewels on the top of the *liṅga* (*śivasyopari*).

Later sources mention that *muktimaṇḍapa* is a place where dying people would receive the liberating initiation (*tārakadīkṣā*) from Śiva. We find a *muktimaṇḍapa* in the Paśupati temple, Kathmandu, as well as in the Jagannātha temple of Puri, Orissa. In the latter, the *muktimaṇḍapa* is located in the southern side of the temple (MOHAPATRA, 2005: 1).

There is a *muktimaṇḍapa*in the vicinity of the Kuśaleśvara temple in Keonjhar, Orissa. (The American Institute of Indian Studies (`http://dsal.uchicago.edu/`), *consulted in January 2011*, has recorded a photograph of this *muktimaṇḍapa*.) The *Devībhāgavata* speaks of four types of *maṇḍapas*, one of which is the *muktimaṇḍapa*—12.12:2a–3b: *śṛṅgāramaṇḍapaś caiko muktimaṇḍapa eva ca* | *jñānamaṇḍapasaṃjñas tu tṛtīyaḥ parikīrtitaḥ* | *ekāṃtamaṇḍapaś caiva caturthaḥ parikīrtitaḥ* |. The text (12.12:8–10b) further states:

> *śṛṅgāramaṇḍape devyo gāyanti vividhaiḥ svaraiḥ* |
> *sabhāsado devavaśā madhye śrījagadaṃbikā* ||
> *muktimaṇḍapamadhye tu mocayaty aniśaṃ śivāḥ* |
> *jñānopadeśaṃ kurute tṛtīye nṛpa maṇḍape* ||
> *caturthamaṇḍape caiva jagadrakṣāvicintanam* |

1:119c–120b If someone daily performs [the rite of] plastering [using] yellow pigment (*rocanā*)[483] and saffron (*kuṅkumam*) on the top of the *liṅga*, he will become a Vidyādhara.

1:120c–121 By besmearing [the *liṅga*] with camphor and and *agaru* for twelve years, people in [this] world who are intently devoted to Śiva [obtain the state of being] a Gaṇa, and by offering bracelets and armbands [for twelve years], they obtain [whatever] supremacy [is] desired by their minds (*manomatam*).

1:122ab If someone offers gems [...] to Śiva.[484]

1:122c–123b [The gift of] even a scentless flower [to Śiva] is of the value of ten gold coins [in heaven?]; a garland is equivalent to one lakh [of gold coins]; if one covers the *liṅga* [with flowers, then the reward is] infinite.

1:123c–124b O best of Brāhmins! I have taught the procedure [of worshipping the *liṅga*] with scentless flowers; listen also to the fruit of

---

The text does not tell us where these pavilions are to be situated, only what function they are intended for. It says that in the *muktimaṇḍapa*, Śaivites obtain liberation.

Bhasmajābālopaniṣad 2.28 states that in the southern side [of a temple in Kāśī], there is a place called the *muktisthāna* which is called *muktimaṇḍapa* where Śiva teaches the liberating mantra. Its description is as follows: *dakṣiṇāyāṃ diśi muktisthānaṃ tan muktimaṇḍapasaṃjñitam | tatrānekagaṇāḥ pālakāḥ sāyudhāḥ pāpaghātakāḥ | tatra ṛṣayaḥ śāṃbhavāḥ pāśupatā mahāśaivā vedāvataṃsaṃ śaivaṃ pañcākṣaraṃ japantas tārakaṃ sapraṇavaṃ modamānās tiṣṭhanti | tatraikā ratnavedikā | tatrāham āsīnaḥ kāśyāṃ tyaktakuṇapāñ chaivān ānīya svasyāṅke saṃniveśya bhasitarudrākṣabhūṣitān upaspṛśya mā bhūd eteṣāṃ janma mṛtiś ceti tārakaṃ śaivaṃ manum upadiśāmi |*.

Cf. also *Śrīpraśnasaṃhitā* 23.192. This passage indicates that it is also known as a place in the late mediæval time where paṇḍits assemble, hold discussions over religious matters, and pronounce judgments (see O'HANLON 2011: 265–266). Note that there is a reference to a *muktimaṇḍala* in a tantric context in *Mūlasūtra* 4.1 ff., and this should not be confused with the *muktimaṇḍapa*. The *muktimaṇḍapa* is a pavilion and the *muktimaṇḍala* is a diagram used in the performance of *dīkṣā*.

483 This translation assumes that what is meant is *gorocanā*.

484 The reading of *Śivadharmasaṅgraha* 5.69 *ratnadānāni divyāni* fills the gap, but its reading is clearly not original since N reads *...kan tu* and K and W read *ratnadā...kan tu*. As Prof. D. ACHARYA suggests, we could conjecture *ratnadāmakam ekaṃ tu*; cf. *keśaradāmakaiḥ* (1.30b). In this case our translation would be: 'if someone offers a garland of jewels.' At least a half verse is probably missing after 122ab; for, before the section on flowers begins in 122cd, we expect the reward of offering gems to Śiva.

[worshipping the *liṅga*] with beautiful [flowers,] divinely fragrant and the like (*divyagandhādyaiḥ*).

1:124c–125b By offering one [fragrant] flower one will not be reborn in misfortune for eighty crores of years:[485] that is the fruit of worshipping the *liṅga* [with one flower].

1:125c–126b This great fruit is taught when the *liṅga* is worshipped without [specific] desire;[486] listen also to the fruit of worshipping the *liṅga* with a [specific] desire.

1:126c–127b Śaṅkara smells all of the four families of flowers: *Agati grandiflora* (*buka*), oleander (*karavīrasya*), milkweed (*arkasya*), and thorn-apple (*unmattakasya*).[487]

1:127c–128b [If one worships the *liṅga*] with *Agati grandiflora* (*buka*), god bestows boons; [if one worships it] with oleander (*karavīra*), [god] bestows wealth; [if one worships it] with milkweed [god] pursues that which is beneficial [for the worshipper] (*priyam anvicchan*); and [if one worships] with thorn-apple (*dhuttūrakeṇa*),[488] [god bestows] liberation.

1:128c–129b If someone worships the excellent *liṅga* by offering blue water lilies, he becomes a *yogin.* [If he worships the *liṅga*] with a lotus (*padmam*), however, [he obtains] a kingdom and [if he worships the *liṅga*] with white lotuses, he [becomes] an emperor (*cakriṇaḥ*).[489]

1:129c–130b [Worshipping the *liṅga*] with the *campaka* flowers [one obtains] all kinds of enjoyments; [worshipping the *liṅga*] with *puṃnāga* and *nāgakeśara* flowers, [he] obtains desired enjoyments;

---

485 Here this apparently nominative plural *aśītikalpakoṭayaḥ* is perhaps intended to be an accusative of duration.

486 In the light of what follows, it seems less likely that this means 'not deliberately'.

487 Verses 1.126c–127f have a parallel in *Skandapurāṇa* 28.31abcd. For further information on this, refer to p. 30 in the introduction to this study.

488 *dhuttūra*, *unmattaka* and *dhattūra* are commonly used as interchangeable synonyms. Surprisingly, *dhuttūra* is not recorded in our dictionaries, but this orthography is common in Bauddha and Śaiva tantras.

489 We understand *cakriṇaḥ* to be used as a masculine nominative singular *cakravartī*. See footnote on *duṣṭacetasaḥ* in the verse 54 above. Another possibility would be to assume that *cakriṇaḥ* means *cakriṇaḥ padaṃ*. In that case our translation would read 'he will achieve the position of Viṣṇu'. To our mind, however, this appears less likely to be the original reading.

similarly (*tathā*) [worshipping the *liṅga*] with *kesara* garlands (*kesaradāmakaiḥ*).[490]

1:130c–131b If someone worships the supreme god with *Solanum* and agasti (*Sesbania grandiflora*) flowers (*bṛhatyāgastipuṣpakaiḥ*)[491] [or] attentively with *siddhaka*?, [he] obtains mastery of mantras.[492]

1:131cd Whoever worships [Śiva] with fragrant flowers obtains all desired objects:

1:132ab [Worshipping the *liṅga*] with musk roses(?) (*kubjakaiḥ*) one obtains great benefit and *vāruṇī*[493] [is said to be used for worshipping the *liṅga*] for good fortune.

1:132c–133b If someone is desirous for a daughter, one should worship the supreme god with *Jasminum grandiflorum* (?) (*jātībhiḥ*); he will obtain a beautiful (*uttamām*) daughter in six months: there is no doubt on this point.

1:133c–134b If someone worships the supreme god with *mallikā* flowers[494] for the sake of knowledge, [he] obtains ultimate knowledge, which destroys the fear of worldly existence.

1:134c–135b In the case of the wish for a son, one should worship [the *liṅga*], after becoming purified, with *kunda* flowers; one will obtain many wealthy and long-lived sons.[495]

1:135c–136b By worshipping [the *liṅga*] with *kuśa* flowers one obtains

---

490 It is not clear whether 125b should be construed with what precedes or with what follows it.

491 This is an instance of vowel-lengthening in the middle of a compound: cf. *Guhyasūtra*: 1.27c, 7.125c; *Niśvāsamukha*: 1.178a etc.

492 The syntax is uncertain here. *Śivadharmasaṅgraha* has obviated the difficulty by changing the word *samāhitaḥ* to *tathaiva hi*.

493 It is not very clear us what exactly *vāruṇī* is. Context strongly suggests the term denotes a type of fragrant flower, quite possibly a type of lotus flower. After all, the latter is commonly described as being 'born from water' (*varuṇād utpannā*). Though APTE has recorded *vāruṇī* as a subtype of *dūrvā* grass, we are not fully confident this would fit the given context.

494 The instrumental *mallikaiḥ* is an irregular instrumental plural for *mallikābhiḥ*.

495 Note that 135ab, relayed but in the *Śivadharmasaṅgraha*, is not syntactically smooth since it appears that *dhanavantam* and *cirāyuṣam*, formally masculine accusative singulars, qualify *bahuputratvam*, and yet describe the sons themselves.

[good] health;[496] union with beloved ones (*priyasaṅgamam*) [comes about from worshipping the *liṅga*] with *aśoka* [flowers]; [if one worships the *liṅga*] with *karṇikāra* flowers one obtains wealth; for the sake of subjugation [of others] the *droṇapuṣpikā* [should be used for worshipping the *liṅga*].

1:136c–137b One should daily (*satatam*) worship the *liṅga* with *kadamba* [flowers], remaining firm in one's observances (*niyatavrataḥ*) for the sake of controlling one's enemies, one should give [a *kadamba* flower] daily (*nityam eva*).

1:137cd The diseases will be destroyed of one who worships [the *liṅga*] with Musta grass (*Cyperus rotundus*).[497]

1:138ab One who is bound will be freed from bondage [by worshipping the *liṅga*] with the flower of *Vitex negundo* (*sinduvārasya*).[498]

1:138c–139b [Flowers of] *Alangium* (*aṅkoṭakāḥ*) and [any] other [flowers] that are known to be scentless and black—such flowers (*tān puṣpān*)[499] one should offer (*kalpayet*) to the god of gods to destroy [one's] enemies.

1:139c–140b Yellow flowers [are understood to be used to worship the *liṅga*] for the sake of nourishment (*puṣṭyarthe*) and victory. If someone offers [them to the *liṅga*] daily, he will obtain all desired objects.

1:140c–141b One should use (*prakalpayet*) fragrant and water-born[500] [flowers] for subjugation. Blue and red flowers always cause attraction.[501]

1:141c–142b Wood-apple (*bilva*) is the bestower of all desired objects, [as well as] the remover of poverty; there is nothing higher than wood-apple (*bilva*) leaves, by which Śaṅkara is pleased.

---

496 Perhaps this passage refers to the broom-like flowers of the *darbha* grass, but it is likewise possible, as recorded in MONIER-WILLIAMS's dictionary, that *kuśapuṣpa* refers to 'a kind of oak-apple'.

497 The reading *arimustakaiḥ* is insecure here.

498 Only the *Śivadharmasaṅgraha*transmits the entirety of this line; it is therefore possible that its wording might not have been identical to what N displayed.

499 *tān puṣpān* is an *aiśa* masculine accusative plural for neuter accusative plural.

500 *saugandhikādyā jalajāḥ* is an *aiśa* masculine plural used instead of the neuter plural, which can equally be translated as 'water-born fragrant [flowers]'.

501 *Ex conj.* Note, however, that *Śivadharmasaṅgraha* reads instead *tāni vaśyakarāṇi tu* (which seems inappropriate since subjugation rituals have been described in the immediately preceding section.

1:142c–143b Damanaka (*Artemisia vulgaris*)[502] [will be suitable] for victory [for one] who worships the supreme god [with it], he conquers all his enemies, if he worships the one who has the bull for his banner.[503]

1:143cd [The offering of] *maruva* [bestows] all kinds of pleasures, and *jambuta*[504] is a bestower of all desired objects.

1:144a–145b [One should use] *Clerodendrum phlomoides* (*tilakaḥ*) [to worship the *liṅga*] for obtaining wealth; and for obtaining cows [one should use] *āṃkulī*.[505] Tabernæmontana (*tagaraḥ*), [if someone uses it for worshipping the *liṅga*, is understood to be] a bestower of good fortune; *kiṃkirāṭa*[506] bestows desired objects, good health and wealth;[507] and panic-seed (*priyaṅguḥ*), [bestows anything] desired.

---

502 The *Śivadharmasaṅgraha* (5.98) reads *damanakam* here and we have adopted this against the testimony of our manuscripts, which give *madanakam*, first on the grounds that the thorn-apple has already been mentioned and, secondly, that the name *damanaka* ('that which tames') is more appropriate to our context here where victory over others is the subject. Accidental metathesis must have produced our reading. The 'Pandanus Database of Plants' (`http://iu.ff.cuni.cz/pandanus/database`, *consulted in March 2013*) gives the Latin name of *damana* as *Artemisia vulgaris L.*, and the English names as Indian wormwood, Fleabane, Mugwort. This database also displays its names in Hindi (*Nāgdonā, Davanā, daunā*); Bengali (*Nāgadānā*); and Tamil (*Mācipattiri, Makkippū, Tirunāmacceṭi*). The botanical information, as the database records it, is as follows: An aromatic shrub, 1-2m. high, yellow or dark red small flowers, grows throughout India in hills up to 2400m elevation.

503 Note that 142c–143b contains otiose repetition which the *Śivadharmasaṅgraha* (5.98) has tried to mend by altering 142cd thus: *vijayārthe damanakaṃ yojayen niyamasthitaḥ.*

504 In fact, one would expect *jambukaḥ* at this juncture, but both N and *Śivadharmasaṅgraha* agree on this reading. Another interpretation might be to take *jambutaḥ* as an ablative of *jambu*, but that results in a loose construction with *kāmadaḥ*.

505 In this (exceptional) instance, N displays an *ā* by adjoining a hook beneath *a*—generally, the scribe of N applies this mode of marking for *u-mātrā* exclusively, although it is a common feature of Licchavi inscriptions to lengthen *a* in such a way (we note this feature in early Nepalese manuscripts, for example in the manuscript of the *Skandapurāṇa*.

Instead of *āṃkulī*, the *Śivadharmasaṅgraha* (5.99) reads *vaṃkulī*, which is not recorded in our dictionaries. Is this *āṃkulī* possibly connected, in any particular way, to *aṅkola* or *aṅkoṭa*?

506 We find only one parallel for this word and that is in the *Mañjuśriyamūlakalpa*, on p. 679 of chapter fifty-five. It is possible that this is the same plant as *kiṅkirāla*, which MONIER-WILLIAMS identifies with *varvūra* ('*Acacia Arabica*').

507 Note that there is in fact no verb governing *ārogyam* and *dhanam* and we have supposed that they are to be understood as things bestowed by using *kiṃkirāṭa*.

1:145cd [When one uses] *Vatica robusta* (*sālaḥ*) [for worshipping the *liṅga*, it] causes pleasure and [when he uses] Flame-of-the-Forest (*kiṃśukaḥ*) it increases [his] life-span.[508]

1:146ab To obtain elephants, horses, and cattle, one should worship Hara with *Wrightia antidysenterica* (*kuṭajena*).

1:146c–147b Camphor and Damaka[509] (*karpūradamakau*) are to be used [to worship the *liṅga*] for the destruction of enemies; [his] enemies will quickly be destroyed by worshipping the god of gods [in this manner].

1:147cd *Śyāmā*[510] always bestows good health; so too does the China Rose Hibiscus (*javāpuṣpaḥ*).[511]

1:148ab [It is taught that one should use] *kerañjaka*[512] flowers to subjugate [others]: [someone who wants to subjugate others] should daily (*nityam*) worship the *liṅga* with [them].

1:148cd *Jasminum auriculatum* (*yūthikā*) is enjoined for worship of the supreme god for the purpose of causing dissension.[513]

1:149ab [The flower of] *Pandanus fascicularis* (*ketakī*) is for destroying enemies. If someone is angry [and wishes to destroy his enemies], he should worship the *liṅga* with [*ketakī* flowers].[514]

1:149c–150b O goddess! This *vyāghra* [flower] (*Pongamia glabra*) is proclaimed (*prakīrtitaḥ*) to be the bestower of all desired objects [when

---

508 We have understood *āyuvarddhanaḥ* as an *aiśa* usage (m.c.) intended to mean the same as *āyurvarddhakaḥ*. Note that the *Śivadharmasaṅgraha* (5.101) has rephrased the sentence to obviate this awkwardness and has instead: *kiṃśukād āyur āpnuyāt*.

509 We find no name recorded for *damaka* in our dictionaries.

510 Monier-Williams records various possible identifications (*gundrā*, *priyaṅgu*, *sārivā*) for this plant and we are not sure which refers to the item intended. If *śyāmā* refers to *śyāmaka* or *śyāmāka*, in that case 'Pandanus Database of Plants' renders its equivalents as follows: Latin—*Panicum sumatrense Roth*; English—Little millet; Hindi—*Sāvan*, *Kumku*, *Kuṭkī* and Tamil—*Cāmai*.

511 Once again, we have an *aiśa* masculine for neuter.

512 Note that *kerañjaka* is not recorded in our dictionaries; *Śivadharmasaṅgraha* 5.103 reads *kuraṇṭaka* instead, which Monier-Williams records as meaning 'yellow Amaranth' or 'a yellow kind of Barleria'.

513 Note that 148cd is syntactically not quite smooth because of the locative *parameśvare*, literally: 'with respect to the supreme god'. In *Śivadharmasaṅgraha* 5.104 the text has been rephrased to mend the section: *vidveṣe yūthikā yojyā devadeve maheśvare*.

514 Note that 149ab is awkwardly structured; yet, in this case, *Śivadharmasaṅgraha* provides no variant.

one uses it in worshipping the *liṅga*]; likewise *jyotsnākārī*[515] [when so used also] always bestows desired objects.

1:150cd One should worship god with *vāsaka* flowers: [by doing so one's] strength (*balam*) and life-span (*āyuḥ*) will be increased.

1:151ab *Jhaṇṭikā* flowers[516] always bestow happiness, so *tathā* [do] *apsara*[517] and *campaka* (*Michelia campaka*)[518] [flowers when they are used for worshipping the *liṅga*].

1:151cd *Ḍimbākṣī*[519] as well as *Aśvakarṇa*[520] [are to be used for worshipping the *liṅga*] for the annihilation of diseases.

1:152 *Sesbania ægyptiaca* (*Jayantī*) is [to be used] for victory (*jayakāmāya*) and [also] white *girikarṇikā*;[521] for [causing] dissension [among people] and driving them away (*vidveṣoccāṭanārthāya*) one should worship with Neem flowers (*nimbapuṣpaiḥ*).[522]

---

515 We have found no identification for this plant; there is however a plant called *jyotiṣmati* which may be a synonym for *jyotsnākārī*. Pandanus Database records the Latin name for *jyotiṣmati* (alternatively called *pītatailā*), *Celastrus paniculatus Willd*; English—climbing staff plant; Tamil— *Vāluḷuvai*; Hindi—*Mālkaṅganī* and *Mālkuṅkī*.

516 MONIER-WILLIAMS does not record this word, but it is possible that it is a variant form of *jhiṇṭikā*, which one manuscript of the *Śivadharmasaṅgraha* transmits here (5.106), and which MONIER-WILLIAMS identifies as *Barleria cristata*, also known as the 'Philippine violet'. It is also possible that *jhaṇṭikā* is simply a copying mistake for *jhiṇṭikā*.

517 Note that our dictionaries do not record any flower known as *apsara*.

518 Note that *apsaracampakam* is an *aiśa samāhāradvandva* compound.

519 No plant of this name is known to us, and the form has been accepted on the authority of the *Śivadharmasaṅgraha* (5.107) alone. Prof. D. ACHARYA, on semantic grounds, observes a possibility of it being corrupted from *ḍitthākṣī*, although this form is also not recorded in the lexicons consulted.

520 MONIER-WILLIAMS identifies this as *Vatica Robusta*, which has already been referred to above under the name *śāla* (1.140).

521 Pandanus Database gives *aparājitā* as a synonym of *girikarṇikā*. The database gives this plant's Latin name as *Clitoria ternatea L.*; English—Clitoria, Butterfly pea; Tamil—*Kaṉṉikkoṭi* and *Kirikaṉṉi*; Hindi—*Aparājit*.The botanical information on the plant according to the Database is as follows: "a perennial twining herb with terete stems and branches, growing throughout India in hedges and thickets, leaves compound, imparipinnate, blue or white flowers, fruits nearly straight, flattened pods, sharply beaked, seeds 6 - 10, yellowish brown."

522 The syntactical difficulty here stems from the fact that no pronoun is provided in conjunction with the relative pronoun. The the *Śivadharmasaṅgraha* (5.108) offers no alternative reading for this segment.

1:153a–154b *Bhaṭī*[523] and also *madayantī*[524] are taught [to be used to worship the *liṅga*] for the act of attraction; *ṛṣipuṣpa* and *rudrajaṭā*, annihilate misfortunes (*nāśayeta upadravān*).[525] Similarly *śaṇapuṣpī* as well as *kokilākṣā*.[526]

1:154cd All white [flowers are to be used to worship the *liṅga*] for peace (*śāntyarthe*) and all yellow [flowers are to be used to worship the *liṅga*] for nourishment (*pauṣṭike*).

1:155 Blue and red flowers,[527] when used in worship, are [respectively] for controlling and for attracting (*vaśyākarṣaṇe*).[528] In this way one may accomplish everything with these [flowers of various colours].

1:156ab One should also offer (*kalpayet*) black flowers to the supreme god for malevolent acts.

1:156c–157b If someone daily offers (*dadyāt*) leaves, flowers, fruit, water, grass and milk (*payaḥ*) to Śaṅkara,[529] he will not not undergo a miserable rebirth (*durgatim*).

---

523 Note that our dictionaries do not record *bhaṭī*, but it is possible that it is a variant form of *bhaṭā*, which MONIER-WILLIAMS identifies as *Coloquintida*. Here the *Śivadharmasaṅgraha* (5.108) instead reads *bhaṇḍī*, which MONIER-WILLIAMS identifies as *Rubia munjista*. We assume that the *m* after *bhaṭī* is intended as a hiatus-breaker; note that the *Śivadharmasaṅgraha* (5.108) has inserted a *ca* to rectify the situation.

524 According to MONIER-WILLIAMS, this is Arabian jasmine, known by its Latin name as *Jasminum sambac*. Note that *yā bhavet* fulfils no particular function in the sentence.

525 Here the *Śivadharmasaṅgraha* (5.109) has normalized the syntax of 153cd by reading *ṛṣipuṣpī rudrajaṭī hanti sarvān upadravān*.

526 *śaṇapuṣpī* is identified by MONIER-WILLIAMS as *Crotolaria Verrucosa*. Note that *kokilākṣā* may be an *aiśa* feminine for masculine ('corrected' in the text of *Śivadharmasaṅgraha* 5.109). This plant is also called *kokilanayana*, in defining which MONIER-WILLIAMS records the following possible identifications: *Capparis spinosa*, *Asteracantha longifolia* and *Barleria longifolia*.

527 Note the use of *aiśa* masculine plurals for neuter plurals.

528 *Ex conj.* We assume that the transmitted *m* was a hiatus-breaker inserted in the course of transmission, but it may in fact have been authorial. The *Śivadharmasaṅgraha* (5.110) appears to have rearranged the text here for improved clarity, but in doing so it appears to have slightly modified the correspondences: there (5.110) red flowers are for attracting and dark flowers are for malevolent rites (*abhicāra*). The categories of *vaśya* and *ākarṣaṇa* are therefore not distinguished, and the following half-line of our text is dropped.

529 Here, as in many other places in this work, the locative is used as a dative. The *Śivadharmasaṅgraha* (5.111), however, has refined the text by reading *śambhave* instead of *śaṅkare*.

1:157c–158b That person, too, reaches the supreme sphere of rebirth (*parāṃ gatim*) of whose tree the leaves, flowers and fruits are offered to Śiva (*mahādevāya*).

1:158c–159 A milkweed (*arka*) is a hundred times better than oleander (*karavīrāt*); a wood-apple (*bilva*), in the same manner [is a hundred times better then an milkweed (*arka*)]; an *Agati grandiflora* (*buka*) is a thousand times better then wood-apple (*bilva*); a thorn-apple [flower] (*dhuttūrakaḥ*) is [yet a thousand] better than *Agati grandiflora* (*buka*). Having thus worshipped the lord of gods [with flowers], one should [next] also offer food.

1:160 By offering food [as] offering (*annanaivedyadānena*) one obtains imperishable happiness. Similarly by offering chewable foods (*bhakṣa-dānāt*) one approaches (*anuprāptiḥ*) the realm of the gods (*devalokam*).

1:161ab The offerer of chewable food as offering (*bhakṣyanaivedyadāyakaḥ*) obtains well-being and prosperity (*śivam aiśvaryam*).[530]

1:161c–162b If someone daily (*sadā*) offers rice-pudding together with ghee [as] the principle offering (*naivedyam*) to Śambhu, he will quickly obtain the state of being a leader of Gaṇas; [if he offers them daily for] twelve years [he will obtain the state of being a leader of Gaṇas] together with his family.[531]

1:162cd If someone makes [offerings] made out of dainty (*khaṇḍakhādya-kṛtam*),[532] he will obtain an excellent sphere of rebirth (*gatim*).[533]

1:163 By offering chewable and unchewable foods (*bhakṣyabhojyāni*)[534] one may indeed (*vai*) obtain all desired objects; by offering rice-gruel

---

530 *Ex conj.* This conjecture is a tentative one.

531 Note that the *Śivadharmasaṅgraha* (5.122) reads *dvādaśābdāt* instead of *dvādaśābdam*. This alteration appears to be intended as a clarificatory improvement.

532 Perhaps the expression refers to lumps of raw sugar cane (*khaṇḍa*) offered as a dainty snack. We are unsure of how to take *kṛtam* at the end of the compound (or °*kṛtān* in the reading of *Śivadharmasaṅgraha* 5.124).

533 The *Śivadharmasaṅgraha* (5.124) has syntactically smoothened the text by providing *dattvā* in place of *dadyāt*.

534 Our text records four divisions of food: *bhakṣya*, *bhojya*, *lehya* and *coṣya*. The last two are recorded in the following verse, 160. The *Śivadharmasaṅgraha* (5.124–26) also mentions this division of food. For the same division, cf. also *Skandapurāṇa* 162.45, *Rāmāyaṇa* 2.85:17 etc. Madhusūdana Sarasvatī on the commentary of *Bhagavad-*

(*yavāgūn*), porridge (*kṛsarām*)[535] and cakes (*pūpān*), one partakes of happiness (*sukhabhāg bhavet*).

1:164a–165b Having offered [to the *liṅga*] rice-gruel (*maṇḍakām*), *susumālān*,[536] pastries and sweets (*śaṣkulyāmodakāni*),[537] [and] other fruits and roots, and whatever is lickable or suckable, one obtains all kinds of pleasures. [He will obtain] infinite pleasures if [he offers] song and music (*gītavādite*).

1:165cd This is the fruit of [offering these things] once; [now] hear from me [the fruit] of playing the lute[538] [in front of god/the *liṅga*].

---

gītā 15.14 defines the four divisions of food as follows: *prāṇibhir bhuktam annaṃ caturvidhaṃ bhakṣaṃ bhojyaṃ lehyaṃ coṣyaṃ ceti | tatra yad dantair avakhāḍyāvakhāḍya bhakṣyate 'pūpādi tad bhakṣyaṃ carvyam iti cocyate | yat tu jihvayā viloḍya nigīryate sūpaudanādi tad bhojyam | yat tu jihvāyāṃ nikṣipya rasāsvādena nigīryate kiṃca dravībhūtaguḍarasālaśikhariṇyādi tal lehyam | yat tu dantair niṣpīḍya rasāṃśaṃ nigīryāvaśiṣṭaṃ tyajyate yathekṣudaṇḍādi tac coṣyam iti bhedaḥ |*. Cf. also the commentary of Nīlakaṇṭha, Śrīdhara on the same verse of *Bhagavadgītā*. However, *Rāmāyaṇa* 2.44:15, *Īśvarasaṃhitā* 5.12 and 13.36, *Jayākhyasaṃhitā* 13.171, *Nāradasaṃhitā* 2.117, *Pārameśvarasaṃhitā* 6.384 etc. mention the four divisions of food as *bhakṣya*, *bhojya*, *peya* and *lehya*. On other occasions we come across only three divisions of food, *bhakṣya*, *bhojya* and *pāna* or *peya*, cf. *Mahābhārata* 3.242:22, 3.265:15, 12.172:27, *Viṣṇudharmottara* 2.54:5, *Pādmasaṃhitā* 11.5, 25.120 etc. We also encounter five divisions of food, *bhakṣya*, *bhojya*, *lehya*, *coṣya* and *peya*, cf. *Mahābhārata* 12.184:16, *Brahmāṇḍapurāṇa* 2.16:49, *Brahmapurāṇa* 215.36, *Nāradapurāṇa* 1.43:117, *Viṣṇudharmottara* 1.209:89, *Nāradasaṃhitā* 19.70, *Sarvajñānottara* 5.60, *Pañcārthabhāṣya* p. 24, *Jayasiṃhakalpadruma* p. 51 etc.

The *Pārameśvarasaṃhitā* (18.386–387) provides an example of these five divisions of food in the following extract: *bhakṣyāṇy apūpapūrvāṇi bhojyāni ca phalāni ca | lehyāni madhupūrvāṇi coṣyāṇy āmrādikāny api | peyāni kṣīrapūrvāṇi anupānānvitāni ca |*. Cf. also *Jayasiṃhakalpadruma* p. 51.

Rājanighaṇṭu 20.72 mentions eight kinds of food as follows: *bhojyaṃ peyaṃ tathā coṣyaṃ lehyaṃ khādyaṃ ca carvaṇam | niṣpeyaṃ caiva bhakṣyaṃ syād annam aṣṭavidhaṃ smṛtam |*. Besides all these divisions, we most commonly find two divisions of food, *bhakṣya* and *bhojya*, often mentioned in the *Mahābhārata*, *Rāmāyaṇa*, Purāṇas, and in Tantras etc.

535 We take this to be an accusative plural. MONIER-WILLIAMS defines *kṛsara* as "a dish consisting of sesamum and grain".

536 It is clear from the context that *susumāla* is a kind of food, but we don't know what it is exactly. Note that our dictionaries do not record the word, quite probably since it might be a corruption of another term.

537 I assume this to be an *aiśa* compound, the first member of which would normally be *śaṣkulī* (cf. the form of the word *Devyāmata*).

538 We have understood *tantrīvādyasya* to mean *tantrīvāditasya*.

1:166ab If he plays (*kṛtvā*)[539] [in front of god/the *liṅga*], the lute player (*tantrīvādyasya vādakaḥ*) attains the state of being a Gaṇa.

1:166c–167b If someone makes (*kurvāṇaḥ*) *huḍuk* sounds (*huḍuk-kārasya*),[540] dances, makes music with [his] mouth and laughs loudly (*mukhavādyasyāṭṭahāsayoḥ*)[541] [as an offering the *liṅga*] three times a day, he will become an excellent Gaṇa.

---

539 We have understood *kṛtvā* to mean *vādanaṃ kṛtvā*.

540 The reading of *huḍuk* remains uncertain. See our note 443 on p. 255.

541 This verse echoes *Pāśupatasūtra* 1.8. The precise meaning of the *mukhavādya* remains uncertain. We may understand *mukhavādya* as a wind instrument such as *śaṅkha*, *bherī* etc. as opposed to *karavādya* 'that which is played by hands'; *Nayasūtra* 2.41 makes it clear that there is a such a division:

tantrīvādyavicitrāṇi karavādyāni yāni ca |
mukhavādyāni ramyāṇi kāṣṭhāyuktāni caiva hi || 41 ||

According to Kṣemarāja, referring to the commentary on *Svacchandatantra* 2.182, *mukhavādya* is a synonym of *huḍḍuṅkāra*: *bhaktivaivaśyonmiṣannādāmarśamayo dhvanir mukhavādyāparaparyāyo huḍḍuṅkāraḥ*; this does not, however, mean that *mukhavādya* should always be taken to mean *huḍḍuṅkāra*. *Śivadharmasaṅgraha* 5.129:

huḍḍuṅkārādikaṃ nityaṃ mukhavādyāṭṭahāsatām |
trikālañ caiva kurvāṇaḥ sa bhaved uttamo gaṇaḥ ||

He who does *huḍḍuṅkāra*, dance, mouth-music (*mukhavādya*) and loud laughter three times a day will attain the state of Gaṇa.

Here *mukhavādya* is definitely to be distinguished from *huḍḍuṅkāra*. Cf. also *Nārada-purāṇa uttarakhaṇḍa* 49.14:

huḍḍuṅkāranamaskārair (corr; *ḍuaṃḍukāranamaskār* ed.) *nṛtyagītais tathaiva ca* |
mukhavādyair anekaiśca stotrair mantrais tathaiva ca ||,

Tīrthavivecanakāṇḍa 8th part, p. 82 reads:

kṣīreṇa madhunā caiva toyena saha sarpiṣā |
tarpayanti paraṃ liṅgam arcayanti devaṃ śubham ||
huḍḍuṅkāranamaskārair (corr; *huḍuṅkāra* ed.) *nṛtyagītais tathaiva ca* |
mukhavādyair anekaiś ca stotramantrais tathaiva ca ||

There are some occurrences of *mukhavādya* which can be interpreted in either way, since there are no commentaries that would help us to understand precisely. Cf. *Śivadharmaśāstra* 5.8:

snānakāle trisandhyāṃ ca yaḥ kuryād geyavādinaḥ |
nṛtyaṃ vā mukhavādyaṃ vā tasya puṇyaphalaṃ śṛṇu |

Hear the meritorious fruit of he who performs singing, playing instruments, dance, or *mukhavādya*.

1:167c–168b Those who always remember the oddly-eyed (*virūpākṣam*) once, twice or three times [a day], they are to be known as lords of Gaṇas.

1:168c–169b Pilgrimage to sixty thousand sites or [even] sixty crore [sites] will not be worth even one-sixteenth part of worshipping the *liṅga* once.

1:169c–f If someone who is ignorant [of the rules] and has not received Śaiva initiation (*śivadīkṣāvivarjitaḥ*) worships [the *liṅga*] in this fashion (*evam*), for him these fruits have been taught (*uddiṣṭam*); in the case of an initiate, [the same worship bestows] liberation (*apavargāya*).[542]

1:170 O Brāhmins! This is what I heard from Hara, who was telling the goddess, and I have recounted it to you, the truth that the Lord has taught.[543]

Cf. also *Śivadharmaśāstra* 9.42–43:

bhūmidānasya yat puṇyaṃ kanyādānasya yat phalam |
mukhavādyena tat puṇyam ubhayaṃ labhate naraḥ ||
tad eva puṇyaṃ gītasya nṛtyasya ca viśeṣataḥ |
tad eva jayaśabdasya tad eva tālakadhvaneḥ ||

We deem it remarkable that in the above verse, *mukhavādya* is given more importance even than an offering of land or of a virgin girl. *Kriyākālaguṇottara* as quoted in the *Netratantra* vol. 2, p. 157, moreover, states:

devagṛhagṛhītasya etad bhavati lakṣaṇam |
gāyate nṛtyate hṛṣṭo mukhavādyaṃ karoti ca ||

Tīrthavivecanakāṇḍa 8th part (p. 64) displays:

gandhadhūpanamaskārair mukhavādyaiś ca sarvaśaḥ |
yo māṃ arcayate tatra tasya tuṣyāmy ahaṃ sadā |

Note that BISSCHOP & GRIFFITHS (2007: 34, fn. 155) mention that in *Carakasaṃhitā*, *Cikitsāsthāna* 9.20 *mukhavādya* is included among the characteristics of one who is possessed by a Gandharva.

542 The *Śivadharmasaṅgraha* (5.133) smoothens the syntax by reading *tasyedaṃ phalam uddiṣṭaṃ nirvāṇaṃ dīkṣitasya tu* | .

543 The remainder of chapter 1 displays a somewhat different character than the antecedent sections, and changes in tone and subject matter suggest a possibility that it might constitute a later addition.

[1.2 The *Liṅgodbhava* myth]

The sages spoke:

1:171 What is the greatness (*māhātmya*) of the *liṅga* here, which you have highly extolled (*ativarṇitam*)?[544] Tell [us] the fruit if someone makes [one]. [And also tell us the fruit] if someone makes [one] every day.[545]

Nandikeśvara spoke:

1:172 There was (*bhavet*)[546] a dispute which (*yat*)[547] took place (*pūrvavṛttam*) between Brahmā and Viṣṇu [in which each claimed]: I am the Cause [of all]. Fiery energy rose up in the water.[548]

1:173 In the midst of the fiery energy there stood a *liṅga* of the size of the thumb's [topmost] joint (*parvāṅguṣṭhapramāṇataḥ*).[549] Both of them were astonished at this (*tatra*). What is this miracle that has occurred?

1:174–175 Then they both started watching the *liṅga* grow, thinking 'it is a miracle', they both went up and down: Viṣṇu went down from there (*tataḥ*)[550] and Brahmā went up from there. And not finding (*paśyantau*) the end of it, both of them became weary.

1:176ab And then having returned back again, [both of them] praised[551] Hara with a hymn.

---

544 It is possible that the scribe of N intended to write the more conventional word *abhivarṇitam*, in which case we might translate simply 'which you have described'. But given that *Śivadharmasaṅgraha* 5.135 (*kiṃ liṅgasya hi māhātmyaṃ tvayā yad iti varṇitam*) has modified the text here, it is perhaps more likely that a slightly odd usage in the *Niśvāsamukha* lay before the redactor.

545 The Sanskrit is elliptical here and some other understanding of the scenario could be imagined.

546 We have understood *bhavet* to mean *abhavat*. The *Liṅgodbhava myth* incepts here, for more details on the latter, consult KAFLE, 2013.

547 This hanging relative pronoun is particularly problematic in this awkward sentence. Note that the *Śivadharmasaṅgraha* (5.136) has rephrased this section in an attempt at clarification.

548 We suppose that *kāraṇakartā* is intended as translated, rather than as a *tatpuruṣa* or *dvandva* compound.

549 Once again, the *Śivadharmasaṅgraha* (5.137) has tightened up the phrasing here, in this case by replacing it with a *bahuvrīhi* compound.

550 This is the suggestion provided by Dr. KAHRS: Viṣṇu descended alongside the downward extension of the *liṅga*, Brahmā ascended alongside its upwards extension. Otherwise we would have to interpret the repeated *tataḥ* to mean simply 'then'.

551 *tuṣṭuve* is an *aiśa* use of the *ātmanepada* perfect third person singular instead of the required dual. Note that the *Śivadharmasaṅgraha* (5.140) has corrected this as required.

1:176c–177b Then, the supreme god, being pleased, in order to bestow boons on both of them (*varan dattvā ubhāvapi*)[552] took the form of a man standing [before them] (*puruṣarūpī sthito bhūtvā*)[553] [and said]: I will give whatever you desire.

1:177c–178 Brahmā said (*vadati*): o you of excellent observances! You yourself be [my] son.[554] So be it, replied god.[555] But you will not be worshipped,[556] since (*yasmād dhi*), o twice born, the boon you desire is inappropriate (*anānurūpam*).[557]

1:179 O Viṣṇu! I certainly will bestow a boon that you desire, tell me! For (*hi*) my speech is not false. Tell me (*vadasva me*) now whatever you desire.

Viṣṇu spoke:

1:180 O god! If you are pleased and want to give me a boon, I will be your devotee and favourite to you (*tvatpriyaḥ*):[558] there is no doubt.

---

552 As translated, the word order suggests that *dattvā* (or perhaps *dattvai* before *sandhi*) may be intended as an infinitive. In that case, we could either have an *aiśa* hiatus within a *pāda*, with *dattvā* irregularly used as an infinitive, or a regular *sandhi* reduction of *dattvai*, in an archaic use of a Vedic infinitive. The syntax of the whole sentence is in any case awkward and once again the *Śivadharmasaṅgraha* (5.140) has rephrased it to 'improve' the text.

553 The *Śivadharmasaṅgraha* (5.141) alters the wording of our text (*svarūpaṃ divyam āsthāya sarvalokanamaskṛtam*) to develop Śiva's anthropomorphism. Chapter 81 of the *Brahmayāmala* records the theomorphic form of Śiva, whereas the myth found in chapter 3 of the *Śivadharmaśāstra* mentions neither Śiva's theomorphic form nor his anthropomorphic counterpart. Phyllis GRANOFF (2006), in her article *Śiva and his Gaṇas: Techniques of Narrative distancing in Purāṇic Stories* ingeniously shows that in early versions of certain Śaiva myths, Śiva is not directly involved in the action; he relies on one of his Gaṇas or one his weapons to accomplish the task at hand. Yet in the later version of the same story, Śiva does become directly involved in the process of rectifying the predicament to be faced. We may observe the same kind of development in the case of the *Liṅgodbhava* myth. We have argued (KAFLE, 2013) that the myth found in the *Śivadharmaśāstra* may be the earliest since it preserves the kernel of the ideas peculiar to early Śaiva myths. Since our text mentions the anthropomorphic form of Śiva, its version of the myth appears one stage further developed from its counterpart in the *Śivadharmaśāstra*.

554 For Brahmā's desire to have Śiva as his son, see *Skandapurāṇa* 4.5.

555 *Ex conj. Niśvāsamukha* 1.178ab is close to the reading of *Śivadharmasaṅgraha* (5.144), the portion *evama* being alone visible in the manuscript N. We have conjectured *evam astv abravīd devaḥ*, thus following *Śivadharmasaṅgraha* as closely as possible.

556 Does this perhaps refer to the paucity of temples dedicated to Brahmā?

557 We assume that the second syllable is lengthened to obviate a metrical fault (the second and third syllable of a *pāda* cannot both be short).

558 Of course this could equally mean 'fond of you'.

Īśvara spoke:

1:181 So be it! May good be with you! All the creatures belong to Rudra and Nārāyaṇa (*rudranārāyaṇī prajā*).[559] There is no difference between the two of them, between Keśava and Hara.

1:182–183 For (*hi*), this very *liṅga*[560] was installed by Brahmā and Viṣṇu,[561] together with the gods including Indra, the Asuras, Yakṣas, Kiṃnaras, Uragas, Rākṣasas, Siddhas, Vidyādharas, Bhūtas, Apsaras, Uragas[562], Piśācas, Grahas, Nakṣatras and the best of the sages (*munisattamaiḥ*).

1:184 Having worshipped the boon-bestowing god and obtained [their desired] boons, they were delighted. 'I have taught (*uktaḥ*)[563] that the *liṅga* bestows all desired wishes, o stainless ones!'[564]

1:185 With minds frightened by the pain of the ocean that is worldly existence, Brahmā, Viṣṇu, Mahendra, snakes, the sages and Yakṣas, together with Vidyādharas [are] devoted to worshipping the *liṅga*. Desirous of boons, they worship [the *liṅga*] daily (*aharahaḥ*),[565] joining their hands together and raising them to [their] foreheads. How is prosperity possible for those mortals who do not worship (*namanti*) the unborn [god] in this form (*īdṛśam*) ?

Thus is the first chapter, concerning worldly duty/religion, in the *Niśvāsamukhatattvasaṃhitā*. Verses 187.

---

559 The same idea is presented in a different context in *Vāyupurāṇa* 20.21 and *Kūrmapurāṇa* 1.14:90.

560 Note that the masculine pronoun *eṣa* is here used in apposition with a neuter noun, a special sort of *aiśa* usage. It does not transpire why the establishment of this *liṅga* by Brahmā and Viṣṇu should be connected to the existence of creatures belonging to Hara and Keśava.

561 *brahmaviṣṇunā* is an *aiśa samāhāradvandva* compound (m.c).

562 It appears '*uragas*' occurs twice in order to pad out the metre.

563 Once again, a masculine is put in apposition with a neuter noun. The *Śivadharmasaṅgraha* (5.155) has mended the problem by treating *liṅga* in every respect as a masculine noun.

564 This plural vocative suggested by the *Śivadharmasaṅgraha* (5.155) seems to be right, since, here it is Nandikeśvara speaking to sages, not Śiva to Devī.

565 Note that our text reads *raharahaḥ* instead of *aharahaḥ* to avoid hiatus with the previous word.

CHAPTER II

[1.3 Temporary *liṅgas*]

The sages spoke:

2:1 What is the fruit of making a *liṅga*? [What is the fruit of] installing it? And what is the fruit that accrues to someone who makes one every day?[566]

Nandi spoke:

2:2 Those children who make a *liṅga* with dust while playing will definitely obtain an unrivalled kingdom without enemies.[567]

2:3 If someone daily makes a [*liṅga*], without knowing this [relevant] rule,[568] relying [just] on devotion, listen also to what is the fruit [that accrues] to him.

2:4 Having made [any *liṅga* without knowing the precise rule], if someone worships Śiva, [he will obtain] wealth, [various] enjoyments and sovereignty; a worshipper of the *liṅga* always enjoys great fortune.

2:5 If one worships a thousand of them, one should know (*vidyāt*) that he will not see hell (*nirayam*); [569] having enjoyed [various] irreproachable enjoyments he will obtain the world of Rudra.

---

[566] Note the grammatical (syntactical) irregularity of the relative pronoun *yat* in the first half-line not being furnished with a correllative pronoun.

[567] This very closely is paralleled by *Śivadharmaśāstra* 3.77c–78b. Refer to p. 97 in the introduction.

[568] The words *vidhim etat* ('this rule') presuppose that a rule had been mentioned before in the text—however, even upon careful scrutiny, it was not possibly to trace such a rule. It is hence likely that this passage has been interpolated from another source. For example, it could be the case that the rule may have been mentioned in the source for the *Niśvāsamukha* in the preceding passage (which has not been borrowed) and would account for inconsistencies in our text. Note that the *Śivadharmasaṅgraha* has entirely rephrased this half-line to avoid the unresolved references. The syntax is irregular here, being an instrumental participle agreeing with the nominative subject and a neuter pronoun agreeing with a masculine accusative noun.

[569] Among the hells (*narakas*) listed in this chapter, the *śilāvarṣa* is not known from any other source, except the *Śivadharmasaṅgraha*. The *medahrada* is also not found anywhere else, if *mahāhrada* in the *Śivadharmottara* is not a corruption of the term.

2:6 If someone makes [and worships a *liṅga*] one hundred thousand times, [the *liṅga*] will become aflame for him one [time(?)]; having seen [that] flaming *liṅga*, he [becomes] an accomplished one (*siddhaḥ*), [and being an accomplished one, he] obtains the state of god.

2:7 [Worshipping the *liṅga*] one million times, he will obtain the state of being Indra; [worshipping the *liṅga*] two million times (*viṃśabhiḥ*)[570] it is [to be] understood that he will obtain the state of Brahmā; worshipping [the *liṅga*] three million times[571] [he will attain] the state of Viṣṇu and [worshipping the *liṅga*] four million times,[572] he will attain the state of Rudra.

2:8 Having cleansed [the ground] with the five products of the cow, one should make a *liṅga* of clay[573]. If someone makes a *liṅga* of cooked rice (*anna*), he will obtain desired fruits.

2:9 Having worshipped a *liṅga* made of jaggery, one obtains the greatest prosperity; one will be the master over a hundred virgins and the ruler of all vassal kingdoms.

2:10 And [if a] woman [makes a *liṅga* out of jaggery and worships it], she, being above all [women[574] and always] surrounded by thousands (*sahasreṇa*) of women on all sides, will obtain incomparable good fortune.

2:11 If a man or a woman (*naranārī vā*)[575] worships a *liṅga* of jaggery daily (*nityaśaḥ*), they will rejoice in children and grandchildren; they will also enjoy happiness greatly (*atyantam*).

2:12 If someone daily worships a *liṅga* having made [it] of refined sugar (*sita*), he will obtain all desired objects within six months; there is no doubt.

---

570 *viṃśabhiḥ* is an *aiśa* shortening for *viṃśatibhiḥ*.

571 *triṃśabhiḥ* is an *aiśa* shortening for *triṃśadbhiḥ*.

572 Context suggests that *caturguṇaiḥ* is intended to mean 'multiplied by forty' even though it literally means 'multiplied by four'.

573 We understand this causative *kārayet* in the sense of *karoti*. The statement of Verse 8ab is incomplete, the reward of the recommended act remaining untold. The *Śivadharmasaṅgraha* does not rectify this problem.

574 Although we have not adopted W's *sarvāsām*, we assume that *sarveṣām* was intended as a feminine genitive plural.

575 *naranārī vā* may be taken as an *aiśa dvandva* compound followed by *vā* connecting its elements; alternatively, *nara* may, for metrical reasons, be taken as a uninflected nominative singular.

2:13 [If someone worships] a *liṅga* made of unclarified butter, he will obtain [any] desired fruit;[576] [by worshipping it] for six months with his self controlled,[577] goes to the world of Śiva.

2:14 If someone daily makes and worships a *liṅga* made of leaves, he will obtain great power and always enjoy [it] remaining in good health.[578]

2:15 One obtains sovereignty on earth by worshipping a *liṅga* made of flowers; without rival one enjoys [sovereignty] and gives [it to others as well?].

2:16 If someone performs worship by means of a *liṅga* [made of] salt, he will obtain the greatest fortune; and if he [worships it] daily, he will obtain eternal and unbroken lordship.

2:17–18 If someone makes[579] [and worships] earthen *liṅga*s made from a mould (*saccakena*)[580] a thousand times, he will certainly (*hi*) obtain the desired fruits. By worshipping [it] ten thousand times, he will obtain the state of Gaṇa, and by worshipping [it] one hundred thousand times, he will obtain (*gacchati*) union with [Śiva] in his own body (*svaśarīreṇa*) and will never come back [to worldly existence] again.

2:19a–20b Having worshipped these [*liṅgas*], gods together with demons and men [become] endowed with all their desires and [they become]

---

[576] Note a hiatus within a *pāda*. The *Śivadharmasaṅgraha* (6.13) has added a semantically meaningless *ca*, that is it reads *cepsitam* instead of *īpsitam* to remedy the problem.

[577] We have accepted the reading of K and *Śivadharmasaṅgraha* against the reading of the original manuscript N and apograph W, *yuktyātmā*. A similar situation appears in the *Nayasūtra* (4.80):

dhyāyate yas tu yuktātmā māsam ekaṃ suyantritaḥ |
prākṛtā jāyate siddhir dvimāsena tu pauruṣī ||

Here too, the old manuscript N and apograph W read *muktyātmā*, which does not fit in the context, and other sources read *yuktātmā*, which is fitting. It is also worth noting that in the *Niśvāsa*-corpus the expression *yuktātmā* appears frequently, but *muktātmā* is found nowhere except in these two cases.

[578] An *aiśa* form for *niruk*, treated as an *a*-stem. This is a reoccurring phenomenon, see for example, 2.91 and 3.89.

[579] Causative is meant for simplex.

[580] Profs. Harunaga Isaacson and D. Acharya point out to us that *saccaka* might be intended for *sañcaka* 'a mound'. We feel no necessity for an emendation from *saccaka* to *sañcaka* since this orthography appears, apart from our text, in the *Śivadharmasaṅgraha* (6.17) and in *Ādikarmapradīpa* (electronic text kindly provided by Prof. Isaacson), where the word appears three times.

freed from pleasure and pain. By the grace of god they play with [the eight yogic powers, namely] *aṇiman* (the supernatural capability to morph into minuscule form) and so forth.[581]

[1.4 Meritorious deeds]

2:20c–21b Those who make a Śiva temple furnished with marked bricks[582] will dwell in heaven until (*yāvat... tāvat*) fourteen Indras [finish their term of office].[583]

2:21c–23b [Having] made [*liṅgas*] of gems, precious stones, corals, crystals, emeralds,[584] glass, gold, silver, copper, bell-metal, brass, iron, lead and tin, and having then (*punaś ca*) worshipped them, after enjoying pleasures one will attain union with Śiva (*śivaṃ vrajet*).[585]

2:23c–24b There is no rebirth for him who installs the *liṅga* on earth; but, if he installs [it] in the middle of a temple, he [becomes equal to] Śiva: there is no doubt on this point.

2:24c–25b He who plants ten mango trees will never see dreadful hells; if someone creates a garden, he will enjoy [everything] in heaven as Indra does.

---

581 The *Śivadharmasaṅgraha* (6.40) reads *prakrīḍaṃty aṇimādibhiḥ* instead of *krīḍante aṇimādibhiḥ* to obviate an *aiśa* use of the *ātmanepada* and *aiśa* hiatus within a *pāda*.

582 From the context it appears that *aṣṭeṣṭaka* means 'marked bricks', but we are not sure what the bricks were marked with: Śiva's names, a *liṅga*, or other emblems of Śiva? A statement parallel to this is found in the *Śivadharmaśāstra* (4.25):

aṣṭeṣṭakāsamāyuktaṃ yaḥ prakuryāc chivālayam |
vidhūya pāpasaṃghātaṃ so 'pi gacchec chivālayam ||

• aṣṭeṣṭakāsamāyuktaṃ] BC; aṣṭoṣṭa kālamāyuktaṃ E_N

See also *Agnipurāṇa* 41.15ab *kumbhān na cālayet teṣu nyased* ***aṣṭeṣṭakāḥ*** *kramāt*, 41.34a–35b *kṛte tu kiṃ punas tasya prāsāde vidhinaiva tu* | *aṣṭeṣṭakasamāyuktaṃ yaḥ kuryyād devatālayam* || *na tasya phalasampattir vaktuṃ śakyeta kenacit* | and 327.19ab *aṣṭeṣṭakasurāgārakārī svargam avāpnuyāt* | ; *Vāyavīyasaṃhitā* of the *Śivapurāṇa* 34.53 *aṣṭeṣṭakābhiḥ prāsādaṃ kṛtvā liṃgaṃ ca mṛnmayam* | *tatrāvāhya mahādevaṃ sāṃbaṃ sagaṇam avyayam* || .

583 This must refer to the time of fourteen Manvantaras, each ruled by one Indra.

584 Inflected nominative singular *sphaṭir* is here meant for a *prātipadika*, meaning *sphaṭika*.

585 Note that 22ab is restored from the *Śivadharmasaṅgraha* (6.42). We assume that this reading is plausible since N reads *kācahema ... tāmrakāsyāni ...*, but K and W has no text transcribed at all.

2:25c–27b Those people who plant (*kurvanti*) trees,[586] such as the fig-tree and others, on a road, they will reach to the house of Yama (*yama-sādanam*) accompanied by cool shadows.[587] For those there will not be [those] dreadful [possible] sorrows of the world of Yama. This is the virtuous act of planting trees [on the way, which] I have told to you (*te*).[588]

2:27c–28b Those who install Viṣṇu, having had a temple constructed [for him], will go to the world of Viṣṇu and rejoice with Him.

2:28c–30b If someone worships[589] [whomsoever among] Brahmā, Skanda, Rudrāṇī, Gaṇeśa, the Mothers, (*mātaram*),[590] Sun, Fire, Indra (*śata-kratum*), the Yakṣas,[591] Vāyu, Dharma, or Varuṇa (*jaleśvaram*) with highest devotion, having installed them in a beautiful temple, he becomes immortal and [achieves] the world of that [particular deity].

2:30c–32b If someone makes a bridge (*saṅkramam*) on a way which is hard to cross (*asaṅkramapathe*), he will go comfortably [down] the path of Yama (*dharmarājapathe*). He will cross (*santaret*) by a bridge the river Vaitaraṇī, with its steaming water (*uṣṇatoyām*),[592] loudly roaring and difficult to traverse because of its deep eddies.

2:32c–33b If someone makes a causeway (*setubandham*) on a terrible muddy path, he will go easily to the city of Yama (*dharmarājapure*), which is so difficult to attain.[593]

---

586 We have understood *vṛkṣāṃ* as an accusative plural, as in other cases we find the ending *āṃ* for *ān*. Note that *Śivadharmasaṅgraha* (6.46) has corrected it to *vṛkṣān*.

587 The *Śivadharmasaṅgraha* (6.46) reads *na te yānti*, which might at first glance appear smoother but in fact makes little sense, since it is then impossible to construe *chāyābhiḥ śītalābhiś ca* with their action, since that action does not take place.

588 Dative singular *te* remains for plural *vaḥ*.

589 Note an irregular elision of the final *t* of the optative.

590 We understand *mātaram* as categorical singular and take it to mean any of the seven or eight mothers. The seven mothers, in general, are: Brāhmī, Māheśvarī, Kaumārī, Vaiṣṇavī/Yāmī, Vārāhī, Aindrī/Indrāṇi/Māhendrī, Cāmuṇḍā; an eighth, added later, is most commonly Mahālakṣmī. For further details, see HATLEY (2007: specifically pp. 33, 44 and 67).

591 As in the case of *mātaram*, we take *yakṣam* as categorical singular. It is possible, however, that Kubera is meant, cf. the translation of verse 3.70 ff. below.

592 The letter *m* preceding this adjective is presumably intended as a hiatus-breaker.

593 Note the unnecessary use of two pronouns. The *Śivadharmasaṅgraha* (6.53) has rephrased 33ab, reading *dharmarājapure mārge durgame sa sukhaṃ vrajet*; 'he will go at ease on the way [which is] difficult to cross (*durgame*) to the city of Yama (*dharma-*

2:33c–34b One who causes the path of a water-channel to flow freely (*nālīmārgaprayāyinaḥ*)[594] passes through the terrible hells, [namely] Paṅkalepa and that of Taptatrapu and Taptajatu (*taptatrapujatuś ca yaḥ*).

2:34c–35 If someone makes (*kāriṇaḥ*)[595] a hut [for an ascetic], an abode (*āvasathasya*), or a pavilion (*maṇḍapasya*), after first going [for judgement] to the city of Yama (*dharmarājapuraṅ gatvā*), [there will be a] golden house [for him] in heaven; there will be no fear of him [falling down] into the [hells called] Taptāṅgāra and Śilāvarṣa (*taptāṅgāra-śilāvarṣe*).[596]

2:36 I have told you all the fruit of [making] a hut, an abode or a pavilion; now listen to the fruit of giving donations (*dānasya*).

[1.5 Donative practices]

2:37a–38b Whoever is a donator of food (*annadātā yo hi*), that man (*asau naraḥ*) will not have a miserable rebirth (*durgatim*): he will obtain the world of Brahmā (*brahmalokagato bhavet*)[597] [and will enjoy] imperishable pleasure. There is no possibility of his being [re]born in the mortal world until Brahmā [himself] is destroyed (*naśyati*).

2:38c–39b If someone gives a place for supplying water to thirst-afflicted passers-by (*pathike jane*) in the hot season (*grīṣme*), his thirst will be quenched in the house of the dead (*pretabhavane*); devoid of thirst and [every possible] pair of extremes [such as hot and cold, pleasure and pain and so forth].[598]

---

rājapure).' In the *Śivadharmasaṅgraha*'s reading, sentence structure is improved and non-standard *sandhi* is avoided.

594 We suppose this to be the sense (cf. *Śivadharmasaṅgraha* 6.54), and we suppose that it may be arrived at by taking *°prayāyinaḥ* as a nominative singular and as having causative sense.

595 This can be interpreted as genitive singular or, alternatively, as nominative plural of singular. See *nālīmārgaprayāyinaḥ* in 2.34b.

596 We find no record of *śilāvarṣa* as a hell except in our text and in the *Śivadharma-saṅgraha*.

597 The *Śivadharmasaṅgraha* (6.57) has tried to make the sentence smoother by replacing *bhavet* (which seems uncomfortably like a non-Sanskritic auxiliary verb) with *naraḥ*.

598 Note that 38c–39b is anacoluthic: we start with a singular subject and finish with a plural one.

2:39c–41b If someone offers sesame and water (*tilodakān*)[599] to the gods and ancestors (*devān pitṝṃ samuddiśya*),[600] [his] ancestors will be satisfied [and] they will be freed (*varjitāḥ*) from the three [following] hells: these men will not sink (*nimajjanti*) in [the hells that are] the pond[s] Pūya, Asṛk and Meda.[601] [Thus] his ancestors will be liberated by the fruit of offering sesame and water (*tilodakaphalena*).

2:41c-43b If someone gives the skin of a black buck filled with sesame seeds, having hooves decorated with silver, horns [decorated] with gold, its body dressed with cloths (*sacailāṅgam*) and having a brazen milk-pail (*kānsadoham*),[602] this giver of a cow of sesame seeds[603] will obtain indestructible worlds. And when that person falls [from those worlds] at the end of the Yuga (*yugānte*), he will be born in a respectable family (*vipule kule*).

2:43c–45b People who, devoted to their ancestors, regularly (*nityam*) perform *śrāddha* [rites], their ancestors as well as (*ca*) they [themselves][604] will certainly be content in the house of Yama (*yamālaye*), and the hell [called] Kumbhīpāka will not be for them;[605] moreover (*ca*), those people who perform the [rites] of *śrāddha* (*śrāddhakārayitā*)[606] will go to the world of the ancestors.

2:45c–46 For one who daily (*nityam*) offers a lamp to gods and

---

599 Note that the *Śivadharmasaṅgraha* (6.65) reads *tilodakam*.

600 Even though it may seem unorthodox that sesame and water would be offered to gods as well, we have taken it in this sense on the strength of the parallel expression *devān pitṝn samuddiśya* or *pitṝn devān samuddiśya* in 2.52c and 2.53a, where the gods and ancestors clearly form two separate groups.

601 These three hells appear together again in *Niśvāsamukha* 4.102 and in a slightly modified form in *Guhyasūtra* 4.38–39.

602 Literally: 'whose milk-pail is of bronze'. *kānsa-* should perhaps be emended to *kāṃsya-*, but cf. 2.58 below, where *kānsadoham* is attested to. This qualification (elsewhere expressed by adjectives such as *sakāṃsyapātra*) is standard in gifts of cows to Brāhmins, such as that described in *Yājñavalkyasmṛti* 1.204 ff.

603 For references to other passages mentioning the gift of a 'sesame-seed cow' (*tiladhenu*) made by filling a black-buck-skin with sesame seeds, see KANE's *History of Dharmaśāstra*, Vol. II, Part 2, pp. 880f. Cf. also *Śivopaniṣad* 6.70.

604 Note that our adopted text actually displays *sa ca tṛpto yamālaye*, which is anacoluthic, but it is conceivable that the singular is 'incorrectly' applied here in order to obviate a possible confusion: if the text displayed *te ca tṛptāḥ*, a reader might have supposed that the ancestors were again being referred to.

605 We take *tasya* to refer to the ancestors as well as the agent of the rite.

606 Note the irregular use of the nominative singular or an agent noun as though it were a plural.

ancestors there will not be the hells [called] Tāmisra and Andhatāmisra.[607] His eyes will become bright and [his] power of sight will [never be] destroyed.

2:47–48 If somebody donates a virtuous [cow with] hoofs decorated with silver, horns [decorated] with gold, [with] a copper milk-pail (*kāṃsyadohanīm*), neck decorated with cloths again and again, his abode (*vāsaḥ*) will be either in the world of cows or in heaven. A cow donator lives (*vasate*) free from all [possible] pair of opposites (*sarvadvandvavinirmuktaḥ*).

2:49 If someone gives a calving cow, which has two beautiful faces (*vaktrobhayasusaṃsthitām*),[608] this [bears the same] fruit as giving land, [and this cow donator] will go to heaven.[609]

2:50 If someone gives bulls (*anaḍvāhāni*)[610] regularly (*bahuśaḥ*) to the best of the twice born (*dvijottame*), by the fruit of that merit [he] will be honoured in heaven (*svargaloke*).

2:51 If someone even with great sins (*bahupātakikaḥ*)[611] offers a golden-haired goat daily (*nityaśaḥ*), he will obtain the world of Fire (*agnilokam*).[612]

2:52 If someone gives a white, red, yellow or a black woollen garment [to a Brāhmin][613] in the name of the gods or [his] ancestors, he will go to the world of the moon.

---

607 The dual subject is here (irregularly) restated as a plural (*narakāḥ*), presumably in order to be able to avoid using a dual verb-form.

608 This presumably means that the calving cow is given away right at the moment when the calf's face appears. The expression *vaktrobhayasusaṃsthitām* is not very common. However, see *Śivadharmasaṅgraha* 10.220ab: *dadyād ubhayamukhīṃ gāṃ śivāyātīvaśobhanām*. *Yājñavalkyasmṛti* 1.206ab *savatsāromatulyāni yugāny ubhayatomukhīm* further supports our idea. The same expression *ubhayatomukhīm* appears in a similar context in *Skandapurāṇa* 111.93, *Nāradapurāṇa pūrvakhaṇḍa* 13.87, and *Viṣṇusmṛti* 88:4.

609 Note that the *Śivadharmasaṅgraha* (6.118) reads *hy etat svargalokābhikāṃkṣiṇām* instead of *hy etat svargalokañ ca gacchati*.

610 Note that the *Śivadharmasaṅgraha* (6.106) reads *anaḍvāho 'pi-* instead of *anaḍvāhāni-*.

611 We take *bahupātakikaḥ* in the sense of *mahāpātakī*.

612 Note that the *Śivadharmasaṅgraha* (6.123) reads *'pi san* instead of *'pi yaḥ* to obviate the problem of having two pronouns.

613 For this suppletion, see the next verse.

2:53 If someone gives a buffalo to a Brāhmin[614] in the name of the gods or [his] ancestors, by the fruit of that merit he will be honoured in the world of Viṣṇu.

2:54–55 One should offer (*prayaccheta*) a white, black or bee-coloured [viz. mottled?] (*bhramarākṛtim*) and well-mannered buffalo (*sudhenu*)[615] to the gods or to the best of the twice born. By offering this kind of buffalo (*mahiṣīm*) he will be honoured in the world of Śiva. Once he falls from the world of Śiva, he will be reborn as a king.

2:56 If someone gives land tilled with a plough, sown with seed (*sabījām*) and grain-garlanded (*sasyamālinīm*),[616] he will remain like the sun as long as the sun-created worlds [exist].[617]

2:57 By giving land one goes to heaven; by giving gems one goes to the world (*puram*) of the sun. He who donates cloth [goes] to the world of the moon and he who donates silver (*tāradaḥ*) [goes] to the world of Viṣṇu (*vaiṣṇave pure*).[618]

2:58 And those who donate sesame seeds and gold will go to the world of Rudra; by giving brass, copper and coral one goes to the world of Indra (*vasoḥ puram*).

2:59 'No matter' (*yāny api*)[619] what kinds of pearls, gems or necklaces one

---

614 Note an irregular optative and the use of the locative in the sense of the dative.

615 Verses 2.54–55 are redundant since the procedure of offering *dhenu*—a cow or a buffalo—has already been mentioned. Here we may have translated *sudhenu* as 'cow' but this translation would not fit with 55a, where we do have clear mention of a buffalo. If we were to translate *sudhenu* as 'cow' then *mahiṣīm*, in 55a would remain problematic. In this case, we expect 55a to feature a term implying a cow—rather than a buffalo; either we understand *mahiṣī* in the sense of 'cow' or we need to replace it by an accusative noun denoting a cow. Note that the *Śivadharmasaṅgraha* does not contain these problematic verses.

616 Cf. *Mahābhārata* 13.61:28ab: *halakṛṣṭāṃ mahīṃ dattvā sabījāṃ saphalām api.*

617 The syntax of the sentence is suboptimal, not only because it is anacoluthic, but also because there seems to be no reason why the worlds created/illuminated by the sun should be in the accusative. The intended meaning may have been 'as long as the light of the Sun remains'. We are not, however, sure how to extract this meaning. Minimally, we need to understand that *āloka* has been reduced to *loka*, perhaps, for metrical reasons.

618 The syntax of the sentence is problematic. Note an *aiśa* use of dative singular for genitive singular and the word *pura* being used in the sense of *loka*.

619 We understood *yāny api* in the sense of *yāni kāny api* 'any'.

gives, one goes to [the world of] the moon (*somapuram*);[620] [and also] for [having offered] an oblation of sesame seeds: there is no doubt.

2:60 If someone daily gives treacle, milk, curds or ghee, he goes to the Yakṣa-world (*yakṣalokapuram*).[621] So too by giving honey.

2:61 By giving sandalwood, *Agallochum*, camphor, *kallokakaḥ*, cloves and other fragrant things, a man will attain the state of being a Gandharva.

2:62 If someone unsolicitedly offers a [virgin] girl[622] having first adorned [her],[623] that man will obtain heaven. So does a donator of grains (*dhānyapradāyakaḥ*).

2:63 Those who daily offer grains [such as] *Phaseolus radiatus*, *Phaseolus mungo* (*māṣamudgādikāṃ*)[624] and others will obtain heaven [after death], as well as those who offer protection (*abhayapradāḥ*)[625] [to living beings].

2:64 [Those who] offer a woman (*striyam*) possessed of beauty and youth and adorned with cloths and ornaments will obtain the state of being a Vidyādhara.

---

620 The *Śivadharmasaṅgraha* (6.126) reads *śakrapuram* 'the world of Indra' instead of *somapuram*, but this does not seem quite right since it reads *śakrapuram* below (71).

621 Here we expect either *yakṣalokam* or *yakṣapuram*, but not both in the same place. Does this refer to the world of Kubera?

622 The *Śivadharmasaṅgraha* (6.129) reads *tv ayācitām* instead of *ayācitām* to obviate an *aiśa* hiatus within a *pāda*. A similar verse appears in the southern recension of *Śivadharmaśāstra* 12.47c-49b (T. 32, p. 146). This passage states that the girl should be offered to a Brāhmin but does not, however, refer to the context. We are not sure whether or not this offering should be made in the context of marriage or not:

kanyām alaṃkṛtāṃ dadyād alaṃ jīvanasaṃyutām ||
dvijāya vedaviduṣe kanyādānaṃ tad ucyate |
śivabhaktāya viprāya dattvā kanyāṃ svalaṃkṛtām ||
kulatrayaṃ samuddhṛtya svargaṃ prāpnoti niścalam |

The offering of a virgin girl mentioned in our text here may refer to the marriage ritual where a father gives his daughter to the groom (cf. *Mahābhārata* (appendix) 13.15:3339 ff.).

623 Note an irregular *ktvā* for *lyap*.

624 Note that *māṣamudgādikāṃ* is intended as an accusative plural, which is what we find in the *Śivadharmasaṅgraha* (6.130).

625 Note that the *Śivadharmasaṅgraha* (6.130) reads *hy abhayapradāḥ* just to avoid a hiatus within a *pāda*.

2:65 Those men who continually (*satatam*) provide (*dāpayet*) a feast of lovemaking (*ratisatram*) among beautiful women (*varanārīṣu*)[626] will rejoice in heaven among companies (*saṃgheṣu*) of celestial nymphs.[627]

2:66 Those who yearly offer (*prativarṣapradāyinaḥ*)[628] a cane-seat or a couch (*vetrāsanañ ca śayyāñ ca*),[629] will rejoice in the Yakṣa-world with thousands of Yakṣiṇīs.

2:67 If someone gives fuel to Brāhmins at the arrival of the cold season, he will become rich, handsome (*rūpasampannaḥ*) and possessed of good fortune (*subhagaḥ*).[630]

2:68 Those people who daily offer[631] shelter, straw (*tṛṇam*), a couch, a blanket, food (*prāvarānnam*)[632] and fire will go to heaven (*svarga-gāminaḥ*).

2:69 For those who regularly offer songs, musical instruments and vehicles to the gods, they will be [re]born to have great enjoyments, [they will regularly be] awakened by songs and instrumental music (*gītavāditra-bodhitāḥ*).

2:70 If someone offers a horse possessed of beauty and youth[633] and adorned

---

626 The syntax is unwieldy here. Firstly, the plural subject has a singular verb (*dāpayet*). Secondly, the relative pronoun is missing. Next, the locative is used in the sense of instrumental. All these problems have been displaced in the *Śivadharmasaṅgraha* (6.132) by reading: *ratisatrañ ca yo dadyād varābhiḥ pramadājanaiḥ | kāmadevapuraṃ yāti jāto 'naṅgasamo bhavet ||* .

627 The *Śivadharmasaṅgraha* (6.132) has rephrased 56cd quite differently by reading *kāmadevapuraṃ yāti jāto 'naṅgasamo bhavet* which means that the giver will obtain the world of Kāmadeva and, once born there, he will become equal to Kāmadeva.

628 Note that the *Śivadharmasaṅgraha* (6.133) has polished the Sanskrit expression *prati-varṣapradāyinaḥ* by reading *pratyabdaṃ yaḥ prayacchati* at the same time making the plural agent singular.

629 We could equally translate *vetrāsanañ ca śayyāñ ca* as 'a cane-seat or a cane-couch' or as 'a cane-seat and a couch (or cane-couch)'.

630 Note that the *Śivadharmasaṅgraha* (6.134) reads *dīptāgniḥ subhago bhavet* 'will become [like] a blazing fire [and] possessed of good fortune' instead of *jāyate subhagas tathā*. We have understand *dīptāgniḥ* 'blazing fire' to mean *dīptāgniprabhaḥ* 'like a blazing fire'.

631 Note that the *Śivadharmasaṅgraha* (6.135) rephrased *prayacchante* to *prayacchanti* in order to normalize the Sanskrit.

632 To avoid this awkward compound the *Śivadharmasaṅgraha* (6.135) reads *puṇyāgniṃ śuddhamānasāḥ* instead of *prāvarānnaṃ hutāśanam*.

633 It is conceivable that we should read instead, with the *Śivadharmasaṅgraha* (6.137),

with golden [ornaments] to Brāhmins, he will obtain the heaven of the Sun (*bradhnasyāpnoti viṣṭapam*).[634]

2:71 By giving a caparisoned (*śārīsaṃyogasaṃyuktam*) elephant with a golden garland one goes to the world of Indra (*śakrapuram*); once one falls from there one will be reborn (*jāyati*)[635] as a king (*bhogavān*).

2:72 By offering an umbrella (*ātapatrapradānena*) this man (*asau naraḥ*) will be[636] endowed with good fortune (*śrīmān*). He will not be afflicted by the heat [on his way] to the world of Yama.[637]

2:73 If someone offers a pair of shoes, he will be freed[638] from all sin, [and] he will have a beautiful horse[639] on the way to [the world of] Yama.

2:74 Also, for one who offers a pair of shoes there will be no torture caused by terrible thorns and the pains of heated sand [on the way to Yama's world].[640]

2:75–76 If someone offers an elephant-[drawn] chariot[641] to a virtuous (*guṇānvite*)[642] Brāhmin, by the merit of that fruit he will be honoured in heaven; he will not fall from heaven until the gods together with Indra (*yāvad devāḥ savāsavāḥ*)[643] [themselves fall down]; and once he falls from there[644] he will be reborn as a pious king.

---

jave yauvanasampannam, where we could perhaps take *jave* as though it were an instrumental: 'possessed of youth and speed'.

634 We find the phrase *bradhnasyāpnoti viṣṭapam* in *Manusmṛti* 9:137, but in a different context.

635 Note an *aiśa parasmaipada*. The *Śivadharmasaṅgraha* (6.154) reads *bhavati* instead of *jāyati* to mend the grammatical problem.

636 Once again, to avoid an *aiśa parasmaipada* problem the *Śivadharmasaṅgraha* (6.154) reads *jāyeta mānavaḥ* instead of *jāyaty asau naraḥ*.

637 Cf. verse 26 above. In this case, however, the *Śivadharmasaṅgraha* (6.154c–155b) has not distorted the meaning.

638 The *Śivadharmasaṅgraha* (6.155) has rephrased the text as *sa tu mucyeta* in order to avoid the irregular form *mucyati*.

639 Note an *aiśa parasmaipada* for *ātmanepada*; to obviate the problem the *Śivadharmasaṅgraha* (6.156) has rephrased the text to read *jāyate śobhano hayaḥ* (instead of *aśvo jāyati śobhanaḥ*).

640 The *Śivadharmasaṅgraha* (6.157) reads *hi dadyād upānahau* instead of *dadāti upānahau* to avoid an *aiśa* hiatus within a *pāda*.

641 The *Śivadharmasaṅgraha* (6.157) has rephrased *gajarathan tu yo dadyād* to read *dadyād rājarathaṃ yas tu*. But this might in part be a secondary corruption, for *rā* and *ga* look similar in old Newari script.

642 The locative adjective is used here to qualify a noun in the dative.

643 Note that this whole line has been adopted from the *Śivadharmasaṅgraha* (6.158). We assume it to be a plausible reading since W also reads *tāvan na cyavate* [[...]].

644 Here we have adopted the reading of the *Śivadharmasaṅgraha* (6.159) *tataś caiva*

2:77–78 By offering a divine horse-[drawn] chariot together with many accoutrements one obtains the world of the Sun; [once one gets there] he will rejoice with him. He will remain like the sun as long as the sun-created worlds [exist]; and once he falls from there will be reborn as a rich [person].

2:79a–80b By offering a bullock-[drawn] cart[645] together with all accoutrements, a man will obtain heaven together with male and female servants.[646] Once he falls from there, he will again (*bhūyaḥ*) invariably (*sadā*) be reborn as a rich person.

2:80c–82b If someone wakes up early in the morning and [daily] gives[647] a mouthful of grass (*grāsaṃ*) to cows while reciting the mantra [that follows below], (*mantreṇaiva samāyuktam*), he will be destined to go to heaven (*svargagāmī ca bhavate*);[648] once he falls [from there, he will be reborn as] a rich person: his birth [will take place] in a family rich in cattle and he will [himself] be rich in cattle.

2:82c–83b "O Surabhi (*surabhī*), world-maintainer, born from the churning of nectar,[649] please accept this mouthful of grass. This is my excellent observance."

2:83c–84b Just as one gives a mouthful of grass to cows, in the same manner one may give to a bull (*saurabheye*). The same fruit is seen

---

instead of K's reading *svargalokāt* since the last letter in W is clearly *va*, and K tends to repair the text imaginatively (whereas W simply copies what he believes he sees).

645 *Ex conj.* We assume that the *Śivadharmasaṅgraha* (6.161) has banalised the text by choosing a more common word.

646 *Ex conj.*: this section is largely drawn from the *Śivadharmasaṅgraha* (6.161), for this portion of text is lost in our manuscripts.

647 The *Śivadharmasaṅgraha* (6.95) has rephrased 80ab to read *gavāṃ grāsaṃ daridreṇa kartavyaṃ prātar eva hi* instead of *gavāṃ grāsan tu yo dadyāt prātar utthāya mānavaḥ*. This gives the extra element *daridreṇa* 'by a pauper', but it means also the loss of *prātar utthāya*, which implies that the gift is to be made on a daily basis.

648 The *ca* appears to be otiose and the *ātmanepada* is irregular; the latter oddity has been corrected in the reading of the *Śivadharmasaṅgraha* (6.96): *svargagāmī ca bhavati*.

649 We have understood the nominative singulars to be intended as vocative singulars. The verse appears in the *Somaśambhupaddhati* (1.6:5), the *Kriyākramadyotikā* (§ 67, p.134) and the *Jñānaratnāvalī* (R 14898, p.144) in the following form: *amṛtamathanotpanne surabhe lokadhāriṇi imaṃ grāsaṃ gṛhāṇa tvam idaṃ me vratam uttamam* |. The *Śivadharmasaṅgraha* (6.98) corrects 82a *amṛtamathanotpannā* to *utpannāmṛtamathane*, but it does not correct 82b, perhaps for metrical reasons.

(*dṛṣṭam*), but the mantra[650] [to be used] is different in each case (*pṛthak pṛthak*).

2:84c–85b 'These (*ete*) [bulls] sustain the entire world and give food to living beings: may they be pleased to accept [this] clump of grass. This is my excellent observance'.[651]

2:85c–86b If someone daily offers [a lump of grass] to another man's cow, adopting this difficult observance, they [viz. the bulls] will protect him from danger and disease; if someone touches (*sparśane*)[652] [them], they (the bulls) will remove his sins.

2:86c–88b If someone lets a bull free[653] at the arrival of an auspicious time (*puṇyakāle tu saṃprāpte*),[654] he will go to the world of Rudra, providing the bullis a black one. If, however, one cannot obtain a black one[655] he will obtain heaven together with his ancestors; once he falls from there will be reborn (*jāyati*)[656] as a king (*bhogavān*).

2:88c–90 By offering the fruit of *Feronia elephantum* (*kapittham*), pomegranate, mango, rose-apple (*jambum*), wood-apple (*bilvam*), bread-fruit (*panasam*), sweet lime (*mātuluṅgam*), coconut, together with banana (*samocakam*), *Clypea hernandifolia*, *Emblica officinalis gaertn*, orange (*prācīnāmalanāraṅgam*), grape and dates (*kharjūram eva ca*)[657] and other nectar-like fruits (*anyāmṛtaphalā ye*)[658] one will

---

650 The word *mantra* is rarely used in the neuter. The *Śivadharmasaṅgraha* (6.99) reads *mantraḥ* instead of *mantram.*

651 This is presumably the mantra to be used when offering grass to a bull.

652 The *Śivadharmasaṅgraha* (6.101) reads *darśane* instead of *sparśane.* The syntax is clumsy and the interpretation of the whole unit is uncertain. Perhaps, since the cow is not one's own, the action is considered altruistic, for one gains no milk or other products from another man's cow.

653 According to KANE (*History of Dharmaśāstra*, Vol. IV, pp. 539 ff.) the bull should preferably be black and have auspicious signs: having intact limbs and so forth. Letting a bull free is prescribed on two occasions; one is on the full moon day of Kārttika or Āśvina, and the 11th (according to *Garuḍapurāṇa*) or 12th (according to *Bhaviṣyapurāṇa*) day after a family member's death.

654 Here, the auspicious time means the full moon day of Kārttika or Āśvina, see KANE's *History of Dharmaśāstra*, Vol. IV, pp. 539f.

655 The *Śivadharmasaṅgraha* (6.104) reads *alābhe nīlaṣaṇḍasya* to obviate the hiatus.

656 An *aiśa parasmaipada* has been used here for metrical reasons. The *Śivadharmasaṅgraha* (6.104) corrects *jāyati* to *bhavati.*

657 Note an *aiśa samāhāradvandva* compound.

658 We assume that the intended meaning here is that of *anyāni cāmṛtarasāṇi phalāni yāni.* The *Śivadharmasaṅgraha* (6.163–164) has rearranged these two verses, adding

be fortunate, have many sons and be endowed with beauty, and [then again] be reborn a very fortunate man.[659]

2:91 One who offers fruits will be [reborn] with all limbs intact (*sampūrṇāṅgaḥ*) and will be healthy. And one who offers teeth-cleaning sticks (*dantadhāvanadātā*) will obtain a beautiful wife.[660]

2:92 By offering fragrant betel and flowers one will become a Pandit and one who offers fragrant substances (*gandhapradāyakaḥ*)[661] will have fragrant breath (*saugandhāsyaḥ*) and eloquence.

2:93ab By offering a sacred thread and a cushion made of *kuśa*-grass one will be born among Brāhmins.[662]

2:93c–94b By offering swords, discuses, [and] weapons, [such as] spears, darts and hatchets (*śaktikuntaparaśvadhān*) one will have no fear of the terrible [hell called] Asipatravana (fierce jungle of sword blades).

2:94c–95 By offering unworked iron (*asaṃskṛtasya lohasya*) one will have no fear of bondage and by offering iron fashioned into utensils (*ghaṭitopaskaram*),[663] there will be no fear from weapons [for him,] and there will never be the hell [called] Lohakāra [for him].[664]

---

more fruits than we have in our text and it has obviated the grammatical problem by reading *anyāni ca phalāny evam*.

659 There is an awkward repetition here of *subhaga*, which the *Śivadharmasaṅgraha* (6.164) has avoided by reading *sukhabhāg* instead of *subhago*.

660 *Śivadharmaśāstra* 12.72 also relates the offering of teeth-cleaning sticks to women. The recipient in the *Śivadharmaśāstra*, however, is a Śivayogin: *dantadhāvanam uddiṣṭaṃ nivedya śivayogine | divyastrībhogasaṃyuktaṃ divi ramyaṃ puraṃ labhet ||*. It is to be noted that our text does not speak of a recipient.

The *Śivadharmasaṅgraha* (6.166) reads *bhāryā bhavati śobhanā* instead of *bhāryāṃ labhati śobhanām*, presumably just to obviate an *aiśa parasmaipada*, but with the unintended result that the *pāda* could then be taken to mean 'will become a beautiful wife'.

661 We have assumed here that this last word is a postponed repetition of the original subject, but one could instead take each verse-half as a separate statement with a separate gift and a separate reward.

662 Literally this means 'in Brāhmin wombs'.

663 This *bahuvrīhi* perhaps more literally means 'out of which utensils have been fashioned'.

664 *lohakāraś ca* is our conjecture on the strength of N's reading [[...]] *kāraś ca*, where K reads *śastrakārāṃś ca*, W reads *lohakāra sa* and the *Śivadharmasaṅgraha* (6.170) reads *lohīpākaś ca*. As mentioned above, this is not a hell that typically features in Śaiva lists (e.g. in the other *sūtras* of the *Niśvāsa* or in *Parākhya* 5), but both

2:96 Offering cups made of clay or a water jar is the best [type of] offering to ascetics; by giving [these] one will obtain pleasures.

2:97 [The offering of] a golden, silver, copper, iron or tin (*āyasatrāpuṣam*) vessel[665] will be an indestructible offering,[666] and [the donor] will have a long life.

2:98 If someone offers a male or female slave[667] to the gods or to Brāhmins,[668] he will be highly fortunate, surrounded by many dependants.

2:99ab By offering rock-salt coming from Sindh (*sindhūttham*) one becomes handsome and highly fortunate.[669]

2:99c–100b By offering *piper longum* (*pipalīm*), ginger, pepper and dry ginger (*viśvabheṣajam*), one obtains good health, and also by [offering] remedies to the sick (*āture*).[670]

2:100cd By restoring health to a sick person one becomes healthy and [acquires] long life (*dīrgham āyuṣam*).[671]

2:101 [By giving] sweet, sour, pungent, bitter, astringent, [things] he becomes a connoisseur of the flavours of all pleasures (*sarvakrīḍārasābhijño*) and a Pandit.

---

occur in *dharmaśāstra* literature: just after *asipatravana*, *Manusmṛti* 4.90 speaks of a hell called *lohadāraka*, *lohacāraka*, *lohāṅgāraka* or *lohakāraka*, etc. depending on which manuscripts are followed (see OLIVELLE 2005: 934). The same hell appears in *Viṣṇusmṛti* 43.22 and perhaps, arguably, in *Parākhya* 5.23.

665 Note that almost the whole line 97ab is reconstructed from the *Śivadharmasaṅgraha* (6.171), but in place of the word °*trāpuṣam*, which is the reading of our manuscripts, the *Śivadharmasaṅgraha* (6.171) reads °*sīsakam*.

666 Presumably it is not the object given that is indestructible, but rather the moral retributive force of the act of giving, which only perishes upon giving its fruit.

667 Note the *aiśa* optative. The *Śivadharmasaṅgraha* (6.172) has obviated this awkwardness by reading *dadāti yaḥ* instead of *ca yo dadet*.

668 *devatābhyo dvijātibhyo* is reconstructed from the *Śivadharmasaṅgraha* (6.172).

669 Presumably this refers to a kind of salt, that is typically but not necessarily found in Sindh. The offering of salt (*lavaṇa*) is implicitly paired here with the acquisition of *lāvaṇya*, 'loveliness'.

670 It is an *aiśa* locative use for dative, to which no *sandhi* has been applied.

671 The *aiśa* use of *āyuṣam* in the sense of *āyuḥ*, which one could take to be a nominative ('[there will be] long life [for him]') or an accusative for which the verb must be supplied. The redactor of the *Śivadharmasaṅgraha* (6.175) has obviated the problem by rewriting the line.

2:102 By offering oil one obtains supreme power (*tejaḥ*);[672] by offering sugar and treacle one will be long lived; by offering thickened curd[673] or buttermilk, one becomes rich in cows if one [also] worships cows.

2:103ab By offering pearl [or] nacreous shells[674] one will have many sons.

2:103c–104b If someone offers cowrie shells, and a stainless [and] bright mirror, he will become handsome, rich and beloved among women.

2:104c–105b If someone daily offers[675] nourishment, expressions of compassion (*hantatim*)[676] or alms (*bhikṣāṃ*), he will become rich; if he does not, he will have a miserable rebirth.[677]

2:105cd This is the injunction of making offerings [that has been] taught. Hear from me also (*ca*) the [injunction] of consummate offering (*atidāna*).[678]

2:106 One should always offer food and water; [as for the offering of] cloths, bed, refuge (*vastraśayyāpratiśrayam*), cows, gold and land—what else among virtuous acts can be greater than this.

---

672 Note that the *Śivadharmasaṅgraha* (6.176) reads *tailāt prāṇā ghṛtāt tejaḥ* 'by offering oil one obtains the breath of life [and] by offering ghee one obtains power' instead of *tailāt sarvādhikaṃ tejaḥ*.

673 This translates *marjjitā*, which might be an error for *mārjitā*, which is in turn listed among milk-products in the *Amarakośa* (sometimes given in the variant form *mārjikā*) 2.9:44.

674 We have assumed that *śaṅkhaśuktīni* is irregularly treated as neuter and that it is intended not as a *dvandva*, but rather as a single unit, meaning 'shells covered with mother of pearl'. One could, of course, take it as a *dvandva*, but there seem to be other usages of the collocation where a *dvandva* analysis is unlikely or impossible, e.g. *Jayākhya* 26.64 and *Īśvarasaṃhitā* 2.26.

675 Note the *aiśa* optative. Note that the *Śivadharmasaṅgraha* (6.179) reads *kṣipet* instead of *dadet* to obviate the problem.

676 We have understand the otherwise unparalleled expression *hantatim* to be intended to mean *hantoktim* on the basis of comparison with the *Śivadharmasaṅgraha* (6.179), which reads *hantakāraṃ*.

677 Here the *Śivadharmasaṅgraha* (6.179) has an anacoluthic sentence (beginning in the plural and ending with a singular), and hiatus.

678 The underlining meaning of the consummate offering (*atidāna*) according to our text (2.109) is the protection of life. In the Pāśupata context, on the basis of Kauṇḍinya's understanding of *Pāśupatasūtra* 2.15 *atidattam atīṣṭam*, the consummate offering refers to offering oneself to god (see Kauṇḍinya's on *Pāśupatasūtra* 2.15). According to *Vasiṣṭhadharmasūtra* 29:19 the consummate offerings are the offering of cows, land and knowledge. Thus, the term *atidāna* refers to different concepts in different traditions.

2:107 Likewise (*tathā*) the offering of knowledge is excellent,[679] but the most excellent is protection of life: if someone protects a living being,[680] that very [protector] (*sa ca*) is understood to be the best [sort of] giver.

2:108 Among all kinds of offerings the gift of the absence of fear to living beings [is the best]. Whoever gives that is verily (*hi*) a 'Giver'; others are beguiled by desire.

2:109 Therefore one should protect all [living beings] when the life of living beings is at risk (*jīvitātyaye*); he who [does] so is a [true] giver, he is a [true] ascetic (*tapasvī*) and will attain the supreme goal.[681]

2:110 I have taught the injunction of consummate offering (*atidānavidhiḥ*) for the benefit of the people. If someone makes offerings every day, hear from me [the fruit of] that offering too.[682]

2:111a–114b If someone offers (*yo dadāti*) teeth-cleaning sticks, betel leaves (*dantadhāvanatāmbūlam*), garlands, incense, ointment (*vilepanam*), yellow orpiment, collyrium, cloths,[683] decoration with wonderful ornaments (*divyālaṅkāramaṇḍanam*), the riding of a horse or elephant (*gajāśvārohaṇam*), vehicles, unguents and massage (*abhyaṅgodvartanan*), bathing with divine perfumes, anointing with sandal paste, agarwood, saffron (*candanāgarukuṅkumaiḥ*) mixed

---

679 The offering of knowledge includes three kinds of notions: "the gifts of book, the gift of icons and the impartation of teachings" (de SIMINI 2016: 290). Most probably *vidyādāna* here refers to the offering of books in the form of manuscripts. The reader is referred to de SIMINI's work (2016a) for full treatment of this subject.

680 The *Niśvāsamukha* has an *ātmanepada* for *parasmaipada* for metrical reasons, while the *Śivadharmasaṅgraha* (6.182) reads *jīvaṃ rakṣati yo nityaṃ sa* instead of *jīvaṃ rakṣayate yo hi sa ca* to obviate the problem.

681 It stands to reason that the protector of living beings in most of the cases is the king. In some instances, however, an ordinary person could also be the agent. Whoever the agent might be, it is clear that protecting life is the best offering according according to our text.

682 Here perhaps starts the section on temple-related offerings. We assume that *dine dine* implies some daily ritual. If the interpretation is right, most likely the capable agent of the following daily offering is the king, which involves the riding of a horse or an elephant and the offering of vehicles together with other expensive objects (2.112).

We have understood *dānan tañ ca* 'that offering too' to mean *taddānaphalaṃ ca* 'the fruit of that offering too'. The *Śivadharmasaṅgraha* (6.185) has rephrased *yo dadyād dānan tañ ca* to read *yad dānaṃ tac cāpi hi*, in order to remove anacoluthon.

683 Note that 111c *rocanāñjanavastrāṇi* is reconstructed from the *Śivadharmasaṅgraha* (6.186).

with camphor, incense together with flowers, gifts of sweets and beverages, a comfortable couch in the night (*sukhaśayyāniśītavān*),[684] he will enjoy the pleasure of amorous enjoyment with most excellent women.[685]

2:114cd If someone does not offer [the above] and [yet] desires it [viz. the pleasure of amorous enjoyment], he will be extremely grieved.

Goddess spoke:

2:115 Who is the best recipient [to offer something to], by giving (*datte*) to whom there is great benefit, [and whereby] the offering will be indestructible? Tell me that o Maheśvara.

[1.6 Hierarchy of recipients]

God spoke:

2:116 Offering to [one's] mother, father, teacher, relatives, a virgin girl (*kanyayaḥ*),[686] the unfortunate, the afflicted , the blind and the poor will be valid for eternity (*ānantāya kalpate*).

2:117 One learned in the Vedas is considered to be better than thousands of foolish Brāhmins;[687] one who has installed the Vedic fires is considered to be better than thousands of men learned in Vedas.

---

684 It is not clear to us what *sukhaśayyāniśītavān* is. We might understand *sukhaśayyāniśītavān* as *sukhaśayyāṃ niśīthe*, but then the *vān* would be meaningless. Alternatively, it might be possible to translate it together with *varanārīratisukham*, and in this case our translation would be 'he will enjoy the pleasure of amorous enjoyment with most excellent women on a comfortable couch at nights'. The *Śivadharmasaṅgraha* (6.188) reads °*niṣīdanam* instead of °*niśītavān*, which could make the compound mean simply '[the gift of] sleeping well on a bed'.

685 Alternatively, *varanārīratisukhaṃ* could be intended to be yet another offering. In this case, we have to imagine that the giver will obtain all of the enumerated items in the other world as the reward of his offering here. Note that 114ab is the reading of the *Śivadharmasaṅgraha* (6.188); our manuscripts have only *varanārīrati*°.

686 The *metri causa* reading *kanyayaḥ* should be understood to mean *kanyāyāḥ*. This understanding is compatible with the understanding of *Śivadharmasaṅgraha* 6.190: *mātāpitṛṣu yad dānaṃ dīnāndhakṛpaṇeṣu ca | gurubandhuṣu kanyāsu tad anantyāya kalpyate* || .

687 Note that the *Śivadharmasaṅgraha* (6.191) reads °*sahasrāṇām* instead of °*sahasrebhyaḥ* in order to smoothen the reading.

2:118 Among thousands of those who have installed the Vedic fires (*āhitāgni*) an *agnihotrī* (one who maintains the sacrificial fire) is considered to be better.[688] Among thousands of *agnihotrī*s, one who knows *brahman* (*brahmavettā*) is considered to be better.[689]

2:119a–120b The [offering] given to him (i.e. *brahmavettā*) will [bear] an eternal [fruit] (*bhave 'nantam*);[690] he is considered the supreme saviour (*trātā*).[691] If someone offers ten thousand times to them [i.e. to those who know *brahman*], [a gift of the same value in terms of merit would be made as if] he had offered once to a [Śiva-]knower (*jñānin*);[692] this [act of giving] to them is not equal; he [viz. the Śiva-knower] is the supreme saviour of all.

2:120c–121b By offering to him there will be no sorrows; givers [to such a recipient] indeed (*hi*) cannot become born [in the rebirths known]

---

688 Sriraman SHARMA, by way of *electronic communication*, dated 5th of December, 2010, clarified the following: *āhitāgni* is he who has installed the Vedic fires, viz. Gārhapatya, Āhavanīya and Dakṣiṇāgni. The moment he installs these fires he will have the right to perform *agnihotra*. He who installs these Vedic fires but cannot continue to sacrifice in them for some reason, such as old age or being widowed, is only *āhitāgni*. An *agnihotrī*, as commonly known, is he who maintains the sacrificial fires by performing sacrifice in them twice a day, morning and evening (e.g. *Aitareya Brāhmaṇa* 5.31:4).

689 The *Śivadharmaśāstra* attests a hierarchy of recipients (7.69–71) that is somewhat similar to our passage here. For further treatment on this topic refer to p. 56, above.

690 Note a double *sandhi* with an elision of final *t*. The *Śivadharmasaṅgraha* (6.192) has rephrased the text by reading *tasmai dattaṃ bhaved dattaṃ* ('what is given to him is [truly] given') instead of *tasya dattaṃ bhave 'nantam* in order to avoid the problem. As for the sense, it could be that this is a hyperbolic expression, since even *svarga* is not eternal, or it could more likely be, as perhaps in earlier passages where *dāna* was said to be *akṣaya* (e.g. in 115 above), a statement to the effect that the pious act of giving will perdure until such time as it bears karmic fruit.

691 Although this word literally means 'protector', it is used here in the sense of *dātā* 'donor'.

692 The knower (*jñānin*) is understood as a Śiva-knower. The text further down (2.121) makes it clear that the intended meaning is a Śiva-knower (*śivajñānine*). For metrical reasons, it is impossible to have (*śivajñānine*) here.

The *Śivadharmasaṅgraha* (6.193) has tried to improve the text by reading *anyeṣāṃ koṭiguṇitaṃ dadyād ekaṃ tu jñānine* instead of *eṣāṃ lakṣaguṇān dadyād ekan dadyāt tu jñānine*. However, this changes the meaning: 'if he gives one [gift] to a [single] knower, he [effectively obtains the merit that he would obtain if he] gave ten million times [that gift] to others.'

as *naraka* and *preta* (*narakapretasambhavāḥ*),[693] [since they are] freed from sin (*vipāpāḥ*) and destined to go to heaven (*svargagāminaḥ*).[694]

2:121cd Therefore among all recipients the knower of Śiva [is certainly] the best of the best (*varo varaḥ*).

2:122 One who desires one's welfare should [always] offer to that [Śaiva] recipient; that [act of] offering will be indestructible, even if (*api*) what is offered is very little (*svalpam alpapi*).[695]

Thus is the second chapter, with regard to worldly duty in the *Niśvāsamukhatattvasaṃhitā*.

---

693 If we were to follow the *Śivadharmasaṅgraha* here, we would translate instead 'by offering to him there will be no sorrows arising from hells or pretas.' This would then simply refer to troubles in hells and troubles from not performing *śrāddha*-rites for deceased ancestors. (Cf. *Śivadharmasaṅgraha* 2.184cd ... *narakapretajair duḥkhais sattvānāṃ kliśyatāṃ bhṛśam.*) But such an interpretation would involve assuming an unlikely *aiśa* switch of gender: *°sambhavāḥ* would have to agree with *duḥkhāni.* Note, however, that the pair *naraka* and *preta* occur together elsewhere in relatively early literature as part of a list of possible rebirths (*yoni*, *gati*), e.g. *Abhidharmakośabhāṣya* at the beginning of the third *kośasthāna.* We therefore think it more likely that the text is referring to those rebirths.

694 Here too, it looks as though the redactor of the *Śivadharmasaṅgraha* (6.195) may have misunderstood the text, taking *vipāpa* to mean 'especially sinful', for he has apparently rephrased this line as follows: *pāpakarmā yadā kaścid dātuṃ notsahate manaḥ*, 'When someone is an evildoer, [his] mind is incapable of giving [to such a recipient].' Such a misunderstanding is perhaps caused by the immediately preceding one.

695 Prof. ISAACSON has presented the possibility that *svalpam alpapi* may be a corruption for (*svalpam aṇv api*), which is what K also has. We decided keep *svalpam alpapi* on the basis of the reading of manuscripts, N and W. We take *alp* as *metri causa* substitution for *alpam.*

CHAPTER III

[1.7 Sacred sites]

Goddess spoke:

3:1 You have taught the merit of donation (*dānadharmaḥ*), [now] teach (*vada*) me the merit of pilgrimage. What will be[696] the virtuous fruit from bathing in each pilgrimage site? (1)

[1.7.1 Rivers]

God spoke:

3:2–7 [1] Gaṅgā,[697] [2] Sarasvatī, [3] Puṇyā, [4] Yamunā, [5] Gomatī, [6] Carmilā,[698] [7] Candrabhāgā, [8] Sarayu, [9] Gaṇḍakī, [10] Jambukā, [11] Śatadrū, [12] Kālikā, [13] Suprabhā, [14] Vitastī, [15] Vipāśā, [15] Narmadā, [16] Punaḥpunā, [17] Godāvarī, [18] Mahāvarttā, [19] Śarkarāvarttā, [20] Arjunī (*śarkarāvarttamarjunī*),[699] [21] Kāverī, [22] Kauśikī, and [23] Tṛtīyā, [24] Mahānadī,,[700] [25] Viṭaṅkā, [26] Pratikūlā, [27] Somanandā, [28] Viśrutā,[701] [29] Karatoyā, [30]

---

696 The text somewhat unexpectedly presents us with two verbs, *syāt* and *bhaviṣyati*. The *Śivadharmasaṅgraha* (7.1) mends this awkwardness by replacing the second verb with *sureśvara* ('o Lord of the gods').

697 Here follows a list of rivers, many of which we are unable to identify. Only few southern rivers are contained in the list: Kāverī, Vasiṣṭhā and Tāmrā. The remainder of the identified rivers run their course in the northern or central part of India. The selection of rivers in this list might suggest that the redactor was more familiar with northern geography than with its southern counterpart, particularly if the list comprises an innovation of the *Niśvāsamukha*. As such lists of rivers are found in a vast range of Indian texts, the actual geographical details are hard to determine for certain.

698 This name of the river occurs also in *Guhyasūtra* 1.31, where it is given the name of 'Carmiṇī'. The name of this river is scarcely attested to in other sources.

699 This is the reading attested to in the *Śivadharmasaṅgraha* (7.4). Note that *śarkarāvarttamarjunī* is an *aiśa* formation with a hiatus breaker *m* in between two words: *śarkarāvartā* and *arjunī*.

700 Alternatively, the Sanskrit original in this way, we might take *mahānadī* as an adjective of *tṛtīyā* and in that case our translation would be [23] 'Tṛtīyā, a great river ...' Let it be noted, at this juncture, that we are aware of two rivers known by the name of 'Mahānadī', one flowing through in Gayā (in modern-day Bihar) as well as in Orissa (DEY 1927: 117); this would buttress our present translation.

701 We might otherwise understand *viśrutā* as an adjective of *somanandā*.

Vetravatī, [31] Reṇukā, [32] Veṇukā, [33] Ātreyagaṅgā, [34] Vaitaraṇī, [35] Karmārī, [36] Hlādanī, [37] Plāvanī, [38] Savarṇā, [39] Kalmāṣā, [40] Sraṃsinī, [41] Śubhā,[702] [42] Vasiṣṭhā, [43] Vipāpā, [44] Sindhuvatī, [45] Aruṇī (*sindhuvatyāruṇī*),[703] [46] Tāmrā, [47] Trisandhyā and [one] known [as] the supreme [48] Mandākinī.[704]

3:8–9 [As also are] [49] Tailakośī, [50] Pārā, [51] Dundubhī, [52] Nalinī, [53] Nīlagaṅgā, [54] Godhā, [55] Pūrṇacandrā and [56] Śaśiprabhā; if someone having first worshipped [his] ancestors and the gods and fasted (*upavāsarataḥ*) bathes in [these] best of rivers,[705] he will be freed from sin.

3:10 This river is of pure water [that] has come from the embodiment of Śiva; whoever bathes [in these waters] (*yaiḥ*) will be liberated; o you who have water as your form! Let there be veneration to you.[706]

3:11 Calling this mantra to mind (*ayaṃ mantram anusmṛtya*)[707] one should bathe in a river (*nadyavagāhanam*); [as a result of doing so] he becomes freed from all sins and goes (*yayau*)[708] to heaven when he abandons his body.

3:12a–13b Having bathed in the Śoṇa [river], Puṣkara [lake?] or Lohitya [river] (*śoṇapuṣkaralohitye*),[709] in [lake] Mānasa, in the place the In-

---

702 We have not been able to trace the following as attested names for rivers: *kamāṣā*, *sraṃsinī*, and *śubhā*. It appears possible that *śubhā* might correctly be understood as an adjective of *śraṃsinī*.

703 We assume this to be an *aiśa* compound where an instrumental singular is treated as a nominative singular: the first member of this would normally be *sindhuvatī* (cf. the form of the word *śaṣkulyāmodakāni* in 1.159).

704 We assume that *mandākinyaḥ* is intended as a singular, and likely is another name.

705 *saridvarām* is presumably a collective feminine accusative singular for locative plural.

706 The text already stated at an earlier juncture (1.32–39), that water is one of the 'eight forms of Śiva'. Note that the verse as a whole comprises a mantra that the practitioner is expected to recite whilst bathing in the aforementioned rivers. Prof. Peter BISSCHOP, during his 2008 presentation at the EFEO at Pondicherry, noted a parallel of this mantra in the *Himavatkhaṇḍa* 88.39 of the *Skandapurāṇa*, although that rendition differs slightly from the representation in our text.

707 As indicated by the correction *imaṃ mantram* in the *Śivadharmasaṅgraha* (7.11), this segment should be understood as an accusative phrase.

708 Note the irregular use of the past perfect form *yayau* which here is employed to denote a future meaning.

709 The river *Lohitya* is more commonly known as *Brahmaputra*.

dus meets the ocean (*sindhusāgare*)[710] or in Brahmāvartta,[711] or Kardamāla[712] or in the salty oceanocean, one [becomes] free from all sins [and] he should [then] worship one's ancestors and the gods.

3:13c–14 It is always (*nityam*) taught (*bhavet*) [that] fire is the womb [and it is] taught [that] Viṣṇu is the seminal fluid; one should know[713] Brahmā to be the father and water is to be known to be a form of Rudra.[714] If someone bathes reciting those[715] [names], he will obtain the highest sphere of rebirth.

3:15a–16b If someone, with desire or without desire, abandons (*samutsṛjya*) his body in female or male rivers (*nadīnadeṣu*), he, his soul pure, will go [directly] to heaven (*svargalokam*) from this world (*iha*).[716] Once he falls from heaven he will be reborn in an excellent family.

---

710 We have understood *sindhusāgare* to mean *sindhusāgarasaṃgame*. Both forms are attested in the *Purāṇas* (e.g. sections 73.8 and 73.71 in the *Skandapurāṇa*). As for the mythological significance of the locality, it is connected to Śaṅkukarṇa, one of Śiva's Gaṇas. According to lore, this is the place where Śiva performed *tapas* while guarded by his Gaṇa, Śaṅkukarṇa. That being the case, we take the phrase *sindhusāgare* as indicative of a particular location where Sindhu supposedly met the ocean (Bisschop 2006: 220). The reader is also referred here to BAKKER (2014: 2, 118, 151 and 173). For the *māhātmya* of Śaṅkukarṇa, see *Skandapurāṇa*, chapter 73.

711 In all likelihood, 'Brahmāvartta' here does not refer to the region in Northern India as identified by the *Manusmṛti* (2.17); instead, it appears to be a place which is imbued with a (religio-cultural) connection to Brahmā. BAKKER (2014: 183–184) assumes that this place, in the *Skandapurāṇa*, could correspond to "the early historical mount at Shyampur Garhi, a small tributary of the Ganges" nearby Haridvāra. This suggests that this is a pilgrimage site, which fits the context of our text. BAKKER (2014: 168) also mentions that the *Mahābhārata* identifies the same place as Kurukṣetra, which clearly identifies it as a pilgrimage site.

712 This is a rare toponym denoting a place located in (modern-day) Gujarāt. The reader is referred to our introduction (p. 27) for the discussion of this locality. The last three terms are names of territories and do not refer to bodies of water, although, in all likelihood, these places were adjacent to, or contained, important bodies of water (e.g. a river, a water-tank, the ocean etc.).

713 If correctly transmitted, this rendition is in an instance of *vindyāt* ('one should find') being used in the sense of 'one should know'.

714 Note that the sentence structure changes in 14a. The *Śivadharmasaṅgraha* (7.13cd) has fused *Niśvāsamukha* 3.13c–14b into one line in the following manner: *agnir yonir viṣṇu retā brahmaṇaḥ pitā rudramūrtir āpaḥ*.

715 Note that N and W give the reading *etān utsmṛtya*, which we believe to be a corruption of *etānusmṛtya*, a contraction of *etān anusmṛtya* implemented on metrical grounds, and attested to in *Śivadharmasaṅgraha* (7.14). K has also tried to correct the text by reading *etān saṃsmṛtya*.

716 We understand *iha* to mean *itaḥ*, it is not clarified, however, whether the person who

3:16c–18 He who always[717] remembers [a certain] pilgrimage site and desires to die (*maraṇaṃ cābhikāṃkṣate*) [there][718] [and] who [therefore] enters the fire [there],[719] following the prescribed injunction (*niyame sthitaḥ*), [that] man (*mānavaḥ*) will obtain the world of Rudra and rejoice [there] with him. Once he falls from the world of Rudra, he will be reborn (*āpnuyāt*) in the world of Fire; having enjoyed the delights of the Fire-world (*vahnimayān bhogān*),[720] he will be reborn as a king (*pṛthivīpatiḥ*).[721]

[1.7.2 The *pañcāṣṭakas*]

3:19–25 [1] Amareśa,[722]

---

commits suicide in these bodies of water transmigrates to heaven. The *Śivadharmasaṅgraha* (7.15) sidesteps the problem presented by *iha* by giving *somalokam iyān naraḥ*, changing the destination the deceased person transmigrates to.

717 *Ex conj.*; *nityam* is reconstructed from the *Śivadharmasaṅgraha* (7.17).

718 The *Śivadharmasaṅgraha* (7.17) tries to clarify the text simply by offering the reading *maranaṃ cātra kāṃkṣate* instead of *maraṇaṃ cābhikāṃkṣate*.

719 An alternative interpretation of his verse would be: 'He who alway remembers [a certain] pilgrimage site and desires to die there [and] who [therefore] enters the fire [anywhere he wishes to do so]...'. These are tentative translations which assume that the text is correctly transmitted here. It is possible, however, that a corruption has taken place. Note that in the *Śivadharmasaṅgraha*, verses 17 and 18 are missing, hence no reference is made to *agnipraveśa*. As a result, the list of *tīrthas*, located directly after the mention of dying in a *tīrtha* (16cd), seamlessly connects with the ensuing text of the *Śivadharmasaṅgraha*. Perhaps, therefore, verses 17 and 18 are an interpolation inserted after the redaction of the *Śivadharmasaṅgraha*. It is also possible that 17 and 18 are original elements of the text and that 16cd initially was situated before these two verses. In that case, 16cd might have been (mistakenly) been resituated after these two verses, in the course of transmission.

720 *Ex conj.*

721 It is to be noted that when a devotee enters a fire in order to commit auto-incineration while calling to mind a certain *tīrtha*—in this case a body of water—he initially transmigrates to the world of Rudra, water being one of the 'forms of Rudra/Śiva'. Once he falls from that world, he is reborn in 'the world of fire'. Śiva. Then the merit of entering fire causes him to stay for a certain time-span in the world of fire. For the attainment of the world of fire by 'abandoning one's body' in the fire see *Mahābhārata* 13.130:51.

722 Here begins a list of 40 worlds, grouped into five ogdoads, known as the *pañcāṣṭaka*. The list of five ogdoads (*pañcāṣṭaka*) features in the *Niśvāsamukha* in the context of places sacred to Śaivas. Some of these places are to be found in the *Mahābhārata* (see BISSCHOP, 2006: 19–22), where they are not yet rebranded as Śaivite. This testifies to the fact that not all of the places named in the list of *pañcāṣṭaka* were originally Śaiva pilgrimage sites. Although the list of *pañcāṣṭaka* does not feature in the *Skandapurāṇa*, it nevertheless very likely was integrated at a rather early stage in

[2] Prabhāsa,[723] [3] Naimiṣa, [4] Puṣkara, [5] ,[724] [6] Diṇḍimuṇḍi, [7] Bhārabhūti,[725] [8] Lākuli, [9] Hariścandra is very secret, [10] Madhyamakeśvara is [also] secret, [11] Śrīparvata is [then] taught, and beyond that [12] Jalpeśvara and [13] Amrātikeśvara,[726] and also [14] Mahākala and [15] Kedāra are excellent secret [pilgrimages], and so is [16] Mahābhairava; [17] Gayā, [18] Kurukṣetra, [19] Nakhala, [20] Kanakhala, [21] Vimala, [22] Aṭṭahāsa, [23] Māhendra and [24] Bhīma [as] the eighth [of that group of eight], [25] Vastrāpada,[727] [26] Rudrakoṭi, [27] Avimukta, [28] Mahābala,[728] [29] Gokarṇa, [30] Bhadrakarṇa, [31] Svarṇākṣa and [32] Sthāṇu [as] the eighth [of that group of eight]; [33] Chagalaṇḍa, [34] Dviraṇḍa, [35] Mākoṭa, [36] Maṇḍaleśvara, [37] Kālañjara[729] is taught [next] [38] Devadāru, [39] Śaṅkukarṇa and

---

the development of Śaiva literature and recast, in time, in the mould of five groups of eight sites. Clearly, the Śaivas, incorporated already existing sites, projecting upon them a Śaiva identity. It is vital to note that the list of the five *aṣṭakas*, as they feature in the *Niśvāsamukha*, are not framed within the Śaiva cosmology explicitly: this fact supports the argument of GOODALL (2004: 15, fn.617) that the five ogdoads are an earlier, not exclusively tantric, conceptual nexus. For further details, consult GOODALL (2004: 315), BISSCHOP, (2006: 27–37), and TAK2 s.v. *guhyāṣṭaka*. See also our introduction p. 72.

723 The *Guhyasūtra* (3.112) reads *prahāsañ ca* instead.

724 The *Guhyasūtra* (3.113) reads *āṣāḍhin* in stead of *āṣāḍha*.

725 *Ex conj.*, we have adopted the reading *bhārabhūtiñ ca* from the *Śivadharmasaṅgraha* (7.18).

726 The *Guhyasūtra* (7:115), which is our conjecture, reads *āmbrātikeśvara*. Our source there read: *ambrā* --- N; *amdhrā* ⊔ K and *ambrātike* ⊔ W.

727 The original toponym of this place, in all likelihood, is Bhastrāpada (BISSCHOP 2006: 31). In contrast, the variant given in *Guhyasūtra* (7.118) is *bhadrāpada*.

728 *Ex conj.* The adopted reading is based on the partially lacunose textual variant in W, *mahāba....* The reading in W is further substantiated by the *Guhyasūtra* (7.117). In many an other Śaiva source, we encounter 'Mahālaya' at the respective juncture—this is the case in the *Śivadharmaśāstra*, the first and earliest book of the *Śivadharma*-corpus. It is also the case in the *Svacchandatantra* (10.887), which borrows extensively from the *Niśvāsa*. Conversely, the *Niśvāsa* records 'Mahābala', for which reason we are not able to ascertain which of these two variants might have been the (more) original reading. A tangent to pursue might be given by BISSCHOP (2006: 208), who noted that the term 'Mahābala' occurs in the *Kāravaṇamāhātmya*, where it features as one of the four names Śiva employed in reference to four *yugas*.

One might have adopted the reading *mahālayam* from the *Śivadharmasaṅgraha* (7.22). After all, the *Skandapurāṇa* presents it as the primary abode of Śiva, which is otherwise known as Rudranātha, Rudrālaya or Rudramahālaya (See BISSCHOP 2006: 177–179).

729 'Kālañjara' rarely occurs outside the list of *pañcāṣṭaka*. It is, however, for example, attested to in the *upodghāta* to the *Rauravasūtrasaṅgraha*, an early Śaiva work.

after that [40] Thaleśvara.[730] By bathing, seeing or performing worship there one becomes free from all sins.

3:26 Those who die in these places go [up], penetrating the [shell of the] egg of Brahmā (*brahmāṇḍam*), to [the respective world in] this divine set of five groups of eight [worlds bearing the same names as the pilgrimage sites], upon reaching which (*yaṃ gatvā*)[731] he will not be reborn [in this world(?)].

3:27 He who stands in Mahāpralaya (*mahāpralayasthāyī*)[732] [is] the creator and agent of grace; from merely (*eva*) seeing [his footprint (*padam*)] in [the sacred site of] Mahālaya, people will attain (*gacchante*)[733] [in the next life] the divine state (*padam*).

3:28a–29a Also by drinking the water of Kedāra one certainly obtains the realm of rebirth (*gatim*) [of attaining] the five sets of eight [i.e. of all forty *bhuvanas*] (*pañcāṣṭamīm*). As for those who possess (*saṃyutāḥ*) the Vidyā-mantra (*vidyayā*)[734] and who drink [this] pure water [of Kedāra], they will obtain (*yānti*) union with Śiva.[735]

---

730 Note that *thaleśvara* is meant for *sthaleśvara*, which is the variant given in the *Guhyasūtra* (7.121).

731 *Ex conj.*; *yaṃ gatvā* is the reading of the *Śivadharmasaṅgraha* (7.24). This portion of the text is lost in our MS of the *Niśvāsamukha*. These five groups of eight sites are divine abodes which correspond to correlated earthly pilgrimage places; the former are both superior to, and located above, the egg of Brahmā. These divine abodes are equated with the permanent state of liberation [from rebirth]. Note that the divine *pañcāṣṭakas* are not presented as part of the cosmology of the *Śivadharmaśāstra* (12.119). The *Śivadharmaśāstra* presents all of the *pañcāṣṭakas* as portals to the world of Rudra (ibid.). The *Niśvāsamukha*'s listing of *pañcāṣṭakas* hints at a a rudimentary cosmological conception and is hence somewhat more complex—and hence *probably* later than—the list displayed in the *Śivadharmaśāstra*, which lacks such a feature. Consult BISSCHOP (2006: 28, fn. 71.)

732 This is perhaps meant to be understood in two ways: 'He who remains [even] in a period of total resorption [of the universe]' and 'He who stands in [the sacred site called] Mahā(pra)laya'.

733 Mahālaya is one of the foremost sacred sites of the Śaivas since it is commonly presented as the place where Mahādeva planted his footprint (BISSCHOP 2006: 22, 177-179).

734 We assume that *vidyayā* refers to the ten-syllable *vidyāmantra* taught in chapter 16 of the *Guhyasūtra*, also referred to as Daśākṣaradeva. (For a summary of the legend, see TAK 3, s.v. *daśākṣara*). Alternatively, *vidyā* could simply mean, as Prof. BAKKER suggests, 'knowledge'. In this case our translation would be 'As for those who are furnished with knowledge ...'.

735 Kedāra is treated as special insofar as it is presented as being imbued with extraordinary features (3.28a–29b). It is to be noted that by dying in each site of the

3:29b–30 Men in all walks of life (*sarvāvasthā''pi mānavāḥ*),[736] by visiting (*dṛṣṭvā*) other secret (*guhyānyāny api*)[737] [places] of god will be freed from all sins; they will obtain the state of being Gaṇas if they die (*nidhanaṅ gatāḥ*) there. [Thus] the greatness of [the sacred sites associated with] Hara has been taught; now hear the greatness of [the sites associated with] Hari from me.

3:31–32 Hari always [resides] in Śālagrāma,[738] Mallakūpa,[739] Saukarava,[740] in Sannidhāna, Mathurā,[741]

---

pañcāṣṭaka one ascends, penetrating the shell of the egg of Brahmā and upon reaching the specific 'divine abode' in question, will not be reborn in this world again.

However, by merely partaking of the water of the sacred site of Kedāra, one can obtain the fruit of attaining the five sets of eight sacred places.

Moreover, if somebody endowed with *vidyā* drinks the water of Kedāra he obtains the union with Śiva, a state that appears loftier than taking one's abode amongst the divine sets of five or the divine abode of Kedāra. The text seems to draw a clear distinction between the reward obtained by an ordinary person and an initiate partaking of the water of Kedāra: in the absence of *vidyā*, an ordinary person does not obtain union with Śiva.

736 This is a tentative interpretation. Note that K reads *sarvāvasthāsu*, which might be the intended meaning, whereas the *Śivadharmasaṅgraha* (6.26) has perhaps tried to correct it by reading *sarvāvasthāś ca*, but this does not appear to further our understanding much.

737 This irregular usage has been supplanted in the *Śivadharmasaṅgraha* (7.27) It is not clear to us which sites are referred to in our text, or which site in the *Śivadharmasaṅgraha* is referred to by the term *guhyāyatanam*.

738 A famous *vaiṣṇava tīrtha*. *Mahābhārata* 3.821:6 speaks of this sacred place thus *tato gaccheta rājendra sthānaṃ nārāyaṇasya tu | sadā saṃnihito yatra harir vasati bhārata | śālagrāma iti khyāto viṣṇor adbhutakarmaṇaḥ | abhigamya trilokeśaṃ varadaṃ viṣṇum avyayam | aśvamedham avāpnoti viṣṇulokaṃ ca gacchati |*. Cf. also *Brahmāṇḍapurāṇa* 2.13:89, 2.25:66; *Brahmapurāṇa* 64.4, 65.89; *Viṣṇudharmottara* 36.15, 70.97; *Nāradapurāṇa* 1.4:50; *Matsyapurāṇa* 22.62; *Kūrmapurāṇa* 2.34:37; *Agnipurāṇa* 219.68, 305.5 380.1 etc. It is a well known fact that *śālagrāma* is also a kind of stone worshiped as a form of Viṣṇu. Here *śālagrāma* is not understood in the sense of pertaining to a form of Viṣṇu, but as a place name. KANE IV: 799 and DEY 1927: 174 mention that it is a sacred place near the shore of the Gaṇḍakī river.

739 As far as we can see, this place sacred to Viṣṇu is attested only in our text and in the *Śivadharmasaṅgraha* (7.41).

740 For this name cf. *Brahmapurāṇa* 228.149. In the same Purāṇa, this place is also called *Śūkarava* and identified as *rūpatīrtha*, see *Brahmapurāṇa* 228.145 *gaccha śūkaravoddeśaṃ rūpatīrtheti viśrutam | siddhiṃ yāsyasi viprendra tatas tvaṃ māṃ avāpsyasi ||* (cf. also the same Purāṇa 25.12). If this *tīrtha* is also known as *śūkaratīrtha* or *sukaratīrtha* then it is the place that KANE IV: 808 says is on the west bank of Gaṅgā between Bareli and Mathurā.

741 It is possible that this is the sacred area known as Saṃnihitā (see KANE IV.2: 801).

as well as in Śvetadvīpa;[742] having seen Viṣṇu [[...]][743] one will be freed from all sins; people deceased in these places will go to that highest abode (*paramaṃ padam*) of Viṣṇu.

3:33a–34b As for Brahmā, Skanda, Gaṇeśa (*brahmaskandagaṇeśasya*), the Lokapālas, the planets (*lokapālagraheṣu*), Devī, the Mothers and Yakṣas (*devyāmātarayakṣeṣu*), Piśācas, and snakes, Rākṣasas: devotees of these will obtain the realms of those (*tadgatim*)[744]

Alternatively, we could conjecture *sannidhāno* and take this, irregularly, as an adjective with the sense of *sannihita*, for which cf., e.g., *Parākhya* 2.25 and 14.61. In the latter case, we might translate: '...[Hari] is present in Mathurā'.

742 Since this place here is listed among localities sacred to Viṣṇu, context suggests the work is referring to an actual, historical place. Unfortunately we are not able to locate the place for lack of evidence. In myth, the region is well known and sacred to Viṣṇu. The *Bhāgavatapurāṇa* (8.4:18) mentions that this is one of the favourite places of Viṣṇu: *kṣīrodaṃ me priyaṃ dhāma śvetadvīpaṃ ca bhāsvaram*|. According to the *Mahābhārata* (12.323:23) it is situated to the north of Kṣīrodadhi where the devotees of Viṣṇu, after performing *tapas* there, attain union with their deity. This island may have been called Śvetadvīpa because the people there are white, resembling the moon (*Mahābhārata* 12.323:31) or the name may refer to the people there who are without *indriyas* i.e. pure. *Mahābhārata* 12.323:19 ff presents us with the description of the Śvetadvīpa as seen by sages Ekata, Dvīta and Trita.

We find references to this place in a wide range of Sanskrit texts: *Mahābhārata*, *Purāṇas*, Āyurveda, Kāvyas, Tantras etc. For instance, cf. *Kūrmapurāṇa* 1.47:39, 2.34:33; *Liṅgapurāṇa* 2.1:43 ff and 2.3:76; *Nāradapurāṇa* 1.62:38; *Vāmanapurāṇa* 34.57; *Kathāsaritsāgara* 11.69, 17.101 etc.; *Vāsavadattā* p. 35; *Bhāratamañjarī* 13.1195; *Īśānagurudevapaddhati* II. 36-35; *Bahmasaṃhitā* 5.6; *Laghubhāgavata* 1.2:41; *Devāmṛtapāñcarātra* 7.3; *Īśvarasaṃhitā* 1.29, 20.52 etc.; *Pādmasaṃhitā* (*jñānapāda*) 2.47; *Rasaratnasamuccaya* 3.2 ff etc.

743 The *Śivadharmasaṅgraha* (7.42) reads *taṃ dṛṣṭvā puruṣavaṭe viṣṇuṃ mucyeta kilbiṣaiḥ*, which suggests that there should be a place called *Puruṣavaṭa*, for which we find no other testimony. We could conjecture something like *pañcāvaṭe*, assuming an irregular lengthening of the vowel in the middle of a compound; after all, *ā* is clearly visible in the manuscript. We know that 'Pañcavaṭī' is the name of the forest where Rāma dwelt during his time in exile (see *Rāmāyaṇa* 3.14:11). This could be a secret place for Vaiṣṇavas, which is what the context demands. The problem is that the our text does not display Pañcāvaṭī, rather it gives Pañcāvaṭa, which is a Śaiva pilgrimage site according to the *Mahābhārata* (3.81:141). We could also consider conjecturing *bhadrāvaṭe* (*Mahābhārata* 3.8:69) or *muñjāvaṭe* (*Mahābhārata* 3.81:18), yet these places are imbued with Śaiva associations, and do not point to any overt conceptual nexi of the Vaiṣṇavas. If we were to accept one of these readings, our translation would be 'having seen Viṣṇu in [the place called] *pañcavaṭa*/ *bhadravaṭe*/ *mundravaṭe* one will be freed'...

744 This part of the text contains a number of problems. Firstly, that the text appears to be incomplete or and structurally misaligned. Secondly, the locative and genitive cases are used interchangeably. Thirdly, members of a compound are used in inflected

by mantra-recitation, oblation into fire and worship (*japahomādya-pūjanaiḥ*).[745]

3:34c–35 If a bad person who has accrued bad *karman* (*pāpasaṃyutaḥ*) undertakes a fast until death (*anāśakaṃ yaḥ kurute*), he too (*ca*), freed from all sins, will go to the world of Viṣṇu. Once he falls from the world of Viṣṇu, he will be reborn as a learned Brāhmin.

[1.8 Observance of fasts]

3:36 By applying the same procedure he will further practice the same [fasting].[746] Thus I have told you all [that]; now listen to the process of fasting.

3:37a–38b If someone observes (*kuryāt*) fasting for one night every month (*māse māse*) after consuming only the five products of the cow having first purified himself—[this] would be Sāntapana.[747] By observing [this

forms: *devyā* for *devī* and *mātara* for *mātṛ*, i.e. the seven (or sometimes eight) mother-goddesses.

745 This is an odd compound in that it has *ādya* in the middle, standing for *ādi*. This oddity has been removed in the *Śivadharmasaṅgraha* (7.44) by reading *japa-homārcanādibhiḥ*.

746 We are unfortunately not sure that we fully grasped the meaning of this line; we believe it may refer to the notion that pious acts in one rebirth tend to lead to further pious acts in subsequent rebirths. Once again, it is worth noting that this return to the theme of Viṣṇuloka has the air of an insertion. Moreover, it is not contained in the *Śivadharmasaṅgraha*, which may mean that it was interpolated here in a version of our text which postdates the version on which the *Śivadharmasaṅgraha* was based. Note that the awkwardness we feel in interpreting this verse may partly stem from the fact that it has been indiscriminately adapted from a well-known cliché about good acts committed lead, in a sort of 'virtuous cycle', to further good acts in later rebirths. A similar half-verse appears quoted in the *Bhāmatī* on *Brahmasūtra-śāṅkarabhāṣya* 2.1:24, p. 482 as:

janmajanma yad abhyastaṃ dānam adhyayanaṃ tapaḥ |
tenaivābhyāsayogena tac caivābhyasate punaḥ |

Cf. also *Viṣṇudharmottara* chapter 98.27. There is also a possibility that some portion of the text has been lost during the process of transmission, and subsequently the redactor of the *Śivadharmasaṅgraha*, upon encountering an incomplete part of this passage, opted not to transmit the problematic section. Alternatively, it is possible that the opaque phrasing of this section led to its being left out by the redactor of the *Śivadharmasaṅgraha*.

747 This verse echoes *Manusmṛti* 11.213: *gomūtraṃ gomayaṃ kṣīraṃ dadhi sarpiḥ kuśo-dakam | ekarātropavāsaś ca kṛcchraṃ sāṃtapanaṃ smṛtam ||*. The commentators of

practice] (*kṛtvā*) for a year, one [becomes] pure and will be honoured in the world of Brahmā.

3:38c–39 Another Sāntapana [is defined as follows]: fasting for twelve days. By doing this [kind of Sāntapana], one will be freed from sins and will not be degraded from Brāhmin-hood.[748] By doing this twelve times a man will certainly obtain a good rebirth.

3:40a–41b Having subdued one's sense faculties, one should, for three days, eat [only] a mouthful and one should fast for three nights. [This kind of religious observance is called] Atikṛccha, for 'purification'.[749] If someone observes (*kuryāt*) [the Atikṛcchra] every fortnight (*pratipakṣaṃ*), he will partake of the fruit of heaven.

3:41c–42 One should drink hot water, hot milk and hot ghee, each for three days, and one should bathe three times a day: [this religious observance is called hot-and-arduous (*taptakṛcchra*)].[750] [In this way] a pure-souled Brāhmin who is devoid of all sin will go to the realm of heaven; [and a Brāhmin who is] a sinner will be purified [from sin].

3:43–44 One should increase [one's food] by a mouthful [a day in the days of] the bright fortnight and should decrease it [in the days] of the dark fortnight [by a mouthful a day] and should bathe three times a day; one should observe this observance for a month in accordance with the change of the moon (*candravṛddhyā*). This is the excellent lunar-observance (*cāndrāyaṇa*), which removes all sins.[751] A sinner will be

---

the *Manusmṛti* vary over the point how this observance is to be practiced; taking two days, consuming the five products of the cow and fasting the other day or consuming the products each for six days and fasting on the seventh. See OLIVELLE's note to the translation of verse 11.213 (2005: 346).

748 According to the *Manusmṛti* this observance is called *parāka*, one of the *sāntapana/kṛcchra* observances. *Manusmṛti* 11.215 presents it as follows: *yatātmano 'pramattasya dvādaśāham abhojanam | parāko nāma kṛcchro 'yaṃ sarvapāpāpanodanaḥ* ||.

749 Alternatively *viśodhane* can be understood in its vocative sense. In this case our translation would be '[This kind of religious observance is called] *atikṛcchra*, [and is especially observed] o pure lady (*viśodhane*)'. Here there is a rather closer verbal echo of Manu, for which one can consult the apparatus.

750 The *taptakṛcchra* as recorded in the *Niśvāsamukha* is slightly different from its appearance in the *Manusmṛti*. The *Manusmṛti* (11.215) records it as *taptakṛcchraṃ caran vipro jalakṣīraghṛtānilān | pratitryahaṃ pibed uṣṇān sakṛtsnāyī samāhitaḥ* ||. 'A Brāhmin should drink hot water, hot milk, hot ghee, and hot air, each for three days and bathe once [a day so as] attentively to observe (*caran*) [the religious practice called] hot-and-arduous (*taptakṛcchra*).'

751 This has the echo of *Manusmṛti* 11.217, for which one can consult the apparatus.

freed from sin [by performing it], and one who has not committed sin will go to heaven.

3:45a–46b One should eat eight rice-lumps at each noon from the sacrificial oblation (*haviṣyeṇa samāyuktān*).[752] By [this religious observance which is called] Yaticāndrāyaṇa one will be freed from all crimes (*sarvapātakaiḥ*); [but] if he is sinless, he will go to heaven.

3:46c–48c A wise man should eat four lumps of rice in the forenoon, and again he should [eat] four lumps of rice after the setting of the sun; this observance which, [is called] Śiśucāndrāyaṇa,[753] destroys [the demerit accrued from] minor transgressions. By observing it for a month (*māsenaikena*)[754] one becomes pure-souled; if someone who is [already] free of sin performs it for three nights, he will go to the realm of heaven.[755]

3:48d–50b Someone who remains constantly (*sarvakālam*) strict in his observance[756] will be freed from all sins by one hundred complete repetitions of it. If someone observes it for a thousand nights,[757] together with mantra-recitation, he will be freed from the great sins.[758] If he is sinless, he will go to heaven and, once he falls [from there], he will be reborn as (*bhavet*) a rich man.

3:50c–51b If someone fasts intermediated by a day [viz. every other day] for twelve years, he will be freed from the great sins; [if he is] a pure soul, he will obtain heaven.

3:51c–52b If somebody [free from sin] fasts for a fortnight [every year][759] (*pakṣopavāsaṃ*) for twelve years, he will attain the realm of heaven; as for a sinner, he will be freed from sin.

---

752 Once again, we have a close verbal echo of the *Manusmṛti* (11.219), for which one could consult the apparatus the apparatus.

753 This also has the echo of the *Manusmṛti* (11.220) for which see the apparatus.

754 *Ex conj.*, this is the reading of the *Śivadharmasaṅgraha* (7.58).

755 The division of the syntactic units here is quite uncertain. Very different statements could be read in the text by applying different textual segmentation through alternative punctuation.

756 *Ex conj.*, this is the reading of the *Śivadharmasaṅgraha* (7.58).

757 *Ex conj.*

758 *Ex conj.*

759 For this suppletion, see 52c below. Alternatively we might conjecture that the intended sense is that one should fast during alternate fortnights; but it might then be difficult to remain alive for 12 years.

3:52c–53 If somebody, having his senses controlled,[760] fasts for one month every year, that man will obtain an excellent realm of rebirth (*gatim uttamāṃ vrajet*) in [this] world; he will be purified from the great sin and he will be [reborn as] a rich man.[761]

3:54 He who eats only one meal [a day] will be reborn as a rich man; if an excellent man (*narottamaḥ*) eats a meal [only] in the evening for a lifetime, that excellent man will be reborn as someone rich in money and grains.

3:55 If someone [being] in a religious observance (*vrate*)[762] eats unsolicited food for a lifetime, he will become a god when he dies (*mṛtaḥ*);[763] [if someone is] sinful (*pātakī*), he will be freed from sin.

3:56 One should not consume intoxicating drink and meat, this is the most excellent observance: whoever always remains thus will obtain an excellent realm of rebirth.

3:57 If someone practises a difficult observance [called] celibacy, together with [his] spouse, he will obtain supernatural power here and hereafter, and he will obtain an excellent realm of rebirth.[764]

---

760 *Ex conj.*, basically this is the reading of the *Śivadharmasaṅgraha* (7.62).

761 The reading *pūjayet* in the *Śivadharmasaṅgraha* (7.63) is perhaps a corruption of *pūjyate*: 'he will also be revered [as] a rich man'.

762 *Ex conj.*, *vrate naraḥ* is the reading of the *Śivadharmasaṅgraha* (7.65); the text is not transmitted in other manuscripts due to lacunose transmission.

763 *Ex conj.*, here N reads --- *to*, and this is the basis for our emendation, whereas K and W are silent; but the *Śivadharmasaṅgraha* (7.66) reads *mṛte*, which, though grammatically wrong, might also be a possible reading. It seems that the practice of eating unsolicited food is somehow related to ascetic behaviour. It is, however, as seen in this text, also meant for householders (see, for example, the *Dharmasūtra* of Āpastambha 1.9.27:7 and *Manusmṛti* 4.5). This observance is sometime called *ayācitavrata* 'the observance of [eating] unsolicited [food]' (see the *Dharmasūtra* of Vasiṣṭha 21.20).

764 Although it is not mentioned when exactly someone is supposed to start the observance of celibacy with his wife, most probably it is after having offspring. The *Śivadharmasaṅgraha* (7.69c) reads *brahmacaryaṃ vrataṃ kaṣṭaṃ*, where we have to understand *vrataṃ* as in apposition to *brahmacaryaṃ*, instead of *brahmacaryavrataṃ kaṣṭaṃ* (37a). Further, the *Śivadharmasaṅgraha* (7.70ab) reads quite differently: *ihaiva mantrāḥ siddhyante gatiṃ vrajati cottamāṃ*. 'Mantras will work for him in this world and he will obtain an excellent rebirth'.

3:58 If somebody gives up the wealth that he has,[765] he will obtain a great reward,[766] and that [reward] will be without end.

3:59 Fish, meat, any spirituous liquor (*surā*) or spirituous liquor distilled from molasses (*sīdhu*) are considered to be the food of Rākṣasas; [767] these should not be offered to a Brāhmin by a noble man who desires [good] realm of rebirth.[768]

[1.9 Worship of different divinities]

Goddess spoke:

3:60 By resorting to which god will fasting bear great fruit? And how should [the god] be worshipped? Tell [me this] by your grace.

God spoke:

3:61–63 If somebody fasts and worships Brahmā[769] on the first day of both lunar fortnights for a year using the mantra *brahmaṇe namaḥ*[770] with fragrance, flowers, and incense, together with *bhakṣya* and *bhojya* (*bhakṣyabhojyasamanvitaiḥ*),[771] he will obtain the fruit of sacrifices [namely]: Aśvamedha (horse sacrifice), Rājasūya, Sauvarṇa and

765 See *Niśvāsamukha* 1.55 for a similar expression. Note that *kuruteti* is perhaps to be seen as an *aiśa sandhi* for *kurute iti*, but the resulting form has the sense of *kurute*; the *Śivadharmasaṅgraha* (7.70) reads *kurute tu yaḥ* to obviate the problem.

766 Note that the text does not describe the great reward.

767 The *Mahābhārata* (9.42:21–22), however, gives the list of *rākṣasānna* as follows:

kṣutakīṭāvapannaṃ ca yac cocchiṣṭāśitaṃ bhavet |
keśāvapannam ādhūtam ārugṇam api yad bhavet |
śvabhiḥ saṃspṛṣṭam annaṃ ca bhāgo 'sau rakṣasām iha ||
tasmāj jñātvā sadā vidvān etāny annāni varjayet |
rākṣasānnam asau bhuṅkte yo bhuṅkte hy annam īdṛśam ||

768 Although the meaning is clear, the construction of *pāda* 59cd is ambiguous. We understand the locative *brāhmaṇe* to stand for the dative *brāhmaṇāya* and *gatim icchan mahātmanām* as *gatiṃ icchatā mahātmanā*. The *Śivadharmasaṅgraha* (7.72) rephrases the first part to read: *tac chāmbhavena moktavyaṃ*, which may mean 'this [type of food] should be given up (*moktavyaṃ*) by a Śaiva devotee'; yet the more problematic *pāda* appears not to have been altered.

769 The *Śivadharmasaṅgraha* (8.2) reads *brahmāṇaṃ pūjayen naraḥ* instead of *brahmāṇaṃ pūjayīta yaḥ* to obviate the problem of having an *aiśa ātmanepada* optative form.

770 The reading *brāhmaṇe namo mantreṇa* is a conjecture based on *Śivadharmasaṅgraha* (8.2). Note that it is not metrical and that it omits a quotative *iti*. We might instead conjecture *brāhmaṇe-nama-mantreṇa*, treating it as a sort of compound.

771 *Ex conj.*; perhaps N's reading, *bhakṣyabhojyasamanvitaiḥ*, could be defended.

Gavāmaya, along with seven Somasaṃsthas[772] together with the Naramedha.

3:64–66 If someone of concentrated mind (*yuktātmā*) worships Brahmā, of infinite splendour, for a year with these names: [1] Brahmā, [2] Svayambhū, [3] Viriñci,[773] [4] Padmayoni, [5] Prajāpati, [6] Caturmukha, [7] Padmahasta, [8] He who is the single syllable Om (*om ity ekākṣaraḥ*), [9] Caturvedadhara, [10] Sraṣṭṛ, [11] Gīrvāṇa and [12] Parameṣṭhin,[774] he will be honoured in heaven; he who does so for a lifetime goes to the world of Brahmā.

3:67–69 If someone worships the Fire-god and pleases him, with nothing other than (*eva*) ghee, on the second day of both halves of the month every month for one year, reciting (*kīrttitam*)[775] his excellent names: [1] Vaiśvānara, [2] Jātavedas, [3] Hutabhuk, [4] Havyavāhana, [5] Devavaktra, [6] Sarvabhakṣa, [7] Ghṛṇin, [8] Jagadāhaka,[776] [9] Vibhāvasuand [10] Saptajihva,[777] he will be pure [and without sin]; [if he does so] for a lifetime, he will [obtain] the world of fire.[778]

3:70–71 If he should worship Yakṣa[779] on the third day in both halves of

[772] The *Dharmasūtra* of Gautama(9.21) mentions the seven Soma sacrifices as: *agniṣṭomo 'tyagniṣṭoma ukthyaḥ ṣoḍaśī vājapeyo 'tirātro 'ptoryāma iti sapta somasaṃsthāḥ.* The same list is found in the *Viṣṇudharmottara* 2.95: 14–16, *Sarvajñānottara* 10.48–49, *Niśvāsakārikā* (for example, T. 150, pp. 190) and *Svacchandatantra* 10.403–4.

[773] *Ex conj.*; the readings of 64ab are basically those of the *Śivadharmasaṅgraha* (8.5).

[774] Note that *parameṣṭhinaḥ* is used as a nominative singular *parameṣṭhī.* The *Śivadharmasaṅgraha* (8.5–6) appears to have rearranged the order of the names to avoid the problem.

[775] We have understood this as present participial *kīrtayan*, but we could also take it as a description: 'who is well known by these names'.

[776] A *metri causa* irregular form for *jagaddāhaka.*

[777] Strictly speaking, we expect twelve names of fire, since one is supposed to worship the fire-god for a year under different names (see 69 below). Even if we count Agni (mentioned 67a) we will have eleven names. We could arrive at twelve names by counting Varanāmā, 'he who has excellent names' as a name of Agni. We are not sure whether or not it is warranted to assume so. The *Śivadharmasaṅgraha* (8.8–10) as well mentions the same list of the names of Agni. In this list of names we have nominative and accusative forms of the neuter and masculine singular used indiscriminately, as though all such forms belonged to the same case and gender.

[778] *yāvajjīvāgnilokatā* is presumably for *yāvajjīvenāgnilokatām.*

[779] Here Yakṣa appears to be a proper name of Kubera rather than an adjective defining a class of semi-divine beings. The names listed below (verses 72–73) clearly suggest that Yakṣa is meant to be Kubera. Kubera, as attested below (verse 72), is generally called the Lord of Yakṣas (see also *Rāmāyaṇa* 4.42:223), not simply Yakṣa. The *Śivadharmasaṅgraha* (8.11) reads *tṛtīye pūjayed yakṣaṃ* instead, changing the metrically incorrect text into metrically correct form.

the month, with fragrances, incense and food-offerings until a year is completed, Kubera, being thoroughly honoured with devotion, will give him wealth here [in this world itself] (*iha*).[780] If he does so for a lifetime, he will go to the world of Kubera (*dhanadasya*).

3:72–73 [He should worship Yakṣa] reciting (*parikīrttitaḥ*) [his names]: [1] Dhanada, [2] Yakṣapati, [3] Vitteśa, [4] Nidhipālaka, [5] Rākṣasādhipati,[781] [6] Piṅgalākṣa,[782] [7] Vimānaga,[783] [8] Rudrasakhā,[784] [9] Kubera, [10] Paulastyakulanandana, [11] Lokapāleśvara[785] and [12] Yakṣendra.

3:74 If someone worships Kubera (*yakṣam*) for a year with devotion, [he will be] rich in wealth and grain; [by doing so] for a lifetime [he will be] the king of Yakṣas.[786]

3:75–76 If someone should worship Gaṇeśa[787] on the fourth day in both halves of the month, with fragrances, flowers, plenty of *bhakṣya* and

---

780 Here, the *Śivadharmasaṅgraha* (8.12) has understood the text differently as *dhanan dāsyanti yakṣā hi dhanadādyāḥ supūjitāḥ* 'Kubera and others, being thoroughly honoured with devotion, will give him wealth'. The plurals are quite problematic and do not fit in either the following and preceding text.

781 The term *adhipati-* may have been used in the sense of king. Kubera is often said to be the lord of the demons, and ruled the city of Laṅkā, which is full of troops of demons (*Mahābhārata* 3.258:16). He obtained the city by the grace of Brahmā (*Mahābhārata* 3.258:15). This name of Kubera might indeed be suggesting that he ruled the city of demons.

782 According to *Rāmāyaṇa* 7.13:19–24, in his visit to god [i.e. Śiva] together with goddess Umā, Kubera was captivated by her unprecedented beauty. He looked at Umā with his right eye and by the power of Goddess that right eye turned tawny.

783 According to *Rāmāyaṇa* 5.7:10–11, Kubera obtains a flying chariot from Brahmā as a result of his (i.e. Kubera's) great *tapas*.

784 Kubera performs one hundred and eight year long *tapas* that Śiva had done previously. Thus, Śiva, being pleased with Kubera's penance, accepts him as his friend. For the story see *Rāmāyaṇa* 7.13:25 ff. See also *Meghadūta*, verse 70.

785 In the post-Vedic period, Kubera is depicted as one of the guardians of the North. He does not appear as a *lokapāla* in the Vedic period; most commonly, Soma is described as being the the lord of the North in this era; sometimes Varuṇa, Dhātṛ, Parjanya, and Rudra substituted Soma in this early phase. Kubera seems to appear for the first time as a *lokapāla* in the *Mānavaśrautasūtra*. From the *Mahābhārata* onwards, he is commonly the standard *lokapāla* of the North. For further details, see Corinna WESSELS-MEVISSEN 2001: 4–17.

786 This phrase is repeated for rhetorical purposes; the same information has been already expressed in verses 70–71 above.

787 The elephant-headed god is addressed as Gaṇeśa. The early *Purāṇas*, such as the Vāyu and the earliest known recension of the *Skandapurāṇa* do not call him Gaṇeśa, but refer to him as Vināyaka. Bhavabhūti, the author of the *Mālatīmādhava* (late

bhojya for a year, he will be purified [from sins]; by doing so for a lifetime (*yāvajjīve*),[788] [he will be reborn as] an excellent Gaṇa. He who worships the lord of the Gaṇas will not be overpowered[789] by demons (*vināyakaiḥ*).

3:77–79 If a religious practitioner of controlled senses worships (*pūjayed yaḥ*) the lord of the Gaṇas with *modakas*, *laḍḍukas* or with delicious roots (*mūlakaiḥ*), using these names: [1] Vighneśvara, [2] Gaṇapati, [3] Ekadanta, [4] Gajānana, [5] Gajakarṇa, [6] Tryakṣa, [7] Nāgayajñopavītin, [8] Caturbhuja, [9] Dhūmrākṣa,[790] [10] Vajratuṇḍa (adamantine-snout),[791] [11] Vināyaka and [12] Mahodara (having a big belly), for him nothing is impossible to obtain.

3:80–81 One should worship serpents on the fifth day in both halves of the month with brilliant, fragrant flowers, incense, perfumes, treacle, milk, milk-rice (*guḍakṣīrasapāyasaiḥ*),[792] flowers,[793] sugar, honey (*śarkaramadhvābhiḥ*);[794] [by doing so] for a year, he will obtain the desired

---

7th to early 8th century) still calls him Vināyaka (TÖRZSÖK 2004: 19–22). The reference of Gaṇeśa here is evidence that this figure is already Gaṇeśa by the time of the *Niśvāsamukha*. Note that *caturthī* has here been used as though it were the inflected form *caturthyām*. This usage is found often in other parts of the corpus, particularly for days of the fortnight.

788 We could take this as a locative, as a curtailed instrumental, as a curtailed optative, or perhaps as an error for *yāvajjīvaṃ*, as K has supposed. Parallels for each could be adduced. Whichever solution is preferred, the sense remains the same.

789 As the rephrasing of the *Śivadharmasaṅgraha* shows (8.17), *abhibhūyet* must be intended to have passive sense, as though it were *abhibhūyeta* (which is metrically impossible here).

790 This is not a commonly known name of Gaṇeśa. He may have been called Dhūmrākṣa 'smokey-eyed' to imply an aggressive colour of the eyes, perhaps. Be that as it may, according to the *Mahābhārata* (3.27:15), Dhūmrākṣa is a demon figure who was killed by Hanumān. In a similar context, the *Garuḍapurāṇa* (1.129:26) refers to Gaṇeśa as Dhūmravarṇa which, most probably, refers to the tone of his skin. This could suggest that *dhūmra*, 'smokey' colour, is somehow connected to Gaṇeśa. Yet, his name 'Dhūmrākṣa' remains out of the ordinary.

791 Except for the *Niśvāsa*, we have not been able to find a single text which refers to *vajratuṇḍa* as a name of Gaṇeśa. It is, however, worth noting that BÖHTLINGK's *Sanskrit-Wörterbuch* attests *vajratuṇḍa* as a name of Gaṇeśa in reference to the *Trikāṇḍakośa*. Both *vakratuṇḍa* and *vakraśuṇḍa* would be more common names for him. The *Śivadharmasaṅgraha* (8.19) here reads *vakraśuṇḍa*.

792 This is an *aiśa dvandva* compound with an otiose *-sa-* in the middle.

793 Note that 'flowers' is mentioned twice.

794 If the conjectured text is correct, we can either interpret this as a shortened form of °*madhvādibhiḥ* or, as we have assumed here, as a case of irregular metrical lengthening before the instrumental ending, perhaps on the analogy of other endings with *bh* in them that are preceded by long vowels: in other words, °*madhvābhiḥ* would stand for

objects; by worshipping [the serpents] for a lifetime, he will obtain the world of the serpents.[795]

3:82a–83b One should fast and worship Skanda on the sixth day of the half month with fragrances, flowers, incense (*gandhapuṣpasadhūpena*),[796] and together with (*saṃyutaḥ*) *bhakṣya* and *bhojya*, worship him concentratedly in both halves of the fortnight.

3:83c–86 [1] Viśākha, [2] Trivarṇa,[797] [3] Umānanda, [4] Agnigarbhaja, [5] Gaṅgāgarbha, [6] Śaradgarbha,[798] [7] Kṛttikāsuta, [8] Ṣaṇmukha, [9] Śaktihasta, [10] Mayūravāhana, [11] Pañcachaṭa[799] and [12] Kumāra: One should worship Skanda[800] every month with these auspicious names, being self-controlled (*yuktātmā*) and with concentration (*samāhitaḥ*) in Mārgaśīrṣa [the month in which the full moon enters the constellation *mṛgaśiras*]. [By doing so] for a year, a man will obtain all desired objects. By worshipping him for a lifetime, he will obtain union with Skanda.

3:87–89 If someone, self-controlled, fasts and worships the Sun on [every] seventh [day], beginning in Mārgaśīrṣa, with flowers, incense, unguents, different kinds of *bhakṣa*, *bhojya* and with oblations, mantra-recitations and so forth for a year, he will be purified [from sins], [and if he is already] freed from sins, he will obtain [his] highest desire. By worshipping him for a lifetime he will go to the world of the Sun.

°*madhubhiḥ*. Note also that *śarkara* too has been metrically shortened: the correct form would be *śarkarā*, as we find in the *Śivadharmasaṅgraha* (8.22).

795 Though there are eight standard names of serpents, to our surprise, they are not mentioned here. Instead they are listed in verse (3.168) below, in the section on the worship of god. It is possible that they may not have been listed here since lists given here feature in the context of the twelve months, and the serpents number only eight.

796 Once again an *aiśa dvandva* compound with an otiose -sa- in the middle.

797 We are not aware of Trivarṇa as a name of Kumāra—maybe that name is here given in reference to three to three topknots of his hair?

798 I am not aware of such a name of Kumāra. It may stand for the commonly known name Śarajanmā or for the less commonly used name Saridgarbha?

799 The *Śivadharmasaṅgraha* (8.26) records Pañcaśikha instead of Pañcachaṭa. We cannot trace any source apart from our text that uses Pañcachaṭa as a name of Skanda.

800 The reason for not counting Skanda as one of the names is that we suspect that 12 names are given for each divinity, one for each month. Note that the *Śivadharmasaṅgraha* (8.25–26), perhaps not following the text precisely, records sixteen names of Kumāra, not mentioning two names which are recorded in our text: Gaṅgāgarbha and Śaradgarbha (we find Pañcaśikha in the *Śivadharmasaṅgraha* in substitution of Pañcachaṭa). Additional names in the *Śivadharmasaṅgraha* are: Devasenāpati, Guha, Naigameśa, Mahāsena, Krauñcāri, and Skanda.

Once he has fallen from there he will be reborn as a rich, healthy and long-lived man.[801]

3:90–91 One should worship [the Sun] with [these] names: [1] Āditya, [2] Savitṛ, [3] Sūrya, [4] Khaga, [5] Pūṣan, [6] Gabhastimat, [7] Hiraṇyagarbha, [8] Triśiras,[802] [9] Tapana, [10] Bhāskara, [11] Ravi and [12] Jagannetra, the witness of the world (*lokasākṣi*).[803] Whoever worships [in this manner] the Sun will obtain all desired objects.

3:92–93 If someone of concentrated mind fasts and worships [1] Śaṅkara while consuming [only] the urine of the cow, on the eighth day of both halves in the month of Mārgaśiras,[804] he will obtain[805] the fruit of the Atirātra. And [by worshipping] with *bhakṣya* and *bhojya* and with beverages, he will obtain this same fruit.

3:94 If someone, undertaking a fast, worships [2] Devadeva[806] in the month of Pauṣa, consuming [only] cow dung, he will obtain the fruit of the Vājapeya.

3:95 If someone fasts and worships [3] Tryambaka in the dark half of the month of Māgha, consuming [only] milk (*payasā*),[807] he will obtain (*lebhe*)[808] the fruit of Aśvamedha (horse sacrifice).

---

801 Masculine plural is functioning as masculine singular.

802 It is not clear to what this name of the sun refers to. Does this allude to the movement of the Sun, which manifests as sunrise, noon, and sunset? We have not been able to find any attestation of this name of the Sun.

803 Alternatively, Lokasākṣi, the eye of the world. *lokasākṣi* has actually been transformed into an *i*-stem noun in the text: the correct form would be *lokasākṣī*, as in the *Śivadharmasaṅgraha* (8.33).

804 *mārgaśire* is an *aiśa* a-stem locative form of *mārgaśiras*. The worship of Śiva is recommended twice: first on the eighth day (verses 83a–107b) and second on the fourteenth day (verses 146–151) of the fortnight. In these two instances we find two slightly different lists of twelve names prescribed for the twelve months' worship. The following names are the same in both lists: Śaṅkara, Tryambaka—replaced by Tryakṣa in the later list, Sthāṇu, Hara, Śiva, Bhava, Rudra, and Īśāna. Instead of the names Devadeva, Nīlakaṇṭha, Piṅgala and Ugra, we find Śarva, Śambhu, Vibhu and Paśupati in the second. The order of the names is also different, except the 10th (Rudra) and 11th (Īśāna).

805 93a is unmetrical, the seventh letter being short. A similar case once again occurs in 94c below. Note that 95c reads *lebhe* to sidestep this problem.

806 Devadeva has not been translated because it is presumably intended as the name of Śiva that is to be used in the month of Pauṣa.

807 If the text is right here (and we do not emend to *payasāṃ* or *payasaḥ*), then perhaps we should literally render this fragment as 'by milk, by eating it'.

808 Although this is formally a perfect, we take it as an optative singular (*labheta*), used

3:96 If someone fasts and worships [4] Sthāṇu in the dark half of Phālguna, consuming [only] curds, he will become pure and obtain the fruit of the Naramedha.

3:97 If someone fasts and worships [5] Hara on the eight day of the dark half of the month of Caitra, consuming [only] clarified butter, becoming pure, he will obtain the fruit of the Rājasūya.

3:98 If someone fasts and worships [6] Śiva in the month of Vaiśākha, consuming [only] water boiled with *kuśa*-grass, he becomes self-controlled and will obtain the fruit of a Sautrāmaṇi.

3:99 If someone fasts and worships, [remaining] pure, [7] Bhava in the month of Jyeṣṭha, consuming water [passed through] the horn of a cow, he will obtain the fruit of all sacrifices.

3:100 One should worship [8] Nīlakaṇṭha on the eighth day of the dark half of the month of Āṣāḍha, drinking [only] water [passed through] a conch;[809] he will obtain the fruit of the Gomedha.

3:101 If someone fasts and worships [9] Piṅgala[810] on the eighth day of the dark half of the month of Śrāvaṇa, drinking [only] mustard-water

---

for the sake of metre. Note that the *Śivadharmasaṅgraha* (8.38) has rephrased the text to obviate the irregular use of the perfect, *lebhe*.

809 Note that the feminine noun *ap* 'water' is—presumably irregularly—treated as a masculine singular noun. As Prof. Sasha LUBOTSKY points out, it is theoretically possible to take *apam/āpam* as a regular feminine singular, since the instrumental singular *apā́* and the genitive-ablative singular *apáḥ* are attested to in the *Ṛgveda*. It needs be mentioned, however, that the accusative singular, in contrast, is not traceable therein. Prof. LUBOTSKY further points out that Avestan even features *āfš* as a nominative singular form. That being the case, he suggests, by way of *electronic communication, dated 25th Feb. 2019*, that the of author our text "correctly created the accusative singular" *apam/āpam* from the feminine stem *āp*.

810 For *Piṅgala* as a name of Śiva cf. *Vāyupurāṇa* 24.122, *Liṅgapurāṇa* 2.18:29, *Haracaritacintāmaṇi* 11.8, 11.8 etc. This term is not widely attested as a name of Śiva. Also note that *piṅgala* can denote a number of phenomena, such as 'sun', 'fire', 'yellow', Yakṣa (*Mahābhārata* 3.221:22: *piṅgalo nāma yakṣendro lokasyānandadāyakaḥ*), attendant of Śiva (*Skandapurāṇa* 135.15: *mahākālaś ca kālābho nandiṣeṇaś ca viśrutaḥ | piṅgalo lohitākṣaś ca somanandī ca vīryavān ||*) etc. The *Anekārthasaṅgraha* (verse 704) records various—though by no means all—possibilities as follows:

piṅgalaḥ kapile vahnau rudre 'rkaparipārśvake |
kapau munau nidher bhede piṅgalā kumudastriyām ||

(*siddhārtham udakam*),[811] he will obtain the fruit of having offered a virgin.

3:102 If someone fasts and worships [10] Rudra in the month of Bhādra, consuming [only] water [mixed] with barley seeds, he will be honoured in the world of Rudra.

3:103 One should worship [11] Īśāna on the eighth day of the dark half of the month of Āśvina, drinking [only] water [mixed] with sesame seeds; [by doing so], he will obtain much gold (*rugma*)[812] as the fruit.

3:104a–106b One should fast and [worship] [12] Ugra on the eighth day of the dark half of the month of Kārttika, drinking [only] water mixed with gold; [by doing so], he will obtain the state of being a lord of Gaṇas (*gāṇāpatyam*). If a man then does [this worship of Śiva every month] for a year, he will obtain [the above] desired objects. [If someone worships] without [particular] desires, he will obtain the fruit of the sacrifices [mentioned],[813] and [if someone worships] with desires, he will obtain the state of being a lord of Gaṇas.[814] This procedure has been described for both halves of the month.

3:106c–110 I shall teach (*pravakṣyāmi*) the worship of Mahādevī on the ninth day. One should fast and worship [Her] with these auspicious names: [1] Umā, [2] The goddess Kātyāyinī,[815] [3] Durgā, [4] Rudrā, [5] Subhadrikā, [6] Kālarātrī, [7] Mahāgaurī, [8] Revatī, [9] Bhūtanāyikā, [10] Āryā, and [11] Prakṛtirūpā, also [12] The leader of Gaṇas (*gaṇānāñ caiva nāyikā*) [i.e. Gaṇanāyikā]. One should worship [Her]

---

811 The syntax is irregular here: we expect a compound.

812 It is, otherwise, more commonly known as *rukma*. Note that *rugma* also occurs in other parts of the *Niśvāsa* (*Nayasūtra* 3.28 and *Guhyasūtra* 6.8).

813 This interpretation is uncertain.

814 Stating 'he will obtain the state of being a lord of Gaṇas' makes little sense, since he already obtained this result from worshipping Ugra in Kārttika. Furthermore, the fruit of the sacrifices is regarded as greater than the state of being a lord of Gaṇas. Instead, it appears more natural to state 'if someone worships without desires, he will obtain the state of being a lord of Gaṇa', as in the case of (3.150). The state of a Gaṇa is certainly a higher reward than the reward of sacrifices in the Śaiva context. The *Śivadharmasaṅgraha* (8.47), in rewriting the account, inverses the hierarchy to the effect that the state of a Gaṇa is regarded lower as the fruit of performing sacrifices.

815 We have taken *devī* as an adjective to *kātyāyinī*. This is probably intended to be one name, since it would not otherwise be a list of twelve, one for each month of the year. There are two other ways of avoiding the problem, [1] we could take *bhūtanāyikā* as an adjective of Revatī or [2] *prakṛtirūpā* as an adjective of *āryā*.

with these names in both halves of the month. One should always worship the boon-giving [goddess] (*varadāṃ*) with fragrance, flowers, incense, cloth, ornaments, decorations, offering of eatables, gifts (*upahāraiḥ*), bulbs, roots and fruits, and various kinds of foods.

3:111a–113b [One should worship the goddess] consuming [only] water, flowers, gruel, parched rice grains (*lājām*) with husks (*sadhānakām*), *kṛsara*,[816] milk, roots, fruits, leaves, green vegetables, sesame seeds [or] sediment of [oil of] sesame seeds (*khalim*). And one may consume mung beans (*mudgāni*) and (*tathā caiva*) [he should] abstain from [all other] food. Having thus eaten these [above mentioned foods], one will obtain all desired objects.

3:113c–114b If someone consumes wet ginger at dawn, eats [only] white [viz. *sāttvika*] food (*śuklabhojin*)[817] and fasts and [worships the goddess] on the ninth day of a fortnight nine times [in a row] (*navamīnavamoṣitaḥ*),[818] he will obtain all desired objects.

3:114c–116b If someone worships [the goddess] nine-times on the ninth day (*navamīnava*)[819] consuming only pepper, he will obtain all desired objects and the goddess will be generous [to him]. If someone worships [the goddess] nine-times on the ninth day sleeping on a bed of *kuśa* grass and consuming the five products of the cow, the goddess will bestow an excellent boon [upon him].

3:116c–121b Venerating Yama on the tenth day of the auspicious month of (*māsi*) Mārgaśiras with flowers, fragrances, incense, together with *bhakṣya* and *bhojya*, one should worship [him] using these names: [1] Yama, [2] Dharmaraja, [3] Mṛtyu, [4] Antaka, [5] Vaivasvata, [6] Kāla, [7] Sarvalokakṣaya, [8] always Ugradaṇḍadhṛt, [9] He who travel sitting on a buffalo (*mahiṣāsanayāyine*), [10] Śāsitṛ and [11] Overlord of the

---

816 According to MONIER-WILLIAMS, this term refers to "a dish consisting of sesamum and grain".

817 This could mean 'eats [only] in the bright half of the month', but that sounds hard to sustain over four and a half months. Note that the previous couple of verses appear to describe pure food.

818 This *aiśa* compound involves an ordinal number *navama* in the sense of a cardinal *nava* and the participle *uṣitaḥ*, 'spent', written as *oṣitaḥ*, is used in the sense of *upoṣitaḥ* 'fasted'. Thus, we have understood the compound to mean something like *nava navamīr upoṣitaḥ*, although the reading remains doubtful.

819 We assume this to be an irregular *tatpuruṣa* compound. It would of course be possible to emend it to *navamīr nava*.

hells (*narakādhipate*),[820] obeisance [to you]! Also one should make a libation to him with water mixed with sesame seeds. If someone [self-]controlled [worships him] in both halves of [each] month for a year, he will be liberated from all sins and there will be no sorrow arising from *naraka* [for him]; worshipping him for a lifetime, the worshipper (*sa*) will obtain an excellent realm of rebirth.

3:121c–125b If someone, of pure observance, worships Dharma[821] on the eleventh day with fragrances, flowers, incense and different kinds of eatables [and] should worship Dharma, [that is to say] Satya, [that is to say] Parākrama, with these names: [1] Dharma, [2] Satya, [3] Dayā, [4] Kṣānti, [5] Śauca, [6] Ācāra, [7] Ahiṃsā, [8] Adambha and [9] Rakṣā,[822] [10] Lokasākṣin, [11] Vṛṣabha,[823] [12] Adṛṣṭa,[824] obeisance [to you]!, being controlled, in both halves [of each month] for a year,

---

[820] The vocative has been used for metrical reasons where we would expect the dative. It seems probable that one name is missing from the list here, for we require 12 names for the 12 months. The redactor of the *Śivadharmasaṅgraha* appears to have responded to this need by reading *ugradaṇḍograhastāya* (8.60). It is likely that there might have been an instance of textual corruption at an earlier stage in this passage as it features in the *Niśvāsamukha*. We take the redundant word *nityaṃ* as indicator of such a possibility.

[821] Some items in the list refer to *yamas* and *niyamas*. The *Yogasūtra* (2.30) records *yamas* as *ahiṃsāsatyāsteyabrahmacaryāparigrahā yamāḥ*, and the *niyamas* as *śauca-saṃtoṣatapaḥsvādhyāyeśvarapraṇidhānāni niyamāḥ* (2.32). In our text, among the twelve names of Dharma, two qualities [vis. *ahiṃśā* and *satya*] of *yamas* and one quality [viz. *śauca*] of *niyama* are shared. The *Mataṅgavidyāpāda* 17.29c–31 gives a list of *yamas* and *niyamas* that also shares the three names [viz. *ahiṃsā*, *satya*, and *śauca*] of Dharma. Furthermore, the *Mataṅgavidyāpāda* (17.29cd) clearly states that the Dharma is of twofold: *yama* and *niyama* (*dharmaś ca dvividhaḥ prokto yamaś ca niyamo 'paraḥ*). The *Parākhya* (4.75–78) contains the same list of *yamas* and *niyamas* as the *Mataṅga* does. The list of *yamas* and *niyamas* is commonly mentioned in the *Purāṇas* and it differs from text to text. For more details, see GOODALL (2004: 253–254).

[822] Note an irregular use of gender.

[823] This depiction of Dharma as a bull is known from other sources, for example *Manu-smṛti* 8.16a (*vṛṣo hi bhagavān dharma*).

[824] It is not clear to us why Dharma is called unseen but it is possible that he has no bodily form, and so is called *adṛṣṭa*. In the Mīmāṃsā system *adṛṣṭa* is a key term and refers to the unseen force produced from the sacrificial act that will provide its reward in the next life. In the Vaiśeṣika system both *dharma* and *adharma* are defined as *atīndrīya* or *adṛṣṭa*. Cf. *Praśastapādabhāṣya* pp. 272–280: *dharmaḥ puruṣaguṇaḥ | kartuḥ priyahitamokṣahetur atīndriyo 'ntyasukhasaṃvijñānavirodhī puruṣāntaḥkaraṇasaṃyogaviśuddhābhisandhijaḥ varṇāśramiṇāṃ pratiniyatasādhananimittaḥ... adharmo 'py ātmaguṇaḥ | kartur ahitapratyavāyahetur atīndriyo 'ntyaduḥkhasaṃvijñānavirodhī |*. Cf. also *Ṣaḍdarśanasaṅgraha* pp. 416–417 *kartṛ-*

he will be freed from the [looming] sorrows of the world of Yama; he will be reborn as a king.

3:125c–126b By worshipping him (*samarcan tan*)[825] and making a libation with water mixed with sesame seeds [in each half of each month] for a lifetime, one obtains an excellent realm of rebirth [in heaven]; once he obtains this [excellent realm of rebirth] he will not return [to this world].

3:126c–127b By worshipping [1] Keśava on the twelfth day of each half of Mārgaśira,[826] while consuming [only] the urine of a cow, a man obtains the fruit of the Agniṣṭoma.[827]

3:127c–128b If someone fasts[828] and worships [2] Nārāyaṇa on the twelfth day [when the sun is] in [the constellation of] *puṣya* [viz. in the month of Pauṣa], consuming [only] cow-dung, he obtains the fruit of the Agniṣṭoma.[829]

3:128c–129b If someone fasts[830] and worships [3] Mādhava on the twelfth day in the month of Māgha, consuming [only] milk, he will obtain the fruit of the Ukthyamedha.[831]

---

phaladāyy ātmaguṇa ātmamanaḥsaṃyogajaḥ svakāryavirodhī dharmādharmarūpatayā bhedavān parokṣo 'dṛṣṭākhyo guṇaḥ | tatra dharmaḥ puruṣaguṇaḥ ....

825 Understand *samarcayaṃs tam.*

826 We find precisely the same list of twelve names of Viṣṇu with reference to the twelve months, starting from Mārgaśīrṣa up to Kārttika, in *Mahābhārata* (appendix) 14.4:2998 ff. The reward of worship, however, is different. The fact that we find this list of twelve names of Viṣṇu also in Vaiṣṇava sources, such as the appendix passage of the *Mahābhārata*, indicates that the *Niśvāsamukha* has appropriated the framework of twelve names in conjunction with their association with twelve months from the Vaiṣṇava traditions.

827 Our text (3.127–133) follows the traditional list of seven *Somasaṃsthās*, basis of a *Soma* sacrifice, in the same order. This shows the author's authoritative knowledge of Vedic sacrifices. KANE II.2:1204 lists the seven *Somasaṃsthās* as follows: Agniṣṭoma, Atyagniṣṭoma, Ukthya, Ṣoḍaśin, Vājapeya, Atirātra and Āptoryāma. This sacrifice may have been called Ṣoḍaśin because in the process of its performance, during the third course ('*savana*'), one should add a *stotra* (a.k.a. *uktha stotra*) and a corresponding *śastra* (known as *uktha śastra*), called Ṣoḍaśin to the fifteen *stotras* and the fifteen śastras of the Ukthya. For more detail see KANE II.2: 1204–1205.

828 Note an *aiśa* hiatus within a *pāda.*

829 Perhaps there is a transmission error here, for we expect the mention of a different soma sacrifice, the Atyagniṣṭoma (see p. 325). On that basis, we could conjecture something like *phalaṃ cātyagniṣṭomasya.* The *Śivadharmasaṅgraha* (8.70) displays 'Jyotiṣṭoma' instead, an unlikely candidate for the original reading.

830 Once again an *aiśa* hiatus within a *pāda.*

831 *Ex conj.* The name Ukthyamedha is not common among Vedic sacrifices, but it most

3:129c–130b If someone fasts and worships [4] Govinda on the twelfth day in the month of Phālguna, consuming [only] curds, he will obtain the fruit of the Ṣoḍaśī.

3:130c–131b If someone fasts and worships [5] Viṣṇu on the twelfth day in the month of Caitra, consuming [only] clarified butter, he will obtain the fruit of the Vājapeya.

3:131c–132b If someone fasts and worships [6] Madhusūdana on the twelfth day in the month of Vaiśākha, consuming [only] water mixed with *kuśa* grass, he will obtain the fruit of the Atirātra.

3:132c–133b If someone fasts and worships [7] Trivikrama on the twelfth day in the month of Jyeṣṭha, consuming [only] water mixed with sesame seeds, he will obtain the fruit of the Āptoryāma.

3:133c–134b By worshipping [8] Vāmana attentively on the twelfth day in the month of Āṣāḍha, consuming [only] fruits, a pure soul will obtain the fruit of the Aśvamedha.

3:134c–135b If someone fasts and worships [9] Śrīdhara on the twelfth day in the month of Śrāvaṇa, consuming [only] leaves, that pure soul will obtain the fruit of the Rājasūya.

3:135c–136b Similarly, by worshipping [10] Hṛṣīkeśa, as prescribed,[832] [on the twelfth day] in the month of Bhādra, the wise man obtains the fruit of the Gavāmaya.[833]

3:136c–137b One should worship the god [11] Padmanābha, in the month of Āśvayuja;[834] [by doing so], a man obtains (*labhati*)[835] the fruit of the Naramedha sacrifice.

---

likely refers merely to the *ukthya*. We conjectured *ukthyamedha°* as all the sources display an initial *uk*, followed by a gap, and completed by *medha* in the end.

832 *Ex conj.* Though the corresponding text is lost in our manuscripts, this reading is attested to in *Śivadharmasaṅgraha* (8.77), wherein the text states *vidhivad*, 'as prescribed'. The *vidhi*, 'method', is not mentioned. Thus, this passage might not be original. Given this section topicalizes observances, we would be expecting a substance listed fit for consumption during the time of the observance (as e.g. at 3.31–33).

833 Cf. *Chāndogyopaniṣad* 4.2:2, *Mahābhārata* 13.109:44 etc.

834 Most commonly known as a *āśvina*.

835 Note an *aiśa parasmaipada* for *ātmanepada*.

3:137c–138b If a man fasts and worships [12] Dāmodara on the twelfth day of each half of the month of Kārttika, he will obtain the fruit of the Bahusuvarṇa.[836]

3:138c–141b By worshipping [Viṣṇu thus] for a year he will obtain all desired fruits. If someone is sinless, he will obtain [the fruit of having performed the above mentioned] sacrifices, [and if someone is sinful, he will] be freed from [possible] destruction. By worshipping [Viṣṇu thus] for a lifetime with flowers, sweet-smelling fragrances, *bhakṣya*, *bhojya*, incense, umbrellas, banners, awnings, divine golden ornaments, various gems and jewels, cloths and performing a splendid worship, one will go to the world of Viṣṇu (literally 'locality of Viṣṇu').

3:141c–145 If someone who knows precepts worships Anaṅga on the thirteenth day of [each] half month with *bhakṣya*, *bhojya*, beverages, fragrances, incense, garlands and the like [and] should worship mighty Kāmadeva with these [of his] names: [1] Anaṅga, [2] Manmatha, [3] Kāma, [4] Īśvara, [5] Mohana, [6] Pañcabāṇa, [7] Dhanurhasta, [8] Unmāda, [9] Vaśaṃkara, [10] Ratipriya, [11] Prītikara [and] [12] Hṛdayāpahārin (*hṛdayasyāpahāriṇam*). By worshipping [him] beginning in the month of Mārgaśira and up until Kārttika, there will be [sexual] good fortune (*saubhāgyam*), wealth, grain and sons and wives [for that worshipper]; one obtains union with Kāmadeva by worshipping [him] for a lifetime.[837]

3:146–150 One should worship god, the supreme lord [=Śiva], again on the fourteenth day [of the fortnight]. One should worship the supreme lord with the prescribed procedure and with these [of his] names: [1] Hara, [2] Śarva, [3] Bhava, [4] Tryakṣa, [5] Śambhu, [6] Vibhu, [7] Śiva, [8] Sthāṇu, [9] Paśupati, [10] Rudra, [11] Īśāna, [12] Śaṅkara [and] practice a religious observance in both halves of the month, beginning in

[836] This sacrifice, as its name suggests, may indicate that it is connected with offering a substantial amount of gold or grains to the priest. SANDERSON, in his unpublished contribution '*Śaivism and Brahmanism in the Early Medieval Peral Period*' (forthcoming, p. 77) relates that Narasiṃhavarman I is reported to have performed a Bahusuvarṇa, which might have been equated to ten Aśvamedhas. He (forthcoming, p. 74–75) takes note of Mādhavavarman who performs Bahusuvarṇa along with other Vedic sacrifices. The occurrence of the Bahusuvarṇa sacrifice is frequent in inscriptions, but not in "technical *Śrauta* literature" (forthcoming, p. 78).

[837] The syntax of the sentence is slightly opaque because the correlative of *yo* in 141d is missing and an unusual genitive *yāvajjīvasya* is used (which could either be understood as *yāvajjīvaṃ* or *yāvajjīvena*).

the month of Mārgaśīrṣa (*mārgaśīrṣasya māsādau*), for a year, with flowers, fragrances, incense, *bhakṣya*, *bhojya*, different kinds of decorations, parasols, banners and awnings. [By doing so,] one will obtain all desired objects; if a concentrated person who has no [worldly] desires worships [the god thus] for a year, he will become a Gaṇa; [by doing so] for a lifetime, he will obtain union with [the supreme god]; [if a worshipper is a] sinful [person], he will be freed from sins.

3:151–153 If someone, on the new moon day (*amāvasyā*) of Mārgaśiras, satisfies [his] ancestors [[...]][838] by means of the ritual called *śrāddha* (*karmaṇā śrāddhayuktena*), [i.e.] by [the act of offering] balls of rice (*piṇḍena*), sesame seeds and water; similarly, if he satisfies [his] ancestors with rice-balls together with sesame seeds and water by the means of the ritual connected to *śrāddha* on the full-moon day, listen to the fruit of that for him: those of his ancestors will be satisfied who dwell in the world of Yama.[839] By doing so for a year, [his] ancestors will be liberated from the punishments [assigned] by Yama.

3:154 If he does so for a lifetime in both halves of the month, he will be freed from sin [if] he is a sinner; if [already] sinless, he will go to heaven.

3:155 In the case of a Brāhmin, the ancestors are [called] Somapās; in the case of a Kṣatriya, Havirbhujas;[840] in the case of a Vaiśya, Ājyapas; and for Śūdra, [they are called] Sukālins.

3:156a–157b [If someone] fasts [and] worships Agni again[841]on the full moon day [[...]], he will obtain the world of Agni. [If someone] is a sinner, he will be freed from sin, and [if someone is already sinless,] he will be reborn as a rich man.

3:157c–158b O Brāhmins, I have taught this procedure of fasting for both halves of a month; now listen to [the procedure of] worshipping gods.[842]

---

[838] Text is lost in the manuscript due to a lacuna incepting after *pitṝṃs tarpa*—the lacuna did not, however, contain anything pivotal for the correct understanding of the sentence. We may conjecture something like *pitṝṃs tarpayate tu yaḥ*.

[839] Hereafter, manuscript N is damaged for the remainder of *pāda*. K leaves a gap that extends over about two *pādas*, and W, which faithfully copies N, leaves no gap. In a number of instances, folios in Wdisplay an incomplete sixth line without marking textual loss in its source, N. For that reason it does not surprise us here that W does not indicate the textual loss in this particular instance.

[840] The *Śivadharmasaṅgraha* (8.109) corrects an irregular plural to a standard plural. For the parallel to this verse see *Manusmṛti* 3.197 and our discussion on page 91.

[841] The word *punaś* in the verse is significant as the text already mentioned an observance of Agni on the second day of the lunar calendar in verses 3.67–69.

[842] The details of the fasts have indeed been given above in every case, whereas no details

3:158c–160b On the new moon day, one should feed Brāhmins after first worshipping Prajāpati, [and one should] make a golden lotus marked with [Prajāpati's] names;[843] then [he] should give it to a Brāhmin having put it in a copper vessel filled with clarified butter; one will get the desired objects. If someone is without desire, he will obtain the world of Brahmā.[844]

3:160c–163 After first worshipping Agni on the second day [of the fortnight], a man should satisfy Brāhmins [i.e. by offering food], and having carefully (*yatnataḥ*) written the names of Agni on a [statuette of] a golden goat (*sauvarṇavaste*), he should put it into a vessel [of] *udumbara* filled with clarified butter;[845] having installed two pots filled with milk together with *bhakṣya* and *bhojya*, one should give this to an excellent Brāhmin[846] in both halves of the month; [by doing so] the Fire[-god] will be the bestower of all desired objects [to the giver] within a year. If one does so for a lifetime he will go to the world of Agni.

3:164 Having first worshipped Yakṣa on the third day [of the fortnight]

of how the *pūjā* of each divinity is to be conducted have as yet been given. Furthermore, it is uncertain who is the speaker here and who has/have been addressed. We could certainly retain the reading of N and W (*dvija*) which would easily agree with *śṛṇu*. If Nandikeśvara is addressing the Brāhmins, we would expect the optative verb in the plural. If Śiva is addressing Devī, the word *dvija, dvijāḥ* is problematic. It is also possible to read 3.157cd separately. In this case we assume that Nandikeśvara is addressing the Brāhmins. In the following lines (3.158a ff.) Śiva is addressing Devī. Then *śṛṇu* in optative third person singular remains unproblematic.

843 Note that the text does not presently specify the names of Prajāpati (*alias* Brahmā), which are to be inscribed on a golden lotus. The appropriate names could be identical to those mentioned in the section of fasting (3.64–5), wherein the twelves names of Brahmā are mentioned.

If this were to be the case, a systematic connection would become apparent between the textual section 3.158–195, topicalizing the worship of divinities that are lords of the different lunar days, and segment 3.61–156, on fasting in the context of the same divinities. As a consequence, the names of the divinities who are alluded to as the lords of the fifteen lunar days in this section of worship (3.158–195) would refer to the names of the same divinities mentioned in the section on fasting (3.61–156).

844 Note that the whole section on worship here seems to be related with the accomplishment (*samāpana*) of fasting as it involves the donation to Brāhmins.

845 Presumably *udumbarejyapūrṇe* is an *aiśa* formulation for *audumbare ājyapūrṇe*. The reading of the *Śivadharmasaṅgraha* (8.118) supports this.

846 Note an *aiśa* use of locative which is used in apposition to a dative noun.

one should give a golden mace[847] [to a Brāhmin] writing the names of [Kubera on it and putting it] in a vessel filled with clarified butter.[848]

3:165–166 On the fourth day [of the fortnight], one should give a [statuette of] a golden elephant[849] marked with the names[850] of the god Vighneśvara placed in [a vessel made of] *udumbara* wood[851] [to a Brāhmin], after first having feasted Brāhmins,[852] and offered pots as well as eatables.[853] Supernatural power will arise for him within a year; by [doing so for] a lifetime, he will obtain the state of being a lord of Gaṇas.

3:167 On the fifth day [of the fortnight], after having feasted Brāhmins, one should give (*dattvā*)[854] a golden lotus (*padma*)[855] marked with the name [of a serpent from among those listed below], putting it in a copper pot filled with clarified butter, [to a Brāhmin].

3:168–169 [1] Ananta, [2] Vāsuki, [3] Takṣaka, [4] Trirekhin, [5] Padma, [6] Mahābja,[856] [7] Śaṅkha,[857] or the great serpent [8] Kulika:[858] one

---

847 The *gadā* is the weapon of Kubera in his function as the Lord of the Northern direction.

848 The syntax of the sentence is opaque and there is no mention of the reward of worshipping Kubera.

849 This evidence shows that Vighneśvara is already identified with *gajavaktra* in this period. The *Śivadharmasaṅgraha* (8.121) reads *radanam* 'tusk' instead of *dantinam* 'elephant'. This reading of the *Śivadharmasaṅgraha* might be secondary.

850 Note an *aiśa* compound having *ca* in between members of the compound.

851 Note that 156d is hypermetrical.

852 Once again *viprāṃ* stands for *viprān.*

853 Could *bhakṣān ghatān* possibly also be understood as 'pots [filled with] eatables'?

854 This presumably stands for *dadyāt.*

855 The occurrence of *padma* here is suspicious. Note that the *Śivadharmasaṅgraha* (8.123) reads *sarpam* instead.

856 Most commonly known as Mahāpadma. For this see our reference to the list of serpents below.

857 Śaṅkha is otherwise called Śaṅkhapāla. Cf. *Brahmāṇḍapurāṇa* 3.20:54, *Ajitāgama* 39.30, *Kāmika Uttarabhāga* 80.70 etc.

858 Kulika is otherwise recorded as Gulika. For the list cf. *Mahābhārata* 1.59:40, *śeṣo 'nanto vāsukiś ca takṣakaś ca bhujaṃgamaḥ | kūrmaś ca kulikaś caiva kādraveyā mahābalāḥ ||* ; *Brahmāṇḍapurāṇa* 3.20:53–54, *ananto vāsukis takṣaḥ karkoṭaḥ padma eva ca || mahāpadmaḥ śaṅkhapālo gulikaḥ subalas tathā | ete nāgeśvarāś caiva nāgakoṭibhir āvṛtāḥ* (We have considered *subala* as an adjective of *gulika*, otherwise we have nine names of serpents). Cf. also *Rājanighaṇṭu* 19.65; *Svacchandatantrodyota* chapter 7, p. 198; *Ajitāgama* 39.29–30; *Kāmika Uttarabhāga* 80.69–70; *Rudrayāmala* 22.68; *Kāraṇa Uttarabhāga* 107.15; *Īśvarasaṃhitā* 10.252–254; *Pādmasaṃhitā* (*caryāpāda*) 10.65–67 etc. Our text provides the standard list of eight serpents with one vari-

should worship one of these with fragrances, incense, garlands, etc., and also with *bhakṣya* and *bhojya* food and beverages; [as a result of this, that serpent will become a] bestower of desired objects, [and] a destroyer of sins.

3:170–172 On the sixth day [of a fortnight], however, having made a [statuette of] a golden peacock marked with the auspicious names of Skanda, one should give it, placed in a pot of *udumbara* filled with ghee, to a Brāhmin [and also one should give] jars filled with milk together with *bhakṣya* and *bhojya*.[859] By giving [thus] in both halves of the month one will obtain the desired objects; a man, [by doing so], for a year will obtain [all] desired objects that are longed for. A sinner will be freed from [his] sins, and a pure soul (i.e. who has not committed sins) will obtain [the world of] Skanda (*skandam āpnuyāt*).

3:173–174 [On the seventh day of a fortnight], a wise man should give a [statuette of] a golden horse marked with the name of Sun-god [to a Brāhmin] in both halves of the month, putting it in a copper vessel filled with clarified butter; [by doing so,] a sinner will be freed from many sins within a year; [by doing so] for a lifetime, he will obtain the world of the Sun (*ādityapadam āpnuyāt*).

3:175a–177b On the eighth day [of a fortnight], one should give a [statuette of a golden] bull marked with the names of Bhava to a Brāhmin in both halves of the month, putting it in a copper vessel filled with clarified butter, together with jars filled with food and with milk; [by doing so,] being purified, one will obtain the desired fruits within a year; if someone worships Hara with [his] names for a lifetime, he will obtain the state of being a Gaṇa.

---

ant, Trirekhin; in its place we generally find Karkoṭa (*Rājanighaṇṭu*), Kārkoṭaka (*Īśvarasaṃhitā*) or Kākoṭa (*Pādmasaṃhitā*). *Trirekhin* alludes to the bodily feature of Kārkoṭaka. According to *Śivadharmaśāstra* 6.188, Karkoṭaka has three lines in his throat.

Note that the *Mahābhārata* presents a different list of eight serpents, including only four of what eventually become their 'standard' names later scriptures—these four are shared by our text: Ananta, Vāsuki, Takṣaka, and Kulika. The *Garuḍapurāṇa* 1.129.29–32, prescribing each to be worshipped in the respective month, records 12 names of serpents: Ananta, Vāsukī, Śaṅkha, Padma, Kumbala, Kārkoṭaka, Nāga, Dhṛtarāṣṭra, Śaṅkhaka, Kālīya,Takṣaka and Piṅgala. Five of these names are to be found in our text: Ananta, Vāsukī, Śaṅkha, Padma and Takṣaka.

[859] Note that 170d is hypermetrical.

3:177c–178b On the ninth day [of a fortnight], [one should give a statuette of a golden] lion [provided] with her name[s after first] worshipping Devī (*abhyarcitena*?), [and] also by giving a copper [container] of ghee and [some] eatables, together with pots filled with milk, [to a Brāhmin]....[860]

3:178c–180 One should give to Yama a [statuette of] a [golden] buffalo covered in ghee, marked with the names [of Yama], and placed in a copper vessel, together with a pot filled with milk and together with [some] eatables on the tenth day [of the fortnight], [and] give [it] to Brāhmins after feeding them. [By doing so], even those who [have committed] great crimes will be freed from [possible] sorrows of the world of Yama; [by doing so] for a year, one will be purified, [and will get] an excellent realm of rebirth after death.[861]

3:181–182 One should give a [statuette of a golden] bull marked with[862] the name of Dharma, [in] a copper pot filled with clarified butter, together with eatables, to an excellent Brāhmin on the eleventh day [of the fortnight]; [by doing so] for a year, [being] purified, he will obtain a wholesome realm of rebirth. A desirous person will obtain desired objects, [and] a desireless person will obtain the realm of Dharma.

3:183–185 On the twelfth day [of the fortnight], one should give a [statuette of a golden] Garuḍa [having installed] two pots filled[863] marked with

---

860 This is a tentative translation, the syntax of the sentence is convoluted and elliptical. It seems that some text is missing in our manuscript, for no reward is mentioned. This would suggest again that this manuscript is a copy of a prior manuscript. Here, the *Śivadharmasaṅgraha* (8.134) reads

> *pūrvoktavidhinā siṃhaṃ devyā nāmāṅkitaṃ śubham |*
> *datvā navamyāṃ viprāya prayāti paramāṅ gatim ||*

> By giving a beautiful lion marked with the name of the goddess to a Brāhmin according to the above mentioned procedure on the ninth day [of the fortnight] (*navamyāṃ*) one will get an excellent rebirth.

This reading may give sense, but it it probably not the original reading.

861 This last half-verse is anacoluthic.

862 We have understood *nāmāṅkam* as *nāmāṅkitam*.

863 Our understanding of *ghaṭam eva vā* rests on verse 3.162a: *toyapūrṇe ghaṭe sthāpya*. The reading *ghaṭam eva*, here, is considered to be the result of a *sandhi* between *ghaṭe* and *eva*, then followed by the insertion of the hiatus breaker *m*. The problem remains with *vā*, 'or', as there seems to be no alternative stated in the verse. Thus, we understand *vā* in the sense of *ca*, 'and.'

the names [of Viṣṇu], placed in a copper vessel,[864] [to a Brāhmin], [and] pots filled with water. [These] should be given in the name of Viṣṇu (*viṣṇor nāmnā*) in both halves of the month. [By doing so] for a year, one becomes purified, [and being sinless] obtain the fruit of sacrifices.[865] But by worshipping [Viṣṇu] for a lifetime with foods together with sacrificial fees [to be given to the same Brāhmins(?)], he will obtain the world of Viṣṇu and rejoice with Viṣṇu.

3:186a–188b Having first worshipped Kāmadeva [on the thirteen day of the fortnight], one should give a golden bow together with five arrows [placed] in a copper vessel filled with clarified butter [to Brāhmins]. He should [also] give pots filled with eatables and water to Brāhmins, having feasted [them].[866] [By doing so], a sinless person certainly will obtain [sexual] good fortune, money and grain;[867] but by worshipping him (i.e. Kāmadeva) [thus] for a lifetime, he will go the world of Kāmadeva.

3:188c–191b After first worshipping the supreme god, one should give a [statuette of a golden] bull on the fourteenth day of the fortnight, having marked it with his names, placed in a copper vessel; one should give it to excellent Brāhmins, after first having feasted them as prescribed, [and he also should give] pots filled with eatables and water in both halves of the month. [By doing so] for a year, one will be freed from [the consequences of] bad deeds; by [continuing for] twelve years, he will be a lord of Gaṇas; and by performing this for a lifetime, [he will obtain] union with Maheśvara.[868]

3:191c–195b On the new-moon and full-moon days of both halves of a month, one should honour [one's] ancestors by giving balls of rice [of]

---

864 *Ex conj.* Cf. 3.179.

865 In 184d, there is a possibility of reading *pāpī* instead of *apāpī* as it is a choice of *sandhi*. We chose the reading *apāpī* on the basis of the fact that N displays an uncertain marking before the word *pāpī* which looks like an *avagraha* and the reading of the *Śivadharmasaṅgraha* (8.141) *vipāpaḥ kratum āpnuyāt*, where the word *vipāpa* is equivalent to *apāpī*. If we were, however, to read *pāpī* our translation would be: '[By doing so] for a year, a sinner will be purified [and] will obtain the fruit of sacrifices'.

866 There are a certain number of familiar irregular usages in 187ab. We have understood it thus: *bhakṣyāmbupūrṇān ghaṭakān viprān saṃbhojya dadyāt*.

867 We assume that *saṃvatsareṇa* 'by worshiping for a year' is missing in the text.

868 We assume that *sāyojyaḥ* is the author's way of saying *sāyujyam* (cf. *Śivadharmasaṅgraha* 8.147), but it is perhaps conceivable that it is intended to refer to 'one who has attained *sāyujya*'.

śrāddha in water.[869] A man, having made a [statuette of a] golden man marked with the name of his ancestor, should give it to excellent Brāhmins, placed in a copper vessel and covered with clarified butter, and by also giving pots filled with eatables and water; he will become sinless. [By doing so] for a year, a concentrated person will become sinless [and obtain] desired objects; [by continuing it] for a lifetime, he will [obtain] the world of ancestors. Once he falls from there, he will be reborn as a prosperous person (*bhogavān*); he[870] will be rich in money, grain and sons.[871]

3:195c–196 O twice-born ones![872] I have taught this procedure for worshipping the gods. I have told [you what I had heard] in the conversation of Devī and Śaṅkara uttered eternally by his Western face,[873] [namely] worldly [religion].

Thus is the third chapter, with regard to worldly duty, in the *Niśvāsamukhatattvasaṃhitā*.

---

869 In this *aiśa* compound, we are assuming that the locative plural *apsu* has been irregularly treated as a stem-form.

870 We assume *so* to be a frozen sandhi form of saḥ occuring in conjunction with *bhavet*, applied here *metri causa*.

871 EINOO (2005) has discussed the *tithis* and their presiding deities in *Purāṇas* and texts that belong to the Gṛhyapariśiṣṭa level. His study shows that the list of the presiding deities varies. Many of the deities mentioned in EINOO's study also appear in our list, although there are variations. The only major difference that occurs in the list of EINOO (2005: 106) when we compare it with ours is the eleventh *tithi*. Our text explicitly associates this *tithi* with Dharma, but EINOO's list provides no such reference. Instead, his list shows an association of this *tithi* with "Munis, Rudra/Śiva, Viśve Devāḥ, Bull, Dhanada", or with Viṣṇu, unless we take 'Bull' to mean 'Dharma', with which the animal is commonly associated.

872 Presumably this plural vocative is intended to remind the reader that it is Nandin speaking to a group of sages, one of which is Mataṅga (see verse 1.22 above).

873 Verse 1.51 suggests that Śiva has already taught the Five Streams at some point in time. We assume that the term *sadā*, 'eternally' bears this connotation. In this text, Śiva is teaching the *vedadharma* with his northern face, the Ādhyātmika with his southern face, the Laukika dharma with his western face, the Mantramārga with his upward-facing face, and the Atimārga with his eastern face.

CHAPTER IV

[2. The Vaidika stream]

Goddess spoke:

4:1 How should the *dharma* prescribed in the Vedas, o god, be practised by one who desires an [excellent] course of rebirth, for the sake of heaven and liberation?[874] Pray tell [me] by [your] grace.

[2.1 Injunctions for Vedic students]

God spoke:

4:2–3 One should[875] wear a girdle (*mekhalī*)[876] and carry a staff (*daṇḍa-dhārī*),[877] [and should be] wholly intent on the observances of the junctions of the day.[878] He should do his daily recitation [of the Veda] (*svādhyāyī*), perform sacrifice, and recite mantras (*homajāpī*).[879] And [he should] subsist on alms and abstain from sexual intercourse,[880] as well as from liquor and meat and [anything] pungent or salty (*sakṣāralavaṇāni*)[881] [He should also refrain] from

---

874 *svargāpavargahetoś ca* is an irregular *dvandva* compound followed by *ca* connecting its elements.

875 Note that the following specifications predate the *Vijñāneśvara*, being attested to in the *Gṛhyasūtras*. *Muñja* and *palāśa* are prescribed in most *Gṛhyasūtras* for Brāhmins, with the bilva fruit functioning as a possible substitute; other materials are to be employed for devotees of the remaining *varṇas*. Note that this distinction presents innovation, since some *Gṛhyasūtras* instead present the Brāhmin's paraphernalia fit for use by all *varṇas*. I would like to credit Prof. LUBIN for this clarification, which reached me *by way of personal communication*, April 7th, 2018.

876 Mitākṣarā, a commentary on *Yājñavalkyasmṛti*, states that the *mekhalā* should be make of *mauñja* grass and the like (see the commentary on verse 1.29ab).

877 Once again the *Mitākṣarā* tells us that the staff should be fashioned of *palāśa* wood (see commentary on 1.29ab).

878 Since this injunction is Vedic, the junctions of the day referred to may be three in number, rather than the four we find in tantric contexts.

879 This is an *aiśa* compound, but we assume that this is the sense.

880 In order to avoid an *aiśa* hiatus within a *pāda*, *Śivadharmasaṅgraha* 9.2 reads *tyakta-maithunī* instead of *ca amaithunī*.

881 Here one would expect *akṣāralavaṇāni ca* instead, since forms with alpha privative

climbing trees[882] and [from] isolation,[883] and he should not eat betel.

4:4 He should avoid (*varjanam*)[884] looking in wells[885] and should not bathe naked.[886] He should not look at women and should avoid garlands and incense.[887]

4:5ab He should avoid ointments and perfumes and should not traverse rugged ground (*viṣamalaṃghanam*).[888]

4:5c–7 The [aforementioned] observance [should last] thirty-six years, and [this] commitment, based on the triple-Veda, [should be carried out] at his teacher's [house]. Alternatively, [it may last] half of that [time] (i.e. eighteen years), or a quarter (i.e. nine years), or until he has learnt

---

are standard in prescriptions for *brahmacarya*, or else *akṣāralavaṇāsi ca* (cf. BGS 1.7.9; BhGS 1.10. I would like to credit Prof. LUBIN for this clarification, which reached me *by way of personal communication, April 7th, 2018.*). Note that we have to construe this expression with *na bhakṣayet* at the end of the verse; yet in case of the two immediately ensuing expressions (4.3c), we have to supply a prohibitory verb form such as *na kuryāt*.

882 Cf. *Kauṣītakagṛhyasūtra* 40.11:26 (*udapānāvekṣaṇavṛkṣārohaṇaphalaprapatanasaṃdhisarpaṇavivṛtasnānaviṣamalaṅghanaśuktavadanasaṃdhyādityaprekṣaṇabhaikṣaṇāni na kuryāt na ha vai snātvā bhikṣetāpaha vai snātvā bhikṣāṃ jayatīti śruteḥ*) and *Pāraskaragṛhyasūtra* 2.7:6 and *Vasiṣṭhadharmasūtra* 12.25. These texts assign this injunction to a 'bath-graduate' *snātaka*. At the same time, it declares that this rule can be observed by anybody. Our text, however, reserves this injunction for a *brahmacārin*, a celibate student.

883 Cf. *Kauṣītakagṛhyasūtra* 40.11:26.

884 If the text is correctly transmitted here, *varjanam* may have the sense of an optative singular, or we may follow the *Śivadharmasaṅgraha* and emend it to *varjayet*.

885 Cf. *Kauṣītakagṛhyasūtra* 40.11:27 and *Pāraskaragṛhyasūtra* 2.7:6. These texts again contextualize this injunction as befitting a *snātaka* ('bath-graduate'), not a *brahmacārin* ('celibate student').

886 Cf. *Pāraskaragṛhyasūtra* 2.7:6, *Baudhāyanadharmasūtra* 2.3.6:24 and *Manusmṛti* 4.45. These sources again mention these injunctions particularly for a *snātaka*. The *Śivadharmasaṅgraha* (9.4) here reads: *varjayet prekṣanaṃ kopam aghṛṣṭvā snānam ācaret*|. In this case perhaps he is enjoined to avoid people or enjoined to refrain from staring at people 'in anger'.

Please be advised that Prof. LUBIN, *by way of personal communication, April 7th, 2018*, noted that it might be the case that "this conflation of the rules for brahmacārin and snātaka suggest that the author really had a bhautika-brahmacārin in mind, rather than a yauvana-, despite the mention of the vrata concluding when the Veda has been learnt (9–36 years)". Prof. LUBIN further noted that in the *Manusmṛti* the *snātaka*'s rules are conflated with the rules for *gṛhastha* (*ibid.*).

887 Cf. similar injunctions in *Manusmṛti* 2.177-178.

888 Cf. *Pāraskaragṛhyasūtra* 2.7:6 for the injunction of not traversing the rugged ground.

them [i.e. the Vedas].[889]This is the *brahmacārin*'s observance, which I have taught previously, o goddess! One who strays from [these rules] will go to hell; observing [them] properly, he will go to the realm of heaven. The *brahmacārin*'s injunction has [now] been taught. [Next,] I will teach the householder's [injunction].

[2.2 Injunctions for householders]

4:8–10 One who is married (*kṛtadāraḥ*) should perform sacrifices[890] at home and [pay] the sacrificial fees [to the officiating priest]. He should study the Vedas daily (*pratyahaḥ*) and perform oblations (*hāvanam*)[891] in the evenings and mornings. He should make Bali offerings and [perform] the *vaiśvadeva* rite and he should venerate [any] uninvited guests. He should observe *darśa*, *paurṇamāsa* and *paśubandha* sacrifices. He should perform the *śrāddha* ritual and [pay] the sacrificial fee [to the officiating priest]. He should go to [his] spouse [for sex] at the seasonal time [of her fertility after menstruation].[892] And he should avoid the wives of others. By observing [these injunctions] one will find an [excellent] realm of rebirth.

4:11–12 [He should adopt] nonviolence and selflessness, and he should refrain from troubling [others] and [from] stealing. He should rid [himself] of desire and anger, and [he should both] respect and greet his religious teachers. Forbearance, self-restraint, compassion, generosity, truthfulness, purity, fortitude (*dhṛtiḥ*), being well-disposed towards others, knowledge, wisdom, and faith are the characteristics of a Brāhmin.[893]

---

889 Cf. *Manusmṛti* 3.1:

ṣaṭtriṃśadābdikaṃ caryaṃ gurau traivedikaṃ vratam |
tadardhikaṃ pādikaṃ vā grahaṇāntikam eva vā ||

890 Once again, what should be filed as feminine accusative singular, *yajñāṃ*, is intended to be understood as a masculine accusative plural.

891 This is an *aiśa* formation for *havanam*.

892 The same injunction is given in *Manusmṛti* (3.45ab) as follows: *ṛtukālābhigāmī syāt svadāraniratah sadā |* "Finding his gratification always in his wife, he should have sex with her during her season." (OLIVELLE 2005: 110)

893 Cf. *Manusmṛti* 6.92:

dhṛtiḥ kṣamā damo 'steyaṃ śaucam indriyanigrahaḥ |
dhīr vidyā satyam akrodho daśakaṃ dharmalakṣaṇam ||

4:13 He who recites the [Vedic] *saṃhitās* everyday will attain accomplishment within a year. He will gain mastery over the GĀYATRĪ-mantra (*gāyatrisiddhiḥ*)[894] within three years; [if he does it for a lifetime],[895] he will obtain the world of Brahmā [after death].

4:14 One should recite daily the *saṃhitās* of *Ṛk*, *Sāman*, *Yajuḥ*, and *Atharvan*.[896] Having conquered his senses and free from possessions, he will go to the world of Brahmā.

4:15 He should live by gleaning or agriculture (*pramṛtena*).[897] Without engaging in trade done by himself he lives without harming living beings.[898]

4:16 He should regularly do mantra-recitation (*japti*) and (*vā*) perform oblations;[899] [by doing so] he will partake of the fruit of heaven. He[900] who does not perform the five sacrifices will certainly go to hell.

4:17–18 The sacrifice to the Veda is teaching; the sacrifice to the ancestors

---

894 We are not sure what *gāyatrisiddhiḥ* means here. It could be understood as referring to mastery of the Vedas or to mastery of the well-known GĀYATRĪ-mantra. Note that the stem-form has been shortened for metrical reasons.

895 *Ex. conj.* We need some time-frame here. Thus we venture to conjecture a lifetime, following *Niśvāsamukha* 3.66cd: *yāvajjīvan tu kurvāṇo brahmalokaṃ sa gacchati* ||.

896 *Ex. conj.* If we are right, *ṛgyajuḥsāmatharvāṇām* contains another *aiśa* shortening of *ā* perhaps for the sake of the metre.

897 For this expression, see *Manusmṛti* 4.4–5:

ṛtāmṛtābhyāṃ jīvet tu mṛtena pramṛtena vā |
satyānṛtābhyām api vā na śvavṛttyā kadā cana ||
ṛtam uñchaśilaṃ jñeyam amṛtaṃ syād ayācitam |
mṛtaṃ tu yācitaṃ bhaikṣaṃ pramṛtaṃ karṣaṇaṃ smṛtam ||

The word order within the compound *śilońcha* is inverted *metri causa* in the *Niśvāsamukha*. In the *Manusmṛti*, gleaning, *uñchaśila*, is the gloss of *ṛtam*. In the *Niśvāsamukha*, *pramṛtena* is understood as agriculture on the strength of the above mentioned passage of the *Manusmṛti*. It seems that the reading of 15ab is fabricated depending on *Manusmṛti* 4.4–5.

898 Cf. *Manusmṛti* 4.2a: *adroheṇaiva bhūtānāṃ*. Perhaps the reading of the *Śivadharmasaṅgraha*, *vāṇijyādi tyajet karma bhūtadrohañ ca sarvadā* is intended here. Furthermore, we have assumed that *asvayaṅkṛtavāṇijye* is intended as an instrumental.

899 An irregular syncope of *japati* for metrical reasons, and *vā* presumably does not stand for option; to obviate these problems the *Śivadharmasaṅgraha* (9.13) reads *japāgnihomasaṃyuktaḥ* instead of *japti juhoti vā nityam*.

900 Here we again encounter a frozen *sandhi*. The *Śivadharmasaṅgraha* (9.14) has rephrased the text as *sa dhruvaṃ vrajet* to do away with the problem.

is the quenching libation; the sacrifice to gods is the burnt offering; the sacrifice to beings is the Bali offering; and the sacrifice to humans is the honouring of guests. If a man never fails to offer these five great sacrifices to the best of his ability, he remains unsullied by the taints of his slaughter-houses in spite of living permanently at home.[901]

4:19 Mortar and pestle, fireplace, water-pot and broom are the five slaughter-houses of [a householder]; these have been taught to you, o beautiful one!

4:20 He, who by means of offering sacred knowledge alone, [effectively] performs sacrifices [involving] sacrificial fees, and he who delights in self-contemplation, that wise person is an expert in the Vedic *dharma*.

4:21 By meditating using the *praṇava*[902] he may attain the state of omnipresence, if he wishes [this] power for himself (*siddhim ātmanaḥ*), by means of the sixteen-spoked wheel (*ṣoḍaśārena cakrena*).[903]

4:22 [He should meditate] with devotion, [his] mind one-pointed, enduring all opposite extremes (*sarvadvandvasahena*), [being] ever with a mind that is not greedy and that sees oneness in all [things].

4:23 If he remains thus regularly engaged in mantra recitation, meditation, worship, and sacrifice, he will not undergo a miserable rebirth; he will go to the world of Brahmā.

---

901 This translation is based on Patrick OLIVELLE's translation of the *Manusmṛti* (2005: 112).

902 This appears to refer to a breath-control type of meditation involving *mantroccāra*, in which the breath is homologised with the mantra in question, namely *oṃ*.

903 This teaching can only be found, as far as we are aware, in tantric sources. We are, however, here in the section on the brahmanical householder, the second stage of life according to the Vedic teachings. Thus, it is unusual to encounter this verse in the present context.

In *Brahmayāmala* 89.10ab, this refers to the sixteen-spoked wheel situated in the middle of the navel: *nābhimadhye paraṃ cakraṃ ṣoḍaśāraṃ* (*ṣoḍaśāraṃ* corr; *ṣoḍaśārāṃ* ed.) *prakīrttitam*. The *Mālinīvijayottaratantra* 19.24–36 also mentions that this *cakra* is located at the navel. The *Tantrasadbhāva* 1.499 states that the sixteen-spoked wheel is situated in the palate (*tālu*). MALLINSON (2007: 236–237), upon consultation of a variety of sources, concludes that commonly the Viśuddhi/Viśuddha *cakra* is located in the throat. The inconsistency with regards to the location of this *cakra* should be noted, for which reason we are unable to determine conclusively where a Yogin is supposed to focus his mind.

4:24 If he should perform works alone and forgo meditation on the Self, thus not attaining the [state of] the omnipresent *brahman*, he will obtain only heaven [as his] reward.[904]

[2.3 Injunctions for forest-dwellers]

4:25 After that [household life], he, together with his spouse, [his] senses mastered, should become a forest-dweller (*vanevāsī*). He should go to the forest and live there by means of [water] drops [that form] on *kuśa* grass.

4:26 He should [sustain himself with] bulbs, roots, fruits, vegetables, black wild rice or *kāṅgu*[905] and make fire sacrifice [every] evening and morning with the same.

4:27 He should satisfy gods and Brāhmins with wild food obtained without [using] the plough. He should satisfy [his] ancestors [and] be always intent upon mantra recitation and sacrifice.[906]

4:28 He should be engaged in benefitting all beings [and] should endure all sufferings. He should accommodate himself to heat and cold [of the weather] (*śītātapāvakāśādi*). [He should attend to] the five-fires [in the hot season, and practice] sleeping in water [in the cold season].

4:29 He should be clothed in *kuśa* grass, or tree-bark, and always wear the skin of a black antelope. [He should] always [observe the penitential practices known as] Kṛcchra, Atikṛcchra, Tapta[kṛcchra], Parāk,[907] Cāndrāyaṇa, and so forth.

4:30a–31c [Mortifying himself,] he should dry himself out[908] by consuming fallen leaves and water [that falls as dew].[909] He should move like a

[904] Note that Prof. LUBIN, by way of personal communication, April 7th, kindly made us aware that one should not take this statement to imply that "the householder state may last until death, without the need to proceed to the further *āśramas*".

[905] Dictionaries record *kaṅgu* as 'a kind of Panic seed', commonly viewed as food for the poor. There is, however, no reference to *kāṅgu*.

[906] *Ex conj.*

[907] *parāk* is an *aiśa* shortening for *parāka*. Seeing the problem, the redactor of the *Śivadharmasaṅgraha* (9.33) opted to note down *parākaiḥ*, although this violates the metre.

[908] Cf. *Manusmṛti* 6.24d *śoṣayed deham ātmanaḥ*.

[909] According to the *Skandapurāṇa* (34.41) Devī seems to have followed these procedures while she was doing her *tapas*: *kadācit sā phalāhārā kadācit* ***parṇabhojanā*** *| kadācid* ***ambubhakṣābhūt*** *kadācid anilāśanā ||* . Cf. also *Haracaritacintāmaṇi* 21.21.

wild animal, not dwell with others (*sahāvāsa*), and resort to a difficult lifestyle. A Brāhmin [who does this] will go to heaven; if he fails [in this observance], he will go to hell. I have explained the religious observance of a forest hermit.

[2.4 Injunctions for ascetics]

4:31d–34b [Now] hear about the fourth *āśrama* [from me]. Having put the [Vedic] fires inside his body, he should place the ether [of the bodily cavities] in the ether, he should place his [bodily] air in the air, [bodily] fire in the fire, [bodily] water in the water, the body in the earth, the mind in the moon [and] the organs of hearing (*śrotrāṇi*)[910] in the quarters; he should deposit the feet in Viṣṇu, energy in Rudra [and] speech in the fire; he should place (*nyasya*) the faculty of excretion in the sun and the penis in Prajāpati.[911]

4:34c–35b Having done [this] depositing in the right order, devoid of anger and greed, abstaining from causing injury to any being, he will see everything in the Self.

4:35c–37 Possessed of a triple-stick, a water pot (*tridaṇḍakuṇḍī*),[912] and being a wanderer (*cakrī*), he should eat from begging, [but] he should not eat food [given] by one person.[913] He should not make use of

---

910 The plural is used for the dual.

911 In *Manusmṛti* 12.120 ff., series of placements are given, but in the reverse direction: the ether is placed in the orifices of the body, and so forth. In *Bhāgavatapurāṇa* 7.12:24 ff., however, we encounter the same direction of placement as stated in our text.

912 Generally, *tridaṇḍakuṇḍin* refers to a class of ascetic (see *Yājñavalkyasmṛti* 3.58) who carries a triple-stick, tied together, to indicate his affiliation. The *Manusmṛti*, however, (12.10) gives the following metaphysical interpretation of the *tridaṇḍin*:

> *vāgdaṇḍo 'tha manodaṇḍaḥ kāyadaṇḍas tathaiva ca |*
> *yasyaite nihitā buddhau tridaṇḍīti sa ucyate ||*
>
> The rod of speech, the rod of mind, and the rod of action–a man in whose intellect these are kept under control is said to be "triple-rodded" (OLIVELLE, 2005: 230).

913 *Manusmṛti* 2.188b (*naikānnādī bhaved vratī*) mentions the injunction. Cf. also *Kūrmapurāṇa* 2.12:60 and 2.28:15, *Nāradapurāṇa* 1.25:29 and 1.27:95, *Nāradaparivrājakopaniṣad* 5.35 and *Saṃnyāsopaniṣad* 2.60. It is likely that the source of our text is the *Manusmṛti* as there are considerable borrowings from the *Manusmṛti*, particularly in the Vedic section.

that which does not belong to him, he should resort to the practice of eating alms-food [only].[914] He should stay [no more than] one night in a village and five nights in a city. During the rainy season, he should stay in one place; he should remain free from arrogance and hypocrisy. He should abstain from contact with the village [people]; he should be free from the fault of attachment.

4:38 He should be the same with regard to all beings; [he should] not undertake [anything], should avoid [causing] harm, [and] should daily delight in meditation on the Self, suffused with the reality of *brahman.*

4:39 Whoever always remains thus, he will go to the world of Brahmā (*brahmalaukikam*).[915] He will rejoice [there] with Brahmā, and (*tu*) will [then] be dissolved in *brahman.*

4:40 If he fails [in this observance], full of desire and greed, he will go to hell. Acting as instructed [and] having *brahman* in his heart (*brahmātmā*), he will go to the world of Brahmā.

4:41 I have taught the *dharma* [prescribed in] the Vedas which is excellent (*paraḥ*), which leads to heaven and the highest good (*svarganaiśreyasaḥ*).[916] I have explained [all this] in brief, specifically (*eva*) with [my] Northern face (i.e. Vāmadeva).

[3. The Ādhyātmika stream]

4:42 [Now] I will teach the [*dharma*] called Ādhyātmika with [my] Southern (Aghora) face: [namely] the great science of the Sāṅkhya, as well as Yoga, o you who observe the *mahāvrata.*[917]

---

[914] This appears to be an otiose repetition. Note that the *Śivadharmasaṅgraha* (9.38) has avoided the repetition by altering the earlier *pāda* that speaks of living off alms to an injunction that he should not eat more than 8 mouthfuls.

[915] This is an odd compound: *brahmalaukikam* is used as though it meant *brahmalokam.*

[916] Of course, the grammatically correct form would be *svarganaiḥśreyasaḥ.*

[917] Alternatively, we could interpret this half-line to mean: "The *sāṅkhya* is truly (*eva*) a great [field of] knowledge and so is the *yoga*, o you of great religious observance!" This is the first time that Devī is addressed as *mahāvrate*, a term with many potential connotations and layers of meaning, and possibly emotionally evocative. However, we are not able to trace what Devī's *mahāvratas* are.

[3.1 Sāṅkhya]

4:43–44 [Regarding] *prakṛti* and *puruṣa*, they are united together in one [[...]][918] as a consequence of which, (*yataḥ*) everything comes into being. [[...]][919] *rajas* and *sattva* arise.[920] [It, viz. *pradhāna*] is endowed with these three qualities; from it (*tataḥ*) the intellect (*buddhiḥ*) is born.

4:45 From the intellect, I-ness comes into being,[921] then the [five] subtle elements arise.[922] In the same manner, sense faculties [arise] here;[923] the gross elements (*bhūtaḥ*)[924] come into being from the [five] subtle elements.[925]

---

918 Irregular neuters *prakṛtiṃ* and *puruṣaṃ* are meant for feminine *prakṛtiḥ* and masculine *puruṣaḥ*. Note that Prof. LUBIN (by way of personal communication, dating April 7th, 2018, voiced his doubt about whether "the author considered these neuters; rather they are accusatives of an implicit verb. This hemistich possibly echoes BhG 13.19ab: *prakṛtiṃ puruṣaṃ caiva viddhy anādī ubhāv api.* Perhaps the author was anticipating a gerund like *yojayitvā* or a finite form, in which case the two accusatives would be in apposition to *ubhau*". We could consider *svargāpavargahetuś ca* as a possible conjecture as we are told (1.52) that the teachings of the five streams are meant for *svarga* and *apavarga*. Furthermore the teaching of the Vedic streams (4.1: *svargāpavargahetoś ca*) is also presented as leading to the attainment of *svarga* and *apavarga*. Although the manuscript, N, is damaged here, we can still see the upper part of the missing letters. These letters do not seem to have contained two *r* particles for the conjecture we proposed *svargāpavargahetuś ca*. Thus, although the conjecture seems logical, it is not likely. An alternative conjecture could be *saṃyogas tatra hetuś ca* 'the union is the reason there' reflecting the *Sāṃkhyakārikā*, 21: *saṃyogas tatkṛtaḥ sargaḥ*. The term *prakṛti/pradhāna* might also have featured in the gap, as this refers to the primordial source out of which the world came into being (*Sāṃkhyakārikā*, 22).

919 It is certain that at least the term *tamas* is missing here as the following verse refers to the three *guṇas*, 'qualities'. For the three qualities see *Sāṃkhyakārikā*, 13. We are not able to propose a likely conjecture here.

920 Present third person singular *prajāyate* stands for dual *prajāyete*.

921 This translation assumes *buddhyahaṃkāras* is not intended as a compound but as a metrically required contraction of *buddher ahaṃkāraḥ*.

922 These elements are: sound (*śabda*), touch (*sparśa*), sight (*rūpa*), taste (*rasa*) and smell (*gandha*). (See Gauḍapāda's commentary on verse 22 of the *Sāṃkhyakārikā*).

923 There are altogether eleven sense faculties in this system. Among these, there are five sense organs (viz. ear, skin, eye, tongue and nose) and five organs of action (viz. tongue, hands, feet, anus and the generative organ) and the mind being the eleventh. (See Gauḍapāda's commentary on verse 22 of the *Sāṃkhyakārikā*).

924 These five gross elements are: sky (*ākāśa*), air (*vāyu*), fire (*agni*), water (*jala*) and earth (*pṛthvī*). (See Gauḍapāda's commentary on verse 22 of the *Sāṃkhyakārikā*)

925 The masculine singular *bhūtaḥ* and °*saṃbhavaḥ* here are used for neuter plural. Verses 45 and 46 seem to be saying the same thing as the *Sāṃkhyakārikā*, 22:

4:46 All [these manifested things] are insentient; [only] the *puruṣa* is considered to be sentient.[926] So long as he maintains a sense of 'mine', so long the person is bound.

4:47 [Knowing] all works are [accomplished] through *prakṛti*, he [[...]][927] should be content. But the non-renouncer (*asaṃnyāsin*) will remain bound [to the cycle of transmigration] for as long as he does not find out *māyā*.[928]

[3.2 Yoga]

4:48a–49b I have taught the knowledge of the Sāṅkhya; hear from me [now] the knowledge of Yoga. [One] who endures all pairs [of extremes], is resolute, devoid of all faults, with a mind troubled by worldly existence, is called a *yogin*.[929]

---

prakṛter mahāṃs tato 'haṃkāras, tasmād gaṇaś ca ṣoḍaśakaḥ |
tasmād api ṣoḍaśakāt pañcabhyaḥ pañca bhūtāni ||

926 Cf. *Sāṃkhyakārikā* 11.

927 We are not certain how to fill the gap here. Perhaps one could assume *sa saṃnyāsī* and interpret the line to mean: '[knowing] all works [are accomplished] by matter, the renunciant becomes happy.' Or alternatively, as suggested by Ramhari TIMALSINA, we could consider emending the text to *prakṛtyā sarvakarmāṇi saṃanyasya sa sukhī bhavet*. In that case, our translation would read: 'renouncing all works to Prakṛti, one becomes happy'. We are not aware of the idea of *saṃnyāsa* attested in Sāṅkhya sources.

928 It is worth noting that the *māyā* is missing in *Sāṃkhya* sources. According to the Sāṅkhya system *puruṣa* is bound so long as he sees *prakṛti* (*Sāṃkhyakārikā*, 61). Could it be the case that *māyā* here refers to *prakṛti* as in the *Śvetāśvataropaniṣad* (4.10): *māyāṃ tu prakṛtiṃ vidyān māyinaṃ tu maheśvaram?*

929 Here begins the yoga section. In this section we are taught the *ṣaḍaṅga* yoga corresponding to the Śaiva Yoga system (VASUDEVA 2004: 367–382 offers an informative introduction to *ṣaḍaṅga* yoga). The *Rauravasūtrasaṅgraha* 7.5 writes:

pratyāhāras tathā dhyānaṃ prāṇāyāmo 'tha dhāraṇā |
tarkaś caiva samādhiś ca ṣaḍaṅgo yoga ucyate ||

However, this is is not to be confused with the *aṣṭāṅga* yoga of Patañjali as it is referred to in the *Yogasūtra* 2.29: *yamaniyamāsanaprāṇāyāmapratyāhāradhāraṇādhyānasamādhayo 'ṣṭāv aṅgāni* | .

4:49c–51 After facing north and then assuming a yogic posture, [such as one of the following:] [1] Svastika,[930] [2] the lotus-posture,[931] [3] Bhadra,[932] [4] Arddhacandra,[933] [5] Prasārita,[934] [6] Sāpāśraya,[935] [7] Añjalika,[936] [8] Yogapaṭṭa,[937] in whatever posture is comfortable [for him],[938] [and] having correctly assumed a yogic posture, with the body

---

930 Vācaspati Miśra in *Tattvavaiśāradī* commenting on *Yogasūtra* 2.46 defines the Svastika posture thus: *savyam ākuñcitaṃ caraṇaṃ dakṣiṇajaṅghorvantare, dakṣiṇaṃ cākuñcitaṃ caraṇaṃ vāmajaṅghorvantare nikṣipet | etat svastikam.* See also GOODALL 2004: 349, fn. 725 and *Pāñcārthabhāṣya* p. 38.

931 The *Yogabhāṣyavivaraṇa* commentary on section 2.46 in the *Yogasūtra* defines this posture as follows: *tatra padmāsanaṃ nāma savyaṃ pādam upasaṃhṛtya dakṣiṇopari nidadhīta | tathaiva dakṣiṇaṃ savyasyopariṣṭāt | kaṭyurogrīvaṃ ca viṣṭabhya mṛ(ga)?tasuptavann nāsikāgranihitadṛṣṭiḥ, samudgakavad apihitoṣṭhasampuṭaḥ dantair dantāgram aparāmṛśan muṣṭimātrāntaraviprakṛṣṭacibukorassthalaḥ rājadantāntara nihitarasanāgraḥ hastau pāṇyor upari kacchapakaṃ brahmāñjaliṃ vā kṛtvā, sakṛd āsthāpitaitthaṃsaṃsthānaḥ punaḥ punaḥ śarīrāvayavaśarīravinyāsaviśeṣaparityaktaprayatnaḥ san yenāsīta tat padmāsanam |* . See also *Pāñcārthabhāṣya*, p. 38.

932 Vācaspati Miśra, in the *Tattvavaiśāradī*, commenting on *Yogasūtra* 2.46, defines this yogic posture as follows: *pādatale vṛṣaṇasamīpe saṃpuṭīkṛtya tasyopari pāṇīkaccapikāṃ kuryāt tad bhadrāsanam.* See also *Pāñcārthabhāṣya* p. 38.

933 This yogic posture is defined in the *Parākhyatantra* 14.6c–7b in the following manner: *dviguṇe jānunī kṛtvā pādāv anyonyasaṃgatau || tadvad bhuvi kṛtāvāse tad bhaved ardhacaṃdrakam |* . See also *Pāñcārthabhāṣya* p. 38. For further details, consult GOODALL (2004: 350, fn. 728).

934 See also *Pāñcārthabhāṣya* p. 38.

935 Kṣemarāja, commenting on *Svacchandatantra*, 7.291a, remarks on this posture: *bhityāśrayāt sāpāśrayam etat.* Although all occurrences of this posture in the *Niśvāsatattvasaṃhitā* appear as 'Sāpāśraya', we assume that the original name of the posture may have been 'Sopāśraya' since *Yogabhāṣya* (see commentary on 2.16) and commentators on it keep the reading 'Sopāśraya'. *Carakasaṃhitāsūtrasthāna* 15.11 mentions the reading 'Sopāśraya' as well as 'Svāpāśraya'.

936 See also *Pāñcārthabhāṣya* p. 38.

937 Kṣemarāja, commenting on *Svacchandatantra* (7.291ab) glosses this posture: *yogārthaṃ paṭṭaṃ parikarabandhāya badhvā etad anyatam āsanam |* .

938 We may count *yathāsukha* as a separate yogic posture as we know there is a well known posture called *sukhāsana*. In this case we will have a list of nine yogic postures. We have a parallel for these postures in *Nayasūtra* 4.14–15

yatra tatra sthito deśe yatra tatrāśrame rataḥ |
svastikaṃ padmakaṃ bhadram arddhacandraṃ prasāritam |
sāpāśrayam añjalikaṃ yogapaṭṭaṃ yathāsukham |
aṣṭāsanāni mukhyāni kīrtitāni samāsataḥ |

The same list of yogic postures occurs again in *Nayasūtra* 4.105; the text explicitly states that the number of yogic postures is eight, which is the reason we do not count *yathāsukha* as a separate yogic posture. The *Yogabhāṣya* on 2.46 does however count

upright, focused, one should place one's tongue on the palate, and

---

yathāsukha as a separate yogic posture. The *Svacchandatantra* 7.290–291 records the list of the six (if we do not count Yathāsukha) or seven yogic postures, sharing its list with our text except that Prasārita and Añjalika are not on its list, thus:

āsanaṃ padmakaṃ badhvā svastikaṃ bhadram āsanam || 290
sāpāśrayam arddhacandraṃ yogapaṭṭaṃ yathāsukham | 291ab

- 290cd āsanaṃ padmakaṃ badhvā svastikaṃ bhadram āsanam] N^{K}_{28}; āsanaṃ svastikaṃ baddhvā padmakaṃ bhadram eva vā KSTS
- 291ab arddhacandraṃ] N^{K}_{28}; sardhacandraṃ KSTS

Kiraṇatantra 58.4–5, however, presents the list of eight *āsanas*—Svastika, Padma, Ardhacandra, Vīra, Yogapaṭṭa, Prasārita, Paryaṅka and Yathāsaṃstha—sharing five *āsanas* with our text:

baddhvāsanaṃ yathābhīṣṭaṃ svastikaṃ padmam eva vā |
ardhacandraṃ ca vīrākhyaṃ yogapaṭṭaṃ prasāritam ||
paryaṅkaṃ ca yathāsaṃsthamāsanāṣṭakamucyate |

The *Sarvajñānottarayogapāda*, verse 9 gives a list of seven *āsanas* of which it shares sharing four with our text:

padmakaṃ svastikaṃ vāpi upasthātyāñjaliṃ tathā |
pīṭhārdham ardhacandraṃ vā sarvatobhadram eva vā ||

The *Parākhyatantra* 14.5 mentions four *āsanas*—Padma, Svastika, Daṇḍa and Ardhacandra—thereof sharing three with our text. The *Makuṭāgama* 11.6cd–7ab mentions six *āsanas*—Gomukha, Svastika Padma, Arddhacandra, Vīra, and Yogāsana(?)—sharing three of them with our text:

gomukhaṃ svastikañ caiva padmañ caivārddhacandrakam ||
vīraṃ yogāsanaṃ proktaṃ ṣaḍvidhañ cāsanaṃ kramāt |

The *Mataṅgayogapāda* 2.13 records six *āsanas*—Paryaṅka, Kamala Bhadra, Svastika, Acala and Dṛḍha—sharing two of them with our text thus:

tataḥ samādhau yogyaḥ syān nānyathā munipuṅgava |
paryaṅkaṃ kamalaṃ bhadraṃ svastikaṃ cācalaṃ dṛḍham ||

Pāśupatasūtra 1.16 mentions eight *āsanas*—Padmaka, Svastika, Upastha, Añjalika, Arddhacandra, Pīṭhaka, Daṇḍāyata and Sarvatobhadra—sharing four with our text. This sketch of the *āsanas* found in Śaiva texts shows that almost every text mentions a different number of *āsanas*, only a few of which are shared. Note that the *Yogabhāṣya*, which might have been the source for other texts, in 2.46 records following thirteen *āsanas*—Padmāsana, Bhadrāsana, Vīrāsana, Svastikāsana, Daṇḍāsana, Sopāśraya, Paryaṅka, Krauñcaniṣadana, Hastiniṣadana, Uṣṭraniṣadana, Samasaṃsthāna, Sthirasukha and Yathāsukha—sharing four *āsanas* with our text.

should not allow [one's upper] teeth to come into contact with [one's lower] teeth.[939]

4:52 With regard to the five [sense-objects], hearing, touch, sight, taste and smell, the group of the senses is unruly; one should restrain [them] with effort.[940]

---

[939] This is what is called *karaṇa* in the context of the yoga which is to be performed once a Yogi has assumed a yogic posture and before he engages in *prāṇāyāma*. Our reading (51cd) is closely paralleled by *Skandapurāṇa* 179.40cd (*tālau jihvāṃ samādhāya dantair dantān na ca spṛśan*). The *Mataṅgayogapāda* (2.22c–28) presents this idea as follows:

karaṇaṃ ca pravakṣyāmi yathāvat tan nibodha me ||
ubhayor jaṅghayor madhye hastāv ānīya tiryagau |
kṛtvottānau samau vidvān vāmasyopari dakṣiṇam ||
nyaset karaṃ yathāṅgulyo dakṣiṇā vāmamūlataḥ |
kiṃcid ākuñcitāṅguṣṭhau kartavyo niyatātmanā ||
uraśconnamya vivataṃ kṛtvā bāhū pariślathau |
pṛṣṭham ākuñcayet skandhadeśam unnamayet sudhīḥ ||
niṣkampāṃ sudṛḍhām ṛjvīṃ nātistabdhāṃ na kuñcitām |
grīvāṃ vidhārayed yatnāc chiraḥ kāryaṃ samaṃ sadā ||
dyāvāpṛthivyābhimukho dṛṅāsāgrasamāśrayā |
kiṃcit sammīlayen netre dantair dantān na saṃspṛśet ||
tālumadhyagatenaiva jihvāgreṇa mahāmune |
karaṇaṃ yogamārgoktaṃ yathāvat parivistarāt ||

The *Triśikhibrāhmaṇopaniṣat* 91–92 presents the same notion without explicitly referring to this practice as *karaṇa*:

badhvā prāg āsanaṃ vipro ṛjukāyaḥ samāhitaḥ |
nāsāgranyastanayano dantair dantān asaṃspṛśan ||
rasanāṃ tāluni nyasya svasthacitto nirāmayaḥ |
ākuñcitaśiraḥ kiṃcin nibadhnan yogamudrayā |
hastau yathoktavidhinā prāṇāyāmaṃ samācaret ||

A portion in the same Upaniṣad (144–146b, especially 146ab: *saṃyamec cendriyagrāmam ātmabuddhyā viśuddhayā*) comes quite close to 4.52ab of our text. Cf. *Sarvajñānottarayogapāda* 250–251, *Svacchandatantra* 4.365–367, *Uttarakāmika* 23.209–210, *Jayottara* 9.19–23, *Vāsudevakalpa* 394–395, Bhojadeva's *Siddhāntasārapaddhati* B 28/19, fol. 39r:1–3 *Bṛhatkālottara* A 43/1, fol. 13v:4–5, *Īśānagurudevapaddhati* V:3, p.185 etc. See also TAK:2 v.s. *karaṇa*.

[940] The *Manusmṛti* (2.99–100) presents this idea as follows: *indriyāṇāṃ tu sarveṣāṃ yady ekaṃ kṣaratīndriyam* | *tenāsya kṣarati prajñā dṛteḥ pādād ivodakam* || *vaśe kṛtvendriyagrāmaṃ saṃyamya ca manas tathā* | *sarvān saṃsādhayedarthānakṣiṇvan yogatastanum* || .

4:53ab When [the senses are] restrained one by one, this is called *pratyāhāra*.[941]

4:53cd All pervading [[...]],[942] whose form is meditation, formless.

4:54ab For the destruction of passion and hatred one should practise meditation (*cintayed dhyānam*) alone.

4:54c–56b Now I will teach controlling of the breath (*prāṇāyāma*): one should practise three varieties. After having first exhaled [and] then inhaled, the retention [of breath] is called Kumbhaka.[943] One should fill one's body [with air] until [it is] completely filled; this is called Pūraka, the second type of breath-control.

4:56c–57b If someone exhales [retained] air from [his] body, [[...]][944] this is called Recaka, which is the third type of breathing exercise.[945]

4:57c–58 One should meditate on the all-pervading, moving air [as being situated] in the tip of one's big toe,[946] and should fill everything

---

941 The *Yogasūtra* 2.54 defines the *pratyāhāra* as follows: *svasviṣayāsamprayoge citta-svarūpānukāra ivendriyāṇāṃ pratyāhāraḥ.* Further, Vyāsa comments on *pratyāhāra* thus: *yathā madhukararājaṃ makṣikā utpatantam anūtpatanti niviśamānam anuniviśante tathā indriyāṇi cittanirodhe niruddhānīti eṣa pratyāhāraḥ* |.

942 We could consider conjecturing *sarvagam ekaniṣṭhaṃ tu* as suggested by Prof. D. ACHARYA. Alternatively, we might consider conjecturing *sarvagam ekacittas tu.*

943 Once again the neuter is used for the masculine.

944 We are not missing the essential part of the text since in this breathing exercise the retained air is exhaled which is what we already have in the existing text. Prof. D. ACHARYA has suggested to conjecture something like *svadehāt tu śanaiḥ śanaiḥ.*

945 These are the commonly known three types of *prāṇāyāmas*. Some other sources, however, mention four kinds of *prāṇāyāmas*. For instance, *Nayasūtra* 4.113, *Svacchandatantra* 7.298 and *Tantrasadbhāva* 27.23 mention the fourth kind of *prāṇāyāma*, known as *supraśānta*. The *Dharmaputrikā* (1.19), a late Śaiva yoga text, also mentions the four kinds of *prāṇāyāma*, the fourth being *praśānta* instead of *supraśānta*:

pūrakaḥ kumbhakaś caiva recakas tadanantaram |
praśāntaś caiva vijñeyaḥ prāṇāyāmaś caturvidhaḥ ||

- 19b recakas tadanantaram] B_7E_N; rekaka tadanantaram C
- 19c praśāntaś caiva] B_7E_N; praśāntaś caiti C

946 Here begins the section on *dhāraṇā*. We have the four types of *dhāraṇā*—air, fire, earth and water, appearing in this order. The *Rauravasūtrasaṅgraha* (7.6–9) mentions four types of *dhāraṇā*: fire (*āgneyī*), moon (*saumyā*), sovereign (*aiśānī*) and nectar (*amṛtā*):

(*viśvam*) with air filled with black dust. He who practices thus, he acts as one who has the nature of air.

4:59 One should meditate [next] on blazing fire which consumes all the quarters;[947] he who mediates thus becomes of the nature of fire.

4:60 Listen to how the earth is situated in the body as something firm in nature: it should be meditated upon as extending up to the ocean, yellow, and having immobility as its defining characteristic.

4:61 If one meditates on flowing water (*varuṇam*) in the uvula (*ghaṇṭikāyām*), he, his sins having been destroyed by [this] mental concentration (*dhāraṇā*), will become of the nature of water.

4:62 One should discriminate the causes of Yoga and wisdom,[948] which are to be discriminated according to the *āgamas*.[949] Confident, he should aim for knowledge of the Self, with a view to that [knowledge] arising.[950]

---

prathamā dhāraṇāgneyī nābhimadhye tu dhārayet |
tasyāṃ vai dhāryamāṇāyāṃ pāpaṃ nirdahati kṣaṇāt |
hṛdaye dhārayed vidvān saumyāṃ somasṛtāṃ kalām |
tasyāṃ vai dhāryamāṇāyāṃ sarvatrāpy āyanaṃ bhavet |
aiśānīṃ dhārayen mūrdhni sarvasiddhikarīṃ nṛṇām |
yayā prayānti vai kṣipraṃ śivasya paramaṃ padam |
amṛtā dhāraṇā yā tu vyāpinī tu śivaṃkarī |
āpyāyayati sarvatra sarvaṃ jñānāmṛtena ca ||

The same list of type of *dhāraṇā*, found in the *Rauravasūtrasaṅgraha*, is also attested to in the *Svāyaṃbhuvasūtrasaṅgraha* (20.4–7). The *Mataṅgayogapāda* (2.38–65) has the list of the four *dhāraṇās*: fire (*āgneyī*), water (*vāruṇī*), sovereign (*aiśānī*) and nectar (*amṛtā*). The list of *dhāraṇā* listed in the *Niśvāsamukha* seems to be unique.

947 Although K and W record the grammatically correct form *sarvatodiśam*, we have retained the reading of N *sarvatodiśām* considering it to be original, not least of all, since N is the oldest extant witness.

948 Once again what appears to be a feminine accusative singular is in fact intended as a masculine accusative plural, used in lieu of a neuter.

949 It is not clear what group of texts this refers to, but presumably it does not refer to *Siddhāntatantras*. *Tarka* 'reasoning/judgement' is one of the most distinguishing characteristics of the Ṣaḍaṅgayoga. VASUDEVA (2004: 173) writes about the latter: "Ṣaḍaṅgayoga is uncompromisingly theistic and distinguished by the presence of 'Judgement' (*ūha, tarka*) as the most important ancillaries".

950 Alternatively, the *m* could be a euphonic glide in the middle of a compound, in which case we could interpret the following: 'he should focus [his attention] for the sake of the arising of complete self-knowledge'.

4:63 He who abides in *samādhi* [will] see amazing [things] [[...]] he should meditate [[...]] until he attains oneness with them.

4:64 Sound, touch, form, taste, and smell as the fifth; he does not perceive (*ajānāti*)[951] any of these when he attains oneness with them.

4:65 He does not experience [the sound of drums and the like] being beaten[952] and he does not see with his eyes; divine sight will arise when he attains oneness with those [elements].

4:66 All kinds of spells (*sarvavidyāḥ*)[953] will function [for him, and] everything will be directly perceptible to him, and he will [be able to] converse with accomplished ones [everywhere], when he attains oneness with [them].[954]

4:67 [[...]][955] and he will be omniscient. By [means of] this very body he will be able to create and destroy.

4:68 All this will work for him who meditates on Īśvara;[956] he will [finally]

---

951 Finite verbs are not usually used with an alpha privative. Prof. Dominic GOODALL writes, in an email dated 26th of September, 2007: "S. A. SRINIVASAN appears inclined to assume that Vācaspatimiśra, in his *Sāṅkhyatattvakaumudī*, may have used the negative *a* without intending to express reproach. He begins his discussion of the privative with this observation (P1.4.5.16, p. 40):

> Das a-[P]rivativum ist sandhigef[ä]hrdet und geht manchmal verloren. Die [Ü]berlieferer tilgen es daher manchmal, oder sie [ä]ndern die Wortstellung, um es vor Verlust zu sch[ü]tzen."

952 Cf. *Kulasāratantra* fol. 38r:3: *tāḍyamānair na vindeta yadā tanmayatāṃ gataḥ* |.

953 Alternatively, this may refer to knowledge.

954 *Ex conj.* 65c–66 echoes *Nayasūtra* 3.21c—22:

> *siddhaś caiva svatantraś ca divyasṛṣṭiḥ prajāyate* ||
> *ṣaṇmāsāddhyānayogena divyasiddhiḥ prajāyate* |
> *trailokye yaḥ pravartteta pratyakṣan tasya jāyate* ||

In light of this reading of the *Nayasūtra*, we may consider emending *divayadṛṣṭi* to *divyasṛṣṭi* in our text, since *sarvaṃ pratyakṣato bhavet* has the same connotation of *divyadṛṣṭi*. Otherwise, either (*sarvaṃ pratyakṣato bhavet* or *divyadṛṣṭi*) is tautologous.

955 In the *Niśvāsa*-corpus *sarvajñaḥ*, when it appears to refer to a state of the aspirant (*sādhaka*), is often accompanied by *śivatulyaḥ* 'equal to Śiva' and *kāmarūpī* 'able to assume form at will'. For example see *Nayasūtra* 3.23. *śivatulyaḥ kāmarūpī* would be a possible conjecture here. Our passage is in the context of general yoga, rather the Śaiva Yoga. Thus, the gap may not have particularly contained the world *śivatulyaḥ*.

956 Given that the text is a Śaiva work, Īśvara is here taken to refer to Śiva; perhaps

obtain the position of Īśvara. Similarly (*ca*), by meditating on Brahmā, he will obtain his (i.e. Brahmā's) position.

4:69a–70a By meditating on Viṣṇu, he will obtain the position of Viṣṇu; by meditation on other [gods], he will obtain [their] positions. Whatever contemplation [he employs], he will obtain the corresponding (*tat tat*) position.[957] I have taught you [the stream of revealed knowledge] relating to the Self (*adhyātmikam*);

[4. The Atimārga stream]

4:70b Now hear as well the Atimārga from me.[958]

[4.1 Atyāśrama: paraphrase of the Pāśupatasūtra]

4:70c–71 [He should bathe ...] with ash,[959]

this is evocative of the *Yogasūtra* (1.23): '*īśvarapraṇidhānād vā*'. According to the *Yogasūtrabhāṣya*, the fruit of fixing [the mind] on Īśvara is equivalent to the result of remaining *samādhi*; however, in our present context, the fruit of concentrating the mind on Īsvara is the obtaining of the position of Īśvara.

957 This cliché *yena yena hi bhāvena* is so well known that the syntax has been left incomplete here. Refer, *inter alias*, to *Manusmṛti* 4.234, *Netratantra* 22.67, *Kubjikāmatatantra* 3.97 and so on. Cf. also *Bhagavadgītā* 4.11ab *ye yathā māṃ prapadyante tāṃs tathaiva bhajāmy aham*, and 9.25 *yānti devavratā devān pitṝn yānti pitṛvratāḥ | bhūtāni yānti bhūtejyā yānti madyājino 'pi mām ||* .

958 The term Atimārga refers to the systems of the Pāśupatas. According to the *Niśvāsamukha*'s classification, Pāśupatas are said to be of two types: Atyāśrama and Lokātīta (*Niśvāsamukha* 4.88). As far as we are aware, there is no earlier parallel for the use of the term Atimārga. Hence, there is a considerable possibility that *Niśvāsamukha* may be responsible for coining the term. The subsequent history of the term has been thoroughly scrutinized by SANDERSON (2006). For a detailed discussion refer to our introduction on p. 78.

959 Here commences a lengthy section constituting a paraphrase of the *Pāśupatasūtra*. Our translation of the *Pāśupatasūtra* and the °*bhāṣya* in the footnotes to this section mainly is based on HARA (1966). Unless otherwise stated, the translation has been provided by ourselves. As our text consists of a paraphrase of the *Pāśupatasūtra*, we have provided a translation but of those *sūtras* which further our understanding of the *Niśvāsamukha*.

Cf. *Pāśupatasūtra* (1.2) *bhasmanā triṣavaṇaṃ snāyīta*. Given that this section consists of a paraphrase of the *Pāśupatasūtras*, one should expect to encounter a reference here to bathing in ash three times a day (*Pāśupatasūtra* 1.2). We may therefore conjecture, although it is hypermetrical, *bhasmanā triṣavaṇasnāyī* or *bhasmanā triṣkālasnāyī* (cf. *Niśvāsamukha* 3.43). Both of these conjectures have been proposed by Prof. D. ACHARYA and to our mind, appear plausible; after all, the consecutive

he should sleep on ash,[960] [and] control his sense faculties;[961] he should wear *nirmālya*,[962] live on alms,[963] [and] frequent secret places.[964] In order to [obtain] a *darśana* of god he should perform worship in those very places.[965]

Pāśupatasūtra (1.3), *bhasmani śayīta*, is paraphrased in *Niśvāsamukha* 4.70d in the same manner as *bhasmaśāyī*. Therefore, we may also conjecture something along the line of *bhasmanā kurute snānam* (cf. *Brahmāṇḍapurāṇa* 1.2:27:123, *Liṅgapurāṇa* 34.18) or *bhaṣmanā digdhasarvāṅgaḥ* (cf. *Skandapurāṇa* 32.115 and 122.78), which would be rather weak since it deviates from the original wording in the *Pāśupatasūtra*. Note that moreover we find a reference to the injunction of bathing in ashes in *Guhyasūtra* 12.9–12.10:

bhasmasnānañ ca śaucañ ca upasaṃhāran tathaiva ca | 9cd
kapālaṃ caiva khaṭvāṅgaṃ bhasmavāsañ ca sarvadā | 10ab

• 9d upasaṃhāran tathaiva] NW(unmetrical); upahāraṃ tathaiva ca K • 10a kapālaṃ caiva] KW; kapālaṃñ caiva N • 10b khaṭvāṅgaṃ] K; khaṭvāga N; khaṭvāṃga W

960 Cf. *Pāśupatasūtra* 1.3 (*bhasmani śayīta*). Kauṇḍinya emphasises the injunction to sleep on ashes during the night: *bhasmany eva rātrau svaptavyam nānyatrety arthaḥ*.

961 The *sūtra* '*jitendriyaḥ*' is not found in the first chapter, but instead is contained in 5.11 of the *Pāśupatasūtra*. It is unlikely that the same *sūtra* would appear twice, for which reason we assume that this cliché is merely a *pādapūraṇa*.

962 Cf. *Pāśupatasūtra* 1.5: *nirmālyam*. This is a technical term most often referring to a collection of flowers that had been offered in worship to an image of Śiva. According to Kauṇḍinya's interpretation, a Pāśupata ascetic should wear *nirmālya* for two reasons. The first is to increase his devotion to his lord and the second is to show his sectarian affiliation: *bhaktivivṛddhyarthaṃ liṅgābhivyaktyarthaṃ ca tad dhāryam ity arthaḥ*. (Kauṇḍinya's commentary and *Pāśupatasūtra* 1.5).

963 The practice of *bhaikṣyam* (living on alms) is not mentioned in the *sūtras* contained in the first chapter of the *Pāśupatasūtra*, but in the *Pāśupatasūtra* 5.14.

964 Although this resembles a *sūtra*, no clear parallel can be found in either the *Pāśupatasūtra* or the *Pāśupatasūtrabhāṣya*. However, it might well be related to *Niśvāsamukha* 3.29cd:

guhyānyānyapi devasya dṛṣṭvā mucyanti kilbiṣaiḥ

by visiting (*dṛṣṭvā*) other secret [places] of god they will be freed from sins.

Unfortunately we are not able to trace the toponyms of the places referred to, here. Might this possibly refer to the Guhyāṣṭaka?

965 There is no clear parallel for the half line (71cd) in either the *Pāśupatasūtra* or the *Pāśupatasūtrabhāṣya*. This is the first time that we encounter the *pūjā*-element among Pāśupata injunctions. For more details, see our introduction p. 82 ff. This element appears to have been added at a later stage among Pāśupata practices.

4:72 He [should take up his] abode in the house of a *liṅga* [i.e. a temple],[966] he should praise with the sound HUḌḌUṄ, sing, dance, [pay] homage with the word *namas* and recite the [five] *brahma* [mantras].[967]

4:73 He should wear one garment,[968] or [be] naked,[969] and he should resort to Dakṣiṇāmūrti.[970]

---

966 Cf. *Pāśupatasūtra* 1.7: *āyatanavāsī.* Although neither the *Pāśupatasūtra* nor the *Pāśupatasūtrabhāṣya* here make mention of the *liṅga*, the *Niśvāsamukha* references the *liṅga* in its paraphrasing of the *Pāśupatasūtra*. Consult p. 80 in the introductory section for more details. According to Kauṇḍinya, the abode should be constructed by others (see Kauṇḍinya's commentary (ad loc.) *Pāśupatasūtra* 1.7). Note that residing in a temple marks the beginning of the first stage of the religious life of a Pāśupata ascetic according to Kauṇḍinya.

967 Cf. *Pāśupatasūtra* 1.8: *hasitagītanṛttaḍuṃḍuṃkāranamaskārajapyopahāreṇopatiṣṭhet.* The *Ratnaṭīkā* (pp. 18–19) refers to the *hasita-gīta* etc. as the 'sixfold deeds' (*ṣaḍaṅgopahāra* 'six-limbed offering') We assume that *ḍuṃḍuṃkāra* is a corruption of *huḍḍuṅkāra.* Thus, we propose this *sūtra* should be read as follows: *hasitagīta-nṛtyahuḍḍuṅkāranamaskārajapyopahāreṇopatiṣṭhet.* This *sūtra* is widespread amongst Śaiva sources, though it sometimes features in more close, at other times as more loose paraphrased formulations. The *Ratnaṭīkā*, p. 18–19; *Sarvadarśanasaṅgraha*, p. 169; *Tīrthavivecanakāṇḍa* p. 82, *Svacchandatantra* 10.588 and the *Śivadharmasaṅgraha* 5.31.

968 Cf. *Pāśupatasūtra* 1.10: *ekavāsāḥ.*

969 Cf. *Pāśupatasūtra* 1.11: *avāsā vā.* Kauṇḍinya, commenting on this sūtra, states that the particle *vā* ('or') in the *sūtra* does not suggest an 'optional choice' between two equally deserving possibilities. Instead, it postulates that one should aspire to roam about naked, and only if one is not able to do so, one should clad oneself in a single piece of clothing (Kauṇḍinya (ad loc.) *Pāśupatasūtra* 1.11).

970 Cf. *Pāśupatasūtra* 1.9: *mahādevasya dakṣiṇāmūrtim* (according to BISSCHOP 2007: 5). BAKKER (2004) argues that the concept of Dakṣiṇāmūrti, which he convincingly shows to be of Vedic origin, comprises two chief elements: first of all, it presents Śiva as the teacher, secondly, it coordinates the seating positions in his vicinity. The teacher, being the protagonist, is understood to face 'eastwards'. His students are to be seated to his right ('south'), facing him (i.e. facing 'north'). This is directly evocative of the seating arrangement in relation to the teacher in the Vedic *upanayana* ritual. BAKKER (2004: 127) bases his presentation of the notion of Dakṣiṇāmūrti on his analysis of the concept as it features in Pāśupata sources:

> The concept of *dakṣṇāmūrti* thus comprises the manifested form (*rūpa*) of God, the (physical) image or body (*mūrti*) in which it may be envisaged, and the right side (*dakṣiṇe pārśve*), which indicates the Pāśupata position with respect to Mahādeva and his embodiment. As such, the term is applicable to every situation in which the Pāśupata enters into contact with his object of worship. And this appears to have been the intention of the author of the *Pāśupatasūtra* when we read PS 1.8-9 coherently (as also the author of the Ṭīkā seems to have done: *upahārasūtra*, above p. 124): "He should worship with offerings of laughter, singing,

He should worship the god of gods with withered, fallen flowers.[971]

---

dancing, bellowing, obeisance, and muttering to the gracious form/body (*dakṣiṇāmūrti*) of Mahādeva". The same idea underlies the *Ratnaṭīkā* at *Gaṇakārikā* 7 (p. 18) where it says that the Pāśupata should consecrate the ashes with mantras in the temple "at Śiva's Dakṣiṇāmūrti," or the *Skandapurāṇa* when it advises that one should offer rice pudding with ghee at the "southern *mūrti*" during one year in order to become like Nandin.

BAKKER (2014) concludes his assessment with stating that

> [i]n sum, the Pāśupata Dakṣiṇāmūrti is a state in which God reveals one quarter of Himself, the form to which He grants access, that is, yoga; it is Śiva's body/form of grace. (BAKKER 2004: 127)

BAKKER's presentation is mostly congruent with Kauṇḍinya's account, who writes in this regard:

> *devasya iti ṣāṣṭhī | svasvāmibhāvaḥ sambandhaḥ | parigrahārtham evādhikurute | atra dakṣiṇeti dikpratavibhāge bhavati | ādityo diśo vibhajati | diśaś ca mūrtiṃ vibhajanti | mūrtir nāma yad etad devasya dakṣiṇe pārśve sthitenodaṅmukhenopānte yad rūpam upalabhyate vṛṣadhvajaśūlapāṇinandimahākālordhvaliṅgādilakṣaṇaṃ, yadvā [yatra] laukikāḥ pratipadyante mahādevasyāyatanam iti tatropastheyam | dakṣināmūrtigrahaṇāt pūrvottarapaścimānāṃ mūrtīnāṃ pratiṣedhaḥ, mūrtiniyogāc ca mūrtyabhāve niyamalopaḥ |*

> "*devasya*" is a genitive. The relation is one of owner and owned; it bears reference to (His) grace (*parigraha*) only. "*Dakṣiṇā*" in the Sūtra has the meaning of a spatial division; the sun divides the quarters and the quarters divide the *mūrti*. (That) which the word "*mūrti*" designates is this form (*rūpa*) which is seen in (His) proximity by one who is facing north while standing at God's right side (*dakṣiṇe pārśve*), (a form) that is characterized by the bull-banner, lance in hand, Nandin, Mahākāla, erect phallus, etc., or it is (that) to which the laymen resort, "the sanctuary of Mahādeva." The object of worship is there. (Bakker 2004: 126)

In the *Guhyasūtra*, this expression occurs not in compound format, but in dissolved form: *dakṣināyāṃ mūrtau*, often preceded by *devasya*. This clarifies that the intended meaning of Dakṣiṇāmūrti here is in reference to the seating position at the right side of god (for example, see *Guhyasūtra* 3.18c–3.20ab, 10.8c–10.10b, 10.50–52, 11.112, 10.22, 10.29, 10.51, 11.59, 11.61, 11.73 and 11.83–85). It is hence neither to be taken as referring to Śiva as the teacher, nor to an iconographical form of Śiva that, as GOODALL (*Tāntrikābhidhānakośa* v.s. Dakṣiṇāmūrti) has shown, appears most commonly on the southern side of temples in South India.

971 Note an irregular compound features here for metrical reasons. We do not find any parallel for this line. It certainly does not originate from the *Pāśupatasūtra*, *Pāśupatasūtrabhāṣya* or *Ratnaṭīkā*. This injunction goes with the Pāśupata concept

4:74 He should not see [[urine and excrement]],[972] and he should not speak to women and Śūdras.[973] If he does see [urine and excrement and speak to women and Śūdras, he should first do] *prāṇāyāma*,[974] and then recite the Aghora [mantra].[975]

4:75 One should see all living beings with an unclouded disposition,[976] [then] the inauspicious [becomes] auspicious,[977] [and] circumambulating to the left [becomes] circumambulating to the right.[978]

---

of harmlessness ('*ahiṃsā*'). By employing fallen flowers one abstains from inflicting harm that would result from plucking them. See also SANDERSON (2014: 10, fn. 38), who shows that this notion has textual parallels in the *Devīkālottara*.

972 *Ex conj.* Cf. *Pāśupatasūtra* 1.12: *mūtrapurīṣaṃ nāvekṣet.* Cf. also *Baudhāyanadharmasūtra* 3.8:17.

973 Cf. *Pāśupatasūtra* 1.13: *strīśūdraṃ nābhibhāṣet.* Cf. also *Manusmṛti* 11.224, *Baudhāyanadharmasūtra* 3.8:17, 4.5:4, *Viṣṇusmṛti* 46.25 etc. For more references, see BISSCHOP & GRIFFITHS (2003: 338, esp. fn. 121).

In the *Niśvāsamukha*, the grammatically irregular optative singular *abhibhāṣet*, which, according to Pāṇinian grammar should be *abhibhāṣeta* in *ātmanepada*, is paraphrased as *abhibhāṣayet*, which is also irregular. For variants of this line with the correct *ātmanepada* form, see *Atharvavedapariśiṣṭa* 40.6:2 in BISSCHOP & GRIFFITHS (2003: 338, esp. fn. 221), *Kāṭhakagṛhyasūtra* 5.3 and *Mahābhārata* 12.36:35.

974 Cf. *Pāśupatasūtra* 1.16: *prāṇāyāmaṃ kṛtvā.* On the basis of this *sūtra*, one could emend *dṛṣṭvā* to *kṛtvā*. But in this case we would miss the main cause in the sentence. For that reason, we have opted to supply the following on the strength of *Pāśupatasūtra* 1.14: *yady avekṣed yady abhibhāṣayet|* 'if one were to look, if one were to speak'.

975 Cf. *Pāśupatasūtra* 1.17: *raudrīṃ gāyatrīṃ bahurūpīṃ vā japet.* Unlike our text, *Pāśupatasūtra* gives the option of reciting either *raudrī gāyatrī* or *bahurūpī gāyatrī.* The *Pāśupatasūtrabhāṣya* (p. 39) tells us that *raudrī* is *tatpuruṣa* and *bahurūpī* is the *aghora* mantra.

976 Cf. *Pāśupatasūtra* 1.18: *akaluṣamateḥ.* Note that the 3rd singular *ātmanepada* optative *paśyeta* remains for 3rd singular *parasmaipada paśyet.*

977 Cf. *Pāśupatasūtra* 2.7: *amaṅgalaṃ cātra maṅgalaṃ bhavati.* Kauṇḍinya mentions that 'inauspicious' here refers to a multitude of transgressive methods (such as nakedness, anti-clockwise circumambulation and so forth) that are 'supposedly inauspicious' yet yield auspicious fruits; he concludes by saying, *kāraṇamūrtau kriyamāṇam amaṅgalaṃ maṅgalaṃ bhavatīty arthaḥ.* "The meaning is, inauspicious [acts] that are performed to the image of the cause (*kāraṇamūrtau*) [of the universe] (i.e. Śiva) become auspicious" (HARA 1966: 272).

978 Cf. *Pāśupatasūtra* 2.8: *apasavyaṃ ca pradakṣiṇam.* Kauṇḍinya glosses, *apasavyaṃ nāma yat savyād viparītam.* '*apasavya*' means that which is 'opposite of counterclockwise'. On clockwise circumambulation, he glosses, *pradakṣiṇaṃ nāma yad anyeṣām apasavyaṃ tad iha pradakṣiṇaṃ dharmaniṣpādakaṃ bhavati.* 'clockwise circumambulation is to say that which is counterclockwise circumambulation for others; in this context (*iha*) it is clockwise circumambulation, and it becomes the accomplishment of *dharma*.'

4:76 Worship as performed for ancestors and worship as performed for gods: one should perform [them] both for the god (i.e. Rudra).[979] The great-souled one should practise intense austerity (*tapaḥ*)[980] with exclusive devotion [for Śiva].[981]

4:77 Through the hardships of cold and heat; water [[...]]. He should always be dedicated to mantra recitation and meditation, and should [have] the capacity for patient endurance of all kinds of pairs [of opposites].[982]

He further says, *na kevalaṃ kāraṇamūrtisāmarthyād amaṅgalaṃ maṅgalām āpadyate, apasavyaṃ ca pradakṣiṇam āpadyata ity arthaḥ.* 'the meaning is—by the strength of the image of Śiva (*kāraṇamūrti*), not only does inauspicious becomes auspicious [but] also left-circumambulation becomes right-circumambulation.'

HARA (1966: 273, fn. 2) points out that *apasavya* means wearing a sacred thread on the left flank i.e. over the right shoulder. He states in a note (ibid.) "[i]t is possible that in giving the etymological sense of *apasavya*, Kauṇḍinya intends it to refer to the wearing of the sacred thread as well as to circumambulation." Although HARA's observation, reiterated, in fact, explicitly in Mitākṣarā glossing *Yājñavalkyasmṛti* (1.132cd), is insightful, the question remains whether a Pāśupata is allowed to wear a sacred thread or not.

979 Cf. *Pāśupatasūtra* 2.9–11; *sūtra* 9 states the following with regards to the worship of gods and ancestors on one hand, and Śiva on the other: *tasmād ubhayathā yaṣṭavyaḥ*. *Sūtra* 10, in turn, indicates that Rudra should be worshipped 'like gods and ancestors': *devavat pitṛvac ca*, the reason being that Rudra/Śiva essentially contains both gods and ancestors: *ubhayaṃ tu rudre devāḥ pitaraś ca* (*Sūtra* 11). According to Kauṇḍinya, 'those who seek the end of suffering (*duḥkhānta*) should not worship gods and ancestors. For this [purpose] one should worship the great god (i.e. Śiva)':

> *tasmād duḥkhāntārthinā te devapitaro na yaṣṭavyāḥ* |
> *tadarthe bhagavān maheśvaro yaṣṭavya ity arthaḥ* |

980 Our text distils the *Pāśupatasūtra* 2.16 *atitaptaṃ tapas tathā*.

981 Cf. *Pāśupatasūtra* 2.20: *nānyabhaktis tu śaṅkare*, which literally means 'no devotion to any other [divinity] but Śaṅkara'.

982 This verse appears to be an elaboration on the previous half-verse's mention of tapas (*Niśvāsamukha* 4.76cd). No other parallel to this line has been traced in the *Pāśupatasūtra*; we do, however, find a similar notion relating to *sarvadvandvasahiṣṇutā* in *Pāñcārthabhāṣya* p. 25: *ihādhyātmikādhibhautikādhidaivikānāṃ sarvadvandvānāṃ manasi śarīre ca upanipatitānāṃ sahiṣṇutvam apratīkāraś ceti* | . "Since in this system forbearance (*sahiṣṇutva*) and absence of retaliation (*apratīkāra*) [are taught] in the face of all the ills that can fall on mind or body from within oneself, from the outside world and from fate." (HARA 1966: 203). The same idea regarding forbearance when subjected to the vagaries of pairs of opposites is likewise mentioned in the *Pāñcārthabhāṣya* p. 121 and 122 as well. It cannot, however, be determined with unwavering certainty that the presentation of patience in the *Niśvāsamukha* is influenced by Kauṇḍinya's *bhāṣya*.

4:78 Being intent upon mantra recitation,[983] and enjoying solitude,[984] [he should be] noticeable [in his deeds] without [any] religious mark;[985] performing transgressive actions, [he should wish to be] censured by people.[986]

4:79 Being ill-treated,[987] he should observe the great Pāśupata observance; [by doing so, he] will give [his] sins to those [who insult him], and take [from them the fruit of their] good deeds.[988]

---

983 We find no direct reference to this line in either the *Pāśupatasūtra* or Kauṇḍinya's *bhāṣya*. Note that the injunction of mantra recitation was mentioned above in 77a (*japadhyānaparo nityam*). Thus, one of the exhortations seems to be redundant. There is, however, a possibility that our text consulted an additional source which is not accessible to us any longer.

984 We find no exact parallel to this segment in *Pāśupatasūtra*. A moderately substantiated connection to *Pāśupatasūtra* 5.39 can be traced: *ekaḥ kṣemī san vītaśokaḥ*. The *Guhyasūtra* (1.21ab) also records forebearance as a characteristic of an ascetic:

ekāntaratiśīlaś ca dayāyukto yatiḥ smṛtaḥ | 121ab

• 121a ekāntaratiśīlaś ca] *em.*; ekāntarati --- N; ekāntaretisaṃ ⊔ K; ekānaratisī — W • 121b yatiḥ] K; yati NW

Cf. also *Brahmayāmala* 55.162 (***ekāntarataśīlas** tu sidhyate vigatāmayaḥ*) and *Mārkaṇḍeyapurāṇa* 41.26

samāhito brahmaparo 'pramādī śucis ***tathaikāntaratir*** *jitendriyaḥ* |
samāpnuyur yogam imaṃ mahādhiyo maharṣayaś caivam aninditāmalāḥ |

This same verse features in *Vāyupurāṇa* 16.23 (albeit *tathaivātmaratiḥ* features in place of *tathaikāntaratiḥ*). It is likewise traceable to *Liṅgapurāṇa* 88.29 with some minor variations.

985 The purport of the *eka*-element in the compound (78b) is not entirely clear. We assume that *°liṅginaḥ* is intended as a nominative singular. Cf. *Pāśupatasūtra* 3.1 *avyaktaliṅgī*, 'without [any] religious mark' and *Pāśupatasūtra* 3.2 *vyaktācāraḥ*, 'noticeable deeds'.

986 78cd is a paraphrase of *Pāśupatasūtra* 3.3–4 *avamata*, 'dishonoured' and *sarvabhūteṣu*, 'among all beings'. Our text rephrases *avamataḥ* as *jugupsita* 'disliked' and *sarvabhūteṣu* as *loka* 'world'.

987 Cf. *Pāśupatasūtra* 3.5: *paribhūyamānaś caret*. This phrase refers to the well-known theory of exchanging good and bad *karma* which is briefly discussed in the *Pāśupatasūtra* (see INGALLS 1962: 287–293). Kauṇḍinya mentions that a Pāśupata ascetic should consider the reception of ill-treatment to be comparable to the consecration of a poor man as a king: *sa paribhavo daridrapuruṣarājābhiṣeka iva draṣṭavyaḥ*.

988 Cf. *Pāśupatasūtra* 3.8–9 *pāpaṃ ca tebhyo dadāti* and *sukṛtaṃ ca teṣām ādatte*. On the strength of *Pāśupatasūtra* 3.8, we must understand that the sense of *ādatte* in our text is similar to the *dadāti* of the *Pāśupatasūtra*. If we were to understand *ādatte* literally as 'he takes away', the following conundrum would ensue: the ascetic would

4:80a–81b He should tremble, yell, limp (*maṇṭe*), or act the fool (*kuṇṭeti*),[989] [engage in] inappropriate behaviour [and] inappropriate speech,[990] he should always apply (*samupakramet*) inappropriate ointments, and always wear inappropriate ornaments on his body.[991]

4:81c–82b Humiliated, practicing harsh *tapas*, and censored everywhere (*sarvalokeṣu*), he becomes great in *tapas*,[992] bereft of respect and

---

take away both sins and the fruit of good deeds from those who ill-treat him. This certainly is not the meaning which we would expect here.

989 Cf. *Pāśupatasūtra* 3.13–14: *spandeta vā* and *maṇṭeta vā*. The *Taittirīyabrāhmaṇa* passage 2.3.9.9 has been pointed out as a model for *Pāśupatasūtra* 3.13–14 by OBERLIES (2000: 178). Prof. D. ACHARYA further holds that the reading of *Pāśupatasūtra* 3.13 and 3.14 might originally have been *spandeteva* and *maṇṭeteva* respectively (D. ACHARYA 2013a: 110). This translation (80ab) is based on Prof. D. ACHARYA's translation (2013a). In our context *spandamānas*, *maṇṭe* and *kuṇṭeti* are formulated in the third person optative singular, causing a number of problems in the reading. The first is *spandamānas*, which is presumably intended to mean *spandeta*; the second is the use of *maṃṭe*, where the last syllable *t* is dropped for the sake of the metre; thirdly, *kuṇṭeti* lacks the final letter, *t*, which would have signalled the third person *parasmaipada* imperative singular; finally, there is an *aiśa sandhi* between *kuṇṭe* and *iti*.

990 These injunctions may be intended as a reflection of *Pāśupatasūtra* 3.16–17 *apitat kuryāt* and *apitad bhāṣet*, "he should act improperly" and "he should speak improperly" (HARA 1966: 327). Kauṇḍinya says on 3.16,

> *yamānām avirodhinām śucirūpakāṇām* (corr/Hara; *śuvirūpakāṇām*) *dravyāṇām kāṣṭhaloṣṭādīnām grahaṇadhāraṇasaṃsparśanādīni kartavyāni | tatas te vaktāro vadanti asamyakkārī śucyaśucyoḥ kāryākāryayor avibhāgajña iti |*
>
> '[a Pāśupata-ascetic] should take or hold or touch an object such as a piece of wood or a lump of clay so that people say of him that he is acting improperly, and he does not know what is pure and what is not and so forth'.

This might be the sense adopted by our text which has been rephrased as *viruddhaceṣṭitam*. In his commentary on the *Pāśupatasūtra* (3.17) Kauṇḍinya mentions that **the ascetic should utter** objectionable phrases, repetitively and contradictory, so that people will say of him that he is speaking ill and so forth: *apārthakaṃ punaruktaṃ vyāhataṃ bhāṣitavyam iti | tatas te vaktāro vadanti asamyagvādī vācyāvācyayor avibhāgajña iti |*. We assume that this is the basic sense of *viruddha vākya* as it features in our text.

991 We do not find any parallel in either the *Pāśupatasūtra* or *Pāśupatasūtrabhāṣya* for *Niśvāsamukha* (80d).

992 Both *kṛchratapā* and *mahātapā* do not display the final *s* and are hence treated as if they had been *n*-stem bahuvrīhi compounds. The segment 81c–82a paraphrases *Pāśupatasūtra* 3.19: *paribhūyamāno hi vidvān kṛtsnatapā bhavati |* 'a wise man, being

benefit (*pūjālābhavivarjitaḥ*).[993]

4:82c–83 He [should be one who carries out] religious observances in secret;[994] [he should] act [as though] mad,[995] contravening ordinary observances.[996] He [should] conquer his senses,[997] be restrained, be forgiving, [and] free from desire.[998] He should [act in the manner of] a cow or an antelope,[999] [but] he [should] never eat the food [that is obtained from] a [single house].[1000]

---

ill-treated accomplishes all *tapas*'. Our text does not mention two elements of *sūtra*: *hi* and *vidvān*. It reads *mahātapas* instead of *kṛtsnatapas*.

993 This word appears to have no clear counterpart in the *Pāśupatasūtra*.

994 Cf. *Pāśupatasūtra* 4.2: *gūḍhavrataḥ*. This marks the beginning of the fourth stage of the religious life of a Pāśupata ascetic according to Kauṇḍinya.

995 Note an *aiśa* double *sandhi*. Cf. *Pāśupatasūtra* 4.6 *unmattavad eko vicareta loke|* 'he must wander about by himself like a madman'. In this case the *Niśvāsamukha* does not rephrase the complete *sūtra*.

996 Alternatively, this half-verse might be translated 'with regards to the practice [called] 'worldly', one conceals one's [own true] observance, acts as though mad and flouts convention (*vilomī*)'. We do not find any parallel to this in either *Pāśupatasūtra* or *Pāśupatasūtrabhāṣya*.

997 Cf. *Pāśupatasūtra* 5.11: *jitendriyaḥ*. According to Kauṇḍinya, the state of having subdued the senses enables one to direct and retain the senses according to one's own will. (*jitendriyatvaṃ nāma utsarganigrahayogyatvam*). *Manusmṛti* 2.98, however, gives athe following definition of a *jitendriya*:

> *śrutvā spṛṣṭvā ca dṛṣṭvā ca bhuktvā ghrātvā ca yo naraḥ|*
> *na hṛṣyati glāyati vā sa vijñeyo jitendriyaḥ|*.
>
> When a man feels neither elation nor revulsion at hearing, touching, seeing, eating or smelling anything, he should be recognised as a man who has mastered his organs (OLIVELLE 2005: 99).

This marks the beginning of the third stage of the religious life of a Pāśupata ascetic according to Kauṇḍinya.

998 We find no parallel to *dāntaś ca kṣamī kāmavivarjitaḥ* in either *Pāśupatasūtra* or *bhāṣya*.

999 Cf. *Pāśupatasūtra* 5.18: *godharmā mṛgadharmā vā*. Kauṇḍinya says that although there exist qualities in a cow and in an antelope, we should understand that the intended meaning here is spiritual qualities such as forbearance when subjected to pairs of opposites and the like (i.e. pain/pleasure etc.): *tayos tu sati dharmabahutve samāno dharmo gṛhyate, ādhyātmikādidvandvasahiṣṇutvam*. Cf. also *Gaṇakārikā* verse 3b ***dvaṃdvajayaḥ*** 'overcoming the pairs of opposites' and the commentary *Ratnaṭīkā* on it (p. 6). For more details, see D. ACHARYA 2013b.

1000 Cf. *Niśvāsamukha* 4.35. and also *Ratnaṭīkā* p. 5. There is, however, no parallel for this line in either *Pāśupatasūtra* or *Pāñcārthabhāṣya*.

4:84 Salt and [[...]] fallen into [his] alms will not be defiled,[1001] he, who practices the observances of the right path eats them.[1002]

4:85 With breath-control (*prāṇāyāmaiḥ*) and meditative fixations (*dhāraṇābhiḥ*),[1003] he should focus his mind on the sound *oṃ*,[1004] living in desolate dwellings or caves,[1005] [and] he should always go to the cremation ground.[1006]

[1001] Perhaps we may conjecture *lavaṇaṃ madhu māṃsaṃ ca*. Cf. *Pāśupatasūtra* 5.14–16: *bhaikṣyam* 'alms', *pātragatam* 'fallen into [his alms] pot' and *māṃsam aduṣyaṃ lavaṇena vā* 'meat is undefiled with salt'. For the proposed supplying of *madhu*, cf. Kauṇḍinya's *avatārikā* of 5.16, which reads: *āha brahmacārikalpe madhumāṃsa-lavaṇavarjanam iti*. Cf. also *Manusmṛti* 2.177 *varjayen madhu māṃsaṃ ca gandhaṃ mālyaṃ rasān striyaḥ | śuktāni yāni sarvāṇi prāṇināṃ caiva hiṃsanam*. D. Acharya suggests that alternatively, we may conjecture *lavaṇaṃ cāpi māṃsaṃ ca* in which case the conjecture is closer to the *Pāśupatasūtra* than to the *Pāñcārthabhāṣya*; this is more likely since *Niśvāsamukha* contains no echo of *Pāñcārthabhāṣya*.

[1002] The syntax is irregular here. Perhaps Ms K is right in correcting to *°cāriṇaḥ*, which could be treated as a nominative. We find no exact parallel for this either in the *Pāśupatasūtra* or in Kauṇḍinya's *Pāśupatasūtrabhāṣya*, yet there is a possibility that *sanmārggavratacāriṇe* is a distant paraphrase of the *Pāśupatasūtra* 4.16–17 *sarva-viśiṣṭo 'yaṃ panthāḥ* 'This path excels all others' and *satpathaḥ* 'The righteous path'.

[1003] Cf. *Pāśupatasūtra* 5.25: *hṛdi kurvīta dhāraṇām* 'he should fix [*oṃ*] in the heart'.

[1004] Cf. *Pāśupatasūtra* 5.24: *oṅkāram abhidhyāyīta*.

[1005] Cf. *Pāśupatasūtra* 5.9: *śūnyāgāraguhāvāsī*.

[1006] Or alternatively 'only (*eva*) when he is permanent[ly in the mental presence of god] (*nityaḥ*)'. This interpretation assumes that the *m* in *nitya-m-eva* is a euphonic glide consonant, and that *nitya* is intended as an adjective describing the ascetic, echoing *Pāśupatasūtra* 5.10: *devanityaḥ* "constantly associated with God" (Hara 1966: 395) .

The *Ratnaṭīkā* (p. 15) notes that the automatic uninterrupted flow of thought directed towards Rudra creates closeness to Rudra and when this very closeness reaches the highest degree, it is called *devanityatva*: *viṣayiṇām iṣṭaviṣayeṣv ivānicchato 'pi rudre cittavṛttipravāhaḥ samīpaṃ, tad evātyantotkarṣāpannaṃ devanityatvam iti* |. The same text (p. 21) commenting on *Gaṇakārikā* 7b *sadārudrasmṛtiḥ*, 'always recalling Rudra', makes a fundamentally identical statement.

Cf. *Pāśupatasūtra* 5.30: *śmaśānavāsī* 'living in a cremation ground'. According to Kauṇḍinya, a Pāśupata ascetic is supposed to live in a cremation ground in the fourth stage. He notes in his comment on *Pāśupatasūtra* 5.30) there are five stages for a Pāśupata ascetic. In the first stage he lives in a temple; in the second he dwells wherever he happens to be (*loke*) (this is an insightful conjecture of Hara's; especially since Śāstrī's edition reads *āyatane* which is undoubtedly wrong since *āyatana* has already been mentioned); in the third stage he lives in an empty house or a cave; in fourth stage in a cremation ground; and in the fifth he lives where the god is. See also *Ratnaṭīkā* pp. 16–17.

4:86–87 If somebody always remains thus,[1007] devoid of pride and greed,[1008] he will obtain [the state of] omniscience,[1009] and also [of divine] hearing and seeing. [There will arise] reflection, purification, wisdom,[1010] and whatever he desires.[1011] Great [[...]],[1012] he will attain union with Rudra.[1013]

4:88a–c An accomplished one will not return [to this world]; if he fails [to practise these observances], he will go to hell. I have taught [you] the *atyāśramavrata*.[1014]

1007 This may reflect *Pāśupatasūtra* 1.19 *carataḥ* 'practising'.

1008 We find no exact parallel to this in either *Pāśupatasūtra* or *Pāśupatasūtrabhāṣya*.

1009 Cf. *Pāśupatasūtra* 1.22 *sarvajñatā*.

1010 Cf. *Pāśupatasūtra* 1.21: *dūradarśanaśravaṇamananavijñānāni cāsya pravartante* 'there comes about for him seeing, hearing, reflection and comprehension of [things that are] far-off'. Our text, if MS K is right in its reading, mentions one extra element: *śodhana* 'purification'. Cf. also *Mūlasūtra* 7.19–20 and *Yogabhāṣya* on 2.43.

1011 Cf. *Pāśupatasūtra* 1.24 *kāmarūpitvaṃ*. Our text does not have the same wording as the *Pāśupatasūtra*.

1012 *Ex. conj.* There may have been a partial paraphrase of *Pāśupatasūtra* 5.26 (*ṛṣir vipro mahān eṣaḥ*), altered to accommodate to the dictates of metre, as this *sūtra* contains the segment '*mahān*'. We could possibly propose *mahāviprarṣi*, assuming an irregular omission of *visarga* implemented due to metrical reasons. Alternatively, it could have been the case that the section constituted a paraphrase of the text of the *Pāśupatasūtra* (5.23) *ato yogaḥ pravartate*. If this were the case, a possible conjecture could be *mahāyogena*. In that case, the translation would be: 'by the means of great yoga' ...

1013 Cf. *Pāśupatasūtra* 5.33: *labhate rudrasāyujyam*.

1014 Literally *atyāśrama* means 'beyond the [fourfold] *āśrama* system'. Already in the *Mahābhārata* the term *atyāśrama* is established with reference to the Pāśupata school. *Mahābhārata* 12.28:405–7 states that *atyāśrama* refers to a Pāśupata system; this system is similar in some respects to the dharma that is practised by *varṇāśramins* (those who adhere to the hierarchy of caste and stage of life) and different in others: *varṇāśramakṛtair dharmair viparītaṃ kvacit samam | gatāntair adhyavasitam atyāśramam idaṃ vratam | mayā pāśupataṃ dakṣa yogam utpāditaṃ purā*. Paurāṇic references also imply that *atyāśrama* refers to the Pāśupata system. For this cf. *Kūrmapurāṇa* 1.13:38 and 2.11:66–68, *Liṅgapurāṇa* 55.26c–27b and *Vāyavīyasaṃhitā* 33.84–84.

In Śaṅkara's commentary on 2.1.23, however, it (*atyāśrama*) refers to the highest ascetic, a.k.a. *paramahaṃsa*: *tathehāpi brahmasaṃsthaśabdo nivṛttasarvakarmatatsādhanaparivrāḍ ekaviṣaye 'tyāśramiṇi paramahaṃsākhye vṛtta iha bhavitum arhati [...] tasmād idaṃ tyaktasarvabāhyaiṣaṇair ananyaśaraṇaiḥ paramahaṃsaparivrājakair atyāśramibhir vedāntavijñānaparair eva vedanīyam*. This word *atyāśrama* occurs in *Śvetāśvataropaniṣad* 6.21, which may stand for the same meaning Śaṅkara follows.

[4.2 Lokātīta: cosmology of the Lākulas]

4:88d–89 Hear now the (Lokātīta).[1015] Touched with the five Brahmamantras and initiated, he should wander. He should carry a skull-topped staff (*khaṭvāṅgī*) and [an alms-bowl fashioned from] a human cranium (*kapālī*). He should have matted locks (*jaṭī*) or have his head shaved (*muṇḍaḥ*).[1016]

4:90 He should wear a sacred thread made from the hair [of the dead] (*vālayajñopavītī*) and he should adorn himself with a chaplet fashioned from human skull-bones. He may wear nothing but a strip of cloth to cover his private parts. He must smear himself with ashes and decorate himself with celestial ornaments.

4:91 Seeing all things as Rudra in essence he should hold firmly to his observance as Rudra's devotee. He may eat and drink anything. No action is forbidden to him. He should remain immersed in contemplation of Rudra.

4:92 [Thinking] 'none but Rudra can save me. He is the deity supreme'. Provided that he has first understood the [Lākula] cosmic hierarchy of eleven [levels] he should practise his observance, remaining free of all inhibition (*nirviśaṅkaḥ*).

4:93–94 On the first [level] is this [lower universe which we call the] Net (*jālam*).[1017] On the second are the Embodiments (*mūrtisaṃjñakam*) [the Śatarudrāḥ, the five Ogdoads (*pañcāṣṭakāni*), the eight Devayonis,

---

[1015] This translation, from 88c–100b, closely follows that of SANDERSON (2006: 164–165). The gloss, which is concerned mainly with the linguistic features of the text, is mine. See SANDERSON (2006: 164 ff.) for more details about the interpretation of this part of the text.

[1016] Note a euphonic glide *m* in *muṇḍameva*; alternatively this might be an *aiśa* use for *muṇḍī eva*.

[1017] Prof. D. ACHARYA has pointed out an interesting discussion in Kauṇḍinya's *Pāśupatasūtrabhāṣya* (on *Pāśupatasūtra* 5.35) where the Net is defined. I quote here his translation of the relevant portion:

> In this system, when demerit is in unaltered state/uniformity, it has not yet begun to produce its effects, till then it is named as 'the cause'. But when by the force of the latent impression of nescience it is consolidated and, by that process, has entered the state of stability and further, it receives the name 'net' (D. ACHARYA 2013b: 18).

the eight Yogas, the three Lines of Gurus (*gurupaṅktitrayam*)]. On the third is the bound soul (*paśuḥ*). On the fourth are the bonds (*pāśaḥ*) (Gahana up to Ananta) and on the fifth are the Vigrahas. These are termed the impure [levels]. I have explained the impure cosmos (*aśuddhamārga*). Hear me now as I teach the pure cosmos (*śuddhamārgaḥ*).

4:95 [First is] the Womb (*yoniḥ*), Vāgeśvarī, from which one is [re]born as Praṇava [the second pure level]. The third is [that of] Dhātṛ and the fourth is [that of] Dhyāna.

4:96 The fifth is called Tejīśa['s] and the sixth is placed as Dhruva['s]. When he has gained knowledge of all this, from the lowest hell (Avīcī) [in the Net] up to [the world of] Dhruva, he attains liberation.

4:97 In order to enable him to accomplish his goal of sporting (*krīḍārthasiddhaye*) [in ever higher levels of the universe, the officiant] should first meditate on the hierarchy of these levels. Then [when he has] purified that hierarchy,[1018] he should initiate [him] by means of the word '*atha*'.

4:98 Initiated through the descent of that word (*athaśabdanipātena*) he will cease to be a soul in bondage. Provided that [the initiate] maintains the observances he attains liberation [at death], even if he is a sinner. Of this there is no doubt. I have now explained the Lokātīta. What else do you wish to know?

Goddess spoke:

4:99 I have learned these eleven levels (*tattvāḥ*) only as names. Explain this matter again in greater detail, o Maheśvara.

Great god spoke:

4:100–106 [1] Avīcī, [2] Kṛminicaya, [3] Vaitaraṇī, [4] Kuṭaśālmalī, [5] Yamala (mount),[1019] [6] Ucchvāsa, [7] Nirucchvāsa and then

---

[1018] *Ex conj.* As the Lākula initiation involves purification of the cosmic hierarchy (SANDERSON, 2006: 192), we are tempted to accept the conjecture of Prof. D. ACHARYA, viz. *sodhya* 'having purified'.

[1019] The *Guhyasūtra* (4.46), however, records *giriyāmala*. Many Śaiva sources record this hell by referencing different appellations. Variation is made possible as it involves two words *giriḥ yāmalaḥ* and the authors could play with the synonyms of both. The *Skandapurāṇa* (BAKKER, BISSCHOP & YOKOCHI (2013: 82, fn. 285) calls it Yamalācala. In *Svacchandatantra* 10.46 it is called Yugmaparvata.

[8] Pūtimāṃsadrava, [9] Trapu, [10] Taptajatu then [11] Paṃkālaya, [12] Asthibhaṅga, [13] Krakacaccheda and [14] Medo'sṛkpūyahrada, [15] Tīkṣṇāyastuṇḍa, then [16] Aṅgārarāśibhuvana, [17] Śakuni, [18] Ambarīṣaka, [19] [[...]], [20] Asitālavana, then [21] Sūcīmukha, [22] Kṣuradhāra, [23] Kālasūtra, then [24] Parvata,[1020] then [25] Padma is taught, then [26] Mahāpadma, then [27] Apāka, [28] Sāra,[1021] [29] Uṣṇa, [30] Sañjīvana, [31] Sujīvana, [32] Śītatamas, [33] Andhatamas, [34] Mahāraurava and [35] Raurava; these thirty-two hells I have taught, o goddess, together with one hundred and eight [[...]] conjoined. [I have] taught these one hundred and forty hells.[1022]

4:107a–111b Now I shall teach the *pātālas*; learn [about them] o famous [one]![1023] The first (*ādau*), called Mahātala, is said [to have] a black

---

1020 The mention of Parvata as a hell is unusual. Thus, *'tha parvataḥ* could be a corruption for *'siparvata* as in the *Guhyasūtra* 4.36. In this case number [24] would be Asiparvata.

1021 We do not know the hells Apāka and Sāra from other sources. It is possible that these two words refer to a single hell.

1022 *Ex conj.* This is a conjecture of SANDERSON's that refers to a Middle Indo-Aryan form (*catālīsa*) for forty. This conjecture appears likely since it is found in the *Guhyasūtra* (4.33c–34b) that the total number of hells is one hundred plus the half of eighty:

tasyopari samākhyātan narakāṇāṃ śataṃ priye || 4.33 ||
aśītyarddhottaraṃ ghoraṃ avīcyādyaṃ bhayaṅkaram |

• 34a aśītyarddho°] N; asī ⊔ ttaraṃ K; aśīya _ W

We find *catālīsa*, meaning 'forty', in the ninth century manuscript of *Pārameśvara* fol. 22r, lin. 1, where its colophon reads *iti pārameśvare mahātantre sāmānyaprakaraṇe samayapaṭalam[|] ślokāḥ ṣaṭ**catālīsa***. It is worth noting that in the *Pāia-sadda-mahaṇṇavo*, the cardinal number forty is called *cattālīsa* (see s.v. *cattālīsa*). If *catālīsa* was indeed the original form behind *catāla*, which is the reading of N and W, then this might have noteworthy consequences in the assessment of the language of our manuscript. The text in its original version may have contained more Prākṛtic forms and they may have disappeared during transmission of the text. This evidence, moreover, provides us with further support for the supposition that this portion of the text must have been composed somewhere in Northern India, as we would not expect Sanskrit written in Southern India to contain such Prākṛtic forms.

Although the text states that there are thirty-two hells, in actual count it records thirty-five of them. A similar list of hells is shared by the *Guhyasūtra* (4.34 ff.). However, a common list of hells consists of twenty-one (BAKKER, BISSCHOP & YOKOCHI, 2013: 81, fn. 279). In the context of Śaiva Siddhānta, the standard list bears thirty-two hells (SANDERSON, 2003-4: 422); GOODALL (2004: 282, fn. 487). The *Skandapurāṇa* attests only thirteen hells (BAKKER, BISSCHOP & YOKOCHI, 2013: 81, fn. 279). It is possible that the Pāśupatas had a different number of hells in their system or, alternatively, their list did not have a fixed number.

1023 Our text records the list of seven *pātālas* which are as follows: [1] Mahātala, [2]

ground;[1024] the second is Rasātala: it is said to be made of white crystal; the third one, Talātala, is [said to] have brazen ground; the fourth one has ground of copper and it is called Nitala. Sutala, which has a silver ground,[1025] is taught as [being] the fifth [*pātāla*]. The sixth, named Vitala, is encrusted with gemstones. The seventh is named Nitala and it is said to be golden. I have taught the seven [*pātālas*] in due sequence; [now] hear about the lords of *pātālas*.[1026]

4:111c–114b Nāgas, Garuḍas, egg-born Kiṃpuruṣas,[1027] Agni, Vāyu, Varuṇa and the lords of demons [viz. Rākṣasas(?)][1028] are the denizens [of these underworlds] (*nivāsinyaḥ*)[1029] have been taught; now hear [about] the earth (*bhūlokam*) which encompasses the seven continents and is bounded by seven oceans, is endowed with land-masses, trees and mountains, is covered with forests and groves, endowed with rivers and seas, filled with throngs of sages and gods, and frequented by Gandharvas and nymphs.

4:114c–115b Virtue (*dharma*), material achievement (*artha*), fulfilment of desires (*kāma*) and liberation (*mokṣa*)—all are rooted in this [world].[1030] This [world] I have taught is the terrestrial world (*bhūr-lokaḥ*); beyond this there is the world [called] *bhuvaḥ*.

Rasātala, [3] Talātala, [4] Nitala, [5] Sutala, [6] Vitala and [7] Nitala. Their respective colour is: [1] black, [2] white crystal, [3] brazen, [4] copper, [5] silver [6] gemstones and [7] golden. KIRFEL (1967: 144) lists the *pātālas* attested in the Purāṇic sources, whereby it swiftly becomes evident that the *pātālas* are attested there also. The order and colour of the *pātālas* mentioned in our text, however, are different from those recorded in Purāṇic sources.

1024 This most likely means that it is made of iron.

1025 *Ex conj.* SANDERSON here (2006: 166) conjectures differently (*raityabhauman tu*), but the sequence of materials suggests that silver would be appropriate.

1026 Probably a portion of the text is lost here as what are mentioned in the following section seem to be the creatures that are the inhabitants of the respective *pātālas* and not the lords of the *pātālas*. Alternatively, the mentioned creatures in the following section can be considered as the lords of *pātālas*. The problem remains that the concerned section starts with *pātālādhipatīṃ śṛṇu* 'hear about the lords of *pātālas*' and ends with *kathitās tu nivāsinyo* 'the inhabitants [of the *pātālas*] have been taught'. This indicates that some form of textual corruption has taken place.

1027 *Ex conj.* SANDERSON here (2006: 166) reads *kimpuruṣāṃtajāḥ*.

1028 Note an irregular genitive plural within the *aluksamāsa*.

1029 We assume that this feminine nominative plural is used in place of the required masculine in order to avoid an undesirable metrical cadence.

1030 This may be intended to asseverate, by implication, that the earth is to be understood as *karmabhūmi*, the plane in which to exercise *karma*. Presumably, all remaining worlds are hence to be classified as *bhogabhūmis*, in which the fruits of actions can be enjoyed but not stored.

4:115c–118 The world [called] *svar* is above that, [then further] the worlds *mahas*, *jana*[1031] and *tapas*, and [further] above [those] the world [called] *satya*, and above that the world of Brahmā; then above [that] the residence of Viṣṇu, and [further] above [that] the city of Śiva. This [that] I have explained is the *brahmāṇḍa* covered in layers of shell. [Beyond that, supporting it, are] the hundred Rudras,[1032] [above them] the five groups of eight [abodes] (*pañcāṣṭau*),[1033] then the eight Devayonis, [above them][1034] the eight Yogas (*yogāṣṭaka*), [above them][1035] Suśiva,[1036] and above [him] the three lineages of Gurus. Above that[1037] is the group of *tattvas* (*tattvasargam*).[1038] Now hear [this] from me as I tell you about it.

4:119a–120b [This consists of] primal nature (*pradhāna*), intellect (*buddhi*), I-ness (*ahaṅkāra*), the [five] subtle elements (*tanmātrāṇi*), the

---

1031 Prof. LUBIN, by way of *personal communication*, dated 7th May, 2018, kindly pointed to the fact that "here, (but normally elsewhere), *janas*, as in the seven *vyāhṛtis* of *Taittirīyāraṇyaka* 10.35.2/*Mahānārāyaṇopaniṣad* 340, ... are taken as the names of seven worlds. *Cf.* *Śivadharma* 6.113: *maharloke janoloke tapoloke sthitāś ca ye* [Pondicherry T860: *janarloke*]; *Atharvaśiras* 2 (southern recension), *Bṛhajjābālopaniṣad.* 8.4, *Devībhāgavatapur.* 7.33.25, *etc.*"

1032 The individual names of these hundred Rudras are listed in *Guhyasūtra* 7.81–110b.

1033 These are the forty *bhuvanas* grouped into five sets of eight that have the same name of the forty pilgrimage sites on earth (*Niśvāsamukha* 3.19 ff.). As far as we can tell, the Lākula sect of Pāśupatas was responsible for including the forty pilgrimage sites into the list of *bhuvanas* of their cosmological system.

1034 According to *Guhyasūtra* 7.126, these eight Devayonis are: Paiśāca, Rākṣasa, Yākṣa, Gāndharva, Indra (which is meant to be Aindra), Prājāpatya, Saumya and Brāhmya. Cf. also *Svacchandatantra* 10.315.

1035 These Yogāṣṭakas are: Akṛta, Kṛta, Raibhava, Brāhma, Vaiṣṇava, Kaumāra, Bhauma and Śrīkaṇṭha (see *Guhyasūtra* 7.134–135). These, according to *Guhyasūtra* 7.135, are the abodes of Yogis.

1036 Suśiva seems to to be employed in lieu of a collective singular noun. After all, the *Guhyasūtra* 7.136–138 and *Svacchandatantra* 10.139-141 record twelve Suśivas. The first two names are not visible in the manuscript due to physical damage. According to the *Svacchandatantra* these two first names are Vāma and Bhīma. The rest of the names recorded in the *Guhyasūtra* are: Bhava, Śarva, Vidyādhipati, Ekavīra, Pracaṇḍadhṛt, Īśāna, Umābhartā, Ajeśa, Ananta and Ekaśiva.

1037 The three lineages of gurus are mentioned with their names in *Guhyasūtra* 7.145–160 and *Svacchandatantra* 10.147–1061. The list of gurus presumably involves eighty-two in number (*Svacchandatantra* ibid.). The first row consists of thirty-three gurus, the second row consists of thirty gurus and the third row consists of twenty-one. It is clear that these teachers are considered to be the Rudras (*Guhyasūtra* 7.144). Note an *aiśa* double *sandhi* between *tataḥ* and *ūrdhvam* in 115c and 116a.

1038 This presumably refers to the ontology of Sāṅkhya which consists of the well-known twenty-five *tattvas*, extrapolated in the verses immediately following. Cf. *Guhyasūtra* 7.160 ff.

[ten] senses (*indriyāṇi*), the five [gross] elements (*bhūtāni*), and the mind (*manas*), which is included among both [organs of action and perception].[1039] These are the twenty-four *tattvas*; *puruṣa* is the twenty-fifth.

4:120c–121b This twenty-fifth (i.e. *puruṣa*) is born out of six *kośa*s, with

---

1039 The assigning of a dual function to the mind is found already in *Sāṅkhyakārikā* 27a: *ubhayātmakam atra manaḥ*, Gauḍapāda (ad loc.) glosses as follows:

> *atra indriyavarge mana ubhayātmakam | buddīndriyeṣu buddhīndriyavat, karmendriyeṣu karmendriyavat | kasmāt, buddhīndriyāṇāṃ pravṛttiṃ kalpayati karmendriyāṇāṃ ca | tasmād ubhayātmakaṃ manaḥ |*

> here in the set of organs, the mind is of the nature of both. Among the organs of sense, it is like an organ of sense; among the organs of action, it is like an organ of action. Why?—[Because] it determines the functioning of the organs of sense and action. Therefore, the mind is of the nature of both (SHARMA, 1933: 40).

Kauṇḍinya's comment on *Pāśupatasūtra* 2.27 (*manomanāya namaḥ*) expresses the idea as follows: *atra manaḥśabdenāntaḥkaraṇaṃ tattantratvāt udāharaṇārthatvāt ca manograhaṇasya ubhayātmakatvāt ca manasaḥ sarvakaraṇagrahaṇānugrahaṇāt ca.* Similarly *Guhyasūtra* 7.165 reads: *buddhīndriyāṇi pañcaiva manaś caivobhayātmakaḥ* | See also *Svacchandatantra* 11.81 and *Parākhya* 4.125. *Mataṅgavidyāpāda* 18.80–82 describes the mind with its presiding deity and activity in detail. For further details, refer to GOODALL (2004: 267, fn. 427).

A second meaning of this expression is the mind's being associated with *dharma* and *adharma* or with *pāpa* and *puṇya*. The *Yogabhāṣya* is very likely the first text to attest the idea. The *Yogabhāṣya* on the *sūtra abhyāsavairāgyābhyāṃ tannirodhaḥ* (1.12) comments as follows: *cittanadī nāma ubhayatovāhinī, vahati kalyāṇāya vahati pāpāya ca | yā tu kaivalyaprāgbhārā vivekaviṣayanimnā sā kalyāṇavahā; saṃsāraprāgbhārāvivekaviṣayanimnā pāpavahā |*

> The stream of mind flows both ways; flows towards good and it flows towards evil. That which flows on to perfect independence (*kaivalya*) down the plane of discriminative knowledge, is named the stream of happiness. That which leads to re-birth and flows down the plane of undiscriminative ignorance, is the stream of sin. PRASĀDA (1998: 26)

For an expression of this idea in our text, see *Niśvāsanaya* 2.14: *manaś caikādaśo jñeyam ubhayor api dhāvati*, 'mind should be understood as the eleventh [sense organ] which runs after both'. That this is intended to refer to *dharma* and *adharma* is implied by *Niśvāsanaya* 2.53ab: *manas tu kathitaṃ hy etad dharmmādharmmanibandhakam.*

[three coming] from the mother [and three] from the father, and nourished with food and liquids.[1040]

4:121c–122 [Above these twenty-five *tattvas* that are known as Sāṅkhya *tattvas*] there is Gahana;[1041] above that is Vigraheśa;[1042] above him is Śivaśaṅkara,[1043] Asādhya, Harirudra,[1044] [and] ten lords

---

A third double function of mind is 'volition and doubt' (*saṅkalpavikalpātmaka*), see *Niśvāsanaya* 2.52cd *saṃkalpāś ca vikalpāś ca daśadhākṣeṣu dhāvati* | '[the mind], for the sake of volition and doubt, engages in sense faculties tenfold'. *Svacchandatantra* 12.31 makes *Niśvāsanaya*'s reading smoother by rephrasing *saṃkalpe ca vikalpe ca* ... instead. Kṣemarāja (ad loc.) glosses *buddhikarmendriyaviṣaye yaḥ idaṃ śritam idam ādadhe iti saṃkalpaḥ, yaś ca idam īdṛdam iti niścayātmā vikalpaḥ*, which means, to him *saṃkalpa* is 'approach' and *vikalpa* is 'resolution'. Cf. also Śaṅkara's commentary on *Īśāvāsyopaniṣad* 4, and *Gītābhāṣya* ad 3.43, 10.22, 12.8 and 12.14.

1040 *Guhyasūtra* 7.161–62 defines this as:

snāyvasthiśukrasaṃghātaṃ paitṛkan trikam ucyate |
tvaṅmāṃsāñ caiva raktañ ca mātṛkan trikam ucyate || 7.161 ||
etad annena satataṃ pānena ca vivarddhitam |
sarvayonyāṃ śarīran tu ṣaṭkauśikam udāhṛtam || 7.162 ||

• 161b trikam] K; tṛkam NW• 161d trikam] K; tṛkam NW• 162a satataṃ] NW; saṃtataṃ K

The group of tendons, bones and marrow is called a triad [coming from] the father; skin, flesh and blood is called a triad coming from the mother. These six elements always come to be enveloped by food and water: the body, in all wombs, is taught—made of six *kośas*.

In the list of the *Suprabhedāgama śukra* is replaced by *majjā*. See *Suprabhedāgama-vidyāpāda* 21.22:

asthi snāyuś ca majjā ca pitṛjaṃs trayam eva tu |
tvaṅmāṃsaśoṇitañ caiva mātṛjaṃ trikam eva ca |
itthaṃ ṣaṭkauśikaṃ proktaṃ śarīrān tais tu jāyate |

For further details, consult GOODALL (2007: 154–155).

1041 Gahana probably refers to Gahaneśa Rudra who is listed among the teachers that are grouped amongst the first row of gurus (GOODALL et al. 2015: 296).

1042 We are not able to identify the position of Vigraheśa. According to GOODALL et al. (2015: 298) "Vigraha refers either to Vigraheśa (cf. *Niśvāsamukha* 4.122, *Guhyasūtra* 1.117, 7.56 and perhaps 7.149) or to the group of eight worlds (*vigrahāṣṭaka*) which he presumably governs (cf. *Guhyasūtra* 7.220-1)."

1043 According to *Guhyasūtra* 7.225–228, this refers to ten Śaṅkaras and ten Śivas with reserved order of two sets.

1044 The reading of *Guhyasūtra* 7.131 and *Svacchandatantra* 10.1113 suggest, by reading the dual *hariharu varau*, that these are two distinct worlds.

(°*daśeśakam*).[1045] Then five pupils, five teachers,[1046] then [above them] three great gods.[1047]

1045 Note an *aiśa dvandva* compound containing a number in between. The ten lords, as recorded in *Guhyasūtra* 7.232–33, are listed as follows:

tasmād api daśeśānāḥ saṃsthitāḥ kāmarūpiṇaḥ |
suhṛṣṭas suprahṛṣṭaś ca surūpo rūpavarddhanaḥ || 232 ||
manonmanas samākhyātaḥ sumanonmana eva ca |
mahāvīras suvīraś ca vīreśo daśamaḥ smṛtaḥ || 233 ||

• 233b sumanonmana] KW; sunonmana N

The *Svacchandatantra* mentions nine of these, referring to them as *vīreśas* (see *Svacchandatantra* 10.1113–114):

suhṛṣṭaḥ suprahṛṣṭaś ca surūpo rūpavardhanaḥ || 1113 ||
manonmano mahādhīraḥ vīreśaḥ parikīrtitaḥ | 1114ab |

• 1113a suhṛṣṭaḥ suprahṛṣṭaś ca] KSTS; suhṛṣṭa suprahṛṣṭañ ca N_{28}^{K}
• 114b vīreśaḥ parikīrtitaḥ] N_{28}^{K}; vīreśāḥ parikīrtitāḥ KSTS

Kṣemarāja, as we know, depends on the Kashmirian recension of *Svacchandatantra* when giving an eightfold count whereby they are referred to as *vīreśas*. *Svacchandatantrodyota* (ad loc.): *yathā niyatikālagatā rudrāḥ śaṅkarāḥ śivāś coktāḥ, tathā ete vīreśā ucyante duṣpariharatvāc caivam uktā* | .

1046 *Guhyasūtra* 7.234–35 lists these five groups of pupils and five groups of teachers as follows:

ata ūrdhvaṃ bhavec chiṣyāḥ kalyāṇā ((du)) --- rmmitāḥ |
kalyāṇaḥ piṅgalo babhrus sarvaḥ suvara eva ca || 234 ||
medhāvī atithiś caiva cchedako dāhakas tathā |
śāstrakārī ca nirddiṣṭā daśaite guravaḥ smṛtāḥ || 235 ||

• 234b sarvaḥ suvara] *em.*; sarva śuvara N; sarva ⊔ vara K; sarva ⊔ W

At first sight, this list may appear to indicate that ten teachers are referred to here (*daśaite guravaḥ smṛtāḥ*). However, it needs to be understood that although they are all in some sense gurus, the first five listed refer to pupils and the second five names refer to teachers. Kṣemarāja, in the commentary of verse 10.1115cd, clarifies this point by stating *ādyāḥ śiṣyāḥ, antyā ācāryā* 'the first [group] are pupils and the second [group] are teachers'. The *Svacchandatantra*, however, records a slightly different list of pupils and teachers than the *Guhyasūtra* does: instead of the two pupils Sarva and Suvara, the *Svacchandatantra* mentions Vīra and Prabha; likewise, instead of Chedaka, it displays Chandaka. See *Svacchandatantra* 1115—6:

kalyāṇaḥ piṅgalo babhrur vīraś ca prabhavas tathā |
medhātithiś cchandakaś ca dāhakaḥ śāstrakāriṇaḥ || 1115
pañca śiṣyās tathācāryā daśaite parikīrttitāḥ | 1116ab

• 115a babhrur] KSTS; babhru N_{28}^{K}• 116b parikīrttitāḥ] N_{28}^{K}; saṃvyavasthitāḥ KSTS

4:123 Then above [them] Gopati, situated in the knot [of *māyā*],[1048] at the head [of the knot of *māyā* are the] five lords (*mūrdhnābhibhavapañcakam*).[1049] [Then above] is Ananta,

---

1047 *Guhyasūtra* 7.236 records the list of three great gods as follows: *vāmo jyeṣṭhaś ca rudraś ca mahādevatrayaṃ smṛtam*, 'Vāma, Jyeṣṭha, and Rudra are understood to be the three great gods'. However, for their part, the *Svacchandatantra* and the *Tantrasadbhāva* (10.1152) give a different list of three gods: Mahādeva, Mahātejā, and Mahājyoti. See *Svacchandatantra* 10.1118–1119:

kalātattve mahādevi mahādevatrayaṃ sthitam || 1118cd ||
mahādevo mahātejo mahājyotiḥ pratāpavān | 1119ab |

• 1119a mahātejo] N^{K}_{28}; mahātejā KSTS

1048 Literally 'he knot of Gopati,' which is not likely to reflect the intended meaning. We would expect simply 'Gopati, situated in the *granthi*' i.e. the *māyāgranthi*. That is what we encounter in the *Guhyasūtra* (1.119): *mahādevatrayaṃ yac ca gopatir granthisaṃsthitāḥ* (perhaps we need to emend it to *granthisaṃsthitāḥ*, or at least, interpret its meaning accordingly). *Guhyasūtra* 7.239, *Uttarasūtra* 1.5, *Niśvāsamūla* 5.12 also confirm that there is not such a thing that is the knot of Gopati. *Svacchandatantra* 10.1124–1125 mentions that the Gopati is situated in the lower part of the *māyā*.

1049 It appears that the instrumental *mūrdhnā* is to be understood as a locative *mūrdhni*. The *Guhyasūtra* lists the constituents of this group of five, even though it does not employ the label *abhibhavapañcaka*: Trikala, Kṣemīśa, Brahman (*brahmaṇo*), Adhipati and Śiva. See *Guhyasūtra* 7.240-241:

granthyordhve saṃsthitaṃ viśvaṃ trikalakṣemīśam eva ca || 240cd ||
brahmaṇo 'dhipatiś caiva śivaś ceti ca pañca vai | 241ab |

• 240cd granthyordhve saṃsthitaṃ viśvaṃ trikalakṣemīśameva ca] *em.*; _ nthyorddha sa --- tṛkalakṣa --- N; ⊔ K; ¯ ndhyorddha saṃsthitaṃ viśvaṃ tṛkalakṣamīśameva ca W

In the uppermost part of the knot is situated the world(?); then Trikala, Kṣemīśa, Brahman (*brahmaṇo*), Adhipati and Śiva. These are the five [Lords].

Niśvāsamūla 5.12 mentions the same list as *Guhyasūtra* 7.240–241 but does not rank them *abhibhava*. *Svacchandatantra* 10.1130–31 records the same list without levelling them, except that it reads *kṣema* instead of *kṣemīśa*. *Niśvāsakārikā*: T. 127 p.159-60 and T. 150 p. 200 record a different name, *suśiva*, instead of *trikala*:

⊔ *kṣemīśaḥ brāhmaṇo 'dhipatis tathā* || 1514cd ||
suśivaś ca śivaś caiva kathitā anupūrvaśaḥ | 1555ab |

and the fetters;[1050] this [group of fetters(?)/totality of the cosmos so far(?)] is called the net.[1051]

4:124–125 [Then above] actions, sufferings, knowledge, instruments and 'truth(s?)' (*tattvam*).[1052] The sixth is that which is to be accomplished (*sādhyam*), sovereignty, and the cause (*kāraṇam*)[1053] is the eighth. I have taught the subject of ignorance;[1054] [now] I shall tell [of] the [subject which is] above the cause. I have explained the impure path, [now] hear [about] the pure path from me.

• 1555b kathitā] T_{127}; adhitā T_{150}

Transcript T. 17, p. 897 records a corrupt version of this list, which mentions only two of them: Trikala and Kṣemīśa. The term *abhibhava* occurs once more in *Guhyasūtra* 1.119, without any mention of individual names.

1050 It is difficult to arrive at anything more than an educated guess about the precise nature of these 'fetters', especially since in the absence of alternative source material, we can resort to but the *Niśvāsa*-corpus in our delineation of the *atimārga* cosmology. It is hence somewhat difficult to fathom what the functionality and significance of the *pāśas* were conceived to be according to that system. SANDERSON's translation (4.93) implies that the cosmological section extending from Gahana to Ananta is to be located above the *pāśas*.

The *Uttarasūtra*, *Niśvāsanaya*, and *Guhyasūtra* all give a different account of *pāśa*, but congrue in placing them above Ananta; this appears to be an alteration stringently applied to the account of Mantramārga cosmology given in these books.

Uttarasūtra 2.28 ff. mentions a list of *pāśas* which is further expounded in *Niśvāsanaya* 1.83–92. *Guhyasūtra* 7.241–2 states that fetters have already been taught which are said to 'persist' (*saṃsthitāḥ*) above Ananta; it is not clear however, where precisely that fact would have already been taught as stated. The *Svacchandatantra* 10.1131–1132 also mentions fetters in the plural in this context and states that these have already been taught. Kṣemarāja (ad loc.) explains: *pūrvam eva puruṣatattvanirūpaṇāvasare* ***'ṃbā ca salilā oghā*** *... | ityādinā tuṣṭisiddhyādyā vidyeśapāśāntā ye pāśā uktāḥ, te iha pararūpeṇa avasthitā ity arthaḥ |*. For this list of fetters, see *Svacchandatantra* 10.1069–1104. This solution of Kṣemarāja also seems implausible since those *pāśas* have already been placed at a lower level.

1051 Perhaps *jālam etat prakīrtitam* rather points forward and identifies the group of eight entities enumerated in the next two half-lines.

1052 This may refer to the group of twenty-five *tattvas* known to the Sāṅkhyas, which were mentioned in *Niśvāsamukha* 4.119–120.

1053 In Kauṇḍinya's Pāśupatism, this is an expression that refers to god, which is echoed by Kṣemarāja, who, commenting on *Svacchandatantra* 10.1089, states it is god, the cause of primordial *tattva*: *kāraṇam iti kāraṇarūpasya pradhānatattvasya utthāpakaṃ devatārūpam ity arthaḥ*. It seems that the cosmology of the Lākulas considers all principles up to the highest reality (*kāraṇam*) of the Pāñcārthikas to be impure. Its cosmology extends further, including what is considered to be the pure path, which is taught in the section immediately following.

1054 We have understood *viṣayam ajñānam* as *viṣayājñānam*.

4:126–128 He who is released from the families of sages and from rebirth, which is difficult to escape, is then born in the womb of Vāgeśī[1055] [and] is called Praṇava. [In due order] Dhātāra, Damana, Īśvara, Dhyāna, and Bhasmīśa is told [of],[1056] then the eight Pramāṇas,[1057] then eight Vidyās,[1058] the eight Mūrtis,[1059] then Tejīśa, then Dhruva.[1060] The numbers of the pure path have been explained in brief. [1061]

4:129 Having resorted to the observance [called] *kapāla* they will go to the realm of Dhruva. I have taught the observance which is called the Lokātīta, the super Pāśupata observance.

4:130 Knowing the cosmography and conduct[1062] one certainly goes to the [respective] state [that he engages with]. If he fails to observe [these observances] he will go to hell [being] devoid of [knowledge of] cosmology and conduct.

4:131 I have taught the Atimārga in two forms, o beautiful-visaged one!

1055 Literally 'born in the womb in Vāgeśī.'

1056 We are not sure who these names refer to. For a discussion on these names see GOODALL et al. (2015: 298 ff.).

1057 The eight Pramāṇas have the same name as the eight scriptures of Lākulas. They seem to be Rudras named after these scriptures (cf. *Svacchandatantrodyota*, p. 477). These are recorded in the *Guhyasūtra* 7.224–225 as: [1] Pañcārtha, [2] Śivaguhya, [3] Rudrāṅkuśa, [4] Hṛdaya, [5] Lakṣaṇa, [6] Vyūha, [7] Ākarṣaka and [8] Ādarśa. For a detailed discussion on these, see SANDERSON (2006: 169 ff.) and GOODALL et al. (2015: 300).

1058 We are not told what these eight *vidyās* are. *Guhyasūtra* 7.246 and *Svacchandatantra* 10.1138 mention *māyā* in this place. Above *māyā*, *Guhyasūtra* 7.246 and *Svacchandatantra* 10.1143 mention *mahāvidyā* which is subdivided into eight divisions. These eight divisions, according to *Svacchandatantrodyota*, p. 484 are the letters: *a, ka, ca, ṭa, ta, pa, ya* and *śa*. We are not sure whether this eightfold division is the intended point of reference in our text. See also the discussion concerning this matter given in GOODALL et al. (2015: 300).

1059 These eight *mūrttis*, according to *Guhyasūtra* 257–258, are: [1] Ananteśa, [2] Sūkṣma, [3] Śivottama, [4] Ekanetra, [5] Ekarudra, [6] Trimūrti, [7] Śrīkaṇṭha and [8] Śikhaṇḍī.

1060 Tejīśa is the highest goal for those who follow the Vimala system of Pāśupatas and Dhruva is the ultimate goal for those who follow the Pramāṇa system of the Pāśupatas. For a detailed discussion on this topic, see SANDERSON (2006: 169 ff.).

1061 The cosmology of the Lākulas is divided into pure and impure levels. Although the cosmology presented in *Guhyasūtra* (ch. 1 and ch. 7) is close to the account of the Lākulas presented in the *Niśvāsamukha*, the *Guhyasūtra* does not divide the universe into a pure and an impure stratum. The *Kiraṇatantra*, however, does include these two categories. For more discussion on the division into pure and impure, see GOODALL et al. (2015: 301) and SANDERSON (2006: 173 ff.).

1062 Note an irregular shortening of the vowel in °*carya* for metrical reasons.

Through the Eastern face I have taught this along with the secret. What further can I teach, o great goddess, o supreme deity?

Goddess spoke:

4:132 You have indicated the Mantramārga, o god, but not described, [that it is] the cause of extirpation of the *saṃsāra*: tell me [of] that o great god.

4:133 Addressed thus by Pārvatī, Hara, the remover of all sins, spoke the sweet words established for the sake of the system of mantras (*mantratantrārthaniścitām*).[1063]

4:134–135 Now then (*tad ato*), o Brāhmins, I shall tell [you] the discourse of the god Śiva (*īśvarasya*) with Umā, called Mantra (*mantrākhyaṃ*), which is settled as the Mantramārga [and] which was formerly related to Devī by the fifth Īśāna face, o best of Brāhmins!

4:136 I told you [about] the four streams, which I heard before by the grace of Devī; [they are] unfailing, o best of Brāhmins.

4:137 But, the fifth is the highest stream [[...]] taught by the god of gods; what else do you want to hear?[1064]

1063 This interpretation assumes that the term *tantra* is meant to refer to 'system' (*śāstra*). We are not absolutely sure about whether the term *mantratantrārthaniścitām* has been understood rightly or not. Literally, it might also mean 'words established by reason of mantra and *tantra*'. This seems to be an unlikely reflection of the author's intent, since it would entail that the god Śiva, supreme authority of the tradition, would be reliant on the very scriptures he is about to to teach for the first time.

1064 To our mind, the author of the *Niśvāsamukha* appears intent upon construing the context for, or at least providing a coherent connection with, the opening passage of the *Mūlasūtra*, the book immediately following in the manuscript. After all, in the inceptive section of the *Mūlasūtra*, the sages proceed to ask the question about the location where the revelation of Śiva-knowledge (*śivajñāna*) took place. Closing the *Niśvāsamukha* with the question concerning the site of the Śaiva teaching seamlessly connects with the scene which is to be explored in *Mūlasūtra* 1.1, to wit: *ṛṣaya ūcuḥ: śivajñānaṃ paraṃ guhyaṃ katham uktaṃ svayambhuvā | kasmiṃ sthāne śrutan devyā prasādād vaktum arhasi* || "The Ṛṣis spoke: How did the self-born [Lord] teach the supreme, secret Śiva-knowledge? In what place did the goddess hear it? Out of [your] grace [you should tell us]" (GOODALL et al., 2015: 233). It is possible that the first verse of the *Mūlasūtra* may have been added by the author of the *Niśvāsamukha*, who could have added it prior to the opening of the textual body of the *Mūlasūtra*. If that possibility were to hold true, the *Mūlasūtra* would originally have incepted with the setting of Mount Kailāsa (1.2), which would would fit both context and the narrative story of the *Mūlasūtra*.

Thus is the fourth chapter in the *Niśvāsamukhatattvasaṃhitā*. One hundred and thirty seven verses. Four streams, verses 643.

On this basis of this analysis, we could attempt to fill the present gap in our text by conjecturing something like *śivajñānaṃ svayaṃbhuvā* or *śivajñānaṃ dvijottamā*.

शिवधर्मसंग्रहे पञ्चमोऽध्यायः॥

ईश्वर उवाच।

अज्ञानार्जितपापानां ब्रवीमि ध्वंसनं प्रिये।
विज्ञायार्जितपापानां न ब्रवीमि कदाचन॥ 5:1॥

न ज्ञानबलमाश्रित्य पापं कुर्वीत संयमी।
लोकाः किम्मृत्युना योज्या बलमाश्रित्य भूभुजाम्॥ 5:2॥

संवृत्तिं ज्ञानिनामेवं युक्तमेवाभिरक्षितुम्।
विरुद्धाशनविच्छित्तिर्भैषजामेव शोभते॥ 5:3॥

वमनै रेचनैः स्वेदैरौषधीनां बलेन च।
रोगार्तान्शमयन्तीति किं सेव्या न हितैषिभिः॥ 5:4॥

दानधर्मं प्रवक्ष्यामि प्रेतलोकार्ग्गलम्परम्।
विधुरध्वान्तमार्तण्डं सोपानं सुरवेश्मनाम्॥ 5:5॥

5:0 ईश्वर उवाच] CE_N; --- श्वर उवाच A **5:1** विज्ञायार्जितपापानां] C; विज्ञायाजितपापानां A; विज्ञानार्जितपापानां E_N **5:1** न ब्रवीमि कदाचन] AE_N; न ब्रवीमि कदाचनः C **5:2** भूभुजाम्] AE_N, लो ⏓ किं मृत्युना यो ⏓ बलमा ⏓ त्य भूभु ⏓⏓ C **5:3** संवृत्तिं ज्ञानिनामेवं] CE_N; संवृत्ति ज्ञानिनामे --- A **5:3** युक्तमेवाभिरक्षितुम्] CE_N; युक्त ⏓ वाभिरक्षितृम् A **5:3** विरुद्धाशनविच्छित्तिर्भैषजामेव] *em.*; विरुद्धाशनविच्छित्तिभैषजामेव A; विरुद्धाशनविच्छित्तिभिषजामेव C; विरुद्धासनविच्छित्तिर्भिषजामेव E_N **5:4** वमनै रेचनैः स्वेदैरौ°] E_N; वमनै विरेचनैः स्वेदैरौ° A (unmetrical); वमनै रेचनैः ⏓ दैरौ° C **5:4** रोगार्तान् शमयन्तीति] C; रोगा ⏓⏓ शमयन्तीति A; रोगार्त्तान् समयन्तीति E_N **5:4** सेव्या न हितैषिभिः] E_N; सेव्याश्च हितैर्षिभिः A; सेव्या न हितेषिभिः C **5:5** दानधर्मं] CE_N; दानधर्म्मं A **5:5** प्रेतलोकार्ग्गलम्परम्] CE_N; प्रेतलोकाग्गल परम् A **5:5** °मार्तण्डं] AC; °मार्तण्ड° E_N **5:5** सुरवेश्मनाम्] E_N; सुरवे --- A; सु ⏓ वे ⏓ मनम् C

इज्याध्ययनदानानि तपः सत्यं क्षमा धृतिः।
अलोभ इति मार्गो ऽयं धर्म्मस्याष्टविधः स्मृतः॥ 5:6॥

तत्र पूर्वश्चतुर्वर्गो दम्भार्थमपि सेव्यते।
ऊर्ध्वश्चोत्तरवर्गस्तु स महात्मसु तिष्ठति॥ 5:7॥

इज्या तपः स्वाध्ययनं दानानि विविधानि च।
दममूलानि सर्वाणि तस्मादुपशमी भवेत्॥ 5:8॥

दानाच्छोषमुपैति वैरजलधिर्द्दानाच्च लोकः प्रियः।
दानात्कीर्तिरतीव रूपविभवः श्रीभोगसम्पत्तथा।
मृत्योर्ल्लोकगतः सुखानि परमाण्याप्नोति दानादपि।
स्वर्गे नन्दति दानतो ऽपि सुचिरन्दानाद्धि सर्वं भवेत्॥ 5:9॥

नागेन्द्रास्तुरगाः पदानि विभवो यानानि वन्दिस्तथा।
दिव्याहारविहारभूषणसुखं सिंहासनञ्चामरम्।
अर्थाशापरिपूरणं युवतयो हर्म्याः शशाङ्कप्रभाः।
प्रज्ञा बोधगुणाः सदा निरुजता प्राग्दानचिह्नं नृणाम्॥ 5:10॥

---

6 Cf., for example, *Hitopadeśa* 1.8–9: इज्याध्ययनदानानि तपः सत्यं धृतिः क्षमा। अलोभ इति मार्गोऽयं धर्मस्याष्टविधः स्मृतः॥ तत्र पूर्वश्चतुर्वर्गो दम्भार्थमपि सेव्यते। उत्तरस्तु चतुर्वर्गो महात्मन्येव तिष्ठति॥

5:6 इज्याध्ययनदानानि] E_N; --- न ⏓⏓ नि A; ⏓⏓ ध्ययन ⏓ नानि C **5:6** स्मृतः] AE_N; ⏓ तः C **5:7** चतुर्वर्गो] CE_N; चतुर्वर्ग्ग A **5:7** दम्भार्थमपि] AC; दम्भाथमपि E_N **5:7** स] E_N; त A^c; ता A^{ac}; ना C **5:8** इज्या तपः स्वाध्ययनं] CE_N; इज्या तप स्वाध्यय A (unmetrical) **5:8** दममूलानि सर्वाणि] *em.*; दमोमूलानि स --- A; दशमूलानि सर्वाणि C; दमो मूलानि सर्वाणि E_N **5:8** तस्मादुपशमी] *em.*; --- मी A; त ⏓ दुपशमी C; तस्यादुदसमी E_N **5:9** दानाच्छोषमुपैति] E_N; दानाशोषमुपैति A; दानाच्छो ⊔ C **5:9** वैरजलधिर्द्दानाच्च] E_N; वैरजलधिदानाच A; ⊔ C **5:9** लोकः प्रियः] *em.*; लोक प्रिये A; ⊔ C; लोकप्रियो E_N **5:9** दानात् कीर्तिरतीवरूपविभवः] *em.*; दाना कीर्त्तिरतीवरूपविभवः A; ⏓ नात् ⏓⏓ रतीव ⊔ C; दानात् कीर्त्तिरतीवरूपविशवः E_N ल्क् स ⏓ त्तथा C **5:9** मृत्योर्ल्लोकगतः] E_N; मृत्योलोकगतः A; मृ ⏓⏓ कगतः C **5:9** परमाण्याप्नोति] CE_N; परमान्याप्नोति A **5:9** नन्दति दानतो ऽपि] AC; नन्दतिदानतो ऽपि E_N **5:9** दानाद्धि सर्वं भवेत्] AE_N; दाना ि ⊔ C **5:10** नागेन्द्रास्तुरगाः पदानि विभवो] E_N; नागे --- भवो A; ⊔ C **5:10** यानानि वन्दिस्तथा] A; ⊔ C; यानानि वन्दी तथा E_N **5:10** दिव्याहारविहारभूषणसुखं सिंहासनञ्चामरम्] AE_N; ⊔ C **5:10** अर्थाशापरिपूरणं युवतयो] AE_N; ⊔ C **5:10** हर्म्याः शशाङ्कप्रभाः] A; ⊔ C; हर्म्यं शशाङ्कप्रभम् E_N **5:10** प्रज्ञा बोधगुणाः सदा निरुजता] E_N; प्रज्ञा बोधगुण सदा निरुजता A; प्रज्ञा ⏓ ध गुणा ⏓ दा ⏓ निरुजता C **5:10** प्राग्दानचिह्नं] CE_N; प्राग्दानचिह्न A

गृहस्थस्योपजीवन्ति वरधेनोश्चतुस्तनान्।
देवताः पितरश्चैव मानुषाश्च गिरीन्द्रजे॥ 5:11॥

स्वाहाकारवषट्कारानुपजीवन्ति देवताः।
स्वधाकारं पितृगणा हन्तकारञ्च मानुषाः॥ 5:12॥

शूद्रो ऽपि पञ्चभिर्यज्ञैर्यजते मन्त्रयोगतः।
अतो ऽन्यथा तु यो भुङ्क्ते स ऋणं नित्यमश्नुते॥ 5:13॥

गृहस्थः सर्वदा कुर्याद्ददातियजतिक्रियाः।
दानधर्ममकुर्वाणो द्रव्ये सति स यात्यधः॥ 5:14॥

उदपानं तु यः कुर्यात्पापात्मा दुष्टचेतसः।
विधूय पापसंघातं पितृभिः सह मोदते॥ 5:15॥

पुष्करिण्याश्च यः कर्त्ता मोदते दिवि शक्रवत्।
कुलैश्च सप्तभिर्युक्तो यावत्कीर्त्तिर्न नश्यति॥ 5:16॥

गृहं द्रव्यसमोपेतं दद्याद्विप्राय यो नरः।
तस्य हेममयं दिव्यं गृहं स्वर्ग्गे प्रजायते॥ 5:17॥

उद्यानं कुरुते यस्तु देवदेवस्य मंदिरे।
तस्य दानफलं यत्तत्पुष्पे पुष्पे निबोध मे॥ 5:18॥

दशसौवर्ण्णिकं पुष्पं माला लक्षेण संमिता।

5:11 गृहस्थस्योपजीवन्ति] AE$_N$; गृहस्थानुपजीवन्ति C **5:11** वरधेनोश्चतुस्तनान्] C; व-रधेनोश्चतुस्त --- A; वत्सो धेनोश्चतुस्तनान् E$_N$ **5:11** देवताः पितरश्चैव] CE$_N$; --- A **5:11** मानुषाश्च गिरीन्द्रजे] E$_N$C; ⏑ नुषश्च गिरीन्द्रजे A **5:12** देवताः] AE$_N$; देव ⏑ C **5:12** स्वधाकारं] E$_N$; स्वाथाकार A; ⊔ C **5:12** हन्तकारञ्च] A; ⊔ C; पाङ्गकारश्च E$_N$ **5:13** शूद्रो ऽपि पञ्चभिर्यज्ञैर्यजते] E$_N$; शूद्रो ऽपि पञ्चभियज्ञैयजन्ते A; ⊔ य ⏑ ⏑ C **5:13** अतो ऽन्यथा तु यो भुङ्क्ते] AE$_N$; ⊔ C **5:13** स ऋणं नित्यमश्नुते] *em.*; स ऋण नित्यमश्नुते A; ⏑ ⏑ ⏑ ˙ नित्य ⏑ नुते C; स त्राणंनित्यमश्नुते E$_N$ **5:14** गृहस्थः सर्वदा कुर्याद्ददातियजतिक्रियाः] CE$_N$; गृहस्थः सर्वदा कु --- A **5:14** दानधर्ममकुर्वाणो] CE$_N$; --- कुर्वाणो A **5:15** यः कुर्यात्] CE$_N$; य कुर्यात् A **5:15** पितृभिः सह मोदते] AE$_N$; पि ⊔ C **5:16** पुष्किरिण्याश्च यः कर्त्ता मोदते दिवि] E$_N$; ⊔ वि C; पुष्किरिण्याश्च यः कर्त्ता मोदते दिवि A **5:16** कुलैश्च सप्तभिर्युक्तो] AE$_N$; कु ⊔ भिर्युक्तो C **5:17** दद्याद्विप्राय यो नरः] E$_N$; दद्य --- A; दद्या विप्राय यो नरः C **5:17** तस्य] CE$_N$; --- स्य A **5:17** स्वर्ग्गे प्रजायते] A; स्वर्ग्गेषु जायते CE$_N$ **5:18** उद्यानं] CE$_N$; उद्यान A **5:18** तस्य दानफलं यत्तत्] Cf. NiMukh; तस्य दानं फल यन्न A; तस्य दानफलं सम्यक् CE$_N$ **5:18** निबोध मे] AC; निबोधमे E$_N$ **5:19** पुष्पं] E$_N$; पुष्प A; ⊔ C **5:19** माला लक्षेण संमिता] AE$_N$; ⊔ C

कोटिर्मालाशतेनाहुरनन्तं लिंगपूरणे॥ 5:19॥

एवं कुर्वन्ति ये नित्यं ते गणा मम चाक्षयाः।
न तेषां मर्त्यभावो हि कल्पकोटिशतैरपि॥ 5:20॥

ऋषय ऊचुः॥
पृच्छन्ति ऋषयो भीताः संसारभयविह्वलाः।
तुष्यते च कथन्देव अर्चितस्य च किम्फलम्॥ 5:21॥

क्षीराज्यदधितोयेन स्नापितस्य च किं फलम्।
पुष्पाणाञ्चैव सर्व्वेषां गन्धधूपस्य किम्फलम्॥ 5:22॥

वस्त्रालङ्कारनैवेद्यैर्ध्वजादर्शवितानकैः।
किं फलं च्छत्रदीपाश्च गवादिमहिषीषु च॥ 5:23॥

अजवारणदानस्य दासीदासस्य यत्फलम्।
सन्माज्र्जने फलं किं स्यात्तथा चैवोपलेपने॥ 5:24॥

गीतनृत्यफलं ब्रूहि तन्त्रीवाद्यफलञ्च यत्।
कृष्णाष्टम्यां चतुर्दश्यां जागरस्य फलं वद॥ 5:25॥

उपवासस्य यत्पुण्यं देवदेवाश्रितस्य तु।
एतत्सर्वं समाख्याहि उपसन्नाः स्म ते वयम्॥ 5:26॥

नन्दिकेश्वर उवाच।
शतं संमार्ज्जने दानं सहस्रमुपलेपने।
निष्काणां प्राप्नुयात्पुण्यं शिवभक्त्या समन्वितः॥ 5:27॥

5:19 कोटिर्मालाशतेनाहु°] *em.*; कोटिमालाशतेनाहु° AE$_N$; ⊔ तनाहु° C **5:20** एवं कुर्वन्ति ये नित्यं] A; एवं कुर्वीत यो नित्यं C **5:20** ते गणा मम चाक्षयाः] *em.*; --- आः A; स गणो मम चाक्षयः CE$_N$ **5:21** ऊचुः] CE$_N$; ऊचु A **5:22** क्षीराज्यदधितोयेन स्नापितस्य च किं फलम्] AE$_N$; क्षीराज्यदधि ⊔ C **5:22** पुष्पाणाञ्चैव सर्व्वेषां] AE$_N$; ⊔ सर्वेषां C **5:22** गन्धधूपस्य किम्फलम्] C; गन्धधूप (?) --- A; गन्धपुष्पस्य किं फलं E$_N$ **5:23** वस्त्रालङ्कारनैवेद्यैर्ध्वजा°] C; --- लंकारनैवेद्यैर्ध्वजा° A; वस्त्रालङ्कारनैवेद्यैर्द्ध्वजा° E$_N$ **5:23** किं फलं च्छत्रदीपाश्च] A; किं फलं च्छत्रदीपेषु CE$_N$ **5:24** अजवारण°] CE$_N$; अजावारण° A **5:24** सन्माज्र्जने] C; सम्मार्जने AE$_N$ **5:24** फलं किं स्यात्तथा चैवोपलेपने] E$_N$; फल किं स्या तथा चैवोपलेपयेत् A; फलं किं स्या तथा चै ⌣ पलेपनेन C **5:25** गीतनृत्यफलं ब्रूहि तन्त्रीवाद्यफलञ्च यत्] AE$_N$; गीतनृत्यफलं ब्रूहि त ⊔ ञ्च यत् C **5:25** कृष्णाष्टम्यां चतुर्दश्यां जागरस्य फलं वद] E$_N$; कृष्णाष्ट --- गरस्य फलं वद A; ⊔ फलं वद C **5:26** देवदेवाश्रितस्य] AC; देवदेवश्रितस्य E$_N$ **5:26** उपसन्ना स्म ते वयम्] A; उपसन्नाः स्म ते वयम् C; उपसत्यः स्म ते वयं E$_N$ **5:27** नन्दि°] A, नन्दी म्स्भ् **5:27** पुण्यं] CE$_N$; पुण्य A

उपलिप्य शिवागारं शुचीभूय समाहितः।
अर्चयेत्सततं देवं ज्ञानदीक्षाविवर्जितः॥ 5:28॥

पत्रपुष्पफलैश्चैव दधिक्षीरघृतादिभिः।
विचित्रैर्भक्तिपूतैश्च यः पूजयति नित्यशः॥ 5:29॥

यस्तु नैवेद्यच्छत्रैश्च ध्वजादर्शवितानकैः।
घण्टाचामरदानेन अलङ्कारौदनेन वा॥ 5:30॥

सुवर्णमणिवस्त्रैश्च गन्धधूपोपलेपनैः।
गीतवादित्रनृत्तैश्च हुडुङ्कारस्तवेन च॥ 5:31॥

वक्ष्यामि सर्वमेवन्तु अपरिज्ञातकारणे।
केवलम्भक्तिमापन्ने शृणुध्वं पूजने फलम्॥ 5:32॥

तोयेन स्नापयेल्लिङ्गं गन्धदिग्धेन चैव हि।
एकरात्रेण मुच्यन्ते मानसात्किल्विषान्नराः॥ 5:33॥

दशरात्रात्कायिकेन महापापेन पक्षतः।
मासेन स्वर्गमाप्नोति अब्दाद्गाणेश्वरीं गतिम्॥ 5:34॥

त्र्यब्देन पितृतां याति पञ्चभिः कुलमुद्धरेत्।
द्विषड्भैरीशसायुज्यं यावज्जीवं शिवं विशेत्॥ 5:35॥

कृष्णाष्टम्याञ्चतुर्दश्यां यो दध्ना स्नापयेच्छिवम्।
यावज्जीवकृतैः पापैर्मुच्यते नात्र संशयः॥ 5:36॥

5:28 उपलिप्य शिवागारं] CE$_N$; --- रं A **5:28** शुचीभूय] A; शुचीर्भूत्वा CE$_N$ **5:28** अर्चयेत्सततं] AC; अर्च्चयन् सततं E$_N$ **5:29** पत्रपुष्पफलैश्चैव] C; पत्रपुष्पफलं चैव A; बभ्रुपुष्पफलञ्चैव E$_N$ **5:29** विचित्रैर्भक्तिपूतैश्च] *em.*; विचित्रैभक्तिपूतैश्च A; विचित्रैभक्तिपूजैश्च C; विचित्रैर्भक्तिपूजैश्च E$_N$ **5:30** घण्टाचामरदानेन अलङ्कारौदनेन वा] CE$_N$; घण्टाचामरदान --- A **5:31** °वस्त्रैश्च] AC; °रत्नैश्च E$_N$ **5:31** हुडुङ्कारस्तवेन] *em.*; हुडुङ्कारास्तवेन A; हंहुंकारस्तवैस्तथा C; हुहुङ्काररैस्तथैव च E$_N$ **5:32** अपरिज्ञातकारणे] C; संपरिज्ञातकारणे C; अपरिज्ञातकारणं E$_N$ **5:32** शृणुध्वं] CE$_N$; शृणुध्व A **5:32** पूजने] *conj.*; पूजते A; पूजा C (unmetrical); पूजया E$_N$ **5:33** स्नापयेल्लिङ्गं] CE$_N$; स्नापये लिङ्गं A **5:33** मानसात्किल्विषान्नराः] CE$_N$, मानसकिल्बि --- म्सा **5:34** दशरात्रात्कायिकेन] CE$_N$; ---कायिकेन A **5:34** अब्दाद्गाणेश्वरीं गतिम्] *conj.*; अब्दांगाणेश्वरी गतिं A; अब्दागाणेश्वरीं गतिम् C; आब्दाद्गाणेश्वरीं गतिं E$_N$ **5:35** याति] CE$_N$; यान्ति A **5:35** द्विषड्भैरीशसायुज्यं] E$_N$; द्विषड्भैरीशसायुज्य A; द्विषड्भैरीशसायोज्यं C **5:35** विशेत्] AE$_N$; शेत् C (unmetrical) **5:36** चतुर्दश्यां] CE$_N$; चतुर्दश्या A **5:36** स्नापयेच्छिवम्] CE$_N$; स्नापये शिवम् A **5:36** यावज्जीवकृतैः पापैर्मुच्यते नात्र संशयः] CE$_N$; यावजीवकृतैः प --- A

प्रत्यहं स्नापयेद्यस्तु मासमेकं शुचिर्नरः।
क्रतूनां फलमाप्नोति भिन्ने देहे सुरालयम्॥ 5:37॥

षण्मासं स्नापयेद्यस्तु सुराणां चोत्तमो भवेत्।
अब्दस्नानेन पितरस्तस्य यान्ति सुरालयम्॥ 5:38॥

त्र्याब्देन रुद्रसायोज्यं द्वादशाब्दैः कुलैः स्वयम्।
घृतेन स्नापयेल्लिङ्गमेकाहमपि मानवः॥ 5:39॥

दग्ध्वा तु सर्वपापानि अश्वमेधमवाप्नुयात्।
दशरात्रात्स्वर्गगतिम्मासाद्गाणेश्वरीङ्गतिम्॥ 5:40॥

पितॄन्नरकगर्तस्थानुद्धरत्यविकल्पतः।
षड्मासं स्नापयेद्यस्तु नित्यं चाभग्नयोगतः॥ 5:41॥

तस्यापि पितरो यान्ति नित्यं गाणेश्वरीङ्गतिम्।
द्विरब्देनैव सायुज्यं व्रजन्ति पितृभिस्सह॥ 5:42॥

घृतस्नानात्परन्नास्ति उद्धरेत्कुलसप्तकम्।
त्रिनेत्राः शूलहस्ताश्च वृषाङ्काश्चन्द्रशेखराः॥ 5:43॥

सर्वज्ञाः सर्वगा नित्या भवन्ति जगदीश्वराः।
कृष्णाष्टम्यां चतुर्दश्यां मधुना स्नापयेच्छिवम्॥ 5:44॥

राजसूयस्य यज्ञस्य फलं प्राप्नोति मानवः।

5:37 मासमेकं शुचिर्नरः] C; मासमेक शुचिनरः A; मासमेकं सुचिर्न्नरः E_N **5:37** क्रतूनां] AC; केतूनां E_N **5:37** भिन्ने देहे] AC; भिन्नदेहे E_N **5:37** सुरालयम्] CE_N; सुरालये ज A **5:38** षण्मासं स्नापयेद्यस्तु] AE_N; षमासं स्नाप यस्तु C **5:38** अब्दस्नानेन पितरस्तस्य] AC; अब्दस्नानेपितरस्तस्य E_N **5:39** त्र्याब्देन रुद्रसायोज्यं] C; त्र्यब्देन रुद्रसायुज्य A; अयब्देन रुद्रसायुज्यं E_N **5:39** द्वादशाब्दैः कुलैः स्वयम्] CE_N; द्वादशाब्दे कुलै स्वयम् A **5:39** घृतेन स्नापयेल्लिङ्गमेकाहमपि मानवः] CE_N; घृतेन स्न --- नवः A **5:40** दग्ध्वा तु सर्वपापानि] AC; दध्वा तु सर्व पापानि E_N **5:40** दशरात्रात्स्वर्गगतिम्] CE_N; दशरात्रा स्वर्गगति A **5:40** मासाद्गाणेश्वरीङ्गतिम्] CE_N; मासाद्गणेश्वरीगतिम् A **5:41** पितॄन्नरकगर्तस्थानुद्धरत्यविकल्पतः] CE_N; पितृं नरकगर्त्तस्थानुद्धरत्वविकल्पतः A **5:42** तस्यापि पितरो] AC; तस्योपरिवरा E_N **5:42** गाणेश्व°] AE_N; गानेश्व° C **5:42** द्विरब्देनैव सायुज्यं व्रजन्ति पितृभिस्सह] *em.*; द्विर --- ⏑̱ स्सह A; दिरब्देनैव सायोज्यं व्रजन्ति पितृभिः सह C; द्विरब्देनैव सायोज्यं व्रजन्ति पितृभिः सह E_N **5:43** घृतस्नानात्परन्नास्ति] C; घृतस्नानपर नास्ति A; घृत स्नानात्परं नास्ति E_N **5:43** उद्धरेत्कुलसप्तकम्] CE_N; उद्धरे कुलसप्तकम् A **5:43** त्रिनेत्राः शूलहस्ताश्च] CE_N; तृणेत्र शूलहस्ताश्च A **5:43** वृषाङ्काश्चन्द्रशेखराः] CE_N; वृषांक चन्द्रशेखरः A **5:44** सर्वज्ञाः सर्वगा नित्या] CE_N; सर्वज्ञा सर्वगा नित्यं A **5:44** स्नापयेच्छिवम्] CE_N; स्नापये शिवम् A **5:45** राजसूयस्य] AE_N; राजसूर्यस्य C

प्रत्यहं स्नापयेद्यस्तु वर्षेणैव गणेश्वरः॥ 5:45॥

पञ्चाब्देन तु सायोज्यं प्रयाति पितृसंयुतः।
प्रत्यहं पञ्चगव्येन यः शिवं स्नपयेन्नरः॥ 5:46॥

न तस्य दृश्यते चान्तं देवलोकञ्च गच्छति।
सम्वत्सरेण शुद्धात्मा शिवसायोज्यतां व्रजेत्॥ 5:47॥

द्विवर्षेण पितॄन्सप्त समुद्धृत्य शिवं व्रजेत्।
गन्धैश्च स्नापयेल्लिङ्गं दिव्यैश्चैव सुगन्धिभिः॥ 5:48॥

वाजपेयस्य यज्ञस्य फलं प्राप्नोति मानवः।
कर्प्पूरव्यतिमिश्रेण चन्दनेन तु लेपयेत्॥ 5:49॥

विद्याधरत्वमाप्नोति रमते सुरपूजितः।
अश्वमेधफलञ्चैव दशरात्रेण चाप्नुयात्॥ 5:50॥

मासेन गणतां याति अब्दात्सायोज्यमाप्नुयात्।
अभग्नयोगो यो दद्यात्प्रत्यहं लिङ्गलेपनम्॥ 5:51॥

पितरस्तस्य सर्वे ते गतिं यस्यन्ति चोत्तमाम्।
अगरुन्दशसाहस्रं षट्साहस्रन्तु चन्दनम्॥ 5:52॥

अनन्तो गुग्गुलश्चैव सहाज्येन सुयोजितः।
द्वे सहस्रे पलानां तु महिषाक्षस्य गुग्गुलोः॥ 5:53॥

प्रदहेत्तद्गतात्मा यः सर्वपापैः प्रमुच्यते।

5:45 प्रत्यहं श्नापयेद्यस्तु वर्षेणैव गणेश्वरः] CE$_N$; प्रत्यहं श्नापयेद्यस्तु व --- A **5:46** सायोज्यं] CE$_N$; सायुज्य A **5:46** यः शिवं श्नपयेन्नरः] CE$_N$; य शिवं श्नपये नरः A **5:47** दृश्यते] AC; दृष्यते E$_N$ **5:47** चान्तं] A^{c}CE$_N$; चिन्तं A^{ac} **5:47** देवलोकञ्च] A; देवलोकं स CE$_N$ **5:47** °सायोज्यतां] C; °सायुज्यतां AE$_N$ **5:48** पितॄन्सप्त] C; पितृ सप्त A; पितृन्सप्त E$_N$ **5:48** स्नापयेल्लिङ्गं दिव्यैश्चैव सुगन्धिभिः] CE$_N$; स्नपये लिंगं --- A **5:49** यज्ञस्य फलं] C; यज्ञस्य फल A; याज्ञस्य फलं E$_N$ **5:49** चन्दनेन] CE$_N$; चन्दनेना A **5:50** अश्वमेधफलञ्चैव] CE$_N$; अश्वमेधफल चैव A **5:50** दशरात्रेण चाप्नुयात्] A; दशरात्रादवाप्नुयात् CE$_N$ **5:51** मासेन गणतां याति] *em.* Cf. NiMukh; मासेन गणता यान्ति A; मासेनैकेन गणतां CE$_N$ म्स्छ्E$_N$; अब्दा सायुज्यमाप्नुयात् A **5:51** अभग्नयोगो यो दद्यात्प्रत्यहं लिङ्गलेपनम्] C; अभग्नयोगो यो --- पनम् A; अहग्नयोगो यो दद्यात्प्रत्यहं लिङ्गलेपनम् E$_N$ **5:52** पितरस्तस्य सर्वे ते गतिं] CE$_N$; पितरस्तस्य सवे ते गति A **5:52** षट्साहस्रन्तु] CE$_N$; षट्सहस्रं तु A **5:53** अनन्तो] CE$_N$; अनंत्यो A **5:53** सहाज्येन] AE$_N$; सहाजेन C **5:53** महिषाक्षस्य गुग्गुलोः] CE$_N$; महिसाखस्च गुगुलोः A **5:54** प्रदहेत्तद्गतात्मा] *conj.*; प्रदहेत्तर्गतानां यः A; प्रदहेत्तङ्गतात्मा यः C; प्रदहेत्तङ्गतात्मायः E$_N$

देवि सम्वत्सरे पूर्णे नन्दीश्वरसमो भवेत्॥ 5:54॥

एकाहं दहते यस्तु देवदेवस्य संनिधौ।
सर्वपापविशुद्धात्मा अग्निष्टोममवाप्नुयात्॥ 5:55॥

भक्तिमान्प्रदहेद्यस्तु धूपं गुग्गुलमुत्तमम्।
मासैकेन समाप्नोति क्रतूनां शतमुत्तमम्॥ 5:56॥

वर्षमेकन्दहेद्यस्तु स गणश्चोत्तमो भवेत्।
न तस्य सम्भवो मर्त्ये पितृभिः सह मोदते॥ 5:57॥

द्व्यब्दं दहति यो देवि शुचीभूय दिने दिने।
स्वकुलञ्चोद्धृतं तेन शिवभक्तेन धीमता॥ 5:58॥

वस्त्रध्वजवितानं वा यो दद्याल्लिङ्गसन्निधौ।
लभते परमैश्वर्यं जायते चोत्तमे कुले॥ 5:59॥

सकृद्दानफलं ह्येतद्द्विस्त्रिधा गतिरुत्तमा।
प्राप्नुयान्मानवः शीघ्रं सोमलोकं न संशयः॥ 5:60॥

शतसाहस्रदानेन गतिर्गाणेश्वरी भवेत्।
पितृभिः संयुतश्चैव लक्षदानान्न संशयः॥ 5:61॥

मेखलाङ्कटिसूत्रञ्च यो दद्याल्लिङ्गमूर्धनि।

5:54 देवि सम्वत्सरे पूर्णे नन्दीश्वरसमो भवेत्] CE$_N$; देवि संवत् --- र समो भवेत् A **5:55** एकाहं दहते यस्तु] C; एकाहो ऽपि दहेद्यस्तु A; एकान्हं दहते यस्तु E$_N$ **5:56** भक्तिमान्] CE$_N$; भक्तिमा A **5:56** मासैकेन] E$_N$; मासैकंन A^c; तमासैकंन A^{ac}; मासेकेन C **5:56** क्रतूनां] AC; क्रतुनां E$_N$ **5:57** वर्षमेकन्दहेद्यस्तु] AC; मासमेकं दहेद्यस्तु E$_N$ **5:57** गणश्चोत्तमो भवेत्] CE$_N$; गणश्चो --- A **5:57** सम्भवो मर्त्ये पितृभिः] CE$_N$; संभव मत्ये पितृभि A **5:58** द्व्यब्दं दहति] A; द्व्यब्दं हति C (unmetrical); व्द्यब्दं दहति E$_N$ **5:58** शुचीभूय] AC; शुचीर्भूतो E$_N$ **5:58** तेन शिवभक्तेन] AE$_N$; तेना सभक्तेन C (unmetrical) **5:59** वस्त्रध्वजवितानं वा] A; वस्त्रध्व ⊔ न चC; वस्त्रध्वजवितानन्तु E$_N$ **5:59** दद्याल्लिङ्गसन्निधौ] CE$_N$; दद्या लिङ्गसंनिधौ A **5:59** लभते परमैश्वर्यं] CE$_N$; लभते परमेश्वर्यं A **5:59** जायते चोत्तमे कुले] CE$_N$; जातः परमके कुले A **5:60** एतद् द्विस्त्रिधा गतिरुत्तमा] *em.*; द्वित्रिधा गतिरुत्तमा C; द्वितृधा गतिरु --- A; °त्रिधागतिरुत्तमां E$_N$ **5:60** प्राप्नुयान्मानवः] E$_N$; प्राप्नुयात्मानवः C; ---नवः A **5:60** सोमलोकं] CE$_N$; सोमलोक A **5:61** गतिर्गाणेश्वरी भवेत्] E$_N$; गतिपाणेश्वरीम्भवेत् A; गतिमार्गाणेश्वरी भवेत् C **5:61** पितृभिः संयुतश्चैव] A^{c}E$_N$; पितृभि संयुतश्चैव A^{ac}; पितृभिः संयुतंश्चैव C **5:61** लक्षदानान्न] CE$_N$; लक्षदानं न A **5:62** मेखलाङ्कटिसूत्रञ्च] C; मेखला कटिसूत्रञ्च A; मेखलां कटिसूत्रश्च E$_N$ **5:62** °मूर्ध्निषु] A; °मूर्धनि CE$_N$

चतुःसागरपर्यन्तक्ष्मायान्तु स भवेन्नृपः॥ 5:62॥

मुकुटं कुण्डलं चैव चित्रपट्टकदायकः।
सकलान्तु महीं भुङ्क्ते अङ्गाभरणदानतः॥ 5:63॥

मुखकोशे तथैवेह पट्टात्प्रादेशिको नृपः।
चित्रके चित्रभोगानि निस्सपत्नमवाप्नुयात्॥ 5:64॥

पुनः पुनश्च यो दद्याद्रत्नाभरणभूषणम्।
गाणापत्यमवाप्नोति अक्षयं परमं ध्रुवम्॥ 5:65॥

मुक्तिमण्डपिकां भक्त्या दत्वा यो ऽर्च्चयते शिवम्।
न तस्य पुनरावृत्तिर्गणश्चैवोत्तमो भवेत्॥ 5:66॥

रोचनां कुंकुमं चैव लिंगस्योपरि यो नरः।
प्रत्यहं लेपनन्दद्यात्स विद्याधरतां व्रजेत्॥ 5:67॥

द्वादशाब्देन गणतां कर्पूरागरुलेपनैः।
कटकेयूरदानेन आधिपत्यं महेच्छताम्॥ 5:68॥

प्राप्नुवन्ति नरा लोके शिवभक्तिपरायणाः।
रत्नदानानि दिव्यानि यो ददाति शिवाय वै॥ 5:69॥

दशसौवर्णिकं पुष्पं निर्ग्गन्धि यदि भाविनि।
शतसाहस्रिका माला अनन्तं लिंगपूरणे॥ 5:70॥

5:62 चतुःसागरपर्यन्तक्षायान्तु स भवेन्नृपः] C; चतुसागरपयन्तं क्षमाया स भवे नृपः A; चतुःसागरपर्यन्त क्षायां नु स भवेन्नृपः E_N **5:63** चित्रपट्टकदायकः] CE_N; चित्रपट्टक --- A **5:63** सकलान्तु महीं भुङ्क्ते] *em.*; --- तु मही भुंक्ते A; सकलान्तु मही भुङ्क्ते C; सकलान्तु महीं मुङ्क्ते E_N **5:63** अङ्गाभरणदानतः] AE_N; अङ्गाभरणदानततः C **5:64** मुखकोशे तथैवेह] AC; मुसकोशेतथैवेह E_N **5:64** पट्टात् प्रादेशिको नृपः] C; पट्टप्रादेशिको नृपः A; षट्टात्प्रादेशिको नृपः E_N **5:64** निस्सपत्नमवाप्नुयात्] *em.*; निस्वपत्नमवाप्नुयात् A; निःसपत्नान्यवाप्नुयात् C; निः सम्पन्नान्यवाप्नुयात् E_N **5:65** गाणापत्यमवाप्नोति] C; गणापत्यमवाप्नोति A; गाणपत्यमवाप्नोति E_N **5:65** अक्षयं] A; चाक्षम् C (unmetrical); चाक्षयं E_N **5:66** मुक्तिमण्डपिकां भक्त्या] *em.*; मुक्तमण्डपिका भक्त्या A; मुक्तामण्डपिकां भक्त्या C; मुक्तिमण्डपिकाभक्त्या E_N **5:66** यो ऽर्च्चयते शिवम्] CE_N; --- A **5:66** °रावृत्तिर्ग°] E_N; °रावृत्तिग° AC **5:67** रोचनां] C; रोचन A; रोचना E_N **5:68** कर्पूरागरु°] C; कपूरागरु° A; कर्पूरागुरु° E_N **5:68** कटकेयूरदानेन] AC; कटकेयूर दानेन E_N **5:69** प्राप्नुवन्ति नरा लोके शिवभक्तिपरायणाः] CE_N; प्राप् --- भक्तिपरायणाः A **5:70** दशसौवर्णिकं] CE_N; दशसौवर्णिक A **5:70** निर्ग्गन्धि] A; निर्गधि C; निर्गन्धं E_N **5:70** भाविनि] A; भामिनि CE_N **5:70** शतसाहस्रिका] AC; शतसाहस्रिकां E_N

निर्गन्धिकुसुमस्यायं विधिः ख्यातो द्विजोत्तमाः।
शोभनैर्दिव्यगन्धाद्यैः शृणु तत्र तु यत्फलम्॥ 5:71॥

एकपुष्पप्रदानेन लिंगेषु प्रतिमासु वा।
अशीतिकल्पकोटीनां दुर्गतिं न नरो व्रजेत्॥ 5:72॥

एवं वै निरयाः सर्वे नियतं शून्यतां गताः।
एकपुष्पप्रदानेन कस्य योगो न विद्यते॥ 5:73॥

वित्तसंपत्तिसंशुद्धं शेषं संपत्तिभावितम्।
तृणमप्युत्तमार्थाय कोटिवेधि रसेन्द्रवत्॥ 5:74॥

नन्दिकेश्वर उवाच।
एकपुष्पप्रदानेन योगः सर्वस्य विद्यते।
न चतुःसम्पदायोगः किं तु सर्वस्य विद्यते॥ 5:75॥

अकामाभ्यर्च्चिते लिङ्गे एतदुक्तं मया फलम्।
कामेनाभ्यर्च्यमानस्य शृणु तस्यापि यत्फलम्॥ 5:76॥

अर्क्कस्य करवीरस्य बुकस्योन्मत्तकस्य च।
चतुर्णां पुष्पजातीनां गन्धं जिघ्रति शंकरः॥ 5:77॥

सुवर्णनिष्कं पुष्पे तु सर्वस्मिन्देवि कथ्यते।
सहस्रे त्वन्यपुष्पाणां दत्ते यत्कथ्यते फलम्॥ 5:78॥

एकस्मिन्करवीरस्य दत्ते पुष्पे हि तत्फलम्।

5:71 निर्गन्धिकुसुमस्यायं विधिः ख्यातो द्विजोत्तमाः] E$_N$; निगन्धिकुसुमस्यैषा विधिः ख्याता द्विजोत्तमाः A; निर्ग्गन्धिकुपुमस्यायं विधिः ख्यातो द्विजोत्तम C **5:71** शोभनैर्दिव्यगन्धाद्यैः शृणु तत्र तु यत्फलम्] CE$_N$; शोभनैदिव्य --- तु यत्फलम् A **5:72** व्रजेत्] CE$_N$; भवेत् A **5:73** निरयाः सर्वे] CE$_N$; वितयं A **5:74** वित्त°] A; वृत्तिं C; वृत्ति° E$_N$ **5:74** °भावितम्] AC; °भाषितं E$_N$ **5:74** तृणमप्युत्तमार्थाय कोटिवेधि रसेन्द्रवत्] C; तृणमप्युत्तमाथा --- A; तृणमप्युत्तमार्थाय कोटिवधिरसेन्द्रवत् E$_N$ **5:75** नन्दिकेश्वर] AE$_N$; नन्दीकेश्वर C **5:75** योगः सर्वस्य विद्यते] CE$_N$; योग सर्वस्य विद्वन्ति A **5:75** चतुःसम्पदायोगः] C; चतुम्पदायोग A; चतुःसम्पदा योगः E$_N$ **5:76** अकामाभ्यर्च्चिते लिङ्गे एतदुक्तं] CE$_N$; अकामाभ्यर्चये लिङ्गमेतदुक्तं A **5:76** कामेनाभ्यर्च्य°] E$_N$; कामेनाभ्यर्च° AC **5:76** यत्फलम्] CE$_N$; यतफलम् A **5:77** चतुर्णां पुष्पजातीनां गन्धं जिघ्रति] E$_N$; चतुणां --- A; चतुर्णां पुष्पजातीनां गन्ध जिघ्रति C **5:78** सुवर्णनिष्कं पुष्पे] *em.*; सुवर्णनिष्कपुष्पे AC; सुवर्णनिष्कं पुष्पं E$_N$ **5:78** सर्वस्मिन्] E$_N$; सर्वस्मिं A; सर्वस्मि C **5:78** सहस्रे त्वन्यपुष्पाणां] C; सहस्रे त्वत्यपुष्पाणां A; सहस्रन्त्वन्यपुष्पाणां E$_N$ **5:78** यत्कथ्यते] CE$_N$; यकथ्यते A **5:79** एकस्मिन्करवीरस्य दत्ते पुष्पे हि तत्फलम्] AC; eyeskip E$_N$

करवीरसहस्रस्य भवेद्दत्तस्य यत्फलम्॥ 5:79॥

तदेकस्य तु पद्मस्य दत्तस्य फलमश्नुते।
पद्मानाञ्च सहस्रस्य मम दत्तस्य यत्फलम्॥ 5:80॥

तत्फलं लभते पत्रे दत्ते बिल्वस्य शोभने।
बिल्वपत्रसहस्रे तु दत्ते मे यत्फलं स्मृतम्॥ 5:81॥

बुकपुष्पे तदेकस्मिन्मम दत्ते लभेत्फलम्।
बुकपुष्पसहस्रे तु दत्ते यत्कीर्तितं फलम्।
पुष्पे दत्ते तदेकस्मिन्लभेद्धुतूरकस्य तु॥ 5:82॥

बुकेन वरदो देवः करवीरैर्द्धनप्रदः।
अर्केण श्रियमाप्नोति मोक्षं धुत्तूरकेन तु॥ 5:83॥

नीलोत्पलैर्भवेद्भोगी यो ऽर्चयेल्लिङ्गमुत्तमम्।
रक्ताब्जैः प्राप्नुयाद्राज्यं पुण्डरीकैश्च चक्रिणम्॥ 5:84॥

चम्पकैः सर्वकामानि पुंनागैर्नागकेशरैः।
ईप्सितांल्लभते कामांस्तथा केशरदामकैः॥ 5:85॥

मन्त्रसिद्धिमवाप्नोति बृहत्यागस्तिपुष्पकैः।
यो ऽर्चयेत्परमेशानं सिद्धकेन तथैव हि॥ 5:86॥

5:79 करवीरसहस्रस्य भवेद्दत्तस्य यत्फलम्] C; करवीरसहस्रस्योम्भवे दत्तस्य यत्फलम् A; करवीरसहस्रस्य भवेत्तदस्य यतफलं E_N **5:80** पद्मस्य] AC; पुष्पस्य E_N **5:80** पद्मानाञ्च] A; पद्मानान्तु CE_N **5:80** सहस्रस्य मम दत्तस्य यत्फलम्] CE_N; स --- फलम् A **5:81** तत्फलं] CE_N; ततफलं A **5:81** बिल्वपत्रसहस्रे तु दत्ते मे यत्फलं] E_N; बिल्वपत्रसहस्रं तु दत्तं मे यतफलं A; बिल्वपत्रसहस्रे तृ दत्ते मे यत्फलं C **5:82** बुकपुष्पे तदेकस्मिन् मम दत्ते लभेत्फलम्] CE_N; बुकपुष्पन्तदेकस्मिं मम दत्ते लभते फलम् A (unmetrical) **5:82** बुकपुष्पसहस्रे तु दत्ते यत्कीर्तितं फलम्] C; बुकपुष्पं सहस्रं तु दत्ते यत्फलम्किर्त्तितम् A; एयेस्किप् E_N **5:82** तदेकस्मिन्] C; च्चदेकस्मिं (?) A; यदेकस्मिन् E_N **5:82** लभेद्धुतूरकस्य] C; लभे धुतूरकस्य A; लभेद्धतुरकस्य E_N **5:83** बुकेन वरदो देवः करवीरैर्द्धनप्रदः] C; बुकेन वरदो दे --- A; वः वुकेन वरदो देवः करवीरैर्द्धनप्रदः E_N **5:83** अर्केण श्रियमाप्नोति] AC; अर्केण प्रियमच्छिन्ने E_N **5:83** धुत्तूरकेन] A; धुत्तुरकेण C; धत्तूरकस्य E_N **5:84** नीलोत्पलैर्भ°] AE_N; नीलोत्पलैभ° C **5:84** यो ऽर्चयेल्लिङ्ग°] CE_N; योर्चये लिङ्ग A **5:84** रक्ताब्जैः] *em.*; रक्ताब्जै A; रक्ताब्दैः C; रक्तार्कैः E_N **5:85** चम्पकैः] CE_N; चम्पकै A **5:85** ईप्सितांल्लभते कामांस्तथा] *conj.*; ईप्सितंल्लभते कामन्तथा A; ईप्सिताल्लभते कामांस्तथा C; ईप्सितां लभते कामांस्तथा E_N **5:86** बृहत्यागस्तिपुष्पकैः] C; --- A; बृहत्यगचस्तिपुष्पकैः E_N (unmetrical) **5:86** सिद्धकेन] *em.*; सिद्धिकेन A; सितार्क्केण CE_N

सर्वकामानवाप्नोति यो ऽर्च्चयेद्गन्धपुष्पकैः।
कुब्जकैर्विपुलो लाभः सौभाग्याय च वारुणी॥ 5:87॥

कन्याकामस्तु जातीभिर्यो ऽर्च्चयेत्परमेश्वरम्।
स लभेच्चोत्तमां कन्यां षण्मासेन न संशयः॥ 5:88॥

मल्लिका ज्ञानकामाय अर्च्चयेद्यो महेश्वरम्।
लभते परमं ज्ञानं संसारभयनाशनम्॥ 5:89॥

पुत्रकामाय कुन्दैस्तु अर्च्चयीत शुचिर्न्नरः।
लभते बहुपुत्रत्वं धनवंतं चिरायुषम्॥ 5:90॥

आरोग्यं कुशपुष्पैस्तु अशोकैः प्रियसङ्गमम्।
कर्ण्णिकारैर्धनं विद्याद्वश्यार्थे द्रोणपुष्पिका॥ 5:91॥

कदम्बेनार्चयेल्लिङ्गं सततं नियतव्रतः।
शत्रूणां वशकामाय नित्यमेव प्रदापयेत्॥ 5:92॥

नश्यन्ति व्याधयस्तस्य यो ऽर्चयेदरिमुस्तकैः।
सिंदुवारस्य पुष्पेण बद्धो मुच्येत बन्धनात्॥ 5:93॥

अंकोटासितवर्ण्णानि निर्गन्धिकुसुमानि च।
तानि शत्रुविनाशाय देवदेवाय कल्पयेत्॥ 5:94॥

5:87 सर्वकामानवाप्नोति] CE$_N$; सर्वकानमावाप्नोति A **5:87** यो ऽर्च्चयेद्गन्धपुष्पकैः] C; यो ऽर्च्चये गन्धपुष्पकैः A; यो ऽउर्चयेद्गन्धपुष्पकैः E$_N$ **5:87** कुब्जकैर्विपुलो लाभः] *conj.*; तूचकै विपुलं लाभं A; कुन्दकैविपुलो लाभः C; कुपुकैर्विपुलोलाभः E$_N$ **5:87** सौभाग्याय च वारुणी] *em.*; सौभाग्यंय च वारुणी A; शौभाग्याय च वारुणी C; सौभाग्याय च वारुणं E$_N$ **5:88** जातीभिर्यो ऽर्च्च°] CE$_N$; जातीभियो ऽर्च्च° A **5:88** स लभेच्चोत्तमां कन्यां] CE$_N$; स लभे चोत्तमां कन्या A **5:89** ज्ञानकामाय अर्च्चयेद्यो महेश्वरम्] *conj.*; ज्ञानकामे य --- A; ज्ञानकामार्थमर्च्चयन्तो महेश्वरम् CE$_N$ **5:89** लभते परमं] *em.*; लभन्ते परमं CE$_N$; लभन्ते तश्वर A **5:90** कुन्दैस्तु अर्च्चयीत शुचिर्न्नरः] C; कुंदेस्तु अर्चये शुचिनरः A; कुन्दैस्तु अर्च्चयीत शुच्चिर्न्नरः E$_N$ **5:90** लभते] CE$_N$; लभन्ते A **5:90** धनवंतं] A; धनवंन्तं C; धनवत्वं E$_N$ **5:91** कुशपुष्पैस्तु] CE$_N$; कुयपुष्पैस्तु A **5:91** कर्ण्णिकारैर्धनं विद्याद्वश्यार्थे द्रोणपुष्पिका] C; कर्ण्णिकारे धनं विद्यांद्वश्यार्थे द्रोणपुष्पिकाः A; कर्णिकारं धनं विद्याद्वश्यार्थे द्रोणपुष्पिकां E$_N$ **5:92** कदम्बेनार्चयेल्लिङ्गं] E$_N$; कदंबेनाच --- A **5:92** सततं नियतव्रतः] C; --- यतव्रतः A; सततं नियते व्रतः E$_N$ **5:92** नित्यमेव] AE$_N$; नित्यमेवं C **5:93** व्याधयस्तस्य] CE$_N$; व्याधयस् सवे A **5:93** यो ऽर्चयेदरिमुस्तकैः] A; यो ऽर्चयेदतिमुस्तकैः C; यो ऽर्चयेदतिमुक्तकैः E$_N$ **5:93** बद्धो] CE$_N$; बधो A (unmetrical) **5:94** अङ्कोटासितवर्ण्णानि] C; अंकोटसितवर्ण्णानि A; अंकोलासितवर्णानि E$_N$ **5:94** निर्गन्धिकुसुमानि च] A; निर्ग्गन्धकुसुमानि च C; निर्गन्धकुसुमा प्रिये E$_N$ **5:94** तानि शत्रुविनाशाय देवदेवाय कल्पयेत्] CE$_N$; तानि शत्रुविनाशाय दे --- A

पीतकानि तु पुष्ट्यर्थे पुष्पाणि विजयाय च।
नित्यमेव तु यो दद्यात्सर्वकाममवाप्नुयात्॥ 5:95॥

जलजानि तु पुष्पाणि वश्यार्थे तु प्रकल्पयेत्।
नीलरक्तानि यो दद्यात्तानि वश्यकराणि तु॥ 5:96॥

सर्वकामप्रदं बिल्वं दारिद्र्यभयनाशनम्।
बिल्वपत्रात्परं नास्ति येन तुष्यति शङ्करः॥ 5:97॥

विजयार्थे दमनकं योजयेन्नियमस्थितः।
विजिताः शत्रवस्तेन यो ऽर्चयेद्वृषभध्वजम्॥ 5:98॥

सुखं मरुवकन्दद्याज्जम्बुटः सर्वकामदः।
तिलको धनकामाय गोकामाय च वंकुली॥ 5:99॥

सौख्यदश्चापि तगरः किङ्कराटश्च कामदः।
आरोग्यञ्च धनञ्चैव फलिनी कामदा स्मृता॥ 5:100॥

शालः प्रियकरश्चैव किंशुकादायुराप्नुयात्।
हस्त्यश्वपशुकामाय कुटजेनार्चयेद्धरम्॥ 5:101॥

कर्पूरदमनं दद्याच्छत्रूणाञ्च विनाशने।
नश्यन्ति शत्रवः शीघ्रं देवदेवस्य पूजनात्॥ 5:102॥

श्यामा चारोग्यदा नित्यं जवापुष्पम्तथैव च।

5:95 पुष्ट्यर्थे पुष्पाणि विजयाय] *conj.*; पुष्ट्यर्थ पुष्पाणि विजयानि A; पुष्ट्यर्थे पुष्पाणि वित्रयाय C; पुष्ट्यर्थं पुष्पाणि विजयाय E_N **5:95** सर्वकाममवाप्नुयात्] A; सतत्काममवाप्नुयात् CE_N **5:96** जलजानि तु पुष्पाणि वश्यार्थे तु] AC; जलजानितु पुष्पाणि वश्यार्थं तु E_N **5:96** यो दद्यात्] *em.*; यो दद्या A; यान्येव CE_N **5:97** सर्वकामप्रदं बिल्वं] CE_N; सर्वकामयद चैवं A **5:97** दारिद्र्यभयनाशनम्] A; दारिद्र्यस्य प्रमोचनम् CE_N **5:97** बिल्वपत्रात्परं नास्ति येन तुष्यति] CE_N; बिल्वप --- A **5:98** विजयार्थे दमनकं] C; विजयार्थन्दवनद्दं A; विजयार्थं दमनकं E_N **5:98** योजयेन्नियमस्थितः] C; योजये नियमस्थितः A; योजयेन्नियमास्थितः E_N **5:98** विजिताः शत्रवस्तेन यो ऽर्चयेद्वृषभध्वजम्] E_N; विजया शत्रुवस्तेन योजयेद्वृषभध्वजः A; विजिताः शस्त्रवस्तेन यो ऽर्च्चयेद्वृषभध्वजम् C **5:99** सुखं मरुवकन्दद्याज्जम्बुटः सर्वकामदः] C; सुखम्मरु (?) वकन्दद्या जम्युट सर्वकामदः A; सुखे मरुवकं दद्याज्जम्बुटः सर्वकामदः E_N **5:99** वंकुली] AC; वंकुलौ E_N **5:100** तगरः] B, तरारः म्सा **5:100** तगरः किङ्कराटश्च] C; तगरङ्किङ्कराटश्च A; तगरः किङ्किरातश्च E_N **5:100** आरोग्यञ्च धनञ्चैव फलिनी कामदा स्मृता] CE_N; आरोग्यञ्च धनं --- A **5:101** किंशुकादायुराप्नुयात्] CE_N; किंशुकारायुदाप्नुयात् A **5:102** कर्पूरदमनं] AC; कर्पूरदमनकौ E_N **5:102** दद्याच्छत्रूणाञ्च] E_N; दद्या शत्रूणाञ्च A; दद्याच्छत्रूणा च C **5:102** शत्रवः] CE_N; तत्रव A **5:103** जवापुष्पम्] AC; जपापुष्पं E_N

कुरण्टकस्य वश्यार्थं नित्यं लिङ्गस्य पूजनात्॥ 5:103॥

विद्वेषे यूथिका योज्या देवदेवे महेश्वरे।
केतकी शत्रुनाशाय क्रुद्धो लिङ्गं तु यो ऽर्चयेत्॥ 5:104॥

सर्वकामप्रदा ह्येषा व्याघ्री देवि प्रकीर्त्तिता।
ज्योत्स्नाकारी तथैवेह नित्यमेव हि कामदा॥ 5:105॥

वासकेनार्चयेद्देवं बलमायुश्च वर्धते।
झिण्टिका सुखदा नित्यं तथा चाप्सरचम्पकम्॥ 5:106॥

डिम्बाक्षी व्याधिनाशार्थमश्वकर्ण्णस्तथैव च।
जयन्ती जयकामाय श्वेता च गिरिकर्णिका॥ 5:107॥

विद्वेषोच्चाटनार्थाय निम्बपुष्पेण यो ऽर्च्चयेत्।
भण्डी चाकर्षणे योज्या मदयन्ती तु या भवेत्॥ 5:108॥

ऋषिपुष्पी रुद्रजटी हन्ति सर्वानुपद्रवान्।
शणपुष्पञ्च यत्प्रोक्तं कोकिलाक्षस्तथैव च॥ 5:109॥

सर्वशुक्लं तु शान्त्यर्थे सर्वपीतन्तु पौष्टिके।
सर्वरक्तन्तु वश्यार्थे कृष्णं चैवाभिचारुके॥ 5:110॥

5:103 कुरण्टकस्य वश्यार्थं] A; कुरुण्टकस्य वश्यार्थ C; कुराण्टकस्य वश्यार्थं E_N **5:103** नित्यं लिङ्गस्य पूजनात्] CE_N; नित्यं --- A **5:104** योज्या देवदेवे महेश्वरे] AE_N; योज्या देवदेवमहेश्वरे C **5:104** शत्रुनाशाय] AE_N; शत्रुनाया C (unmetrical) **5:105** सर्वकामप्रदा ह्येषा] C; सवकामपदो ह्येषा A; सर्वकामप्रदा ह्यैषा E_N **5:105** व्याघ्री देवि प्रकीर्त्तिता] *em.*; व्याघ्री देवि प्रकीर्त्तिताः A; व्याघ्री देवी प्रकीर्त्तिता CE_N **5:105** ज्योत्स्नाकारी तथैवेह] A; ज्योत्स्नाकरी तथैवेह C; ज्योत्स्नाकरी तथैवाह E_N **5:106** वासकेनार्चयेद्देवं] AE_N; वाशकेनार्चयेद्देवं C **5:106** बलमायुश्च वर्धते] CE_N; बलमायुश्च वधते A **5:106** झिण्टिका सुखदा नित्यं] C; गण्टिका सुखदा नित्य --- म्सा; किण्टिका सुखदा नित्यं E_N **5:106** तथा चाप्सरचम्पकम्] CE_N; --- A **5:107** डिम्बाक्षी व्याधिनाशार्थमश्वकर्ण्णस्तथैव च] C; डिम्बाथी व्याधिनाशार्थ अश्वकर्ण्णस्तथैव च A; डिम्बाक्षी व्याधिनाशार्थमश्वकर्ण्णस्तथैव च E_N **5:107** गिरिकर्णिका] CE_N; गिरिकर्णि A (unmetrical) **5:108** विद्वेषोच्चाटनार्थाय निम्बपुष्पेण यो ऽर्च्चयेत्] CE_N; विद्वेषोचाटनाथन्तु निम्बपुष्पानि योचयेत् A **5:108** भण्डी चाकर्षणे योज्या] *em.*; भण्डी चाकर्षणे योज्य AC; भण्डीचाकर्षणे योज्या E_N **5:108** तु] A; च CE_N **5:109** हन्ति सर्वानुपद्रवान्] E_N; हन्ति सर्वान्तुपद्रवात् A; हन्ती सर्वानुपद्रवान् C **5:109** सणपुष्पञ्च यत्प्रोक्तं] E_N; शतपुष्पञ्च य --- A; सणपुष्पञ्च यत्प्रोक्तं C **5:109** कोकिलाक्षस्तथैव च] CE_N; --- व च A **5:110** सर्वशुक्लं तु] AC; सर्वं शुक्लंन्तु E_N **5:110** सर्वपीतन्तु] AC; सर्वं पीतन्तु E_N **5:110** सर्वरक्तन्तु वश्यार्थे कृष्णं चैवाभिचारुके] *em.*; सर्वरक्तन्तु वश्यार्थे कृष्ण चैवाभिचारुके A; कृष्णञ्चैवाभिचारे च देवदेवाय कल्पयेत् CE_N

पत्रं पुष्पं फलं तोयं तृणञ्चैव तथा पयः।
प्रत्यहं शम्भवे दद्यान्नासौ दुर्गतिमाप्नुयात्॥ 5:111॥

यस्य वृक्षस्य पुष्पाणि पत्राणि च फलानि च।
महादेवोपयुक्तानि सो ऽपि याति पराङ्गतिम्॥ 5:112॥

नास्ति पापसमः शत्रुर्न च धर्मसमः सखा।
नैव रुद्रात्परो देवो न पुष्पं कनकादपि॥ 5:113॥

बुकेनाभ्यर्च्यमानस्तु वरदो भवति प्रभुः।
सप्तरात्रं निवेद्यस्तु बुको रुद्राय धीमता॥ 5:114॥

दिने दिने तु दातव्यं शौचयित्वा पुनः पुनः।
सप्तरात्रमतिक्रम्य निर्माल्यत्वं प्रपद्यते॥ 5:115॥

सकृद्दत्ते बुके देवि गोसहस्रफलं लभेत्।
पक्षेण योगी भवति मासेन तु दिवं व्रजेत्॥ 5:116॥

मासद्वयेन चाप्नोति क्रतूनां फलमुत्तमम्।
त्रिभिर्मासैः प्रपद्येत ब्रह्मलोकमनुत्तमम्॥ 5:117॥

चतुर्भिः सिद्धिमाप्नोति योगसिद्धिञ्च पञ्चभिः।
षण्मासेन नरो याति रुद्रलोकं न संशयः॥ 5:118॥

रुद्राकृतिधरो भूत्वा चन्द्रार्द्धकृतशेखरः।
प्रयाति वृषयानेन द्वितीय इव शूलधृक्॥ 5:119॥

एवमभ्यर्च्य देवेशं नैवेद्यम्परिकल्पयेत्।
अन्ननैवेद्यदानेन लभते सुखमक्षयम्॥ 5:120॥

5:111 पत्रं पुष्पं फलं तोयं] CE$_N$; पत्रं पुष्प फलन्तोय A **5:111** दद्यान्नासौ] CE$_N$; दद्यातसौ A **5:112** महादेवोपयुक्तानि] C; महादे --- A; महादेवाय युक्तानि E$_N$ **5:112** सो ऽपि याति पराङ्गतिम्] E$_N$; --- यान्ति पराङ्गतिम् A; सो ऽपि याति परा गतिम् C **5:113** पापसमः शत्रुर्न च धर्मसमः] CE$_N$; पापसम शत्रुन च धर्मसम A **5:113** रुद्रात्परो देवो न पुष्पं] CE$_N$; रुद्रपरो देवो न पुष्प A **5:115** शौचयित्वा पुनः पुनः] C; शौचयित्वा पुनः पु --- A; शोचयित्वा पुनः पुनः E$_N$ **5:115** सप्तरात्रमतिक्रम्य] CE$_N$; --- मतिक्रम्य A **5:117** क्रतूनां] AE$_N$; क्रतूना C **5:117** त्रिभिर्मासैः] CE$_N$; तृभिमासैः A **5:118** चतुर्भिः सिद्धिमाप्नोति] CE$_N$; चतुभि दिसिमाप्नोति A **5:118** योगसिद्धिञ्च पञ्चभिः] C; योगसिद्धिञ्च पञ्च --- A; योगसिद्धिश्च पञ्चभिः E$_N$ **5:118** याति रुद्रलोकं न संशयः] CE$_N$; यान्ति रुद्रलोक न संशय A **5:119** ◦धरो] AC; ◦नरो E$_N$ **5:120** ◦नैवेद्य◦] AE$_N$; नेवेद्य C

देवलोकमनुप्राप्तो भक्ष्यदानान्नरोत्तमः।
विद्याधरपतिर्भूत्वा मोदते दिवि देववत्॥ 5:121॥

सघृतं पायसं दद्यान्नैवेद्यं शंभवे सदा।
गाणापत्यं भवेच्छ्रीघ्रं द्वादशाब्दात्कुलैः सह॥ 5:122॥

घृतपूपं तु सगुडं मम दक्षिणमूर्तिषु।
निवेदयति यो मर्त्यो नन्दीश्वरसमो भवेत्॥ 5:123॥

खण्डखाद्यकृतान्दत्वा प्राप्नुयाद्गतिमुत्तमाम्।
भक्ष्यभोज्यादिकं दत्वा सर्वकामानवाप्नुयात्॥ 5:124॥

यवागूं कृसराम्पूपान्दत्वा तु सुखभाग्भवेत्।
मण्डकासिद्धिपिण्डांश्च शष्कुलीमोदकानि च॥ 5:125॥

दत्वान्यफलमूलञ्च लेह्यचोष्याणि यानि च।
दत्वा सर्वसुखावाप्तिरनन्तं गीतवादने॥ 5:126॥

निराहाराः क्षमायुक्ताः सत्यार्जवपरायणाः।
मद्भक्ता ये हि नृत्येयुस्ते स्युः प्राणसमा गणाः॥ 5:127॥

सकृत्कृत्वा फलं ह्येतत्तन्त्रीवाद्यस्य मे शृणु।
कृत्वासौ गणतां याति तन्त्रीवाद्यस्य वादकः॥ 5:128॥

5:121 देवलोकमनुप्राप्तो भक्ष्यदानान्नरोत्तमः] C; देवलोकमनुप्रा --- त्तमः A; देवलोकमनुप्राप्ता भक्ष्यपानान्नरोत्तमाः E_N **5:121 विद्याधरपतिर्भूत्वा**] E_N; विद्याधरपतिभूत्वा AC **5:122 दद्यान्नैवेद्यं**] E_N; दद्या नैवेद्य A; दद्यान्नेवेद्यं C **5:122 सदा**] CE_N; त्सन्दा A **5:122 गाणापत्यं भवेच्छ्रीघ्रं**] C; गाणापत्य भवे शीघ्रं A; गाणपत्यं भवेच्छ्रीघ्रं E_N **5:122 द्वादशाब्दात्कुलैः सह**] E_N; द्वादशाब्द् कुलैस्सहः A; द्वादशाब्दा कुलैः सह C **5:123 घृतपूपं**] CE_N; घृतदीपं A **5:123 मर्त्यो**] CE_N; मन्ये A **5:124 खण्डखाद्यकृतान्दत्वा प्राप्नुयाद्गतिमुत्तमाम्**] CE_N; खण्ड --- प या गतिमुत्तमात् A **5:124 भक्ष्यभोज्यादिकं**] AC; भक्ष्य भोज्यादिकं E_N **5:124 सर्वकामानवाप्नुयात्**] CE_N; सर्वा कामानवाप्नुयात् A **5:125 यवागूं कृसराम्पूपान्**] C; यवागूकृसरपूपा A; यवागूकृशराः पूपा E_N **5:125 मण्डकासिद्धिपिण्डांश्च**] *conj.*; मण्डका सिद्धपिण्डाश्च A; मण्डका सिद्धपिण्डाश्च C; मण्दकान् सिद्धपिण्डाश्च E_N **5:125 शष्कुलीमोदकानि च**] *em.*; शंकुलीमोदकानि च A; षष्कुलीमोदकानि तु C; शष्कुलीमोदकानि तु E_N **5:126 दत्वान्यफलमूलञ्च**] AE_N; दत्वान्यन्फलमूलञ्च C **5:126 दत्वा सर्वसुखावाप्तिरनन्तं गीतवादने**] CE_N; सर्व सह --- द ⪯ A **5:127 सत्यार्जव°**] AC; सत्यर्जव° E_N **5:127 मद्भक्ता ये हि नृत्येयुस्ते स्युः प्राणसमा गणाः**] CE_N; मद्भक्त यो हि नृत्येयुस्ते स्युः प्राणसमो गणः A **5:128 सकृत्कृत्वा फलं ह्येतत्**] C; सकृ दत्वा फलं ह्येत A; सकृद्दत्वा फलं ह्येतत् E_N **5:128 तन्त्रीवाद्यस्य वादकः**] A; तन्त्रीवादस्य वादकः C; तन्त्रीवाद्यस्य वा देवः E_N

हुडुङ्कारादिकं नित्यं मुखवाद्याट्टहासताम्।
त्रिकालञ्चैव कुर्वाणः स भवेदुत्तमो गणः॥ 5:129॥

एककालं द्विकालं वा त्रिष्कालं वापि नित्यशः।
ये स्मरन्ति विरूपाक्षं विज्ञेयास्ते गणेश्वराः॥ 5:130॥

षष्टितीर्थसहस्राणि षष्टिकोटिस्तथैव च।
लिङ्गप्रणामस्यैकस्य कलां नार्घन्ति षोडशीम्॥ 5:131॥

एको ऽपि लिंगे सुकृतप्रणामी दशाश्वमेधादधिकानि योगात्।
दशाश्वमेधी पुनरभ्युपैति लिङ्गप्रणामी त्वपुनर्भवो हि॥ 5:132॥

एवं यः पूजयेदज्ञः शिवदीक्षाविवर्जितः।
तस्येदं फलमुद्दिष्टं निर्वाणं दीक्षितस्य तु॥ 5:133॥

श्रुतमेतन्मया विप्रा देव्यै कथयतो हरात्।
मयापि वः समाख्यातं सत्यमीशानभाषितम्॥ 5:134॥

ऋषय ऊचुः।
किं लिङ्गस्य हि माहात्म्यं त्वया यदिति वर्णितम्।
कृत्वा चैव फलं ब्रूहि यः करोति दिने दिने॥ 5:135॥

नन्दिकेश्वर उवाच।
ब्रह्माब्रवीदहं कर्त्ता तथैवाह गदाधरः।

5:129 हुडुङ्कारादिकं] *em.*; हुन्नुकारादिक हिन्नें (?) A; हुंदुंकारादिकं नित्यं C; हुंहुंकारादिकं नित्यं E_N **5:129** मुखवाद्याट्टहासताम्] CE_N; मुख --- A **5:129** त्रिकालञ्चैव कुर्वाणः] C; तृकालञ्चैव कुर्वाण A; त्रिष्कालञ्चैव कुर्वाणः E_N **5:130** एककालं वापि] CE_N; एककाल वापिA **5:130** त्रिष्कालं वापि] C; तृष्कालं वापि A; त्रिकालंवापि E_N **5:131** षष्टितीर्थसहस्राणि] E_N; षष्ठित्तीर्थसहस्राणि A; षष्ठिन्तीर्थे सहस्राणि C **5:131** षष्टिकोटिस्तथैव च] *conj.*; षष्ठिं कोटिस्तथैव च A; षष्टिकोट्यस्तथैव च C; षष्टिकोट्यस्तथैव च E_N **5:131** लिङ्गप्रणामस्यैकस्य] E_N; लिङ्गप्रमाणसमेकस्य A; लिङ्गप्रसौमस्यैकस्य (?) C **5:131** कलां नार्घन्ति षोडशीम्] C; कला नार्घन्ति षोडशीम् A; कलान्नार्गन्ति षोडशीं E_N **5:132** सुकृतप्रणामी] C; सुकृतः प्रण --- A; सुकृतः प्रणामो E_N **5:132** दशाश्वमेधादधिकानि योगात्] C; ---कानि योगात् A; दशाश्वमेधादधिको नियोगात् E_N **5:132** पुनरभ्युपैति] AE_N; पुनरभ्यपैति C **5:132** त्वपुनर्भवो] CE_N; त्वपुनभवो A **5:133** पूजयेदज्ञः] AE_N; पूजयेत्तज्ञः C **5:133** तु] AE_N; च C **5:134** श्रुतमेतन्मया] AE_N; श्रुतमेतत्मया C **5:134** वः समाख्यातं] CE_N; व समाख्यात A **5:134** सत्यमीशानभाषितम्] *em.*; सत्यमीशान --- म्सा; सत्यमीश्वरभाषितम् CE_N **5:135** ऋषय ऊचुः] E_N; --- चु A; ऋषय ऊचु C **5:135** माहात्म्यं] CE_N; माहात्म्य A **5:136** नन्दिकेश्वर] AE_N; नन्दीकेश्वर C **5:136** °ब्रवीदहं] A; ब्रतीत्यहं C; ब्रवीत्यहं E_N **5:136** तथैवाह] AC; तथैवाहः E_N

इत्येवं वदतोरग्रे प्रादुरासीज्जले विभुः॥ 5:136॥

तेजोमध्ये स्थितं लिङ्गं पर्वाङ्गुष्ठप्रमाणकम्।
उभौ तौ विस्मितौ तत्र किञ्चेदमिति चाहतुः॥ 5:137॥

उभौ तौ द्रष्टुमारब्धौ वर्द्धमानस्ततो विभुः।
आश्चर्यमिति सञ्चिन्त्य अध ऊर्द्धङ्गतावुभौ॥ 5:138॥

अधो गतस्ततो विष्णुरूर्द्धं ब्रह्मा जगाम च।
अन्तश्चास्य न पश्यन्तौ खिन्नावेतौ सुरोत्तमौ॥ 5:139॥

पुनश्चैव समागम्य स्तोत्रैस्तुष्टुवतुर्हरम्।
ततस्तुष्टो महादेवो ब्रह्माणमिदमब्रवीत्॥ 5:140॥

स्वरूपं दिव्यमास्थाय सर्वलोकनमस्कृतम्।
किमिच्छसि वरं विप्र ब्रूहि यत्ते ऽभिकांक्षितम्॥ 5:141॥

एवंवादिनि देवेशे ब्रह्मा पप्रच्छ केशवम्।
वरं किं याचयाम्येनं देवदेवञ्जगत्पतिम्॥ 5:142॥

अवादीन्माधवस्तस्मै पुत्रत्वं याचय द्रुतम्।
यदा ते सम्भवेत्पुत्रो भवानेव तदा प्रभुः॥ 5:143॥

तथैवाह तथा ब्रह्मा पुत्रो मे भव इत्यमुम्।
तथास्त्वित्यब्रवीद्देवः किंत्वपूज्यो भविष्यसि॥ 5:144॥

अनानुरूपं यस्माद्धि वरं ते कांक्षितं द्विज।

5:136 इत्येवं] CE_N; इत्येव E_N **5:136 विभुः**] A; प्रभुः CE_N **5:137 तेजोमध्ये**] AE_N; तेजोमध्य C **5:137 पर्वाङ्गुष्ठ°**] CE_N; पर्वागुष्ठ° A **5:137 उभौ तौ विस्मितौ तत्र किञ्चेदमिति चाहतुः**] CE_N; --- तत्र किचेदमि वाहतु A **5:138 द्रष्टुमारब्धौ**] A; द्रष्टमारब्दौ C; द्रुष्टुमारब्धौ E_N **5:138 वर्द्धमानस्ततो विभुः**] AC; वर्द्धमानं ततो विभुं E_N **5:138 आश्चर्यमिति सञ्चिन्त्य अध**] E_N; आश्चयमिति सञ्चिन्त्य अधर्म A; आचर्यमिति संचिन्त्य अध C **5:139 गतस्ततो विष्णुरूर्द्धं ब्रह्मा**] CE_N; गतास्ततो विष्णु उर्द्ध ब्रह्म A **5:139 पश्यन्तौ**] CE_N; पश्येतौ A **5:139 खिन्नावेतौ**] AC; क्षितावेतौ E_N **5:139 सुरोत्तमौ**] AE_N; सुचोत्तमौ C **5:140 स्तोत्रैस्तुष्टुवतुर्हरम्**] CE_N; स्तोत्रैस्तुष्टुवतु --- म्सा **5:140 ततस्तुष्टो**] CE_N; --- A **5:141 स्वरूपं**] CE_N; स्वरूप A **5:141 किमिच्छसि**] CE_N; किमिच्छस्व A **5:142 ब्रह्मा**] CE_N; ब्रह्म A **5:143 तस्मै**] AE_N; तस्मे C **5:143 पुत्रत्वं**] AC; पुत्रस्त्वं (त्वं) E_N **5:143 यदा ते सम्भवेत्पुत्रो भवानेव**] C; --- ता ⏓ ⏓ व A; यदा ते शम्भवे पुत्रो भवते वा E_N **5:144 ब्रह्मा**] CE_N; ब्रह्म A **5:144 तथास्त्वित्यब्रवीद्देवः**] C; तथास्त्वित्यब्रवीद्देव A; तथास्मि(स्त्वित्व)त्यब्रवीद्देवः E_N **5:145 अनानुरूपं यस्माद्धि**] A; अनुरूपन्न यस्माद्धि CE_N **5:145 द्विज**] C; द्विजः AE_N

तथैवमुक्तो देवेन विषण्णवदनः स्वभूः॥ 5:145॥

शार्ङ्गिणं शापयामास क्रोधसंरक्तलोचनः।
भवन्तं ये ऽर्चयिष्यन्ति ते यान्तु निरयं ध्रुवम्॥ 5:146॥

ब्रह्मणाथैवमुक्तस्तु विष्णुराह महेश्वरम्।
इत्थं शप्तो ऽस्मि देवेश ब्रह्मणा परमेष्ठिना।
उपायो ऽस्ति यदीशान तद्भवान् वक्तुमर्हति॥ 5:147॥

देवदेव उवाच।
पितेत्युक्तो मया ह्येष न तस्य वितथं वचः।
किन्तु क्षीणयुगे घोरे सुगतस्त्वं भविष्यसि॥ 5:148॥

तस्मिन्त्वां ये ऽर्चयिष्यन्ति मूढाः पण्डितमानिनः।
ते यान्ति निरयं घोरं अन्ये यान्तु परां गतिम्॥ 5:149॥

विष्णो ददामि ते वत्स वरमिष्टं वदस्व मे।
मम वाक्यममिथ्या हि ब्रूहि यत्ते ऽभिकांक्षितम्॥ 5:150॥

विष्णुरुवाच।
यदि तुष्टो ऽसि मे देव वरं दातुमिहेच्छसि।
त्वद्भक्तस्त्वत्प्रियश्चैव भविष्यामि न संशयः॥ 5:151॥

महेश्वर उवाच।
एवं भवतु भद्रन्ते रुद्रनारायणी प्रजा।
आवयोरन्तरं नास्ति मरुदंबरयोरिव॥ 5:152॥

5:145 तथैवमुक्तो] A; अथैवमुक्तो C; अथैवमुक्तो E_N **5:145** विषण्णवदनः] CE_N; विषण्णवदन A **5:146** क्रोधसंरक्तलोचनः] CE_N; क्रोधसंरक्तलोचनम् A **5:146** °यिष्यन्ति ते यान्तु निरयं ध्रुवम्] CE_N; यिष्य --- A **5:147** ब्रह्मणाथैवमुक्तस्तु] C; ब्रह्मणेनैवमुक्तस्तु A; ब्रह्मणाप्येवमुक्तस्तु E_N **5:147** इत्थं] CE_N; इथं A **5:147** तद्भवान् वक्तुमर्हति] C; तद्भवां वक्तुमर्हसि A; स भवान् वक्तुमर्हति E_N **5:148** तस्य वितथं वचः] C; तस्य वितथ वच A; तथ्यं वितथं वचः E_N **5:148** क्षीणयुगे] AE_N; क्षीणे युगे C **5:149** तस्मिन्त्वां ये ऽर्चयिष्यन्ति मूढाः पण्डितमानिनः] C; यस्मिं त्वं ये ऽर्च --- तमानिनः A; तस्मिंस्त्वां ये ऽर्चयिष्यन्ति मूढाः पण्डित मानिनः E_N **5:149** ते यान्ति निरयं घोरं अन्ये] A; ते यान्तु निरयं घोरमन्ये CE_N **5:151** दातुमिहेच्छसि] CE_N; दातुमेहेशुसि A **5:151** त्वद्भक्तस्त्वत्प्रियश्चैव] CE_N; त्वद्भक्तः त्वत्प्रियश्चैव A **5:152** महेश्वर उवाच] CE_N; --- A **5:152** °नारायणी प्रजा] CE_N; °नारायणो प्रजाः A **5:152** आवयोरन्तरं] CE_N; आवयोरन्तर A **5:152** मरुदंबरयोरिव] *conj. Acharya*; वरदंबरयोरिव A; मरुवंवरयोरिव C; मेरुदुम्बरयोरिव E_N

एष एव हि लिङ्गो हि स्थापितं ब्रह्मविष्णुना।
इन्द्रादिभिः सुरैर्दैत्यैः सयक्षोरगराक्षसैः॥ 5:153॥

सिद्धैर्विद्याधरैर्भूतैरप्सरोगणकिन्नरैः।
पिशाचैर्ग्रहनक्षत्रैस्तथैव मुनिसत्तमैः॥ 5:154॥

संपूज्य वरदं देवं वरं लब्ध्वा तु रेमिरे।
सर्वकामप्रदो लिङ्ग एष उक्तो मयानघाः॥ 5:155॥

ब्रह्मोपेन्द्रमहेन्द्रनागमुनयो यक्षाः सविद्याधराः
संसारार्णवदुःखभीतमनसो लिंगार्चने तत्पराः।
भक्तिप्रह्वधिय स्तुवन्त्यहरहः कृत्वाञ्जलिं मस्तके
ये मर्त्या न नमन्ति तं सुरगुरुं ते घ्नन्ति स्वं मुष्टिभिः॥ 5:156॥

॥ ⊗॥ इति शिवधर्म्मसंग्रहे पञ्चमो ऽध्यायः॥ ⊗॥

5:153 स्थापितं] A; स्थापितो CE$_N$ **5:153** सुरैर्दैत्यैः] E$_N$; सुरैदैत्यैः AC **5:154** सिद्धै विद्याधरै भूतैरप्सरोगणकिन्नरैः] CE$_N$; सिद्धैर्विद्याधरैर्भूतै साप्सरोगणकिंनरैः A **5:154** पिशाचैर्ग्रहनक्षत्रैस्तथैव मुनिसत्तमैः] C; पिशाचैन्नहनक्षत्रैस्त --- A; पिशाचैर्नेहनक्षत्रैस्तथैव मुनिसत्तमैः E$_N$ **5:155** वरं लब्ध्वा तु रेमिरे] E$_N$; वर लब्धा तु रेमिरे A; वर लब्धा तु रे ⊔ C **5:155** सर्वकामप्रदो लिङ्ग एष उक्तो मयानघाः] C; सर्वकामप्रदो लिङ्गो एष उक्तो मयानघः A; सर्वकामप्रदोलिङ्ग एष उक्तो मयानघाः E$_N$ **5:156** ब्रह्मोपेन्द्र॰] CE$_N$; ब्रह्मेपेन्द्र॰ A **5:156** यक्षाः] CE$_N$; यक्षा A **5:156** सविद्याधराः] CA; सविद्याधरा E$_N$ **5:156** मनसो लिंगार्चने] AC; मनसोलिङ्गार्चने E$_N$ **5:156** कृत्वाञ्जलिं] CE$_N$; कृत्वाञ्जलि A **5:156** ये मर्त्या न नमन्ति तं सुरगुरुं] CE$_N$; --- रगुरुं A **5:156** स्वं] *em.*; स्व A; सं C; खं E$_N$ **5:156** इति शिवधर्म्मसंग्रहे पञ्चमो ऽध्यायः] CE$_N$; इति शिवधर्म्मसंग्रहे पुष्पविधिलिंगोत्पत्तिः पञ्चमो ऽध्यायः पटलः A

शिवधर्मसंग्रहे षष्ठोऽध्यायः॥

ऋषय ऊचुः।

कृतस्यैव तु लिंगस्य स्थापितस्य तु यत्फलम्।
प्रत्यहं कुरुते यस्तु किन्तस्यापि फलं भवेत्॥ 6:1॥

नन्दिकेश्वर उवाच।
क्रीडन्तो ऽपि च ये बाला लिङ्गं कुर्वन्ति पांशुना।
लभन्ते राज्यमेकान्ते निस्सपत्नमकण्टकम्॥ 6:2॥

प्रत्यहम्विधिहीनं तु लिङ्गं यः कुरुते नरः।
केवलम्भक्तिमालम्ब्य शृणु तस्यापि यत्फलम्॥ 6:3॥

धनं भोग्यं तथा राज्यं यः कृत्वा पूजयेत्सदा।
लिङ्गं पूजयिता नित्यं महतीं श्रियमश्नुते॥ 6:4॥

सहस्रमर्च्चयन्विद्वान्निरयं तु न पश्यति।
रुद्रलोकमवाप्नोति भुक्त्वा भोगाननिन्दितान्॥ 6:5॥

लक्षं तु कुरुते यस्तु तस्यैकं ज्वलति ध्रुवम्।
दृष्ट्वा लिङ्गं ज्वलन्तञ्च सिद्धो देवत्वमाप्नुयात्॥ 6:6॥

6:0 ऊचुः] E_N; ऊचु A; उवाच C **6:1** भवेत्] AE_N; लभेत् C **6:2** नन्दिकेश्वर उवाच] E_N; नन्दिकेश्व --- A; नन्दीकेश्वर उवाच C **6:2** क्रीडन्तो ऽपि] CE_N; --- ⏑̆ A **6:2** राज्यमेकान्ते] AE_N; राजमेकान्ते C **6:2** निस्सपन्नमकण्टकम्] CE_N; निसपतमकण्टकम् A **6:3** लिङ्गं यः कुरुते नरः] CE_N; लिङ्ग य कुरुते नरः A **6:3** °मालम्ब्य] AE_N; °मालम्ब्यं C **6:4** यः कृत्वा पूजयेत्] CE_N; य --- A **6:4** लिङ्गपूजयिता] A; लिङ्गं पूजयिता CE_N **6:4** नित्यं महतीं] E_N; नित्यं महती A; नित्य महती C **6:5** सहस्रमर्चयन्विद्यान्] CE_N; सहस्रमर्चयं विद्या A **6:5** निरयं तु न] A; निरयन्न तु CE_N **6:5** भुक्त्वा भोगाननिन्दितान्] C; भुक्त्वा भोगाननिन्दितां A; भुक्त्वाभोगाननिन्दितान् E_N **6:6** तस्यैकं ज्वलति] C; तस्यैकं ज्वलिति A; तस्यैको ज्वलति E_N **6:6** ज्वलन्तञ्च] CE_N; ज्वल --- A **6:6** सिद्धो देवत्वमाप्नुयात्] C; --- A; सिद्धे देवत्वमाप्नुयात् E_N

लक्षैर्द्दशभिरिन्द्रत्वं स्कन्दं विंशतिभिः स्मृतम्।
त्रिंशल्लक्षैः मुरारित्वं रुद्रत्वं तु चतुर्गुणैः॥ 6:7॥

पञ्चगव्येन संमार्ज्य यदा लिङ्गं तु पूजयेत्।
अन्नलिङ्गञ्च कुर्वाणो लभते कामिकं फलम्॥ 6:8॥

गुडलिङ्गं समभ्यर्च्य परं सौभाग्यमाप्नुयात्।
कन्याशतपतिश्चैव प्रातिराज्येश्वरो भवेत्॥ 6:9॥

नारी च स्त्रीसहस्रेण सापत्नैः परिवारिता।
लभेत्सौभाग्यमतुलं सर्वेषामुपरि स्थिता॥ 6:10॥

रमते पुत्रपौत्रैस्तु सुखमानन्त्यमश्नुते।
अर्च्चयेन्नरनारी वा खण्डलिङ्गञ्च नित्यशः॥ 6:11॥

सितेन कृत्वा लिङ्गन्तु प्रत्यहं यः समर्च्चयेत्।
सर्वकामानवाप्नोति षड्भिर्मासैर्न संशयः॥ 6:12॥

नवनीतमये लिङ्गे लभते चेप्सितं फलम्।
षण्मासेनैव युक्तात्मा शिवलोकञ्च गच्छति॥ 6:13॥

प्रत्यहं पत्रलिङ्गन्तु यः कृत्वा तु समर्च्चयेत्।
लभेच्चोत्तममैश्वर्यं स भुंक्ते निरुजः सदा॥ 6:14॥

6:7 लक्षैर्द्दशभिरिन्द्रत्वं] E$_N$; लक्षै दशभिरिन्द्रत्वं A; लक्षैर्दशभिरिन्द्रत्व C **6:7** स्कन्दं] CE$_N$; कन्धं A **6:7** त्रिंशल्लक्षैः मुरारित्वं] *em.*; त्रिंशलक्षैः सुरारित्व A; त्रिंशल्लक्षैः स-रारित्वं C; त्रिंशल्लक्षैर्म्मुरारित्वं E$_N$ **6:7** रुद्रत्वं तु चतुर्गुणैः] *em.*; रुद्रत्वं तु चतुगुणैः A; रुद्रत्व तु चतुर्गुणैः C; रुद्रत्वं तु चतुर्गुनः E$_N$ **6:8** पञ्चगव्येन संमार्ज्य] AC; पञ्च गव्येन संयोज्य E$_N$ **6:8** अन्नलिङ्गञ्च कुर्वाणो लभते कामिकं फलम्] C; अन्नलिङ्गञ्च कुवाणो लभत्ते कामिक फलम् A; अन्ते (न्नैः) लिङ्गञ्च कुर्वणो लभते कामिकं फलं E$_N$ **6:9** गुडलिङ्गं] CE$_N$; गुडलिङ्ग A **6:9** कन्याशतपतिश्चैव] CE$_N$; --- व A **6:9** प्राति°] AC; प्रति° E$_N$ **6:10** नारी च स्त्रीसहस्रेण सापत्नैः परिवारिता] CE$_N$; वरस्त्रीभिः सहस्रेण सापनैः पंरिवा-रिता A **6:10** लभेत्] CE$_N$; ⏑̆ भेत् A **6:10** स्थिता] CE$_N$; स्थिताः A **6:11** रमते पुत्रपौत्रैस्तु] E$_N$; लभते पुत्रपौत्रस्तु A; पमते पुत्रपौत्रेषु C **6:11** सुखमानन्त्यमश्नुते] CE$_N$; सुखश्चामंनमश्नुते A **6:11** अर्च्चयेन्नरनारी] CE$_N$; अर्चये नरनारी A **6:11** खण्ड°] AC; खड्ग° E$_N$ **6:12** सितेन कृत्वा लिङ्गन्तु] E$_N$; सितेन कृत्वा ⊔ A; शितेन कृत्वा लिङ्गन्तु C **6:12** प्रत्यहं यः समर्च्चयेत्] CE$_N$; --- त् A **6:12** षड्भिर्मासैर्न] CE$_N$; षड्भिर्मासैन A **6:13** नवनीतमये लिङ्गे] AC; नवनीतमयं लिङ्गं E$_N$ **6:13** शिवलोकञ्च] A; शिवलोकं स CE$_N$ **6:14** पत्रलिङ्गन्तु] AC; यत्र लिङ्गन्तु E$_N$ **6:14** तु समर्च्चयेत्] A; सम्यगर्च्चयेत् CE$_N$ **6:14** लभेच्चोत्तममैश्वर्यं] CE$_N$; लभेच्चोत्तममैश्वयं E$_N$ **6:14** स भुंक्ते] C; स भुक्ते A; स भुङ्क्ते° E$_N$

पृथिव्यामाधिपत्यञ्च पुष्पलिङ्गस्य पूजनात्।
लभते निःसपत्नन्तु भुङ्क्ते चैव ददाति च॥ 6:15॥

लावणेन तु लिंगेन भवेत्सौभाग्यमुत्तमम्।
नित्यैश्वर्यमखण्डञ्च प्रत्यहं यो ऽभिपूजयेत्॥ 6:16॥

सच्चकेन तु लिङ्गनि पार्थिवानि तु कारयेत्।
सहस्रपूजनात्सो हि लभते चेप्सितं फलम्।
लक्षेणैकेन गणतां कोट्यामभ्यर्च्य गच्छति॥ 6:17॥

दधीचिरुवाच।
किं फलम्बालुकालिङ्गस्यार्च्चनादपि किं भवेत्।
कथं वा पूजयेत्कर्म व्रतञ्चैव कथम्भवेत्॥ 6:18॥

महेश्वर उवाच।
शृणु मे कथयिष्यामि बालुकालिङ्गमर्चनम्।
व्रतञ्च ब्रह्मचर्यञ्च जितक्रोधो जितेन्द्रियः॥ 6:19॥

अर्च्चितानां नदीं गत्वा बालुकां शोध्य यत्नतः।
अभ्युक्ष्य गन्धतोयेन मन्त्रयुक्तेन बुद्धिमान्॥ 6:20॥

प्रतिलिङ्गं शुभं कृत्वा सुसंपूर्ण्णं सुलक्षणम्।
ताम्रं वा दन्तिकाशृङ्गं काष्ठेनापि च शोभनम्॥ 6:21॥

बालुकां पूरयित्वा च बीजमन्त्रसमन्विताम्।
सद्योजातेन देवेन तद्भूम्यां परिशोधयेत्॥ 6:22॥

वामदेवेन शोध्येत बालुका येन यत्नतः।
अघोरेण तु देवेन सिञ्चेच्चत्वारि वारिणा॥ 6:23॥

तत्पुरुषेण देवेन प्रतिलिङ्गानि मन्त्रयेत्।
ईशानेन तु देवेन बालुकां परिपूरयेत्॥ 6:24॥

6:15 पुष्पलिङ्गस्य पूजनात्] CE$_N$; पु --- A **6:15** लभते निःसपत्नन्तु] E$_N$; लभते निसपनं तु A; लभते निःपत्नन्तु C (unmetrical) **6:15** चैव] E$_N$; चै ⏓ A; चेव C **6:16** लावणेन] C; लवणेन AE$_N$ **6:16** नित्यैश्वर्य°] CE$_N$; नित्यैश्वय° A **6:17** सच्चकेन] C; सचकेन A; सङ्कक्तेन E$_N$ **6:17** पार्थिवानि] CE$_N$; पार्थियवानि A **6:17** सो हि] A; सो ऽपि CE$_N$ **6:17** कोट्यामभ्यर्च्य गच्छति] *em.*; कोट्या माहात्म्यमर्च्छति C; मभ्यर्च्य गच्छ --- A; कोट्या माहात्म्यमृच्छति E$_N$ **6:19** °मर्चनम्] *conj.*; °मर्च्चयेत् C **6:21** सुसंपूर्ण्णं] C; सुसंपूर्णं E$_N$ **6:24** प्रति लिङ्गानि मन्त्रयेत्] C; प्रतिलिङ्गाभिमन्त्रयेत् E$_N$ **6:24** ईशानेन] E$_N$; इशानेन C **6:24** बालुकां] E$_N$; बालुका C

भगवन्पञ्चब्रह्मेण प्रतिष्ठाप्य हृदा तथा।
अनेनैव तु मन्त्रेण पूजयित्वा सदाशिवम्॥ 6:25॥

करन्यासान्तःकरणं षडध्वाङ्गञ्च शोधनम्।
कृत्वा चासनसान्निध्यं शक्तिशंभुं ततो ऽर्चयेत्॥ 6:26॥

होमकर्म च जाप्यञ्च साधनम्मन्त्रमेव च।
शान्तिकं पौष्टिकारोग्यं वश्याकर्षणकामदम्॥ 6:27॥

अनेनैव तु मन्त्रेण सिद्ध्यते साधनाद्बुधः।
शुचौ प्रतिष्ठितं लिङ्गमेकैकं बालुकान्नरः॥ 6:28॥

अहोरात्रकृतैः पापैर्मुच्यते नात्र संशयः।
पञ्चरात्रकृतात्पापान्मुच्यते द्विकृतार्च्चनात्॥ 6:29॥

दशरात्रकृतात्पापान्मुच्यते त्रिःकृतार्चनात्।
विंशद्रात्रकृतं पापञ्चतुर्लिङ्गेन मुच्यते॥ 6:30॥

पञ्चकृत्वार्च्चनो यस्तु मुक्तः पञ्चोपपातकात्।
सर्वशान्तिकमाप्नोति षट्कृतं लिङ्गमर्च्चनात्॥ 6:31॥

पुष्टिकार्थी लभेत्पुष्टिं सप्तकृत्वार्च्चनाद्द्विजः।
अष्टप्रतिष्ठिताल्लिङ्गाद्बालुकाविकृतान्नरः॥ 6:32॥

इच्छाकाममवाप्नोति सर्वरोगविवर्जितः।
अष्टाविंशं प्रतिष्ठाप्य बालुकेन तु यो नरः॥ 6:33॥

सर्वपापैः प्रमुच्येत सर्ववित्स भवेत्ततः।
शुद्धस्फटिकसाहस्रजापी विघ्नैः प्रमुच्यते॥ 6:34॥

शते प्रतिष्ठिते लिङ्गे रुद्रकोटीर्जपेत्फलम्।

6:26 षडध्वाङ्गञ्च] C; षडर्ध्वाङ्गञ्च E_N **6:26** चासनसान्नैध्यं] E_N; चासनसानैध्यं C **6:26** शक्तिशंभुं] C; शक्तिं शंभुं E_N **6:27** होमकर्म च] E_N; होमं कर्म च C **6:27** शान्तिकं पौष्टिकारोग्यं] C; शान्तिकापौष्टिकारोग्यं E_N **6:28** शुचौ] C; गुरौ E_N **6:28** बालुकान्नरः] E_N; बालुकं नरः C **6:29** °पान्मुच्यते] E_N; °पात् मुच्यते C **6:30** °पान्मुच्यते त्रिःकृतार्चनात्] E_N; °पात् मुच्यते त्रिकृतार्चनात् C **6:30** विंशद्रात्रकृतं पापञ्चतुर्लिङ्गेन] C; विंशद्रात्रकृतंपापं चतुर्लिङ्गं न E_N **6:31** पञ्चकृत्वार्च्चनो यस्तु मुक्तः] C; पञ्चकृत्वार्चनो यस्तु मुक्ता E_N **6:31** षट्कृतं] C; षट् कृतं E_N **6:32** सप्तकृत्वार्च्चनाद्द्विजः] C; सप्तकृत्वार्च्चनाद् द्विजः E_N **6:32** अष्टप्रतिष्ठिताल्लिङ्गाद्] C; अष्टप्रतिष्ठितं लिङ्गं E_N **6:33** अष्टाविंशं] C; अष्टाविंश° E_N **6:34** °जापी] C; °जापो E_N **6:35** रुद्रकोटीर्ज°] *em.*; रुद्रकोटीज° C; रुद्रकोटिज° E_N

सहस्रं तत्प्रतिष्ठाप्य जाप्यकोटीसहस्रिकम्॥ 6:35॥

लभेच्च लक्षलिङ्गेन रुद्रस्य चतुरो महत्।
कोटीप्रतिष्ठिते लिङ्गे मनोमयपरं पदम्॥ 6:36॥

निष्कण्टकं पुत्रपौत्रं राज्यप्राप्तिः शताधिका।
ओं रुद्राक्षं मा भव शिव स्वाहा सर्वाङ्गसंयुतम्॥ 6:37॥

पताकाधूपसंयुक्तं बालुकालिङ्गमर्च्चनम्।
एतत्पुरा मया ख्यातं न देयं यस्य कस्यचित्॥ 6:38॥

स्वशरीरेण सायोज्यं पुनश्च न निवर्त्तते।
एतान्येव समभ्यर्च्य सदेवासुरमानुषाः॥ 6:39॥

सर्वकामसमृद्धाश्च सर्वदुःखविवर्जिताः।
ईश्वरस्य प्रसादेन प्रक्रीडंत्यणिमादिभिः॥ 6:40॥

अष्टेष्टकसमायुक्तं ये कुर्वन्ति शिवालयम्।
तावत्ते दिवि तिष्टन्ति यावदिन्द्राश्चतुर्दश॥ 6:41॥

मणिरत्नप्रवालानि स्फटिकमरकतानि च।
काचहेमजरौप्याणि ताम्रकांस्यानि यानि तु॥ 6:42॥

रैत्यलोहकसैस्यानि त्रापुषाणि तथैव च।
पुनश्चैतान्समभ्यर्च्य भुक्त्वा कामाञ्छिवं व्रजेत्॥ 6:43॥

न तस्य पुनरावृत्तिर्यो लिङ्गं स्थापयेद्भुवि।
कृत्वा प्रासादमध्ये तु स शिवो नात्र संशयः॥ 6:44॥

6:35 जाप्यकोटीसहस्रिकम्] *em.*; जाप्यकोटीसहश्रिकम् C; जापकोटिसहस्रकम् E_N **6:36** रुद्रस्य] $C^c E_N$; रुस्य C^{ac} (unmetrical) **6:36** मनोमय°] C; मनामय° E_N **6:37** शताधिका] E_N; शताब्दिका C **6:37** ओं रुद्राक्षं] C; अरुद्राय E_N **6:38** कस्यचित्] C; कस्य चित् E_N **6:39** स्वशरीरेण सायोज्यं] CE_N; --- सायुज्यं A **6:40** °विवर्जिताः] CE_N; °विवर्ज्जिता A **6:40** प्रक्रीडंत्यणिमादिभिः] AC; प्रक्रीडन्नणिमादिभिः E_N **6:41** अष्टेष्टकसमायुक्तं] *conj.*; अष्टेष्टकसमायुक्त A; अष्टेष्टकासमायुक्तं C; अष्टाष्टकसमायुक्तं E_N **6:41** कुर्वन्ति] AE_N; कुर्वीत C **6:41** चतुर्दश] CE_N; चतुर्द्दशः A **6:42** मणिरत्नप्रवालानि] E_N; मणिर --- A; मनिरत्नप्रवालानि C **6:42** स्फटिकमरकतानि च] *conj.* (unmetrical); --- मरकतानि च A; स्फटिकमरकतानि च C; स्फटिकं मरकतानि च E_N (unmetrical) **6:42** °रौप्याणि] CE_N; °रप्याणां A **6:43** °सैस्यानि] AE_N; °शैस्यानि C **6:43** त्रापुषाणि] C; त्रपुषाणि AE_N **6:43** पुनश्चैतान्] CE_N; पुनश्चैता A **6:43** कामाञ्छिवं व्रजेत्] E_N; कामा सिवं व्रजेत् A; कामाच्छिवं व्रजेत् C **6:44** पुनरावृत्तिर्यो] CE_N; पुनरावृत्ति यो A

दशाम्रवापी नरकानतिघोरान्न पश्यति।
आरामस्य च यः कर्ता स्वर्ग्गे मोदति इन्द्रवत्॥ 6:45॥

स्रक्षादींश्च तथा वृक्षान्पथि कुर्वन्ति ये नराः।
छायाभिश्शीतलाभिश्च न ते यान्ति यमालयम्॥ 6:46॥

याम्यदुःखानि घोराणि न च तेषां भवन्ति हि।
वृक्षवापनधर्म्मो ऽयमेष ते परिकीर्त्तितः॥ 6:47॥

प्रासादं कारयित्वा तु विष्णुं ये स्थापयन्ति हि।
विष्णुलोकं व्रजन्त्येते मोदन्ते विष्णुना सह॥ 6:48॥

ब्रह्माणीस्कन्दरुद्राणीं मातॄन्गणपतिं रविम्।
वह्निं शतक्रतुं यक्षं वायुं धर्म्मं जलेश्वरम्॥ 6:49॥

यो यं स्थापयते धीमान्प्रासादे च सुशोभने।
पूजयेत्परया भक्त्या स मृतस्तत्पदं व्रजेत्॥ 6:50॥

अचंक्रमपथे यस्तु संक्रमं कारयिष्यति।
धर्मराजपथं सो हि सुपथेनैव गच्छति॥ 6:51॥

नदीं वैतरणीं घोरामुष्णतोयां महार्ण्णवाम्।
गम्भीरावर्त्तदुस्तारां सन्तरेत्संक्रमेण तु॥ 6:52॥

सेतुबन्धश्च यः कुर्यात्कर्दमे पथि दारुणे।

6:45 दशाम्रवापी] C; दशास्रवापी A; दशास्त्रवाणी E_N **6:45 यः**] CE_N; य A **6:45 इन्द्रवत्**] A; रुद्रवत् CE_N **6:46 स्रक्षादींश्च तथा वृक्षान्**] E_N; स्रक्षादींश्च तथा वृक्षात् C; पक्षादीश्च तथा वृक्षं A **6:46 न ते यान्ति**] CE_N; ये न यान्ति A **6:47 च तेषां भवन्ति हि**] CE_N; तेषां यु भवन्ति हि A **6:47 वृक्षवापनधर्म्मो**] Cf. NiMukh; वक्षवापनधर्म्मो A; वृक्षारोपणधर्मो CE_N **6:47 परिकीर्त्तितः**] CE_N; परिकीर्त्तिताः A **6:48 प्रासादं कारयित्वा तु**] E_N; प्रासादं कारयित्वा --- A; प्रासाद कारयित्वा तु C **6:48 विष्णुं ये स्थापयन्ति हि**] CE_N; --- A **6:48 विष्णुलोकं व्रजन्त्येते मोदन्ते विष्णुना सह**] C; --- ष्णुलोक व्रजंत्येते मोदते विष्णुना सह A; विष्णुलोकं व्रजन्तेते मोदन्ते विष्णुना सह E_N **6:49 ब्रह्माणीस्कन्दरुदाणीं**] E_N; ब्रह्मणस्कन्दरुदाणी A; ब्रह्मानीस्कन्दरुदाणी C **6:49 मातॄन् गणपतिं**] *conj.*; मातृं गणपतिं A; मातृगणपतिं C; मातृ गणपतिं E_N **6:49 यक्षं वायुं धर्म्मं**] AE_N; यक्ष वायु धर्मं C **6:50 धीमान्**] CE_N; धीमां A **6:50 पूजयेत्**] CE_N; पूजेत् A (unmetrical) **6:50 स मृतस्तत्पदं**] CE_N; संमृतस्तत्पदं A **6:51 अचंक्रमपथे**] AC; असंक्रमपथे E_N **6:51 कारयिष्यति**] CE_N; यः प्रकुर्वति A **6:51 धर्मराजपथं**] CE_N; --- A **6:51 सो हि**] A; सो ऽपि CE_N **6:52 नदीं वैतरणीं घोरामुष्णतोयां**] E_N; नदी वैतरणी घोरामुष्णतोया A; नदीं वैतरणी घोरां उष्णतोयां C **6:52 सन्तरेत्संक्रमेण तु**] *em.*; स तरेत्संक्रमेण तु A; सत्तरेत्संक्रमेण तु C; सन्तरेत्स क्रमेण तु E_N **6:53 कुर्यात्**] CE_N; कुर्या A

धर्मराजपुरे मार्गे दुर्गमे स सुखं व्रजेत्॥ 6:53॥

पङ्कलेपश्च नरकस्तप्तत्रपुजतूनि च।
सन्तरेत्तानि घोराणि नदीमार्ग्गप्रदायकः॥ 6:54॥

मठस्यावसथस्यैव मण्डपस्य च कारकः।
त्यक्त्वा यमपुरं स्वर्ग्गे तस्य हेमगृहं भवेत्॥ 6:55॥

तप्ताङ्गारशिलावर्षे न भयन्तस्य जायते।
अन्नदाता नरो यो हि नासौ नरकमाप्नुयात्॥ 6:56॥

अक्षयं सुखमाप्नोति ब्रह्मलोकगतो नरः।
न तस्य संभवो मर्त्ये यावद्ब्रह्मा न नश्यति॥ 6:57॥

न चास्ति रैत्यकं दानमन्नदानात्परं प्रिये।
देहिनामन्नदानेन जीवन्दत्तं न संशयः॥ 6:58॥

यस्तु ग्रीष्मे प्रपां दद्यात्तृषार्ते पथिके जने।
ते तृप्ताः प्रेतभवने तृषाद्वंद्वविवर्जिताः॥ 6:59॥

देव्युवाच।
दरिद्रान्वीक्ष्य चेतो मे दीर्यते कृपया विभो।
किमकृत्वा दरिद्रः स्यादेतदाख्यातुमर्हसि॥ 6:60॥

भगवानुवाच।
तीर्थान्यगत्वा क्षितिहेमधेनुं कृष्णाजिनं कृष्णतिलान्न दत्वा।

6:53 स सुखं] CE_N; सुखसं A **6:54** पङ्कलेपश्च नरकस्तप्तत्रपुजतूनि च] C; पङ्कलेपश्च नरकस्तप्तत्रपुजंतूनि च A; पङ्कलेपश्च नरकस्तप्तत्र पुजनूनि च E_N **6:54** सन्तरेत्तानि घोराणि] C; सन्तरेत्तानि घो --- A; सन्तरेहानि घोराणि E_N **6:54** नदीमार्ग्गप्रदायकः] CE_N; --- यकः A **6:55** हेमगृहं] N; हेमपुरं CE_N **6:56** तप्ताङ्गारशिलावर्षे न] *conj.*; तप्ताङ्गारशिलावर्षान्न C; तप्ताङ्गारशिलावर्ष न A; तप्ताङ्गारशित्लावर्षान्न E_N **6:56** अन्नदाता] CE_N; अंनदात A **6:57** न तस्य संभवो मर्त्ये] CE_N; न तस्य सम्भवं मर्त्ये A **6:57** यावद्ब्रह्मा न नश्यति] CE_N; --- A **6:58** रैत्यकं दानमन्नदानात्परं प्रिये] *em.*; रैत्यकन्दनमन्नदानात्पर प्रियम् A; न चास्ति रेत्यकं दानं मन्नदानात्परं प्रिये C; नैत्यकन्दानमन्नदानात्परं प्रिये E_N **6:58** जीवन्दत्तं न] E_N; जीवन्दत्त न A; जीवंदत्तन्न C **6:59** प्रपां दद्यात्तृषार्ते] C; प्रपान्दद्या तृषात्ते A; प्रपान्दद्यातृषार्त्ते E_N **6:59** ते तृप्ताः प्रेतभवने] A; तृसप्तः प्रेतभवने C; स तृप्तः प्रेत भवने E_N **6:59** तृषाद्वंद्वविवर्जिताः] A; तृषद्वंद्वविवर्जितः CE_N **6:60** दरिद्रान्वीक्ष्य चेतो मे] C; दरिद्रवीक्ष्य चेतो मे A; दरिद्रान्वीक्ष्य चेतोमे E_N **6:60** दीर्यते कृपया विभो] CE_N; दीयत्ते कृपया विभो A **6:60** किमकृत्वा दरिद्रः स्यादेतदाख्यातुमर्हसि] CE_N; कि --- ख्यातुमर्हसि A **6:61** तीर्थान्यगत्वा क्षितिहेमधेनुं] C; तीर्थान्यगत्वा क्षितिहेमधेनु A; तीर्थात्यगत्वा क्षितिहेमधेनुं E_N **6:61** कृष्णतिलान्न दत्वा] E_N; कृष्णतिलं न दत्वा A; कृष्णतिलानदत्वा C

त्रिवासरं चाप्यनुपोष्य जन्तुर्जायेत दारिद्र्यजराभिभूतः॥ 6:61॥

देव्युवाच।
किं तिलस्य च माहात्म्यं किन्तु कृष्णाजिनस्य वा।
सुवर्णस्य गवाञ्चैव भूदानस्य च मे वद॥ 6:62॥

भगवानुवाच।
नमुचिर्नाम दैत्येन्द्रं युद्धे वीक्ष्य पुराच्युतः।
उद्वेजयन्तं गीर्वाणं क्रोधतामगमत्तदा॥ 6:63॥

क्रोधात्स्वेदलवास्तस्य निष्पेतुर्धरणीतले।
ते बभूवुस्तिलाः कृष्णास्तस्मात्ते पावनाः स्मृताः॥ 6:64॥

देवान्पितॄंसमुद्दिश्य यो ददाति तिलोदकम्।
तृप्यन्ति पितरस्तस्य वर्जिता नरकैस्त्रिभिः॥ 6:65॥

मेदोऽसृक्पूयगर्तेषु न निमज्जन्ति ते नराः।
पितरश्च विमुक्ताः स्युस्तिलोदकफलेन वै॥ 6:66॥

श्राद्धं कुर्वन्ति ये नित्यं पितृभक्ताश्च मानवाः।
तेषां तृप्ता हि पितरः स च तृप्तो यमालये॥ 6:67॥

कुम्भीपाकस्तु निरयो न तेषां प्रभविष्यति।
पितृलोकञ्च यास्यन्ति श्राद्धकारयिता नराः॥ 6:68॥

6:61 जन्तुर्जायेत] CE$_N$; जंतुजायेत A **6:61** दारिद्र्यजराभिभूतः] *em.*; दारिद्रजराभिभूतः A; दारिद्र्यरुजाभिभूतः CE$_N$ **6:62** तिलस्य च माहात्म्यं] A; तिलस्य च माहात्म्य C; तिलस्यमाहात्म्यं E$_N$ **6:62** गवाञ्चैव भूदानस्य च मे वद] CE$_N$; ग ⏑̆ --- A **6:63** नमुचिर्नाम दैतेन्द्रं] CE$_N$; नमुचिनाम दैतेन्द्र A **6:63** पुराच्युतः] AC; पुरा ऽच्युतः E$_N$ **6:63** क्रोधतामगमत्तदा] CE$_N$; क्रोधत्रा (?) म्रगमत्तदा A^{c}; क्रोधत्रा (?) म्रगमत्तमदा A^{ac} (unmetrical) **6:64** क्रोधात्स्वेदलवास्तस्य] CE$_N$; क्रोधा स्वेदलवाप्तस्य A **6:64** निष्पेतुर्धरणीतले] *em.*; निष्पेतुद्धरणीतले AC; निष्पेतूर्द्धरणीतले E$_N$ **6:64** कृष्णास्तस्मात्ते] E$_N$; कृष्णा तस्मात्ते A; कृष्णास्तस्मान्ते C **6:65** देवान्पितॄंसमुद्दिश्य] *em.*; देवां पितॄं समुद्दिश्य A; देवान्पितॄन्समुदिश्य C; देवान् पितॄन् समभ्यर्च्य E$_N$ **6:65** तृप्यन्ति पितरस्तस्य] CE$_N$; तृ --- A **6:65** त्रिभिः] CE$_N$; तृभिः A **6:66** मेदोऽसृक्पूयगर्तेषु] E$_N$; मेदोऽसृकूयगर्त्तेषु C **6:66** पितरश्च विमुक्ताः स्युस्ति॰] CE$_N$; पितरस्य विमक्तस्यस्ति॰ A **6:67** श्राद्धं] CE$_N$; श्राद्ध A **6:67** नित्यं] AE$_N$; गित्यं C **6:67** मानवाः] C; मानवा A; ये नराः E$_N$ **6:67** तेषां तृप्ता हि पितरः] E$_N$; तेषां तृप्ता हि पितर A; तेषा तृप्ति हि पितरः C **6:67** च तृप्तो] AE$_N$; च तृप्ता C **6:68** कुम्भीपाकस्तु निरयो] CE$_N$; कुम्भीपाकं तु निरये A **6:68** प्रभविष्यति] CE$_N$; प्रभविष्य --- A **6:68** पितृलोकञ्च यास्यन्ति] CE$_N$; --- यास्यन्ति A **6:68** श्राद्धकारयिता] AC; श्राद्धं कारयिता E$_N$

पितॄन्देवान्समुद्दिश्य नित्यं दीपप्रदायिनः।
तामिस्रश्चान्धतामिस्रौ नरकौ न भविष्यतः॥ 6:69॥

लोचने च शुभे तेषां दृक्शक्तिश्च न नश्यति।
उपानच्छत्रसंयुक्तं तिलपात्रं ददाति यः॥ 6:70॥

स्वच्छशीताम्बुपूर्णेन करकेण च संयुतम्।
द्विजेभ्यः शिवभक्तेभ्यस्स न याति यमालयम्॥ 6:71॥

विद्याधरपदं प्राप्य मोदते सुचिरं दिवि।
कालान्तरे यदा मर्त्यमागच्छति नरोत्तमः॥ 6:72॥

उदितोदितवंशे ऽस्मिन्जन्म तस्य भवेद्ध्रुवम्।
एतत्तिलस्य माहात्म्यं कथितं वरवर्ण्णिनि॥ 6:73॥

कृष्णाजिनस्य माहात्म्यं कथयाम्यधुना शृणु।
यत्कृष्णं तदृचां रूपं यद्बभ्रु यजुषां स्मृतम्॥ 6:74॥

यच्छुक्लं तद्भवेत्साम्नां कृष्णसारस्य सुन्दरि।
अतस्तदजिनं पुण्यन्त्रैविद्येनाभ्यलंकृतम्॥ 6:75॥

तस्माद्देयं प्रयत्नेन कुम्भीनरकभीरुभिः।

6:69 पितॄन्देवान्समुद्दिश्य] *conj.*; पितृं देवा समुदिश्य A; पितृदेवान्समुद्दिस्य C; पितृन् देवान् समुद्धिश्य E_N **6:69** नित्यं दीपप्रदायिनः] C; नित्यदीपप्रदायिनः A; नित्यं दीप प्रदायिनः E_N **6:69** तामिस्रश्चान्धतामिस्रौ नरकौ न भविष्यतः] *conj.*; तामिस्रौ चान्धतामिस्रौ नरकौ न भविष्यति A; तामिस्रश्चान्धतामिस्रो नरको न भविष्यतिः C; तामिस्रश्चान्धतामिस्रौ नरकौ न भ-विष्यतः E_N **6:70** दृक्शक्तिश्च न] AC; दृक्शक्तिश्चन E_N **6:70** °संयुक्तं तिलपात्रं ददाति यः] E_N; °संयुक्ततिलपात्रं ददाति यः C; °संयुक्तं तिलपात्र ददाति यः A **6:71** स्वच्छशीताम्बुपू-र्णेन करकेण च संयुतम्] *em.*; स्वच्छशीताम्बुपूर्णेन क --- A; स्वच्छशीताम्बुपूर्णेन करकेन च संयुतम् C; स्वच्छशीताम्बुपूर्णे नरकं न च संयुतं E_N **6:71** द्विजेभ्यः शिवभक्तेभ्यस्स न] *em.*; द्विजेभ्य शिवभक्तेभ्यस्स न A; द्विजेभ्यः शिवभक्तेभ्यो न स CE_N **6:72** मर्त्यमागच्छति नरोत्तमः] C; मर्त्यामागच्छन्ति नरोत्तमः A; मर्त्यमागच्छन्ति नरोत्तमाः E_N **6:73** उ-दितोदितवंशे ऽस्मिन् जन्म] E_N; उदितोदितवशे ऽस्मिं जन्म A; उदितोदितवंशो ऽस्मिंज्ञन्म C **6:73** एतत्तिलस्य] A; एतत् तिलानां CE_N **6:73** वरवर्ण्णिनि] AC; वर वर्ण्णिनि E_N **6:74** कृष्णाजिनस्य माहात्म्यं कथयाम्यधुना शृणु] C; कृष्ण --- म्यधुना शृणु A; कृष्णाजिनस्य माहात्म्यं कथयाम्य धुना शृणु E_N **6:74** यत्कृष्णं तदृचां रूपं] *em.*; यत्कृष्ण तदृचा रूपं A; यत्कृष्णं तदृचां रापं C; यत्कृष्णंतदृचां रूपं E_N **6:74** यद्बभ्रु यजुषां स्मृतम्] C; यद्बभ्रु यजुषा स्मृतम् A; यद् बभ्रं यजुषां स्मृतं E_N **6:75** यच्छुक्लं तद्भवेत्साम्नां] E_N; य शुक्लन्तद्भवेत्सा-म्ना A; यत्च्छुक्लत्तद्भवेत्साम्नां C **6:75** °भ्यलंकृतम्] A; °भ्यलकृतम् C; °प्यलङ्कृतं E_N **6:76** प्रयत्नेन कुम्भीनरकभीरुभिः] CE_N; प्रयंनेंन पुंभि नरकभीरुभिः A

अजिनन्तिलपूर्णं तु दद्याद्रौप्यमयं खुरम्॥ 6:76॥

हेमशृङ्गं सुचैलाङ्गं कांस्यदोहं द्विजन्मने।
चतुःसागरपर्यन्ता सशैलवनकानना॥ 6:77॥

दत्तानेन भवेत्पृथ्वी दत्वा त्रिभुवनेश्वरि।
अक्षयं लभते लोकन्तिलधेनुप्रदायकः।
युगान्ते च परिभ्रष्टो जायते पृथिवीपतिः॥ 6:78॥

भगवानुवाच।
भीतैस्तारकतः सुतस्सुरगणैर्मत्तः पुरा याचितः।
तद्धेतोः कृपया मया तु मदनादुत्पाद्यमाने सुते।
सत्तेजो ऽग्निरपादुपेत्य तदभूद्वह्नेः कुमारः प्रभुः।
तच्छेषं कनकं बभूव गिरिजे तेनातिपुण्यं स्मृतम्॥ 6:79॥

विप्रेभ्यः शिवभक्तेभ्यो मासि मासि तिलान्ददत्।
नानादुःखप्रदं घोरं नरकं न स पश्यति॥ 6:80॥

माधव्यां पञ्चदश्यां तु तिलान्मधुसमन्वितान्।
सप्तभ्यो वाथ पञ्चभ्यो ब्राह्मणेभ्यः सदक्षिणान्॥ 6:81॥

धर्मराजस्तु सुप्रीत इति दद्याद्वरं ध्रुवम्।
पापं विहाय स श्रीमान्निर्मलत्वं प्रजायते॥ 6:82॥

6:76 अजिनन्तिलपूर्णं तु दद्याद्रौप्यमयं खुरम्] C; अजिनन्तिलपूर्णत्तु दद्याद्रौप्य --- A; अजिनं तिलपूर्णं तु दद्याद्रौप्यमयं क्षुरम् E_N **6:77** हेमशृङ्गं सुचैलाङ्गं कांस्यदोहं द्विजन्मने] *em.*; --- सुचैलाङ्गं कान्सदोहां द्विजन्मने A; हेमशृङ्ग सुचैलाङ्ग कांस्यदोहं द्विजातये C; हेमशृङ्गं सुचैलाङ्गं कांस्यदोहं द्विजातये E_N **6:77** चतुःसागरपर्यन्ता सशैलवनकानना] CE_N; चतुसागरपर्यन्तं सशैलवनकानना A **6:78** दत्तानेन भवेत्पृथ्वी दत्वा त्रिभुवनेश्वरि] *em.*; दत्तानेन भवेत्पृथ्वी दत्वा त्रिभुवनेश्वरी C; दद्यात्तेन भवेत्पृथ्वी दत्त्वा तृभुवनेश्वरीं A; दत्ता तेन भवेत्पृथ्वी द-त्ता त्रिभुवनेश्वरि E_N **6:78** लोकन्तिलधेनुप्रदायकः] CE_N; लोका तिलधेनोः प्रदायकः A **6:79** सुतस्सुरगणैर्मत्तः पुरा याचितः] C; सु --- त्तः पुरा याचितः A; सुतः सुरगणैर्मत्तः पुरा याचित E_N **6:79** मदनादुत्पाद्यमाने सुते] C; मदनादुत्पाद्यमानो सुते A; मदना दुत्पाद्यमाने सुते E_N **6:79** तच्छेषं कनकं बभूव गिरिजे] C; तच्छेषं कनक षुभूव गिरिजे A; यच्छेषं कनकं बभूव गिरिजे E_N **6:80** तिलान्ददत्] CE_N; तिला ददत् A **6:80** नानादुःखप्रदं घोरं नरकं] E_N; नाना --- रकं A; नानादुःखपदं घोरन्नरकं C **6:81** माधव्यां पञ्चदश्यां तु] A; वैशाख्यां पञ्चदश्यान्तु C; वैशाख्यां पञ्चशश्यान्तु E_N **6:81** तिलान्मधुसमन्वितान्] C; तिलां मधुसमन्वितम् A; तिलान्मधु समन्वितान् E_N **6:81** सदक्षिणान्] C; सदक्षिणाम् AE_N **6:82** दद्याद्वरं] CE_N; दद्यां नरो A **6:82** निर्मलत्वं] AC; निर्म्मलश्च E_N

यमाय धर्म्मराजाय मृत्यवे चान्तकाय च।
वैवस्वताय कालाय सर्वलोकक्षयाय च॥ 6:83॥

उग्रदण्डोग्रहस्ताय महिषासनगामिने।
शासित्रे च नमस्तुभ्यं नरकाधिपतये नमः॥ 6:84॥

एकैकस्य पदस्यापि तिलमिश्रञ्जलाञ्जलिम्।
त्रींस्त्रीन्कृष्णचतुर्दश्यां नदीङ्गत्वा तु निर्वपेत्॥ 6:85॥

हविष्यैकाशनः शान्तस्त्रयोदश्यां समाहितः।
आजन्मचरितं पापं दहत्याशु न संशयः।
युगान्ते च परिभ्रष्टो जायते पृथिवीपतिः॥ 6:86॥

भगवानुवाच।
गावः प्रजज्ञिरे पुण्या मथ्यमाने ऽमृते पुरा।
माननीया महाभागा देवानामपि नित्यशः॥ 6:87॥

तासां गात्रेषु सर्वेषु विबुधाः पर्यवस्थिताः।
तस्मात्पुण्यतमा ज्ञेयास्तासां दानाद्दिवं व्रजेत्॥ 6:88॥

हेमशृंगां रौप्यक्षुरां रत्नाङ्गीं कांस्यदोहिनीम्।
सचैलघण्टाङ्गान्दद्याच्छिवभक्तद्विजन्मने॥ 6:89॥

गोलोके स्वर्ग्गलोके वा वासस्तेषां भविष्यति।
सर्वद्वन्द्वविनिर्मुक्ता वसेयुर्गोप्रदायिनः॥ 6:90॥

6:83 मृत्यवे चान्तकाय च] CE$_N$; --- च A **6:84** उग्रदण्डोग्रहस्ताय] C; उग्रदण्डाय ह-स्ताय E$_N$ **6:84** नमस्तुभ्यं] C; नमस्तु भ्यं E$_N$ **6:85** एकैकस्य पदस्यापि] *em.*; एकैकस्य पदस्यपि A; एकैकस्य पदस्यास्य C; एकैकस्य प्रमादस्य E$_N$ **6:85** तिलमिश्रञ्जलाञ्जलिम्] *conj.*; तिलमिश्रजलाञ्जलिम् A; तिलमिश्रं लाञ्जलिम् C (unmetrical); तिलमिश्रंजलाञ्जलिं E$_N$ **6:85** त्रींस्त्रीन्कृष्णचतुर्दश्यां] C; त्रींस्त्रीन्कृष्णचतु ⏓ दश्यान् A; त्रिस्त्रिः कृष्णचतुर्द्दश्यां E$_N$ **6:85** नदिङ्गत्वा] CE$_N$; नदि गत्वा A **6:86** हविष्यैकाशनः शान्तस्त्र°] E$_N$; हविष्यै-काशन शान्त त्र° A; हविष्यकाशनः शान्तस्त्र° C **6:86** पापं] CE$_N$; पापः A **6:86** जायते पृथिवीपतिः] CE$_N$; --- A **6:87** मथ्यमाने] CE$_N$; चक्ष्यमाने (?) A **6:88** पर्यवस्थिताः] CE$_N$; पयवस्थिताः A **6:88** तस्मात्पुण्यतमा ज्ञेयास्तासां दानाद्दिवं] C; तस्मा पुण्यतमा ज्ञेया तासां दाना दिवं A; तस्मात्पुण्यतमा ज्ञेयास्तासां दाने दिवं E$_N$ **6:89** रौप्यक्षुरां] *em.*; रौप्यखुरां E$_N$; रौप्यक्षुरा (?) A; रोप्यखुरां C **6:89** कांस्यदोहिनीम्] CE$_N$; --- A **6:89** सचैलघण्टाङ्गान्दद्याच्छिवभक्तद्विजन्मने] E$_N$; --- ⏓ ⏓ घ⏓ ⏓ गान्दत्य गिवभक्ति-द्विजन्मने A; सचैलघण्तां गान्दद्याच्छिवभक्तद्विजन्मने C **6:90** गोलोके] CE$_N$; गोलोकः A **6:90** °मुक्ता] CE$_N$; °मुक्त A **6:90** वसेयुर्गो°] CE$_N$; वसेयुगो° A

स्वपापप्रग्रहैर्बद्धाः पतन्ति निरयांबुधौ।
नौरिवानिलविक्षिप्ता दातृंस्तारयते हि गौः॥ 6:91॥

देव्युवाच।
दरिद्रेण कथं कृत्यं गोप्रदानं सुरोत्तम।
कथं वा स्वर्गमाप्नोति तद्भवान्वक्तुमर्हति॥ 6:92॥

भगवानुवाच।
दद्यादाज्यमयीं धेनुं दरिद्रो द्रविणैः सह।
स मृतो ऽमृतवाहिन्यां सुरै रमत इच्छया॥ 6:93॥

आज्यालाभे जलमयीं दद्याद्धेनुं सदक्षिणाम्।
पिपासादि महादुःखं हित्वा यात्यमरालयम्॥ 6:94॥

गवां ग्रासं दरिद्रेण कर्तव्यं प्रातरेव हि।
मन्त्रेणैव समायुक्तो मुच्यते सर्वकिल्बिषैः॥ 6:95॥

स्वर्गगामी च भवति परिभ्रष्टो महाधनी।
गवाढ्ये च भवेज्जन्म गवाढ्यश्च भवत्यसौ॥ 6:96॥

अग्निहोत्रं हुतन्तेन पितृदेवाश्च तर्प्पिताः।
स स्नातः सर्वतीर्थेषु यो ददाति गवाह्निकम्॥ 6:97॥

उत्पन्नामृतमथने सुरभी लोकधारिणी।
इदं ग्रासं गृहाण त्वमिदं मे व्रतमुत्तमम्॥ 6:98॥

6:91 °ग्रहैर्बद्धाः] C; ग्रहैबद्धा A; ग्रहैर्वध्दाः E_N **6:91** निरयांबुधौ] AE_N; निरयाबुधौ C **6:91** नौरिवा°] CE_N; न्वौरिवा° A **6:91** दातृंस्तारयते] E_N; दातृ तारयते A; दातॄस्तारयते C **6:92** कथं कृत्यं गोप्रदानं सुरोत्तम] C; --- सुरोत्तमः A; कथं कार्यं गोप्रदानं सुरोत्तम E_N **6:92** स्वर्गमाप्नोति] AC; स्वर्गमानोति E_N **6:92** तद्भवान्व°] CE_N; तद्भवा व° A **6:93** दद्यादाज्यमयीं धेनुं] E_N; दद्यादाज्यमयी धेनु A; दद्यादाज्यमयीम्धनुं C **6:93** सुरै] A; नद्यां CE_N **6:94** आज्यालाभे जलमयीं] *em.*; आज्यलाभे जलमयी A; आज्यलाभे जलमयीं C; आज्यालाभेजलमयीं E_N **6:94** धेनुं सदक्षिणाम्] CE_N; धेनु सदक्षिणम् A **6:94** महादुःखं] AE_N; महद्दुःखं C **6:94** यात्यमरालयम्] CE_N; यात्यमरा --- A **6:95** गवां ग्रासं] C; --- ग्रास A; गवां घासं E_N **6:95** मन्त्रेणैव] *em.*; मत्रेणैव C; सत्रेणैव E_NA **6:95** °किल्बिषैः] A; °पातकैः CE_N **6:96** महाधनी] *conj.*; महाधने] ; AC; महामुने E_N **6:96** गवाढ्ये च] AC; गवाद्येच E_N **6:96** भवेज्जन्म] C; भवेजन्म A; भवेन्म E_N **6:97** अग्निहोत्रं] C; अग्निहोत्र A; अग्नि होत्रं E_N **6:97** ददाति] AE_N; दद्याति C **6:97** स स्नातः] AC; सुस्नातः E_N **6:97** गवाह्निकम्] CE_N; --- A **6:98** उत्पन्ना°] CE_N; --- त्पना° A **6:98** इदं] A; इमं CE_N **6:98** गृहाण त्वमिदं] *em.*; गृहाण त्वंमिदं AC^{ac}; गृहाण त्वं इदं C^{c}; गृहाणाम्ब E_N

गवां ग्रासं यथा देयं सौरभेये तथैव च।
तुल्यमेव फलं दृष्टं किन्तु मन्त्रः पृथक्पृथक्॥ 6:99॥

सर्वलोकधरा ह्येते जीवितान्नप्रदायकाः।
ग्रासं गृह्णन्तु तुष्टास्तु एतन्मे व्रतमुत्तमम्॥ 6:100॥

नित्यं परगवे दद्याद्गृहीत्वा दुर्लभं व्रतम्।
रक्षन्ति च भयाद्घोराद्दर्शने पापनाशनाः॥ 6:101॥

गवां कण्डूयनं कुर्याद्ग्रासं दत्वा नगात्मजे।
प्रदक्षिणत्रयं कृत्वा गोप्रदानफलं लभेत्॥ 6:102॥

पुण्यकाले तु संप्राप्ते वृषोत्सर्गं करोति यः।
स याति रुद्रलोकं तु यदि नीलो भविष्यति॥ 6:103॥

अलाभे नीलषण्डस्य पितृभिः सह संयुतः।
स्वर्ग्गलोकमवाप्नोति भ्रष्टो भवति भोगवान्॥ 6:104॥

लांगूलाग्रं सितं यस्य क्षुरं शृंगञ्च सुव्रते।
लोहितानि च गात्राणि नीलषण्ढः स उच्यते॥ 6:105॥

अनड्वाहो ऽपि बहुशो यः प्रयच्छेद्द्विजोत्तमे।
तेन पुण्यफलेनैव स्वर्ग्गलोके महीयते॥ 6:106॥

भगवानुवाच।
द्रव्याणां यावतां योनिः क्षितिरेव विधीयते।

6:99 गवां] C; गंवा A **6:99** दृष्टं किन्तु मन्त्रः] CE$_N$; दृष्ट किंतु मन्त्र A **6:99** पृथक्पृथक्] AC; पृथक्पथृक् E$_N$ **6:100** सर्वलोकधरा] AC; सर्वलोक धरा E$_N$ **6:100** जीवितान्नप्रदायकाः] C; जीवितान्नप्रदायकः A; जीवितानां प्रदायकाः E$_N$ **6:100** ग्रासं गृह्णन्तु तुष्टास्तु एतन्मे व्रतमुत्तमम्] C; ग्रास गृह्णंन्तु दृष्टा तु एतन्मे --- A; ग्रासं गृह्णन्तु तुष्टास्तु एतन्मेव्रतमुत्तमम् E$_N$ **6:101** नित्यं परगवे दद्याद्] C; --- त्यं परगवे दद्यां A; नित्यं परगवे दद्या E$_N$ **6:102** नगात्मजे] CE$_N$; नगात्मजा A **6:102** गोप्रदानफलं] C; गोप्रदानं फलं A; गो प्रदानफलं E$_N$ **6:103** वृषोत्सर्गं] E$_N$; वृषोत्सर्ग्ग A; वृषोत्सग्गं C **6:103** भविष्यति] CE$_N$; भ --- A **6:104** अलाभे नील°] CE$_N$; --- ल A **6:104** °स्षण्डस्य] A; °सण्ढस्य CE$_N$ **6:104** पितृभिः सह संयुतः] CE$_N$; पितृभि षह संयुतः A **6:104** स्वर्ग्गलोकमवाप्नोति] AC; स्वर्गलोक मवाप्नोति E$_N$ **6:105** लांगूलाग्रं सितं] CE$_N$; लांगूलाश्रितं A **6:105** क्षुरं शृंगञ्च सुव्रते] *em.*; क्षुर शृंगञ्च सुव्रते A; खुरं शृंगञ्च सुव्रते C; खुराः शृङ्गे च सुव्रते E$_N$ **6:105** नीलषण्ढः स] CE$_N$; नीलषण्ढस्य A **6:106** बहुशो] CE$_N$; बहुषो A **6:106** द्विजोत्तमे] CE$_N$; द्विजोत्तमः A **6:106** महीयते] CE$_N$; महीय --- A **6:107** योनिः] CE$_N$; योनि A

किञ्च तेन न दत्तं स्याद्यः प्रयच्छति गां प्रिये॥ 6:107॥

ममैषा प्रथमा मूर्तिरिति तस्या महत्फलम्।
करोटीगतमप्यम्भः क्षितौ गत्वा शुचीभवेत्॥ 6:108॥

निवर्तनसहस्राढ्यामवनीं सस्यशालिनीम्।
शिवभक्ताय विप्राय दद्याच्छतमखो भवेत्॥ 6:109॥

ये हरन्ति महीं दत्तामात्मनाथ परेण वा।
दिव्यवर्षसहस्राणि रौरवे निवसन्त्यघाः॥ 6:110॥

परमाक्षरजापेन प्राणायामशतेन च।
ध्यानधारणयोगाच्च क्षितिहर्त्ता न शुद्ध्यति॥ 6:111॥

देव्युवाच।
निवर्तनसहस्राढ्यामवनीं सस्यमालिनीम्।
कथं दरिद्रा दास्यन्ति तदुपायं ब्रवीहि मे॥ 6:112॥

भगवानुवाच।
गोचर्ममात्रमपि गां यो ददाति शुचिस्मिते।
स भविष्यति सुव्यक्तमिन्द्रस्यार्धासनातिथिः॥ 6:113॥

देव्युवाच।
गोचर्ममात्रमपि गां यदा दातुं न शक्यते।

6:107 यः प्रयच्छति गां प्रिये] AC; यःप्रय च्छति गां प्रियेः E_N **6:108** तस्या महत्फलम्] A; तस्याः फलं महत् C; तस्याःफलं महत् E_N **6:108** करोटीगतमप्यम्भः] AC; करोटीगतमप्यम्मः E_N **6:108** शुचीभवेत्] C; शुचीम्भवेत् A; शुची भवेत् E_N **6:109** निवर्तनसहस्राढ्यामवनीं] *conj.*; निवर्त्तनसहस्राढ्यामवनी A; निवर्तनसहस्राद्यामवतीं C; निवर्तनसहस्राढचामवनी E_N (unmetrical) **6:109** सस्यमालिनीम्] AC; सस्यशालिनी E_N **6:109** शिवभक्ताय विप्राय दद्याच्छतमखो] CE_N; --- दद्या शतमखो A **6:110** महीं दत्तामात्मनाथ] *conj.*; मही दत्वामात्मनाथ A; महीं दत्तां स्वयम्वाथ CE_N **6:110** दिव्यवर्षसहस्राणि रौरवे निवसन्त्यघाः] C; दिव्यं वर्षसहस्राणि रौरवे निवसंत्यघा A; दिव्यवर्षसहस्राणि रौरबे निवसन्त्यघः E_N **6:111** °जापेन] CE_N; °जाप्योवो (?) A **6:111** ध्यानधारणयोगाच्च क्षितिहर्त्ता] C; ध्यानधारणयोगा च क्षितिहत्ता A; ध्यान धारण योगाच्च क्षितिहर्त्ता E_N **6:112** निवर्तनसहस्राढ्यामवनीं सस्यमालिनीम्] C; निवर्तनसहस्राढ्यमवनी सस्यमालिनी A; निवर्तन सहस्राढयामवनीं सस्यशालिनीं E_N (unmetrical) **6:112** कथं दरिद्रा दास्यन्ति तदुपायं ब्रवीहि मे] C;--- तदुपाय ब्रवीमि हे A; कथं दरिद्रा दास्यन्ति तदुपायं व्रवीहिमे E_N **6:113** गोचर्ममात्रमपि] A; गोचर्ममात्रां यपि CE_N **6:113** सुव्यक्तमिन्द्रस्यार्धासनातिथिः] C; सुव्यक्तमिन्द्रस्यार्धसनातिथि A; सुव्यक्त मिन्द्रस्यार्ध्दासनातिथिः E_N **6:114** देव्युवाच] CE_N; देव्यूवाच A **6:114** यदा] CE_N; कदा A

तदा किं तु दरिद्रेण कर्तव्यञ्जगतांपते॥ 6:114॥

भगवानुवाच।
शुचावुद्धृत्य मृद्भारं सुगन्धीकृत्य यत्नतः।
दद्याद्गुणवते नित्यं भूदानफलमाप्नुयात्॥ 6:115॥

एकछत्रां महीं कृत्वा महादेवाय शम्भवे।
शिवभक्तद्विजेभ्यो वा दत्वा रुद्रसमो भवेत्॥ 6:116॥

देव्युवाच।
एकछत्रां वसुमतीं कथन्दद्यात्पृथग्जनः।
तस्याः प्रतिनिधिम्ब्रूहि यथा याति परां गतिम्॥ 6:117॥

भगवानुवाच।
प्रसवन्तीञ्च गान्दद्याद्वक्रोभयसुसंस्थिताम्।
पृथ्वीदानफलं ह्येतत्स्वर्ग्गलोकाभिकांक्षिणाम्॥ 6:118॥

एकजन्मानुगाः सर्वे दानधर्म्मफलोदयाः।
गोमहीकनकानान्तु सप्तजन्मानुगाः प्रिये॥ 6:119॥

देव्युवाच।
बालवृद्धातुराल्पाङ्गैर्भगवन्शक्यते कथम्।
उपवासत्रयं कर्तुन्तदुपायञ्च मे वद॥ 6:120॥

भगवानुवाच।

6:114 पते] AE_N; परे C **6:115** शुचावुद्धृत्य मृद्भारं सुगन्धीकृत्य यत्नतः] C; शुचावु ⏑̆ --- ⏑̆ तः A; शुचावुद्धृत्यमृद्भारं सुगन्धी कृत्य यत्नतः E_N **6:115** दद्याद्गुणवते नित्यं] C; दद्याद्गु ⏑̆ वते नित्य A; दद्या द्गुणवते नित्यं E_N **6:115** भूदानफलमाप्नुयात्] AC; भू-दान फलमाप्नुयात् E_N **6:116** महीं] E_N; मही AC **6:116** शम्भवे] AE_N; संभवे C **6:116** शिवभक्तद्विजेभ्यो] AC; शिवभक्त द्विजेभ्यो E_N **6:117** वसुमतीं] CE_N; वसुमती A **6:117** दद्यात्पृथग्जनः] CE_N; दद्यात्पृथग्जनैः A **6:117** प्रतिनिधिम्ब्रूहि] AC; प्रतिनिधिंब्रू-हि E_N **6:117** यथा याति परां गतिम्] C; यथा याति प --- A; यथायान्ति परां गतिम् E_N **6:118** भगवानुवाच] CE_N; भ --- A **6:118** प्रसवन्तीञ्च गान्दद्याद्वक्रोभयसुसंस्थिताम्] C; --- गा दद्यद्वक्रोभयसुसंस्थिताम् A; प्रसवन्तीश्च गान्दद्याद् बक्रोभयसुसंस्थितां E_N **6:118** ह्येत-त्स्वर्ग्ग°] CE_N; ह्येत स्वर्ग्ग° A **6:118** °लोकाभिकांक्षिणाम्] A; °लोकेभिकांक्षिणाम् C; °लोकाभिकांक्षिणा E_N **6:119** एकजन्मानुगाः] CE_N; एकजन्मानुगा A **6:119** °दयाः] CE_N; °दया A **6:119** सप्तजन्मानुगाः] CE_N; सप्तजन्मानुगां A **6:120** बालवृद्धातुरा-ल्पाङ्गैर्भगवन् शक्यते] E_N; बालवृद्धातुराल्पांगै भगवं शक्यते A; बालवृद्धातुराल्पाङ्गैर्भगन् ⏑̆ क्यते C (unmetrical) **6:120** उपवासत्रयं कर्तुन्तदुपायञ्च] E_N; उपवासं त्रयं कर्तुं तदुपायञ्च A; उपवासत्रयं कर्तुत्तदुपायञ्च C **6:121** भगवानुवाच] *em.*; भ --- A; देवदेव उवाच CE_N

यः पृथ्वीभाजनं कृत्वा भुंक्ते पर्वसु यत्नतः।
अहोरात्रेण चैकेन त्रिरात्रफलमश्नुते॥ 6:121॥

एतदुक्तं मया देवि शक्तिहीनहिताय वै।
शक्तानां तु भवेन्नैवं विधिः सर्वत्र सुन्दरि॥ 6:122॥

हेमवर्णमजं दत्वा शिवभक्तद्विजन्मने।
अग्निलोकमवाप्नोति बहुपापात्मिको ऽपि सन्॥ 6:123॥

भूमिदानाद्भवेत्स्वर्गो रत्नदानाद्रवेः पुरम्।
वस्त्रदः शशिलोकं तु तारदो वैष्णवं पुरम्॥ 6:124॥

तिलहेमप्रदातारो यान्ति रुद्रस्य चालयम्।
कांस्यताम्रप्रवालानि दत्त्वैति वसुमन्दिरम्॥ 6:125॥

मुक्तामणिविचित्राणि हीनजातीनि यान्यपि।
दत्वा शक्रपुरं यांति तिलहोमाच्च मानवाः॥ 6:126॥

दधि क्षीरं गुडं सर्पिर्यः प्रयच्छति नित्यशः।
यक्षलोकपुरं याति मधुदानेन चैव हि॥ 6:127॥

चन्दनागरुकर्प्पूरकक्कोलकलवङ्गकान्।

6:121 यः पृथ्वीभाजनं कृत्वा] C; --- थ्वी भाजन कुया A; यः पृथ्वी भाजनं कृत्वा E_N **6:121** त्रिरात्र°] CE_N; तृरात्र° A **6:122** एतदुक्तं मया देवि शक्तिहीनहिताय] AC; एतदुक्तंमया देवि शक्ति ही नहिताय E_N **6:122** भवेन्नैवं विधिः] C; भवे नैव विधि A; भवेन्नैव विधिः E_N **6:123** शिवभक्तद्विजन्मने] AC; शिवभक्त द्विजन्मने E_N **6:123** अग्निलोकमवाप्नोति बहुपापात्मिको ऽपि सन्] C; अग्निलोकमवाप्नोति बहुपापात्मतामपि A; अग्निलोकमवाप्नोतिबहुपापात्मिको ऽपि सन् E_N **6:124** भूमिदानाद्भवेत्स्वर्गो] E_N; भूमिदानाद्भवे --- म्सा; भूमिदानाल्लभेत्स्वर्ग्गं C **6:124** रत्नदानाद्रवेः पुरम्] C; --- पुरं A; रत्नदानाद्रवे:पुरं E_N **6:124** तारदो वैष्णवं पुरम्] C; तारदो वैष्णवे पुरे A; तारदोवैष्णवं पुरं E_N **6:125** कांस्यताम्रप्रवालानि दत्वैति वसुमन्दिरम्] C; कांसताम्रप्रवालानि दत्वैति वचुमुन्दत्रि A; कांस्यताम्रप्रवालानि दतेति वसुमन्दिरम् E_N **6:126** मुक्तामणिविचित्राणि] *em.*; मुक्तमणिविचित्राणि A; मुक्तामनिविचित्राणि C; मुक्तामणि विचित्राणि E_N **6:126** शक्रपुरं] C; स्वर्ग्गपुरं A; शुक्रपुरं E_N **6:126** तिलहोमाच्च] C; तिलहोमा च A; तिलहोमाश्च E_N **6:127** दधि क्षीरं गुडं सर्पिर्यः] *em.*; दधि क्षीर गुडं सर्प्पि यः A; दधि क्षीरं गुडं सार्प्पः यः C; दधिक्षीरगुडं सर्पि र्यं E_N **6:127** नित्यशः] CE_N; नित्य ⏓ --- A **6:127** यक्षलोकपुरं याति] C; --- न्ति A; यक्षलोकपुरं यान्ति E_N **6:127** मधुदानेन चैव हि] *conj.*; दधिदानेन चैव हि C; दधिदानेव चेव हि A; दधिदानेन चैव हि E_N **6:128** चन्दनागरुकर्प्पूरकक्कोलकलवङ्गकान्] *conj.*; चन्दनागरुकपूरः ककोलकलवङ्गकाम् A; चन्दनागरुकर्प्पूरकक्कोलकलवङ्गकम् CE_N

दत्वान्यानि सुगन्धीनि व्रजेद्गन्धर्वतान्नरः॥ 6:128॥

अलङ्कृत्य च ये कन्यां प्रयच्छन्ति त्वयाचिताम्।
ते नराः स्वर्गमेष्यन्ति ये च धान्यप्रदायिनः॥ 6:129॥

माषमुद्गादिकान्व्रीहीन्ये ददत्यसकृन्नराः।
ते ऽपि स्वर्गङ्गमिष्यन्ति ये चान्ये ह्यभयप्रदाः॥ 6:130॥

रूपयौवनसम्पन्नां वस्त्राभरणभूषिताम्।
युवतीं ये प्रयच्छन्ति यान्ति वैद्याधरं पदम्॥ 6:131॥

रतिसत्रञ्च यो दद्याद्वराभिः प्रमदाजनैः।
कामदेवपुरं याति जातो ऽनङ्गसमो भवेत्॥ 6:132॥

वेत्रासनञ्च शय्याञ्च प्रत्यब्दं यः प्रयच्छति।
मोदते यक्षलोकेषु यक्षिणीभिः समन्वितः॥ 6:133॥

इन्धनानि च यो दद्याद्विप्रेभ्यः शिशिरागमे।
धनवान्रूपसंपंनो दीप्ताग्निः सुभगो भवेत्॥ 6:134॥

प्रतिश्रयं तृणं शय्याम्पुण्याग्निं शुद्धमानसाः।
प्रत्यहं ये प्रयच्छन्ति ते नराः स्वर्गगामिनः॥ 6:135॥

गीतवादित्रयानानि देवानां नित्यदायिनः।
जायन्ते ते च भोगाढ्या गीतवादित्रबोधकाः॥ 6:136॥

---

134 Cf. *Garuḍapurāṇa* 1.51.27ab: इन्धनानां प्रदानेन दीप्ताग्निर्जायते नरः।

6:128 दत्वान्यानि सुगन्धीनि] CE$_N$; दद्याद्यानि सुगन्दानि A **6:128** व्रजेद्गन्धर्वतान्नरः] CE$_N$; व्रजे गन्धर्वतां नरः A **6:129** अलङ्कृत्य च ये कन्यां प्रयच्छन्ति त्वयाचिताम्] C; अलंकृत्य च यः कन्या संप्रयच्छत्यायाचितां A; अलङ्कृत्यच ये कन्यां प्रयच्छन्ति त्वयाचितां E$_N$ **6:129** स्वर्गमेष्यन्ति] CE$_N$; स्वर्ग्गयेष्यन्ति A **6:130** माषमुद्गादिकान् व्रीहीन्] *conj.*; मासमुद्गादिकां व्रीहीं A; मुद्गमाषादिकां व्रीहीन् C; मुद्गमाषादिकान्नानि E$_N$ **6:130** ददत्यसकृन्नराः:लेम् CE$_N$; ददत्यसकृनरः A **6:130** ते ऽपि स्वर्गङ्गमिष्यन्ति ये चान्ये ह्यभयप्रदाः] CE$_N$; तिपि --- न्ये ह्यभयप्रदा A **6:131** रूपयौवनसम्पन्नां] E$_N$; रूपयौवनसम्पन्न A; रूपयौवन्नसम्पन्नां C **6:132** वराभिः] *conj.*; वाराणि A; आरिभिः CE$_N$ **6:132** कामदेवपुरं याति] C^{c}E$_N$; कामदेवपुरा यान्ति A; कामदेवपुरं यान्ति C^{ac} **6:133** मोदते यक्षलोकेषु यक्षिणीभिः समन्वितः] E$_N$; मोदते य --- ⏓ ⏓ ⏓ न्वन्तं A; मोदते यक्षलोकेषु यक्षिणीभिःर्समन्वितः C **6:134** दीप्ताग्निः] CE$_N$; दीप्ताग्नि A **6:135** प्रतिश्रयं तृणं शय्याम्पुण्याग्निं शुद्धमानसाः] C; प्रतिश्रय तृणं शय्य पुण्याग्निं शुद्धमानसा A; प्रतिश्रयं तृणं शय्याम्पुण्याग्निं शुध्दमानसाः E$_N$ **6:136** जायन्ते ते च भोगाढ्या गीतवादित्रबोधकाः] C; जयन्ति ते म --- धैका +:+A; जायन्ते ते च भोगाद्या गातवादित्रबोधकाः E$_N$

जवे यौवनसम्पन्नं सप्तिं हेमविभूषितम् ।
प्रयच्छेद्द्विजमुख्येभ्यो ब्रध्नस्याप्नोति पिष्टपम् ॥ 6 : 137 ॥

पुण्येन धनमाप्नोति सन्ततिं श्राद्धकर्मणा ।
†तृणासिनां †भवेद्राज्यं नित्यस्नानेन यक्षताम् ॥ 6 : 138 ॥

प्रदानादुपभोग्यं स्यात्सौभाग्यं रसवर्ज्जनात् ।
व्याधिशोकौ न जायेते सान्त्वदस्य महात्मनः ॥ 6 : 139 ॥

ब्रह्मचारी चिरायुर्वै स्वर्ग्गः पर्णाशनेन तु ।
गुरुशुश्रूषया विद्वान्सुचक्षुर्दीपदानतः ॥ 6 : 140 ॥

भृगुप्रपतनाद्राज्यं पयोभक्षस्त्वरेद्दिवि ।
अग्निप्रवेशेन नरः प्रयाति ब्रह्मणः पदम् ॥ 6 : 141 ॥

उपवासाद्गदाधीशो मौनेनाज्ञाप्रदो भवेत् ।
सर्वकामसमृद्धिस्तु जायते ऽन्नप्रदानतः ॥ 6 : 142 ॥

दानेन प्रेक्षणीयस्य मेधावी स्मृतिमान्भवेत् ।
लभते छत्रदानेन रम्याणि भवनानि च ॥ 6 : 143 ॥

गृहदानेन सुव्यक्तं नगरं लभते नरः ।
उपानहप्रदानेन प्राप्नुयाद्यानमुत्तमम् ॥ 6 : 144 ॥

6:137 जवे यौवनसम्पन्नं सप्तिं हेमविभूषितम्] A; जवे यौवनसम्पन्नं सप्तिं हेमावभूषितम् C; नवयौवनसम्पन्नं सप्तिहेमविभूषि E_N (unmetrical) **6:137** प्रयच्छेद्द्विजमुख्येभ्यो] A; यो दद्याद्द्विजमुख्येभ्यो CE_N **6:137** ब्रध्नस्याप्नोति पिष्टपम्] C; बद्ध्रस्याप्नोतृ पिष्टपं A; ब्रध्नस्याप्नोति विष्टपम् E_N **6:138** सन्ततिं श्राद्धकर्मणा] *em.*; सन्तत्रिं शाद्धकर्मणा A; सन्ततिं शाद्धकर्मणा C; सन्ततिं श्राध्दकर्मणा E_N **6:138** तृणासिनां] A; तृणसिनां C; तृणासिना E_N **6:138** भवेद्राज्यं] CE_N; भवेद्राज्य A **6:138** नित्यस्नानेन यक्षताम्] A; नित्यं स्नानेन यक्षताम् C; नित्यस्नानेन यक्षता E_N **6:139** °पभोग्यं] C; °पभोगं A; °पभोग्य E_N **6:139** व्याधिशोकौ न जायेते सान्त्वदस्य महात्मनः] CE_N; व्याधिशोको न --- हात्मनः A **6:140** चिरायुर्वै] E_N; चिरायु वै AC **6:140** स्वर्ग्गः] A; स्वर्ग्ग C; स्वर्गं E_N **6:140** गुरुशुश्रूषया विद्वान्] C; गुरुशुश्रूषया विद्यो A; गुरुशुश्रूषयाविद्वान् E_N **6:140** सुचक्षुर्दीपदानतः] CE_N; सुचक्षु दीपदानतः A **6:141** भृगुप्रपतनाद्राज्यं] CE_N; भृगुप्रपतने द्रज्य A **6:141** अग्निप्रवेशेन नरः प्रयाति ब्रह्मणः पदम्] AC; अग्निप्रवेशन नरः प्रयाति ब्रह्मः पदम् E_N **6:142** गदाधीशो] A; गजाधीशो CE_N **6:142** मौनेनाज्ञाप्रदो] AC; मौनेन ज्ञानदो E_N **6:142** सर्वकामसमृद्धिस्तु जायते ऽन्नप्रदानतः] C; सर्वकामस --- दानतः A; सर्वकामसमृध्दिस्तु जायते ऽन्नप्रदानतः E_N **6:143** स्मृतिमान्] CE_N; स्मृतिमां A **6:143** रम्याणि] E_N; रम्यानि AC **6:144** उपानहप्रदानेन] A; उपानहः प्रदानेन CE_N

हरशुश्रूषया राज्यं फलमूलाशिनामपि।
विप्रायाश्वयुजे सर्पिर्दत्वा भवति रूपवान्॥ 6:145॥

त्रिसन्ध्यासु जपन्देवि द्विजो भवति रूपवान्।
द्रव्याणि भृत्यवर्गांश्च क्षेत्राणि च गृहाणि च॥ 6:146॥

ब्रह्मदेयां सुतान्दत्वा प्राप्नोत्याभरणानि च।
इन्द्रत्वं वायुभक्षेण नीरोगत्वमहिंसया॥ 6:147॥

महीमधिशयानस्य दिव्यशय्यागृहं भवेत्।
पुष्पाढ्यं वा फलाढ्यं वा दत्वा विप्राय पादपम्॥ 6:148॥

दिव्यस्त्रीधनपूर्णानि गृहाण्याप्नोति मानवः।
शिवदीक्षांबुपूताय विप्रायाचमनाय च॥ 6:149॥

कमण्डलुमपां पूर्णं दत्वा प्रेत्य सुखी भवेत्।
पूजयन्ति दिवि प्रीता विबुधाः सत्यवादिनः॥ 6:150॥

सलिलस्य प्रदानेन तृप्तिर्भवति सर्वदा।
बलीवर्दसहस्राणां दृढानाम्फलवाहिनाम्॥ 6:151॥

गुणवत्पात्रदत्तानां फलं कन्याप्रदानतः।
तिलान्ददतः पानीयं दीपमन्नं प्रतिश्रयम्॥ 6:152॥

6:145 फलमूलाशिनामपि] CE$_N$; फलमूलाशनामपि A **6:145** सर्पिर्दत्वा भवति रूपवान्] *em.*; सर्प्पि --- A; सर्पिदत्वा भवति रूपवान् CE$_N$ **6:146** त्रिसन्ध्यासु जपन्देवि द्विजो भवति रूपवान्] A; त्रिसन्ध्यासु जपन्देवि द्विजो भवति नान्यथा C; त्रिसन्ध्यन्तु जपेद्देवि द्विजो भवति नान्यथा E$_N$ **6:146** द्रव्याणि भृत्यवर्गांश्च] *em.*; द्रव्याणि भृत्यवग्गांश्च AE$_N$; द्रव्यानि भृत्यवग्गांश्च C **6:147** ब्रह्मदेयां सुतान्दत्वा] AC; ब्रह्मदेयात्सुतान्दत्वा E$_N$ **6:147** इन्द्रत्वं वायुभक्षेण] AC; इन्दुत्वं वायुभक्ष्येण E$_N$ **6:147** नीरोगत्वमहिंसया] CE$_N$; निरोगत्वमहिंसया A **6:148** महीमधिशयानस्य] CE$_N$; महीमधशयानस्य A **6:148** फलाढ्यं] AC; फलाढयं E$_N$ **6:148** विप्राय पादपम्] CE$_N$; --- A **6:149** दिव्यस्त्रीधनपूर्णानि] CE$_N$; ⏑ व्यस्त्रीधनपूर्णानि A **6:149** गृहाण्याप्नोति] *em.*; गृहानाप्नोति A; गृहान्याप्नोति C; गृहाव्याप्नोति E$_N$ **6:149** च] *em.*; चः A; यः C; य E$_N$ **6:150** कमण्डलुमपां पूर्णं दत्वा प्रेत्य] C; कमण्डलुमयां पूर्णन्दत्वा वेत्य A; कामनास्तु मया पूर्णं दत्त्वा प्रेत्य E$_N$ **6:150** विबुधाः सत्यवादिनः] C; विबुधा सत्यवादिनः A; विबुधाः सत्यवादिनं E$_N$ **6:151** तृप्तिर्भवति] C; तृप्तिं भवति A; तृप्तिर्भबति E$_N$ **6:151** बलीवर्दसहस्राणां] E$_N$; बलीवद्दसहस्राणां A; बलीवर्दसहस्राणां C **6:151** फलवाहिनाम्] C; चलवाहिनाम् A; फलवाहिनं E$_N$ **6:152** तिलान्ददतः] *em.*; तिलान्ददथ E$_N$; तिलां ददत A; तिलान्दद्रथ C **6:152** दीपमन्नं प्रतिश्रयम्] C; दीपमंन प्रतिश्रयम् A; दीपमन्त्र प्रतिज्ञया E$_N$

बान्धवैस्सह मोदन्ति एतत्प्रेत्य सुदुर्लभम्।
शारीसंयोगसंयुक्तमिभङ्काञ्चनमालया॥ 6:153॥

दत्वा शक्रपुरं याति भ्रष्टो भवति भोगवान्।
आतपत्रप्रदानेन श्रीमाञ्जायेत मानवः॥ 6:154॥

धर्मराजपुरं गच्छन्नातपेनानुपीड्यते।
उपानहौ तु यो दद्यात्स तु मुच्येत किल्बिषात्॥ 6:155॥

धर्मराजपथे तस्य जायते शोभनो हयः।
तप्तसैकतदुःखाग्रैः कण्टकैश्च सुदारुणैः॥ 6:156॥

न च तस्य भवेत्पीडा यो हि दद्यादुपानहौ।
दद्याद्राजरथं यस्तु ब्राह्मणाय गुणान्विते॥ 6:157॥

तेन पुण्यफलेनैव स्वर्गलोके महीयते।
तावन्न च्यवते स्वर्गाद्यावद्देवास्सवासवाः॥ 6:158॥

ततश्चैव परिभ्रष्टो राजा भव+ति+ धार्मिकः।
दत्वा चाश्वरथं दिव्यं बहुद्रव्यसमन्वितम्॥ 6:159॥

सूर्यलोकमवाप्नोति तेनैव सह मोदते।
यावत्सूर्यकृता लोकास्तावत्तिष्ठेत्स सूर्यवत्॥ 6:160॥

तत्र चैव परिभ्रष्टो धनवाञ्जायते पुनः।

6:153 मोदन्ति एतत्प्रेत्य सुदुर्लभम्] E_N; मोदध्वमेतत्प्रेत्य सुदुर्लूभं A; मोदध्वमेतत्प्रेत्य सुदुलभम् C **6:153** शारीरयोगसंयुक्तम्] C; शरीरसंयोगसंयुक्तं A; शारीरयोगसंयुक्त E_N **6:153** इभङ्काञ्चनमालया] AC; नितंकाञ्चन मालया E_N **6:154** भवति भोगवान्] CE_N; --- A **6:154** जायेत] AE_N; जायेत् C **6:155** गच्छन्नातपेनानुपीड्यते] C; गच्छं आतपेनानुपीड्यते A; गच्छन्नातपैनानु पीड्यते E_N **6:155** तु यो] CE_N; च यो A **6:155** किल्बिषात्] CE_N; किल्बिषां A **6:156** धर्मराजपथे तस्य] A; धर्मराजस्य मार्ग्गे ऽस्य CE_N **6:156** हयः] AC; हयाः E_N **6:156** तप्तसैकतदुःखाग्रैः] AC; तप्तसैकत दुःखाद्रैः E_N **6:156** कण्टकैश्च] CE_N; कष्टोकैश्च A **6:157** न च तस्य भवेत्पीडा यो हि दद्यादुपानहौ] CE_N; न च त --- द्यादुपानहौ A **6:157** ब्राह्मणाय] AC; ब्राह्मणा E_N (unmetrical) **6:158** तावन्न च्यवते] CE_N; तावं न च्यते A (unmetrical) **6:158** देवास्सवासवाः] $A^{c}CE_N$; देवात्सस्सवासवाः A^{ac} (unmetrical) **6:159** परिभ्रष्टो राजा भवति धार्मिकः] AE_N; परिभ्रष्टा रास भवन्ति धार्मिकाः C **6:159** दत्वा वाश्वरथं] CE_N; दत्वा क्काश्वरथं (?) A **6:159** दिव्यं] CE_N; दिव्यां A **6:159** बहुद्रव्यसमन्वितम्] CE_N; बहुद्रव्यसम --- A **6:160** सूर्यलोकमवाप्नोति तेनैव] CE_N; --- प्नोति तेननैव A (unmetrical) **6:160** यावत्सूर्यकृता लोकास्तावत्तिष्ठेत्स सूर्यवत्] C; यावत्सूयकृता लोकात्ताव तिष्ठन्ति सूयवत् A; यावत्सूर्यकृतालोकास्तावत्तिष्ठेत्स सूर्यवत् E_N **6:161** तत्र चैव] A; ततश्चैव CE_N

बलीवर्दरथं दत्वा सर्वद्रव्यसमन्वितम्॥ 6:161॥

दासीदाससमोपेतः स्वर्गमाप्नोति मानवः।
परिभ्रष्टस्तु तद्भूयो धनवाञ्जायते सदा॥ 6:162॥

कपित्थं दाडिमञ्चैव पनसं बीजपूरकम्।
नालिकेरकनारङ्गं प्राचीनामलमोचकम्॥ 6:163॥

श्रीफलं चूतजम्बीरन्द्राक्षा खर्जूरमेव च।
अन्यानि च फलान्येवं दत्वा तु सुखभाग्भवेत्॥ 6:164॥

बहुप्रजश्च रूपाढ्यः सुभगश्चैव जायते।
संपूर्णाङ्गश्च निरुजो भवेच्च फलदायकः॥ 6:165॥

दन्तधावनदानाच्च भार्या भवति शोभना।
तांबूलं शोभितं पुष्पं दत्वा जायेत पण्डितः॥ 6:166॥

सुगन्धास्यश्च भवति वाग्मी गन्धप्रदायकः।
उपवीतं वृतं दत्वा जायते ब्रह्मयोनिषु॥ 6:167॥

खड्गचक्रायुधन्दत्वा शक्तिकुन्तपरश्वधान्।
असिपत्रवनाद्घोरान्न भयं तस्य जायते॥ 6:168॥

असंस्कृतस्य लोहस्य दानाद्बन्धभयं न च।

6:161 बलीवर्दरथं दत्वा] *em.*; बलीवर्द्धरथन्दत्वा A; बलीवर्द्धरथं दद्यात् C; वलीवर्दरथं दद्यात् E$_N$ **6:161** सर्वद्रव्यसमन्वितम्] AE$_N$; सर्वधर्मसमन्वितम् C **6:162** °समोपेतः] CE$_N$; °समोपेत A **6:162** स्वर्गमाप्नोति] A; स्वर्गप्राप्नोति C; स्वर्गं प्राप्नोति E$_N$ **6:162** परिभ्रष्टस्तु तद्भूयो धनवाञ्जायते सदा] CE$_N$; परिभ्रष्टस्तु तं भूयो --- A **6:163** कपित्थं दाडिमञ्चैव पनसं] CE$_N$; कपिथं दातिमञ्चैड पवोसं (?) A **6:163** बीजपूरकम्] AC; वीजपूरकम् E$_N$ **6:163** नालिकेरकनारङ्गं] CE$_N$; नालिकेरकनारंगा A **6:164** चूतजम्बीरन्द्राक्षा खर्जूरमेव] C; चूतजंबीर द्राक्ष खर्जूरमेव A; चूतजम्बीरं द्राक्षाखर्ज्जूर मेव E$_N$ **6:164** दत्वा तु] C; दद्या तु A; दत्त्वातु E$_N$ **6:165** बहुप्रजश्च रूपाढ्यः] C; बहुप्रजाश्च रूपाढ्य A; वहुप्रजश्च रूपाढ्य E$_N$ **6:165** सुभगश्चैव] AE$_N$; शुभगश्चैव C **6:165** संपूर्णाङ्गश्च] CE$_N$; संपूर्णाङ्गांश्च A **6:165** भवेच्च फलदायकः] CE$_N$; भवे ⏑̄ --- A **6:166** दन्तधावनदानाच्च] E$_N$; ---वनदाजा च A; दन्तधावनदाना च C **6:166** शोभितं पुष्पं] A; सुरभिं पुष्पं C; सुरभिपुष्पं E$_N$ **6:167** °दायकः] AC; °दायक E$_N$ **6:167** वृतं दत्वा] C; वृतन्दवा Aवृषन्दत्वा E$_N$ **6:168** परश्वधान्] C; परश्वधम् A; परश्वधाम् E$_N$ **6:168** असिपत्रवनाद्घोरान्न] E$_N$; असिपत्रवनं द्वोर न A; अशिपत्रवनाद्घोरान्न C **6:168** भयं तस्य जायते] CE$_N$; भय --- A **6:169** असंस्कृतस्य] CE$_N$; --- तस्य A **6:169** बन्धभयं न] *conj.*; द्वन्द्वभयं न A; बंन्धभयन्न C; द्वन्द्व भयन्न E$_N$

घटितोपस्करं लोहं दत्वा शस्त्रभयन्न च॥ 6:169॥

लोहीपाकश्च नरको न कदाचिद्भविष्यति।
मृन्मयानि कपालानि दत्वा चैव कमण्डलुम्॥ 6:170॥

यतिदानमिदं श्रेष्ठं दत्वा तु सुखभाग्भवेत्।
काञ्चनं रजतं ताम्रं भाण्डमायससीसकम्॥ 6:171॥

अक्षयन्तद्भवेद्दानं दीर्घमायुश्च जायते।
देवताभ्यो द्विजातिभ्यो दासीदासां ददाति यः॥ 6:172॥

ते लभन्ते महाभोगान्बहुभृत्यजनावृताः।
सिन्धूत्थं लवणं दत्वा रूपवान्सुभगो भवेत्॥ 6:173॥

पिप्पलीं शृङ्गवेरञ्च मरिचम्भैषजानि च।
दत्वा निरुजतां याति आतुरायौषधानि च॥ 6:174॥

आतुरं निरुजं कुर्यादायुष्मान्निरुजो भवेत्।
मधुराम्लानि तिक्तानि कषायलवणानि च॥ 6:175॥

सर्वक्रीडारसाभिज्ञो विद्वाञ्जायेत मानवः।
तैलात्प्राणा घृतात्तेज आयुः शर्करखण्डयोः॥ 6:176॥

मर्जिता तक्रदानेन गवाढ्यो गोप्रपूजनात्।
मौक्तिकं शङ्खशुक्तीनि दत्वा बहुसुतो भवेत्॥ 6:177॥

6:169 घटितोपस्करं लोहं] E_N; घटितोपस्कर लोह A; घटितोंपस्करं लोड्गं C **6:170** लोहीपाकश्च नरको] AC; लोहीपाके ऽथ नरके E_N **6:170** मृन्मयानि] AC; मृण्मयानि E_N **6:170** चैव] CE_N; नैव A **6:171** श्रेष्ठं] C; श्रेष्ठ A; प्रोक्तं E_N **6:171** तु सुखभाग्भवेत्] A; सुखमवाप्नुयात् CE_N **6:171** रजतं ताम्रं भाण्डमायससीसकम्] CE_N; रजत --- सीसकं A **6:172** दानं] CE_N; दान A **6:173** लभन्ते महाभोगान्] *em.*; लभन्ते महाभोगा A; लभन्ति महाभोगान् CE_N **6:173** °वृताः] C; °वृता A; °कुलाः E_N **6:173** सिन्धूत्थं लवणं] *em.*; सिंधूथ लवणन् A; सिन्धूच्छं लवनं C; सिंधूथ लवणान् **6:173** दत्वा रूपवान्] C; दत्वा रूपवा A; दद्याद् रूपवान् E_N **6:174** पिप्पलीं] C; पिप्पली AE_N **6:174** शृङ्गवेरञ्च मरिचम्भैषजानि] C; शृङ्गवेरञ्च मरिच ⏑̱ --- A; शृङ्गवेरश्च मरिचं भेषजानि E_N **6:174** निरुजतां] AC; नीरुजतां E_N **6:175** निरुजं] AC; नीरुजं E_N **6:175** कुर्यादायुष्मान्] *conj.*; कुर्या आयुंष्मां A; कृत्वा आष्मान् CE_N **6:175** निरुजो] CE_N; निरुजा A **6:175** तिक्तानि] AC; तिक्तानी E_N **6:176** जायेत] AC; जाये त E_N **6:176** तैलात्प्राणा घृतात्तेज] C; तैलात्प्राणमिक्ष्योस्तेज A; तैलात् प्राणान् धनात्तेज E_N **6:176** आयुः] CE_N; आयु A **6:177** मर्जिता] C; अजिता E_N **6:177** गोप्रपूजनात्] C; गो प्रपूजनात् E_N **6:177** मौक्तिकं] AC; मौक्रिकं E_N

कपर्दकानि यो दद्याद्दर्प्पणं निर्मलं तथा।
रूपवान्धनसम्पन्नो जायते स्त्रीषु वल्लभः॥ 6:178॥

पोषणं हन्तकारञ्च भिक्षां वा प्रत्यहं क्षिपेत्।
धनिनस्ते प्रजायन्ति अन्यथा दुर्ग्गतिं व्रजेत्॥ 6:179॥

एष दानविधिः ख्यातो ह्यन्नदानञ्च मे शृणु।
अन्नपानं सदा दद्याद्वस्त्रं शय्यां प्रतिश्रयम्॥ 6:180॥

गां सुवर्ण्णन्तथा भूमिं धर्मेण किमतः परम्।
विद्यादानं परं श्रेष्ठमतिश्रेष्ठञ्च रक्षणम्॥ 6:181॥

जीवं रक्षति यो नित्यं स दाता परमः स्मृतः।
सर्वेषामेव दानानां भूतेष्वभयदक्षिणाम्॥ 6:182॥

यो ददाति स दाता हि ये चान्ये काममोहिताः।
तस्माद्रक्षन्ति सत्वानि प्राणिनाञ्जीवितात्यये॥ 6:183॥

स च दाता तपस्वी च स याति परमं पदम्।
इति दानविधिश्चोक्तो लोकानां हितकाम्यया॥ 6:184॥

दिने दिने च यद्दानं तच्चापि हि निबोध मे।
दन्तधावनताम्बूलं स्रग्धूपञ्च विलेपनम्॥ 6:185॥

6:178 निर्मलं तथा] A; निर्मलन्तथा CE$_N$ **6:178** रूपवान्] CE$_N$; रूपवांन् A **6:178** स्त्रीषु वल्लभः] C; स्त्रीषु वलभः A; स्त्रीषुबल्लभः E$_N$ **6:179** हन्तकारञ्च भिक्षां] CE$_N$; हतकिंचैव भिक्ष A **6:179** धनिनस्ते प्रजायन्ति अन्यथा दुर्ग्गतिं व्रजेत्] A; प्रजायते स धनवानन्यथा दुर्ग्गतिं लभेत् C; प्रजायते स धनवानन्यथा दुर्गति लभेत् E$_N$ **6:180** ह्यन्नदानञ्च] CE$_N$; अन्नदा --- A **6:180** मे शृणु] CE$_N$; --- A **6:180** अन्नपानं] C; अंनपाने A; अन्नदानं E$_N$ **6:180** वस्त्रं शय्यां प्रतिश्रयम्] *em.*; वस्त्र शय्या प्रतिश्रयं A; वस्त्रं शय्या प्रतिश्रयम् C; वस्त्रं शय्यां प्रतिश्रयं E$_N$ **6:181** सुवर्ण्णन्तथा] AE$_N$; सुवर्ण्णत्तथा C **6:181** भूमिं धर्मेण] E$_N$; भूमिं धर्म्मेण A; भूमिं धर्मेणं A **6:181** परं] CE$_N$; पर A **6:181** श्रेष्ठमति] AC; श्रेष्ठं अति° E$_N$ **6:181** रक्षणम्] AC; लक्षणं E$_N$ **6:182** यो नित्यं] C; यो नित्य A; योनित्यं E$_N$ **6:182** परमः स्मृतः] AC; परमःस्मृतः E$_N$ **6:182** भूतेष्वभयदक्षिणाम्] AC; भूतेष्व भयदक्षिणम् E$_N$ **6:183** चान्ये काममोहिताः] CE$_N$; --- ताः A **6:183** तस्माद्रक्षन्ति सत्वानि प्राणिनाञ्जीवितात्यये] E$_N$; तस्माद्रक्षन्ति सत्वानि प्राणिनां जीवतात्यये C; तस्माद्रक्षन्ति सत्वा हि प्राणिनो जीवितान्यये A **6:184** परमं पदम्] A; परमां गतिम् CE$_N$ **6:184** °चोक्तो] CE$_N$; °चोक्त A **6:185** दानं तच्चापि] CE$_N$; दान तचापि A **6:185** निबोध] AC; निवोध E$_N$ **6:185** दन्तधावनताम्बूलं] *conj.*; दन्तधावनतांबूल° AE$_N$; द्रण्तधावनताम्बूलं C **6:185** स्रग्धूपञ्च विलेपनम्] A; श्रग्धूपञ्च विलेपनम् C; स्रग्धूपश्च विलेपनम् E$_N$

रोचनाञ्जनवस्त्राणि दिव्यालंकारमण्डनम्।
गजाश्वारोहणं यानमभ्यङ्गोद्वर्तनन्तथा॥ 6:186॥

स्नानं दिव्यसुगन्धैश्च चन्दनागरुकुंकुमैः।
कर्पूरव्यतिमिश्रैश्च लेपं धूपं सपुष्पकम्॥ 6:187॥

मृष्टान्नपानदानानि सुखशय्यानिषीदनम्।
वरनारीरतिसुखं यो ददाति स चाश्नुते।
अदत्त्वा यो ऽभिकांक्षेत स च दुःखी परो भवेत्॥ 6:188॥

देव्युवाच।
किन्तत्पात्रं भवेच्छ्रेयं यस्य दत्तम्महत्फलम्।
अक्षयञ्च भवेद्दानं तन्मे ब्रूहि महेश्वर॥ 6:189॥

ईश्वर उवाच।
मातापितृषु यद्दानं दीनान्धकृपणेषु च।
गुरुबन्धुषु कन्यासु तदनन्त्याय कल्प्यते॥ 6:190॥

मूर्खविप्रसहस्राणां वेदाध्यायी वरः स्मृतः।
वेदाध्यायिसहस्राणामाहिताग्निस्ततो ऽधिकः॥ 6:191॥

आहिताग्निसहस्राणां ब्रह्मवेत्ता ततो ऽधिकः।
तस्मै दत्तं भवेद्दत्तं स वै त्राता वरः स्मृतः॥ 6:192॥

अन्येषां कोटिगुणितं दद्यादेकं तु ज्ञानिने।

6:186 रोचनाञ्जनवस्त्राणि] AC; लोचनाञ्जनवस्त्राणि E_N **6:186** दिव्यालंकारमण्ड°] CE_N; --- A **6:186** गजाश्वारोहणं] A; गजाश्वारोहनं C; गजाश्वारोहनं° E_N **6:186** यानमभ्यङ्गोद्वर्तनन्तथा] CE_N; यानमम्वङ्गोद्वर्त्तनन्तथा A **6:187** °गरुकुंकुमैः] AC; °गुरुकुंकुमैः E_N **6:187** कर्पूरव्यतिमिश्रैश्च] A; कर्पूरव्यतिमिश्रेण CE_N **6:187** लेपं धूपं सपुष्पकम्] C; लेप धूप सपुष्पकम् A; लेपधूपं सपुष्पकं E_N **6:188** मृष्टान्नपानदानानि] CE_N; मृष्टानपानदानानि A **6:188** सुखशय्यानिषीदनम्] CE_N; सुखशय्यानिसीदत A **6:188** °सुखं] AC; °सौख्यं E_N **6:188** स चाश्नुते] AC; सचाश्नुते E_N **6:188** यो ऽभिकांक्षेत स च दुःखी] C; यो --- A; यो ऽभिकांक्षेत सच दुःखी E_N **6:188** परो भवेत्] A; परोदये CE_N **6:189** भवेच्छ्रेयं] *em.*; भवे श्रेयं A; भवेच्छ्रेष्टं C; भवेच्छेष्ठं E_N **6:189** अक्षयञ्च भवेद्दानं] CE_N; अक्षञ्च भवे दाने A **6:189** तन्मे ब्रूहि महेश्वर] E_N; तत् मे ब्रूहि महेश्वर C; तत् मे ब्रूहि महेश्वरः A **6:190** दीनान्धकृपणेषु च] CE_N; दीना ⏑̱ --- A **6:190** गुरुबन्धुषु कन्यासु तदनन्त्याय] C; --- धुषु कन्यासु तदनंन्याय A; गुरुबन्धुषु कन्यासु तदानन्त्याय E_N **6:190** कल्प्यते] AC; कल्पते E_N **6:191** वरः] AC; परः E_N **6:191** °स्राणामाहिता°] CE_N; °स्राणांमाहिता° A **6:192** ब्रह्मवेत्ता] C; ब्रह्मवेता A; व्रह्मवेत्ता E_N **6:192** वरः] A; परः CE_N **6:193** अन्येषां] CE_N; अन्येषा A **6:193** कोटिगुणितं] *em.*; कोटि --- A; लक्षगुणितं CE_N **6:193** दद्यादेकं तु] CE_N; --- A

न तेषां तुल्यमेवं हि स वै त्राता परो वरः॥ 6:193॥

यद्दानशक्त्या दुःखानि नरकप्रेतजान्यपि।
अन्यानि च सुघोराणि न भवन्तीह दातरि॥ 6:194॥

पापकर्मा यदा कश्चिद्दातुं नोत्सहते मनः।
अपात्रं मन्यते पात्रं तस्य पापस्य तत्फलम्।
धर्माक्षेपेण दुष्टानां सञ्चयं पापलक्षणम्॥ 6:195॥

॥ ⊗॥ इति शिवधर्म्मसंग्रहे षष्ठो ऽध्यायः॥ ⊗॥

6:193 न तेषां तुल्यमेवं हि स वै] A; न तेषा तुल्यमेव हि स वै C; न तेषान्तुल्यमेवं हि सबै E_N **6:194** यद्दान°] CE_N; यदान° A **6:194** नरकप्रेतजान्यपि] CE_N; नरकः प्रेत्यजान्यपि A **6:194** च] CE_N; चा A **6:194** दातरि] CE_N; दातरिम् A **6:195** तस्य पापस्य तत्फलम्] C; तस्य पापस्य त --- A; न भवेत्तस्य तत्फलम् E_N **6:195** धर्माक्षेपेण दुष्टानां सञ्चयं] C; धर्मक्षेयेण दुष्टानां सञ्चयः E_N **6:195** इति शिवधर्म्मसंग्रहे षष्ठो ऽध्यायः] CE_N; इति शिवधर्म्मसंग्रहे दानधर्मो नामाध्यायः षष्टपटलः A

शिवधर्मसंग्रहे सप्तमोऽध्यायः॥

देव्युवाच।

दानधर्मस्त्वया ख्यातस्तीर्थधर्मञ्च मे वद।
स्नाने पुण्यफलं किं स्यात्तीर्थे तीर्थे सुरेश्वर॥ 7:1॥

ईश्वर उवाच।
गंगा सरस्वती पुण्या यमुना गोमती तथा।
चर्मिला चन्द्रभागा च सरयूर्गण्डकी तथा॥ 7:2॥

जम्बूका च शतद्रू च कालिका सुप्रभा तथा।
वितस्ती च विपाशा च नर्मदा च पुनःपुना॥ 7:3॥

गोदावरी महावर्त्ता शर्करावर्त्तमर्जुनी।
कावेरी कौशिकी चैव तृतीया च महानदी॥ 7:4॥

वटङ्का प्रतिकूला च सोमनन्दा च विश्रुता।
करतोया वेत्रवती रेणुका वेणुका च या॥ 7:5॥

7:0 देव्युवाच] A; पार्वत्युवाच CE$_N$ **7:1** धर्मस्त्वया] C; धर्म्म त्वया A; हर्म्मस्त्वयं E$_N$ **7:1** वद] AE$_N$; वदः C **7:1** स्नाने] CE$_N$; स्वीन॰ A **7:1** सुरेश्वर] C; सुरेश्वरः AE$_N$ **7:2** सरस्वती] AE$_N$; श्वरस्वती C **7:2** गोमती तथा] C; गोम --- A; गोमती हिमा E$_N$ **7:2** चर्मिला] C; --- A; चर्मिरा E$_N$ **7:2** चन्द्रभागा च] E$_N$; --- सू ⏓ पुण्या A; चन्दभागा च C **7:2** सरयूर्गण्डकी] *em.*; सरयू गण्डकी ACE$_N$ **7:2** तथा] AC; तिला E$_N$ **7:3** च शतद्रू च] AC; च शतद्रु च E$_N$ **7:3** कालिका सुप्रभा तथा] AC; कास्तिका शारदा जवा E$_N$ **7:3** पुनःपुना] *conj.*; कूलं पुनः A; कुलम्पुनः C; मालिका सिता E$_N$ **7:4** गोदावरी महावर्त्ता शर्करावर्त्तसर्जनी] AE$_N$; गो ⏓ ⏓ ⏓ ⏓ ⏓ ⏓ ⏓ शर्करावर्तसर्जुनी C **7:4** कावेरी] *em.*; कावीरी A; कोवेरी C; कौबेरी E$_N$ **7:4** चैव तृतीया च महानदी] A; चैव तृतीया च महोनदी C; वृद्धा मार्कण्डेयी महानदी E$_N$ **7:5** सोमनन्दा च विश्रुता] C; सोम --- A; सोमनन्दा त्रिशूलिका E$_N$ **7:5** रेणुका] A; धेनुका CE$_N$ **7:5** च या] A; च ⊔ C; प्रभा E$_N$

आत्रेयगंगा वैतरणी कौशिकी ह्लादनी च या।
स्रावनी च सवर्णा सा कल्माषस्रंसनी शुभा॥ 7:6॥

वशिष्ठा च अपापा च सिन्धुवत्यारुणी तथा।
ताम्रा चैव त्रिसन्ध्या च मन्दाकिन्यः पराः स्मृताः॥ 7:7॥

वाग्वती तैलकोशी च दुन्दुभी नलिनी तथा।
नीलगंगा च बोधा च पूर्णचन्द्रा शशिप्रभा॥ 7:8॥

उपवासरतस्तासु यः स्नायाद्धि सरित्स्विह।
समभ्यर्च्य पितॄन्देवान्स तु मुच्येत किल्बिषात्॥ 7:9॥

नद्येषा पूतसलिला हरमूर्तिरियं स्मृता।
स्नातो यैस्तु विशुद्ध्येत जलमूर्ति नमो ऽस्तु ते॥ 7:10॥

इमं मन्त्रमनुस्मृत्य कुर्यान्नद्यवगाहनम्।
सर्वपापविशुद्धात्मा देहत्यागे दिवं ययौ॥ 7:11॥

शोणपुष्करलोहित्ये मानसे सिन्धुसागरे।
ब्रह्मावर्ते कर्द्दमाले स्नात्वा च लवणोदधौ॥ 7:12॥

सर्वपापविशुद्धात्मा पितृदेवांश्च पूजयेत्।

7:6 कौशिकी ह्लादनी च या] AC; ह्लादिनी स्रावनी शिवा E_N **7:6** स्रावनी च] AC; मात्स्येन्द्री च E_N **7:6** सवर्णा सा] Cf. *Niśvāsamukha* 3.6c; सवास्रावां A; सचानासाC; सवानासा E_N **7:6** कल्माषस्रंसनी शुभा] A; ⊔ श्रंसनी शुभा C; कल्माषा कमला ऽमला E_N **7:7** वसिष्ठा च अपापा च] A; ⊔ स्ठा च अपापा च C; अपापा च वशिष्ठा च E_N **7:7** सिन्धुवत्यारुणी] CE_N; सिन्धवत्यारुणी A **7:7** ताम्रा चैव त्रिसन्ध्या च] C; ताम्रा चैव तृसांध्या च A; सीता तापी त्रिसन्ध्या च E_N **7:7** मन्दाकिन्यः पराः स्मृताः स्मृताः] A; मन्दाकिन्य परा स्मृता C; मन्दाकिन्यमरावती E_N **7:8** वाग्वती तैलकौशी च दुन्दुभी] Cतै वाग्वती --- भी A; वाग्वती तैल कौशीक्षुरिन्द्राणी E_N **7:8** नलिनी तथा] E_N; नलिन तथा A; नलना तथा C **7:8** बोधा] AC; वोधा E_N **7:9** उपवासरतस्तासु] C; उपवासरतस्त्वेष A; उपवासरतस्त्वासु E_N **7:9** यः स्नायाद्धि सरित्स्विह] C; य स्नायाद्धि सरित्विहः A; यः स्नायद्धिसरित्स्विह E_N **7:9** समभ्यर्च्य पितॄन्देवान्] *conj.*; समभ्यर्च्य पितृं देवा A; पितॄन् देवान् समभ्यर्च्य C; पितृदेवान् समभ्यर्च्य E_N **7:10** स्मृता] CE_N; स्मृताः A **7:10** यैस्तु] AC; यस्तु E_N **7:10** नमो ऽस्तु ते] C; नमो --- A; नमो ऽस्तुते E_N **7:11** इमं मन्त्रमनुस्मृत्य] C; --- मनुस्मृत्य A; इदं मन्त्रमनुस्मृत्य E_N **7:11** देहत्यागे दिवं ययौ] AC; देहत्यागे दिवं व्रजेत् E_N **7:12** शोणपुष्करलोहित्ये] *em.*; षोणपुष्करलोहित्ये A; शोनपुष्करलोहित्ये C; शोणपुष्कर लौहित्ये E_N **7:12** लवणोदधौ] CE_N; लणोदधौ A **7:13** °विशुद्धात्मा] AC; विशुद्धातृमा E_N **7:13** पितृदेवांश्च] *em.*; पितृदेवाश्च A; ⊔ श्च C; पितृदेवांश्च E_N

अग्निर्योनिर्विष्णु रेता ब्रह्मणः पिता रुद्रमूर्तिरापः॥ 7:13॥

एताननुस्मृत्य यः स्नायात्स याति परमां गतिम्।
नदीनदेषु यो देहं कामतो वाप्यकामतः॥ 7:14॥

समुत्सृज्य विशुद्धात्मा सोमलोकमियान्नरः।
चन्द्रकान्तिविमानेन सोमकन्याभिरावृतः॥ 7:15॥

सुरूपः सोमवत्सौम्यो विचरेत्स यथासुखम्।
सोमलोकात्परिभ्रष्टो जायते विपुले कुले॥ 7:16॥

तत्तीर्थं संस्मरेन्नित्यं मरणं चात्र कांक्षते।
अमरेशं प्रभासञ्च नैमिषं पुष्करन्तथा॥ 7:17॥

आषाढिं दिण्डिमुण्डिञ्च भारभूतिञ्च लाकुलिम्।
हरिश्चन्द्रं परं गुह्यं गुह्यं मध्यमकेश्वरम्॥ 7:18॥

श्रीपर्वतं समाख्यातं जल्पेश्वरमतः परम्।
आम्रातिकेश्वरञ्चैव महाकालन्तथैव च॥ 7:19॥

केदारमुत्तमं गुह्यं महारौरवमेव च।
गयां चैव कुरुक्षेत्रं नखलं कनखलं तथा॥ 7:20॥

विमलञ्चाट्टहासञ्च माहेन्द्रं भीममष्टमम्।

7:13 अग्निर्योनिर्विष्णु रेता] C; अग्नियोनि --- A; अग्निर्योनिर्विष्णुरेतो E_N **7:13** ब्रह्मणः] C; --- A; ब्रह्म E_N **7:14** एताननुस्मृत्य] C (unmetrical); एतामनुस्मृत्य A; एताः संत्स्मृत्य E_N **7:14** यः स्नायात्स] *em.*; यः स्नात्वा A; यो स्नाया स E_N **7:14** परमां गतिं] E_N; परमं पदम् AC **7:15** सोमलोकमियान्नरः] A; सोमलोकं स गच्छति CE_N **7:15** चन्द्रकान्तिविमानेन] A; ⏑⏑ कान्तिविमानेन C; चन्द्रकान्ति विमानेन E_N **7:16** सोमवत्सौम्यो] *em.*; --- A; सामेसाम्यमा ⏑ (?) C; सोमबत्सौम्यो E_N **7:16** विचरेत्स] CE_N; --- ⏑ ⏑ A **7:16** सोमलोकात्परिभ्रष्टो] A; सोमलोकपरिभ्रष्टो CE_N **7:17** संस्मरेन्नित्यं] CE_N; संस्मरे नित्यं A **7:17** मरणं चात्र] AC; मरणंचात्र E_N **7:17** कांक्षते] E_N; काक्षते AC **7:17** अमरेशं] CE_N; अमरेश्वरं A (unmetrical) **7:18** आषाढिं] CE_N; अषढि A **7:18** लाकुलिम्] CE_N; लांगुलिम् A **7:18** हरिश्चन्द्रं परं] CE_N; हरिश्चन्द्रपरं A **7:18** गुह्यं मध्यमकेश्वरम्] A; गुह्यं मध्यमकेश्वर C; गुह्यमध्यमकेश्वरं E_N **7:19** श्रीपर्वतं समाख्यातं] E_N; श्रीप --- A; ⊔ तं समाख्यातं C **7:19** जल्पेश्वरमतः परम्] CE_N; --- परम् A **7:19** आम्रातिकेश्वरञ्चैव] AC; आम्रातकेश्वरश्चैव E_N **7:19** तथैव च] A; तथापि वा C; अथापि वा E_N **7:20** केदारमुत्तमं] AC; केदारं पशुपं E_N **7:20** महारौरवमेव] AC; महाभैरवमेव E_N **7:20** गयां चैव] AC; गयां भीमं E_N **7:21** माहेन्द्रं] CE_N; माहेन्द्र A

छगलण्डन्द्विरण्डञ्च माकोटं मण्डलेश्वरम्॥ 7:21॥

भस्त्रापदं रुद्रकोटिमविमुक्तं महालयम्।
गोकर्ण्णं भद्रकर्ण्णञ्च स्वर्णाक्षं स्थाणुमष्टमम्॥ 7:22॥

स्नानदर्शनपूजाभिर्मुच्यते सर्वकिल्बिषैः।
गच्छन्ति भित्वा ब्रह्माण्डमेषु स्थानेषु ये मृताः॥ 7:23॥

पञ्चाष्टकपदं दिव्यं यं गत्वा न निवर्तते।
प्रलयस्थायिनो दिव्याः स्थित्यनुग्रहकारिणः॥ 7:24॥

दर्शनादेव गच्छन्ति पदं दिव्यं महालये।
केदारोदकपानाच्च गतिः पञ्चाष्टकी ध्रुवा॥ 7:25॥

विद्यया संयुता ये तु पिबन्ति च शुभं जलम्।
शिवसायोज्यतां यान्ति सर्वावस्थाश्च मानवाः॥ 7:26॥

गुह्यायतनमीशस्य मुच्यते वीक्ष्य किल्बिषैः।
प्राप्नुवन्ति गणत्वं हि ये तत्र निधनङ्गताः॥ 7:27॥

स्थानेष्वेतेषु मनुजः कुर्यादनशनं व्रतम्।
अलाभे ऽन्यत्र वा कुर्यात्स्वयंभूर्यत्र शङ्करः॥ 7:28॥

देव्युवाच।
प्रब्रूह्यनशनस्यापि विधिं सम्यग्महेश्वर।

7:21 छगलण्डन्द्विरण्डञ्च] A; छगलण्ड ⊔ ⏑ C; छगलाण्डधिरण्डञ्च E_N **7:21** माकोटं] E_N; मकोतम् A; ⏑ कोटं C **7:22** भस्त्रापदं] AC; भद्रपदं E_N **7:22** रुद्रकोटिमविमुक्तं महालयम्] CE_N; रुद्रको --- A **7:22** गोकर्ण्णं भद्रकर्ण्णञ्च] CE_N; --- ञ्च A **7:22** स्वर्णाक्षं स्थाणुमष्टमम्] AC; स्वणाख्यं वैद्यनाथकं E_N **7:23** पूजाभिर्मुच्यते] AE_N; पूजाभिम्मुच्यते C **7:23** °किल्बिषैः] AC; °किल्विषैः E_N **7:23** भित्वा] CE_N; हित्वा A **7:24** पञ्चाष्टकपदं] AC; पञ्चाष्टक (शैलबान्) पदं E_N **7:24** दिव्यं] CE_N; दिव्य A **7:24** प्रलयस्थायिनो दिव्या] AC; प्रलये स्थापिता दिव्याः E_N **7:24** स्थित्यनुग्रहकारिणः] AC; क्षित्यनुग्रहकारिणा E_N **7:25** दिव्यं महालये] CE_N; दि --- A **7:25** केदारोदकपानाच्च] C; --- रोदकपानाच A; के परोदक्षपालाच्च E_N **7:25** ध्रुवा] C; ध्रुवाः A; ध्रुवं E_N **7:26** शुभं] CE_N; शुभ A **7:26** शिवसायोज्यतां] C; शिवसायुज्यतां AE_N **7:26** यान्ति] CE_N; याति A **7:26** सर्वावस्थाश्च मानवाः] C; सर्वावस्था च मानवाः A; सर्वावस्थाश्च मानवांः E_N **7:27** किल्बिषैः] AC; किल्विषैः E_N **7:27** तत्र] CE_N; तत्तृ A **7:28** मनुजः] CE_N; मनुज A **7:28** अनशनं] AE_N; अनशन° म्स्छ् **7:28** व्रतम्] C; --- A; व्रतंः E_N **7:28** अलाभे ऽन्यत्र] CE_N; --- A **7:28** स्वयंभूर्यत्र] C; स्वयम्भू यत्र A; स्वयंम्भूर्यत्र E_N **7:29** विधिं] CE_N; विधि A **7:29** सम्यग्महेश्वर] C; सम्यग्महेश्वरः A; सम्यङ्महेश्वर E_N

किं वास्य फलमुद्दिष्टं तच्च कीदृक्तपः स्मृतम्॥ 7:29॥

ईश्वर उवाच।
स्वपद्भ्यामेव गन्तव्यं यथोक्तविधिमिच्छता।
अनिवर्तकयोगेन संपूज्य द्विजदेवताम्॥ 7:30॥

द्वात्रिंशत्पिण्डमश्नीयाद्धविष्यं प्रथमे ऽहनि।
एकैकं ह्रासयेत्पिण्डं यावन्निरशनान्तिकम्॥ 7:31॥

पूजयेत्परमेशानं त्रिस्नायी जपतत्परः।
तमेव संस्मरन् विद्वांस्त्यजेत्प्राणान्यतात्मवान्॥ 7:32॥

न केदारसमं तोयन्नाश्वमेधसमः क्रतुः।
न च शैवसमं शास्त्रं न तपो ऽनशनात्परम्॥ 7:33॥

नश्यन्त्यनशनेनाशु पापानि सुतराण्यपि।
रविरश्मिनिपातेन हिमानीव वरानने॥ 7:34॥

सन्यस्तो ऽस्मीति यो ब्रूयात्प्राणैः कण्ठगतैरपि।
न तत्र यान्ति यज्वानो यत्रैत्यनशनी जनः॥ 7:35॥

यदह्ना सुसमारभ्य करोत्यनशनं नरः।
स्वर्गे मणिपुरन्तस्य तदह्नादेव जायते॥ 7:36॥

हैमं विमानं संगृह्य गन्धर्वाप्सरसां गणाः।
एकचित्ताः प्रतीक्षन्ते स्वामिनं सेवका इव॥ 7:37॥

7:29 किं वास्य] AC; किञ्चास्य E_N **7:29** फलमुद्दिष्टं] AE_N; फलद्दिष्टं C (unmetrical) **7:29** तच्च] CE_N; तच A **7:29** तपः स्मृतम्] C; तपः स्मृतः A; त्वया स्मृतं E_N **7:30** ईश्वर] A; महेश्वर CE_N **7:30** स्वपद्भ्यामेव गन्तव्यं] E_N; सपद्भ्यामेव गन्तव्य A; स्वपद्भ्यामेव गन्तंव्यं C **7:30** °योगेन] CE_N; °योगे च A **7:30** द्विजदेवताम्] A; द्विजदेवताः C; स्वेष्टदेवतां E_N **7:31** द्वात्रिंशत्पिण्डमश्नीयाद्धविष्यं] CE_N; द्वात्रिंश --- विस्य (?) A **7:31** यावन्निरशनान्तिकम्] CE_N; यावनिरशनान्तिकम् A **7:32** त्रिस्नायी] C; तृस्नायी A; त्रिःस्नायी E_N **7:32** तमेव] AC; तमेवं E_N **7:32** संस्मरन्] C; सस्मरेद् A; संस्मरेद् E_N **7:32** विद्वांस्त्यजेत्] E_N; विद्वांत्यजेत् A; विद्वां त्यजेत् C **7:32** प्राणान्] CE_N; प्राणन् A **7:33** केदारसमं] CE_N; केदारसंम A **7:33** °समः क्रतुः] CE_N; °सम क्रतुः A **7:34** नश्यन्त्यनशनेनाशु] CE_N; --- शनेनाशुः A **7:35** सन्यस्तो ऽस्मीति] AC; सत्यस्थो ऽस्मीति **7:35** प्राणैः] E_N; प्राणः A; प्राणेः C **7:35** जनः] CE_N; जनाः A **7:36** यदह्ना] AC; यदन्हात् E_N **7:36** तदह्नादेव] AC; तदन्हादेव E_N **7:37** हैमं विमानं संगृह्य] C; --- ⏑̄ A; हंसविमानं सङ्गृह्य E_N **7:37** गन्धर्वाप्सरसां गणाः] CE_N; गन्धवाप्सरसां गणाः A **7:37** एकचित्ताः] CE_N; एकचिताः A

दिवि सप्तसहस्राणि वर्षाण्यप्सु मृतो भवेत्।
दश वह्निप्रवेशेषु पतनेषु च षोडश॥ 7:38॥

महाप्रस्थानयानेषु सहस्राण्यैकविंशतिः।
चतुःषष्टिसहस्राणि युधि संत्यक्तविग्रहः॥ 7:39॥

अवध्यत्वं पतत्येष जायते विपुले कुले।
मृतो ऽनाशकयोगेन नासौ च्यवति मानवः॥ 7:40॥

उक्तं हरस्य माहात्म्यं हरेश्चापि निबोध मे।
शालग्रामे मल्लकूपे नित्यं सौकरवे हरिः॥ 7:41॥

मथुरायां स्थितः साक्षाच्छ्वेतद्वीपे तथैव च।
तं दृष्ट्वा पुरुषवटे विष्णुम्मुच्येत किल्बिषैः॥ 7:42॥

स्थानेष्वेषु मृतो यायात्तद्विष्णोः परमं पदम्।
ब्रह्मस्कन्दगणेशानां लोकपालग्रहेषु च॥ 7:43॥

उमाया मातृयक्षाणां पिशाचोरगराक्षसाम्।
ये भक्तास्तद्गतिं यान्ति जपहोमार्चनादिभिः॥ 7:44॥

एतत्ते सर्वमाख्यातमुपवासविधिं शृणु।
मासि मासि च यः कुर्यादेकरात्रमुपोषितः॥ 7:45॥

7:38 मृतो भवेत्] CA; मृतोभवेत् E_N **7:38** वह्निप्रवेशेषु] A; वह्निप्रवेशे तु C; वन्हिपवेशे तु E_N **7:39** महाप्रस्थानयानेषु] AC; महाप्रस्थानयानेन E_N **7:39** सहस्राण्यैकविंशतिः] C; सहस्राण्यैकविंशति A; सहस्राण्येकविंशतिः E_N **7:39** चतुःषष्टिसहस्राणि] AC; चतुः षष्टिसहस्राणि E_N **7:39** °विग्रहः] CE_N; °विग्रह --- A **7:40** अवध्यत्वं पतत्येष] C; --- ष A; अवध्यत्वं पतत्येव E_N **7:40** मृतो] AE_N; मृता C **7:40** नाशकयोगेन नासौ] C; नाशनयोगेन नासौ A; नासकयोगेन नासो E_N **7:41** हरेश्चापि] AC; हरश्चापि E_N **7:41** मल्लकूपे] CE_N; मलकूपे A **7:41** सौकरवे हरिः] E_N; सौकरवे हरि A; शौकरवे हरिः C **7:42** मथुरायां स्थितः साक्षाच्छ्वेतद्वीपे तथैव च] C; मृथुराया स्थित सात्क्ष स्वेतद्वीप तथैव च A; मथुरायां स्थितः साक्षाच्छ्रएतद्वीपतथैव च E_N **7:42** मुच्येत किल्बिषैः] AC; मुच्येतकिल्विषैः E_N **7:43** स्थानेष्वेषु] C; --- A; स्थानेष्वेतेषु E_N (unmetrical) **7:43** मृतो यायात् तद्विष्णोः] E_N; --- वि ⏑̱ A; मृता यान्ति तद्विष्णोः C **7:43** ब्रह्मस्कन्दगणेशानां] E_N; ब्रह्मस्कन्दगणेशस्य A; ब्रह्मस्कन्दगनेशानां C **7:43** लोकपालग्रहेषु च] C; लोकपालग्रहस्य च A; लोकपालगृहेषु च E_N **7:44** तद्गतिं] AC; तां गतिं E_N **7:44** जप°] CE_N; जाप° A **7:45** एतत्ते सर्वमाख्यातमुपवासविधिं शृणु] A; एतत्ते सर्वमाख्यातामुपवासविधिं शृणु C; एवन्ते सर्वमाख्यातमुपवासविधिं शृणुः E_N **7:45** यः कुर्यादेकरात्रमुपोषितम्] *em.*; वै (?) कुर्यादेकरात्रमु ⏑̱ ष ⏑̱ A; दाः कुर्यादेकरात्रमुपोषितम् C; यः कुर्यादेकरात्रमुपोषितः E_N

पञ्चगव्यं शुचिर्भूत्वा पीत्वा मुच्येत पातकैः।
त्र्यहं त्र्यहञ्च भुञ्जीत प्रातः सायमयाचितम्॥ 7:46॥

उपवासं त्र्यहं कुर्यात्प्राजापत्यविधिं चरन्।
एकैकञ्च तथैवाद्यात्पिण्डं पिण्डं स संयमी॥ 7:47॥

अतिकृच्छ्रम्भवेदेतदशेषपापनोदनम्।
त्र्यहन्तप्तोदकं पीत्वा तप्तक्षीरं त्र्यहं पिबेत्॥ 7:48॥

त्र्यहं चाज्यं प्रतप्तन्तु वातादो वासरत्रयम्।
तप्तकृच्छ्रं तदुच्येत रेतोमूत्रादिभक्षणे॥ 7:49॥

कथितं देवदेवेन गाढपापविशोधनम्।
त्रिःस्नायी हरयाजी च जपमौनी सुयन्त्रितः॥ 7:50॥

ब्रह्मचारी हविर्भोजी नियमानि समाचरेत्।
अनेनैव विधानेन जितक्रोधो जितेन्द्रियः।
पराकं तु चरेद्विद्वान्द्वादशाहमभोजनम्॥ 7:51॥

गोमूत्रगोमयपयोदधिसर्पिषा च।
दर्भाम्बुना निरशनेन दिनानि सप्त।
पीत्वा पितृभ्य उपपादितदक्षिणान्तम्।
एतद्भवेत्पवनसान्तपनं शिवोक्तम्॥ 7:52॥

एकैकं वर्द्धयेत्पिण्डं शुक्ले कृष्णे च ह्रासयेत्।
त्रिस्नायी मासमेकन्तु चन्द्रवृद्ध्या व्रतञ्चरेत्॥ 7:53॥

चान्द्रायणमिदं श्रेष्ठं सर्वपापापनोदनम्।

7:46 पञ्चगव्यं शुचिर्भूत्वा] CE$_N$; --- ⏑̄ A **7:46** प्रातः सायमयाचितम्] C; प्रात सायमयाचितम् A; प्रातः समय याचितम् E$_N$ **7:47** उपवासं त्र्यहं कुर्यात्] A; उपवास त्र्यंह कुर्यात् C; उपवासं त्रयहं कुर्य्यात् E$_N$ **7:47** प्राजापत्यविधिं चरन्] C; प्रजापत्यविधिञ्चरेत् A; प्राजापत्यविधिञ्चरेत् E$_N$ **7:47** पिण्डं पिण्डं] *em.*; पिण्डं प्रस्त A; पिण्डं C (unmetrical); पिण्डं पिण्ड॰ E$_N$ **7:47** स संयमी] AC; ॰समं यमी E$_N$ **7:48** अशेषपापनोदनम्] AC; अशेषं पापनोदनं E$_N$ **7:48** त्र्यहं पिबेत्] E$_N$; --- A; त्यहं पिबेत् C **7:49** त्र्यहं चाज्यं प्रतप्तन्तु वातादो वासरत्रयम्] CE$_N$; --- वातादो व --- ह A **7:51** द्वादशाहमभोजनम्] CE$_N$; --- A **7:52** गोमूत्र॰] CE$_N$; --- A **7:52** ॰सर्पिषा च] AC; ॰सर्पिषाच E$_N$ **7:52** सप्त] CE$_N$; सप्तः A **7:52** पितृभ्य उपपादितदक्षिणान्तम्] CE$_N$; पवित्र-उपदाद्य सदक्षिणा ते A **7:52** भवेत्] CE$_N$; भवे A **7:53** वर्द्धयेत्] A; वर्द्धयात् C; बह्क्षयेत् (वर्धयेत्) E$_N$ **7:53** चन्द्रवृद्ध्या व्रतञ्चरेत्] AC; चन्द्रवृद्ध्याव्रतञ्चरेत् E$_N$ **7:54** श्रेष्ठं सर्वपापापनोदनम्] CE$_N$; --- A

पापी मुच्येत पापेन अपापी स्वर्ग्गगो भवेत्॥ 7:54॥

अष्टावष्टौ समश्नीयात्पिण्डान्मध्यन्दिने स्थिते।
हविष्येण समायुक्तं मुच्यते सर्वपातकैः॥ 7:55॥

अपापी स्वर्ग्गमाप्नोति यतिचान्द्रायणान्नरः।
चतुरो भक्षयेत्पिण्डान्पूर्वाह्ने तु विचक्षणः॥ 7:56॥

सूर्यस्यास्तमने वापि चतुरो भक्षयेत्पुनः।
शिशुचान्द्रायणं ह्येतदुपपातकनाशनम्॥ 7:57॥

मासेनैकेन शुद्धात्मा अपापी स्वर्गतिं व्रजेत्।
त्रिरात्राणि च यः कुर्यात्सर्वकालं शुचिव्रतः॥ 7:58॥

शतेनैकेन पूर्ण्णेन मुच्यते सर्वकिल्बिषैः।
सहस्रेण महापापैर्मुच्यते नात्र संशयः॥ 7:59॥

अपापी स्वर्गमाप्नोति च्युतश्च धनवान्भवेत्।
एकान्तरोपवासन्तु द्वादशाब्दं करोति यः॥ 7:60॥

महतो मुच्यते पापाच्छुद्धात्मा स्वर्गमाप्नुयात्।
पक्षोपवासं यः कुर्याद्द्वादशाब्दं विकल्मषः॥ 7:61॥

स स्वर्गगतिमाप्नोति पापात्मा तु विकल्मषः।
प्रतिवर्षं तु यः कुर्यान्मासैकं संयतेन्द्रियः॥ 7:62॥

उपवासं नरो लोके स गतिञ्चोत्तमां व्रजेत्।

7:54 पापी मुच्येत पापेन] CE$_N$; पा । पेन A **7:55** समश्नीयात्] CE$_N$; समश्नीया A **7:55** मध्यन्दिने स्थिते] A; माध्यंदिने स्थिते C; मध्यन्दिनेस्थिते E$_N$ **7:55** हविष्येण समायुक्तं] AE$_N$; हवि ⏓ ⊔ मायुक्तं C **7:56** यतिचान्द्रायणान्नरः] C; यतिचान्द्रायणं नरः A; यति चान्द्रायणन्नरः E$_N$ **7:56** भक्षयेत्पिण्डान्] CE$_N$; भक्षयेत्पिण्डं A **7:56** पूर्वाह्ने तु] A; पूर्वाह्ने च C; पूर्वाह्लेच E$_N$ **7:57** सूर्यस्यास्तमने वापि चतुरो भक्षयेत्पुनः] CE$_N$; सूर्य --- भ ⏓ येत्पुनः A **7:58** अपापी स्वर्गतिं व्रजेत्] AC; अपापीस्वर्गतिंव्रजेत् E$_N$ **7:58** कुर्यात्] CE$_N$; कुर्या A **7:58** शुचिव्रतः] AC; शुचिब्रतः E$_N$ **7:59** सर्वकिल्बिषैः] AC; सर्वकिल्विषैः E$_N$ **7:59** महापा॰] AC; महत्पा॰ E$_N$ **7:59** संशयः] CE$_N$; --- A **7:60** अपापी स्वर्गमाप्नोति] E$_N$; --- ति A; अपापा स्वर्ग्गमाप्नोति C **7:61** पापाच्छुद्धात्मा] CE$_N$; पापा शुद्धात्मा A **7:61** स्वर्गमाप्नुयात्] AC; योगमाप्नुयात् E$_N$ **7:61** पक्षोपवासं] AE$_N$; पक्षोपवास C **7:61** वादशाब्दं] AE$_N$; वादशाब्दंम् C **7:62** स स्वर्गगतिमाप्नोति पापात्मा तु विकल्मषः] AC; *om.* E$_N$ **7:62** कुर्यान्मासैकं संयतेन्द्रियः] E$_N$; कुर्या --- A; कुर्यात् मासैकं संयतेन्द्रियः C **7:63** उपवासं नरो लोके] C; उपवा ⏓ ⏓ रो लोके A; उपवासं नरोलोके E$_N$

महत्पापं विशुद्ध्येत धनवानपि पूजयेत्॥ 7:63॥

एकाह्नश्चैव भुञ्जानो धनवान्जायते नरः।
यावज्जीवं तु यो भुङ्क्ते नक्तमन्नं नरोत्तमः॥ 7:64॥

धनधान्यसमृद्धः स्यादुत्तमो जायते नरः।
अयाचितं तु भुंजानो यावज्जीवं व्रते नरः॥ 7:65॥

मृते देवत्वमाप्नोति पापान्मुच्येत पातकी।
मधु मांसन्न भक्षेत व्रतमेतदनुत्तमम्॥ 7:66॥

एवं यो वर्त्तते नित्यं स याति परमां गतिम्।
न वीरुधो न वृक्षाग्रान्नाकाशात्पर्वतादपि॥ 7:67॥

मांसं भवति सुश्रोणि शरीरादेव जायते।
परमांसैः स्वमांसानि यो वर्द्धयितुमिच्छति॥ 7:68॥

व्यक्तो ऽसौ राक्षसो ज्ञेयो मांसन्तस्मान्न भक्षयेत्।
ब्रह्मचर्यं व्रतं कष्टं यश्चरेत्स्त्रीसमन्वितः॥ 7:69॥

इहैव मन्त्राः सिध्यन्ते गतिं व्रजति चोत्तमाम्।
द्रव्यस्य विद्यमानस्य निवृत्तिङ्कुरुते तु यः॥ 7:70॥

स महत्फलमाप्नोति तच्चानन्त्यं भविष्यति।
मत्स्या मांसं सुरा सीधु राक्षसान्नमिदं स्मृतम्॥ 7:71॥

तच्छाम्भवेन मोक्तव्यं गतिमिच्छन्महात्मनाम्।

7:64 एकाह्नश्चैव भुञ्जानो] AC; एकान्हे चैव भुञ्जाने E_N **7:64** यावज्जीवं तु] A; यावज्जीवञ्च CE_N **7:64** भुङ्क्ते] AC; भुङ्क्ते E_N **7:65** धनधान्यसमृद्धः स्यादुत्तमो जायते] AC; धनधान्यसमध्दःस्यादुत्तमोजायते E_N **7:65** यावज्जीवं व्रते नरः] C; --- A; यावज्जीवंब्रजेन्नरः E_N **7:66** मृते देवत्वमाप्नोति] CE_N; --- देवत्वमा --- A **7:66** पापान् मुच्येत पातकी] C; ⏑ पान्मुच्येत पातकी A; पापान्मुच्येत पातकैः E_N **7:66** मधु मांसन्न] AC; मधुमांसं न E_N **7:66** एतदनुत्तमम्] AC; एततन्महत्तमं E_N **7:67** नित्यं] AE_N; नित्य C **7:67** स याति] AC; स याति E_N **7:67** वीरुधो] AC; विरुधो E_N **7:67** वृक्षा°] AC; बृक्षा° E_N **7:68** वर्द्धयितुमिच्छति] CE_N; व --- A **7:69** व्यक्तो ऽसौ] CE_N; --- सौ A **7:69** ब्रह्मचर्यं व्रतं] *em.*; ब्रह्मचर्यं व्रत AC; ब्रह्मचर्यव्रतं E_N **7:70** सिध्यन्ते] A; सिध्यन्ति C; सिध्द्यन्ति E_N **7:70** चोत्तमाम्] CE_N; चोत्तमात् A **7:71** तच्चानन्त्यं] *em.*; तच्चानन्त्ये A; तच्च नान्त्यं C; तच्चनान्त्यं E_N **7:71** मत्स्या मांसं सुरा सीधु] A; मांसं मत्स्याः सुरा सीधु C; मांसमत्स्यसुरासिन्धु E_N **7:71** राक्षसान्नमिदं स्मृतम्] CE_N; रा --- A **7:72** तच्छाम्भवेन मोक्तव्यं] AC; तच्छाम्भवे न भोक्तव्यं E_N **7:72** गतिमिच्छन्महात्मनाम्] AC; गतिमिच्छेन्न्महात्मनां E_N

किन्तस्य दुर्लभं लोके यो ऽनुतिष्ठेत सुव्रतम्॥ 7 : 72॥

कुरुध्वं सुव्रतं सम्यग्यदि वाञ्छत सद्गतिम्।
पौर्ण्णमास्याममावास्यां चतुर्द्दश्यष्टमीषु च॥ 7 : 73॥

संक्रान्तौ च युगादौ च विषुवे ऽप्ययने तथा।
यथेप्सया च कर्त्तव्यं ज्येष्ठमध्यमकन्यसम्॥ 7 : 74॥

रुद्रत्वञ्च गणत्वञ्च चक्रवर्त्तित्वमेव च।
आद्यन्तवासरे ज्येष्ठे ब्रह्मचारी निरामिषः॥ 7 : 75॥

एकाहारो जितक्रोधो मध्ये नक्तं प्रकल्पयेत्।
तथैव नक्तहीनं तु मध्यमं समुदाहृतम्॥ 7 : 76॥

आद्यन्तव्रतहीनं तु नक्तन्तदपि मध्यमम्।
नक्तं विना तथैवान्नं कन्यसन्तं विदुर्बुधाः॥ 7 : 77॥

सातत्यमेव कर्त्तव्यं चक्रवर्तित्वकांक्षिणा।
आचार्यस्याग्रतो गन्धैः कृत्वा मण्डलकं शुभम्॥ 7 : 78॥

पुष्पधूपैः समभ्यर्च्य पञ्चाङ्गेन महीं स्पृशेत्।
यद्यदाचार्यवक्त्रेण निष्क्रमत्यक्षरं स्फुटम्।
तत्तदुच्चारयेत्स्पष्टं गृह्णीयाद्व्रतमुत्तमम्॥ 7 : 79॥

देव्युवाच।
नक्षत्रदानं प्रब्रूहि हिताय जगतो विभो।
कस्मिन्कस्मिंश्च नक्षत्रे किं किन्दानं प्रशस्यते॥ 7 : 80॥

7:72 दुर्लभं लोके] AC; दुर्लभंलोके E_N **7:72** यो ऽनुतिष्ठेत सुव्रतम्] A; यो ऽनुतिष्ठति सुव्रतम् C; रातु (अनु) तिष्ठति सुव्रतं E_N **7:73** सुव्रतं] CE_N; सुव्रत A **7:73** वाञ्छत सद्गतिम्] C; वांछति सद्गतिम् A; वाञ्छेत सदग्तिं E_N **7:73** पौर्ण्णमास्याममा°] CE_N; पौर्ण्णमास्यांममा° A **7:73** चतुर्द्दश्यष्टमीषु च] A; चतुर्दश्यष्टमीदिने CE_N **7:74** विषुवे ऽप्ययने] AC; विषुवेष्वययने E_N **7:74** ज्येष्ठमध्यमकन्यसम्] CE_N; ⏓ --- A **7:75** रुद्रत्वञ्च गणत्वञ्च] CE_N; ⏓ द्रत्वञ्च ग ⏓ त्वञ्च A **7:76** मध्ये नक्तं] AC; मध्यनक्तं E_N **7:77** आद्यन्तव्रतहीनं तु] AC; आद्यन्तं व्रतहीनन् E_N (unmetrical) **7:77** कन्यसं तं विदुर्बुधाः] CE_N; कन्यस --- A **7:78** सातत्यमेव कर्तव्यं] CE_N; ⏓ ⏓ ⏓ A **7:78** °कांक्षिणा] AE_N; °कांक्षिणाम् C **7:78** गन्धैः] C; गन्धै A; बन्धैः E_N **7:78** मण्डलकं] CE_N; मण्डलक A **7:79** पुष्पधूपैः] CE_N; पुष्पै धूपै A **7:79** पञ्चाङ्गेन महीं स्पृशेत्] C; पञ्चगेन मही स्पृशं A; पञ्चाङ्गेन महींस्पृशेत् E_N **7:79** °दुच्चारयेत्] CE_N; °दुचारये A **7:79** गृह्णीयाद्] CE_N; गृह्णीया A **7:80** हिताय जगतो विभो] E_N; जग --- A; हिताय गतो विभो C (unmetrical) **7:80** कस्मिन् कस्मिंश्च नक्षत्रे किं किन्दानं प्रशस्यते] CE_N; --- नक्षत्रे --- दान प्रशस्यते A

भगवानुवाच।
पायसं सर्प्पिषाप्लुत्य कृत्तिकासु सदक्षिणम्।
शिवभक्ताय विप्राय दत्वा यान्त्यमरावतीम्॥ 7:81॥

माषाक्षतेन रोहिण्यां शालिभक्तं घृतान्वितम्।
क्षीरपानन्ततः पश्चाद्देयं स्वर्गमभीच्छता॥ 7:82॥

सवत्सां देवि गां दद्यान्नक्षत्रे मृगशीर्षके।
विहाय मानुषं लोकं याति पौरन्दरं पुरम्॥ 7:83॥

सतैलं कृसरं दद्यान्नक्षत्रे रुद्रदैवते।
उपोष्य नरकान्नेति क्षुरधारान्सुदुस्तरान्॥ 7:84॥

दद्यात्पुनर्वसौ पूपां ब्राह्मणाय तपस्विने।
स्वर्ग्गं भुक्त्वा परिभ्रष्टो जायते विपुले कुले॥ 7:85॥

दद्याच्चामीकरं पुष्ये मङ्गक्तायाग्रजन्मने।
अत्यन्धकारे लोके ऽपि भ्राजते सों अशुमानिव॥ 7:86॥

वृषमश्लेषया दद्यात्ताराघटितमेव वा।
अरातीन्दुर्जयान्जित्वा देहपाते सुखी भवेत्॥ 7:87॥

वर्द्धनीतिलपात्राणि यो मघासु प्रयच्छति।
स्वर्ग्गलोकपरिभ्रष्टो गोमान्भवति मानवः॥ 7:88॥

उपोष्य शैवविप्राय शर्करां यः प्रयच्छति।

7:81 सर्प्पिषाप्लुत्य] AC; सर्प्पिषा प्लुत्य E_N **7:81** सदक्षिणम्] C; सदक्षिणः A; सदक्षिणां E_N **7:82** माषाक्षतेन] E_N; मांसाक्षतेन AC **7:82** क्षीरपानन्ततः] CE_N; क्षीरपाणं ततः A **7:82** °मभीच्छता] C; °मभीच्छताम् A; °मभीप्सता E_N **7:83** सवत्सां देवि गां दद्यान्नक्षत्रे मृगशीर्षके] CE_N; स --- क्षेत्रे मृगशीर्षके A **7:83** पौरन्दरं पुरम्] A; पौरं प्रन्दरम् CE_N **7:84** दद्यान्नक्षत्रे] C; दद्या नक्षत्रे A; दद्यान्नक्षत्रे° E_N **7:84** रुद्रदैवते] *em.*; रुद्रदेवते A; शर्वदेवते C; °शर्वदेवते E_N **7:84** क्षुरधारान्] *em.*; क्षुरधारा A; खुरधारान् C; क्षुरधारां E_N **7:84** सुदुस्तरान्] AC; सुदुस्तरां E_N **7:85** पूपां ब्राह्मणाय] A; पूपां ब्रह्मणाय C; धुपंब्राह्मणाय E_N **7:85** विपुले कुले] C; विपु --- A; विपुलेकुले E_N **7:86** दद्याच्चामीकरं पुष्ये मङ्गक्ताया°] CE_N; --- करं पुष्ये भक्ताया° A **7:86** अत्यन्धकारे] CE_N; अन्धकारे A (unmetrical) **7:86** सों अशुमानिव] CE_N; साशुमानिव A **7:87** वृषमश्लेषया] E_N; वृषश्लेषया A (unmetrical); वृषमशेषया C **7:87** ताराघटितमेव] C; ताराघट्टिकमेव A; तारघटितमेव E_N **7:87** अरातीन् दुर्जयान्] CE_N; अरातीं दुर्ज्जया A **7:87** देहपाते] CE_N; देहपातो A **7:88** वर्द्धनीतिलपात्राणि] AC; वर्द्धनीस्तिलपात्राणि E_N **7:88** मघासु] AC; मद्यासु E_N **7:88** गोमान् भवति मानवः] CE_N; --- A **7:89** शैवविप्राय] CE_N; शैव्यविप्राय A **7:89** शर्करां] E_N; शर्क्करा AC

फाल्गुणीषु गुडैः सार्द्धं धनसौभाग्यकांक्षया॥ 7:89॥

नानाव्यंजनसंयुक्तमुत्तरासु घृतान्वितम्।
दद्यात्षष्टिकभक्तन्तु शक्रलोकमवाप्नुयात्॥ 7:90॥

स्रङ्गा (?) प्रदीयते पुम्भिरुत्तरासु सुलोचने।
अत्यद्भुतफलावाप्तिर्भवतीति किमद्भुतम्॥ 7:91॥

उपोष्य करिणां दद्याद्रथं हस्तेन भामिनि।
पिष्टकेन कृतं वापि दत्वा यात्यमरालयम्॥ 7:92॥

रूपिणीं वृषलीन्दद्याच्चित्रायां त्रिदशेश्वरि।
रमते नन्दनवने गन्धर्वाप्सरसावृतः॥ 7:93॥

यद्यदिष्टतमं द्रव्यं स्वातौ दद्यान्नरोत्तमः।
अक्षयान्प्राप्नुयाल्लोकान्दानस्यास्य प्रभावतः॥ 7:94॥

पयस्विनीञ्च गां दद्यादनड्वाहमथापि वा।
शकटं ये प्रयच्छन्ति सधान्यं वाससावृतम्॥ 7:95॥

विशाखायां पितॄन्देवान्प्रीणयंत्यविकल्पितः।
नरकेषु महादुःखं न प्राप्नोति सुलोचने॥ 7:96॥

दद्यात्प्रावरणं वस्त्रं समुपोष्यानुराधया।
तिष्ठेद्युगशतन्देवि शक्रलोके यथेच्छया॥ 7:97॥

ज्येष्ठायां मूलकन्दद्याद्ब्राह्मणेभ्यः सपानकम्।

7:89 फाल्गुणीषु] A; फल्गुणीषु C; फाल्गुनीषु E_N **7:89** गुडैः सार्द्धं] CE_N; गुडै सार्द्ध A **7:90** °संयुक्तमुत्तरासु] *em.*; °संयुक्तंमुत्तरासु A; °सयुक्तमुत्तरासु C; °संयुक्त मुत्तरासु E_N **7:90** दद्यात्षष्टिक°] CE_N; दद्याच्छष्टीक° A **7:91** स्रङ्गा (?) प्रदीयते] A; दद्यात्प्रदीयते C; दद्यात्प्रदीपते E_N **7:91** पुम्भिरुत्तरासु] AC; प्रमिरुचरास E_N **7:91** अत्यद्भुतफला+वा+प्तिर्भवतीति किमद्भुतम्] C; अत्य --- तीति कि --- तं A; अत्यदभु तफलावाप्तिर्मवतीति किमदभुम E_N **7:92** करिणां] AC; करिणं E_N **7:92** यात्यमरालयम्] CE_N; यांत्यमरालयम् A **7:93** दद्याच्चित्रायां] CE_N; दद्या चित्रायां A **7:93** त्रिदशेश्वरि] AC; त्रिदशेश्वरी E_N **7:93** °सरसावृतः] CE_N; °सरसां वृतः A **7:94** दद्यान्नरोत्तमः] CE_N; दद्या नरोत्तमः A **7:94** प्राप्नुयाल्लोकान्] CE_N; प्राप्नुया लोका A **7:95** अनड्वाहमथापि] AC; अनड्वाह मथापि E_N **7:95** शकटं] CE_N; शाकटां A **7:96** पितॄन् देवान्] *em.*; पितॄन् देवा A; पितॄं देवान् C; पितृदेवान् E_N **7:96** प्रीणयंत्यविकल्पितः] A; प्रीणयत्यविकल्पतः CE_N **7:97** दद्यात्प्रावरणं वस्त्रं समुपोष्यानुराधया] C; दद्या --- पोष्यं ⪯ नुराधया A; दद्यात्प्रावरणंवस्त्रं समुपोष्यानुराधया E_N **7:97** यथेच्छया] A; यथेप्सया CE_N **7:98** ब्राह्मणेभ्यः] E_N; ब्राह्मणेभ्य A; ब्रह्मणेभ्यः C

प्रीयन्ते तेन पितरो गच्छेत्स्वर्गमपि ध्रुवम्॥ 7:98॥

दद्यान्मूलफलं मूले ब्राह्मणेभ्यः सदक्षिणम्।
तेनापि पितरस्तृप्ताः स्वर्ग्गं तु प्रविशन्ति ते॥ 7:99॥

पूर्वाषाढासु च दधि प्रदद्यादन्नमेव च।
स्वर्गलोकपरिभ्रष्टो गवाढ्यं कुलमाप्नुयात्॥ 7:100॥

घृतं चैवोदमंथञ्च भूरिशो मधुफाणितम्।
उत्तराषाढविषये सर्वकामविवृद्धये॥ 7:101॥

पायसं चाभिजात्यां तु दद्याद्घृतगुडान्वितम्।
स धर्मपुष्कलं प्राप्य नाकपृष्ठे विराजते॥ 7:102॥

आविकं श्रावणे दद्यात्प्रावारं वस्त्रसंयुतम्।
उपोष्य स्वर्ग्गतिङ्गच्छेच्छ्वेतयानेन मानवः॥ 7:103॥

गोभिर्युक्तन्धनिष्ठासु यानं विप्राय कल्पयेत्।
वस्त्रप्रग्रहसंयुक्तं जायते स नरेश्वरः॥ 7:104॥

छत्रञ्च पादुके गन्धन्दद्यात्सागरुचन्दनम्।
दत्वा शतभिषायोगे स्थानमप्सरसां व्रजेत्॥ 7:105॥

समांसमोदनं दत्वा पूर्वप्रोष्ठपदे प्रिये।
सर्वभक्षफलोपेतं स मृतः सुखभाग्भवेत्॥ 7:106॥

7:98 गच्छेत्] CE$_N$; गच्छे A **7:99** मूलफलं मूले] C^{c}E$_N$; मूलफल मूल A; मूलफलं C^{ac} (unmetrical) **7:99** सदक्षिणम्] AC; सदक्षिणाम् E$_N$ **7:99** तेनापि पितरस्तृप्ताः] AE$_N$; तेनापि तरस्तृप्ताः C (unmetrical) **7:99** स्वर्ग्गं तु प्रविशन्ति ते] CE$_N$; --- ते A **7:100** पूर्वाषाढासु] AE$_N$; पूर्वाशाढासु C **7:100** गवाढ्यं] C; गवाढ्य° A; गवाद्य° E$_N$ **7:101** घृतं] C; घृत A; घृतं° E$_N$ **7:101** चैवोदमंथञ्च] A; चैवोदमन्थनञ्च C; चैवोदमत्थञ्च E$_N$ **7:101** भूरिशो मधुफाणितम्] C; भूरिषो मधुफाणितम् A; भूरिसोमधुफाणितम् E$_N$ **7:101** °विषये] AC; विसये E$_N$ **7:101** सर्वकाम°] AC; सेवाकाम° E$_N$ **7:102** पायसं चाभिजात्यां तु दद्याद्घृतगुडान्वितम्] CE$_N$; पयांस्याभिजितौ दद्या गुडाजेन सन्त ि A **7:102** स धर्मपुष्कलं प्राप्य] *conj.*; --- प्य A; स धर्मपुष्कल प्राप्य C; स धर्म पुष्कलं प्राप्य E$_N$ **7:103** प्रावारं] AC; प्राकरं E$_N$ **7:103** स्वर्ग्गतिङ्ग°] AC; सग्दतिङ्ग° E$_N$ **7:104** गोभिर्युक्तन्] AE$_N$; गोभ्रुक्त° C **7:104** यानं] CE$_N$; यान A **7:104** वस्त्रप्रग्रहसंयुक्तं] AC; वस्त्र प्रग्रहसंयुक्तं E$_N$ **7:105** छत्रञ्च पादुके गन्धन्दद्यात्सागरुचन्दनम्] C; छत्र पादुके गन्ध दद्या सागरुचन्दनं A; छत्रञ्च पादुके गन्धन्दद्यात्सागुरुचन्दनम् E$_N$ **7:105** दत्वा शतभिषायोगे स्थानमप्सरसां] C; द --- सा A; दत्वा शतभिषायोगे स्थानमप्स ⏑̱ सो E$_N$ **7:106** समांसम्] AC; समाषम् E$_N$ **7:106** स मृतः] AC; समृतः E$_N$

दत्त्वा उत्तरयोगेसु मांसं सौरभमोदनम्।
प्रीणन्ति पितरस्तस्य मृतेन तत्फलं भवेत्॥ 7:107॥

धेनुं प्रदद्याद्रेवत्यां कामदोहां सवाससीम्।
सा प्रीणयति दातारं कामैर्बहुभिरुत्तमैः॥ 7:108॥

अश्विन्यामश्वसंयुक्तं रथं दद्याद्द्विजन्मने।
गजवाजिसमाकीर्णन्तेजस्विकुलमाप्नुयात्॥ 7:109॥

शिवभक्ताय विप्राय भरण्यां तिलधेनुकाम्।
कामधेनुमवाप्नोति यमलोके यशस्विनि॥ 7:110॥

देव्युवाच।
कियन्तं किं फलारूढं कस्मिन्पर्वणि पर्वणि।
दानधर्मस्य देवेश ज्ञातुमिच्छामि कृत्स्नशः॥ 7:111॥

भगवानुवाच।
शतमिन्दुक्षये दानं सहस्रं वासरक्षये।
अक्षयं विषुवे ऽप्याहुर्व्यतीपाते तथैव च॥ 7:112॥

युगादौ कोटिदानं स्याद्दशकोट्ययनद्वये।
चन्द्रग्रहे ऽर्बुदं विद्धि सूर्यग्रासे तदक्षयम्॥ 7:113॥

7:107 दत्त्वा उत्तरयोगेसु] A; दद्यादुत्तरयोगेस C; दद्यादुत्तरयोगेन E_N **7:107** मांसं] E_N; मान्स A; मांस C **7:107** सौरभमोदनम्] AC; दध्ना सहौदनं E_N **7:107** प्रीणन्ति पितरस्तस्य] CE_N; प्रीयन्ति पिकरस्तस्य A **7:107** मृतेन तत्फलं] A; मृतेनन्तत्फलं C; अनेतैतत्फलं भवेत् E_N **7:108** रेवत्यां] AE_N; रैवत्यां C **7:108** सा] CE_N; स A **7:108** प्रीणयति] AE_N; प्रीणयदि C **7:108** कामैर्बहुभिरुत्तमैः] CE_N; --- त्तमैः A **7:109** गजवाजिसमाकीर्णन्तेजस्विकुलमाप्नुयात्] A; गजवाजिसमायुक्तं तेजस्विकुलमाप्नुयात् C; गवां वाजिसमायुक्त तेजस्वी कुलमाप्नुयात् E_N **7:110** कामधेनुमवाप्नोति] AC; कामधेनु मवाप्नोति E_N **7:111** कियन्तं किं फलारूढं कस्मिन् पर्वणि पर्वणि] C; कियत्कि यतफलारूढि कस्मिन् धर्वणि पर्वणि A; कियन्त किं फलारुढं कस्मिन् पर्वणि पर्वणि E_N **7:111** दानधर्मस्य देवेश ज्ञातुमिच्छामि कृत्स्नशः] C; दा --- तुमिच्छामि कृत्स्नशः A; दानधर्मस्य देवेश ज्ञातुमिच्छामि कृत्सनशः E_N (unmetrical) **7:112** शतमिन्दुक्षये दानं] C; शतन्मिन्द्रिक्षये A; शतमिन्दुक्षये दान° E_N **7:112** सहस्रं वासरक्षये] A; सहस्रं तु दिनक्षये C; सहस्न्तु दिनक्षये E_N **7:112** अक्षयं विषुवे ऽप्याहुर्व्य] *conj.*; अक्षय विषुव न्याहु व्य° A; अक्षये विषुवे प्राहुर्व्य° E_N **7:112** च] AE_N; हि C **7:113** युगादौ कोटिदानं स्याद्] *em.*; युगादैः कोटिदान स्या A; युगादैः कोटिदान स्याद् E_N **7:113** दशकोट्ययनद्वये] AC; दशकोत्ययनर्द्वये E_N **7:113** चन्द्रग्रहे ऽर्बुदं विद्धि] C; चन्द्रग्रहे ऽबुंध विद्धि A; चन्द्रग्रहेवेदविध्दि E_N **7:113** सूर्यग्रासे तदक्षयम्] A; सूर्यग्रासे तदक्षयत् C; सूर्यग्रासे तक्षयं E_N (unmetrical)

दशकोटिर्भवेद्दानं षडशीतिमुखेषु च।
निखर्वं विष्णुपदयोः स्याद्विगायनयोरपि॥ 7:114॥

देव्युवाच।
केन धर्मविपाकेन नरो जातिस्मरो भवेत्।
एतदिच्छामि विज्ञातुं भगवन्वक्तुमर्हसि॥ 7:115॥

भगवानुवाच।
क्षीरस्य पूर्णममलांबुजरुद्धवक्रम्-
औदुम्बरं सकनकं कलशं यतात्मा।
प्रीतो ऽस्तु सोमतनुरीश इति ब्रुवाण
उद्यत्यनुष्णरुचि कार्तिकपौर्णमास्याम्॥ 7:116॥

सन्तर्पिताय विप्राय दत्वा जातिस्मरो भवेत्।
अथ स्नानविधिं पुण्यं प्रवक्ष्याम्यनुपूर्वशः॥ 7:117॥

यत्कृत्वा देवि पापेभ्यो मुच्यते कर्मणादपि।
नदीं प्राक्स्रवनीङ्गत्वा यः करोति हि सेचनम्॥ 7:118॥

दक्षिणावर्त्तशंखेन तिलाक्षतयुतेन च।
प्रविश्य नाभिमात्राम्बु प्राङ्मुखः शुचिमानसः॥ 7:119॥

शिवं संस्मृत्य मतिमान्सर्वपापैः प्रमुच्यते।
अलाभे दक्षिणावर्त्तशंखस्य शृणु भामिनि॥ 7:120॥

पूर्वोक्तविधिमास्थाय शुक्लवासाः शिवं स्मरेत्।

7:114 दशकोटिर्भवेद्दानं] *conj.*; दशकोटि भवे दानं A; दशकोटि भवेद्दानं C; दशकोटिम्भवेद्दानं E_N **7:114** षडशीतिमुखेषु च] *conj.*; षडाशीति ⏓ --- A; षडाशीतिमुखेसु च C; षडशीतिसुखेषुच E_N **7:114** निखर्वं विष्णुपदयोः] C; --- र्वं विष्णुपदयोः A; निषर्णविष्णुपदयोः E_N **7:115** केन] A; येन CE_N **7:115** भगवन्] CE_N; भगवन A **7:116** °रुद्धवक्रम्] म्साC; °रुध्दवक्र E_N **7:116** सकनकं] CE_N; सकनक A **7:116** सोमतनुरीश इति ब्रुवाण] C; --- वाण A; सोमतनुरीश इतिब्रुवाण E_N **7:116** उद्यत्यनुष्णरुचि कार्तिकपौर्णमास्यां] A; उद्यत्यनुष्णरु चिकार्तिकपुर्णमास्यां C; उद्यत्यनुष्णरुचि कार्तिक पौर्णमास्यां E_N **7:117** अनुपूर्वशः] AC; अनुपूर्वः E_N (unmetrical) **7:118** यत्कृत्वा] AE_N; यं कृत्वा C **7:118** कर्मणादपि] A; तत्क्षणादपि CE_N **7:118** नदीं] E_N; नदी AC **7:118** करोति हि सेचनम्] *em.*; करोति हि षेचनम् A; करोत्यभिषेचनम् CE_N **7:119** °शंखेन] E_N; --- A; संखेन C **7:119** तिलाक्षतयुतेन च] CE_N; --- न च A **7:120** शिवं] CE_N; शिव A **7:120** मतिमान्] E_N; मतिमां CA **7:120** सर्वपापैः प्रमुच्यते] A; स पापैः परिमुच्यते CE_N **7:121** शुक्लवासाः] C; शुक्लवासा A; शुक्लवास E_N **7:121** स्मरेत्] AE_N; स्मरन् C

निच्छिद्रभोजपत्रेण कर्तव्यमभिषेचनम्॥ 7:121॥

पुष्परत्नाम्बुपूर्णेन सो ऽपि निर्मलतां व्रजेत्।
स्नात्वा तीर्थे विपापः स्याद्गोपुच्छोद्धृतवारिणा॥ 7:122॥

प्रस्रावेण च रोहिण्यां श्रद्धया परयान्वितः।
यो धत्ते स्तनतो धारां क्षीरस्य शिरसा नरः॥ 7:123॥

शिवञ्च सुरभीञ्चैव स्मरन्पापैः प्रमुच्यते।
य एवं कुरुते स्नानमिहैव धनवान्भवेत्।
नश्यंत्युपद्रवाः सर्वे परतः स्वर्गमाप्नुयात्॥ 7:124॥

॥ ⊗ ॥ इति शिवधर्मसङ्ग्रहे सप्तमो ऽध्यायः॥ ⊗ ॥

7:121 निच्छिद्रभोजपत्रेण] C; निच्छिद्रयोजपत्रेण A; निश्छिद्राम्भोजपत्रेण E_N **7:121** अभि-षेचनम्] CE_N; अभिसेचनम् A **7:122** पुष्परत्नाम्बुपूर्णेन] C; पुष्प --- A; पुष्परत्नाम्बु पूर्णेषु E_N **7:122** व्रजेत्] AC; ब्रजेत् E_N **7:122** तीर्थे विपापः] AC; तीर्थमपापः **7:122** स्याद्] CE_N; स्या A **7:122** गोपुच्छोद्धृतवारिणा] AC; गोपुच्छो धृतवारिणा E_N **7:123** प्रस्रावेण च रोहिण्यां] *conj.*; प्रस्रावेण च रोहिण्याः C; प्रस्रावेन च रोहिण्या A; प्रस्रवेण च रोहिण्याः E_N **7:123** श्रद्धया परयान्वितः] C; प्रश्रया परियान्वितः A; श्रध्दया परयान्वितः E_N **7:123** यो धत्ते] C; ये धत्ते A; योधत्ते E_N **7:123** धारां] CE_N; धारा A **7:124** सु-रभीञ्चैव स्मरन्] C; सुरभि चैव स्मरं A; सुरभिञ्चैव स्मरन् E_N **7:124** य एवं] C; य एव A; एवं यः E_N **7:124** इहैव] AE_N; इहेव E_N **7:124** धनवान् भवेत्] CE_N; --- A **7:124** उपद्रवाः] CE_N; उपद्रवा A **7:124** परतः] CE_N; परत A **7:124** शिवधर्मसङ्ग्रहे सप्तमो ऽध्यायः] C; शिवधर्मसङ्ग्रहे सप्तमो ऽध्यायः पटलः A; शिव धर्म संग्रहे सप्तमोध्यायः E_N

शिवधर्मसंग्रहेऽष्टमोऽध्यायः॥

देव्युवाच।
कतरं देवमाश्रित्य उपवासफलम्महत्।
कथं वा पूजनीयास्ते ब्रवीहि परमेश्वर॥ 8:1॥

ईश्वर उवाच।
प्रतिपत्सूपवासी तु ब्रह्माणं पूजयेन्नरः।
ब्रह्मणे नम इत्येवमुभयोरपि पक्षयोः॥ 8:2॥

गन्धपुष्पैश्च धूपैश्च भक्ष्यभोज्यसमन्वितम्।
अब्दमेकं समभ्यर्च्य क्रतूनां फलमाप्नुयात्॥ 8:3॥

अश्वमेधं राजसूयं सौवर्णञ्च गवामयम्।
सप्तभिः सोमसंस्थैश्च नरमेधसमन्वितैः॥ 8:4॥

ब्रह्मा स्वयंभूर्विरिञ्चिः पद्मयोनिः प्रजापतिः।
गीर्वाणः पद्महस्तश्च ओमित्येकाक्षरः प्रभुः॥ 8:5॥

चतुर्वेदधरः स्रष्टा परमेष्ठी चतुर्मुखः।

8:1 कतरं] CE_N; तरम् A (unmetrical) **8:1** ब्रवीहि परमेश्वर] CE_N; प्रब्रवीमि महेश्वरः A **8:2** ईश्वर उवाच] A; भगवानुवाच CE_N **8:2** प्रतिपत्सूपवासी तु ब्रह्माणं] *conj.*; प्रति --- ह्मणं A; प्रतिपत्सोपवासी तु ब्राह्मणं C; प्रतिपत्सोपवासीतु ब्राह्मणम् E_N **8:2** पूजयेन्नरः] A; भोजयेन्नरः CE_N **8:2** ब्रह्मणे नम इत्येवम्] C; ब्रह्मणे भूय इत्येवम् A; ब्रह्मणे नम इत्येषम् E_N **8:3** गन्धपुष्पैश्च धूपैश्च] A; गन्धधूपैश्च पुष्पैश्च CE_N **8:3** °समन्वितम्] AC; °समन्वितम्ः E_N **8:3** अब्दमेकं समभ्यर्च्य क्रतूनां] CE_N; अब्दमेक समंभ्यर्च्य क्रतूना A **8:4** अश्वमेधं] CE_N; अश्वमेध A **8:4** सप्तभिः सोमसंस्थैश्च] CE_N; --- श्च A **8:5** ब्रह्मा स्वयंभूर्विरिञ्चिः] C; ब्रह्मा स्वयंभूविरिञ्चि A; ब्रह्मा स्वयंभूर्विरीञ्चः E_N **8:5** गीर्वाणः पद्महस्तश्च] A; ग्रीर्वाणः पद्मभूतश्च CE_N **8:5** ओमित्येकाक्षरः] CE_N; ओमित्येकाक्षर A

संज्ञाभिः पूजयेदाभिर्ब्रह्माणममितद्युतिम्॥ 8:6॥

सम्वत्सरेण युक्तात्मा स्वर्ग्गलोके महीयते।
यावज्जीवन्तु कुर्वाणो ब्रह्मलोके महीयते॥ 8:7॥

द्वितीये पूजयेदग्निमाज्येनैव तु तर्प्पयेत्।
वैश्वानरो जातवेदा हुतभुग्घव्यवाहनः॥ 8:8॥

देववक्त्रः सर्वभक्षो घृणी च जगदाहकः।
विभावसुः सप्तजिह्वो वरनामेति कीर्त्तितम्॥ 8:9॥

प्रतिमासं समभ्यर्च्य पक्षयोरुभयोरपि।
वर्षेणैकेन शुद्धात्मा स गच्छेदग्निलोकताम्॥ 8:10॥

तृतीये पूजयेद्यक्षं गन्धधूपनिवेदनैः।
उभाभ्यामपि पक्षाभ्यां यावदब्दं भवेदिह॥ 8:11॥

धनन्दास्यन्ति यक्षा हि धनदाद्याः सुपूजिताः।
यावज्जीवन्तु कुर्वाणो धनदस्य पदं व्रजेत्॥ 8:12॥

धनदो यक्षराजश्च वित्तेशो निधिपालकः।
राक्षसाधिपतिश्चैव पिंगलाक्षो विमानगः॥ 8:13॥

रुद्रसखः कुवेरश्च पौलस्त्यकुलनन्दनः।
लोकपालेश्वरश्चैव यक्षेन्द्रः परिकीर्त्तितः॥ 8:14॥

अब्दन्तु पूजयेद्यस्तु यक्षभक्तिसमाश्रितः।

8:6 संज्ञाभिः पूजयेदेभिर्ब्रह्माणममितद्युतिम्] *conj.*; संज्ञाभि पूजयेदेभिब्रह्मणममितद्युतिम् A; संज्ञाभिः पूजयेदाभिर्ब्रह्माणममितद्युतिम् C; संज्ञाभिः पूजयेदेभिब्रह्न्णममितं द्युति E_N **8:7** सम्वत्सरेण युक्तात्मा स्वर्गलोके महीयते] CE_N; ⏓ ⏓ ⏓ ⏓ ⏓ A **8:7** ब्रह्मलोके] AC; ब्रह्यलोके E_N **8:8** पूजयेदग्निमाज्येनैव] E_N; पूजये देवि आज्येनैव A; पूजयेदग्निमोजेनैव C **8:8** हुतभुग्घव्यवाहनः] A; हुतभुग् हव्यवाहनः C; हुत भुग्भव्यवाहनः E_N **8:9** जगदाहकः] AC; जगद्दाहकः E_N **8:9** विभावसुः] CE_N; विभावसु A **8:9** सप्तजिह्वो वरनामेति कीर्त्तितम्] C; सप्तजिह्वो वर ⏓ म्सा; सप्तजिह्व वरनामेतिकीर्तनम् E_N **8:11** तृतीये] C; त्रितीये A; तृतीयं E_N **8:11** पूजयेद्यक्षं] A; ल्क् ⏓ न् C; यक्षाङ्° E_N **8:11** गन्धधूपनिवेदनैः] AC; गन्धधूपैर्निवेदनैः E_N **8:11** उभाभ्यामपि] CE_N; उभाभ्यांमपि A **8:11** यावदब्धं] CE_N; यावदब्ध A **8:12** धनदाद्याः] CE_N; धनदद्या? A **8:12** धनदस्य पदं व्रजेत्] CE_N; ⏓ --- A **8:14** रुद्रसखः] AE_N; रुद्रशख C **8:14** पौलस्त्यकुलनन्दनः] C; पौलस्त्रोकुवनन्दनः A; पौलस्त्यः कुलनन्दनः E_N **8:14** लोकपालेश्वरश्चैव] AE_N; लोकपालेश्वराश्चैव C **8:15** यक्षभक्तिसमाश्रितः] AC; *om.* E_N

धनधान्यसमृद्धस्तु यावज्जीवं स यक्षराट्॥ 8:15॥

गणेशं पूजयेद्यस्तु गन्धपुष्पसमन्वितः।
भक्ष्यभोज्यसमाकीर्ण्णं चतुर्थ्युभयपक्षयोः॥ 8:16॥

अब्देनैकेन शुद्धात्मा स याति गणमन्दिरम्।
विघ्नैश्च नाभिभूयेत यो ऽर्चयेद्गणनायकम्॥ 8:17॥

विघ्नेश्वरं गणपतिमेकदन्तङ्गजाननम्।
गजकर्ण्णन्तथा त्र्यक्षन्नागयज्ञोपवीतिनम्॥ 8:18॥

चतुर्भुजञ्च धूम्राक्षं वक्रशुण्डम्विनायकम्।
महोदरञ्च संज्ञाभिः साधकः संयतेन्द्रियः॥ 8:19॥

मोदकैर्लड्डुकैश्चैव मूलकैश्चापि शोभनैः।
न तस्य दुर्लभं किञ्चित्पूजयेद्यो गणाधिपम्॥ 8:20॥

पञ्चम्यां पूजयेन्नागान्पुष्पैः सुरभिशोभनैः।
धूपैः सुरभिगन्धैश्च गुडक्षीरैः सपायसैः॥ 8:21॥

शर्करामधुपुष्पैश्च पक्षयोरुभयोरपि।
सम्वत्सरेण कामानि लभते कांक्षितानि तु॥ 8:22॥

यावज्जीवं समभ्यर्च्य नागलोकमवाप्नुयात्।
स्कन्दं षष्ठ्यां तु संपूज्य उपवाससमन्वितः॥ 8:23॥

गन्धपुष्पसुधूपेन भक्ष्यभोज्येन संयुतः।

8:15 धनधान्यसमृद्धस्तु] C; धनधान्यस --- A; *om.* E_N **8:15** यावज्जीवं स यक्षराट्] C; --- क्षराट् A; यावज्जीबं स यक्षराट् E_N **8:16** चतुर्थ्यु॰] AC; चतुर्थ्यो॰ E_N **8:17** अब्देनैकेन] A; अब्देनेकेन C; अब्दैनैकेन E_N **8:18** विघ्नेश्वरं] AC^cE_N; विघ्नश्वरं C^{ac} **8:18** गणपतिमेकदन्तङ्गजाननम्] E_N; गणपतिमेकदन्त --- A; गणपतिमेकदन्तगजाननम् C **8:18** गजकर्ण्णन्तथा त्र्यक्षन्नागयज्ञोपवीतिनम्] C; --- ज्ञोपवीतिनम् A; गजकर्ण्णन्तथा यक्षं नागयज्ञोपवीतिनम् E_N **8:19** चतुर्भुजञ्च] AC; चतुभुजश्च E_N **8:19** धूम्राक्षं] CE_N; धूम्राक्ष A **8:19** महोदरञ्च] AC; महोदरश्च E_N **8:19** संज्ञाभिः साधकः] CE_N; संज्ञाभि साधक A **8:20** लड्डुकैश्चैव] AC; न्लड्कैश्चैव E_N (unmetrical) **8:20** यो गणाधिपम्] AC; योगणाधिपम् E_N **8:21** नागान् पुष्पैः सुरभिशोभनैः] CE_N; नागा --- A **8:21** गुडक्षीरैः सपायसैः] C; गुडक्षीरसपायसैः A; गुडक्षीरैःसपायसैः E_N **8:22** ॰मधुपुष्पैश्च] A; ॰मधुधूपैश्च C; ॰मधुपूपैश्च E_N **8:22** कामानि लभते] AC; कामानिलभते E_N **8:23** उपवाससमन्वितः] AC; उपवास समन्वितः E_N **8:24** गन्धपुष्पसुधूपेन भक्ष्यभोज्येन संयुतः] C; गन्धपुष्प --- A; गन्धधूपेषु धूपेन भक्ष्यभोज्येन संयुतं E_N

उभाभ्यामपि यक्षाभ्यां पूजयित्वा समाहितः॥ 8:24॥

स्कन्दो विशाखः क्रोञ्चारिरुमानन्दो ऽग्निगर्ब्भजः।
नैगमेशो महासेनस्त्रिवर्णः कृत्तिकासुतः॥ 8:25॥

पञ्चच्छटः कुमारश्च देवसेनापतिर्गुहः।
षड्मुखः शक्तिहस्तश्च मयूरवरवाहनः॥ 8:26॥

नामभिः पूजयेदेभिः संयतो मार्ग्गशीर्षतः।
सर्वकामानवाप्नोति वर्षेणैकेन मानवः॥ 8:27॥

स्कन्दाग्निं जुहुयाद्यस्तु पक्षयोरुभयोरपि।
यावज्जीवं समभ्यर्च्य स्कन्दसायुज्यतां व्रजेत्॥ 8:28॥

सप्तम्यां मार्ग्गशीर्षादौ भास्करं पूजयेच्छुचिः।
उपवासेन युक्तात्मा पुष्पधूपविलेपनैः॥ 8:29॥

भक्ष्यभोज्यैश्च विविधैस्तथा होमजपादिभिः।
सम्वत्सरेण युक्तात्मा निर्मलः काममाप्नुयात्॥ 8:30॥

सूर्यलोकं व्रजत्याशु यावज्जीवं प्रपूजनात्।
च्युता धनाढ्या जायन्ते निरुजा दीर्घजीविनः॥ 8:31॥

आदित्यः सविता सूर्यः खगः पूषा गभस्तिमान्।
हिरण्यगर्भस्त्रिशिखस्तपनो भास्करो रविः॥ 8:32॥

8:24 उभाभ्यामपि] CE$_N$; --- मपि A **8:25** विशाखः] CE$_N$; विशाख A **8:25** ०नन्दो ऽग्निगर्ब्भजः] AC; ०नन्दाग्निगर्ब्भजः E$_N$ **8:25** नैगमेशो] CE$_N$; नैगमेवो A **8:25** महासेनस्त्रिवर्णः] CE$_N$; महासेन तृवर्ण्णः A **8:26** पञ्चच्छटः] C; पञ्चशिख A; पञ्चशिखा० E$_N$ **8:26** देवसेनापतिर्गुहः] CE$_N$; देवसेनापति गुहः A **8:26** षड्मुखः] AE$_N$; षण्मख C **8:27** मार्ग्गशीर्षतः] CE$_N$; --- A **8:27** सर्वकामानवाप्नोति] *em.*; सर्वकाममवाप्नोति C; --- र्वकाममवाप्नोति A; सर्वकाममवाप्नति E$_N$ **8:28** स्कन्दाग्निं जुहुयाद्यस्तु पक्षयोरुभ०] AC; जुदृयाघस्तु पक्षयोरुम० E$_N$ **8:28** यावज्जीवं समभ्यर्च्य] C; यावज्जीव समभ्यर्च्य स्कन्दसायुज्यतां व्रजेत् A; स्कन्दाग्निं समभ्यर्चय E$_N$ (unmetrical) **8:29** मार्ग्गशीर्षादौ] CE$_N$; मार्ग्गशीषादौ A **8:29** पूजयेच्छुचिः] CE$_N$; पूजये शुचिः A **8:30** भक्ष्यभोज्यैश्च वि०] AC; भक्ष्यभोज्यैश्चवि० E$_N$ **8:30** होमजपादिभिः] CE$_N$; --- A **8:30** युक्तात्मा निर्मलः] C; युक्तात्मा निर्म्मल A; युक्तात्म निर्मलाः E$_N$ **8:31** सूर्यलोकं] CE$_N$; सूर्यलोक A **8:31** यावज्जीवं] CE$_N$; यावज्जीव A **8:31** धनाढ्या] C; धनाढ A; धनादया E$_N$ (unmetrical) **8:31** निरुजा दीर्घजीविनः] AC; निरुजादीर्घजीविनः E$_N$ **8:32** आदित्यः] CE$_N$; आदित्य A **8:32** त्रिशिखस्तपनो] CE$_N$; तृशिखा ⏑̲ स्तपनो (unmetrical)

लोकसाक्षी जगन्नेत्रं नामभिस्त्वेभिरर्चयेत्।
सर्वकामानवाप्नोति पूजयेद्यो दिवाकरम्॥ 8:33॥

अष्टम्यां मार्गशीर्षस्य शिवनामानमर्चयेत्।
उपवासेन युक्तात्मा गोमूत्रप्राशनेन च॥ 8:34॥

अतिरात्रफलन्तस्य पक्षयोरुभयोरपि।
भक्ष्यभोज्यान्नपानाद्यैरेतत्फलमवाप्नुयात्॥ 8:35॥

देवदेवं समभ्यर्च्य मासे पौषे उपोषितः।
वाजपेयमवाप्नोति गोशकृत्प्राशनेन तु॥ 8:36॥

त्र्यम्बकं पूजयित्वा तु माघे कृष्णे ह्युपोषितः।
लभते हयमेधन्तु पयःसंप्राशनेन तु॥ 8:37॥

स्थाणुं फाल्गुनमासे तु पूजयेदुपवासितः।
दधि प्राश्य विशुद्धात्मा नृमेधफलमाप्नुयात्॥ 8:38॥

हरश्चैत्रे तु सम्पूज्य कृष्णाष्टम्यामुपोषितः।
आज्यं प्राश्य शुचिर्भूत्वा राजसूयमवाप्नुयात्॥ 8:39॥

वैशाखे शंकरं पूज्य उपवासी कुशोदकम्।
प्राशयित्वा जितक्रोधः सौत्रामणिफलं लभेत्॥ 8:40॥

भवं ज्येष्ठे तु संपूज्य सोपवासी शुचिव्रतः।
प्राश्य शृङ्गोदकं गोस्तु सर्वयज्ञफलं लभेत्॥ 8:41॥

8:33 लोकसाक्षी जगन्नेत्रं नामभिस्त्वेभिरर्चयेत्] CE$_N$; --- त्वेभिरर्चयेत् A **8:33** सर्वकामानवाप्नोति] *conj.*; सर्वकाममवाप्नोति ACE$_N$ **8:34** गोमूत्र॰] CE$_N$; गोमूत्रा॰ A **8:35** भक्ष्यभोज्यान्नपानाद्यैरेतत्फलमवाप्नुयात्] C; भक्ष्यभोज्यानपानाद्यैरेतत्फलमाप् --- A; भक्ष्यभोज्यान्न पानाद्यैरेतत्फलमवाप्नुयात् E$_N$ **8:36** देवदेवं समभ्यर्च्य] E$_N$; --- A; देवन्देव समभ्यर्च्य C **8:36** उपोषितः] A; ह्युपोषितः C; हयुपोषित E$_N$ (unmetrical) **8:37** त्र्यम्बकं] A; त्र्यम्बकं C; यम्बकं E$_N$ **8:37** माघे कृष्णे] AC; माघेकृष्णे E$_N$ **8:37** ह्युपोषितः] E$_N$; मुपोषितः A; ह्युशोदकः C **8:37** लभते हयमेधन्तु पयःसंप्राशनेन तु] C; लभते हयमेधन्तु पीयसंप्राशनेन तु A; *om.* E$_N$ **8:38** स्थाणुं फाल्गुनमासे तु] *em.*; स्थाणुं फाल्गुणमासे तु C; स्तृ?णुं फाल्गुणमासे तु A; स्थाणुं फाल्गुन मासेतु E$_N$ **8:38** दधि प्राश्य विशुद्धात्मा नृमेधफलमाप्नुयात्] C; दधि प्राश्य विशुद्धात्मा नृमेधफलमाप्नु --- A; दधिप्राश्य विशुद्धात्मानृमेघपुल माप्नुयात् E$_N$ **8:39** हरश्चैत्रे तु सम्पूज्य] C; --- ज्य A; हरश्चैत्रेतु सम्पूज्य E$_N$ **8:39** आज्यं प्राश्य शुचिर्भूत्वा राजसूयमवाप्नुयात्] C; आज्यं प्राश्य विशुद्धात्मा निर्मलकाममाप्नुयात् A; आज्यं पाइय शुचिर्भूत्वा राजसूय मच्छाप्नुयात् E$_N$ (unmetrical) **8:40** शंकरं] CE$_N$; शङ्कर A **8:40** ॰फलं लभेत्] AC; ॰मवाप्नुयात् E$_N$ **8:41** भवं] AC; शिवं E$_N$ **8:41** शृङ्गोदकं गोस्तु] C; शृङ्गोदक ⏑̲ स्तु A; शृङ्गोदकं यस्तु E$_N$

आषाढे नीलकण्ठन्तु कृष्णाष्टम्यां समर्च्चयेत्।
शङ्खस्यापस्ततः पीत्वा गोसहस्रफलं भवेत्॥ 8:42॥

पिङ्गलं श्रावणे पूज्य कृष्णाष्टम्यामुपोषितः।
सिद्धार्थमुदकं पीत्वा कन्यादानफलं लभेत्॥ 8:43॥

मासे भाद्रपदे रुद्रं पूजयित्वा ह्युपोषितः।
यवोदकं प्राशयित्वा रुद्रलोके महीयते॥ 8:44॥

ईशानञ्चाश्विने मासे कृष्णाष्टम्यां तु पूजयेत्।
तिलोदकं प्राशयित्वा बहुसौवर्णिकं फलम्॥ 8:45॥

उग्रन्तु कार्त्तिके मासे कृष्णाष्टम्यामुपोषितः।
सौवर्णमुदकं पीत्वा गाणापत्यमवाप्नुयात्॥ 8:46॥

सम्वत्सरन्ततः कृत्वा इष्टकामांल्लभेत सः।
भवेत्क्रतुफलं कामाद्गाणापत्यमकामतः॥ 8:47॥

उभाभ्यामपि पक्षाभ्यां विधिरेष प्रकीर्त्तितः।
नवम्यां संप्रवक्ष्यामि महादेव्याः प्रपूजनम्॥ 8:48॥

उपवासेन संयुक्तः पूजयेन्नामभिः शुभैः।
उमा कात्यायनी देवी दुर्ग्गा भद्रा सुभद्रिका॥ 8:49॥

कालरात्री महागौरी रैवती भूतनायिका।
आर्या प्रकृतिरूपा च गणानाञ्चैव नायिका॥ 8:50॥

8:42 आषाढे नीलकण्ठन्तु] CE$_N$; ⏓ --- A **8:42** कृष्णाष्टम्यां समर्चयेत्] C; --- ष्णष्टम्या समर्चयेत् A; कृष्णाष्टम्यामुपोषितः E$_N$ **8:42** पीत्वा गोसहस्रफलं] AC; पीत्वागोसहस्रफलं E$_N$ **8:42** भवेत्] A; लभेत् CE$_N$ **8:43** पिङ्गलं] AC; पिङ्गाक्षं E$_N$ **8:43** सिद्धार्थमुदकं] CE$_N$; सिद्धर्थमुदक A **8:44** रुद्रं] AE$_N$; रु ⏓ C **8:44** रुद्रलोके महीयते] CE$_N$; रुद्रलो --- A **8:45** ईशानञ्चाश्विने मासे] CE$_N$; --- शानञ्चाश्विनो मासे A **8:45** कृष्णाष्टम्यां तु पूजयेत्] A; कृष्णाष्टम्यां समर्चयेत् CE$_N$ **8:45** तिलोदकं] CE$_N$; तिलोदक A **8:45** फलम्] CE$_N$; लभेत् A **8:46** कृष्णाष्टम्यामुपोषितः] C; कृष्णाष्टम्यांमुपोषितः A; कृष्णाष्टम्यमामुपोषितः E$_N$ (unmetrical) **8:46** सौवर्णमुदकं] CE$_N$; सुवर्ण्णमुदक A **8:46** गाणापत्य°] AC; गाणपत्य° E$_N$ **8:47** इष्टकामांल्लभेत] *em.*; इष्टकामा लभेत A; इष्टान् कामान् लभेत C; इष्टान् कामांल्लभेत E$_N$ **8:47** भवेत्क्रतुफलं कामाद्गाणापत्यमकामतः] C; भवेत्क्रतु --- त्यमकामतः A; भवेत् क्रतुफलं कामाग्दाणपत्यमकामतः E$_N$ **8:48** विधिरेष प्रकीर्त्तितः] C; विधिरेषा प्रकीर्त्तिता A; विधिरेषः प्रकीर्तितः E$_N$ **8:48** संप्रवक्षामि] AC; संप्रवक्षामिः E$_N$ **8:49** संयुक्तः] CE$_N$; संयुक्त A **8:49** दुग्र्गा भद्रा] A; दुग्र्गा रुद्रा C; दुग्र्गारुद्रा E$_N$ **8:50** रैवती भूतनायिका] C; रैवती भूत ⏓ --- A; दैवती भूतनायिका E$_N$ **8:50** आर्या प्रकृतिरूपा च] C; --- कृतिपूपा तु A; आर्या प्रकृतिरूपाच E$_N$

नामभिः पूजयेदेभिः पक्षयोरुभयोरपि।
पुष्पैर्धूपैश्च गन्धैश्च वस्त्रालङ्कारभूषणैः॥ 8:51॥

नैवेद्यैश्चोपहारैश्च कन्दमूलफलैस्तथा।
प्राशनैश्च विचित्रैश्च वरदां पूजयेत्सदा॥ 8:52॥

उदकं कुसुमं प्राश्य सक्तुलाजं सधानकम्।
कृसराञ्च पयो मूलं फलं पर्णन्तथैव च॥ 8:53॥

शाकानि च फलञ्चैव तिलानाञ्च खलिन्ततः।
मुद्गानपि समश्नीयात्तथा चैव निरश्नता॥ 8:54॥

प्राशयित्वा तथैतानि सर्वकामानवाप्नुयात्।
आर्द्रकं प्राशयित्वा तु शुक्लभोजी तथा पुनः॥ 8:55॥

लभते सर्वकामांस्तु नवमीसमुपोषितः।
मरिचं प्राशनं कृत्वा नवमीन्नव यो ऽर्चयेत्॥ 8:56॥

सर्वकामानवाप्नोति देवी च वरदा भवेत्।
कुशप्रस्तरशायी च पञ्चगव्यकृताशनः॥ 8:57॥

नवमी नव संपूज्य देवी दद्याद्वरोत्तमम्।
यमन्दशम्यां संपूज्य मासे वै मार्गशीर्षके॥ 8:58॥

पुष्पैर्गन्धैश्च धूपैश्च भक्ष्यभोज्यसमन्वितैः।
यमाय धर्मराजाय मृत्यवे चान्तकाय च॥ 8:59॥

8:51 पूजयेदेभिः] CE$_N$; पूजयेदेदि A **8:51** पुष्पैर्धूपैश्च] A; पुष्पै धूपैश्च C; पुष्पैर्घूपैश्च E$_N$ **8:51** वस्त्रालङ्कारभूषणैः] CE$_N$; वस्त्राभरणभूषणैः A **8:52** वरदां] CE$_N$; वरदा A **8:53** कुसुमं] AC; कुशुमं E$_N$ **8:53** सक्तुलाजं] A; सक्तुलांज C; सकुलाजं E$_N$ **8:53** सधानकम्] CE$_N$; सधा --- A **8:53** कृसराञ्च पयो मूलं] C; --- पयो मूल A; कृशराश्च पयोमूलं E$_N$ **8:53** फलं पर्णन्तथैव] E$_N$; फलपर्ण्णन्तथैव A; फलं पर्ण्णतथैव C **8:54** खलिन्ततः] CE$_N$; बलन्ततः A **8:54** समश्नीयात्तथा] CE$_N$; समश्नीया तथा A **8:55** सर्वकामान्] A; सर्वान्कामान् CE$_N$ **8:55** आर्द्रकं] E$_N$; आद्रकं AC **8:55** प्राशयित्वा तु] AC; प्राशयित्वातु E$_N$ **8:56** सर्वकामांस्तु] C; सर्वकामन्तु A; सर्वकामास्तु E$_N$ **8:56** नवमीसमुपोषितः] C; नवमीसमु --- A; नवमी समुपोषितः E$_N$ **8:56** मरिचं प्राशनं कृत्वा] CE$_N$; --- चं प्राशयित्वा तु A **8:56** नवमीन्नव यो ऽर्चयेत्] A; नवमी नव यो ऽर्च्चयेत् C; नवमीं न तु यो ऽर्चयेत् E$_N$ **8:57** सर्वकामानवाप्नोति] CE$_N$; सर्वकाममवाप्नोति A **8:58** देवी दद्याद्] CE$_N$; देवी दद्या A **8:58** दशम्यां संपूज्य] C; दशम्या सपूज्य A; दशम्यां सम्पूज्य E$_N$ **8:59** पुष्पैर्गन्धैश्च धूपैश्च भक्ष्यभोज्यसमन्वितैः] *conj.*; पुष्पै गन्धैश्च धूपैश्च --- तैः A; पुष्पैर्गन्धैश्च संपूज्य भक्ष्यभोज्यसमन्वितम् C; पुष्पैर्गन्धैश्च सम्पूज्य भक्ष्य भोज्यसमन्वितः E$_N$ **8:59** चान्तकाय] CE$_N$; चान्तरा?य A

वैवस्वताय कालाय सर्वलोकक्षयाय च।
उग्रदण्डोग्रहस्ताय महिषासनयायिने॥ 8:60॥

शासित्रे च नमस्तुभ्यं नरकाधिपतये नमः।
नामभिः पूजयेदेभिस्तर्प्पयेच्च तिलोदकैः॥ 8:61॥

उभाभ्यामपि पक्षाभ्यां अब्दमेकं सुयन्त्रितः।
मुच्यते सर्वपापैस्तु न दुःखं नरकोद्भवम्॥ 8:62॥

यावज्जीवार्चनं कृत्वा स गच्छेत्परमाङ्गतिम्।
एकादश्यां तु यो धर्मं पूजयेत शुचिव्रतः॥ 8:63॥

गन्धैर्धूपैश्च पुष्पैश्च भक्षैर्न्नानाविधैस्तथा।
धर्मः सत्यं दया क्षान्तिः शौचमाचारमेव च॥ 8:64॥

अहिंसा चाप्यदम्भश्च रक्षा लोकस्य साक्षिणे।
वृषभाय नमस्तुभ्यमदृष्टाय नमो नमः॥ 8:65॥

नामभिः पूजयेदेभिर्धर्मं सत्यं पराक्रमम्।
उभयोः पक्षयोश्चैव वर्षमेकं सुयन्त्रितः॥ 8:66॥

याम्यदुःखैर्विमुक्तस्तु जायते पृथिवीश्वरः।
यावज्जीवं समभ्यर्च्य तर्पयेच्च तिलोदकैः॥ 8:67॥

उत्तमां गतिमाप्नोति याङ्गत्वा न निवर्त्तते।
केशवं पूजयित्वा तु मार्गशीर्षे नरोत्तमः॥ 8:68॥

8:60 सर्वलोकक्षयाय] AC; सर्वलोक क्षयाय E_N **8:60** °दण्डोग्रहस्ताय] AC; °दण्दोग्रहस्ताय E_N **8:60** °यायिने] A; °गामिने CE_N **8:61** शासित्रे च नमस्तुभ्यं नरकाधिपतये नमः] E_N (unmetrical); शासितारं नमस्तुभ्यं नरकाधिपताय च A; शासित्रे च नमस्तुभ्यं नरकायिपतये नमः C (unmetrical) **8:61** पूजयेदेभिस्तर्प्पयेच्च तिलोदकैः] CE_N; पूजयेदेविस्तर्प्पयेच तिलोकदकैः A (unmetrical) **8:62** उभाभ्यामपि पक्षाभ्यां अब्दमेकं सुयन्त्रितः] CE_N; उभा ⏓ --- ब्दमेक सुयन्त्रितं A **8:62** °पापैस्तु] A; °पापैश्च CE_N **8:62** नरकोद्भवम्] AC; नरके भवेत् E_N **8:63** परमाङ्गतिम्] AC; पर माङ्गतिम् E_N **8:63** पूजयेत] A; पूजयेच्च CE_N **8:64** गन्धैर्धूपैश्च] E_N; गन्धैधूपैश्च A; गन्धधूपैश्च C **8:64** भक्षैर्न्नाना°] E_N; भक्षैनाना° AC **8:64** धर्मः] AC; धर्मं E_N **8:64** शौचमाचारमेव च] *conj.*; शौचमा? ⏑ ⏑ A; शौचमाचार एव च C; शौचमाहारमेव च E_N **8:65** अहिंसा] CE_N; --- A **8:65** रक्षा लोकस्य साक्षिणे] AC; रक्षालोकश्च सक्षिणे E_N **8:66** सत्यं] CE_N; सत्य A **8:66** उभयोः] CE_N; उभयो A **8:66** वर्षमेकं] CE_N; वर्षमेक A **8:67** याम्यदुःखैर्विमुक्तस्तु] CE_N; यम्यदुःखैविमुक्तस्तु A **8:67** तर्पयेच्च तिलोदकैः] C; तर्पयेच तिलोदकैः A; तर्पयेच्चतिलोदकैः E_N **8:68** उत्तमां गतिमाप्नोति] CE_N; --- प्नोति A **8:68** तु] AC; च E_N

द्वादश्यां प्राश्य गोमूत्रं अग्निष्टोमफलं लभेत्।
पौषे नारायणं पूज्य द्वादश्यामुपवासितः॥ 8:69॥

ज्योतिष्टोमफलन्तस्य कृत्वा गोमयभक्षणम्।
माधवं माघमासे तु द्वादश्यां समुपोषितः॥ 8:70॥

पूजयित्वा पयः प्राश्य अश्वमेधफलं लभेत्।
गोविन्दं फाल्गुने ऽभ्यर्च्य द्वादश्यामुपवासितः॥ 8:71॥

षोडशीफलमाप्नोति कृत्वा तु दधिभक्षणम्।
चैत्रे विष्णुं समभ्यर्च्य द्वादश्यां समुपोषितः॥ 8:72॥

आज्यं वै प्राशयित्वा तु वाजपेयफलं लभेत्।
उपोषितस्तु वैशाखे पूजयेन्मधुसूदनम्॥ 8:73॥

द्वादश्यां प्राश्य दर्भोदमतिरात्रफलं लभेत्।
ज्येष्ठे त्रिविक्रमं पूज्य द्वादश्यामुपवासितः॥ 8:74॥

तिलोदकं प्राशयित्वा आप्तोर्यामफलं लभेत्।
आषाढे वामनं पूज्य द्वादश्यामुपवासितः॥ 8:75॥

फलं प्राश्य विशुद्धात्मा अश्वमेधफलं लभेत्।
श्रावणे श्रीधरं पूज्य द्वादश्यां समुपोषितः॥ 8:76॥

पर्णं प्राश्य विशुद्धात्मा राजसूयफलं लभेत्।
तथा भाद्रे हृषीकेशं संपूज्य विधिवद्बुधः॥ 8:77॥

गवामयस्य यज्ञस्य ततः फलमवाप्नुयात्।

8:69 गोमूत्रं अग्निष्टोम] A; गोमूत्रमग्निष्टोम CE$_N$ **8:69** नारायणं] E$_N$; नारायण A; नारायनं C **8:69** द्वादश्यामुपवासितः] A; द्वादश्यां समुपोषितः CE$_N$ **8:70** द्वादश्यां समुपोषितः] CE$_N$; द्वादश्य --- A **8:71** लभेत्] AC; लभेत E$_N$ **8:71** गोविन्दं फाल्गुने ऽभ्यर्च्य] C; गोविन्द फाल्गुणे ऽभ्यर्च्य A; फाल्गुनेमासि गोविन्दं E$_N$ **8:71** द्वादश्यामुपवासितः] A; द्वादश्यां समुपोषितः CE$_N$ **8:72** षोडशीफलमाप्नोति] AC; षोडशी फलमाप्नोति E$_N$ **8:72** विष्णुं] CE$_N$; विष्णु A **8:73** वाजपेयफलं] C; वाजपेयफल A; वाजपेय फलं E$_N$ **8:73** उपोषितस्तु वैशाखे पूजयेन्म°] CE$_N$; उपोषि --- जयेन्म° A **8:74** दर्भोदमतिरात्रफलं] CE$_N$; दभोदमतिरात्रफल A **8:74** लभेत्] AC; भवेत् E$_N$ **8:74** द्वादश्यामुपवासितः] A; द्वादश्यां समुपोषितः CE$_N$ **8:75** आप्तोर्यामफलं] C; आप्तोयामफल A; आप्तोर्योमफलं E$_N$ **8:75** वामनं] CE$_N$; वामन A **8:75** द्वादश्यामुपवासितः] A; द्वादश्यां सुसमाहितः CE$_N$ **8:76** अश्वमेधफलं लभेत्] CE$_N$; अश्व --- त् A **8:77** पर्णं] CE$_N$; पर्ण्णं A **8:77** राजसूयफलं] AC; राजसूय फलं E$_N$ **8:77** तथा भाद्रे हृषीकेशं] CE$_N$; हृषीकेशं भाद्रपदे A **8:78** ततः फलमवाप्नुयात्] AE$_N$; तद्बुः फलं लन्भते फलं C

मासे चाश्वयुजे देवं पद्मनाभन्तु पूजयेत्॥ 8 : 78॥

नरमेधस्य यज्ञस्य फलं लभति मानवः।
दामोदरन्तु संपूज्य कार्तिके मासि यो नरः॥ 8 : 79॥

उपोषितस्तु द्वादश्यां बहुसौवर्णिकं फलम्।
सम्वत्सरन्तु संपूज्य सर्वकामानवाप्नुयात्॥ 8 : 80॥

अपापी क्रतुमाप्नोति पापात्मा मुच्यतें ऽहसा।
यावज्जीवं समभ्यर्च्य पुष्पैर्गन्धैः सुगन्धकैः॥ 8 : 81॥

भक्ष्यभोज्यैश्च धूपैश्च छत्रध्वजवितानकैः।
हेमजैर्भूषणैर्दिव्यैर्मणिरत्नविचित्रकैः॥ 8 : 82॥

वस्त्रैः पूजां विचित्रैश्च कृत्वा विष्णुपदम्व्रजेत्।
अनङ्गन्तु त्रयोदश्यां पूजयेद्यो विधानवित्॥ 8 : 83॥

भक्ष्यभोज्यान्नपानैश्च गन्धधूपस्रगादिभिः।
अनङ्गं मन्मथं काममीशारिं मोहनन्तथा॥ 8 : 84॥

पञ्चबाणम्धनुर्हस्तमुन्मादञ्च वशङ्करम्।
रतिप्रियं प्रीतिकरं हृदयस्यापहारिणम्॥ 8 : 85॥

नामभिः पूजयेदेभिः कामदेवं महाबलम्।

8:78 देवं] CE$_N$; देव E$_N$ **8:78** पूजयेत्] CE$_N$; पूजये --- A **8:79** नरमेधस्य यज्ञस्य फलं लभति मानवः] C; --- ⏓ य ⏓ ⏓ ⏓ ⏓ ⏓ मानवः A; नरमेधस्य यज्ञस्य फलं भवति मानवः E$_N$ **8:80** उपोषितस्तु द्वादश्यां] AC; उपोषितस्तुद्वादश्यां E$_N$ **8:80** फलम्] CE$_N$; भवेत्A **8:80** सर्वकामानवाप्नुयात्] C; सर्वकाममवाप्नुयात् A; सर्वकामवाप्नुयात् E$_N$ (unmetrical) **8:81** अपापी क्रतुमाप्नोति] AC; सुयाजी क्रतु माप्नोती E$_N$ **8:81** पापात्मा मुच्यतें ऽहसा] CE$_N$; पापात्मा मुच्यते तुसा A **8:81** यावज्जीवं समभ्यर्च्य] C; यावज्जाव समभ्यच्य A; याज्जीवं समभ्यर्च्य E$_N$ (unmetrical) **8:81** पुष्पैर्गन्धैः सुगन्धकैः] E$_N$; पुष्पै गन्धै सुगन्ध --- A; पुष्पैगन्धैः सुगन्धकैः C **8:82** भक्ष्यभोज्यैश्च] CE$_N$; --- श्च A **8:82** छत्र-ध्वजवितानकैः] AC; छत्र ध्वजवितानकैः E$_N$ **8:82** हेमजैर्भूषणैर्दिव्यैर्मणिरत्नविचित्रकैः] C; होमजै भूषणै दिव्यै मणिरत्नविचित्रकैः A; हेमजैर्भूषणैर्दिव्यैर्मणिरत्न विचित्रकैः E$_N$ **8:83** वस्त्रैः पूजां विचित्रैश्च] *conj.*; वस्त्रपूज्यविचित्रैश्च A; वस्त्रपूजाविचित्रैश्च CE$_N$ **8:83** अनङ्गन्तु] A; अनङ्गञ्च A; अनङ्गश्च E$_N$ **8:84** भक्ष्यभोज्यान्नपानैश्च] A; भक्ष्यभोज्यन्नपानैश्च C; भ-क्ष्यभोज्यान्नपानैष्नैश्च E$_N$ (unmetrical) **8:84** गन्धधूपस्रगादिभिः] AC; गन्ध धूपस्रगादिभिः E$_N$ **8:84** अनङ्गं मन्मथं काममीशारिं मोहनन्तथा] CE$_N$; अनङ्ग मन्मथ कामं ईशा --- A **8:85** पञ्चबाणम्धनुर्हस्तमुन्मादञ्च] C; पञ्चबाणम्धनुहस्तमुन्मादञ्च A; पञ्चवाणधनुर्हस्त उन्मादश्च E$_N$ **8:85** हृदयस्यापहारिणम्] AC; हृदयं पापहारिणम् E$_N$ **8:86** कामदेवं] E$_N$; कामदेव AC

मासे मार्गशिरस्यादौ यावत्कार्त्तिकमेव च॥ 8:86॥

सौभाग्यं धनधान्यञ्च पुत्रदारा भवन्ति च।
कामदेवस्य सायुज्यं यवज्जीवस्य पूजनात्॥ 8:87॥

चतुर्दश्यां पुनर्देवं पूजयेत्परमेश्वरम्।
हरं शर्वं भवं त्र्यक्षं शम्भुञ्चैव विभुं शिवम्॥ 8:88॥

स्थाणुञ्चाप्यथ रुद्रञ्च ईशानं शङ्करन्तथा।
पूजयेदेभिः संज्ञाभिर्देवदेवं वृषध्वजम्॥ 8:89॥

मार्गशीर्षात्समारभ्य यावदब्दं व्रतञ्चरेत्।
पुष्पैर्धूपैश्च गन्धैश्च भक्ष्यभोज्यैः सुशोभनैः॥ 8:90॥

अलंकारैश्च विविधैश्छत्रध्वजवितानकैः।
उभयोः पक्षयोश्चैव सर्वकामानवाप्नुयात्॥ 8:91॥

सम्वत्सरेण युक्तात्मा निष्कामस्तु गणो भवेत्।
यावज्जीवेन सायोज्यं पापी मुच्येत किल्बिषैः॥ 8:92॥

अमावास्यां पितॄणां हि मासे वै मार्ग्गशीर्षके।
कर्मणा श्राद्धयुक्तेन पिण्डेन च तिलोदकैः॥ 8:93॥

उद्दिश्य पितरं यस्तु विप्रान्श्राद्धे निमन्त्रयेत्।
आहिताग्नीनधीयानान्सुवृत्तान्सुपथे स्थितम्॥ 8:94॥

8:86 मासे] CE$_N$; मासि A **8:87** सौभाग्यं धनधान्यञ्च] AC; सौभाग्यधन धान्यं च E$_N$ **8:87** पुत्रदारा भवन्ति च] C; पुत्रदार भवन्ति च AE$_N$ **8:87** सायुज्यं] *em.*; सा --- A; सायोज्यं CE$_N$ **8:87** यवज्जीवस्य] CE$_N$; --- A **8:88** पुनर्देवं] CE$_N$; पुनदेवं A **8:88** हरं शर्वं] CE$_N$; हर शर्व A **8:88** शम्भुञ्चैव] CE$_N$; शम्भु चैव A **8:88** विभुं शिवम्] A; शिवं विभुम् C; रिभुं शिवम् E$_N$ **8:89** शङ्करन्तथा] AE$_N$; शकंरन्तथा C **8:89** रुद्रञ्च ईशानं] C; रुद्रञ्च ईशान A; रुद्रयं च ईशानं E$_N$ (unmetrical) **8:89** पूजयेदेभिः संज्ञाभिर्देवदेवं] *conj.*; पूजयेदेभि संज्ञाभिदेवदेवं A; संज्ञाभि पूजयेदाभि देवदेवं C; संज्ञाभिः पूजयेदेभिर्देवदेवं E$_N$ **8:90** मार्गशीर्षात्समारभ्य] E$_N$; मार्गशीर्षे समारभ्यः A; मार्गशीषात्समारभ्य C **8:90** यावदब्दं] CE$_N$; यावदब्द A **8:90** पुष्पैर्धूपैश्च गन्धैश्च भक्ष्यभोज्यैः] CE$_N$; पुष्पै --- भोज्यैः A **8:91** विविधैश्छत्रध्वजवितानकैः] C; विविधैः छत्रध्वजवितानकैः A; विविधैश्छत्र ध्वजवितानकैः E$_N$ **8:91** सर्वकामानवाप्नुयात्] *conj.*; सवकाममवाप्नुयात् A; सर्वकाममवाप्नुयात् C; सर्वकामनवाप्नुयात् E$_N$ **8:92** सायोज्यं] CE$_N$; सायुज्य A **8:93** पितॄणां हि] *em.*; पितृणां हि A; पितृणान्तु CE$_N$ **8:93** मासे वै मार्ग्गशीर्षके] CE$_N$; --- के A **8:93** श्राद्धयुक्तेन] AC; श्राध्दयुक्तेन E$_N$ **8:94** उद्दिश्य] E$_N$; उदिश्य AC **8:94** विप्रान्] C; विप्रां A; विप्रान E$_N$ (unmetrical) **8:94** आहिताग्नीनधीयानान् सुवृत्तान् सुपथे स्थितम्] C; आहिताग्नीमधीयानं सुवृत्तं सुपथे स्थितम् A; आहिताग्नी न धीयाना सुवृत्तान सुपथे स्थितान् E$_N$

हीनाङ्गानतिरिक्ताङ्गान्चक्षुहीनाञ्च वर्ज्जयेत्।
विप्रान्श्रेष्ठतमान्श्राद्धे सर्वरोगविवर्ज्जितान्॥ 8:95॥

आसने कुतपास्तीर्ण्णे नियुञ्जीतोत्तरामुखम्।
भूमौ दर्भोत्तरीयायान्त्रीन्पिण्डान्देवि निर्वपेत्॥ 8:96॥

प्रथमं पितरं मन्ये द्वितीयञ्च पितामहम्।
तृतीयं चैव कर्त्तव्यमेष मे प्रपितामहः॥ 8:97॥

एवं सम्भावयित्वा तु यस्तु भोजयते द्विजान्।
भोजनं खड्गमांसेन पायसं मधुसर्पिषा॥ 8:98॥

सुवर्ण्णं दक्षिणां दद्यादमावास्यान्तिलोदकम्।
पिण्डनिर्वपणञ्चैव कर्त्तव्यं दर्भसंस्तरे॥ 8:99॥

हुत्वाग्निं सर्पिषा तत्र येन मन्त्रेण तच्छृणु।
ओं अग्नये कव्यवाहनाय स्वधायाङ्गिरसे नमः॥ 8:100॥

ओं सोमाय च पितृपतये स्वधायांगिरसे नमः।
ओं यमायाग्निरोचिषे स्वधायाङ्गिरसे नमः॥ 8:101॥

अनेन विधिना पूर्वं हुत्वा सम्यग्घुतासनम्।
पिण्डनिर्वपणं कुर्यादवसव्येन पाणिना॥ 8:102॥

8:95 हीनाङ्गानतिरिक्ताङ्गान् चक्षुहीनाञ्च वर्जयेत्] C; हीनांगानतिब्दक्ताङ्गां चक्षुहीनाञ्च वर्ज्जयेत् A; हीनाङ्गानतिरिक्ताङ्गांचक्षुर्हीनांच वर्जयेत् E_N **8:95** विप्रान् श्रेष्ठतमान् श्राद्धे सर्वरोगविवर्जितान्] C; विप्रां श्रेष्ठतमां श्राद्धे सर्वरोगविवर्ज्जिताम् A; विप्रान् श्रेष्ठतमान् श्राध्देसर्वरोगविवर्जितान् E_N **8:96** नियुञ्जितोत्तरामुखम्] CE_N; नियुञ्जितोत्तरामुखे A **8:96** भूमौ] AE_N; भूमो C **8:96** दर्भोत्तरीयायान्त्रीन् पिण्डान्देवि निर्वपेत्] C; दर्भत्तरीयायां त्रीं पिण्डान्देवि निर्वपेत् A; दर्भोत्तरीयायां त्रीन् पिण्डान् वि निर्वदेत् E_N (unmetrical) **8:97** कर्त्तव्यमेष] *em.*; कर्त्तव्यंमेष A; मन्तव्यमेष C; मन्तव्य एष E_N **8:97** प्रपितामहः] CE_N; प्रपितामहम् A **8:98** भोजयते] CE_N; भोजयति A **8:98** खड्गमांसेन] CE_N; खड्गमासेन A **8:98** मधुसर्पिषा] C; मधुस --- म्सा; मधु सर्पिषा E_N **8:99** सुवर्ण्णं दक्षिणां दद्यादमावास्यान्] C; --- दक्षिणा दद्यामावास्या A; सुवणं दक्षिणान्दद्यादमावास्यान् E_N **8:99** पिण्डनिर्वपणञ्चैव कर्त्तव्यं] C; पिण्डनिर्वापन चैव कर्त्तव्य A; पिण्डनिर्वपणश्चैव कर्त्तव्यं E_N **8:100** तच्छृणु] CE_N; तशृणु A **8:101** पितृपतये] CE_N; पितृमते A **8:101** यमायाग्निरोचिषे] CE_N; यमायाग्निरो --- A **8:101** स्वधायाङ्गिरसे] CE_N; --- रसे A **8:102** पूर्वं] CE_N; पूर्व A **8:102** सम्यग्घुतासनम्] *em.*; सम्यक् तासनः A (unmetrical); सम्य ⏑ हुतासनम् C; सम्यक हुतासनम् E_N (unmetrical) **8:102** पिण्डनिर्वपणं कुर्यादवसव्येन] C; पिण्डनिर्वापण कुर्यादवसव्येन A; पिण्डनिर्वापणं कुर्यादपसव्येन E_N

प्रथमं निर्वपेत्पिण्डमुद्दिश्य पितरन्नरः ।
पितामहं ततः पिण्डं निर्वपेत द्वितीयकम् ॥ 8:103 ॥

तृतीयं निर्वपेत्पिण्डमुद्दिश्य प्रपितामहम् ।
तिलोदकेन तान्सिञ्चेत्प्रणम्य शिरसा क्षितौ ॥ 8:104 ॥

अनेन विधिना दत्वा स्पृष्ट्वा वामेन दक्षिणम् ।
श्राद्धेन पितरस्तेन यावदासप्तमं कुलम् ॥ 8:105 ॥

उद्धृत्य नरकाद्देवि स्वयं स्वर्ग्गे महीयते ।
येषां पुत्रा दुराचाराः पितृदेवविवर्ज्जिताः ॥ 8:106 ॥

न च तीर्थानि सेवन्ते ते नराः पापकर्मिणः ।
ते मृता नरकं यान्ति दुःखानि प्राप्नुवन्ति ते ॥ 8:107 ॥

नरके पच्यमानानां त्राता तेषां न विद्यते ।
पापकर्मक्षयो येषां मोक्षन्तु नरकाद्भवेत् ॥ 8:108 ॥

पितरः सोमपा विप्रे क्षत्रिये तु हविर्भुजः ।
आज्यपा वैश्ययोनौ तु शूद्राणां तु सुकालिनः ॥ 8:109 ॥

यावज्जीवन्तु कुर्वाणः पक्षयोरुभयोरपि ।
पापात्मा मुच्यते पापैरपापी स्वर्गमाप्नुयात् ॥ 8:110 ॥

वसवः पितरो ज्ञेया रुद्राश्चैव पितामहाः ।
प्रपितामहास्तथादित्या एवं सञ्चिन्त्य पूजयेत् ॥ 8:111 ॥

पौर्णमास्यां दधि प्राश्यं यावकं ताम्रभाजने ।

8:103 पिण्डमुद्दिश्य पितरं नरः] E$_N$; पिण्डंमुद्दिश्य पित्तरन्नरः A; पिण्डमुद्दिश्य पितरे नरः C **8:103** पितामहं ततः पिण्डं] *conj.*; पितामहं ततो पिम्य? A; पि ⊔ C; पितामहं समुद्दिश्य E$_N$ **8:103** निर्वपेत] AC; निर्वपेच्च E$_N$ **8:104** तिलोदकेन तान् सिञ्चेत्] CE$_N$; ति --- A **8:105** स्पृष्ट्वा] AC; स्पृत्वा E$_N$ **8:106** उद्धृत्य] AC; उध्दृत्य E$_N$ **8:106** स्वर्ग्गे महीयते] AE$_N$; ⊔ ते C **8:106** दुराचाराः] CE$_N$; दुराचारा A **8:107** सेवन्ते] CE$_N$; सेवन्ति A **8:107** पापकर्मिणः] E$_N$; --- A; पापकारिणः C **8:107** मृता नरकं] AC; मृतानरकं E$_N$ **8:107** ते] A; च CE$_N$ **8:108** तेषां] AE$_N$; तेषा C **8:108** मोक्षन्तु] A; विमोक्षो CE$_N$ **8:109** हविर्भुजः] AC; हविर्भूजः E$_N$ **8:109** वैश्ययोनौ] AC; वैश्ययोन्यै E$_N$ **8:110** कुर्वाणः] CE$_N$; कुर्वाण A **8:111** पितरो ज्ञेया] AC; पितरश्चैव E$_N$ **8:111** पितामहाः] CE$_N$; पितामहा A **8:111** एवं] CE$_N$; एव A **8:112** पौर्णमास्यां दधिप्रायं यावकं] E$_N$; पौर्ण्णमास्या दधिप्राश्य यावक A; पौर्णमास्यां दधिप्रायं यावकं C

सङ्गृह्योद्गच्छते दद्याद्भक्त्या चन्द्रमसे नरः॥ 8:112॥

तेन दानेन भगवान्प्रीयते मृगलाञ्छनः।
प्रीयन्ते च सुराः सर्वे सोमस्यैति सलोकताम्॥ 8:113॥

शीतांशवे नमस्तुभ्यं महादेवस्य मूर्त्तये।
इदं बलिं गृहाण त्वं मामप्यनुगृहाण च॥ 8:114॥

प्रतिपदि भोजयेद्द्विप्रान्पूजयित्वा प्रजापतिम्।
सौवर्णमरविन्दन्तु कुर्यान्नामाङ्कितं ततः॥ 8:115॥

ताम्रपात्रे घृतापूर्णे क्षिप्त्वा दद्याद्द्विजन्मने।
ईप्सितं लभते कामं निष्कामो ब्रह्मलोकताम्॥ 8:116॥

सम्पूज्याग्निं द्वितीयायां ब्राह्मणांस्तर्पयेत्पुनः।
तानि नामानि सौवर्णे वह्नेरालिख्य यत्नतः॥ 8:117॥

ताम्रिके सर्पिषा पूर्णे भाजने प्रक्षिपेत च।
तोयपूर्ण्णे घटे स्थाप्य भक्ष्यभोज्यसमन्विते॥ 8:118॥

उभाभ्यामपि पक्षाभ्यां दद्याद्द्विप्राय शोभने।
सर्वकामप्रदो वह्निरब्देकेन भविष्यति॥ 8:119॥

यावज्जीवं कृतेनैव प्रयात्यनलमन्दिरम्।

8:112 सङ्गृह्योद्गच्छते दद्याद्भक्त्या चन्द्रमसे नरः] C; सं --- द्याद्भक्त्या चन्द्रमसे नरः A; सङ्गृह्ये-ऋ-दग्छते दद्याद्भक्त्या चन्द्रमसेनरः E_N **8:113** भगवान्] CE_N; भगवां A **8:113** मृगलाञ्छनः] CE_N; मृगलांच्छणः A **8:113** प्रीयन्ते] CE_N; प्रीयेते A **8:114** शीतांशवे] AC; शीतङ्गवे E_N **8:114** इदं] A; अमुं C; इमं E_N **8:114** बलिं त्वं] CE_N; बेलि त्वं A **8:114** मामप्यनुगृहाण च] E_N; मामप्यनुग्रहाय च A; मामप्यनुगृहान च C **8:115** प्रतिपदि भोजयेद्द्विप्रान्] CE_N; प्रतिद्भोजये विप्रां A **8:115** पूजयित्वा प्रजापतिम्] CE_N; पू --- ति A **8:115** सौवर्णमरविन्दन्तु] AC; सौवर्णमरविन्दस्तु E_N **8:115** कुर्यान्नामाङ्कितं] CE_N; कुर्यानामाकितं A **8:115** ततः] A; तथा CE_N **8:116** घृतापूर्णे] CE_N; घृतपूर्ण A **8:116** क्षिप्त्वा दद्याद्] AC; क्षिप्तादद्याद् E_N **8:116** ईप्सितं लभते कामं निष्कामो] A; इप्सितान् लभते कामानकामो C; इप्सितांल्लभते कामान्निकामो E_N **8:117** सम्पूज्याग्निं द्वितीयायां] CE_N; सम्पूज्याग्नि द्वितीयं स्या A **8:117** ब्राह्मणांस्तर्पयेत्पुनः] E_N; ब्राह्मणन्तर्पयेत्पुनः AC **8:117** वह्नेरालिख्य यत्नतः] C; वह्नेरालि --- A; वन्हे रालिख्थ यत्नतः E_N **8:118** ताम्रिके सर्पिषा पूर्णे] CE_N; --- म्रिके सर्पिषा पूर्णे A **8:118** प्रक्षिपेत च] CE_N; प्रक्षिपेव च ह A (unmetrical) **8:118** घटे] AC; घृते E_N **8:118** °समन्विते] CE_N; °समन्वितैः A **8:119** उभाभ्यामपि] CE_N; उभांभ्यामपि A **8:119** सर्वकामप्रदो वह्निरब्देकेन] C; सर्वकामपदो वह्निरब्देकेन A; सर्वकामप्रदोबन्हिरब्देकेन E_N **8:120** यावज्जीवं] *conj.*; यावज्जीव° ACE_N **8:120** अनलमन्दिरम्] AC; अमरमन्दिरम् E_N

संपूज्यैलविलन्तस्य नामाङ्काङ्काञ्चनीं गदाम्॥ 8:120॥

क्षिप्त्वा दद्यात्तृतीयायां सघृते ताम्रभाजने।
चतुर्थ्यां रदनं दद्याद्धेमं नामाङ्कितं शुभम्॥ 8:121॥

विघ्नेश्वरस्य देवस्य ताम्रपात्रे घृतान्विते।
विप्रान्सुभोजितान्कृत्वा दद्याद्भक्षं घटानपि॥ 8:122॥

सम्वत्सरेण सिद्धिः स्याद्यावज्जीवं गणेशता।
पञ्चम्यां हेमजं सर्पं दद्याद्विप्राय भोजिते॥ 8:123॥

घृतप्लुतं तु नामाङ्कं ताम्रभाजनसंस्थितम्।
अनन्तं वासुकिं वापि तक्षकं वा त्रिरेखिणम्॥ 8:124॥

पद्मं महाब्जं शंखं वा कुलिकं च महोरगम्।
संपूज्यान्यतमं वापि गन्धधूपस्रगादिभिः॥ 8:125॥

भक्ष्यभोज्यान्नपानैश्च कामदं पापहारिणम्।
मयूरं हेमजं कृत्वा स्कन्दनामाङ्कितं शुभम्॥ 8:126॥

षष्ठ्यां दद्याच्च विप्राय ताम्रपात्रे घृतान्विते।
तोयपूर्णांश्च कलशान्भक्ष्यभोज्यसमन्वितान्॥ 8:127॥

दत्वा कामानवाप्नोति पक्षयोरुभयोरपि।

8:120 संपूज्यैलविलन्तस्य] CE$_N$; संपूज्य भविलन्तस्य A **8:120** नामाङ्काङ्काञ्चनीं गदाम्] CE$_N$; नामाअ --- A **8:121** क्षिप्त्वा दद्यात्तृतीयायां सघृते ताम्रभाजने] E$_N$; क्षिप्त्वा दद्यात्तृतीयस्यां सघृतं ताम्रभाजने A; ⊔ C **8:121** चतुर्थ्यां रदनं दद्याद्धेमं] C; चतुर्थ्या वरदं द्याद्धेम A; चतुर्थ्यां रदनन्दद्यादेध्मन् E$_N$ **8:122** विघ्नेश्वरस्य] AC; विघ्नेवारस्य E$_N$ **8:122** घृतान्विते] CE$_N$; घृताज्जिने A **8:122** विप्राअन् सुभोजितान् कृत्वा] *em.*; विप्रां सुभोजितां कृत्वा A; विप्रां सुभोजितं कृत्वा C; विप्रञ्च भोजितं कृत्वा° E$_N$ **8:122** दद्याद्भक्षं घटानपि] C; दद्याद्भक्षघटानपि A; दद्याद्भक्त्या घृतानपि E$_N$ **8:123** सिद्धिः स्याद्यावज्जीवं] C; सिद्धि स्या यावज्जीव A; सिध्दिः स्पाद्यावज्जीवं E$_N$ **8:123** गणेशता] C; गणेशताम् AE$_N$ **8:123** हेमजं सर्पं] E$_N$; हेमजं सर्प A; हेमज सर्प्पं C **8:123** भोजिते] E$_N$; --- AC **8:124** घृतप्लुतं तु] E$_N$; --- तन्तु A; ⊔ ⏑ स्च्छ **8:124** नामाङ्कं] AC; नामाङ्क E$_N$ **8:124** ताम्रभाजनसंस्थितम्] CE$_N$; ताम्रभाजनसस्थितम् A **8:124** अनन्तं] CE$_N$; अनन्त A **8:124** त्रिरेखिणम्] C; त्रिरेखिनम् AE$_N$ **8:125** महाब्जं] C; महापद्मजं A (unmetrical); महाकुलं E$_N$ **8:125** संपूज्यान्यतमं वापि] C; संपूज्यन्यतमं वापि A; संपूज्य च शतवापि E$_N$ **8:125** गन्धधूपस्रगादिभिः] A; गन्धपुष्पस्रगादिभिः CE$_N$ **8:126** कामदं पापहारिणम्] AC; कामदर्पापहारिणम् E$_N$ **8:126** मयूरं] CE$_N$; मयूर A **8:126** °नामाङ्कितं शुभम्] CE$_N$; °ना --- A **8:127** षष्ठ्यां दद्याच्च] CE$_N$; षष्ठ्यान्तद्यातु A **8:127** तोयपूर्णांश्च कलशान्] E$_N$; तोयपूर्णश्च कलशां A; ⏑ यपूर्णांश्च कलशान् C **8:127** °समन्वितान्] CE$_N$; °समन्वितम् A

सम्वत्सरेण कामांस्तु चिन्तितांल्लभते नरः॥ 8:128॥

पापी मुच्येत पापेन शुद्धात्मा स्कन्दमाप्नुयात्।
अश्वं हेममयं दद्याद्रवेर्नामाङ्कितं बुधः॥ 8:129॥

पक्षयोरुभयोश्चैव सघृते ताम्रभाजने।
वर्षेणैकेन शुद्धात्मा मुच्यते सर्वकिल्बिषैः॥ 8:130॥

यावज्जीवकृतेनैव आदित्यपदमाप्नुयात्।
अष्टम्यां भवनामांकं वृषं दद्याद्द्विजन्मने॥ 8:131॥

उभाभ्यामपि पक्षाभ्यां सघृते ताम्रभाजने।
कलशैर्भक्ष्यसंयुक्तैः पयसा च सुपूरितैः॥ 8:132॥

सम्वत्सरेण शुद्धात्मा प्राप्नुयादीप्सितं फलम्।
यावज्जीवेन गणतां यो ऽर्चयेन्नामभिर्हरम्॥ 8:133॥

पूर्वोक्तविधिना सिंहं देव्या नामाङ्कितं शुभम्।
दत्वा नवम्यां विप्राय प्रयाति परमाङ्गतिम्॥ 8:134॥

यमनामाङ्कितं हेमं महिषं ताम्रभाजने।
आज्यपूर्णे विनिक्षिप्य पयोघटसमन्विते॥ 8:135॥

दत्त्वा दशम्यां विप्राय भोजिताय तपस्विने।
याम्यदुःखेन मुच्यन्ते महापातकिनो ऽपि ये॥ 8:136॥

8:128 सम्वत्सरेण कामांस्तु] *conj.*; सम्वत्सरेण कामस्तु A; सम्वत्सरेणकामांस्तु E_N **8:128** चिन्तितांल्लभते] E_N; चिन्तितं लभते A; चिन्तितान् लभते C **8:129** हेममयं] CE_N; हिममयं A **8:129** दद्याद्रवेर्नामाङ्कितं बुधः] E_N; दद्या ⏑̱ --- बुधः A; दद्याद्द्वेर्नामाङ्कितं बुधः C **8:130** वर्षेणैकेन शुद्धात्मा] AE_N; ⊔ त्मा C **8:131** आदित्य°] CE_N; मादित्य° A **8:131** भवनामांकं] AC; भव नामांकं E_N **8:131** दद्याद्द्विजात्मने] CE_N; दद्याविजात्मने A **8:132** पक्षाभ्यां] CE_N; पक्षाभ्या A **8:132** कलशैर्भक्ष्यसंयुक्तैः] CE_N; कलशैभक्ष्यसम्यु --- A **8:132** पयसा च सुपूरितैः] C; --- सुपूरितैः A; पयसा च उपूरि तैः E_N **8:133** प्राप्नुयादीप्सितं फलम्] A; --- प्सितं फलम् C; प्राप्नुयादीप्सितंफलम् E_N **8:133** यो ऽर्चयेन्नामभिर्हरम्] CE_N; यो ऽर्चये नामभिहरम् A **8:134** सिंहं] CE_N; सिंहा A **8:134** प्रयाति] A; स याति CE_N **8:135** यमनामाङ्कितं] CE_N; यमनामाकितं A **8:135** महिषं] CE_N; महिष A **8:135** आज्यपूर्णे] C; आज्यपू ⏑̱ A; आज्यपूर्णं E_N **8:135** पयोघटसमन्विते] A; पयोघटसमन्वितम् C; पयाघृतसमन्वितम् E_N **8:136** दत्त्वा दशम्यां विप्राय भोजिताय तपस्विने] E_N; दत्त्वा दशम्या विप्राय भोजिताय तपस्विने A; दत्त्वा दशम्या विप्रा ⊔ C **8:136** याम्यदुःखेन मुच्यन्ते] A; याम्यदुःखैः प्रमुच्यन्ते CE_N **8:136** महापातकिनो ऽपि ये] AE_N; महापातकिनो प्रिये C

सम्वत्सरेण युक्तात्मा जीवान्ते गतिरुत्तमा।
एकादश्यान्तु धर्मस्य वृषं दद्याद्विजन्मने॥ 8:137॥

नामाङ्कं सघृतं न्यस्य ताम्रपात्रे घृतान्विते।
स धर्मगतिमाप्नोति शुद्धः सम्वत्सरेण तु॥ 8:138॥

कामी च लभते कामान्निष्कामी धर्मलोकताम्।
द्वादश्यां गरुडं दद्यान्नानाभक्ष्यसमन्वितम्॥ 8:139॥

पूर्वोक्तेन विधानेन पयोघटसमन्वितम्।
विष्णोर्नाम समुच्चार्य पक्षयोरुभयोरपि॥ 8:140॥

सम्वत्सरेण शुद्धात्मा विपापः क्रतुमाप्नुयात्।
यावज्जीवन्तु संपूज्य भोजनैश्च सदक्षिणैः॥ 8:141॥

विष्णुलोकमवाप्नोति विष्णुना सह मोदते।
सौवर्णन्धनुषं कृत्वा पञ्चबाणसमन्वितम्॥ 8:142॥

कामदेवं समभ्यर्च्य सघृते ताम्रभाजने।
भक्ष्याम्बुपूर्णघटकां विप्रान्संभोज्य दापयेत्॥ 8:143॥

सौभाग्यं धनधान्यञ्च विपाप्मा लभते ध्रुवम्।
यावज्जीवं च सम्पूज्य कामदेवपुरं व्रजेत्॥ 8:144॥

चतुर्दश्यां वृषन्दद्यात्सम्पूज्य परमेश्वरम्।

8:137 जीवान्ते गतिरुत्तमा] C; जीवन्ते गतिरुत्तमाः A; जीवान्ते गतिमुत्तमाम् E_N **8:137** दद्याद्विजन्मने] CE_N; दद्याद्विजन्मने A **8:138** नामाङ्कं सघृतं] AE_N; नामाकं सघृते A **8:138** घृतान्विते] CE_N; येपा? --- A **8:138** स धर्मगतिमाप्नोति शुद्धः सम्वत्सरेण तु] E_N; स धर्मगतिमा ⊔ सरेण तु C; --- तिमाप्नोति शुद्धं संवत्सरेण तु A **8:139** कामान् निष्कामी] *conj.*; कामं निष्कामी A; कामनकामी C; कामं निःकामी E_N **8:139** दद्यान्नानाभक्ष्यसमन्वितम्] C; दद्या नानाभक्षसमन्वितम् A; दद्यान्नानाभक्षसमन्वितम् E_N **8:140** °समन्वितम्] AC; °संमन्वितम् E_N **8:140** विष्णो नाम समुच्चार्य] C; विष्णोर्नाम समुचार्य A; विष्णुर्नाम समुच्चार्य E_N **8:141** यावज्जीवन्तु संपूज्य] CE_N; --- A **8:142** सह मोदते] AC; सहमोदते E_N **8:142** कृत्वा] A; दत्त्वा CE_N **8:142** °बाण°] CE_N; °बान° A **8:143** कामदेवं] CE_N; कामदेव A **8:143** ताम्रभाजने] AC; ताम्र भाजने E_N **8:143** भक्ष्याम्बुपूर्णघटकां विप्रान् संभोज्य दापयेत्] *conj.*; भक्षाम्बुपूर्णघटकां विप्रां संभोज्य दार्पयेत A (unmetrical); भक्ष्याम्बुपूर्णघटकं विप्रान् संभोज्य चार्चयेत् C; भक्षाम्बुपूर्णं घटकं विप्रान्संभोज्य चार्चयेत् E_N **8:144** विपाप्मा लभते] *em.*; विपापा लभते A; विप्राप्मा लभते C; विपाप्मालभते E_N **8:144** च सम्पूज्य कामदेवपुरं] C; --- पुरं A; च सम्पूज्य कामदेव पुरं E_N **8:145** चतुर्दश्यां] CE_N; चतुद्दश्या A **8:145** वृषन्दद्यात्सम्पूज्य] C; वृषन्दद्यात्सपूज्य A; वृषंदद्यात्सम्पूज्य E_N

तस्य नामाङ्कितं कृत्वा ताम्रभाजनसंस्थितम्॥ 8:145॥

प्रदद्याद्विप्रमुख्येभ्यो भोजयित्वा यथाविधि।
उभाभ्यामपि पक्षाभ्यां घटं भक्ष्याम्बुपूरितम्॥ 8:146॥

अब्दात्पापविशुद्धिः स्याद्द्वादशाब्दैर्गणेश्वरः।
यावज्जीवकृतेनैव सायोज्यन्तु महेश्वरे॥ 8:147॥

पौर्ण्णमास्याममावास्यां पक्षयोरुभयोरपि।
श्राद्धपिण्डाप्सुदानेन पितॄन्सन्तर्पयेन्नरः॥ 8:148॥

सौवर्णं पुरुषं कृत्वा पितृनामाङ्कितं बुधः।
प्रदद्याद्विप्रमुख्येभ्यः ताम्रस्थन्तु घृतप्लुतम्॥ 8:149॥

भक्ष्याम्बुपूर्णघटकान्दत्वा चैव विकल्मषः।
अब्देनैकेन युक्तात्मा विपापी काममीप्सितम्॥ 8:150॥

यावज्जीवकृतेनैव सुतृप्ताः पितरो भवेत्।
पितॄणां पदमाप्नोति भ्रष्टो भवति चोत्तमः॥ 8:151॥

धनधान्यसमृद्धस्तु बहुपुत्रः प्रजायते।
देवानां पूजने ह्येष विधिरुक्तो मयानघाः।
देव्याशंकरसंवादं तन्मया परिकीर्त्तितम्॥ 8:152॥

8:145 ताम्रभाजनसंस्थितम्] AC; ताम्र भाजनसंस्थितं E_N **8:146** भोजयित्वा] CE_N; योजयित्वा A **8:146** घटं भक्ष्याम्बुपूरितम्] A; घटान् भक्ष्याम्बुपूरितान् C; घटान् भक्ष्याम्बुपूरितान् E_N **8:147** अब्दात्पापविशुद्धिः स्याद्] C; अब्दात्पापविशुद्धि स्यां A; अष्दात्पापविशुद्धिः स्याद् E_N **8:147** द्वादशाब्दैर्गणेश्वरः] E_N; द्वादशाब्दै गणेश्वरः AC **8:147** यावज्जीवकृतेनैव] CE_N; यावज्जीव --- A **8:147** सायोज्यन्तु] C; --- A; सायुज्यन्तु E_N **8:147** महेश्वरे] E_N; --- श्वरे A; महेश्वरः C **8:148** श्राद्धपिण्डाप्सुदानेन] C; श्राद्धपिण्डासदानेन A; श्राध्दपिण्डासुदानेन E_N **8:148** पितॄन् सन्तर्पयेन्नरः] C; पितॄ तर्प्पयेन्नरः A; पितृन् सन्तर्पयेन्नरः E_N **8:149** सौवर्णं पुरुषं] *em.*; सौवर्ण पुरुषं AC; सौवर्णपुरुषं E_N **8:149** ताम्रस्थन्तु घृतप्लुतम्] C; ताम्रंस्थन्तु घृतप्लुतम् A; ताम्रस्थन्तु घटप्लुतम् E_N **8:150** भक्ष्याम्बुपूर्णघटकान्] *conj.*; भक्षाबुपूर्णन्सटका? A; भक्ष्याम्बुपूर्णघटकं C; भक्षाम्बुपूर्णघटकं E_N **8:150** विकल्मषः] AE_N; विकल्मकः C **8:150** अब्देनैकेन युक्तात्मा विपापी काममीप्सितम्] CE_N; अब्देनै ⏑ --- काममीप्सित A **8:151** यावज्जीवकृतेनैव] CE_N; याज्जीवकृतेन तु A **8:151** सुतृप्ताः पितरो भवेत्] A; भोजनैश्च सदक्षिणैः CE_N **8:152** °समृद्धस्तु] C; °समृद्धिस्तु A; °समृध्दन्तु E_N **8:152** देवानां पूजने ह्येष] A; देवाना पूजने ह्येष C; देवानां पूजयेद्धेष E_N **8:152** मयानघाः] *em.*; मयानघः A; मयानघ C; मयानद्याः E_N **8:152** देव्याशंकरसंवादं] AC; देव्या शंकरसंवाद E_N

॥ ⊗ ॥ इति शिवधर्मसंग्रहे ऽष्टमो ऽध्यायः ॥ ⊗ ॥

8:152 इति शिवधर्मसंग्रहे] C; --- सङ्गृहे A; इति शिव धर्मसङ्गृहे E_N **8:152** °हे ऽष्टमो ऽध्यायः] CE_N; °हे ऽष्टमपटलः A

शिवधर्मसंग्रहे नवमोऽध्यायः॥

देव्युवाच।

वेदधर्मः कथं देव कर्त्तव्यो विधिमिच्छता।
स्वर्गापवर्गहेतोश्च प्रसादाद्वक्तुमर्हसि॥ 9:1॥

ईश्वर उवाच।
मेखली दण्डधारी च सन्ध्योपासनतत्परः।
स्वाध्यायी होमजापी च भिक्षाशी त्यक्तमैथुनी॥ 9:2॥

मधुमांसनिवृत्तश्च सक्षारलवणानि च।
वृक्षारोहणमेकान्तं ताम्बूलञ्च न भक्षयेत्॥ 9:3॥

वर्जयेत्प्रेक्षणं कोपमघृष्ट्वा स्नानमाचरेत्।
स्त्रीप्रेक्षणन्न कुर्वीत माल्यधूपञ्च वर्जयेत्॥ 9:4॥

वर्जयेदञ्जनं गन्धन्तथा विषमलंघनम्।
षट्त्रिंशदब्दिका चर्या गुरोस्त्रैवेदिकं व्रतम्॥ 9:5॥

तदर्धिकं पादिकं वा ग्रहणान्तिकमेव वा।

9:1 कर्त्तव्यो विधिमिच्छता] C; कर्त्तव्यो विधिपृच्छता A; कर्त्तव्योविधिमिच्छता E_N **9:1** वक्तुमर्हसि] AC; बक्तुमर्हसि E_N **9:2** सन्ध्योपासन°] CE_N; सन्धोपासन° A **9:2** होमजापी च] CE_N; जप --- A **9:2** भिक्षाशी त्यक्तमैथुनी] C; शि त्यक्तमैथुनी A; भिक्षाशीत्यक्तमैथुनः E_N **9:3** मधुमांसनिवृत्तश्च] E_N; मधुमान्सनिवृत्तिश्च A; मधुमांसनिवृर्त्तिश्च C **9:3** सक्षारलवणानि च] *conj.*; अक्षालवणानि च A; अक्षारलवणानि च CE_N **9:3** °मेकान्तं] C; मेकान्त A; °मेकान्तां E_N **9:4** कोपमघृष्ट्वा] C; कोपमघृष्टा AE_N **9:4** स्त्रीप्रेक्षणन्न कुर्वीत] C; स्त्रीपेक्षणं न कुर्वीत A; स्त्रीप्रेक्षणं न कुर्कीत E_N **9:4** माल्यधूपञ्च] CE_N; माल्यपुष्पञ्च A **9:5** वर्जयेदञ्जनं गन्धन्तथा विषमलंघनम्] CE_N; वर्जयेद्व्ञ्चन --- लंघनम् A **9:5** षट्त्रिंशदब्दिका चर्या] *conj.*; षट्त्रिंशदाब्दिकाञ्चर्या A; षट्त्रिंशदब्दिकाञ्चर्यां C; षडिवंशदब्दिकां E_N (unmetrical) **9:5** गुरोस्त्रैवेदिकं] CE_N; गुरोस्त्रैवेदिक A

ब्रह्मचारिव्रतं ह्येतदुक्तमेव मया पुरा॥ 9:6॥

विस्रुतो नरकं याति आचारात्स्वर्ग्गतिं व्रजेत्।
कृतदारो गृहे यस्तु यजेद्यज्ञं सदक्षिणम्॥ 9:7॥

स्वाध्यायं सततं कुर्यात्सायं प्रातश्च हावनम्।
बलिञ्च वैश्वदेवानामतिथेश्चैव भोजनम्॥ 9:8॥

दर्शञ्च पौर्ण्णमासञ्च पशुबन्धेष्टिमेव च।
श्राद्धं सदक्षिणं कुर्यादृतुकाले स्त्रियं व्रजेत्॥ 9:9॥

वर्ज्जयेत्परदारादीनाचाराद्गतिमाप्नुयात्।
अहिंसा निर्मलत्वं हि तस्तस्तेयविवर्जनात्॥ 9:10॥

कामक्रोधनिवृत्तिश्च गुरुपूजनमेव च।
क्षमा दमो दया दानं सत्यं शौचं धृतिर्घृणा॥ 9:11॥

विद्या विज्ञानमास्तिक्यमेतद्ब्राह्मणलक्षणम्।
जीवेच्छिलोञ्छवृत्त्यैव प्रमृतेनैव वा पुनः॥ 9:12॥

वाणिज्यादि त्यजेत्कर्म भूतद्रोहञ्च सर्वदा।
जपाग्निहोमसंयुक्तः स स्वर्ग्गफलभाग्भवेत्॥ 9:13॥

पञ्चयज्ञमकुर्वाणो नरकं स ध्रुवं व्रजेत्।
अष्टम्याञ्च चतुर्दश्यामुपोष्य प्रयतात्मवान्॥ 9:14॥

9:6 ह्येतदुक्तमेव] CE$_N$; ह्येततदुक्तमे A **9:7** विस्रुतो नरकं याति] C; विस्रतो नरकं यान्ति A; विस्रुता नरकं यान्ति E$_N$ **9:7** आचारात्स्वर्ग्गतिं] CE$_N$; आचारा स्वर्ग्गति A **9:7** यजेद्यज्ञं सदक्षिणम्] CE$_N$; यजेद्यस्तुज्ञ सदक्षिण A (unmetrical) **9:8** सततं कुर्यात्सायं प्रातश्च] CE$_N$; तं कुर्या? सायं प्रातश्च A **9:8** हावनम्] AE$_N$; हानवम् C **9:8** °मतिथेश्चैव] E$_N$; °मतिथिश्चैव AC **9:9** दर्शञ्च] C; दर्शनं AE$_N$ **9:9** पौर्ण्णमासञ्च] *conj.*; पौर्णमास्याञ्च A; पौर्णमास्यान्तु CE$_N$ **9:9** श्राद्धं] CE$_N$; श्राद्ध A **9:10** आचाराद्गतिमाप्नुयात्] *em.*; आचारागतिमाप्नुयात् A; आराद्गतिमाप्नुयात् C (unmetrical); स्वाचाराद्गतिमाप्नुयात् E$_N$ **9:10** अहिंसा निर्मलत्वं हि] C; अहिंसा निर्मल --- A; अहिंसानिर्मलत्वं हि E$_N$ **9:10** तस्तस्तेयविवर्जनात्] C; --- विवर्जनात् A; तमस्तेयविवर्जनात् E$_N$ **9:11** शौचं धृतिर्घृणा] C; शौच धृतिघृणा A; शौचं धृतिर्घृणा कृपा (unmetrical) **9:12** °आस्तिक्यम्] CE$_N$; आस्तिक्य A **9:12** एतद्ब्राह्मणलक्षणम्] E$_N$; एतद्ब्राह्मणवक्षणम् A; एद्ब्राह्मणलक्षणम् C (unmetrical) **9:12** जीवेच्छिलोञ्छवृत्त्यैव] CE$_N$; जीवे शिलांच्छवृत्येव A **9:12** प्रमृतेनैव] AC; प्रसृतेनैव E$_N$ **9:13** वाणिज्यादि] AE$_N$; वानिज्यादि C **9:13** जपाग्निहोमसंयुक्तः] CE$_N$; जपाग्निहोत्रसंयु --- A **9:13** स स्वर्ग्गफलभाग्भवेत्] CE$_N$; --- भाग्भवेत् A **9:14** पञ्चयज्ञमकुर्वाणो] AC; पञ्च यज्ञमकुर्वाणो E$_N$ **9:14** नरकं] CE$_N$; नरक A **9:14** चतुर्दश्यामुपोष्य] CE$_N$; चतुर्दश्यां मुपोष्य A

बह्वृचं शिवसंकल्पं जपेत्संपूज्य शंकरम्।
एवं सम्वत्सरैकन्तु भक्त्या यः कुरुते द्विजः॥ 9:15॥

सर्पनिर्मोकवत्पापैर्मुच्यते नात्र संशयः।
तथैवैकादशं रुद्रञ्जपेदध्वपुरोहितः॥ 9:16॥

दक्षिणायां स्थितो मूर्त्तौ संपूज्य परमेश्वरम्।
स सर्वकलुषैर्मुक्तः शुद्धस्फटिकनिर्मलः॥ 9:17॥

रत्नालोकविमानेन याति माहेश्वरं पदम्।
अथवोद्धृत्य तत्रैव मानस्तोकशतं शतम्॥ 9:18॥

प्रत्यहं तु जपेद्देवि गणत्वं यो ऽभिवाञ्छति।
वामदेवं जपेत्सोमं देवव्रतमथापि वा॥ 9:19॥

पूर्वोक्तविधिमास्थाय च्छन्दोगः शुचिमानसः।
दिवाकर इव व्योम्नि भ्राजमानः स्वतेजसा॥ 9:20॥

स गच्छेत्परमं स्थानं यत्र यान्ति बहुश्रुताः।
जपेद्रुद्रगणान्विद्वानथर्वशिर एव वा॥ 9:21॥

अथवाभ्यर्च्य देवेशं याति माहेश्वरम्पदम्।
विविक्षुर्देवदेवस्य शरीरं ब्रह्मवित्तमः॥ 9:22॥

पवित्रं परमं पुण्यं व्रतं भौतिकमाचरेत्।
यज्ञब्रह्मार्पणेनैव यजेद्यज्ञं सदक्षिणं॥ 9:23॥

9:15 बह्वृचं शिवसंकल्पं जपेत्संपूज्य] C; ब्रह्मत्य शिवसंकल्प जपेत्सपूज्य A; बह्व वं शिवसङ्कल्पञ्जपेत्सपूज्य E_N **9:15 एवं सम्वत्सरैकन्तु**] E_N; एवं सम्वत्सरैक तु A; एवं सत्सरैकं तु C (unmetrical) **9:15 भक्त्या यः**] CE_N; भिक्षा य A **9:16 सर्पनिर्मोकवत्पापैर्मुच्यते नात्र संशयः**] E_N; सर्प्पनिर्मोचकवत्पापै मुच्यते नात्र सशयः A; सर्पनिर्मोचकवत्पापैर्मुच्यते नात्र संशयः C (unmetrical) **9:16 तथैवैकादशं**] E_N; त --- A; तथैवेकादशं C **9:16 रुद्रञ्जपेदध्वपुरोहितः**] CE_N; --- द्रं जपेदधुत्पुराहितः A **9:17 दक्षिणायां स्थितो मूर्त्तौ**] *conj.*; दक्षिणांगस्थितो मूत्तौ A; दक्षिणायां स्थितो मूर्त्ते C; दक्षिणायां स्थितं मूर्त्तौ E_N **9:17 °कलुषैर्मुक्तः**] C; °कलुषै मुक्तः A; °कलुषर्मुक्तः E_N **9:17 शुद्धस्फटिकनिर्मलः**] AC; शुद्धः स्फटिकनिर्मलः E_N **9:19 तु जपेद्देवि**] *em.*; तज्जपेद्देवि CE_N **9:19 यो ऽभिवाञ्छति**] CE_N; यो ऽभिवाञ् --- A **9:19 वामदेवं जपेत्सोमं**] CE_N; --- ञ्जपेद्साम A **9:20 पूर्वोक्त°**] AC; पूर्वोक्ति° E_N **9:20 च्छन्दोगः**] CE_N; च्छन्दोग A **9:20 भ्राजमानः**] CE_N; भ्राजमान A **9:21 परमं**] CE_N; परम A **9:21 °गणान्**] CE_N; °गण A **9:22 याति**] CE_N; यान्ति A **9:22 माहेश्वरम्पदम्**] CE_N; माहेश्वर --- A **9:22 विविक्षुर्देवदेवस्य शरीरं**] CE_N; --- देवदेवस्य शरीर A **9:23 यज्ञब्रह्मार्पणेनैव**] CE_N: यज्ञबर्पणेनैव A (unmetrical) **9:23 यजेद्यज्ञं सदक्षिणं**] AC; यजेद्यज्ञान् सदक्षिणान् E_N

आत्मध्यानरतश्चैव सिद्ध्यते देवधर्मवित्।
ध्यायन्प्रणवयोगेन सर्वगं ब्रह्म सर्वदा॥ 9:24॥

षोडशारेण चक्रेण यदिच्छेत्सिद्धिमात्मनः।
श्रद्धया चैकचित्तेन सर्वद्वंद्वसहेन च॥ 9:25॥

नित्यञ्चालुब्धचित्तेन सर्वमेकत्वदर्शिना।
एवं यो वर्तते नित्यञ्जपध्यानाग्निकर्म्मसु॥ 9:26॥

न चासौ दुर्गतिं याति ब्रह्मलोकञ्च गच्छति।
केवलं कर्मकारी स्यादात्मध्यानविवर्जितः॥ 9:27॥

अजित्वा सर्वगं ब्रह्म स्वर्गमात्रफलं लभेत्।
अत ऊर्ध्वं वनेवासी जितक्रोधो जितेन्द्रियः॥ 9:28॥

वसेद्वनगतो विद्वान्वर्तयन्कुशबिन्दुना।
कन्दमूलफलैः शाकैः श्यामानीवारकङ्गुभिः॥ 9:29॥

सायं प्रातश्च तैरेव होमयेज्जातवेदसम्।
अफालकृष्टैर्वनजैर्देवब्राह्मणतर्पणम्॥ 9:30॥

पितॄणान्तर्प्पणञ्चैव जपहोमरतः सदा।
सर्वभूतहितो नित्यं सर्वदुःखसहिष्णुकः॥ 9:31॥

अभ्रावकाश्यं शीतोष्णे पञ्चाग्निर्जलशायिता।

9:24 आत्मध्यान°] AC; आत्मज्ञान° E_N **9:24** ध्यायन्प्रणवयोगेन सर्वगं] *conj.*; ध्यायं प्रणवां योगेन सर्वत्मा A; ध्यायेत्प्रणवयोगेन सर्वगं C; ध्या॒येन् प्रणवयोगेन सर्वगं E_N **9:25** यदिच्छेत्सिद्धिमात्मनः] *conj.*; यदि ⏑̱ --- A; यदीच्छेत्सिद्धिमात्मनः CE_N **9:25** चैकचित्तेन] CE_N; --- चित्तेन A **9:25** सर्वद्वंद्वसहेन च] AC; सर्व द्वंद्वसहेन च E_N **9:26** °चालुब्धचित्तेन] CE_N; °चालुप्तचित्तेन A **9:26** °दर्शिना] AC; °दशिना E_N **9:27** कर्मकारी स्यादात्मध्यानविवर्जितः] C; धर्मकारी स्यादात्मध्यानविवर्जितः A; कर्मकारीस्यादात्मध्यान विवर्जितः E_N **9:28** °फलं लभेत्] CE_N; --- A **9:28** अत] CE_N; --- A **9:29** वनगतो] AC; बनगतो E_N **9:29** वर्तयन्कुशबिन्दुना] C; वर्तय कुशबिन्दुना A; वर्तयन् कुशविन्दुना E_N **9:29** कन्दमूलफलैः शाकैः] CE_N; कन्दमूलफलै शाकै A **9:29** °कङ्गुभिः] CE_N; °कोङ्गुभिः A **9:30** तैरेव] AE_N; तेरेव C **9:30** होमयेज्] CE_N; होमये A **9:30** अफालकृष्टैर्वनजैर्देवब्राह्मणतर्पणम्] *conj.*; अफलकृष्टैर्वनक्षै देवब्राह्मणतर्प्पणाम् A; अट्टालकृष्टैर्व्वनजैर्देवव्राह्मणतर्पणैः E_N **9:31** पितॄणान्तर्प्पणञ्चैव] CE_N; पितॄणान्तर्प्पण चैव A **9:31** जपहोमरतः सदा] CE_N; जापहोमरत सादा A **9:31** सर्वभूतहितो नित्यं] CE_N; --- त्यं A **9:32** अभ्रावकाश्यं शीतोष्णे] C; अभ्रावकाशा सातोष्ण A; अभ्रावकाश्यं शीतोष्णौ E_N **9:32** पञ्चाग्निर्जलशायिता] C; पञ्चाग्निजलशायिता A; पञ्चाग्निर्ज्जलशायि वा E_N

कुशवल्कलवासांसि कृष्णाजिनधरः सदा॥ 9:32॥

कृच्छ्रातिकृच्छ्रतप्तादिपराकैश्चान्द्रायणैस्तथा।
शीर्णपर्णोदकाहारैरात्मानं परिशोधयेत्॥ 9:33॥

मृगचारी वसेत्तैस्तु कष्टां वृत्तिं समास्थितः।
ब्राह्मणः स्वर्गगामी स्याद्विप्लुतो नरकं व्रजेत्॥ 9:34॥

कायस्थमग्निं कृत्वा तु खमाकाशे तु विन्यसेत्।
चेष्टायां विन्यसेद्वायुमनले ऽग्निं पयो ऽम्भसि॥ 9:35॥

कायं भूमौ मनश्चन्द्रे दिक्षु श्रोत्रे तु विन्यसेत्।
विष्णुं पादे गले रुद्रं अग्निं वाचि विनिक्षिपेत्॥ 9:36॥

मित्रे पाय्विन्द्रियं न्यास्य शिश्ने चैव प्रजापतिम्।
संन्यासन्तु ततः कृत्वा लोभक्रोधादिवर्जितः॥ 9:37॥

अद्रोहः सर्वभूतानां सर्वमात्मनि पश्यति।
त्रिदण्डी कुण्डिपात्री च भैक्षग्रासाष्टभुक्सदा॥ 9:38॥

न शश्वदुपभुञ्जीत भैक्षवृत्तिसमाश्रितः।
ग्रामैकरात्रमुषितो न वसेत्पञ्चरात्रिकः॥ 9:39॥

9:32 °वासांसि कृष्णाजिनधरः] CE$_N$; वासांस्या कृष्णाजिनधर A **9:33** कृच्छ्रातिकृच्छ्रतप्तादिपराकैश्चान्द्रायणैस्तथा] C (unmetrical); कृच्छ्रादिकृच्छतप्तादिपराकेन्तापणैस्तथा A; कृच्छ्रातिकृच्छ्रतप्तादिपराश्चान्द्रायणैस्तथा E$_N$ **9:33** शीर्ण°] AC; शा-ई-र्ण° E$_N$ **9:33** आत्मानं] CE$_N$; आत्मान A **9:34** वसेत्तैस्तु कष्टां वृत्तिं समास्थितः] E$_N$; वसेचैस्तु कष्टवृत्ति समास्थिता A; वसेत्तैस्तु कष्टा वृत्ति समास्थितः C **9:34** ब्राह्मणः स्वर्गगामी स्याद्विप्लुतो नरकं व्रजेत्] E$_N$; --- र्गगामी स्याद्विप्लुतो नरकं व्रजेत् A; ब्राह्मणः स्वर्गगामी स्याद्विप्लुतो नरक् व्रजेत् C **9:35** कायस्थमग्निं कृत्वा तु] A; अग्निं कृत्वा तु कायस्थं CE$_N$ **9:35** खमाकाशे] CE$_N$; क्षमांसाख्ये A **9:35** चेष्टायां] AE$_N$; चेष्टाया C **9:35** पयो ऽम्भसि] CE$_N$; पयो भसि A **9:36** श्रोत्रे] AE$_N$; श्रोत्त C **9:36** विन्यसेत्] AC; विक्षिपेत् E$_N$ **9:36** विष्णुं] C; विष्णु A; *om.* E$_N$ **9:36** पादे गले रुद्रं अग्निं वाचि विनिक्षिपेत्] AC; *om.* E$_N$ **9:37** पाय्विन्द्रियं] C; पाय्वीन्द्रिय A; पथ्विन्द्रि E$_N$ **9:37** शिश्ने चैव प्रजापतिम्] CE$_N$; शि --- ति A **9:37** संन्यासन्तु] *em.*; सन्यासन्तु ACE$_N$ **9:37** कृत्वा लोभक्रोधादिवर्जितः] *em.*; कृत्वा लोभक्रोधादिवर्जितं A; कृत्वा लोभमोहविवर्जितः C; कृत्वालोभमोहविवर्जितः E$_N$ **9:38** अद्रोहः सर्वभूतानां] E$_N$; अद्रोह सर्वभूताना A; अद्रोहस्य वभूताना C **9:38** भैक्षग्रासाष्टभुक् सदा] *conj.*; भैक्षग्रासाष्टस्सदा A; भैक्षस्यष्टभुक सदा C (unmetrical); भैक्षग्रासाष्टतुट् सदा E$_N$ **9:39** समाश्रितः] AE$_N$; समाश्रितिः C **9:39** उपभुञ्जीत] CE$_N$; उपयुञ्जीत A **9:39** भैक्षवृत्ति°] AC; भैक्षवृत्तिं E$_N$ **9:39** ग्रामैक°] AE$_N$; ग्राषैक° C **9:39** °रात्रिकः] E$_N$; °रात्रिकं A; °रात्रकः C

वर्षास्वेकत्र संवासी नगरे पञ्चरात्रिकः।
दम्भकल्कविनिर्मुक्तः सर्वद्वंद्वसहिष्णुकः॥ 9 : 40॥

ग्रामसङ्गविवर्ज्जी स्यात्सङ्गदोषविवर्जितः।
समः सर्वेषु भूतेषु अनारंभी अहिंसकः॥ 9 : 41॥

आत्मध्यानरतिर्नित्यं ब्रह्मभावसमन्वितः।
एवं यो वर्तते नित्यं स याति ब्रह्मलौकिकम्॥ 9 : 42॥

ब्रह्मणा सह मोदेत ब्रह्मण्येव तु लीयते।
विप्लुतो नरकं याति कामलोभसमन्वितः॥ 9 : 43॥

यथोक्तकारी ब्रह्मात्मा ब्रह्मलोकञ्च गच्छति।
वेदधर्मो मया प्रोक्तः स्वर्गनैश्रेयसः पदम्।
उत्तरेणैव वक्त्रेण व्याख्यातश्च समासतः॥ 9 : 44॥

॥ ⊗॥ इति शिवधर्मसंग्रहे नवमो ऽध्यायः॥ ⊗॥

9:40 संवासी नगरे पञ्चरात्रिकः] C; --- पञ्चरात्रिकः A; सन्न्यासी नगरे पञ्चरात्रिकः E_N **9:40** दम्भकल्कविनिर्मुक्तः] CE_N; दंभकर्ण्णविनिर्मुक्तः A **9:40** सर्वद्वंद्वसहिष्णुकः] AE_N; सर्वद्वंद्वसहिष्णुकः C **9:41** ग्रामसङ्गविवर्ज्जी स्यात्] C; ग्रामकर्मविवर्जी स्यात् E_N; ग्रामसङ्गविवजी स्या A **9:41** सङ्गदोषविवर्जितः] CE_N; संगदोषविवर्जिता A **9:41** समः सर्वेषु भूतेषु] C; सम सर्वेषु भूतेषु A; दयालु सर्वभूतेषु E_N **9:41** अनारंभी] AC; अनासक्ति E_N **9:42** आत्मध्यानरतिर्नित्यं] *em.*; आत्मध्यानरति नित्यं A; आत्मभावरतिर्नित्यं CE_N **9:42** स याति ब्रह्मलौकिकम्] AC; सयाति ब्रह्मलोकिकं E_N **9:43** ब्रह्मणा सह मोदेत] C; --- न्ते A; ब्रह्मणा सह मोदन्ते E_N **9:43** कामलोभसमन्वितः] AC; कामलोभ समन्वितः E_N **9:44** यथोक्तकारी] AC; यण्थोक्तकारी E_N **9:44** ब्रह्मात्मा] AE_N; ब्रह्मत्मा C **9:44** ब्रह्मलोकञ्च] A; ब्रह्मलोकं स CE_N **9:44** वेदधर्मो मया प्रोक्तः] C; वेदधर्म मया प्रोक्तः A; वेदधर्म मया प्रोक्ताः E_N **9:44** स्वर्गनैश्रेयसः पदम्] A; स्वग्र्गनैश्रेयसम्पदम् C; स्वर्ग नैश्रेयसम्पदम् E_N **9:44** व्याख्यातश्च समासतः] CE_N; व्याख्याता च समास्सतः A **9:44** इति शिवधर्मसंग्रहे] CE_N; इति शिवधर्म --- A **9:44** नवमो ऽध्यायः] C; --- पटलः A; नवमो ऽध्याय E_N

WORKS CONSULTED

Abbreviations

BORI	Bhandarkar Oriental Research Institute
CUP	Cambridge University Press
EFEO	Ecole française d'Extrême-Orient
EI	*Epigraphia Indica*
GOML	Government Oriental Manuscripts Library, Madras
IFI	Institut Français d'Indologie (misnomer used in old publications)
IFP	Institut Français de Pondichéry/French Institute of Pondicherry
KSTS	Kashmir Series of Texts and Studies
NAK	National Archives of Kathmandu
NGMPP	Nepal-German Manuscript Preservation Project
NM	Niśvāsamukha
ŚiDhS	Śivadharmasaṅgraha
T	Transcript
ZDMG	Zeitschrift der Deutschen Morgenländischen Gesellschaft

Manuscripts

ĀTMĀRTHAPŪJĀPADDHATI
of Vedajñānaguru II. IFP MS Transcript T. 323.

BRAHMAYĀMALA,
NAK MS 3–370, NGMPP Reel No. A 42/6. Palm-leaf, Newari script. (I have also consulted an electronic transcription prepared by Dr. Shaman HATLEY.)

BṚHATKĀLOTTARA,
NAK MS 5–778, NGMPP Reel No. A 42/8. Palm-leaf, Newari script. NAK MS 4–131, NGMPP Reel No. A 43/1. Palm-leaf, Devanāgarī script.

DEVYĀMATAM,
(also called *Niśvāsākhyamahātantra*). NAK MS 5–446, NGMPP Reel No. A 41/13. Palm-leaf, Nandīnāgarī script.

DHARMAPUTRIKĀ,
NAK MS 5–738, NGMPP Reel No. A 11/3. Palm-leaf, Newari script. NAK MS 1–1075, NGMPP Reel No. B 7/3. Palm-leaf Newari script. Cambridge University Library MS Add. 1445. Palm-leaf, Newari script. Printed in *Śivadharma Paśupatimatam Śivadharmamahāśāstram Paśupatināthadarśanam* ed. Yogin Narahari NĀTHA 1998 (saṃvat 2055). (I have also consulted an electronic text prepared by Dr. Anil Kumar ACHARYA.)

Jñānaratnāvalī
of Jñānaśiva. GOML MS R 14898 and its apograph IFP MS T. 231, as well as pp. 13–60 of IFP MS T. 106 (the latter giving the text of what is probably a manual based upon the *Jñānaratnāvalī*, cf. Goodall 2000: 209, fn. 11), paper transcripts in Devanāgarī.

Kulasāratantra,
NAK MS 4–137, NGMPP Reel No. A 40/11. Palm-leaf, Nandīnāgari script.

Lalitavistara,
NAK MS 5–738, NGMPP Reel No. A 11/3. Palm-leaf, Newari script. NAK MS 1–1075, NGMPP Reel No. B 7/3. Palm-leaf, Newari script. Cambridge University Library MS Add. 1445. Palm-leaf, Newari script. Also IFP T. 32, and 514. Paper transcripts in Devanāgarī. (I have also consulted an electronic transcription prepared by Dr. Anil Kumar Acharya.)

Mṛgendrapaddhati
of Aghoraśiva with the commentary (-ṭīkā) of Vaktraśambhu. IFP T. 1021. Paper transcript in Devanāgarī.

Niśvāsakārikā,
IFP paper transcripts: T. 17, T. 127 and T. 150.

Niśvāsākhyamahātantra
See *Devyāmatam*.

Pārameśvaratantra,
Cambridge University Library MS Add. 1049. Palm-leaf, early Nepalese 'Licchavi' script. Also NAK MS 4-892, NGMPP Reel No. A 1280/2 (paper manuscript in Newari); IFP T. 249, paper transcript in Devanāgarī.

Prāyaścittasamuccaya
of Hṛdayaśiva. Cambridge University Library MS Add. 2833. Palm-leaf, early Newari script. Also NAK MS 1-1297, NGMPP Reel No. A 521/6 (paper manuscript in Newari script); NAK MS 5-2402, NGMPP Reel No. B 427/2 (paper manuscript in Devanāgarī).

Note that a complete transcription of the Cambridge MS is contained in the appendix to the work of R. Sathyanārāyanan and Dominic Goodall (2015: 355–499).

Sarvadarśanasaṁgraha
of Sāyaṇa Mādhava, edited with an original commentary in Sanskrit by Vāsudev Śāstrī Abhyaṅkara. Government Oriental (Hindu) Series no. 1. Poona: Bhandarkar Oriental Research, 1924.

Sarvajñānottaratantra,
NAK MS 1–1692, NGMPP Reel No. A 43/12. Palm-leaf, early Nepalese 'Licchavi' script. Described by Śāstri (1905:lxxiv–lxxv and 85–6). Also IFP T. Nos. 334, 760, paper transcripts in Devanāgarī. (I have also consulted an electronic transcription prepared by Prof. Dominic Goodall.)

Sarvajñānottaravṛtti
of Aghoraśivācārya. Oriental Research Institute and Manuscripts Library, Trivandrum MS 6578, palm-leaf (palmyra) manuscript from Madurai in

Grantha script (listed by BHASKARAN, 1986:6). Also IFP 39818, palm-leaf (palmyra) manuscript in Grantha script; IFP 47818 and IFP 47828, paper manuscripts in Grantha script; Hoshiarpur MS 5987, palm-leaf (palmyra) manuscript in Grantha script; and IFP T. Nos. 83 and 985, paper transcripts in Devanāgarī. (I have used the electronic transcription prepared by Prof. Dominic GOODALL.)

SIDDHĀNTASAMUCCAYA
of Trilocanaśiva. IFP MS T. 284, pp. 127–74 and IFP MS T. 206, pp. 56–111. Paper transcripts in Devanāgarī.

ŚIVADHARMASAṄGRAHA,
NAK MS 5–738, NGMPP Reel No. A 11/3. Palm-leaf, Newari script. NAK MS 1–1075, NGMPP Reel No. B 7/3. Palm-leaf, Newari script. The Asiatic Society Manuscript Number G 4077/3, Newari script. Also Cambridge University Library MS Add. 1445. Palm-leaf, Newari script. Printed in *Śivadharma Paśupatimatam Śivadharmamahāśāstram Paśupatināthadarśanam* ed. Yogin Narahari NĀTHA 1998 (saṃvat 2055). (I have also consulted an electronic transcription prepared by Dr. Anil Kumar ACHARYA.)

ŚIVADHARMAŚĀSTRA,
NAK MS 5–738, NGMPP Reel No. A 11/3. Palm-leaf, Newari script. NAK MS 1–1075, NGMPP Reel No. B 7/3. Palm-leaf, Newari script. Cambridge University Library MS Add. 1445. Palm-leaf, Newari script. Also IFP T. 32, and 514. Paper transcripts in Devanāgarī. Printed in *Śivadharma Paśupatimatam Śivadharmamahāśāstram Paśupatināthadarśanam* ed. Yogin Narahari NĀTHA 1998 (saṃvat 2055). (I have consulted an electronic transcription prepared by Dr. Anil Kumar ACHARYA.)

ŚIVADHARMOTTARA,
NAK MS 5–738, NGMPP Reel No. A 11/3. Palm-leaf, Newari script. NAK MS 1–1075, NGMPP Reel No. B 7/3. Palm-leaf, Newari script. The Asiatic Society Manuscript Number G 4077/3, Newari script. Also Cambridge University Library MS Add. 1445. Printed in *Śivadharma Paśupatimatam Śivadharmamahāśāstram Paśupatināthadarśanam* ed. Yogin Narahari NĀTHA 1998 (saṃvat 2055).

TANTRASADBHĀVA,
NAK MS 1–363, NGMPP Reel No. A 44/1. Palm-leaf, Newari script. (I have also consulted the electronic transcription prepared by Prof. Mark S. G. DYCZKOWSKI.)

UMĀMAHEŚVARASAṂVĀDA,
NAK MS 5–738, NGMPP Reel No. A 11/3. Palm-leaf, Newari script. NAK MS 1–1075, NGMPP Reel No. B 7/3. Palm-leaf, Newari script. Cambridge University Library MS Add. 1445. Palm-leaf, Newari script. Printed in *Śivadharma Paśupatimatam Śivadharmamahāśāstram Paśupatināthadarśanam* ed. Yogin Narahari NĀTHA 1998 (saṃvat 2055). (I have also consulted an electronic text prepared by Dr. Anil KUMAR ACHARYA.)

UTTAROTTARAMAHĀSAṂVĀDA/ UMOTTARA,
NAK MS 5–738, NGMPP Reel No. A 11/3. Palm-leaf, Newari script. NAK

MS 1-1075, NGMPP Reel No. B 7/3. Palm-leaf, Newari script. Cambridge University Library MS Add. 1445. Palm-leaf, Newari script. Printed in *Śivadharma Paśupatimatam Śivadharmamahāśāstram Paśupatināthadarśanam* ed. Yogin Narahari NĀTHA 1998 (saṃvat 2055). (I have also consulted an electronic text prepared by Dr. Anil Kumar ACHARYA.)

Printed Sources

AGNIPURĀṆA,
ed. Jivānanda Vidyāsāgara BHAṬṬA. Colakatta, 1883.

AJITAMAHĀTANTRAM,
edited with annotated translation by N.R. BHATT and Jean FILLIOZAT in five vols. Delhi: Indira Gandhi National Centre For The Arts and Motilal Banarsidass, 2005.

AJITĀGAMA.
See *Ajitamahātantram* above.

ATHARVAVEDAPARIŚIṢṬA.
See BISSCHOP & GRIFFITHS 2003.

ANEKĀRTHASAṄGRAHA
of Ācharya Hema Candra, ed. Jagannāth ŚĀSTRI with an alphabetical index prepared by Chanānanda PĀṆḌEYA and Janārdana JOSHI. Benares: Vidya Vilas Press, 1929.

ABHIJÑĀNAŚĀKUNTALAM
of Kālidāsa (based on Mss. in Maithili script) with commentaries of Śankara and Narahari ed. Ramanath JAH. Darbhanga Mithila Institute of Post-Graduate Studies and Research in Sanskrit Learning, 1957.

ABHIDHARMAKOŚABHĀṢYA
of Vasubandhu, ed. P. PRADHAN. Tibetan Sanskrit Works Series vol. 8. Patna: K. P. Jayaswal Research Institute, 1967.

AMARAKOŚA.

1997 *Amarakośa* with the commentary (VYĀKHYĀSUDHĀ or RĀMĀŚRAMĪ) of Bhānujidīkṣita, ed. Sivadatta DĀDHIMATHA and rev. Vāsudeva Laksmana PANAŚĪKARA. Brajajivan Prachyabharati Granthamala 1. Delhi: Chaukhamba Sanskrit Pratishthan, 1997 (3rd impression).

1971– *Amarakośa with the unpublished South Indian Commentaries*, ed. A. A. RAMANATHAN. 3 vols. The Adyar Library Series, Volume 101. Madras: Adyar Library and Research Centre, 1971, 1978, 1983.

AṢṬĀDHYĀYĪ
of Pāṇini. See VASU, Śrīśa Candra 1891.

ĀDIKARMAPRADĪPA
by Anupamavajra, ed. Louis de la VALLÉE POUSSIN, in *Études et Matériaux*. Bruxelles/London, 1898. pp. p. 177–232. (I have consulted an e-text prepared by Prof. Harunaga ISAACSON.)

ĪŚĀDYAṢṬOTTARAŚATOPANIṢADAḤ.
īśādyaṣṭottaraśatopaniṣadaḥ with various readings. ed. Vāsudeva ŚARMĀ. Mombay: Nirṇaya Sāgar Press, 1932.

ĪŚĀNAŚIVAGURUDEVAPADDHATI
of Īśānasivagurudeva, ed. T. Gaṇapati Śāstrī, 4 Vols. Delhi: Bharatiya Vidya Prakashan, 1990. (Reprinted, but with a substantial new introduction dated to 1987 by N. P. UNNI, from Trivandrum Sanskrit Series Nos. 69, 72, 77 and 83, Trivandrum, 1920, 1921, 1922, 1925.)

ĪŚĀVĀSYOPANIṢAD.
Īśāvāsyopaniṣad with introduction, Sanskrit text, Śāṅkara bhāṣya, Prose-order Hindi translation, Explanation, Notes, and English translation. ed. Shashi TIWARI. Delhi: Bharatiya Vidya Bhavan, 1986.

ĪŚVARASAṂHITĀ,
ed. P. B. Anantacharya SWAMI. Śāstramuktāvalī 45. Kanchipuram: Sudarsana Press, 1923.

UTTARASŪTRA.
See GOODALL et al. 2015.

AITAREYA BRĀHMAṆA.
The Aitareya Brahmanam of the Rigveda, Containing the Earliest Speculations of the Brahmans on the Meaning of the Sacrifcial Prayers, and on the Origin, Performance, and Sense of the Rites of the Vedic Religion, ed. Martin HAUG. Vol. I: Sanscrit Text, with Preface, Introductory Essay, and a Map of the Sacrifcial Compound at the Soma Sacrifce. Vol. 2: Translation, with Notes. Bombay-London, 1863. Reprint: Bharatiya Publishing House, Delhi, 1976 and 1977.

KATHĀSARITSĀGARA,
of Somadeva Bhatta, ed. by Pandit DURGĀPRASĀD & Kāśināth Pāndurang PARAB and revised by Vāsudev Laxman SHĀSTRI Pansikar. Bombay: Nirṇaya Sāgar Press,1915 (third edition).

KARMAKĀṆḌAKRAMĀVALĪ
of Somaśambhu, ed. Jagaddhar ZADOO. KSTS 73. Srinagar, 1947.
See also SOMAŚAMBHUPADDHATI and BRUNNER 1963, 1968, 1977.

KĀṬHAKAGṚHYASŪTRA.
The Kāṭhakagṛhyasūtra with extracts from three commentaries, an appendix and indexes, ed. Willem CALAND. Dayānanda Mahāvidyālaya Saṃskṛta Granthamālā saṃ 9. Lahore: Research Department D.A.V. College, 1925.

KĀMIKĀGAMA,
PŪRVABHĀGA and UTTARABHĀGA. No editor accredited. Published by C. Swaminatha GURUKKAL. Madras: South Indian Archaka Association, 1975 and 1988.

KIRAṆATANTRA,

1932 ed. Ti. Rā. Pañcāpageśaśivācārya and K. M. Subrahmaṇyaśāstrī. Śivāgamasiddhāntaparipālanasaṅgha Vol. No. 16. (=edD) Devakōṭṭai, 1932.

1998 See GOODALL 1998.

KUBJĪKĀMATATANTRA,
The Kubjikāmatatantra: Kulālikāmnāya version, ed. T. GOUDRIAAN and J. A. SCHOTERMAN. Orientalia Rheno-Traiectina. E. J. Brill: Leiden, New York, København and Köln, 1988.

KUMĀRASAMBHAVA
of Kālidāsa with the commentary of Vallabhadeva. *Vallabhadeva's Kommentar (Śāradā Version) zum Kumārasambhava des Kālidāsa,* ed. M. S. NARAYANA MURTI. Verzeichnis der orientalischen Handschriften in Deutschland, Supplementband 20,1. Wiesbaden: Franz Steiner Verlag, 1980.

KŪRMAPŪRĀṆA.
The Kurma Purana critically edited by Ānandasvarūpa GUPTA. Varanasi: All-India Kashiraj Trust, 1971.

KṚTYAKALPATARU.
See *Tīrthavivecanakāṇḍa aṣṭamo bhāgaḥ.*

KAIVALYOPANIṢAD,
ed. Vāsudeva ŚARMĀ, 1932. See *Īśādyaṣṭottaraśatopaniṣadaḥ* or ŚARMĀ Vāsudeva 1932.

KAUṆḌINYA'S BHĀṢYA.
See *Pāśupatasūtra.*

KAUṢĪTAKAGṚHYASŪTRA.
The Kauṣītakagṛhyasūtras with the commentary of Bhavatrāta, ed. T. R. CHINTAMANI. Madras university Sanskrit series no. 15. University of Madras, 1944.

KRIYĀKRAMADYOTIKĀ
of Aghoraśivācārya with the commentary (PRABHĀVYĀKHYĀ) of Nirmalamaṇi, ed. Rāmaśāstrin and AMBALAVĀNAJÑĀNASAMBANDHAPARĀŚAKTISVĀMIN. Chidambaram, 1927.

KHECARĪVIDYĀ.
The Khecarīvidyā of Ādinātha. A critical edition and annotated translation of an early text ot haṭhayoga by James Mallinson, ed. Gavin FLOOD. Routledge Studies in Tantric Tradition Series. Routledge: London and New YorK, 2007.

GAṆAKĀRIKĀ
of Bhāsarvarvajña with the commentary *Ratnaṭīkā*, ed. C. D. DALAL. Gaekwad's Oriental Series No. XV. Baroda: Central Library, 1920.

GARUḌAPURĀṆA.
Śrīgaruḍamahāpurāṇam, ed. Khemarāja ŚRĪKṚṢṆADĀSA. Delhi: Nag Publishers, 1984. [Reprint of the Venkatesvara Press]

GĪTĀBHĀṢYA.
See *Bhagavadgītā.*

GUHYASŪTRA.
An electronic transcription of the NGMPP A 41/14.

GAUTAMADHARMASŪTRA
with the commentary *maskari*, ed. L. SRINIVASACHARYA. Mysore: Government branch Press, 1917.

CARAKASAṂHITĀ.
THE CARAKASAṂHITA BY AGNIVEŚA revised by Caraka and Dṛdhabala, with the Āyurveda-Dīpikā commentary of Cakrapāṇi DATTA, ed. Yādava SHARMA. Bombay: Nirṇaya Śāgar Press,1941 (third edition).

CHĀNDOGYOPANIṢAD.
The Chandogya Upanisahad of the Samaveda with the commentary of Sankara Charya and the gloss of Ananda Giri, ed. Jibananda VIDYASAGARA. Calcutta: Sucharoo Press, 1873.

JAYASIṂHAKALPADRUMA,
ed. Harināyāyaṇa ŚARMAN. Bombay, 1903. (I have also consulted an electronic text provided by Prof. Diwakar ACHARYA.)

JAYĀKHYASAṂHITĀ.
Jayākhyasaṃhitā, critically edited with an introduction in Sanskrit, indices etc. by Embar KṚṢṆAMĀCĀRYA. Gaekwad's Oriental Series, No. 54. Baroda: Oriental Institute, 1967.

JAYOTTARA.
An electronic transcription prepared by Prof. Diwakar ACHARYA.

JĀBĀLOPANIṢAD,
ed. Vāsudeva Śarmā, 1932. See *Īśādyaṣṭottaraśatopaniṣadaḥ* and ŚARMĀ Vāsudeva 1932.

TATTVAVAIŚĀRADĪ.
See *Pātañjalayogasūtrāṇi* and [WOODS] James HAUGHTON 1927.

TANTRASAMUCCAYA.
The Tantrasamuccaya of Nārāyaṇa with the commentary Vimarśinī of Saṅkara ed. T. Ganapati ŚĀSTRĪ. Trivandrum Sanskrit Series. Delhi: Nag Publishers, 1990 (first edition 1921).

TANTRASĀRA
of Abhinavagupta. ed. Mukund Rām SHĀSTRĪ. KSTS XVII. Bombay and Srinagar, 1918.

TANTRĀLOKA
of Abhinavagupta with commentary (-VIVEKA) of Rājānaka Jayaratha, ed. Madhusūdan Kaul ŚĀSTRĪ. KSTS 23, 28, 30, 35, 29, 41, 47, 59, 52, 57 and 58. Bombay and Srinagar, 1918–38.

TANTRĀLOKAVIVEKA.
See *Tantrāloka.*

TĪRTHAVIVECANAKĀṆḌA AṢṬAMO BHĀGAḤ
of Bhaṭṭa Śrīlakṣmīdhara's *Kṛtyakalpataru,* ed. K. V. RANGASVAMI AIYANGAR. Borada: Oriental Institute, 1942.

TAITTIRĪYĀRAṆYAKA
with the commentary of Sāyaṇācārya. Ed. by Rājendralāl MITRA. Calcutta: 1871. Bibliotheca Indica LII.

TRIŚIKHIBRĀHMAṆOPANIṢAD,
ed. Vāsudeva ŚARMĀ, 1932. See *Īśādyaṣṭottaraśatopaniṣadaḥ* or ŚARMĀ Vāsudeva 1932.

DIVYĀVADĀNA,
ed. Paraśurāma Lakṣmaṇa VAIDYA. Buddhist Sanskrit texts 20. Mithila Institute of Postgraduate Studies and Research in Sanskrit Learning. Darbhanga, 1959.

DEVĪBHĀGAVATAPURĀṆA
Śrīmaddevībhāgavatapurāṇa, ed. Kumar Pushpendra and transl. by Śriścandra Rai BAHADUR, 2 vols. Delhi: Eastern Books Linkers, 2006.

DHARMASŪTRAS.
The law codes of Āpastamba, Gautama, Baudhāyana, and Vasiṣṭha with annotated text and translation. ed. Patrick OLIVELLE. Delhi: Motilal Banarasidas, 2000.

DHĀTURATNĀKARA
of Munilāvaṇyavijaya sūri. 7 Vols. No editor accredited. Delhi: Dimond Printers, 1994. [reprint of 1867 Saka = 1945/6]

NAYASŪTRA.
See GOODALL et al. 2015.

NĀRADAPARIVRĀJAKOPANIṢAD,
ed. Vāsudeva ŚARMĀ, 1932. See *Īśādyaṣṭottaraśatopaniṣadaḥ* and ŚARMĀ Vāsudeva 1932.

NĀRADAPURĀṆA
Nāradīyapurāṇam, ed. by Khemarāja ŚRĪKṚṢṆADĀSA. Venkatesvara Press, Bombay V.S. 1962 [AD 1905]. (2nd edition. Bombay AD 1923) [Reprinted, with an Introduction by Carudeva ŚĀSTRIN and a Ślokānukramaṇī by Nāgaśaraṇa SIṂHA. Nag Publishers, Delhi 1984 (1995^2).

No editor accredited. Bombay: Veṅkaṭeśvara press, 1980.

NĀRADĪYASAṂHITĀ,
ed. Rāghava Prasāda CHAUDHARY. Kendriya Sanskrit Vidyapetha Series No. 15. Tirupati: Kendriya Sanskrit Vidyapetha, 1917.

NIŚVĀSATATTVASAṂHITĀ
The Niśvāsatattvasaṃhitā. The Earliest Surviving Śaiva Tantra. Volume 1. A Critical Edition & Annotated Translation of the Mūlasūtra, Uttarasūtra & Nayasūtra, ed. Dominic Goodall in collaboration with Alexis Sanderson & Harunaga. Isaacson with contributions of Nirajan Kafle, Diwakar Acharya & others. Pondichéry, Hamburg: Institut français d'Indologie, École française d'Extrême-Orient, Asien-Afrika-Institut, Universität Hamburg, 2015.

NETRATANTRA
with the commentary (UDDYOTA) of Kṣemarāja, ed. Madhusudan KAUL. KSTS 46 and 61. Bombay, 1926 and 1939.

PARAMAHAṂSAPARIVRĀJAKOPANIṢAD,
ed. Vāsudeva ŚARMĀ, 1932. See *Īśādyaṣṭottaraśatopaniṣadaḥ* or Śarmā Vāsudeva 1932.

PARĀKHYATANTRA.
See GOODALL 2004.

PĀIA-SADDA-MAHAṆṆAVO,
ed. Hargovind DAS T. Varanasi: Prakrit Text Society, 1963.

PĀTAÑJALAYOGASŪTRĀṆI,

1904 together with *Vyāsabhāṣya* of Vyāsa, *Tattvavaiśāradī* of Vācaspati Miśra and *Bhojavṛtti* of Bhojadeva, ed. Kāśīnātha ŚĀSTRĪ. Ānandāśrama Sanskrit Series No. 47. Poona: Ānandāśrama Press, 1904.

1912 (1998) *Pātañjali's Yoga Sūtras: with the commentary of Vyāsa and the gloss of Vāchaspati Miśra*, translated by Rāma Prasāda with an introduction from Rai Bahadur Śrīśa Chandra Vasu. Delhi: Munshiram Manoharlal Publishers (1998 reprint of the 1912 edition).

1952 together with *Vyāsabhāṣya* of Vyāsa and *Vivaraṇa* of Śaṅkara. Critically edited with introduction by Rama ŚĀSTRI and Krisnamurthi ŚĀSTRĪ. Madras: Government Oriental Manuscripts Library, 1952.

2000 together with *Vyāsabhāṣya* of Vyāsa, Hindi translation and Hindi commentary *Suviśada* of Hariharānanda Āraṇya, ed. Rāmaśaṃkara BHAṬṬĀCĀRYA. Delhi: Motilal Banarsidass, 2000 (reprint).

PĀDMASAṂHITĀ.

1974 *Padma Samhita* part I, Critically edited by Seetha PADMANABHAN and R.N. SAMPATH. PPPS 3. Madras.

1982 *Padma Samhita* Part II, Critically edited by Seetha PADMANABHAN and V. VARADACHARI. PPPS 4. Madras.

PĀRAMEŚVARASAṂHITĀ,
ed. Govindācārya. Tiruchi: Kalyāṇa Press, 1953.

PĀRASKARAGṚIHYASŪTRA
of Pāraskara, with five commentaries of Karka Upādhyāya, Jayarām, Harihar, Gadādhar and Vishvanāth ed. Mahādeva Gaṅgādhara BĀKRE. New Delhi: Munshiram Manoharlal 1982 (reprint of 1917).

PĀŚUPATASŪTRA
with the commentary (PĀÑCĀRTHABHĀṢYA) of Kauḍinya, ed. Ananthakrishna SASTRI. Trivandrum Sanskrit Series No. CXLIII. Trivandrum: The Oriental Manuscript Library of the University of Travancore, 1940.

PĀŚUPATASŪTRABHĀṢYA.
See *Pāśupatasūtra*.

PRAYOGAMAÑJARĪ
of Ravi, ed. Si. Ke. Rāman NAMPIYĀR with Ke. ACYUTAPPOTUVĀL. Trippunithura: Sanskrit College, 1953–54.

PRAŚASTAPĀDABHĀṢYA
together with the *Nyāyakandalī* of Śrīdhara, ed. Vindhyesvarīpradāda DVIVEDIN. Vol. IV. Vizianagram Sanskrit Serise No. 6. Benares: E. J. Lazarus & Co., 1895.

PRĀYAŚCITTAVIDHI.
An edition and translation of Diwakar ACHARYA, a work in progress.

BṚHADĀRAṆYAKOPANIṢAD
with the commentary of Śaṅkara and Ānandagiri. ed. Kāśinātha ŚĀSTRĪ. Ānandāśrama Sanskrit Series 15. Poona: Ānandāśrama Press, 1953.

BAUDHĀYANADHARMASŪTRA,
ed. OLIVELLE, Patrick, 2000. See *Dharmasūtras* of Olivelle Patrick, 2000.

BRAHMAPURĀṆA.
Vol 1, *Sanskrit Indices and text of the Brahmapurāṇa* by Peter SCHREINER and Renate SÖHNEN. Vol 2, Brahmapurāṇa. Summary of Contents, with Index of Names and Motifs by Renate SÖHNEN and Peter SCHREINER. Wiesbaden 1987, 1989.2 vols. Purāṇa Research Publications Tübingen 1 and 2.

BRAHMASŪTRAŚĀṂKARABHĀṢYAM
with the commentaries (BHĀṢYARATNAPRABHĀ, BHĀMATĪ and NYĀYANIRṆAYA of Govindānanda, Vācaspatimiśra and Ānandagiri. ed. J. L. SHASTRI. Delhi: Motilal Banarasidas, 2000 (reprint of 1st edition of 1980).

BRAHMĀṆḌAPURĀṆA.
Srīvyasamaharṣiprokta *Brahmāṇḍapurāṇa* with Introduction in Sanskrit and English and an Alphabetical Index of Verses, ed. J.L. SHASTRI. Delhi, 1973. [Reprint of the Venkatesvara edition of AD 1912]

BHAGAVADGĪTĀ
Śrīmadbhagavadgītā with the commentaries *Gītābhāṣya* of Śaṅkara, *Ānandagirivyākhyā* of Ānandagiri, *Bhagavadgītāprakāśa* of Nīlakaṇṭha, *Gūḍhārthadīpikā* of Madhusūdanasarasvatī *Bhāṣyotkarṣadīpikā* of Dhanapati, *Subodhinī* of Śrīdhara, *Gītārthasaṅgraha* of Abhinavagupta and *Gūḍhārthatattvāloka* of Dharmadatta Śarmā, ed. Vāsudeva ŚARMĀ. Bombay: Nirṇayasāgar Press, 1936 (second edition).

BHASMAJĀBĀLOPANIṢAD,
ed. Vāsudeva ŚARMĀ, 1932. See *Īśādyaṣṭottaraśatopaniṣadaḥ* and ŚARMĀ Vāsudeva 1932.

BHĀGAVATAPURĀṆAM.
Śrīmadbhāgavatapurāṇam with the commentary *Bhāvārthabodhinī* of Śrīdhara, ed. Jagadīśalāla ŚĀSTRĪ. Delhi: Motilal Banarasidas, 1983.

BHĀMATĪ.
See *Brahmasūtraśāṃkarabhāṣyam.*

BHĀRATAMAÑJARĪ.
The Bhāratamañjarî of Kshemendra, ed. PAṆḌITA Śivadatta and Kāśīnātha Pāṇḍuraṅga PARABA. Kāvyamālā, 65. Nirnaya Sagara Press: Bombay, 1898 (reprint Delhi, 1984).

MAKUṬĀGAMA.
Part 1, chapters 1 to 11. An e-text prepared by Muktabodha under the supervision of Mark S. G. DYCZKOWSKI. The text was originally published in Grantha script by C. Swaminatha GURUKKAL.

MAÑJUŚRIYAMŪLAKALPA,
(entitled: *Āryamanjusrīmūlakalpa*) ed. Mahāpahopādhyāya T. Gaṇapati ŚĀSTRĪ, 3 Vols. Trivandrum Sanskrit Series No. LXX (70). Trivandrum: Government Press, 1920, 1922 and 1925.

MATAṄGAPĀRAMEŚVARĀGAMA,

1977 (VIDYĀPĀDA) with commentary -VṚTTI of Bhaṭṭa Rāmakaṇṭha. ed. N. R. BHATT. Publications de l'IFI No. 56. Pondicherry: IFI, 1977.

1982 *kriyāpāda, caryāpāda* and *yogapāda*, with the commentary (*-vṛtti*) of Bhaṭṭa Rāmakaṇṭha up to KRIYĀPĀDA 11:12b, ed. N. R. BHATT. Publications de l'IFI No. 65. Pondicherry: IFI, 1982.

MATSYAPURĀṆA.
The Matsya Mahāpurāṇa edited with introduction & verse index by Pushpendra. Delhi: Meharchand Lachhmandas, 1984 (reprint from the edition of Khemraj Shrikrishna DAS, Venkateshwar Stem Press, Bombay).

MANUSMṚTI,

1932 *Manusmṛti with the Manubhāṣya of Medhātithi*, ed. by Gaṅgānātha JHĀ. Allahabad: Asiatic Society of Bengal.

1946 *Manusmṛti with the Commentary Manvarthamuktāvali of Kullūka*, ed. by Nārāyaṇ Rām ĀCHĀRYA. (tenth edition). Bombay: Nirṇaya Śāgar Press.

2005 *Manusmṛti, with critical edition and translation ed. Patrick Olivelle with the editorial assistance of Suman Olivelle*. Delhi: Oxford University Press.

MAHĀBHĀRATA,
ed. V. SUKTHANKAR, with the cooperation of S. K. BELVALKAR, A. B. GAJENDRAGADKAR, V. KANE, R. D. KARMARKAR, P. L. VAIDYA, S. WINTERNITZ, R. ZIMMERMAN, and other scholars and illustrated by Shrimant Balasaheb Pant Pratinidhi. (Since 1943 ed. S. BELVALKAR). 19 Vols. Poona: BORI, 1927–1959.

MAHĀVASTU AVADĀNAM,
ed. Vasāka, Rādhāgovinda. Calcutta Sanskrit college research series vol. 21, 30 and 43. Texts no. 12, 16 and 21.

MĀRKAṆḌEYAPURĀṆA.
The *Márkaṇḍeyapuráṇa* in the original Sanscrit, ed. K. M. Banerjea. Bibliotheca Indica 29. Calcutta 1855-62. [Reprinted by Biblio Verlag, Osnabrück 1988]

MĀLINĪVIJAYOTTARATANTRA,
ed. Madhusūdan Kaul Śāstrī. KSTS 37. Srinagar, 1922.

MITĀKṢARĀ.
See *Yājñavalkyasmṛti*.

MŪLASŪTRA.
See GOODALL et al. 2015.

MEGHADŪTA
of Kālidāsa. Edited from Manuscripts with the Commentary of Vallabhadeva and provided with a Complete Sanskrit-English Vocabulary by E. Hultzsch. Prize Publications Fund Vol. III. London 1911.

MṚGENDRAVṚTTIDĪPIKĀ
of Aghoraśivācārya. ed. Nā. KṚṢṆAŚĀSTRIN and K. M. SUBRAHMAṆYAŚĀSTRIN. Śivāgamasiddhāntaparipālanasaṅgha Publication No. 12. Devakōṭṭai: Śivāgamasiddhāntaparipālanasaṅgha, 1928.

MṚGENDRĀGAMA [= *Mṛgendratantra,*]
kriyāpāda and incomplete *caryāpāda* with the commentary (*-vṛtti*) of Bhaṭṭa Nārāyaṇakaṇṭha, ed. N. R. Bhatt. Publications de l'IFI No. 23. Pondicherry: IFI, 1962.

YĀJÑAVALKYASMṚTI

1949 of Yājñavalkya with the commentary (*mitākṣarā*) of Vijñāneśvara, ed. Śāstrī Ram ACHARYA. 5th edition. Bombay: Veṅkaṭeśvara press, 1949.

2003 (*ācārādhyāya*) with the commentary of Vijñānaśena called the *Mitākṣarā* and notes from the gloss of Bālaṃbhaṭṭa, translated into English by Rai Bahadur Srisa Chandra VIDYĀRṆAVA along with *Mitākṣarā* Sanskrit commentary, ed. Laxman Sharstri Panshikar. Chowkhamba Sanskrit Studies CXXIII. Varanasi: Caukhamba Sanskrit Series Office, 2003 (reprint).

YĀJÑAVALKYOPANIṢAD,
ed. Vāsudeva ŚARMĀ, 1932. See *Īśādyaṣṭottaraśatopaniṣadaḥ* or Śarmā Vāsudeva 1932.

YOGABHĀṢYAVIVARAṆA.
Pātañjalayogasūtrabhāṣya Vivaraṇa of Śaṅkara-Bhagavatpāda, critically edited with introduction by Polakam Śrī Rama SASTRI and S. R. Krishnamurthi SASTRI. Madras: Government Oriental Manuscripts Library, 1952.

YOGASŪTRA.
See *Pātañjalayogasūtrāṇi* above.

RATNAṬĪKĀ.
See *Gaṇakārikā*.

RASARATNASAMUCCAYA,
ed. V. A. DOLE with translation and commentary in English. Varanasi: Chowkhamba Sanskrit Series Office, 2006.

RĀJANIGHAṆṬU
(also called Nighaṇṭurāja, or Abhidhānacūḍāmaṇi) of Narahari Paṇḍita. Calcutta, 1933.

RĀMĀYAṆA of Vālmīki.

1914– *Rāmāyaṇa of Vālmīki with the commentaries Tilaka of Rāma, Rāmāyaṇaśiromaṇi of Śivasahāya and Bhūṣaṇa of Govindarāja,* ed. Shrinivasa Katti MUDHOLAKARA. Parimal Sanskrit Series No. 11. 8 vols. New Delhi: meharchand Lacchmandas, 1983 (reprint of edition in 7 vols. Bombay: Gujarati Printing Press, 1914–1920).

1960– *The Vālmīki-Rāmāyaṇa.* Critically edited for the First Time, ed. G. H. BHATT, P. L. VAIDYA, P. C. DIVANJI, D. R. MANKAD, G. C. JHALA, Umakant Premanand SHAH. 7 vols. Baroda: Oriental Institute, 1960–1975.

RAURAVASŪTRASAṄGRAHA.
Printed at the beginning of the (pp. 1–16) and as Appendices I (pp. 173–194) of volume 1 of the *Rauravāgama* (see below).

RAURAVĀGAMA,
ed. N. R. BHATT. 3 Vols. Publications de l'IFI No. 24. Pondicherry: IFI, 1972, 1985 and 1988.

LIṄGAPURĀṆA
with Hindi translation, ed. Dvārakāprasād ŚĀSTRĪ. Caukhamba Sanskrit series 129. Varanasi: Chaukhambha Sanskrit Sansthan, 2008.

VASIṢṬHADHARMASŪTRA,
ed. OLIVELLE Patrick, 2000. See *Dharmasūtras* of Olivelle Patrick, 2000.

VĀKYAPADĪYA
of Bhartṛhari. *Bhartṛharis Vākyapadīya: die mūlakārikās nach den Handschriften herausgegeben und mit einem Pāda-Index versehen*, ed. Wilhelm RAU. Wiesbaden: Deutsche Morgenländische Gesellschaft/Kommissionsverlag Franz Steiner Gmbh, 1977.

VĀMANAPURĀṆA.
The Vāmana Purāṇa. Critically edited by Anand Swarup GUPTA. Varanasi: All-India Kashiraj Trust, 1967.

VĀYAVĪYASAṂHITĀ.
See *Śivapurāṇa*.

VĀYUPURĀṆA,
Veṅkaṭeśvara Steam Press edition, with verse preface, verse-Index and textual corrections, ed. Khemarāja ŚRĪKṚṢṆADĀSA. Delhi: Nag Publishers, 1983. [Reprint of the Veṅkaṭeśvara edition of AD 1895]

VĀSAVADATTĀ

1879 ed. Rājendra Lal MIŚRA. Calakatta: The Asiatic Society, 1879.

1966 of Subandhu, edited by Jaydev Mohanlal SHUKLA. Rājasthāna Purātana Granthamālā 28. Jodhpur, 1966.

VIṢṆUDHARMOTTARAMAHĀPURĀṆA
in three volumes, [ed. Kṣemarāja ŚRĪKṚṢṆADĀSA] Bombay: Veṅkaṭeśvara Steam press, Bombay V.S. 1969 [1911 AD].

VIṢṆUPURĀṆAM,
critically edited by M. M. PATHAK, 2 Vols. Vadodara: Oriental Institute, 1997 and 1999.

VIṢṆUSMṚTI
with the commentary Keśavavaijayantī of Nandapaṇḍita, ed. V. KRISHNAMACARYA. Madras: The Adyar Library And Research Centre, 1964.

ŚATAPATHABRĀHMAṆA
with Sanskrit text, English translation, notes, introduction and index by Julius EGGELING, ed. Jeet Ram BHATT, 3 vols. Delhi: Eastern Book Linkers, 2009.

ŚATARATNASAṄGRAHA
of Umāpati Śivācārya with an anonymous commenatry (-Ullekhinī), ed. Pancanana SASTRI. Arthur Avalon's Tantrik Texts XXII. Calcutta, 1943.

ŚĀṄKHĀYANAGṚHYASUTRA,
ed. Hermann OLDENBERG, in *Indische Studien, XV, pp.13-116* Fünfzehnter Band, 1878

ŚIVAPURĀṆA.
Śrī-Śivamahāpurāṇa, ed. Khemarāja ŚRĪKṚṢṆADĀSA. Venkatesvara Press, Bombay V.S. 2011 [= 1954]

ŚIVOPANIṢAD.
Published under *Un-published Upanishadas*, ed. The pandits of Adyar Library under the supervision of C. Kunhan Raja. For The Adyar Library (Theosophical Society), 1933. pp. 324– 378.

ŚIŚUPĀLAVADHA
of Māgha with the commentary of Sarvaṅkaṣā, ed. Durgā Prasāda and Śivadatta, revised by Vāsudeva ŚĀSTRIN. Bombay: Nirṇaya Sagar Press, 1933 (10th edition).

ŚRĪPRAŚNASAṂHITĀ,
ed. Sītā PADMANĀBHANĀ with the foreword of V. RAGHAVAN. Kendriya Sanskrit Vidyapeetha series No. 12. Tirupati : Kendriya Sanskrit Vidyapeetha, 1969.

ŚVETĀŚVATAROPANIṢAD,
ed. Vāsudeva ŚARMĀ, 1932. See *Īśādyaṣṭottaraśatopaniṣadaḥ* and ŚARMĀ Vāsudeva 1932.

ṢAḌDARŚANASAMUCCAYA
of Haribhadra with the commentary *Tarkarahasyadīpikā* of Guṇaratnasūri, *Laghuvṛtti* of Somatilaka Sūri and an *Avacūrṇi* ed. Mahendra Kumar JAIN with the introduction of Dalasukh MALAVANIYA. Jñānapīṭha Mūrtidevī Bhāratīya Jaina Granthamālā: Sanskrit Grantha No. 36. Delhi: Bhāratīya Jñānapīṭha, 1969.

SARVAJÑĀNOTTARĀGAMAḤ
(*vidyāpāda* and *yogapāda*). Ed. K. Rāmacandra SARMA (revised by R. Thagasvami SARMA). The Adyar Library Pamphlet Series No. 53. Chennai: The Adyar Library And Research Centre, 1998 (Reprinted from the Adyar library Bulletin Vol. 62).

SĀṂKHYAKĀRIKĀ.
Sāṃkhyakārikā of Īśvarakṛṣṇa critically edited with the commentary of Gauḍapāda together with introduction, translation and notes. Poona Oriental Series, vol. 9, ed. Haradatta SHARMA. Poona: The Oriental Book Agency, 1933.

SĀRDHATRIŚATIKĀLOTTARĀGAMA
with commentary (*-vṛtti*) of Bhaṭṭa Rāmakaṇṭha, ed. N. R. BHATT. Publications de l'IFI No. 61. Pondicherry: IFI, 1979.

SUPRABHEDĀGAMA,
printed by Mayilai-Aḻakappa Mudaliyār. No editor accredited. Madras (Cintātiripēṭṭai): Civañānapotayantracālai, 1908 (Kaliyuga 5009).

SOMAŚAṂBHUPADDHATI,
ed. K. M. Subrahmaṇyaśāstrin. Devakōṭṭai: Śivāgamasiddhāntaparipālanasaṅgraha, 1931. See also BRUNNER 1963, 1968, 1977 and *Karmakāṇḍakramāvalī*.

SKANDAPURĀṆA,

1998 Volume I. *Adhyāyas* 1–25. Critically Edited with Prolegomena and English Synopsis by R. ADRIAENSEN, H.T. BAKKER & H. ISAACSON. Groningen 1998. Supplement to Groningen Oriental Studies.

2004 Volume II A, *Adhyāyas* 26–31.14: The Vārāṇasī Cycle. Critical Edition with an Introduction, English Synopsis & Philological and Historical Commentary by Hans T. BAKKER & Harunaga ISAACSON. Groningen 2004. Supplement to Groningen Oriental Studies.

2013 Volume III. *Adhyāyas* 34.1–61, 53–69. Critically Edited with Introduction and English Synopsis by Yuko YOKOCHI. Groningen/Leiden 2013.

2014 Volume II B, *Adhyāyas* 31–52: The Vāhana and Naraka Cycles. Critical Edition with an Introduction & Annotated English Synopsis by Hans. T. BAKKER, Peter C. BISSCHOP &,Yoko YOKOCHI in cooperation with Nina MIRNIG and Judit TÖRZSÖK. Leiden/Boston 2014.

2018 Volume IV, *Adhyāyas* 70–95: The Start of the Skanda and Andhaka Cycles. Critical Edition with an Introduction & Annotated English Synopsis by Peter C. BISSCHOP & Yoko YOKOCHI in cooperation with Diwakar ACHARYA and Judit TÖRZSÖK. Leiden/Boston 2018. Supplement to Groningen Oriental Studies.

SKANDAPURĀṆASYA AMBIKĀKHAṆḌAḤ,
ed. Kṛṣṇaprasād BHAṬṬARĀĪ. Kathmandu, 1988. Mahendraratnagranthamālā 2.

SVACCHANDATANTRA
with the commentary (-UDDYOTA) of Rājānaka Kṣemarāja, ed. Madhusūdan Kaul ŚĀSTRĪ. KSTS 31, 38, 44, 48, 51, 53, and 56. Bombay 1921–35.

SVĀYAMBHUVASŪTRASAṄGRAHA,

1937 ed. VEṄKAṬASUBRAHMAṆYAŚĀSTRĪ, Mysore, 1937.

1991 with the *vṛtti* of Sadyojyotiḥ, see FILIOZAT 1991.

HARACARITACINTĀMAṆI
of Rājānaka Jayadratha, ed. PAṆḌITA Śivadatta and Kāśināth Pāṇḍurang PARAB. Kāvyamālā 61. Bombay, 1897.

HARṢACARITA.
Śrīharṣacaritamahākāvyām of Bāṇa Bhaṭṭa with Śaṅkara's commentary, *Saṅketa*, ed. A. A. FÜHRER. Bombay Sanskrit and Prakrit Series, No. LXVI. Bombay: Government Central Press, 1909. See also COWELL, E. B. and THOMAS, F. W. 1983.

HITOPADEŚA,
the Sanskrit text, with a grammatical analysis, alphabetically arranged, ed. Francis JOHNSON. London: WM. H. Allen and Co.; Hertford: Stephen Austin, 1847.

Secondary Material

ACHARYA, Anil Kumar

2009* '*Śivadharmasaṅgrahasya ādyādhyāyatrayasya samīkṣātmakapāṭhasampādanam adhyayanañ ca*'. Doctoral Thesis submitted to the University of Pondicherry.

ACHARYA, Diwakar

2007 'The Saṃskāravidhi: A Manual on the Transformatory Rite of the Lakulīśa-Pāśupatas' in *Tantric Studies in Memory of Hélène Brunner*. ed. Dominic GOODALL & André *Padoux*. Collection Indologie 106. Pondicherry: Institut Français de Pondichéry, EFEO, pp. 27–48.

2010 'The Anteṣṭividhi: A manual on the last rite of the Lakulīśa Pāśupatas', *Journal Asiatique* 298.1 (2010), pp. 133–156.

2013A 'How to Behave like a Bull? New Insight into the Origin and Religious Practices of Pāśupatas', *Indo-Iranian Journal* 56 (2013), pp. 101–131.

2013B 'On the Śaiva Concept of Innate Impurity (*mala*) and the Function of the Rite of Initiation', *Journal of Indian Philosophy* 42 (2013), pp. 9–25.

forthc. 'The Pātravidhi: A Lakulīśa Pāśupata Manual on Purification and Use of the Initiate's Vessel', in *Saṃskṛtasādhutā: Studies in Honour of Professor Ashok N. Aklujkar*, ed. C. WATANABE, M. DESMARAIS, and Y. HONDA. New Delhi: D. K. Printworld, pp. 1–28.

APTE, Vaman Shivaram

1957 *The Practical Sanskrit-English Dictionary, Revised and Enlarged Edition.* Ed. P. K. GODE, C. G. KARVE. Poona: Prasad Prakashan.

BAGCHI, P. C.

1929 'On Some Tantrik texts studied in Ancient Kambuja I', *The Indian Historical Quarterly* 5.4 (1929), pp. 754–769.

BAKKER, Hans

2002 'Sources for reconstructing ancient forms of Śiva worship,' pp. 397–419 in *Les sources et le temps. Sources and Time. A colloquium. Pondicherry 11–13 January 1997*, ed. F. GRIMAL. Pondicherry: Institut Français de Pondichéry, EFEO, 2001 [appeared 2002].

2004 'At the Right Side of the Teacher: Imagination, Imagery, and Image in Vedic and Śaiva Initiation.' pp. 117–148 in *Images in Asian Religions: Texts and Contexts*, ed. Phyllis GRANOFF and Koichi SHINOHARA. Asian Religions and Society. Vancouver: UBC Press, 2004 [appeared 2005].

2014 *The World of the Skandapurāṇa: Northern India in the Sixth and Seventh Centuries*. Leiden/Boston: Brill, 2014 [appeared 2015].

BAKKER, Hans & BISSCHOP, Peter

forthc. 'Kauṇḍinya's Commentary on the Pāśupatasūtras 1.7-9'.

BENTON, Catherine

2006 *God of Desire: Tales of Kāmadeva in Sanskrit Literature*. Albany: State University of New York Press.

BHAṬṬĀCĀRYA, Kamaleśvara

1966 'Liṅga-Kośa', in: *Essays offered to G. H. Luce by His Colleagues and Friends in Honour of His Seventy-Fifth-Birthday*. Vol 2: *Papers on Asian Art and Archaeology. Artibus Asiæ. Supplementum* 23.2. Zurich: Artibus Asiæ Publishers, 6–13.

BISSCHOP, Peter

2006 *Early Śaivism and the Skandapurāṇa Sects and Centres*, Groningen Oriental Studies, vol. XXI. Groningen: Egbert Forsten.

2007 'The Sūtrapāṭha of the Pāśupatasūtra', *Indo-Iranian Journal* 49 (2007), pp. 1–21.

2014 'Invoking the Powers that Be: The *Śivadharma*'s Mahāśānti Mantra,' *South Asian Studies* 30.2 (2014), pp. 133–141

2016 'India and the Making of Hinduism: The contribution of the Purāṇas' in: *Religion and Orientalism in Asian Studies*, ed. Kiri PARAMORE. London/New York/Delhi: Bloomsbury, pp. 39–50.

2018 *Universal Śaivism: The Appeasement of All Gods and Powers in the* Śāntyadhyāya *of the* Śivadharmaśāstra. Leiden: Brill.

BISSCHOP, Peter & GRIFFITHS, Arlo

2003 'The Pāśupata Observance (*Atharvavedapariśiṣṭa 40*)', *Indo-Iranian Journal* (2003) 46, pp. 315–348.

2007 'The Practice involving the Ucchuṣmas (*Atharvavedapariśiṣṭ* 36)', *Studien zur Indologie und Iranistik* 24, (2007), pp. 1–46.

BÖHTLINGK, Otto & Rudolf ROTH (PW)

1853– *Sanskrit Wörterbuch nebst allen Nachträgen*, 6 vols., St. Petersburg: Imperatorskaja Akademija Nauk, 1853-75.

BRUNNER, G. OBERHAMMER, G. and PADOUX, A.

2000 *Tāntrikābhidhānakośa I. Dictionnaire des termes techniques de la littérature hindoue tantrique. A Dictionary of Technical Terms from Hindu Tantric Literature. Wörterbuch zur Terminologie hinduistischer Tantren*, eds H. BRUNNER, G. OBERHAMMER, A. PADOUX. Österreichische Akademie der Wissenschaften, Philosophisch-historische Klasse, Sitzungsberichte, vol. 681.*Beiträge zur Kultur- und Geistesgeschichte Asiens* 35. Vienna: Verlag der österreichischen Akademie der Wissenschaften.

2004 *Tāntrikābhidhānakośa II. Dictionnaire des termes techniques de la littérature hindoue tantrique. A Dictionary of Technical Terms from Hindu Tantric Literature. Wörterbuch zur Terminologie hinduistischer Tantren. sous la direction de H. Brunner, G. Oberhammer et A. Padoux.* Österreichische Akademie der Wissenschaften, Philosophisch-historische Klasse, Sitzungsberichte, 714. Band. Beiträge zur Kultur- und Geistesgeschichte Asiens 44. Vienna: Verlag derösterreichischen Akademie der Wissenschaften.

2013 *Tāntrikābhidhānakośa III. Dictionnaire des termes tech- niques de la littérature hindoue tantrique. A Dictionary of Techni- cal Terms from Hindu Tantric Literature. Wörterbuch zur Terminologie hinduistischer Tantren. Fondé sous la direction de Hélène Brunner, Gerhard Oberhammer et André Padoux. Direction éditoriale du troisième volume:* Dominic GOODALL *et Marion* Rastelli. Philosophisch-historische Klasse Sitzungsberichte, 839. Band. Beiträge zur Kultur- und Geistesgeschichte Asiens Nr. 76. Vienna: Verlag der Österreichische Akademie der Wissenschaften.

BRUNNER, Hélène,

1963– ed. and trans. 1963, 1968, 1977, 1998. *Somaśambhupaddhati.* 4 vols: *Première Partie. Le rituel quotidien dans la tradition śivaïte de l'Inde du Sud selon Somaśambhu; Deuxième Partie. Rituel Occasionnels dans la tradition śivaïte de l'Inde du Sud selon Somaśambhu I : Pavitrārohaṇa, Damanapūjā et Prāyaścitta*; and *Troisième Partie. Rituels occasionels dans la tradition śivaïte de l'Inde du Sud selon Somaśambhu II : dīkṣā, abhiṣeka, vratoddhāra, antyeṣṭi, śrāddha*; and *Rituels dans la tradition sivaïte selon Somaśambhu. Quatrième partie : rituels optionnels : pratiṣṭhā.* Publications de l'IFI No. 25. Pondicherry: IFI.

COWELL, E. B. and THOMAS, F. W.

1983 *The Harṣacarita of Bāṇa.* Delhi: Motilal Banasari Das.

DEUSSEN, Paul

1917 'Über das Devadāruvanam', *ZDMG*, vol. 71. Wiesbaden: Harrassowitz, pp. 119–20.

DEY, Nundo Lal

1971 The Geographical Dictionary of Ancient and Mediaeval India. Delhi. [3rd edition]

EDGERTON, Franklin

1953 Buddhist hybrid Sanskrit grammar and dictionary, Vol. I: Grammar, Vol. II: Dictionary. New Haven: Yale University Press.

EINOO, Shingo

2005 'Ritual calender. Change in the conception of time and space', pp. 99–124, in *Jounal Asiatique 293.1.* Paris: Société Asiatique.

FILLIOZAT, Vasundhara

2001 'Kālāmukha and Pāśupata Temples in Dharwar.' Chennai: The Kuppusvami Sastri Research Institute.

FISHER, Elaine M.

2017 *Hindu Pluralism: Religion and the Public Sphere in Early Modern South India.* Oakland: University of California Press.

GARG, Gaṅgā Rām

1992 *Encyclopaedia of the Hindu world.* Volume 2. Delhi: Ashok Kumar Mittal Concept Publishing Company.

GOLZIO, Karl-Heinz,

2004 *Inscriptions of Campā based on the editions and translations of Abel Bergaigne, Étienne Aymonier, Louis Finot, Édouard Huber and other French scholars and of the work of R. C. Majumdar. Newly presented, with minor corrections of texts and translations, together with calculations of given dates.* Aachen: Shaker Verlag.

GONDA, Jan

1963 *The Vision of the Vedic Poets.* The Hague: Mouton & co.

GOODALL, Dominic

1998 *Bhaṭṭa Rāmakaṇṭha's commentary on the Kiraṇatantra. Chapters 1-6. Critical edition and annotated translation.* Vol. 1. Pondicherry: Institut Français de Pondichéry, EFEO.

2004 *The Parākhyatantra. A Scripture of the Śaiva Siddhānta. A critical edition and annotated translation by D.G.* Pondicherry: Institut Français de Pondichéry, EFEO.

2007 'A first edition of the [Śatika-]Kālajñāna, the shortest of the non-eclectic recensions of the Kālottara' in: *Mélanges tantriques à la mémoire d'Hélène Brunner (Tantric studies in memory of Hélène Brunner)*, eds. Dominic GOODALL & André PADOUX. Pondicherry: Institut Français de Pondichéry, EFEO.

2016 'How the Tattvas of Tantric Śaivism Came to Be 36: The Evidence of the Niśvāsatattvasaṃhitā' in *Tantric Studies: Fruits of a Franco-German Collaboration on Early Tantra*, eds. Dominic GOODALL and Harunaga ISAACSON. Collection Indologie, vol. 131. Early Tantra Series № 4. Pondicherry: Institut Français de Pondichéry, EFEO, pp. 77–111.

GOODALL Dominic et al.

2015 *The Niśvāsatattvasaṃhitā The Earliest surviving Śaiva Tantra. A critical edition of the Mūlasūtra, Uttarasūtra & Nayasūtra,* ed. Dominic GOODALL in collaboration with Alexis SANDERSON & Harunaga ISAACSON. With contributions of Nirajan KAFLE and Diwakar ACHARYA and Others. Vol. 1. Pondicherry: Institut Français de Pondichéry, EFEO. See also Niśvāsatattvasaṃhitā.

GOODALL, Dominic and ISAACSON, Harunaga

2003 *The Raghupañcikā of Vallabhadeva being the earliest commentary on the Raghuvaṃśa of Kālidāsa. Critical Edition with Introduction and Notes.* Vol. I. Groningen: Egbert Forsten.

2007 'Workshop on the *Niśvāsatattvasaṃhitā*: The Earliest Surviving Śaiva Tantra?' in: *Newsletter of the NGMCP*, № 3, pp. 4–6.

2011 'Tantric Traditions'. In *The Continuum Companion to Hindu Studies*, ed. Jessica Frazier. London/New York: Continuum, pp. 122–37, 189–91, 361–400.[1065]

GOODALL, Dominic, KATAOKA, Kei, ACHARYA, Diwakar, YOKOCHI, Yoko

2008 *A First Edition and Translation of Bhaṭṭa Rāmakaṇṭha's* Tattvatrayanirṇayavivṛti, *A Treatise on Śiva, Sols and Māyā, with Detailed Treatment of Mala.* South Asian Classical Studies № 3. Kyushu University: Department of Indology, pp. 311—384.

GOODALL, Dominic, ROUT, Nibedita, SATHYANARAYANAN, R., SARMA, S. A. S., GANESAN, T., SAMBANDHASIVACARYA, S.

2005 *The Pañcāvaraṇastava of Aghoraśivācārya: A twelfth-century South Indian prescription for the visualisation of Sadāśiva and his retinue.* Collection Indologie, vol. 102. Pondicherry: Institut Français de Pondichéry, EFEO.

GOUDRIAAN, Teun and GUPTA Sanjukta

1981 *Hindu Tantric and Śākta Literature.* A History of Indian Literature, vol. 2, fasc. 2. Wiesbaden: Harrassowitz.

GRANOFF, Phyllis

2006 'Śiva and his Gaṇas: Techniques of Narrative distancing in Purāṇic Stories', in: *Voice of the Orient. A Tribute to Prof. Upendranath Dahl*, ed. Raghunath PANDA and Madhusudan MISHRA. Delhi: Eastern Books Linkers, pp. 77–103.

GUY, John

2009 'Artistic Exchange, Regional Dialogue and the Cham Territories' in *Champa and the Archaeology of Mỹ Sơn (Vietnam)*, ed. [HARDY,] Andrew, [CUCARZI,] Mauro and [ZOLESE,] Patrizia. Singapore: Nus Press, pp. 127–154.

2018 "Cham-Khmer Interactions in 1113–1220 CE", in *Vibrancy in Stone: Masterpieces of the Đà Nẵng Museum of Cham Sculpture*, eds. Trần Kỳ Phương, Võ Văn Thắng, and Peter D. SHARROCK. Bangkok: River Books, pp. 111–19.

[1065] As noted by GOODALL (2015: 574, fn. 252), pagination of this volume has been somewhat compromised by "muddled endnotes" to the effect that the present entry spans from pp. 122–137 (main body), 189–91 (notes), 361–400 (bibliography, joint for the whole volume).

HACKER, Paul

1983 *Inklusivismus. Eine indische Denkform*, ed. Gerhard OBERHAMMER. Publications of the De Nobili Research Library, Occasional Papers, vol. 2. Vienna: Institut für Indologie der Universität Wien, pp. 11–28.

HARA, Minoru

1966* *Materials for the study of Pāśupata Śaivism.* Unpublished doctoral thesis to the department of Sanskrit and Indian studies, Harvard University Cambridge, Massachusetts.

2002 *Pāśupata Concept of Ahiṃsā.* Pāśupata Studies, ed. Jun TAKASHIMA. Vienna 2002: Sammlung de Nobili, ISTB. Delhi: Motilal Banarsidass.

HARIMOTO, Kengo

2014 'Nepalese Manuscripts of Suśrutasaṃhitā', *Journal of Indian and Buddhist Studies*, 62.3 (2014), pp. 1087–1093.

HATLEY, Shaman

2007* *The* Brahmayāmalatantra *and early* Śaiva*cult of Yoginīs.* Unpublished thesis submitted to the University of Pennsylvania.

forthc. 'Brahmayāmala *XXXIX: the* Srotanirṇayapaṭala *(chapter of the Verdict on the Streams of Revelation), verses 1–46, 91–93.'* Provisional title. Submitted for inclusion in '*Tantric Śaivism*', ed. Somadeva VASUDEVA' (*forthcoming*). Submitted in May 2010*, publication status unknown).

2018 *The Brahmayāmala or Picumata, Volume I: Chapters 1-2, 39-40, & 83. Revelation, Ritual, and Material Culture in an Early Śaiva Tantra.* Pondichéry, Hamburg: Institut Français d'Indologie/École française d'Extrême-Orient/Universität Hamburg.

HAZRA, R. C.

1940 *Studies in the Purāṇic records on Hindu rites and customs.* Calcutta: General Printers and Publishers Ltd.

1952–3 'The Śivadharma', *Journal of the Ganganath Jha Research Institute, Allahabad*, vol. XIII, pp. 282–299.

HILTEBEITEL, Alf

2001 *Rethinking the Mahābhārata: A reader's Guide to the Education of the Dharma King.* Chicago and London: The University of Chicago Press.

INGALLS, Daniel H. H.

1962 'Cynics and Pāśupatas. The Seeking of Dishonor', *Harvard Teological Review* 55.4 (1962), pp. 281–298.

JAHN, Wilhelm

1915 'Die Legende vom Devadāruvana I', *ZDMG*, vol. 69. Wiesbaden: Harrassowitz, 529–557.

1916 'Die Legende vom Devadāruvana II',*ZDMG*, vol. 70. Wiesbaden: Harrassowitz, 301–320.

JAIN, K. Sharad, [AGARWAL,] K. Pushpendra and [SINGH,] P. Vijay

2007 *Hydrology and water resources of India.* Water Science and Technology Library. Electronic book. Springer.

KAFLE, Nirajan

2013 The Liṅgodbhava myth in early Śaiva sources in *Puṣpikā. Tracing Ancient India Through Texts and Traditions. Contributions to Current Research in Indology*, vol. 1. Proceedings of the International Indology Graduate Research Symposium. Ed. Nina MIRNIG, Péter-Dániel SZÁNTÓ and Michael WILLIAMS. Oxford/Philadelphia: Oxbow books, pp. 241–262.

KANE, P. V.

1930– *History of Dharmaśāstra (Ancient and Medieval Religious and Civil Law in India).* 5 vols. Poona: Bhandarkar Oriental Research Institute, 1930–1962.

KIRFEL, Willibald

1967 *Die Kosmographie der Inder nach Quellen dargestellt.* Reprint, Darmstadt. [*Original publication* Schroeder: Bonn & Leipzig, 1920].

KISS, Csaba

2015 *The Brahmayāmalatantra or Picumata. Volume II. The Religious Observances and the Sexual Rituals of the Tantric Practitioner: Chapters 3, 21, and 45.* Collection Indologie 130 / Early Tantra Series 3. Pondicherry: Institut Français de Pondichéry / École Française d'Extrême-Orient / Asien-Afrika-Institut, Universität Hamburg.

LORENZEN, David N.

1999 *Who Invented Hinduism?* Comparative Studies in Society and History, vol. 41, № 4. Cambridge: CUP, pp. 630–659.

MAGNONE, Paolo

2005 '*Śivadharmottarapurāṇa.* A Survey', in *Epics, Khilas, and Purāṇas: Continuities and Ruptures: Proceedings of the Third Dubrovnik International Conference on the Sanskrit Epics and Purāṇas September 2002*, ed. Petteri KOSKIKALLIO. Zagreb: 2005, pp. 575–596.

MALLINSON, James

2007 See *Khecarīvidyā*.

MICHAELS, Axel

2004 *Hinduism: Past and Present*, transl. HARSHAV, Barbara (2003). 2nd ed. Princeton/New Jersey: Princeton University Press (2004 reprint of the 1998 edition).

MOHAPATRA, Sarat Chandra

2005 "Brāhmin Śāsan Villages Around Puri." in *Orissa Review* (www.orissa.gov.in/e-magazine/Orissareview), December.

MONIER-WILLIAMS, Monier

1899 *A Sanskṛit-English Dictionary, Etymologically and Philologically Arranged with special reference to Cognate Indo-European Languages.* Oxford: Clarendon Press.

NATH, Vijaya

1987 *Dāna: Gift System in Ancient India (c. 600–c. A.D. 300), a socio-economic perspective.* New Delhi: Munshiram Manoharlal Publishers.

NICHOLSON J. Andrew

2010 *Unifying Hinduism: Philosophy and Identity in Indian Intellectual History.* New York: Columbia University Press.

O'HANLON, Rosalind

2011 'Speaking from Siva's temple: Banaras scholar households and Brahman 'ecumene' of Mughal India', *South Asian History and Culture*, vol. 2.2. Oxford: Faculty of Oriental Studies. Online publication date: March 21st, 2011.

OBERLIES, Thomas

2003 *A Grammar of Epic Sanskrit.* Indian Philoloy and South Asian Studies, vol. 5. Berlin/New York: Walter de Gruyter.

OLIVELLE, Patrick

2000 See *Dharmasūtras.*

2005 See *Manusmṛti.*

ROCHER, Ludo

1986 'The Purāṇas,' in *A History of Indian Literature*, ed. Jan GONDA, vol. II, fasc. 3. Wiesbaden: Otto Harrassowitz.

SALOMON, Richard

1986 'The Viṣṇu Purāṇa as a Specimen of Vernacular Sanskrit.' WZKS 30 (1986), pp. 39–56.

SANDERSON, Alexis

1995 'Meaning in Tantric Ritual', in: *Essais sur le rituel III. Colloque du centenaire de la section des sciences religieuses de l'Ecole Pratique des Hautes Etudes*, eds. Anne-Marie BLONDEAU and Kristofer SCHIPPER. Louvain, Paris: Peeters.

1988 'Saivism and the Tantric Traditions', in: *The World's Religions*, ed. S. SUTHERLAND, L. HOULDEN; P. CLARKE and F. HARDY. London: Routledge, pp. 660-704.

2002 'History through Textual Criticism in the Study of Śaivism, the Pañcarātra and the Buddhist Yoginītantras', in: *Les sources et le temps. Sources and Time. A colloquium. Pondicherry 11–13 January 1997*, ed. François Grimal. Publications du département d'indologie 91. Pondicherry: Institut Français de Pondichéry, EFEO, 2001 [appeared 2002], pp. 1–47.

2003–4 'The Śaiva Religion among the Khmers. Part I', *Bulletin de l'Ecole française d'Extrême-Orient* 90–91 (2003–4), pp. 349-462.

2006 'The Lakulas: New evidence of a system intermediate between Pāñcārthika Pāśupatism and Āgamic Śaivism.' Ramalinga Reddy Memorial Lectures, 1997, in: *The Indian Philosophical Annual* 24 (2006), pp. 143 - 217.

2009 The Śaiva Age: An Explanation of the Rise and Dominance of Śaivism during the Early Medieval Period, in *Genesis and Development of Tantrism*, ed. Shingo Einoo. Tokyo: Institute of Oriental Culture, University of Tokyo, pp. 41–349.

2014 'The Śaiva Literature', in *Journal of Indological Studies,* vols 24–25 (2012–2013), pp. 1–113.

forthc. '*Śaivism and Brahmanism in the Early Medieval Period*'. Draft version, currently dated Oct. 4, 2006.

SARMA, Vāsudeva

1932 *One hundred and eight Upaniṣadas (Īśa and others) with various readings.* Bombay: Nirṇaya Sāgar Press.

SASTRI, Ananthakrishna

1940 See *Pāśupatasūtra.*

ŚĀSTRĪ, H. P.

1905 *A Catalogue of Palm-leaf & Selected Paper MSS belonging to the Durbar Library, Nepal.* Vol I. Calcutta: Asiatic Society.

1915 *A Catalogue of Palm-leaf & Selected Paper MSS belonging to the Durbar Library, Nepal.* Vol II. Calcutta: Asiatic Society.

SATHYANĀRĀYANAN, R.

2007 'Eight Forms of Śiva and Their Correlation with the Eight Names. The Evidence of Inscriptions Contrasted with that of Other Texts', in: *Journal of the Gaṅgānātha Jhā Kendrīya Sanskrit Vidyāpītha*, LXII (1–4), ed. Goparaju Rama. Allahabad: Rashtriya Sanskrit Samsthan, pp. 397–404.

2015 '*Śaiva Rites of Expiation: A First Edition and Translation of Trilocanaśiva's Twelfth-Century Prāyaścittasamuccaya. Critically Edited and Translated by R. Sathyanarayanan with an Introduction by Dominic Goodall*'. Collection Indologie, vol. 127. Pondicherry: Institut Français de Pondichéry, EFEO.

SCHREINER, Peter, et al.

1997 *Nārāyaṇīya-Studien*. Wiesbaden: Harrassowitz.

SFERRA, Francesco

2008 'Sanskrit Manuscripts and Photographs of Sanskrit Manuscripts in Giuseppe Tucci's Collection', in *Sanskrit Texts from Giuseppe Tucci's Collection Part I*, Asien-Afrika-Institut Hamburg in cooperation with Istituto Italiano per L'Africa e L'Oriente, Università degli Studi di Napoli "L'Orientale". *Manuscripta Buddhica* 1, ed. Francesco SFERRA. Rome: Istituto Italiano per L'Africa e L'Oriente, pp. 15–78.

SHARMA, Haradatta

1933 See *Sāṃkhyakārikā*.

DE SIMINI, Florinda

2016A *Of Gods and Books Ritual and Knowledge Transmission in the Manuscript Cultures of Premodern India*. Studies in Manuscript Cultures, vol. 8, ed. Michael FRIEDRICH, Harunaga ISAACSON and Jörg B. QUENZER. Berlin/Boston: de Gruyter.

2016B 'Śivadharma Manuscripts from Nepal and the Making of a Śaiva Corpus', in: *Studies in Manuscript Cultures* 9, ed. Michael FRIEDRICH, Harunaga ISAACSON and Jörg B. QUENZER. Berlin/Boston: de Gruyter. 233–280.

DE SIMINI, Florinda and Nina MIRNIG

2017 'Umā and Śiva's Playful Talks in Detail (*Lalitavistara*): On the Production of Śaiva Works and their Manuscripts in Medieval Nepal', published by De Gruyter, 587–653.

SIRCAR, D. C.

1971 *Studies in the geography of ancient and medieval India*. Second edition: revised and enlarged. Delhi: Motilal Banarasidas.

SRINIVASAN, S. A.

1967 *Vācaspatimiśras* Tattvakaumudī *Ein Beitrag zur Textkritik bei kontaminierter Ueberlieferung, Alt- und Neu-Indische Studien* 12. Hamburg: Gram/de Gruyter.

STIETENCRON VON, Heinrich

1995 'Religious Configurations in Pre-Muslim India and the Modern Concept of Hinduism' in: *Representing Hinduism. Construction of Religious Traditions and National Identity*, ed. V. DALMIA and H. von STIETENCRON. Thousand Oaks: Sage Publications.

SWEETMAN, Will

2001 'Unity and Plurality: Hinduism and the Religions of India in Early European Scholarship', *Religion*, vol. 31, № 3, pp. 209–224.

2003 *Mapping Hinduism. "Hinduism" and the Study of Indian Religions, 1600–1776.* Wiesbaden: Harrassowitz.

TÖRZSÖK, Judit

1999* *The Doctrine of Magic Female Spirits. A critical edition of selected chapters of the Siddhayogeśvarīmata(tantra) with annotated translation and analysis.* Unpublished doctoral thesis submitted to Merton College, Oxford University.

2004 'Three Chapters of *Śaiva* Material Added to the Earliest Known Recension of the Skandapurāṇa', in: *Origin and Growth of the Purāṇic Text Corpus, with special reference to the* Skandapurāṇa. Papers of the 12th World Sanskrit Conference, vol. 3.2, ed. Hans T. BAKKER. Delhi: Motilal Banarasidass.

2013 'The Heads of the Godhead. The Number of Heads/Faces of Yoginīs and Bhairavas in Early Śaiva Tantras,' in *Indo-Iranian Journal* 56.2, pp. 133–155. Leiden: Brill.

VASU, Śrīśa Candra

1891 *The Aṣṭādhyāyī of Pāṇini. Critically edited and translated into English*, 2 vols. Allahabad. [Reprint via Kessinger Publications (23. May 2010)].

VASUDEVA, Somadeva

1997 *Sārasvatamate Bhairavamaṅgalā.* Electronic transcription of the Nepalese manuscript, B27/21.

2004 *The Yoga of The Mālinīvijayottaratantra.* Collection Indologie, vol. 97. Pondicherry: Institut Français de Pondichéry, EFEO.

WESSELS-MEVISSEN, Corinna

2001 *The gods of the directions in ancient India; origin and early development in art and literature (until c. 1000 A.D.)* Berlin: Dietrich Reimer Verlag.

WOODS, James Haughton

1927 *The Yoga-System of Patañjali or the Ancient Hindu Doctrine of Concentration of Mind Embracing The Mnemonic Rules, called Yoga-Sūtras of Patañjali and The Commentary, called Yoga-Bhāshya, Attributed to Veda-Vyāsa and The Explanation, Called Tattva-vaiśāradī of Vācaspati-Miśra*, ed. Charles Rockwell LANMAN. (second edition) *Harvard Oriental Series*17. Massachusetts: The Harvard University Press.

INDEX OF PĀDAS

In the following index of *pāda*s, brackets indicating editorial suppletions and the like have been removed; *pāda*s whose beginnings are missing are omitted.

आज्यं प्राश्य शुचिर्भूत्वा 3:97c
आज्यं वै प्राशयित्वा तु 3:131a
आज्यपा वैश्ययोनौ तु 3:155c
आज्येनैव तु तर्पयेत् 3:67b
आज्ञान्दत्त्वा तु नन्दिने 1:13d
आतपत्रप्रदानेन 2:72a
आतुरं निरुजङ्कृत्वा 2:100c
आतुरे ओषधानि च 2:100b
आत्मध्यानरतश्चैव 4:20c
आत्मध्यानरतो नित्यं 4:38c
आत्मध्यानविवर्जितः 4:24b
आत्मनः श्रेय इच्छता 2:122b
आत्मा यजति यज्ञानि 1:36a
आत्मानम्परिशोषयेत् 4:30b
आत्रेयगङ्गा वैतरणी 3:6a
आदित्यपदमाप्नुयात् 3:174d
आदित्यस्सविता सूर्यो 3:90a
आदौ महातलन्नाम 4:107c
आधिपत्यं मनोमतम् 1:121b
आध्यात्मिकं प्रवक्ष्यामि 4:42a
आपरूपः प्रजायेत 4:61c
आप्तोर्यामफलं लभेत् 3:133b
आयुः शर्क्करखण्डयोः 2:102b
आरामस्यैव यः कर्ता 2:25a
आरोग्यं कुशपुष्पैस्तु 1:135c
आरोग्यञ्च धनञ्चैव 1:145a
आर्द्रकम्प्राशयित्वा तु 3:113c
आर्या प्रकृतिरूपा च 3:108c
आलब्धः पञ्चभिर्गुह्यैर् 4:89a
आहिताग्निसहस्रेषु 2:118a
आश्चर्यमिति सञ्चिन्त्य 1:174c
आषाढन्दिण्डिमुण्डिञ्च 3:19c
आषाढे नीलकण्ठञ्च 3:100a
आषाढे वामनम्पूज्य 3:133c
इति सङ्ख्याः समासेन 4:128c
इदङ्ग्रासङ्गृहाण त्वम् 2:83a
इदम्मे व्रतमुत्तमम् 2:83b
इन्द्रियाणि तथैवेह 4:45c
इन्धनानि तु यो दद्याद् 2:67a
इभं काञ्चनमालिनम् 2:71b
इहामुत्र च सिद्ध्येत 3:57c
इष्टकामांल्लभेन्नरः 3:105b
इष्टानां विप्रयोगैश्च 1:48c
ईदृशञ्चामरं दत्वा 1:111c
ईदृशीम्महिषीन्दत्त्वा 2:55a
ईप्सितं लभते फलम् 3:176d
ईप्सितांल्लभते कामांस् 1:130a
ईप्सितांल्लभते कामान् 3:160a
ईश्वरं ध्यानमेव च 4:127b
ईश्वरं ध्यायमानस्य 4:68a
ईश्वरम्पदमाप्नोति 4:68c
ईश्वरम्मोहनन्तथा 3:142d
ईश्वरस्य तु देवस्य 4:134c
ईश्वरस्य प्रसादेन 2:20a
ईशानं शङ्करन्तथा 3:147b
ईशानञ्चाश्विने मासे 3:103a
ईशानेन द्विजोत्तमाः 4:135b
उक्तं हरस्य माहात्म्यं 3:30c
उक्तन्देवि मया पुरा 4:6d
उक्थ्यमेधफलं लभेत् 3:129b
उग्रदण्डधृते नित्यं 3:118c
उग्रन्तु कार्त्तिके मासे 3:104a
उत्तमाङ्गतिमाप्नोति 3:126a
उत्तमो जायते नरः 3:54t
उत्तरेणैव वक्त्रेण 4:41c
उत्तराभिमुखो भूत्वा 4:49c
उत्पानं कुरुते यस्तु 1:58a

तद्गत्वा मुच्यते पापैर् 3:39a
तच्चैवाभ्यसते पुनः 3:36b
तच्चानन्तम्भविष्यति 3:58d
ततस्तुष्टो महादेवो 1:176c
ततश्चैव परिभ्रष्टो 2:76c
ततः फलमवाप्नुयात् 3:136b
ततो बुद्धिश्च जायते 4:44d
ततो लिङ्गं विवर्द्धितम् 1:174b
तत्तत्पदमवाप्नुयात् 4:69d
तत्त्वसर्गमतोर्ध्वन्तु 4:118c
तत्र चैव परिभ्रष्टो 2:78c
तत्रैव दीक्षितो ब्रह्मा 1:7a
तत्सर्व्वङ्कथितन्तुभ्यं 1:64c
तथा कथय सर्वन्तु 1:17c
तथा किम्पुरुषाण्डजाः 4:111d
तथा कुरु प्रसादा वा 1:23c
तथा केसरदामकैः 1:130b
तथा च मुनिसत्तमैः 1:183d
तथा चैव निरश्नता 3:112d
तथा चैवोपलेपने 1:68d
तथा चाप्सरचम्पकम् 1:151b
तथा भाद्रे हृषीकेशं 3:135c
तथा वक्ष्यामि विप्रेन्द्र 1:19c
तथा वक्ष्यामि विप्रेन्द्राः 1:29c
तथा विषमलंघनम् 4:5b
तथा होमजपादिभिः 3:88b
तथाध्यात्मिकमेव च 1:26d
तथानशनमेव च 1:54d
तदर्धिकं पादिकं वा 4:6a
तदुपायं वदस्व मे 1:50d
तद्ब्राह्मणे न दातव्यं 3:59c
तद्भक्तास्तद्गतिं यान्ति 3:34a
तदानन्त्याय कल्पते 2:116d
तन्त्रीवाद्यफलञ्च यत् 1:69b
तन्त्रीवाद्यस्य मे शृणु 1:165d
तन्त्रीवाद्यस्य वादकः 1:166b
तन्दृष्ट्वा कौतुकान्वितः 1:1d
तन्निबोध यथार्थतः 1:52b
तन्मया परिकीर्त्तितम् 3:196b
तन्मात्राणि ततो 'भवन् 4:45b
-तन्मात्राणीन्द्रियाणि च 4:119b
तन्मे ब्रूहि महेश्वर 2:115d
तप उग्रम्महात्मना 4:76d
तपनो भास्करो रविः 3:90d
तपःखेदितगात्राय 1:25a
तप्तत्रपुजतुश्च यः 2:33d
तप्तवालुकदुःखैस्तु 2:74a
तप्ताङ्गारशिलावर्षे 2:35c
तमोगुणाभिभूते तु 4:44a
तमाचक्ष्व महेश्वर 4:132d
तर्पयंश्च तिलोदकैः 3:125d
तर्प्पयेच्च तिलोदकैः 3:119d
तलातलन्तृतीयन्तु 4:108c
तस्मिन्पात्रे सदा देयम् 2:122a
तस्मात्सर्वेषु पात्रेषु 2:121c
तस्माद्रक्षेत सर्वाणि 2:109a
तस्य दत्तम्भवे 'नन्तं 2:119a
तस्य नामाङ्कितङ्कृत्वा 3:189a
तस्य पुण्यफलं यत्तत् 1:61c
तस्य यान्ति शिवालयम् 1:82d
तस्य हेममयन्दिव्यङ् 1:60c
तस्येदं फलमुद्दिष्टम् 1:169e
तस्यैकं ज्वलते ध्रुवम् 2:6b
तस्यापि पितरो यान्ति 1:86a
तांस्तु विस्तरतो मे 'द्य 1:57c
ताडितश्च न विन्देत 4:65a
तान् पुष्पाञ्छत्रुनाशाय 1:139a

नागलोकमवाप्नुयात् 3:81t
नागाश्च गरुडाश्चैव 4:111c
नातपेन तु पीड्यते 2:72d
नान्यस्त्राता भवेद्देव 1:25c
नामभिस्तु प्रपूजयेत् 3:91b
नामभिः पूजयेदेभिर् 3:124a
नामभिः पूजयेदेभिस् 3:119c
नामभिः पूजयेदेभिः 3:109a
नामभिः पूजयेदेभिः 3:144a
नाममात्रेण मे श्रुताः 4:99b
नामाङ्कं घटमेव वा 3:183b
नामाङ्कं सघृतन्ताम्रं 3:181c
नामाङ्कन्तु घृतप्लुतम् 3:178d
नामान्यालिख्य दातव्या 3:164c
नारिकेलं समोचकम् 2:89b
नारी च स्त्रीसहस्रेण 2:10a
नालीमार्गप्रयायिनः 2:34b
नासौ दुर्ग्गतिमाप्नुयात् 1:157b
नासौ दुर्ग्गतिमाप्नुयात् 2:37b
नाशयेत उपद्रवान् 1:153d
निष्क्रामयति यो वायुं 4:56c
निष्कामस्तु गणो भवेत् 3:150b
निष्कामो धर्म्मलोकताम् 3:182d
निष्कामो ब्रह्मलोकताम् 3:160b
निष्काणाम्प्राप्नुयाच्चैव 1:71c
नित्यं गाणेश्वरीङ्गतिम् 1:86b
नित्यं चाभग्नयोगतः 1:85d
नित्यं लिङ्गं प्रपूजयेत् 1:148b
नित्यं सौकरवे हरिः 3:31b
नित्यन्दीपप्रदायिनः 2:45d
नित्यमेव प्रदापयेत् 1:137b
नित्यमेव प्रदायिनः 2:63b
नित्यमेवन्तु यो दद्यात् 1:140a
नित्यमेव श्मशानगः 4:85d
नित्यमेव हि कामदा 1:150b
नित्यम्परगवे दद्याद् 2:85c
नित्यञ्चालुब्धचित्तेन 4:22c
नित्यैश्वर्यमखण्डञ्च 2:16c
नित्याकर्षकराणि तु 1:141b
निबोधय यशस्विनि 4:107b
निम्बपुष्पैस्तु यो 'र्चयेत् 1:152d
निरयन्न तु पश्यति 2:5b
निरुच्छ्वासो ह्यथापरः 4:100d
निरुजो दीर्घजीविनः 3:89d
निर्गन्धञ्चैव यद्भवेत् 1:122d
निर्ग्गन्धकुसुमैरेष 1:123c
निर्जिताः शत्रवस्तेन 1:143a
निर्माल्यधारी भिक्षाशी 4:71a
निर्विशङ्कः समाचरेत् 4:92d
निर्व्याधिर्दीर्घमायुषम् 2:100d
निर्व्वाणे योजिताः परे 1:27d
निवृत्तिं कुरुतेति यः 3:58b
निस्सन्दिग्धा द्विजोत्तमाः 4:136d
निस्सपत्नमकंटकम् 2:2d
निःसपत्नानि भुंजते 1:117b
नीलगङ्गा च गोधा च 3:8c
नीलरक्तानि पुष्पाणि 1:141a
नीलरक्तास्तु ये पुष्पा 1:155a
नीलस्यैव अलाभे तु 2:87c
नीलोत्पलैर्भवेद्योगी 1:127c
नृयज्ञो 'तिथिपूजनम् 4:17d
नैकान्नादस्स भैक्षभुक् 4:35d
नैकान्नादः कदाचन 4:83d
नैमि षारण्यवासिभिः 1:6d
नैमिषं पुष्करन्तथा 3:19b
नैमिषे वसमानैस्तु 1:5c
नैमिषारण्य - - - 1:2c

भक्षाम्बुपूर्णघटकां 3:187a
भक्तियुक्तं सुपूजितः 3:71b
भक्त्या तु यो 'र्चयेच्छिवम् 1:118d
भगवन्सर्व्वमेतत्तु 1:3c
भगवान्नन्दिकेश्वरः 1:18b
भवं ज्येष्ठे तु संपूज्य 3:99a
भवति स महाभागः 2:98c
भवनामाङ्कितं द्विजे 3:175b
भविष्यामि न संशयः 1:180d
भवेत्फलप्रदायकः 2:91b
भवेद्गणः स चोत्तमः 1:167b
भस्मना - - - 4:70c
भस्मशायी जितेन्द्रियः 4:70d
भस्मीशश्च समाख्यातं 4:127c
भिक्षां वा प्रत्यहन्ददेत् 2:104d
भिक्षायां पतितं सदा 4:84b
भिन्ने देहे शिवालयम् 1:81d
भुङ्क्ते च निरुजः सदा 2:14d
भुङ्क्ते चैव ददाति च 2:15d
भुक्त्वा कामाञ्छिवम्व्रजेत् 2:23b
भुक्त्वा भोगाननिन्दितान् 2:5d
भुक्त्वा वह्निमयान्भोगाञ् 3:18c
भुवर्लोकमतः परम् 4:115b
भैक्षवृत्तिसमाश्रितः 4:36b
भैक्षाशी च अमैथुनी 4:2d
भोगापवर्गहेतुश्च 4:43c
भोजनैश्च सदक्षिणैः 3:185b
भोजयित्वा यथाविधि 3:189d
भ्रष्टो जायति भोगवान् 2:71d
भ्रष्टो जायति भोगवान् 2:88b
भ्रष्टो भवति भोगवान् 3:194d
भाजने घृतपूरिते 3:164d
भाजने प्रक्षिपेत्तु तम् 3:161d
भारभूतिश्च लाकुलिम् 3:19d
भार्यां लभति शोभनाम् 2:91d
भाण्डमायसत्रापुषम् 2:97b
भूतस्तन्मात्रसम्भवः 4:45d
भूतेष्वभयदक्षिणा 2:108b
भूताद्रोहेण जीवते 4:15d
भूतानि च तथा पञ्च 4:119c
भूमिदानाद्भवेत्स्वर्ग्गो 2:57a
भूयो भूयो गुणान्विताम् 2:47d
भूर्लोकः कथितो ह्येष 4:115a
भूलोकमधुना शृणु 4:112d
मंटे कुण्टेति वा पुनः 4:80b
मठस्यावसथस्यैव 2:34c
मठस्यावसथस्यैव 2:36a
मणिरत्नविचित्रकैः 3:140d
मत्स्यं मान्सं सुरा सीधु 3:59a
मदयन्ती च या भवेत् 1:153b
मधु मान्सन्न भक्षेत 3:56a
मधुदानात्तथैव च 2:60d
मधुना स्नापयेल्लिङ्गङ् 1:93a
मधुमांसनिवृत्तश्च 4:3a
मधुराम्लकटुतिक्तानि 2:101a
मननं शोधनं चैव 4:87a
मनश्चैवोभयात्मकम् 4:119d
मन्त्रतन्त्रार्थनिश्चिताम् 4:133d
मन्त्रमार्गं व्यवस्थितम् 4:134d
मन्त्रमार्गन्त्वया देव 4:132a
मन्त्रसिद्धिमवाप्नोति 1:130c
मन्त्रेणैव समायुक्तम् 2:81a
मन्त्राख्यं कथयिष्यामि 4:135c
मन्त्राख्याश्च तथा शैवा 1:56e
मन्दाकिन्यः पराः स्मृताः 3:7d
मम वाक्यममिथ्यं हि 1:179c

यावदब्दं व्रतञ्चरेत् 3:148b
यावदिन्द्राश्चतुर्द्दश 2:21b
यावद्देवास्सवासवाः 2:76b
यावद्ब्रह्मा न नश्यति 2:38b
यावदापूरितम्भवेत् 4:55d
यावन्ममत्वं कुरुते 4:46c
यावन्मायान्न विन्दति 4:47d
युगान्ते च परिभ्रष्टो 2:43a
ये कुर्व्वन्ति शिवालयम् 2:20d
ये चान्ये अभयप्रदाः 2:63d
ये तत्र निधनङ्गताः 3:30b
ये मर्त्या न नमन्ति ईदृशमजं क्षेमस्तु तेषां कुतः 1:185d
ये वसन्ति यमालये 3:153b
ये स्मरन्ति विरूपाक्षं 1:168a
येन तुष्यति शङ्करः 1:142b
येन येन हि भावेन 4:69c
येन वेत्सि मतङ्ग त्वम् 1:4d
येन स्वर्गं व्रजन्ति ते 1:52d
येनोपायेन देवेश 1:50c
यो ’र्चयेदरिमुस्तकैः 1:137d
यो ’र्चयेद्गंधपुष्पकैः 1:131d
यो ’र्चयेल्लिङ्गमुत्तमम् 1:128d
यो ’र्च्चयेत वृषध्वजम् 1:143b
यो ’र्च्चयेत्परमेश्वरम् 1:132d
यो ’र्च्चयेत्परमेश्वरम् 1:142d
यो ’र्च्चयेत्परमेशानं 1:131a
यो ’र्च्चयेन्नामभिर्हरम् 3:177b
योग - - - 1:9 b
योगज्ञानञ्च मे शृणु 4:48b
योगपट्टं यथासुखम् 4:50d
योगविज्ञानकारणाम् 4:62b
योगञ्चापि महाव्रते 4:42d
योगाष्टकञ्च सुशिवं 4:118a
योद्धरेत्कुलसप्तकम् 1:87b
यो दद्याल्लिङ्गमूर्धनि 1:114d
यो दद्याल्लिङ्गसन्निधौ 1:104d
यो ददाति उपानहौ 2:74d
यो ददाति तिलोदकान् 2:39d
यो ददाति स चाश्नुते 2:114b
यो ददाति स दाता हि 2:108c
यो ददाति शिवस्य तु 1:107d
यो ददाति शिवस्य तु 1:122b
योनिर्वागेश्वरी देवी 4:95a
योन्याञ्चाप्यथ वागेश्यां 4:126c
यो यस्य स्थापनङ्कुर्यात् 2:29c
यो लिङ्गं स्थापयेद्भुवि 2:23d
रक्षन्ति च भयाद्घोरात् 2:86a
रक्षा लोकस्य साक्षिणे 3:123b
रजःसत्त्वौ प्रजायते 4:44b
रतिप्रियम्प्रीतिकरं 3:143c
रतिसत्रन्तु सततं 2:65a
रत्नदा - - - कन्तु 1:122a
रत्नदानाद्रवेः पुरम् 2:57b
रत्नशर्क्करसञ्चितम् 4:110b
रत्नाङ्गीं कांस्यदोहनीम् 2:47b
रत्नाभरणभूषणम् 1:117d
रवेर्न्नामाङ्कितं बुधः 3:173b
रसं गन्धञ्च पञ्चमम् 4:64b
रसे गन्धे च पञ्चसु 4:52b
रसातलन्द्वितीयन्तु 4:108a
राक्षसाधिपतिश्चैव 3:72c
राक्षसान्नमिदं स्मृतम् 3:59b
रागद्वेषविनाशाय 4:54a
राजसूयफलं लभेत् 3:135b
राजसूयफलं लभेत् 3:97d
राजसूयस्य यज्ञस्य 1:93c

षट्त्रिंशदब्दिका चर्या 4:5c
षण्मुखं शक्तिहस्तञ्च 3:84c
षण्मासं स्नापयेद्यस्तु 1:82a
षण्मासं स्नापयेद्यस्तु 1:85c
षण्मासन्तन्दहेद्यस्तु 1:102c
षण्मासेन न संशयः 1:133b
षण्मासेनैव युक्तात्मा 2:13c
षण्मासान् स्नापयेद्यस्तु 1:90a
षष्टिकोटिस्तथैव च 1:168d
षष्टितीर्त्थसहस्राणि 1:168c
षष्ठं वितलसञ्ज्ञन्तु 4:110a
षष्ठं साध्यं तथैश्वर्यं 4:124c
षष्ठ्यान्दद्यात्तु विप्राय 3:170c
षोडशारेण चक्रेण 4:21c
षोडशीफलमाप्नोति 3:130a
स - - - सुखी भवेत् 4:47b
संवत्सरेण शुद्धात्मा 1:96a
संवत्सरेण शुद्धात्मा 3:180c
संवत्सरेण शुद्धात्मा 3:184c
संवत्सरेण शुद्धात्मा 3:88c
संवादमुमया सह 4:134b
संसारभयनाशनम् 1:134b
संसारभयपीडिताः 1:65b
संसारोच्छित्तिकरणं 1:22a
संसारोच्छित्तिकरणन् 4:132c
संसारोद्विग्नचित्तस्तु 4:49a
संसाराच्च दुरत्ययात् 4:126b
संसाराद्दुद्धरस्व माम् 1:40d
संसारार्णवदुःखभीतमनसो लिङ्गार्च्चने तत्पराः 1:185b
संध्योपासनतत्परः 4:2b
संन्यासं तु क्रमङ्कृत्वा 4:34c
संपूज्य वरदं देवं 1:184a
संपूज्य विधिवद्बुधः 3:135d
सकलान्तु महीम्भुङ्क्ते 1:116a
सकृत्कृत्वा फलं ह्येतत् 1:165c
सकृद्दानफलं ह्येतद् 1:105c
सकृद्धूपेन प्राप्नोति 1:101a
स गच्छेत्परमाङ्गतिम् 3:121b
स गतिमुत्तमाम्व्रजेत् 3:53b
स गणश्चोत्तमो भवेत् 1:102d
स गणश्चोत्तमो भवेत् 1:82b
स गणश्चोत्तमो भवेत् 1:90b
स च तृप्तो यमालये 2:44b
स च दुःखी परो भवेत् 2:114d
स च दाता परः स्मृतः 2:107d
स जटी मुण्डमेव वा 4:89d
स तु मुच्येत किल्बिषात् 3:9d
स दाता स तपस्वी च 2:109c
स धर्म्मगतिमाप्नोति 3:182a
स नरः स्वर्ग्गमायाति 2:62c
स महाफलमाप्नोति 3:58c
स याति परमं पदम् 2:109d
स याति परमाङ्गतिम् 3:14d
स याति परमाङ्गतिम् 3:56d
स याति ब्रह्मलौकिकम् 4:39b
स याति रुद्रलोकन्तु 2:87a
स योगी परिकीर्त्तितः 4:49b
स रेचकस्समाख्यातः 4:57a
स लभेत्परमैश्वर्यं 1:105a
स लभेदुत्तमां कन्यां 1:133a
स विद्याधरतां व्रजेत् 1:120b
स विद्वान् वेदधर्म्मवित् 4:20d
स विधूय स्वकं पापं 1:58c
स वै त्राता परः स्मृतः 2:119b
स वै त्राता वरो वरः 2:120b
स सर्वः स्वर्गगोचरः 1:109d

सर्वकामप्रदो ह्येष 1:149c
सर्वकामसमृद्धाश्च 2:19c
सर्वकामानवाप्नुयात् 3:113b
सर्वकामानवाप्नुयात् 3:138d
सर्वकामानवाप्नुयात् 3:149d
सर्वकामानवाप्नोति 1:131c
सर्वकामानवाप्नोति 2:12c
सर्वकामानवाप्नोति 3:115a
सर्वकामानवाप्नोति 3:86a
सर्वकामानवाप्नोति 3:91c
सर्वकालं शुचिव्रतः 3:48d
सर्वगं क्षितिरूपन्तु 1:32c
सर्वगं जलरूपन्तु 1:33c
सर्वगं यज्ञरूपं तु 1:36c
सर्वगं वायुरूपन्तु 1:34c
सर्वगं सोमरूपं तु 1:38c
सर्वगं सूर्यरूपं तु 1:39c
सर्वगत्वं स चाप्नुयात् 4:21b
सर्वगमग्निरूपं तु 1:35c
सर्वगमे - - - तु 4:53c
सर्वगस्सर्वरूपो 'सि 1:42c
सर्वज्ञ नन्दिकेश्वर 1:17d
सर्वज्ञ शिवतेजसा 1:21b
सर्वज्ञश्चैककारणः 1:42d
सर्वज्ञश्चैव जायते 4:67b
सर्वज्ञाता च भवते 4:86c
सर्वज्ञानामृतोत्तमम् 1:22b
सर्वदुःखसहिष्णुश्च 4:28b
सर्वदोषविवर्जितः 4:48d
सर्वद्रव्यसमन्वितम् 2:79b
सर्वद्वन्द्वविनिर्मुक्तो 2:48c
सर्वद्वन्द्वसहिष्णुता 4:77d
सर्वद्वन्द्वसहेन च 4:22b
सर्वद्वन्द्वसहो धीरस् 4:48c
सर्वदा समुपक्रमेत् 4:81b
सर्वपापविनिर्मुक्तो 3:35a
सर्वपापविवर्जितः 3:42b
सर्वपापविशुद्धात्मा 3:11c
सर्वपापविशुद्धात्मा 3:13a
सर्वपापसमन्वितः 1:89b
सर्वपापहरो हरः 4:133b
सर्वपापापनोदनम् 3:44b
सर्वभूतहिते युक्तस् 4:28a
सर्वमस्मिन् प्रतिष्ठितम् 4:114d
सर्वमेकत्वदर्शिना 4:22d
सर्वमेतत्प्रवर्त्तते 4:68b
सर्वमेतद्भवेदिह 1:114b
सर्वम्प्रत्यक्षतो भवेत् 4:66b
सर्वमाघ्राति शङ्करः 1:127b
सर्वमात्मनि पश्यति 4:35b
सर्वयज्ञफलं लभेत् 3:99d
सर्वरोगसमावृताः 1:48d
सर्वलोकक्षयाय च 3:118b
सर्वलोकधरा ह्येते 2:84c
सर्वलोकेषु निन्दितः 4:81d
सर्वविद्याः प्रवर्तन्ते 4:66a
सर्वे शुक्लास्तु शान्त्यर्थे 1:154c
सर्वेषामुपरि स्थिता 2:10d
सर्वेषामेव दानानां 2:108a
सर्व्वकामानवाप्नुयात् 1:140b
सर्व्वकामानवाप्नुयात् 1:163b
सर्व्वदुःखहरो हरः 1:29b
सर्व्वन्तैः परिकल्पयेत् 1:155d
सर्व्वपापविनिर्म्मुक्तः 1:41c
सर्व्वशास्त्रविशारदाः 1:8b
सर्व्वे पीतास्तु पौष्टिके 1:154d
सर्वादस्सर्वचेष्टश्च 4:91c

सौभाग्यन्धनधान्यञ्च 3:187c
सौभाग्याय च वारुणी 1:132b
सौरभेये तथैव च 2:83d
सौवर्णन्धनुषन्दद्यात् 3:186a
सौवर्णन्तदुदाहृतम् 4:110d
सौवर्णन्नाम-चाङ्कितम् 3:165b
सौवर्णम्पुरुषङ्कृत्वा 3:192c
सौवर्णवस्ते नामानि 3:161a
सौवर्णञ्च गवामयम् 3:63b
सौवर्णञ्चारविन्दन्तु 3:159a
स्कन्दं षष्ठ्यां पूजयेत्तु 3:82a
स्कन्दं विशाखन्त्रिवर्णं 3:83c
स्कन्दनामाङ्कितं शुभम् 3:170b
स्कन्दसायोज्यमाप्नुयात् 3:86d
स्तुत्वा नन्दिं शिवात्मजम् 1:20d
स्तुन्वन्ते च वरार्थिनो -र्-अहरहः
कृत्वाञ्जलिम्मस्तके 1:185c
स्तोत्रमेवमुदीरयेत् 1:30d
स्तोत्रेण तुष्टुवे हरम् 1:176b
स्त्रियश्चैव प्रयच्छन्ति 2:64c
स्त्रीप्रेक्षणन्न कुर्वीत 4:4c
स्त्रीशूद्रन्नाभिभाषयेत् 4:74b
स्थानेष्वेषु मृता यान्ति 3:32c
स्थापितं ब्रह्मविष्णुना 1:182b
स्थापितस्य तु यत्फलम् 2:1b
स्थाणुं पशुपतिं रुद्रं 3:147a
स्थाणुं फाल्गुनकृष्णे तु 3:96a
स्नातो यैस्तु विमुच्येत 3:10c
स्नात्वा च लवणोदधौ 3:12d
स्नानं दिव्यसुगन्धैश्च 2:112c
स्नानदर्शनपूजाभिर् 3:25c
स्नाने पुण्यफलं यत्स्यात् 3:1c
स्नापितस्य च किम्फलम् 1:66b
स्पन्दमानस्तु विक्रोशेन् 4:80a
स्पर्शने पापनाशनाः 2:86b
स्फटिम्मर्रकतानि च 2:21d
स्फाटिकन्तत्प्रकीर्त्तितम् 4:108b
स्रष्टा धर्त्ता च हर्त्ता च 1:43a
स्रष्टानुग्रहकारकः 3:27b
स्रग्धूपञ्च विलेपनम् 2:111b
स्वकुलञ्चोद्धृतन्तेन 1:104a
स्वगृहे 'पि वसन्नित्यं 4:18c
स्वदेहा - - - 4:56d
स्वपरिज्ञानमुत्पत्तौ 4:62c
स्वर्गगामी च भवते 2:81c
स्वर्गनैश्रेयसः परः 4:41b
स्वर्गमात्रफलं लभेत् 4:24d
स्वर्गमाप्नोति मानवः 2:79d
स्वर्गलोकमवाप्नोति 2:88a
स्वर्गलोकञ्च गच्छति 2:49d
स्वर्गलोकात्परिभ्रष्टो 1:110a
स्वर्ग्गलोकम्व्रजेदिह 3:15d
स्वर्ग्गलोके महीयते 2:50d
स्वर्ग्गलोके महीयते 2:75d
स्वर्ग्गलोके महीयते 3:66b
स्वर्ग्गलोकात्परिभ्रष्टो 3:16a
स्वर्ग्गे मोदति चेन्द्रवत् 2:25b
स्वर्ग्गे हेममयङ्गृहम् 2:35b
स्वर्ग्गापवर्ग्गहेतोश्च 1:52a
स्वर्गापवर्गहेतोश्च 4:1c
स्वर्लोकन्तु ततोर्ध्वन्तु 4:115c
स्वर्णाक्षं स्थाणुमष्टमम् 3:23d
स्वस्तिकं पद्मकं भद्रं 4:50a
स्वस्थानन्तु गताः सर्व्वे 1:13c
स्वशरीरेण सायोज्यं 2:18c
स्वाचरन् स्वर्ग्गतिम्व्रजेत् 4:7b

General Index